Progression**Series**

Journalism, Broadcasting, Media Production and Performing Arts

For entry to university, college and conservatoire in 2012

Published by: UCAS Rosehill New Barn Lane Cheltenham GL52 3LZ

Produced in conjunction with GTI MEDIA LTD

© UCAS 2011

UCAS, a company limited by guarantee, is registered in England and Wales number: 2839815
Registered charity number: 1024741 (England and Wales) and SC038598 (Scotland)

UCAS reference number: PU038012
Publication reference: 11_080
ISBN: 978-1-908077-05-9
Price £15.99

We have made all reasonable efforts to ensure that the information in this publication was correct at time of publication. We will not, however, accept any liability for errors, omissions or changes to information since publication. Wherever possible any changes will be updated on the UCAS website (www.ucas.com).

UCAS and its trading subsidiary, UCAS Media Limited, accept advertising for publications that promote products and services relating to higher education and career progression. Revenue generated by advertising is invested by UCAS in order to enhance our applications services and to keep the cost to applicants as low as possible. Neither UCAS nor UCAS Media Limited endorse the products and services of other organisations that appear in this publication.

Further copies available from UCAS (p&p charges apply):

Contact Publication Services PO Box 130 Cheltenham GL52 3ZF

email: publicationservices@ucas.ac.uk or fax: 01242 544806

For further information about the UCAS application process go to www.ucas.com.
further information about the CUKAS application process is available at www.cukas.ac.uk

If you need to contact us, details can be found at www.ucas.com/about_us/contact_us or at CUKAS www.cukas.ac.uk/aboutus/contactus

UCAS QUALITY AWARDS

Foreword

THINKING ABOUT JOURNALISM, MEDIA AND PERFORMING ARTS?

Finding the course that's right for you at the right university, college or conservatoire can take time and it's important that you use all the resources available to you in making this important decision. We at UCAS have teamed up with GTI Media Ltd to provide you with *Progression to Journalism, Broadcasting, Media Production and Performing Arts* to show you how you can progress from being a student to careers in journalism, media and performing arts. You will find information on what the subject includes, entry routes and real-life case studies showing how it worked out for others.

Once you know which subject area you might be interested in, you can use the listings of all the full-time higher education courses in journalism, media and performing arts to see where you can study your subject. The course entry requirements are listed so you can check if getting in would be achievable for you. There's also advice on applying through UCAS and the Conservatoires UK Admissions Service (CUKAS), telling you what you need to know at each stage of the application process in just six easy steps to starting at a university, college or conservatoire.

We hope you find this publication helps you to choose and make your application to a course and university, college or conservatoire that is right for you.

On behalf of UCAS and GTI Media Ltd, I wish you every success in your research.

Mary Curnock Cook, Chief Executive, UCAS

www.ucas.com
www.cukas.ac.uk

at the heart of connecting people to higher education

Introducing journalism, media and performing arts

ProgressionSeries

It could be you...

... presenting a popular arts programme	– television presenter
... writing a monthly column for a top women's magazine	– features editor
... performing *La Traviata* around the world	– opera singer
... becoming the new JK Rowling	– writer
... performing with the Royal Ballet Company	– dancer
... receiving an Oscar in Hollywood	– film director

... and lots more besides. Could a career in journalism, media and performing arts be for you? The aim of this guide is to help you decide. For the purposes of this book 'journalism, media and performing arts' includes broadcasting and media production

A CAREER IN JOURNALISM, MEDIA AND PERFORMING ARTS?

- Your experience counts more than your degree subject – see **Which area?** starting on page 19
- Admissions tutors look for creativity, self-confidence and an ability to entertain – see **The career for you?** starting on page 51
- Despite the low pay, graduates love their work – see **Case studies** starting on page 61

JOURNALISM, MEDIA AND PERFORMING ARTS IN CONTEXT

Say the words 'journalism, media and performing arts' to people outside the sector, and they'll invariably start talking about TV shows, films and tabloid journalists. But those on the inside know it's a much more diverse field than this, with a myriad of roles, sectors and sub-sectors.

Under the previous government much money was invested in the arts, to great effect. Currently funding to the arts, from museums to theatres, and orchestras to university arts courses, is facing cuts from all directions, although the most recent funding cuts announced by Arts Council England are less dramatic than was expected. Nevertheless, these, as well as cuts from other organisations, will have an impact on career prospects in the sector for the time being.

However, this should not put you off pursuing your interest in working in journalism, media and arts. In spite of the recent economic downturn, the arts have continued to make a considerable contribution to the British economy. For example, a recent study of the arts sector in the Lancaster region showed that the sector was thriving: contributing £50 million annually to the local economy, supporting up to 2,400 jobs and providing thousands of activities for young people.

In the current economic climate, the arts may suffer some funding shortages, especially due to cuts at local authority level. Nevertheless, all political parties claim to recognise the contribution of the arts to British economic and social life, so determined candidates should not be put off pursuing a career in journalism, media and performing arts.

If you're interested in a possible career in journalism, media and performing arts, then this guide can help you. Read on to discover:

- the main roles on offer
- the skills admissions tutors look for
- how to get in and the routes to qualification
- advice from journalism, media and performing arts graduates in different sectors.

Why journalism, media and performing arts?

Choose a career that is...

CREATIVE

Few careers can claim to be as creative as journalism, media and performing arts. You will be paid to think creatively at all times. There is also an unrivalled sense of satisfaction and achievement in seeing your ideas come to life in the finished product.

VARIED

Your journalism, media and performing arts background will enable you to work in a huge variety of careers sectors, from magazine journalism to web-based writing and from theatrical production to broadcast journalism. Read **Which area?** beginning on page 19 to find out more about the full range of journalism, media and performing arts careers.

FUN

Read the case studies of the journalism, media and performing arts graduates in this book and you'll find that they all really love their work. Being 'creative' and 'artistic' is something they have developed a special interest in during their studies, pursued as a hobby, or have always enjoyed doing as they grew up. And now they're getting paid to do it! As well as being a fun career, journalism, media and performing arts also make things fun for other people – whether it's making authors such as Jane Austen accessible or popularising history from the Romans to the Tudors.

A STRONG INFLUENCE ON OUR DAY-TO-DAY LIVES

Journalism, media and performing arts have a crucial influence on what we wear, read, sit on, look at, enjoy, and almost everything we buy. We read about the latest health and beauty trends in magazines like *Cosmopolitan* or *FHM* and find out about current affairs through the television or radio. As a new student in higher education, you'll probably enjoy going to the cinema or theatre with your friends.

ADDING 'VALUE'

This may seem a little obscure at first, but the journalism, media and performing arts sector is also 'valued' by people. For example, an uplifting theatrical or television production can enthral viewers or encourage people to start reading pieces of literature that they never dreamed they would like. Newspaper or magazine articles and reports help keep us informed about what is happening on a local, national and international scale, often prompting us to take action, for example in helping to save the environment. Finally, we have an innate appreciation of journalism, media and performing arts; a song or a film can give pleasure and uplift the senses.

WHAT IS SO GOOD ABOUT A CAREER IN JOURNALISM, MEDIA AND PERFORMING ARTS?

I loved the way that, through words and storytelling, radio could transport you to another world, and was excited by how it was starting to develop digitally and interactively.
Abbie Cunliffe, commercial programmer

Making a living from photography now is especially difficult and people will try to put you off. In my opinion, it's still one of the most exciting and creative careers possible and full of opportunity. You just have to be prepared to work hard for it.
Martin Scott Powell, freelance photographer

Working in news journalism can also be really exciting when you get to bring new information to light, or report on something that everyone in the country is talking about.
Hollie Clemence, reporter

Working with many different people, both in-house and externally, in the UK and abroad, is one of the highlights of my job.
Emma Hawes, production editor

Be enthusiastic and assertive – production environments can be very busy places and you can easily get lost in the crowd.
Mark Wright, final-year media production studies student

A career in journalism, media and performing arts

A career in journalism, media and performing arts

Thousands of students are accepted onto journalism, media and performing arts degrees in the UK each year. On graduating, many immediately start employment within the UK, though interestingly only 24% of journalism graduates, 23% of performing arts graduates and 15% of media studies graduates work in a field directly relevant to their degree six months after graduation. Many can be found in what may be considered more temporary jobs such as clerical, catering and retail. This reflects the fact that there are more applicants than there are places and that many aspiring performers and writers must do casual work while looking for their big break. Since working in the media or performing arts is more a vocation – a 'calling' if you like – than a career, these individuals are happy to do this to try to reach their goal.

WHERE THEY WORK

Freelance/self-employed

This is the most common employment option in journalism, media and performing arts and in many ways is one of the hardest paths to follow early on in your career. It relies on the reputation you build for yourself to ensure a continuous stream of work, and when you're fairly new to a profession, gaining valuable contacts can take a while. Freelancing is a common route among writers, producers, editors, photographers, actors and musicians, all of whom rely on the strength of their portfolio to secure new work and need to maintain a good relationship with current and past clients.

Large national companies

Major TV, radio, newspaper and magazine companies are recruiters of graduates, and a few offer training schemes to recruit new blood each year. Competition for places is extremely fierce so you will need excellent experience, heaps of motivation and plenty of ideas to be considered.

Smaller organisations and voluntary groups

On a more regional level, some people find work in local theatres, radio stations and newspapers. You may find yourself mucking in and doing all sorts of odd jobs while waiting for your big break, and salaries can vary from being on the minimum wage to being non-existent! Supplementing your monthly pay cheque with proceeds from another job is a fairly common experience among graduates trying to make it on their own.

WHICH AREA?

There are so many career paths to choose from in this sector that in many ways journalism, media and performing arts students are spoilt for choice.

Many of the skills required for some of the key roles are also highly transferable; for example, an actor could decide to use his or her years of experience to start directing plays or films. That said, the skills required for each particular profession are in many ways becoming more precise, which means that, in many media and performing arts sectors, the further down one route you go, the harder it could be to transfer across to other fields. It is rare for a fine art photographer to work as a newspaper photographer in a war zone, for instance. You would therefore be wise to take time at this stage to find out the key differences in each of the main journalism, media and performing arts sectors before embarking on your course. Have a look at the **Which area?** section, starting on page 19, to read outlines of some of the main fields in which you can specialise.

JOURNALISM, MEDIA AND PERFORMING ARTS STATISTICS

Typical journalism graduate destinations

Retail, catering, waiting and bar staff	24%
Art, design, culture and sports professionals	15%
Clerical and secretarial occupations	15%
Marketing, sales and advertising professionals	14%
Other occupations	10%

Typical media studies graduate destinations

Retail, catering, waiting and bar staff	30%
Other occupations	15%
Clerical and secretarial occupations	15%
Arts, design, culture and sports professionals	15%
Commercial, industrial and public sector managers	8%

Typical performing arts graduate destinations

Arts, design, culture and sports professionals	23%
Retail, catering, waiting and bar staff	22%
Education professionals	13%
Clerical and secretarial occupations	9%
Commercial, industrial and public sector managers	6%

Reproduced with kind permission of HECSU/AGCAS, What do graduates do? 2010
All data comes from the HESA Destination of Leavers of Higher Education Survey 2008/9

Trends

Different parts of the journalism, media and performing arts sector are subject to different trends and pressures.

ECONOMIC

Like most areas of work, journalism, media and performing arts are dependent on the state of the economy to flourish or flounder. In an economic downturn, people will still buy newspapers and magazines, watch the television and listen to the radio, and go to the cinema or theatre, although perhaps not so much. However, most of the organisations that produce these media depend for much or some of their income on advertisers, who may decrease or cut their advertising spend. This means that newspapers, magazines, TV companies and so on have to find the money from elsewhere and potentially make cutbacks.

In the current economic climate, the arts are also being severely affected by funding cuts by the government, local authorities, the Arts Council and other arts organisations. Inevitably this will affect opportunities in the sector for everyone, new graduates included. However, artists are creative, innovative types, so if you're really determined to succeed in this sector, don't let the current situation put you off pursuing your ambitions.

TECHNOLOGY

Technology plays a huge role these days in the ways films are made, television and radio programmes are broadcast and compiled, and music is produced. Photographers have largely changed from film to digital software, while film editors are increasingly using digital techniques rather than splicing. Anyone hoping for a career in this sector must be prepared to learn about the relevant and rapidly changing technology.

TASTE

Of all the things that affect journalism, media and performing arts, trends in popular and critical taste are of vital importance. Think about musicals, for example. These experienced something of a slump until a couple of recent BBC reality TV shows sparked the nation's interest by searching for the next Maria and Joseph. Films too are subject to audience preferences: consider the trend for adapting children's classic books into films that rely on fantastic computer-generated animation such as *The Lord of the Rings*, *The Chronicles of Narnia* and *The Golden Compass*.

PAY

Salaries vary greatly in this diverse employment sector. At the bottom end, it is common for those starting out to work voluntarily (for free) or just for expenses on internships or work placements in order to get a foot in the door, to build their portfolio and make good contacts. Many people in this sector are also self-employed or work on a freelance basis, charging hourly, daily, or on a contract basis. Rates depend on the sector, location and experience of the person; for example, an actor in a repertory theatre may be paid a minimum of £380 per week, according to Equity guidelines (2010-11 rates). Regional newspaper journalists can often start off on a very low rate, at £12,000 for example, although their salary will increase with experience.

WORKING CONDITIONS

Your work will vary greatly according to the sector and nature of the job you do. And just because you're self-employed or freelance doesn't mean that you can set your own hours; writers often can do so but theatre directors, actors, dancers, musicians and producers, for example, will need to work the hours a project dictates. In most fields, the working hours are long, erratic and unsocial with frequent late-night, early-morning, weekend and holiday working. Travelling and working away from home is a common occurrence and flexibility over where you work is essential.

Unistats®

from universities and colleges in the UK

Which university is right for you?

Compare by:
- Student satisfaction
- Job prospects
- UCAS points

 HIGHER EDUCATION FUNDING COUNCIL FOR ENGLAND

UCAS

Visit www.direct.gov.uk/unistat
The official university comparison sit

Which area?

Progression**Series**

Actor

WHAT DO THEY DO?

Actors portray a writer's character through their words, body language and movements, normally according to the instructions of a director, although some work is based on improvisation. Their work is incredibly varied, from performing each night on a stage to television and radio serials or film acting. Typical activities include:

- attending auditions and rehearsals
- researching to prepare themselves for their role
- working with other cast members and the director to interpret a script
- performing either for an audience or in front of a camera
- doing 'voice-overs' for commercials or recording talking books
- helping out behind the scenes.

It's easy to romanticise the working life of an actor but the reality is that nearly 80% of an actor's time is spent between acting jobs. Therefore they will need other sources of income to pay the rent, such as taking on casual jobs (waiting on tables or temporary admin roles, for example), which give them the freedom to stop at short notice if a role comes their way.

WHERE DO THEY WORK?

Many actors work in theatres or in television or film studios, but sometimes outdoor scenes are necessary, which can be in any weather and at any temperature. Working hours tend to be long and unsocial, rehearsing during the day and performing at night in theatres, while on film or TV sets actors typically start early and finish late. Actors typically work all over the UK, sometimes touring abroad. Auditions are often held at very short notice so you will need to be prepared to travel without much warning. Spending time away from home is common and a normal social life is impossible during projects.

WHAT SKILLS DO THEY NEED?

Apart from the ability to 'act', the following skills are also essential:

- good communication skills
- empathy
- flexibility
- a proactive approach
- punctuality and reliability
- teamwork skills
- a thick skin to take criticism from directors, critics and the audience
- self-confidence
- stamina and self-motivation.

Other skills and talents may be developed on the job, such as singing, dancing or playing a musical instrument, and these can help boost employment prospects.

ROUTES TO QUALIFICATION

Experience, talent, hard work and – if we're being totally honest here – *luck* are as important than qualifications in this field. Work experience in theatres or television production companies can help you gain a better understanding of the industry as a whole and could provide good contacts for the future. Or why not consider working as an entertainer in a holiday camp or resort to gain some much-needed experience?

A performing arts degree may help your chances but many top actors have done well without one.

Participation in a drama society at school or university is essential, while work experience as an 'extra' can give you an insight into what the profession is like, although people who make a living as an extra rarely go on to become fully fledged actors.

PROSPECTS

It is difficult to define a standard career route for actors. Some will spend their entire career moving from one job to the next without further responsibility or pay, whereas others will gain fame and fortune and will be at the top of their profession.

FURTHER INFORMATION

- Equity **www.equity.org.uk**
- The London Academy of Music and Dramatic Art (LAMDA) **www.lamda.org.uk**
- National Council for Drama Training **www.ncdt.co.uk**

Broadcast journalist

WHAT DO THEY DO?

Broadcast journalists investigate and report on current affairs for news programmes on the television and radio, taking a neutral and unbiased stance in order to reflect the news as honestly as possible to a wide audience. They are involved in various media roles, such as editing, reporting and presenting. Typical duties can include the following:

- coming up with ideas for stories and features
- following up leads from many different sources
- researching and writing their stories
- gathering evidence
- advising their crews on what to film or record
- pitching their ideas to editors
- presenting their stories 'on air'
- interviewing experts and the general public.

WHERE DO THEY WORK?

News happens at all times of the day and night, and of course at weekends, so you'll have to be prepared to work long and unsocial hours, usually in shifts. These can start in the early morning or late evening, on weekdays, weekends and during public holidays.

This industry is unpredictable, with most people employed on short-term contracts or as freelancers, which means you may have to travel to find work. Opportunities are available throughout the UK, although if you want to work for one of the major networks you must be prepared to work in London or large regional cities.

WHAT SKILLS DO THEY NEED?

You will need great physical and emotional stamina to cope with work that is unpredictable, stressful and subject to tight deadlines. You will also need to have the following skills and attributes:

- an interest in the news (obviously!)
- good general knowledge
- excellent written and oral communication skills
- self-confidence
- resilience under pressure
- analytical skills to sort through different sources of information
- an ability to present often complex information in a comprehensible way
- an understanding of technical equipment
- sensitivity, empathy and tact
- creativity and originality.

A great way to get a foot in the door is through (often unpaid) work experience. Both the BBC and Independent Television (ITV) offer small journalism traineeship schemes but competition is fierce for places. You may want to contact editors and producers directly to ask for a work experience placement or the chance to shadow them for a short period of time. The local press is also a good place to start – try your newspaper or your local hospital radio – and don't forget to get involved with any student media opportunities.

Routes to qualification

There are three different ways to get into broadcast journalism:

- a traineeship directly after graduating
- moving from print journalism after a few years' experience
- by completing a postgraduate qualification in journalism, with the National Council for the Training of Journalists (NCTJ) or the Broadcast Journalism Training Council (BJTC). This is the most common route.

PROSPECTS

In TV you will normally start as a newsroom assistant or researcher and then progress into a reporting role, specialising in a particular field once you've gained more experience or even moving into a presenting role. Another possible option is to go into investigative or documentary journalism, or if you'd prefer to stay behind the camera you can work as a programme editor or sub-editor.

In radio, trainees receive greater responsibility earlier on, and may even be solely responsible for a newsroom from the very beginning. The most natural career progression would be to join a large commercial or network station, or to go into TV work.

FURTHER INFORMATION

- Broadcast Journalism Training Council **www.bjtc.org.uk**
- The National Council for the Training of Journalists (NCTJ) **www.nctj.com**
- Skillset (The Sector Skills Council for Creative Media) **www.skillset.org**

Commissioning editor

WHAT DO THEY DO?

Commissioning editors in the book publishing industry identify potential authors and support them from the commissioning stage right through to publication. Thus they play an important role in creating and constantly adding to a publishing house's booklists and, subsequently, helping their profits. To do this effectively, commissioning editors must know their field inside-out. They do this by attending book fairs, looking at catalogues and lists, and even by conducting surveys to see what sort of books are currently in demand.

Magazine commissioning editors ask writers to produce articles and features according to the remit of their magazine. They must ensure that the work they commission is of interest to their readers and is completed on time.

In both book and magazine publishing, this is not an entry-level job: you will need proven experience and ability in order to do it well. Commissioning editors normally start off in a junior position and work their way up within the company or by switching employers.

WHERE DO THEY WORK?

Commissioning editors normally work in an office environment, with occasional trips out to meetings or fairs, both in the UK and abroad. Working hours can often be long when leading up to a deadline, particularly in magazine publishing where such deadlines can occur once a week or month. The publishing world is mainly centred around the South East, with London, Oxford and Cambridge being hotspots.

WHAT SKILLS DO THEY NEED?

Commissioning editors need the following skills:

- a great knowledge of, and enthusiasm for, the field in which they work
- an eye for spotting talent
- business sense
- great interpersonal skills
- self-motivation
- the ability to plan and work to deadlines
- IT ability
- organisational skills
- an eye for detail.

While you may have gained such skills in other settings, work experience and entry-level experience are essential to get a job as a commissioning editor. Many publishing houses and magazines offer work experience schemes or placements, which can be a great source of contacts – essential in this very competitive field.

ROUTES TO QUALIFICATION

Any graduates can work in publishing, but scientific and academic publishers often stipulate that candidates have a degree in the relevant field. Publishing degrees and masters can help you get your foot in the door, as they are evidence of your commitment to working in a very competitive sector and will give you skills to set you apart from other applicants. Check out and apply for postgraduate courses at **www.ukpass.ac.uk**.

An entry-level post in a publishing house will normally be that of an editorial assistant, where you will carry out everyday tasks such as copy-editing, proofreading and writing text for book jackets. You may then move on to work as a desk editor or associate editor before finally becoming a commissioning editor.

In the magazine world, a degree in publishing is not essential. A postgraduate qualification in journalism might help improve your chances but nothing is as important as contacts, so make this a priority. Normally you would start off as a junior writer on a magazine, before perhaps taking a post as deputy features editor before becoming a features or commissioning editor.

PROSPECTS

Successful commissioning editors in publishing houses can work up the career ladder to become publishers. Commissioning editors working on magazines, meanwhile, can eventually become editors, responsible for the overall look and content of their product.

FURTHER INFORMATION

- Society for Editors and Proofreaders **www.sfep.org.uk**
- National Council for the Training of Journalists (NCTJ) **www.nctj.com**

Copy-editor/ proofreader

WHAT DO THEY DO?

Publishing copy-editors and proofreaders check that books, newspapers and other texts are suitable for publication by ensuring the accuracy and accessibility of their information, language and grammar. This may involve correcting typos, checking that facts are correct, ensuring that the publication's house style and tone are adhered to, and rewriting anything that isn't quite right or doesn't meet the appropriate standards. It can also involve preparing documents for the design stage by flagging up codes for the designers and suggesting images and photographs. This role can be done in-house, especially in smaller publishing houses, but increasingly work is being farmed out to specialist freelancers.

WHERE DO THEY WORK?

If you work as an in-house copy-editor or proofreader, you will normally be based in an office environment, while freelancers work from home. The latter situation gives you much more flexibility as to when you actually work, as long as you meet deadlines. Freelancers can work in most parts of the country but most in-house opportunities are found in London and the South East. Working hours can be long when a deadline is approaching. Those employed on a freelance basis might find that projects have extremely tight deadlines – publishers often tend to contact you at the very last minute and expect a quick turnaround!

If you decide to go down the freelance route, it's worth bearing in mind that it can be difficult to gain sufficient work to earn a living. Publishing houses often have a list of preferred copy-editors and proofreaders, often with staff who have gone from working in-house to working at home, so perseverance is essential to get started in this field. Additionally, working on your own can be quite lonely and you may miss the buzz and camaraderie of an office.

WHAT SKILLS DO THEY NEED?

Successful copy-editors and proofreaders have the following skills and attributes:

- an excellent knowledge of English
- a methodical approach
- great attention to detail: you're employed to pick up other people's mistakes, but there's no one to correct yours
- accuracy and concentration
- the ability to multitask as you may be working on several projects at once
- a tactful manner to suggest corrections to authors
- self-motivation, especially for freelancers, to get the work done
- IT and computer skills (much editing and proofreading these days is done on-screen)
- business and numerical skills (for example, to deal with tax returns, National Insurance contributions and negotiating pay rates).

ROUTES TO QUALIFICATION

Any graduate can work in this field, although some scientific or academic publishers require a degree in a relevant field. A degree or postgraduate qualification in either publishing or the media may improve your chances.

Experience is extremely important, so try to get involved with university magazines or find some work experience at bookshops, libraries and publishers. Some graduates will start in a junior role in a publishing house – for example, as an editorial assistant – and then work their way up, often going freelance once their careers are more firmly established.

PROSPECTS

The salary you receive will depend on what type of work you do and for which company. Understandably, larger publishers tend to pay better rates although this is not always the case.

If you become quite experienced in your field and build up a good rapport with your company or clients, you may be offered project management roles. This would involve seeing a publication through from concept to finish and can command higher fees because of the increased responsibility.

FURTHER INFORMATION

- The Society for Editors and Proofreaders **www.sfep.org.uk**

Dancer

WHAT DO THEY DO?

Dancers are like actors in that they portray characters, but they do so primarily through movement, often to music, with the guidance of a choreographer or through improvisation. There are a huge variety of dance genres, from ballet and tap to contemporary and jazz dance. As well as performing, dancers often become involved with education and therapy.

This job is extremely competitive and physical and tends to have a short shelf-life – dancers rarely go on performing professionally beyond their forties. As with all performing arts careers, dancers must promote themselves in order to get work, at least until they are an established name. It is also a career marked by periods of unemployment in which dancers will need to take on other jobs to bring home money. Performance itself makes up a fairly small part of a dancer's life. Instead, they will usually combine dancing with fields such as teaching, arts promotion and administration, normally to fit around their dancing commitments.

WHERE DO THEY WORK?

Dancers work in a variety of settings, from gyms and dance halls, where they practise nearly every day, to theatres and other performance centres, when they are part of a production. Working hours are very antisocial, with performances typically taking place in the evenings and at weekends, six or even seven days a week. Contract work is common and offered on a short-term basis so you can expect periods of intensive work followed by quieter times when you will need to look for further contracts.

Travel is almost an essential part of a dancer's career, with opportunities both in the UK and abroad. Most work is available in large cities rather than smaller communities.

WHAT SKILLS DO THEY NEED?

Dancers need the following skills to succeed:

- a thorough training in dance
- physical stamina to cope with daily rehearsals and performances
- perseverance to find work and maintain contacts
- the ability to work both as part of a team and on an individual basis.

ROUTES TO QUALIFICATION

Most dancers start training at a very young age; this is usually not a profession that you can enter later in life and it's unlikely that you will be able to start a career after graduating if you have not followed a dancing path. Dance degrees are normally offered at specialist colleges or universities and focus on the theoretical side of dance, although performance forms a part of the course.

PROSPECTS

After a dancing career, a popular choice is teaching, either on a private basis or for public-sector organisations. Other possible areas include choreography and dance administration, or working in a community to run workshops for groups of people such as young people or those with disabilities.

FURTHER INFORMATION

- British Theatre Dance Association **www.btda.org.uk**
- National Dance Teachers' Association **www.ndta.org.uk**
- young-dancers **www.young-dancers.org**

Film/video editor

WHAT DO THEY DO?

Film or video editors take a variety of raw camera footage, dialogue, sound effects and graphics, select which ones they want and put them together to make a final 'cut', which is the version you will see on television or at the cinema. Much of the editing is done with computer or digital technology within a special suite, often beside a director to ensure the final product meets their vision. However, some production companies still use the more traditional method of cutting film and then arranging shots into the desired order.

WHERE DO THEY WORK?

Editors in these fields often work on a freelance basis, on short-term contracts for post-production studios and TV companies. They will work either alone or as part of a small team, often in very small, enclosed surroundings. Freelance editors can work from home in their own editing suites.

Working hours can vary. If you work in-house then you can expect a steadier stream of work and normal nine-to-five hours, but long hours and weekend work are common when a deadline approaches. Freelancers tend to work in shorter, more intense bursts, with shorter deadlines. However, they can also experience periods of unemployment until the next project comes in.

WHAT SKILLS DO THEY NEED?

Film and video editors must be able to competently use editing software packages. Without this, you can forget a career in this area, so look out for courses on the AVID, Lightworks or Final Cut Pro packages. While these can be expensive, they will provide you with the specific skills required for the industry. You will also need the following skills:

- a keen eye for detail
- a creative approach
- good listening skills
- teamwork
- self-motivation
- organisational and self-management skills
- oral and written communication skills.

ROUTES TO QUALIFICATION

Graduates from all degrees can in theory pursue a career in this field but courses in media and communication, photography, television, film, fine art and information technology could increase your chances. Experience is vital, as you will need to show that you have had experience of working in a film/video environment, either in production or post-production. Most film or video editors do not step straight into this role either – they tend to start out as runners and work their way up.

PROSPECTS

Gaining experience before trying to get a job is advisable, for example by joining a student film-making society (or starting one!) or undertaking voluntary placements with relevant employers. As a graduate your first job may be as a runner or trainee, so you need to be positive about working your way up from the bottom, learning new skills quickly and networking. The next stage could be to secure an assistant editor post, before becoming an editor. Structured career paths exist in some of the larger organisations, although there is huge competition for a relatively small number of jobs.

Freelance film or video editors tend to work on smaller projects to begin with. With increasing experience they will be able to find work on larger, more complex productions. In general, success in this career depends to a large extent on your practical experience, evidence of your achievements and personal contacts.

FURTHER INFORMATION

- British Film Institute **www.bfi.org.uk**
- Skillset (The Sector Skills Council for Creative Media) **www.skillset.org**

Features editor

WHAT DO THEY DO?

Features editors work for magazines, newspapers and websites, and are responsible for coming up with ideas for features on a weekly or monthly basis. Magazines and websites can vary in size from specialist publications on particular topics to glossy women's magazines and gossip 'mags'. Larger consumer magazines include features on fashion, beauty and lifestyle, as well as celebrity interviews, while specialist publications look at news and developments in their particular field.

Typically, features editors will do some or all of the following tasks:

- attend regular features meetings to come up with ideas for future editions
- plan each issue's features
- manage and commission both in-house and freelance writers
- draw up and send out briefs for features to writers
- edit features and ensure that they are accurate and that they meet house style
- write features
- liaise with the design department on layouts and illustrations
- proofread their pages before going to press.

WHERE DO THEY WORK?

Features editors mainly work in an office environment, although they sometimes will attend photoshoots and meetings. If writing is involved as part of their job, they may also take trips to research a topic or to interview relevant people.

Working hours tend to be fairly regular, particularly on

magazines, with an average day lasting from 9am until 6pm. However, be prepared to work longer hours in the days running up to print, especially in newspapers and weekly magazines. While newspapers and magazines are based throughout the UK, the majority are in London so you may have to consider living in the capital.

WHAT SKILLS DO THEY NEED?

Since all media professions are popular, potential candidates have to prove their worth to get the job over hundreds of others. Typical skills include:

- top-notch organisation skills; often you'll be planning future issues while finishing current ones
- determination to get the job done on time and to an excellent standard
- the ability to take criticism... and often to give it
- strong interpersonal skills and a sociable nature
- creativity and an eye for an idea
- natural curiosity and an interest in people
- self-confidence and a professional approach.

Getting a foot on the career ladder can be tough. Make the most of any school or university vacations to seek work experience in the local and national press, as well as in any student-led magazines and newspapers. While much of this will be unpaid, you will be gaining invaluable contacts and an insight into the industry.

ROUTES TO QUALIFICATION

Most features editors are graduates who have worked their way up in journalism to get to this senior post: most have at least five years' experience in a writing capacity or as a deputy features editor before they move into this role. Degree discipline is usually not important, unless you are working on highly specialist magazines; recruiters view experience as more valuable than qualifications. However, a postgraduate qualification in journalism is often valued highly.

PROSPECTS

You'll probably start your career as a junior writer, working up to senior writer and then possibly deputy editor before becoming a features editor. This career route can take at least three to five years and you might have to move from one publication to another as positions arise. A features editor can then aim for the highest job as editor but this can take a long time to achieve as there are relatively few positions at the top.

FURTHER INFORMATION

- National Council for the Training of Journalists (NCTJ) **www.nctj.com**
- Periodical Publishers Association (PPA) **www.ppa.co.uk**

Magazine journalist

WHAT DO THEY DO?

Magazine journalists research and write both news articles and features for local, national and sometimes international magazines. There are thousands of magazines in the UK, ranging from women's lifestyle glossies to specialist titles on areas such as fly-fishing, so the articles that magazine journalists write must reflect the interests of their readers.

Magazine journalists may specialise in writing either news or features, and are normally also involved in sub-editing, in which they take another person's article and make amendments. While the work is predominantly focused on paper-based products, web writing is becoming increasingly popular. In whatever medium they work, magazine journalists will typically research a subject or story and talk to the appropriate people, and then write an article based on their findings.

WHERE DO THEY WORK?

Magazine journalists work in a variety of places. Those employed directly by magazines or websites are based in an office environment, while those who work as freelancers (around 80% of features are written by freelancers) are home-based. All journalists will frequently go out to meetings to interview people or carry out research relevant to their feature.

Regular working hours are not common in this industry, with tight deadlines meaning that you are unlikely to enjoy a nine-to-five existence. Long and unsocial hours are common. While most major magazines are based in London and the South East, the availability of freelance work means that you can work from all over the UK.

WHAT SKILLS DO THEY NEED?

Successful magazine journalists need to be:

- literate
- curious
- good with technology (eg computers)
- up-to-date with current affairs
- good at working with other people
- interested in whatever magazine(s) they write for.

The best way to get noticed by employers is to find relevant work experience. Try writing for your student newspaper or magazine and, during the holidays, try to organise work experience placements on local, regional and national newspapers and magazines.

If you are considering a career as a freelancer, you may have to do some unpaid work first in order to build up a portfolio that you can then show to potential commissioning editors. Alternatively you could start as a staff writer and then go freelance.

ROUTES TO QUALIFICATION

Most features writers are graduates so a degree really is a prerequisite. If you want to write for a specialist field, you will often need to have a degree in that area in order to be considered. Postgraduate diplomas in journalism are not essential but they can be helpful in giving you an awareness of the industry and some skills that are required.

PROSPECTS

Career progression depends on a variety of factors. If you are working for an employer, you could start off as a staff writer, progressing to sub-editor. With a few years' experience under your belt, you may be able to land a job as chief editor. Thanks to the writing skills and commercial nous you'll develop, you could also move into related areas of work such as PR or marketing. Freelancers have more flexibility but must be highly proactive networkers, keep up with technological developments and produce good work to deadline to keep bringing the work in.

FURTHER INFORMATION

- National Council for the Training of Journalists (NCTJ) **www.nctj.com**

Musician

WHAT DO THEY DO?

Musicians can work in several different fields within the music industry – as an instrumental performer, as a composer and as a singer. Normally they will specialise in a particular type of music such as pop, classical, jazz, etc. Some musicians are employed as part of a regular group (for example, in orchestras), while others will freelance and play whenever demand dictates. This often involves performing live or in a recording studio, either in a group or on their own. Practising on a daily basis is as important as performance to ensure that their skills and talents are always at the top of their field.

WHERE DO THEY WORK?

Musicians commonly work on a self-employed basis, although some are employed in orchestras and other groups of musicians. Freelance musicians will testify to the unreliability of their work – taking on a part-time job to pay the bills is often part and parcel of a music career. Musicians tend to practise at home and then perform in theatres or recording studios, at any time of the day and night. Unsociable working hours are common as performances tend to be in the evenings and at weekends. Working in holiday seasons is also unavoidable.

If your main passion is to play in an orchestra or perhaps as part of a backing group for a pop star, you will normally need to be based in London or another big city, where opportunities are most prevalent. Travel is common, as musicians often go on tour both in the UK and abroad.

WHAT SKILLS DO THEY NEED?

To get ahead in the music industry you need to know how to network. This involves making contacts and keeping in touch with them so they think of you when they are planning their next musical project. Experience is essential to attract the attention of musical directors. Other desirable skills include:

- **teamwork**: to get on in large and small groups of musicians
- **accuracy**: to play a piece of music well
- **confidence**: to perform in front of large audiences
- **stamina**: to cope with the amount of rehearsals and performances
- **language skills**: to be able to sing in other languages (if opera's your thing).

To build up your portfolio of experience, make the most of opportunities at school and university to perform with amateur orchestras and groups. Talk to musicians currently working in your preferred field to see what they have to say about getting your career off the ground, and ask if they can introduce you to anyone of influence.

ROUTES TO QUALIFICATION

Many musicians and composers have a degree in music but this is not always essential – talent and ability in your chosen instrument is of greater importance. However, music degrees do give you the opportunity to develop performance skills as well as concentrating heavily on the theory side of music. If you want to play in an orchestra or sing in an opera house you will normally need to attend an audition and then work for them for a trial period. Unfortunately contracts aren't always offered at the end, even if you have played well, and trials can last from a few sessions to a few years.

PROSPECTS

There are so many different kinds of music, and hence of musicians, that it is impossible to describe a typical career path. Many musicians, whatever genre they specialise in, will be self-employed, and may need to make ends meet by taking on regular part-time work, which could be related to music – for example, teaching music or working in arts administration. Self-employment is not the only option: there are permanent positions, for example in orchestras, in teaching (whether private tuition, in schools or in further or higher education), and in arts administration or management. People don't tend to go into music for the pay – only a few famous soloists (instrumental or singers) can command considerable pay packets.

FURTHER INFORMATION

- Musicians' Union **www.musiciansunion.org.uk**
- Association of British Orchestras **www.abo.org.uk**
- Incorporated Society of Musicians (ISM) **www.ism.org**

Newspaper journalist

WHAT DO THEY DO?

Newspaper journalists carry out a similar role to magazine journalists except that they work for newspapers. They can be found working in the local, regional, national and sometimes international press. Journalists normally start off as a junior reporter and are given work from the news desk as stories roll in. The juicier topics tend to be snapped up by the more senior reporters but it is the journalist's task to make even the most dull, everyday story interesting. Topics covered include news, culture, sport and science, local and national events, and entertainment. Contacts in such areas as the police and emergency services are essential as they provide a much-needed stream of ideas.

WHERE DO THEY WORK?

Newspaper journalists will work from a central office but will often be out and about researching stories and talking to sources. There are opportunities with regional and local papers throughout the UK but if you want to work for one of the nationals, you'll probably have to move to London. Generally you will need to be flexible about where you're based in this career, particularly when you're starting out.

Hours can be very long and unsocial, as you will have to be ready to investigate a story when it happens, often at the drop of a hat. Early on in your career, particularly, you will often work on a shift basis – early and late shifts are common.

WHAT SKILLS DO THEY NEED?

It's often said that journalists need a thick skin and a dogged sense of determination to get ahead in this field. This is true, of course! You will also need the following skills and attributes:

- excellent written and oral communication skills
- an eye for a good story and the ability to write it up in an interesting manner
- the ability to keep to strict deadlines
- stamina to cope with long hours and often stressful conditions
- self-motivation.

Some national and regional newspaper groups offer a small number of traineeships but competition for these is extremely fierce, so prior experience is essential to even be considered. Try working for student publications and use your holidays to arrange work experience placements or work-shadowing possibilities. These can be in other forms of media such as radio and television.

ROUTES TO QUALIFICATION

Gone are the days when you could become a hack by starting off as a tea boy and working your way to the top. Most newspaper journalists now have degrees and many also take a postgraduate qualification in journalism. Some newspapers offer places on graduate training schemes, in which you will spend two years learning on the job.

PROSPECTS

The most common career route is to start as a general reporter on a local or regional newspaper and then move your way up the career ladder to specialise in a certain area. Other journalists may leave the regional press and start in a more junior job with the nationals. Another alternative would be to join a news desk or to work in production.

FURTHER INFORMATION

- National Council for the Training of Journalists (NCTJ) **www.nctj.com**

Photographer

WHAT DO THEY DO?

Photographers take pictures of people, objects and places in order to capture their essence or to convey a particular message through the image. The work varies from portraits of individuals and groups, to capturing the horror of war or photographing an aesthetically pleasing plate of food. However, it is rare for a photographer to be a jack of all trades – he or she will almost always specialise in a particular area such as fine art, fashion or advertising.

Many photographers are self-employed, although some work for such different employers as media companies, publishers and in education. Typical tasks include:

- liaising with clients about what they want from the photos
- researching sites for photoshoots in advance
- using a wide variety of technical equipment, such as lenses, cameras and computers
- advising human subjects on how to pose
- arranging still-life objects according to a brief.

Many graduates start out as a photographer's assistant, which tends to involve doing much of the photographer's admin work.

WHERE DO THEY WORK?

Photographers work in many different settings – from an office in a workplace or at home to attending shoots in studios or even outside... and in all weathers! Hours can be very long on projects and you may experience the two opposite states of being too busy one moment and twiddling your thumbs the next. During quiet periods, it is essential to keep motivated to look for work and network with any contacts you have made.

Working conditions themselves can be uncomfortable (a photoshoot in the snow, for instance) and even downright dangerous (for example, taking photos in a war zone). Most work can be found in London but there are opportunities throughout the UK, depending on your specialism.

WHAT SKILLS DO THEY NEED?

To be a top photographer, you need to be able to work as part of a team, as well as on your own. You will also need to be:

- **personable** – to get on with a wide range of people
- **dedicated** – to keep looking for jobs
- **technically minded** – the digital world has reached photography now and image manipulation is popular.

To stand a chance of getting regular, well-paid work you will need a portfolio to show potential employers and clients. Websites are proving a popular marketing tool these days too. To gain experience and build your portfolio, join any photographic societies and take your own pictures as often as possible. Read relevant magazines and check out the displays at local and national galleries. Work experience with a photographer can be both an insight into the industry and a way to get a foot in the door.

ROUTES TO QUALIFICATION

Graduates of any degree discipline can work in photography if they have the talent. However, art and design, digital imaging, graphics, media studies and photography can all help. Postgraduate courses are not essential but in specialist fields such as fashion and advertising it can be advantageous to do a further qualification in a relevant area of photography.

PROSPECTS

Some will decide to start their photographic career by building valuable experience working as a photographic assistant or in a photographic picture library. There are a relatively small number of opportunities for photographers to work for an employer, including as a staff photographer on a newspaper or in highly specialised capacities such as a museum or medical photographer.

Most photographers are self-employed. The decision then is whether to specialise and build up your reputation in a particular niche – for example, portraits, fashion or reportage – or whether to be more flexible and generalist. Keeping up-to-date with the latest equipment and technology is vital.

FURTHER INFORMATION

- British Institute of Professional Photography (BIPP) **www.bipp.com**
- The Association of Photographers (AOP) **www.the-aop.org**
- The British Press Photographers' Association (BPPA) **www.thebppa.com**

Presenter – radio and television

WHAT DO THEY DO?

Presenters of radio and television are the voices and faces of news, current affairs and popular culture. Radio presenters will host their own shows, which may have a theme (Eddie Mair's news programme on BBC Radio 4, for example), or will play music according to what their listeners will like, such as Radio 1's breakfast show with Chris Moyles. Television presenters normally work on shorter programmes and will specialise in a very particular field. Areas include news programmes, chat shows, children's entertainment, game shows and consumer programmes.

Presenters don't just start work when the cameras roll, or the microphone is turned on, however. A good deal of preparation goes on behind the scenes for several hours before the programme begins, with presenters rehearsing what they are going to say and often writing a script to follow. After their programme there may be meetings to plan for the next show, too.

WHERE DO THEY WORK?

Radio presenters work in studios within radio stations, although occasionally they may do outside broadcasts from live events. The same applies to television presenters, who will work in television studios, sometimes in front of a live studio audience.

Hours can be long and unsocial, particularly if you are doing early morning or late night shows. Both the radio and television operate throughout the night and during weekends and holidays, so chances are you will be working at some periods when your friends and family are at home.

WHAT SKILLS DO THEY NEED?

Presenting is often viewed as a glamorous career and therefore competition for places can be hard. Normally the following skills and attributes are required:

- a smart appearance (for television)
- a pleasant speaking voice (for TV and radio)
- good interpersonal skills to deal with audience members and interviewees
- determination to get this far in the first place
- an unflappable nature – television and radio are often live and mistakes or problems happen. You need to be able to deal with issues as and when they arise and cope with the director shouting into your earpiece.

To stand a chance of a career in this area, get as much experience as possible while you're studying. Write to major broadcasters and local radio stations and ask for work experience or work-shadowing opportunities. Try to build up a good network of contacts to whom you can turn when you start your job search. A stint working on local or hospital radio can be invaluable and will give you the opportunity of recording your show to play to potential employers. Drama experience is helpful for teaching you how to present, so join a student theatre company or go on a short course if you can.

ROUTES TO QUALIFICATION

While there is no definitive route to becoming a presenter, most do have degrees. Subject matter is normally not important but a media or performing arts degree may give a small advantage. What's more important is enthusiasm for the area plus relevant experience and good contacts.

Most presenters start out as journalists or researchers, while some have had previous experience in another field of the arts such as acting or music. Some may be experts in the area in which they present, such as sports, politics or the arts.

PROSPECTS

There is no structured career path for radio and TV presenters. Looking for voluntary opportunities can be a useful way of building up experience and showing your commitment (for example, working for a hospital or local community radio station). New presenters often start on the least popular slots – the early morning or late evening ones. Career development may then be a case of working their way to prime time slots once they establish a reputation. However, it is a very competitive industry that is under pressure due to the current economic climate, so achieving success will require a great deal of determination, the ability to spot opportunities and a gift for networking.

FURTHER INFORMATION

- Broadcasting Entertainment Cinematograph and Theatre Union (BECTU) **www.bectu.org.uk**
- Broadcast Journalism Training Council **www.bjtc.org.uk**
- National Council for the Training of Journalists (NCTJ) **www.nctj.com**
- Skillset (The Sector Skills Council for Creative Media) **www.skillset.org**

Producer – radio

WHAT DO THEY DO?

Radio producers are the people behind the scenes who provide the ideas and content for the broadcasts that presenters give on the radio and internet. They also manage the audience response to these programmes and work with presenters, DJs and sound engineers. Sometimes they may find themselves covering other roles in presenting and reporting.

WHERE DO THEY WORK?

Broadcasting roughly falls into three main areas: public radio, commercial radio and voluntary radio, and opportunities for producers exist in each. Studio-based work is the norm but producers often go out on location to interview people, research a programme and cover live events. Hours can be long, unsocial and unpredictable and travel away from home is not uncommon.

Half of the people working in radio are based in London but that also means that half the opportunities are in other areas. Local, regional and voluntary radio exists in cities throughout the UK although you may have to relocate to a larger place to get the bigger jobs.

WHAT SKILLS DO THEY NEED?

Radio producers need many skills, which include the following:

- self-confidence
- strong written and spoken communication skills
- organisation
- the ability to cope under pressure and work to tight deadlines
- curiosity and an eye for a good feature
- teamwork and the ability to work independently
- a talkative and lively nature
- a willingness to use different forms of technology.

ROUTES TO QUALIFICATION

Any graduate can have a career in this area but broadcast journalism and journalism graduates may have a slight edge. You could always opt for a postgraduate diploma or MA in radio production but don't forget that experience and excellent skills matter more than a piece of paper. Training takes place on the job in all aspects of radio production, from technical aspects to presenting and editing.

PROSPECTS

Progression is possible in this field but it must be driven by you. Since many producers work on a freelance basis, they will often move from one job to another and undertake short-term projects, although long-term opportunities are available. To find out about these you will need to set up a good network of contacts as jobs are rarely advertised. You will probably also end up specialising in a particular field such as news, culture or sport.

FURTHER INFORMATION

- Skillset (The Sector Skills Council for Creative Media) **www.skillset.org**
- Broadcast Journalism Training Council **www.bjtc.org.uk**

Producer
– television/film

WHAT DO THEY DO?

Producers are the head honchos in television, film and video. They will often come up with the idea for a project and they will see it through from conception until distribution. This will involve working with directors, other production staff and sometimes actors to get the job done, and it is becoming more and more common for producers to offer directing skills too. Fundraising to finance a project is also an important task, as is ensuring that a film doesn't stray too much from its proposed budget.

The difference between a producer and a director is mainly that producers deal with the practical aspects of a project, while a director is more focused on the artistic and interpretative side.

WHERE DO THEY WORK?

Working environments are incredibly varied, with producers being based in offices, studios and on location – often all in the same day! Hours are irregular and long and will involve weekend, evening and early morning work. Most of the jobs are in London but there are large production companies based in regional cities such as Birmingham, Manchester, Cardiff, Edinburgh and Glasgow. Working away from home is common. There are good opportunities for those who want to work on a freelance or self-employed basis but this does entail low job security.

WHAT SKILLS DO THEY NEED?

This is not an entry-level job: it requires a good deal of experience within the relevant industry, perhaps as an assistant producer, a researcher or a scriptwriter. Knowledge of programme- or film-making techniques is essential, as are directing and editing skills. The following are also vital:

- self-confidence
- excellent communication skills
- management skills
- creativity
- time-management skills
- leadership ability
- networking skills – jobs are rarely advertised and mostly gained from word of mouth
- stamina to cope with often long spells of stressful and intense working.

Be prepared for fierce competition and don't underestimate the importance of building up your own network of contacts. Try to gain much-valued experience by contacting production companies and asking to spend some time observing what goes on. Keep track of what's happening in the industry and look out for jobs as a runner in the first instance. Join any student film or theatre societies and if possible make a reel of the work you have contributed to as evidence of your capabilities.

ROUTES TO QUALIFICATION

Careers in this field are not subject-dependent but subjects focusing on media studies, photography, film, IT, multimedia and broadcasting can confer a certain advantage because they normally teach practical skills in production. If you opt for a degree in a non-related field, consider a postgraduate qualification to boost your chances and improve your skills. However, most of the training is on the job.

PROSPECTS

Most programme-makers and producers in television, film and video are self-employed and work on short-term contracts, whose length will depend on the project at hand. It is possible to move between film, video and television as the skills are often transferable. Some producers will start their own production company once they have built a good reputation and made enough contacts.

FURTHER INFORMATION

- Skillset (The Sector Skills Council for Creative Media) **www.skillset.org**

Theatre director

WHAT DO THEY DO?

Theatre directors interpret scripts for plays or musical scores in order to bring them to life on the stage. They do this by working closely with their creative and production teams and, to a certain extent, are dictated to by their budget. Most work on a freelance basis or on fixed-term contracts, although some are employed as 'resident' directors in some repertory companies.

Large theatre companies decide in advance which plays they wish to put on and then consider which directors they would like to use to do this. In smaller companies, the theatre director will do this in addition to his or her creative job. It is normal to start out as an assistant director or as an actor, writer, designer, stage manager or producer.

WHERE DO THEY WORK?

Directors work in theatres, predominantly, unless they are putting on performances in other places such as outdoor theatres or other theatrical settings. Working hours are unsocial by nature as performances occur when people are out of work and school and able to attend. It is not unusual for directors to put in more hours than they have been contracted to do, from rehearsals right through to the first performance. Typical contracts can last from one to three years. You need to be flexible about where you're willing to work as travel is common, both within the UK and abroad.

WHAT SKILLS DO THEY NEED?

Directors need the following skills to succeed:

- creativity
- artistic vision, to bring a play from page to stage
- teamwork
- time-management skills
- tact and diplomacy (many actors have fragile egos)
- an understanding of the technical aspects of stage performance
- research skills
- interpersonal skills
- practical acting and stage management experience.

Experience is vital so take any opportunity to become involved in the theatre, from amateur dramatic groups to student societies. Try to gain some work experience at your local theatre, or why not aim for a visit to one of the nationals? See as many productions as possible and make notes about aspects of the performances that you enjoyed or ways you could do things differently. By working behind the scenes at a theatre you will be in a good position to understand how a theatre runs and the many different aspects a director needs to take into account.

ROUTES TO QUALIFICATION

Any graduate can work within this field but the following degrees might help your prospects:

- drama/theatre studies
- music
- creative/performing arts
- English
- languages.

You don't need to have a postgraduate qualification under your belt if you have a relevant degree or practical experience. If you do decide to go for a postgraduate qualification, make sure that the course you choose places an emphasis on practical skills.

PROSPECTS

It is not uncommon for directors to start their careers by setting up their own small theatre company, or by directing a production for a touring company. To apply for senior roles with established theatre companies a director would need several years' experience. A good head for business is also essential, as it's often necessary to apply for funding as well as make sure productions bring in enough money to assure the future of the organisation one is working for. An experienced director could start a new company or work as a director in an already established company, overseeing the annual cycle of productions. With enough experience, another option would be to move into directing in television or film.

FURTHER INFORMATION

- The Independent Theatre Council **www.itc-arts.org**
- Theatrical Management Association (TMA) **www.tmauk.org**

TARGETjobs.co.uk

The UK's leading graduate jobsite.

At targetjobs.co.uk you will find everything you need to get your career off to a flying start including;

- Thousands of jobs, internships and placements
- Advice on how to get into every major industry sector
- Unique employer insights and bespoke career planning tools

The career for you?

ProgressionSeries

Is journalism, media and performing arts for you?

Building a successful career in journalism, media and performing arts requires more than the ability to act, sing, dance, write or produce. It also requires certain skills and personal qualities or 'attributes'. To help you decide if a career in journalism, media and performing arts is for you, we suggest you think about the following three areas:

- what **you** want from your future work
- what a journalism, media and performing arts course typically involves
- which skills and qualities admissions tutors in this field typically seek in new recruits.

WHAT DO YOU WANT IN YOUR FUTURE WORK?

You may not have an instant answer for this, but your current studies, work experience and even your hobbies can help give you clues about the kind of work you enjoy and the skills you have already started to develop. Start with a blank sheet of paper and note down the answers to the questions opposite to help get you thinking. Be as brutally honest with yourself as you can – don't write what you think will impress your teachers or parents. Write what really matters to you, and you'll start to see a pattern emerge.

ANSWERING THESE QUESTIONS MAY HELP YOU TO CHOOSE YOUR CAREER

- When you think of your future, in what kind of environment do you see yourself working? For example in an office, outdoors, nine-to-five, relaxed or high-pressured?
- What are your favourite hobbies outside school?
- What is it about them you enjoy? For example working with people, figuring out how things work?
- What are your favourite subjects in school and what is it about them that you enjoy most? For example being able to create something new, or working with people?
- What do you dislike about the other subjects you're studying? ('The teacher' doesn't count!)
- Which aspects of your work experience have you most enjoyed?

WHAT DO JOURNALISM, MEDIA AND PERFORMING ARTS COURSES INVOLVE?

Not surprisingly, the skills you'll require for a successful career in journalism, performing arts or media will also be required at various stages of your studies. Therefore, it is important to know what journalism, media and performing arts courses entail before you apply to be sure it's the kind of work you will enjoy. For example, one common misconception about media and performing arts courses is that they are purely practically based. While it's true that most courses include some practical tasks and assessments, you'll have to study the theoretical and historical side of media and performing arts – precisely how much will depend on the individual course syllabus.

WHAT SKILLS WILL YOU NEED?

Despite the many differences in journalism, media and performing arts sectors, the underpinning skillset they all require is broadly the same: talent, which employers will mostly discern from your portfolio and other experience. Beyond this, the following are the other key skills required of any potential journalism, media and performing arts student.

- **Creativity** – not just the artistic skill, but the capacity to use it to produce new perspectives or new productions.
- **Capacity for sustained effort** – working in this sector involves not just creating, but the patience and perseverance to rework and change your work, not once, but often many times, until you or your client are happy with the finished product.
- **A thick skin and a self-critical attitude** – in this field, your work – your *self* – will be on display, not just to your peers and tutors but also to the wider public and eventually the wider community. Therefore it is important from the outset that you learn to turn even the sharpest of criticisms into constructive feedback that you can use to improve your work.

- **Perseverance** – many, if not most, of the people working in this sector do so on a freelance basis. That means a lot of people compete for the same job, the same contract, the same writing slot. As any writer, editor, actor, dancer or musician will tell you, rejection is far too common for their liking! However, rather than sitting and brooding on it, you need to keep trying to find work and not become downhearted or dejected.

In addition to these general skills shared and sought by all fields in journalism, media and performing arts, admissions tutors will also look for sector-specific skills related to their field. For example:

- would-be **musicians** will need to have excellent performance skills and be able to sight-read
- if you're planning on making a career as a **dancer**, you must have a high level of personal fitness and plenty of years' experience behind you – most dancers have been studying since they were tiny tots
- **writers** must be brimming with ideas and have excellent literary knowledge
- potential **directors** must also be keen actors and have bold creative visions that they are not scared of sharing with an audience.

Alternative careers

If you're looking for something a little less mainstream, a journalism, media and performing arts qualification can open the door to some alternative career paths.

MUSIC THERAPIST

Music therapists are allied health professionals who typically work as part of a therapeutic team headed by a psychiatrist. They are usually employed in health authorities, hospitals, schools, prisons and mental health centres. Their aim is to help in treatment by encouraging self-expression through music. To qualify, you typically need to take a postgraduate diploma. In addition to the formal qualifications, you'll also need great emotional sensitivity for this work, which is conducted on a one-to-one or small group basis over long periods of time.

Further information
British Society for Music Therapy **www.bsmt.org**

TEACHER

As a teacher, you can influence future generations of actors, musicians, writers, and so on. It is usually preferable to have some experience of your own to draw upon, and many teachers in this area combine teaching with performance or writing. As a teacher, you will work with students to interpret plays, novels and music, as well as helping them to come up with their own creations, stage their own performances or find outlets for their writings. All state sector schools require a postgraduate qualification in teaching, which can be done either as a one-year, full-time course or as on-the-job training. Private schools do not ask for this qualification although increasingly they prefer candidates who offer it. University lecturers will normally have a relevant postgraduate qualification plus experience in their field.

Further information
Training and Development Agency for Schools
www.tda.gov.uk

Professional bodies

Professional bodies are responsible for overseeing a particular profession or career area, ensuring that people who work in the area are fully trained and meet ethical guidelines. Professional bodies may be known as institutions, societies and associations. They generally have regulatory roles: they make sure that members of the profession are able to work successfully in their jobs without endangering lives or abusing their position.

Professional bodies are often involved in training and career development, so courses and workplace training may have to follow the body's guidelines. In order to be fully qualified and licensed to work in your profession of choice, you will have to follow the professional training route. In many areas of work, completion of the professional training results in gaining chartered status – and the addition of some extra letters after your name. Other institutions may award other types of certification once certain criteria have been met. Chartered or certified members will usually need to take further courses and training to ensure their skills are kept up-to-date.

WHAT PROFESSIONAL BODIES ARE THERE?

Not all career areas have professional bodies. Those jobs that require extensive learning and training are likely to have bodies with a regulatory focus. This includes careers such as engineering, law, construction, health and finance. If you want to work in one of these areas, it's important to make sure your degree course is accredited by the professional body – otherwise you may have to undertake further study or training later on.

Other bodies may play more of a supportive role, looking after the interests of people who work in the sector. This includes journalism, management and arts-based careers. Professional bodies may also be learned bodies, providing opportunities for further learning and promoting the development of knowledge in the field.

CAN I JOIN AS A STUDENT?

Many professional bodies offer student membership – sometimes free or for reduced fees. Membership can be extremely valuable as a source of advice, information and resources. You'll have the opportunity to meet other students in the field, as well as experienced professionals. It will also look good on your CV, when you come to apply for jobs.

See below for a list of professional bodies and other useful organisations in the fields of journalism, media and performing arts.

ALL SECTORS

Arts Council England
www.artscouncil.org.uk

Arts Council of Northern Ireland
www.artscouncil-ni.org

Arts Council of Wales
www.artswales.org.uk

Creative Scotland
www.creativescotland.com

Skillset (The Sector Skills Council for Creative Media)
www.skillset.org

PUBLISHING

National Council for the Training of Journalists (NCTJ)
www.nctj.com

Periodical Publishers Association (PPA)
www.ppa.co.uk

Society for Editors and Proofreaders (SfEP)
www.sfep.org.uk

Society of Young Publishers
www.thesyp.org.uk

JOURNALISM

Chartered Institute of Journalists
http://cioj.co.uk

Broadcast Journalism Training Council (BJTC)
www.bjtc.org.uk

National Council for the Training of Journalists (NCTJ)
www.nctj.com

National Union of Journalists (NUJ)
www.nuj.org.uk

CREATIVE WRITING

The Society of Authors
www.societyofauthors.org

The Writers' Guild of Great Britain
www.writersguild.org.uk

BROADCASTING, FILM AND VIDEO

Broadcasting Entertainment Cinematographic and Theatre Union (BECTU)
www.bectu.org.uk

Directors Guild of Great Britain
www.dggb.org

Stage Management Association
www.stagemanagementassociation.co.uk

Student Radio Association
www.studentradio.org.uk

THEATRE

Broadcasting Entertainment Cinematographic and Theatre Union (BECTU)
www.bectu.org.uk

Directors Guild of Great Britain
www.dggb.org

Equity - The British Actors Union
www.equity.org.uk

National Council for Drama Training
www.ncdt.co.uk

The Society of British Theatre Designers
www.theatredesign.org.uk

PERFORMANCE

Arts & Humanities Research Council (AHRC)
www.ahrc.ac.uk

Associated Board of the Royal Schools of Music (ABRSM)
www.abrsm.org

Association of British Choral Directors
www.abcd.org.uk

Association of British Orchestras
www.abo.org.uk

The British Association of Teachers of Dancing
www.batd.co.uk

British Dance Council
www.british-dance-council.org

Council for Dance Education & Training (CDET)
www.cdet.org.uk

Dance UK
www.danceuk.org

Equity - The British Actors Union
www.equity.org.uk

Incorporated Society of Musicians
www.ism.org

Musicians' Union
www.musiciansunion.org.uk

National Association of Youth Theatres (NAYT)
www.nayt.org.uk

National Council for Drama Training
www.ncdt.co.uk

National Dance Teachers' Association
www.ndta.org.uk

Graduate destinations

Journalism, media and performing arts
HESA Destination of Leavers of Higher Education Survey

Each year, comprehensive statistics are collected on what graduates are doing six months after they complete their course. The survey is co-ordinated by the Higher Education Statistics Agency (HESA) and provides information about how many graduates move into employment (and what type of career) or further study and how many are believed to be unemployed.

The full results across all subject areas are published by the Higher Education Careers Service Unit (HECSU) and the Association of Graduate Careers Advisory Services (AGCAS) in *What Do Graduates Do?*, which is available from **www.ucasbooks.com**.

	Journalism, media & performing arts
In UK employment	60.1%
In overseas employment	1.6%
Working and studying	5.9%
Studying in the UK for a higher degree	6.4%
Studying in the UK for a teaching qualification	2.9%
Undertaking other further study or training in the UK	3.2%
Studying overseas	0.2%
Not available for employment, study or training	3.4%
Assumed to be unemployed	11.2%
Other	5.0%

> THE CAREER FOR YOU?

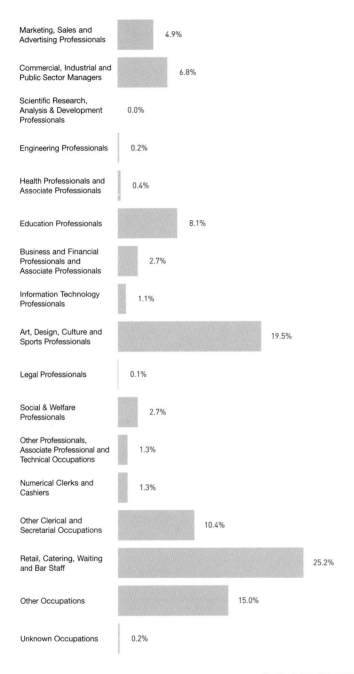

Occupation	Percentage
Marketing, Sales and Advertising Professionals	4.9%
Commercial, Industrial and Public Sector Managers	6.8%
Scientific Research, Analysis & Development Professionals	0.0%
Engineering Professionals	0.2%
Health Professionals and Associate Professionals	0.4%
Education Professionals	8.1%
Business and Financial Professionals and Associate Professionals	2.7%
Information Technology Professionals	1.1%
Art, Design, Culture and Sports Professionals	19.5%
Legal Professionals	0.1%
Social & Welfare Professionals	2.7%
Other Professionals, Associate Professional and Technical Occupations	1.3%
Numerical Clerks and Cashiers	1.3%
Other Clerical and Secretarial Occupations	10.4%
Retail, Catering, Waiting and Bar Staff	25.2%
Other Occupations	15.0%
Unknown Occupations	0.2%

Reproduced with the kind permission of HECSU/AGCAS, *What Do Graduates Do? 2010*.
Data from the HESA Destinations of Leavers from Higher Education Survey 08/09

Case studies

Just what can you do with a journalism, media and performing arts degree? The following graduate profiles show you the wealth of exciting careers awaiting you!

Reporter

Jane's Police Review

HOLLIE CLEMENCE

Route into journalism:
A levels - English, history, drama, art (2004); BA English literature and cultural criticism, Cardiff University (2007); MA magazine journalism, City University, London (2010)

WHY JOURNALISM?

I have always loved writing and talking to people so a job where I get to do both every day is perfect for me. Working in news journalism can also be really exciting when you get to bring new information to light, or report on something that everyone in the country is talking about.

HOW DID YOU GET WHERE YOU ARE TODAY?

As an undergraduate I wrote for the university newspaper and did work experience at local newspapers. The more experience I had, the more I was certain that journalism was the career for me.

After university I went straight into an internship at a specialist magazine publishers and ended up staying there for over a year as an editorial assistant. This was a great first job as I received training in proofreading, sub-editing, feature writing and writing for the web, which all comes in useful as a journalist.

In September 2008 I left to go travelling. I desperately wanted to go abroad but I also wanted to get more work experience in journalism – so I decided to combine the two. I worked on a lifestyle magazine in Shanghai, stayed in a village in Thailand teaching children and building a community centre, and spent three months in Ghana working on their national newspaper and for a local radio station. It was an amazing chance to write news and features, as well as reading the international news on breakfast and lunchtime radio in Ghana. I freelanced on an entertainment magazine, interviewing TV celebrities on set and going to shows in the evenings.

When I returned I began my master's in London, which was really hard work – but it was worth every minute (and every penny!). As part of the course we had to do seven weeks of work experience. Through this, I ended up with two job interviews and secured a job as a reporter on *Police Review*.

WHAT DOES YOUR JOB INVOLVE?

Police Review is an independent weekly magazine aimed at police officers, covering anything from grassroots stories about bobbies on the beat, to nationwide investigations and policy changes within the police service.

I help the editorial team fill the pages with news and features. A lot of our interviews are done over the phone, but we also travel to meet officers from different police forces or go along to meetings and press conferences. I work in quite a small team but we do get to speak to different people all day every day, from frontline police constables to chiefs and politicians. Features I have written range from meeting the police officers responsible for the Papal visit; visiting a gypsy site to interview a special police team who work with gypsies and travellers; and writing a case study on how detectives caught the murderer of an elderly couple in Devon.

WHAT HAS BEEN YOUR BIGGEST CHALLENGE?

Learning shorthand was pretty tough – like learning a new language. It got a bit easier once I figured out that transcribing my favourite television programmes was good practice!

WHAT DO YOU LIKE MOST ABOUT YOUR JOB?

The best feeling of each week is just after the magazine goes to press, when you finally appreciate the excitement of getting all your news in and the rush of the deadline. Overall, going out to meet people and getting an insight into how the country is kept in order – particularly when it is something everyone is talking about, such as the student protests or a high profile murder case.

HOLLIE'S TOP TIPS

If you are keen to get into journalism read as much news as you possibly can – from many different sources.

Production editor

Oxford University Press

EMMA HAWES

Route into publishing:
A levels – English, art, psychology (2005); BA publishing with communication, media and culture,
Oxford Brookes University (2009)

WHY PUBLISHING?

I've always been interested in books and magazines, so a degree in communication, media, and culture was a natural choice for me. In my first year I had the opportunity to study some modules on publishing. I enjoyed these so much that I ended up changing my degree to majoring in publishing, with a minor in communication, media, and culture. By the end of the course I was keen to develop a career within the publishing industry.

HOW DID YOU GET WHERE YOU ARE TODAY?

During my degree I learnt a lot about the publishing industry and was also given the chance to apply this knowledge through practical assignments. I designed a magazine, developed a new idea for a book series, produced a production schedule and analysed a marketing campaign.

In my second year, encouraged by my tutor, I took a module in publishing production. I began to apply for work experience at publishing companies and secured three weeks' unpaid work experience at Oxford University Press. I really enjoyed my time and this spurred me on to apply for production roles. Two months before the end of my degree I started job hunting. It was a lot of additional work, during what was already a stressful time. But it definitely paid off, as I started in my current job one week after graduation.

WHAT DOES YOUR JOB INVOLVE?

Oxford University Press publishes academic and educational material to further the work of the University of Oxford. I am a production editor in the law section, and my responsibility is to ensure that a manuscript is turned into a book, to schedule and to budget.

On a daily basis, I organise the copy-editing, proofreading, indexing, typesetting and printing of books on my law list. A lot of my time can also be spent problem solving and dealing with issues as they arise during the production process. I am the main point of contact for in-house colleagues, external freelancers, suppliers and authors, while the book is in production.

WHAT HAS BEEN YOUR BIGGEST CHALLENGE?

There is quite a lot to learn in terms of processes and systems. However, my publishing degree and work experience has allowed me to come into this job with a really good knowledge of the industry and to pick things up more quickly. On a day-to-day basis, there is always a lot to do so I need to manage my time effectively.

WHAT DO YOU LIKE MOST ABOUT YOUR JOB?

Working with many different people, both in-house and externally, in the UK and abroad, is one of the highlights of my job. It is also very rewarding to see the printed book at the end of the process, knowing six months earlier it was just a series of electronic files.

EMMA'S TOP TIPS

Get as much work experience as you can: it looks really good on your CV, it allows you to gain knowledge of the industry and you can also try out jobs before you commit to a career. Also, make use of your tutors! They are happy to help you out and they want you to succeed; they have often worked in the industry, so their knowledge is invaluable.

Final-year media production studies student

Liverpool John Moores University

MARK WRIGHT

Route into media production:
A levels – English language, economics, geography, general studies (2007); BA media professional studies with television, Liverpool John Moores University (current)

WHY MEDIA PRODUCTION?

In my final year at school I was assistant producer on my school's adaptation of the *X Factor* and loved it. During my gap year I worked as an extra at Lime Pictures, an independent media production company. The experience of being on set and witnessing the production process confirmed what I knew already – that media production was what I wanted to do.

HOW DID YOU GET WHERE YOU ARE TODAY?

Before I started my degree I had very little experience of the media industry, so I made a conscious effort to try as many different roles in university production assignments as possible. This helped me to decide on pursuing a career in camerawork.

My course involved outside projects, where I was involved in filming live band footage for a local music promotions company and a 10 minute documentary for Glyndwr University students.

Recently, I have secured work as a freelance camera assistant at Lime Pictures. I also run my own music entertainment business and work part-time for a music entertainment agency.

WHAT DID YOUR PLACEMENT INVOLVE?

Lime Pictures is a large, independent media production company, best known for its production of the Channel 4 soap opera *Hollyoaks*. My role, as camera assistant, was to ensure that all equipment was set up and working properly on set.

Each morning we collected the camera equipment and took it to the shoot location to begin rigging. After each shot was filmed my job was to reposition the camera, tripods and camera boxes for the next shot. I also had to set up production cables, lay camera track, change and clean camera lenses and filters, and set up and position external monitors. I also did some chasing around, retrieving equipment that was needed. After the final shot of the day we de-rigged the equipment and stored it away or took it to the location for the next day's shoot.

Normal working hours at Lime Pictures were 8am to 7pm, but I also worked on a number of evening shoots, some of which ran from 6pm to 6am! I spent most of my time on set with a small camera crew, a director of photography, a camera operator and another camera assistant.

WHAT HAS BEEN YOUR BIGGEST CHALLENGE?

Working under time constraints. Though you may have all of the skills necessary for your role, the realisation that you have to complete them in the shortest time possible adds a huge amount of pressure!

WHAT DID YOU LIKE MOST ABOUT YOUR PLACEMENT?

I really enjoyed both acquiring new skills and developing existing ones under the guidance of a highly qualified shoot crew. I was also fortunate to learn 'gripping' skills: laying camera track and manoeuvring camera dollies, as well as standard camera assistant duties. The placement resulted in my current freelance work as a camera assistant.

MARK'S TOP TIPS

Be enthusiastic and assertive – production environments can be very busy places and you can easily get lost in the crowd. Use your colleagues' knowledge to your advantage: don't be afraid to ask those more experienced than you how to perform tasks correctly. Be organised – you then stand a better chance of coping with the pressure of time constraints. Lastly, understand the importance of teamwork: individuality will only get you so far in the media industry!

Commercial programmer

Global Radio

ABBIE CUNLIFFE

Route into radio:

A levels – drama, art and English literature (1998); BA drama, theatre and TV studies, University of Winchester (2001); MA radio production, Bournemouth University (2005)

WHY RADIO?

My degree involved community work projects, using theatre and TV, and from these I became interested in how media affects people. I took an active part in the university radio station, including becoming a DJ.

After my degree I did an eight-week radio training course with an organisation called Earshot, based in the 107.6 Juice FM building, my local radio station in Brighton. I loved the way that, through words and storytelling, radio could transport you to another world, and was excited by how it was starting to develop digitally and interactively.

HOW DID YOU GET WHERE YOU ARE TODAY?

My MA in radio production was focused on getting employment in radio and included forums with visiting professionals. We were able to question them about their jobs and were encouraged to keep them as contacts. The course included a four-week work placement at talkSport, where I was asked to stay on, firstly as a volunteer and then I was offered paid work as an assistant producer. I followed this by working at WRN (World Radio Network) as a product development manager, where I set up the podcasting service and experienced my first taste of working for commercial clients. I then worked for GCap, which became Global Radio.

WHAT DOES YOUR JOB INVOLVE?

I am a commercial programmer - a middleman between commercial output and programming output. My role is to ensure the client's message is conveyed to the audience and the commercial content is engaging for the listener. I manage campaigns that involve competitions, giveaways and promotional events. I plan campaigns and manage on-air activity, such as briefing the production team.

The hours can be long, especially just before we launch a campaign, and there is occasional weekend and evening work. I am based at the Global Radio head office in Leicester Square and sometimes get to travel; we recently took 200 listeners to Disneyland Paris. I work with many different people including producers, presenters and the production team and commercial teams, including sales directors and account managers.

WHAT HAS BEEN YOUR BIGGEST CHALLENGE?

My current project: the Heart Breakfast & McCain Family of the Month campaign! This is a five-month project running across all 17 Heart radio stations. It involves recruiting families to take part in exciting activities such as learning to dance with Arlene Phillips at Pineapple Studios, or becoming safari rangers for the day. I am in charge of the day-to-day running of the campaign, making sure that everything comes together successfully. It is a challenge to manage a campaign of this scale, making sure everything runs smoothly and ensuring the radio output is engaging to listen to.

WHAT DO YOU LIKE MOST ABOUT YOUR JOB?

The interesting and inspiring people I meet, and the fact that I am always learning something new. Turning on the radio and hearing my campaign is totally rewarding – and makes me smile!

ABBIE'S TOP TIPS

You've got to be motivated and persistent to find a job in radio; I was sending out 15 to 20 applications a day at one stage. Get work experience, even if unpaid, at your local radio station as this may lead to paid work. And most importantly, stay positive: it goes a long way!

Freelance photographer

MARTIN SCOTT POWELL

Route into photography:
Standard grades – seven subjects including art; BA photography, film and imaging, Napier University (2008)

WHY PHOTOGRAPHY?

When I turned 21 I asked for an SLR camera for my birthday; I was planning to travel around the world the following year and wanted to have a decent camera to capture my journey. At the time I had no inclination of turning professional, but knew that I was interested in much more than the occasional snapshot. During my trip I was fascinated by the way in which the camera helped and developed how I engaged with people and places. From this experience I knew it was something I was interested in studying further.

HOW DID YOU GET WHERE YOU ARE TODAY?

I left school at 17 and trained and worked as a jewellery designer and goldsmith, before leaving to embark on my world trip. A year later, and full of enthusiasm for photography, I got a place on the photography, film and imaging degree at Napier University.

In my second year I specialised in photography and focused on narrative-driven imagery: becoming interested in how viewers engage with the photographic image. For a short while I flirted with the idea of switching to film, but decided that continuing to study the photographic image would give me a solid understanding that could possibly lead to a career in either field.

When I graduated I worked as a photographer's assistant for six months and then moved to New York. I have assisted some amazing photographers and now I am beginning to build up my own client base in Manhattan. As a photographer it was always a dream to live and work in New York and it really lives up to every expectation.

WHAT DOES YOUR JOB INVOLVE?

I am a freelance fashion, portrait and fine art photographer. On a daily basis I do anything from taking photographs and editing shoot images to retouching photos, updating portfolios, contacting clients and galleries, fishing for new work and organising upcoming photo shoots, including booking crew members and casting for models.

I try to keep regular hours if I'm working on portfolios or editing, but shoot days usually start much earlier. That said, I feel as though I'm working all the time; I always think about work! That's the bug of being self-employed.

I have a small studio space at home that I work from and the spaces we shoot in are usually rented. One of the great perks of the job is that you meet and work with so many talented people.

WHAT HAS BEEN YOUR BIGGEST CHALLENGE?

I can never say no to a job so the biggest challenges are new clients and taking on the unknown.

WHAT DO YOU LIKE MOST ABOUT YOUR JOB?

I love everything about being a photographer, even difficult clients and the butterflies before each shoot.

MARTIN'S TOP TIPS

Always believe in your ability to succeed, work hard, and never think that anything will just fall into your fingers. Go out and meet people that can help you progress and don't be afraid of making mistakes or asking people in the industry for help. Making a living from photography now is especially difficult and people will try to put you off. In my opinion, it's still one of the most exciting and creative careers possible and full of opportunity. You just have to be prepared to work hard for it.

Entry routes

Entry routes

UNDERGRADUATE COURSES

Unlike in many other professions, there is no single route that all students must follow to be successful in these career sectors – most degrees are acceptable, although relevant journalism, arts and media degrees can sometimes give an advantage. Some graduates will have done a degree in a relevant area, some will have done something entirely different while pursuing their artistic interests in their spare time, and others will have stopped studying altogether to try to join the workforce. That said, very few people go straight from school into journalism, media and performing arts careers nowadays, as most employers look for individuals who have gained nationally recognised qualifications alongside any relevant experience. Take a look at the 'Routes to qualification' information in each area of work (pages 19–49) to read about any specific subject requirements.

Don't let the vast range of courses on offer confuse you. Most courses on the same subject will follow a similar syllabus but institutions may vary in how they allocate time to each particular topic. On some courses, for example, students study subjects one after another, while others prefer to teach numerous aspects of the course simultaneously through projects that last several weeks. Most courses last for three years, full-time, with some institutions offering a four-year course if you combine journalism, media or performing arts with a language.

POSTGRADUATE COURSES

Most students will leave their studies after completing their undergraduate degree (or HND) to get their foot on the first rung of the journalism, media and performing arts career ladder. However, most of those who stay on to complete postgraduate studies do so for one of three main reasons.

- **To specialise in a particular field** – for example, an actor or director wishing to specialise in performance practice.
- **To stand out from the crowd** – a postgraduate qualification is one way to give yourself an edge over other applicants in particularly competitive fields, such as journalism.
- **To gain a teaching qualification** – for example, a Professional/Postgraduate Certificate in Education (PGCE) in drama, media, performing arts or related fields.

If you are considering a postgraduate degree, you can research and apply for a range of postgraduate courses at different higher education institutions at **www.ukpass.ac.uk**.

However, the possible advantage a postgraduate qualification may give you should be weighed against not only the additional cost, but also the additional time you will spend away from the job market.

Connect with us...

 www.facebook.com/ucasonline

 www.twitter.com/ucas_online

 www.youtube.com/ucasonline

What others say...

ProgressionSeries

What others say…

These are extracts from case studies in previous editions of this book. They give some insights into the experiences and thoughts of people who were once in the same position as you.

JESSICA LEE - TV SCRIPTWRITER

At school I'd always loved English and drama. I joined a youth theatre, took extra performing arts classes out of school hours and spent all my spare time doing what I loved. Even at youth theatre there were people writing plays and getting them onto the smaller theatres in Liverpool. It was a great inspiration.

I'm self-employed and work mostly, but not exclusively, for *Hollyoaks*. My job is to generate fresh, exciting stories, and to deliver scripts on time. I spend two days every three weeks at a story conference, where all 20 or so writers sit around the table with producers, editors, storyliners etc. Here we pitch stories and plan the main headlines of what will happen to each character for the next three weeks. After this, we will be assigned an episode to write and given about two weeks to do a first draft. The script goes through about three or four drafts before it is finally signed off.

Embrace criticism. If you want to be a writer you have to turn the negative into a positive on a daily basis. Not all writers have an agent but it helps: the *Writers' and Artists' Yearbook* lists them all and advises on how to approach one. Get a 'calling card' script to send out to anyone and everyone – a film, a one-off drama, anything that you're proud of and shows off your voice.

COLIN PARKER – CHIEF REPORTER

After leaving university I didn't have a clue what career to pursue. I decided to travel, and realised that no matter where I was I could always read a newspaper. I loved current affairs so decided to try journalism.

The life of a journalist is varied. One day I could be attending council meetings, the next day court, and the following day knocking on the door of a family whose son has just died in a car accident. Often it's putting up with the humdrum of village fayres, but we live for truly exciting stories that hit the newsroom.

AMANDA WHITING – FREELANCE MUSICIAN

My work is extremely varied. I usually spend a few hours each week giving harp lessons, both to adults and children. I am the harpist at a local hotel, and regularly play for up to 700 guests at mealtimes. My weekends are often taken up with performing at weddings and recitals, and I also play at corporate events. If I am playing for a concert, I prepare with several hours practice daily. I also play with a jazz trio once a month.

You have to be very business-minded if you are freelance. It's nice to think that you can just go and play, but at the end of the day you're running a business and you have to do your accounts and paperwork properly, and be very organised.

EMILY ROGERS - DESIGNER

During the first two years of my graphic communication degree I did a range of modules, from advertising to book design to typography. This allowed me to see where my strengths were and which areas I enjoyed the most. My final project, designing a new children's publication, confirmed that I wanted to go into children's publishing.

After graduating I focused on creating a great portfolio demonstrating my abilities in creating publications for children, and making sure my CV was the best it could be. I chose work samples to send to employers and looked into all the publishing companies in the area in the *Yellow Pages*, as well as regularly looking at job websites for vacancies with children's publishing.

CHRIS COX – PRODUCER AT RADIO 1

My drama, theatre, film and television degree was a very practical course. I worked for BBC Bristol throughout my degree, initially as a volunteer. By my final year I was taken on as a freelancer, working five nights a week.

When I graduated, I was offered a part-time job at BBC Radio 1 as a broadcast assistant. This was a fairly administrative role, but it was a great way of building up my experience. I have been lucky enough to work on some substantial shows, including nine months on the *Chris Moyles Show*: that was a big challenge.

Many people want to work in this sector and it is very competitive. Everyone has to start at the bottom, so it's worth getting involved as early as possible by doing work experience both at school and during your degree: you will then be in a much better position when you leave university. When doing work experience, try to do as many different things as you can to develop transferable media skills, always show enthusiasm and make yourself useful, so that they will be keen to have you back!

ANNA WRIGHT – ASSISTANT EDITOR

I wanted to work in a literary environment, and chose academic publishing specifically because I wanted to retain some connection with academia, intellectuals and cutting-edge ideas.

Try to get as much work experience as you can to get a taster of all aspects of the publishing process. Though a publishing degree or qualification is useful to some extent, it's not necessary if you're able to learn quickly and train as you go. Note that although the money isn't amazing, the job can be highly satisfying and you still have time to have a life outside of work.

ANGAHARAD HARROP – LECTURER IN DANCE

In my first year at university, studying for a degree in dance, I was given the opportunity to perform with a well established British improviser. This sparked my interest in improvisation as performance, which I pursued throughout my degree. We also had many guest lecturers and were given the opportunity to interview and take workshops with them. I became fascinated with choreographic processes, and started to research my own methods.

I enjoy creating new performances with all the different people I meet. Working with students is extremely rewarding as I can share my passion with them and see them develop their own. I enjoy the variety: one day I might be working on choreographing a rock-climbing piece and the next day I might be teaching parent and toddler classes.

DAVID HUTCHINSON – ACTOR AND DIRECTOR

While studying for a degree in acting I learned as many additional skills as I could, from singing and juggling, to directing and producing. While there were academic components, the course was very practical: from day one we were encouraged to be creative and make things happen. All this helped when it came to finding a way to put our skills to use in the real world.

Even though the theatre is a very competitive industry, there are no limits to what you can do if you have determination and flexibility. Being able to work successfully with people is key, as you are much stronger in a group than by yourself.

LISA HOGAN – PR AND MARKETING ADVISER

My degree in public relations required me to do placement modules in two PR settings, and I hated the agency placement I did in my second year. I started to wonder if PR was right for me, but decided to try an in-house role as soon as I could, and secured a two-week unpaid summer placement in the University of Sunderland's PR office. On finishing the placement I was offered a full-time paid job for the whole of the summer, so I did my third year placement there, and worked as a paid member of staff every Wednesday as well. If you want to work in PR, get experience of working in agency and in-house environments to help you decide the direction that is right for you.

SINEAD MCMILLAN – SELF-EMPLOYED MUSICIAN

I studied classical piano for two years before realising that I needed a broader creative experience in the music world. While I loved classical music I always knew I needed to be more experimental and create my own music, so I am now moving into electronic music.

Get as much work experience in the area of music that interests you, even if you're not being paid for it. It's a way of getting your foot in the door. It's also useful to take extra courses and make contact with like-minded people. If you're making your own music don't be afraid of sending it to as many important people as possible!

SION GRIFFITHS – FILM STUDIES PHD STUDENT, CHWAREL TELEVISION EMPLOYEE

The hardest aspect is juggling my PhD research and studio work. Working in the media is rarely a nine-to-five job and can be very unpredictable: you may not know where you've got to be, or how long you've got to be there, until the last minute. The best part is seeing something you have contributed to come together – hearing people discussing a TV show you've helped produce is really cool.

Take any opportunities to work in a media environment that come your way. Be flexible and have back-up plans. To work in film you will need great communication skills and the ability to work well in a team.

Applicant
journey

SIX EASY STEPS TO A UNIVERSITY, COLLEGE OR CONSERVATOIRE

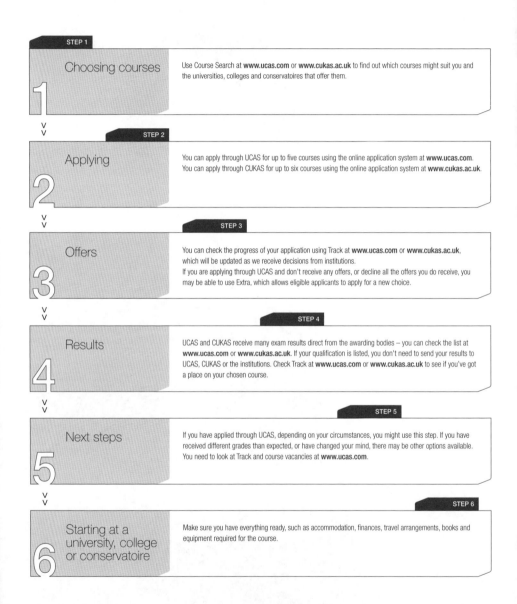

STEP 1

1 Choosing courses

Use Course Search at **www.ucas.com** or **www.cukas.ac.uk** to find out which courses might suit you and the universities, colleges and conservatoires that offer them.

STEP 2

2 Applying

You can apply through UCAS for up to five courses using the online application system at **www.ucas.com**. You can apply through CUKAS for up to six courses using the online application system at **www.cukas.ac.uk**.

STEP 3

3 Offers

You can check the progress of your application using Track at **www.ucas.com** or **www.cukas.ac.uk**, which will be updated as we receive decisions from institutions.

If you are applying through UCAS and don't receive any offers, or decline all the offers you do receive, you may be able to use Extra, which allows eligible applicants to apply for a new choice.

STEP 4

4 Results

UCAS and CUKAS receive many exam results direct from the awarding bodies – you can check the list at **www.ucas.com** or **www.cukas.ac.uk**. If your qualification is listed, you don't need to send your results to UCAS, CUKAS or the institutions. Check Track at **www.ucas.com** or **www.cukas.ac.uk** to see if you've got a place on your chosen course.

STEP 5

5 Next steps

If you have applied through UCAS, depending on your circumstances, you might use this step. If you have received different grades than expected, or have changed your mind, there may be other options available. You need to look at Track and course vacancies at **www.ucas.com**.

STEP 6

6 Starting at a university, college or conservatoire

Make sure you have everything ready, such as accommodation, finances, travel arrangements, books and equipment required for the course.

Choosing courses

1

Step 1 – Planning your application

Planning your application is the start of your journey to finding a place at a university, college or conservatoire.

This section will help you decide what course to study and how to choose a university, college or conservatoire where you'll enjoy living and studying. Find out about qualifications, degree options, how they'll assess you, and coping with the costs of higher education.

ENTRY REQUIREMENTS

This section covers routes into journalism, media and performing arts from qualifications such as A levels and Scottish Highers.

Which subjects?

The good news for would-be performers and media professionals is that the range and number of subjects you need to take at sixth form level is quite flexible. However, you will usually need to offer a minimum of two – and preferably three – A levels, and at least one of these should be in an arts subject. Many drama, theatre studies and performing arts courses require an A level in one of these areas. Other useful A level subjects include English literature and languages, while science subjects can be helpful for people interested in scientific writing or programme making. However, we strongly advise that you check with the admissions tutors at your shortlisted institutions on their preferred subjects and grades.

Get ahead

Sign up for the FREE UCAS Card if you're in Year 12, S5 or equivalent and thinking about higher education to receive all these benefits . . .

cdWOW!

TOPSHOP

Ryman

BELLA ITALIA
Caffe • Bar • Ristorante

TOPMAN

BSM

Domino's Pizza

SAVE
a packet on the high street with your card.*

INFO
about the courses and universities you're interested in.

FREE
monthly newsletters providing advice on the application process.

EXPERT
help from our UCAS advisers with all the reminders, hints and tips.

CHAT
with other students on yougofurther.co.uk, the UCAS student network

Which grades?

The sort of grades you will need for a degree in a media studies or performing arts-related area varies from one institution to the next. Some institutions require a minimum of two A levels but three is the norm. Offers can be made either using the Tariff (see page 124 for further details) or through specified grades. Since competition for places on courses is very competitive, good grades will boost your chances of being offered a place, though you won't be expected to achieve as highly as candidates for areas such as law and medicine.

UCAS CARD

If you're in Year 12, S5 or equivalent and thinking about higher education, the UCAS Card's for you. Sign up and you'll receive all these benefits...

- Save money on the high street with your UCAS discount card.
- Information about the courses and universities you're interested in.
- Free monthly newsletters providing advice on the application process.
- Expert help from our UCAS advisers with all the reminders, hints and tips.
- Chat with other students on **www.ucas.com/yougo** the UCAS student network.

Receive your free UCAS Card and all that goes with it by registering at **www.ucas.com/ucascard**.

1

Choosing courses

Choosing courses

USE COURSE SEARCH AT WWW.UCAS.COM AND WWW.CUKAS.AC.UK TO FIND OUT WHICH COURSES MIGHT SUIT YOU, AND THE UNIVERSITIES, COLLEGES AND CONSERVATOIRES THAT OFFER THEM.

Start thinking about what you want to study and where you want to go. This section will help you, and see what courses are available where in the listings (starting on page 150). Check the entry requirements required for each course meet your academic expectations.

Use the UCAS and CUKAS websites – www.ucas.com and **www.cukas.ac.uk** have lots of advice on how to find a course. CUKAS (the Conservatoires UK Admissions Service) processes applications for practice-based music courses, and some drama and dance courses, at seven of the UK's conservatoires. Go to the students' section of the websites for the best advice or go straight to Course Search to see all the courses available through UCAS or CUKAS. See the section on Entry Profiles on pages 92-93 which explains what they are and how to use them. Our maps of the UK at **www.ucas.com/students/choosingcourses/choosinguni/map/** and **www.cukas.ac.uk/students/choosingcourses/choosingaconsandcourse/map** show you where all the universities, colleges and conservatoires are located.

Watch UCAStv – at **www.ucas.tv** there are videos for UCAS applicants on *How to choose your course* and *Attending events* as well as case studies and video diaries from students talking about their experiences of finding a course at university or college.

Attend UCAS conventions – UCAS conventions are held throughout the country. Universities and colleges have exhibition stands where their staff offer information about their courses and institutions. Details of when the conventions are happening are shown at **www.ucas.com/events/conventions.** The Compose your future event provides a fantastic opportunity for those interested in performing arts, music, dance, drama, broadcasting and multimedia production - see page 90 for details.

Look at websites and prospectuses – universities, colleges and conservatoires have prospectuses and course-specific leaflets on their courses. Your school or college library may have copies or go to the university's or conservatoire's website to download a copy, or ask them to send one to you.

Go to university, college and conservatoire open days – most institutions offer open days to anyone who wants to attend. See the institution information pages on Course Search and the UCAS *Open Days* publications (see the Essential reading chapter) for information on when they are taking place. Aim to visit all of the universities, colleges or conservatoires you are interested in before you apply. It will help with your expectations of studying there and make sure the course is the right one for you.

League tables – these can be helpful but bear in mind that they attempt to rank institutions in an overall order reflecting the views of those that produce them. They may not reflect your views and needs. Examples can be found at **www.thecompleteuniversityguide.co.uk**, **www.guardian.co.uk/education/universityguide**, **www.thetimes.co.uk/gug** (subscription service) and **www.thesundaytimes.co.uk/universityguide** (subscription service).

Visit the Unistats website at www.direct.gov.uk/unistats – it includes results from the National Student Survey and enables you to compare students' views of universities, colleges and conservatoires, and the subjects they offer.

Do your research – speak and refer to as many trusted sources as you can find. Talk to someone already doing the job you have in mind. The section on 'Which area?' on page 19 will help you identify the different areas of journalism, media and performing arts you might want to enter.

DECIDING ON YOUR COURSE CHOICES

Through UCAS you can initially apply for up to five courses. Remember you don't have to make five course choices. Only apply for a course if you're completely happy with both the course and the university or college and you would definitely be prepared to accept a place.

Through CUKAS you can apply for a maximum of six courses. You only need to apply to the highest level of course in which you are interested through CUKAS. If you are not sure which level of course you should apply for, please contact the conservatoire direct to discuss.

How do you find out more information to make an informed decision and narrow down your course choices? First of all, look up course details in this book or online on **www.ucas.com** or **www.cukas.ac.uk**.

This will give you an idea of the full range of courses and topics on offer. You may want to study a specific area of journalism, media or performing arts by itself, but there are also many courses which also include additional options, such as a modern language (check out the degree subjects studied by our case studies). You'll quickly be able to eliminate institutions that don't offer the right course, or you can choose a 'hit list' of institutions first, and then see what they have to offer.

Once you've made a short(er) list, read the institution Entry Profiles (see page 92) to find out what particular courses offer. You can then follow this up by looking at university, college and conservatoire websites, and generally finding out as much as you can about the course, department and institution. Don't be afraid to contact them to ask for more information, request their prospectus or arrange an open day visit.

YOUR CHANCE TO CHECK OUT THE COURSES

If you don't fancy reading through endless prospectuses, why not visit the 'Compose your future' exhibition offered at the Manchester Central Convention Complex on 17 October 2011.

This event offers you a fantastic opportunity to chat to course leaders and those involved in performing arts, music, dance, drama, broadcast and multimedia production courses. You can also watch live performances given by current undergraduates within further and higher education or attend interactive workshops. This is an unrivalled opportunity for you to meet representatives from major providers of media and performing arts in the UK, and to collect as much information as possible.

For further details, please visit the Compose your future website, **www.ucasevents.com/compose** or contact UCAS Media Events tel: 01242 544 979, email: events@ucas.ac.uk.

wondering
how much
higher education
costs?

need information
about
student finance?

Visit www.ucas.com/students/studentfinance and find sources for all the information on student money matters you need.

With access to up-to-date information on bursaries, scholarships and variable fees, plus our online budget calculator. Visit us today and get the full picture.

www.ucas.com/students/studentfinance

Choosing courses

1

Entry Profiles

WHAT ARE THEY?

Entry Profiles give potential applicants to higher education specific information to help them make informed decisions about the courses they apply for. Detailed knowledge about the course, formal entry requirements and the qualities and experiences institutions are looking for in their applicants can help ensure that every applicant finds their way onto the right course. Entry Profiles are published on the UCAS and CUKAS websites and can be reached using Course Search. They are available for all potential applicants and their advisers to see as they start making important decisions about where to apply. All course providers are asked to contribute Entry Profiles for the UCAS and CUKAS Course Search facilities.

WHY USE THEM?

Courses can vary at different universities, colleges and conservatoires even though they have the same name. Differences in course content, structure, optional modules, and the department's approach to teaching and learning can make the experience of studying any subject very different for students at different institutions, even before the size and location of the institution are taken into account.

It is important that you are fully informed about the courses and the institutions offering them before you apply, and that you know what academic qualifications and personal qualities are being sought in an applicant. Then you can avoid mistakes and make fully informed choices.

HOW DO I USE ENTRY PROFILES?

When you find courses that interest you, look for the **EP** symbol after the course title on Course Search at **www.ucas.com** or the **I** symbol on **www.cukas.ac.uk**. This means the course has an Entry Profile.

- First, read the information about the course. Does it cover subjects that interest you, and what career opportunities would be open to you? Does the Entry Profile tell you about the personal qualities the university, college or conservatoire is looking for in its students, or any experience that would be beneficial?
- Check the academic entry requirements. Are you studying the right subjects to be accepted onto this course? Will you meet the grades or Tariff points required? (See page 124 for information about the Tariff.)

- Make sure that you know where the course will be taught - sometimes it is not at the main campus. Could you travel to lectures and tutorials easily?
- Do you need to take an admissions test? If so, you need to find out how to apply for it, if there is a fee and where and when it will take place.
- Look for comments written by current or former students. What they have to say will help you get a feel for what it is like to be a student at that university or conservatoire, or on that course.

If you don't find all the information you need in Course Search, check the universities', colleges' and conservatoires' websites, or contact them direct with any questions you may have.

TOP TIP

Don't be afraid to pick up the phone – admissions officers welcome enquiries directly from students, rather than careers officers phoning on your behalf. It shows you're genuinely interested and committed to your own career early on.

1

Choosing courses

Choosing your institution

Different people look for different things from their university, college or conservatoire course, but the checklist on the next page sets out the kinds of factors all prospective students should consider when choosing their institution. Keep this list in mind on open days, when talking to friends about their experiences, or while reading prospectuses and websites.

WHAT TO CONSIDER WHEN CHOOSING YOUR MEDIA AND PERFORMING ARTS COURSE	
Location	Do you want to stay close to home? Would you prefer to study at a city or campus university, at a college or a conservatoire?
Grades required	Use the Course Search facilities on the UCAS and CUKAS websites, **www.ucas.com** and **www.cukas.ac.uk**; to view entry requirements for courses you are interested in. Also, check out the institution's website or call up the admissions office. Some institutions specify grades required, eg AAB, while others specify points required, eg 340. If they ask for points, it means they're using the UCAS Tariff system, which awards points to different types and levels of qualification. For example, an A grade at A level = 120 points; a B grade at A level = 100 points. The full Tariff tables are available on pages 124-133 and at **www.ucas.com**.
Employer links	Ask the course tutor or department about links with employers, such as theatres, publishing houses, magazines etc. Find out if the course involves visiting lecturers from the professional side of the industry, and where they typically come from.
Graduate prospects	Ask the careers office for their list of graduate destinations.
Cost	Ask the admissions office about variable tuition fees and financial assistance. Also find out what fees are charged for studio time and/or equipment.
Degree type	Do you want to study music, drama or media etc on its own (single honours degree) or 50/50 with another subject (joint degree) or as one of a few subjects (combined degree)?
Coursework	How is the course taught? Ask about the number of lectures and tutorials per week, the amount of one-to-one work, and how you will build a portfolio of achievement or be involved in project work. Also ask about the split between practical and contextual work.
Course assessment	What proportion of the assessment is based on your project work and how much is based on written assignments? Do you have to do a performance as part of your final assessment?
Facilities for media and performing arts	Check out their musical and theatrical facilities; unlike most subjects, where most time is spent in lecture theatres and seminars etc, media and performing arts courses involve a lot of hands-on work in workshops. Also, find out if there is a university or college careers adviser dedicated to media and performing arts.
'Fit'	Even if all the above criteria stack up, this one relies on gut feel – go and visit the department if you can, and see if it's 'you'. For example, check out any end-of-year performances or recitals to give you a good idea of the type and level of work the course produces. Also ask about lecturers' own particular interests; many will have personal web pages somewhere on the departmental website.

Choosing courses

1

How will they choose you?

Universities, colleges and conservatoires receive thousands of applications each year for only a limited number of places. So how can you make your UCAS or CUKAS application stand out from the others?

ACADEMIC ABILITY

Degrees can be intellectually demanding. Not only will you possibly be learning about the basics of your chosen discipline(s) for the very first time but you will also be expected to work on them in greater analytical depth than you have been used to before at GCSE and A level (or equivalent). Therefore, in order for admissions tutors to be certain that you have what it takes to cope with the course, you will have to show you have the academic ability to take on new ideas.

SELF-MOTIVATION AND SELF-DISCIPLINE

Studying at a university, college or conservatoire is very different from school and sixth form. In these settings, you will have followed a set course, normally following a study pattern suggested by your teachers. Homework set each night will have ensured that you completed your study regularly and on time.

In higher education, tutors and lecturers do not have the time to keep tabs on their students in the same way. Whereas your A level teachers will have helped motivate you to finish your work on time, university tutors will hand out reading lists and essay titles in advance and will expect you to complete them on time without constant reminders.

This can, understandably, be daunting for some people. Certainly, time management and self-motivation are skills you hone in higher education but it also helps if your referee can write about any instances where you have shown an ability to work well on your own, as this is how you will be studying throughout your undergraduate course.

DEVOTION TO YOUR CHOSEN SUBJECT

Make no mistake about it, people who choose to work in either the media or performing arts do so because they love what they do. Financial rewards can be low not just at the start but for years to come. You also may have to face the reality that, while you love acting or dancing or writing, you might never be a George Clooney or JK Rowling. Acknowledgement of this and a proven love of your subject (through writing for student newspapers, undertaking unpaid work experience or working at your local theatre) will help convince admissions tutors that you are devoted to their subject.

The tutors who select students on to their courses also want to see evidence that you have carefully considered what a degree in performing arts and the media will involve and why it appeals to you so much. After all, you don't necessarily need a degree in these areas to get a job in them, so why have you chosen to specialise in media even earlier than some of your peers? Only you will know the reasons why you're fascinated by these subject areas and it's your job to convey this enthusiasm in your UCAS or CUKAS application.

DO SOME READING

This is related to the previous point. A good way to prove to potential admissions tutors that you have an interest in their field is to find out their specialist academic areas and do some reading into these, potentially from books or academic papers that they have written. Additionally, contact the relevant department and ask for their first-year reading list, if this is not available online. You do not need to read everything on it but if you choose two or three books that most appeal to you and read them in some depth it will show a commitment to both the subject and the relevant institution's course.

Be warned, though: don't think that merely mentioning a few key books will automatically get you through. Admissions tutors will know if you're lying, so unless you can make a few valid points about why you enjoyed their books, don't bother: it could do more harm than good.

WORK EXPERIENCE

While relevant work experience is not essential to gain a place in media and the performing arts, if you have had any, do include details of it in your personal statement (see below). A job working as an usher at a theatre, or perhaps work shadowing a journalist, can give you valuable insight into these sorts of careers, as well as real inspiration to study what it is that drives them. Relevant work experience can be of real interest to admissions tutors so make sure you give details of anything you learned during the time and explain how it has led you to make the decisions you are taking today. Please see page 117 for more information about work experience.

YOUR PERSONAL STATEMENT

Your personal statement can really enhance your application. It is here that you can show evidence of all the above issues – academic attainment, self-discipline, work experience, a desire for your chosen subject. Most institutions place much importance on personal statements as this is where your own voice comes through, so make the most of it and use it to your advantage. Be honest but not over-friendly and give well-reasoned statements. And above all make sure it's free from mistakes and easy to read. There's nothing more offputting for an admissions tutor than an application and personal statement that have glaring grammatical and spelling mistakes.

As this is such an important part of your application, it's worth drafting it a few times. Ask your family or friends and teacher to check it, not only for mistakes but also to see if you're leaving anything out that should be in... or equally if there's anything that should come out.

Please see page 115 for more advice about your personal statement.

AUDITION

CUKAS applicants will normally need to have auditions before the conservatoires can make their decisions. This usually involves giving a live audition at the conservatoire, but in some cases applicants are allowed to send in recordings or videos. Some conservatoires have audition centres in other countries to cater for international applications.

The audition process will vary between conservatoires. When conservatoires invite applicants to audition they will provide advice on what the audition will include and what kinds of pieces should be prepared.

For further information to help you perpare for auditions, download the Conservatoires UK advice leaflet *Making the Most of Your Audition* from **www.cukas.ac.uk**.

Choosing courses

1

The cost of higher education

The information in this section was up-to-date when this book was published. You should visit the websites mentioned in the section for the very latest information.

THE COST OF STUDYING IN THE UK

As a student, you will usually have to pay for two things: tuition fees for your course, which for most students do not need to be paid for up front, and living costs such as rent, food, books, transport and entertainment. Fees charged vary between courses, as well as between universities and colleges, so it's important to check these before you apply. The 2012 entry UCAS Course Search at **www.ucas.com/students/coursesearch** will be available from mid-May 2011. Course fee information will be added in mid-July for each course, or you can contact the universities and colleges direct.

If you're studying in Scotland and already live there, check the Student Awards Agency for Scotland (SAAS) website **www.saas.gov.uk** for further information.

STUDENT LOANS

The purpose of student loans from the Government is to help cover the costs of your tuition fees and basic living costs (rent, bills, food and so on). Two types are available: a tuition fee loan to cover the tuition charges and a maintenance loan to help with accommodation and other living costs. Both types of student loan are available to all students who meet the basic eligibility requirements. Interest will be charged at inflation (RPI) plus 3% while you are studying. In addition, many other commercial loans are available to students studying at university or college but the interest rate can vary considerably.

Find out more information from the relevant sites below:

England: Student Finance England -
www.direct.gov.uk/studentfinance

Northern Ireland: Student Finance Northern Ireland -
www.studentfinanceni.co.uk

Scotland: Student Awards Agency for Scotland -
www.saas.gov.uk

Wales: Student Finance Wales -
www.studentfinancewales.co.uk

Important information for students entering English universities and colleges from 1 September 2012
At the time of writing, the Department for Business, Innovation and Skills (BIS) has announced changes to student finance, subject to parliamentary approval:

- Any university or college will be able to charge up to £6,000 a year for their courses. In exceptional cases, universities will be able to charge up to £9,000, subject to meeting much tougher conditions on widening participation and fair access.

- As is the case now, students in England will not have to pay up-front for their tuition, as Government loans will be available to most students. Students only start to repay these loans once they are earning over £21,000 per year.

- A new £150m National Scholarships Programme will be targeted at bright potential students from poor backgrounds.

- Students from families with incomes of up to £25,000 will be entitled to a non-repayable grant of £3,250 to help with living costs and those from families with incomes up to £42,600 will be entitled to a partial non-repayable grant.

- Loans to help with living costs will be available for all eligible students, irrespective of family income.

- Many universities and colleges will also offer non-repayable scholarships and bursaries to help students cover tuition and living costs whilst studying.

- All eligible part-time undergraduates who study for at least 25% of their time will be able to apply for a loan to cover the costs of their tuition, which means they no longer have to pay up front.

There will be extra support for disabled students and students with child or adult dependants.

For more information on the proposed changes in England please visit
www.direct.gov.uk/studentfinance.

Choosing courses

1

International students

APPLYING TO STUDY IN THE UK

Deciding to study in the UK is very exciting. You need to think about what course to do, where to study, and how much it will cost. The decisions you make can have a huge effect on your future but UCAS and CUKAS are here to help.

How to apply

Whatever your age or qualifications, if you want to apply for any of the 40,000 courses listed at over 300 universities and colleges on the UCAS website, you must apply through UCAS at **www.ucas.com**. If you are unsure, your school, college, adviser, or local British Council office will be able to help. Further advice and a video guide for international students can be found on the non-UK students' section of the website **www.ucas.com/international/**.

What is CUKAS?

The Conservatoires UK Admissions Service (CUKAS) is an admissions service operated by UCAS. CUKAS provides a central application service for practice-based music courses, and some drama and dance courses, at seven conservatoires in the UK. CUKAS processes applications for the following types of full-time and part-time courses in music:

- undergraduate degree level courses
- postgraduate degree level courses
- postgraduate certificate and diploma courses
- courses with no award.

Applicants must apply through CUKAS for any courses listed on Course Search on the CUKAS website **www.cukas.ac.uk**. Further advice for international students can be found on the non-UK section of the website at **www.cukas.ac.uk/students/wheretostart/ nonukstudents**.

UCAS applicants may apply on their own or through their school, college, adviser, or local British Council if they are registered to use Apply. If you choose to use an education agent's services, check with the British Council to see if they hold a list of certificated or registered agents in your country. Check also on any charges you may need to pay. UCAS charges only the application fee (see below) but agents may charge for additional services.

When you apply through CUKAS you can apply for up to six choices. All CUKAS applications are made online, and students apply on their own rather than through a centre.

How much will my application cost?

UCAS – If you choose to apply to more than one course, university or college you need to pay £22 GBP when you apply. If you only apply to one course at one university or college, you pay £11 GBP.

CUKAS – All applicants have to pay an application fee of £16 GBP to CUKAS to cover the processing of their applications. This fee applies to single and multiple choices. CUKAS applicants also have to pay audition fees – the fees vary between conservatoires. All the conservatoires in the CUKAS application system, except Leeds College of Music, require you to pay your audition fees at the time of application. Leeds College of Music require you to pay once you have been invited to audition. Please see page 102 'How to apply through CUKAS' for more information.

What level of English?

UCAS provides a list of English language qualifications and grades that are acceptable to most UK universities and colleges, however you are advised to contact the institutions directly as each have their own entry requirement in English. For more information go to **www.ucas.com/students/wheretostart/ nonukstudents/englangprof**.

Links to information on conservatoires' websites about English language requirements can be found at **www.cukas.ac.uk/students/wheretostart/ nonukstudents/englishlang**.

INTERNATIONAL STUDENT FEES

If you study in the UK, your fee status (whether you pay full-cost fees or a subsidised fee rate) will be decided by the UK institution you plan to attend. Before you decide which university, college or conservatoire to attend, you need to be absolutely certain that you can pay the full cost of:

- your tuition fees (the amount is set by institutions, so contact them for more information - visit their websites where many list their fees. Fee details will also be included on Course Search at **www.ucas.com** and **www.cukas.ac.uk** from mid-July)
- the everyday living expenses for you (and your family) for the whole time that you are in the UK, including accommodation, food, heat, light, clothes, travel
- books and equipment for your course
- travel to and from your country.

You must include everything when you work out how much it will cost. You can get information to help you do this accurately from the international offices at universities, colleges and conservatoires, UKCISA (UK Council for International Student Affairs) and the British Council. There is a useful website tool to help you manage your money - **www.studentcalculator.org.uk**.

Scholarships and bursaries are offered at some institutions and you should contact them for more information. In addition, you should check with your local British Council for additional scholarships available to students from your country who want to study in the UK.

LEGAL DOCUMENTS YOU WILL NEED

As you prepare to study in the UK, it is very important to think about the legal documents you will need to enter the country.

Everyone who comes to study in the UK needs a valid passport. If you do not have one, you should apply for one as soon as possible. People from certain countries also need visas before they come into the UK. They are known as 'visa nationals'. You can check if you require a visa to travel to the UK by visiting the UK Border Agency website and selecting 'Studying in the UK?' so, please check the UK Border Agency website at **www.ukba.homeoffice.gov.uk** for the most up-to-date guidance and information about the United Kingdom's visa requirements.

When you apply for your visa you need to make sure you have the following documents:

- A confirmation of acceptance for studies (CAS) number from the university, college or conservatoire where you are going to study. The institution must be on the UKBA Register of Sponsors in order to accept international students.

- A valid passport.
- Evidence that you have enough money to pay for your course and living costs.
- Certificates for all qualifications you have that are relevant to the course you have been accepted for and for any English language qualifications.

You will also have to give your biometric data.

Do check for further information from your local British Embassy or High Commission. Guidance information for international students is also available from UKCISA and from UKBA.

ADDITIONAL RESOURCES

There are a number of organisations that can provide further guidance and information to you as you prepare to study in the UK:

- British Council
  www.britishcouncil.org
- Education UK (British Council website dealing with educational matters)
  www.educationuk.org
- English UK (British Council accredited website listing English language courses in the UK)
  www.englishuk.com
- UK Border Agency (provides information on visa requirements and applications)
  www.ukvisas.gov.uk
- UKCISA (UK Council for International Student Affairs)
  www.ukcisa.org.uk
- BIS (Department for Business, Innovation and Skills)
  www.bis.gov.uk
- Prepare for Success
  www.prepareforsuccess.org.uk

Applying

2

Step 2 – Applying through UCAS

You apply through UCAS using the online application system, called Apply, at **www.ucas.com**. You can apply for a maximum of five choices, but you don't have to use them all if you don't want to. If you apply for fewer than five choices, you can add more at a later date if you want to. But be aware of the course application deadlines.

IMPORTANT DATES FOR 2012 ENTRY	
Early June 2011	UCAS Apply opens for 2012 entry registration.
Mid-September 2011	Applications can be sent to UCAS.
15 October 2011	Application deadline for the receipt at UCAS of applications for all medicine, dentistry, veterinary medicine and veterinary science courses and for all courses at the universities of Oxford and Cambridge.
15 January 2012	Application deadline for the receipt at UCAS of applications for all courses except those listed above with a 15 October deadline, and some art and design courses with a 24 March deadline.
24 February 2012	Extra starts (see page 122 for more information about Extra).
24 March 2012	Application deadline for the receipt at UCAS of applications for art and design courses except those listed on Course Search at **www.ucas.com** with a 15 January deadline.
31 March 2012	If you apply by 15 January, the universities and colleges should aim to have sent their decisions by this date (but they can take longer).
10 May 2012	If you apply by 15 January, universities and colleges need to send their decisions by this date. If they don't, UCAS will make any outstanding choices unsuccessful on their behalf.
30 June 2012	Applications received after this date are entered into Clearing and are not automatically sent to universities and colleges (see page 136 for more information about Clearing).
4 July 2012	Last date to apply through Extra.
August 2012 (date to be confirmed)	Scottish Qualifications Authority (SQA) results are published.
16 August 2012	GCE and Advanced Diploma results are published (often known as 'A level results day'). Adjustment opens for registration (see page 137 for more information about Adjustment).

DON'T FORGET...

Universities and colleges guarantee to consider your application only if we receive it by the appropriate deadline. Check application deadlines for your courses on Course Search at **www.ucas.com**.

If you send it to UCAS after the deadline but before 30 June 2012, universities and colleges will consider your application only if they still have places available.

See page 112 for when to apply through CUKAS.

Applying

2

How to apply through UCAS

You apply online at **www.ucas.com** through Apply – a secure, web-based application service that is designed for all our applicants, whether they are applying through a UCAS-registered centre or as an individual, anywhere in the world. Apply is:

- easy to access – all you need is an internet connection
- easy to use – you don't have to complete your application all in one go: you can save the sections as you complete them and come back to it later
- easy to monitor – once you've applied, you can use Track to check the progress of your application, including any decisions from universities or colleges. You can also reply to your offers using Track.

Watch the UCAStv guide to applying through UCAS at **www.ucas.tv**.

DEFERRED ENTRY

If you want to apply for deferred entry in 2013, perhaps because you want to take a year out between school or college and higher education, you should check that the university or college will accept a deferred entry application. Occasionally, tutors are not happy to accept students who take a gap year, because it interrupts the flow of their learning. If you apply for deferred entry, you must meet the conditions of any offers by 31 August 2012 unless otherwise agreed by the university or college. If you accept a place for 2013 entry and then change your mind, you cannot reapply through us in the 2013 entry cycle unless you withdraw your original application.

INVISIBILITY OF CHOICES

Universities and colleges cannot see details of the other choices on your application until you reply to any offers or you have not been successful at any of your choices. **You can submit only one UCAS application in each year's application cycle.**

APPLYING THROUGH YOUR SCHOOL OR COLLEGE

1 GET SCHOOL OR COLLEGE 'BUZZWORD'

Ask your UCAS application coordinator (may be your sixth form tutor) for your school or college UCAS 'buzzword'. This is a password for the school or college.

2 REGISTER

Go to **www.ucas.com/students/apply** and click on **Register/Log in to use Apply** and then **register**. After you have entered your registration details, the online system will automatically generate a username for you, but you'll have to come up with a password and answers to security questions.

3 COMPLETE SEVEN SECTIONS

Complete the sections of the application. To access any section, click on the section name at the top of the screen and follow the instructions. The sections are:

Personal details – contact details, residential status, disability status

Additional information – only UK applicants need to complete this section

Student finance – for UK students only

Choices – which courses you'd like to apply for

Education – your education and qualifications

Employment – for example, work experience, holiday jobs

Personal statement – see page 115

Before you can send your application you need to go to the 'view all' screen and tick the 'section complete' box.

4 PASS TO REFEREE

Once you've completed all the sections, send your application electronically to your referee (normally your form tutor). They'll check it, approve it and add their reference to it, and will then send it to UCAS on your behalf.

USEFUL INFORMATION ABOUT APPLY

- Important details like date of birth and course codes will be checked by Apply. It will alert you if they are not valid.
- The text for your personal statement and reference can be copied and pasted into your application.
- From 2012 entry, if you want to, you will be able to enter European characters into certain areas of Apply
- You can change your application at any time before it is completed and sent to UCAS.
- You can print and preview your application at any time. Before you send it you need to go to the 'view all' screen and tick the 'section complete' box.
- Your school, college or centre can choose different payment methods. For example, they may want us to bill them, or you may be able to pay online by debit or credit card.

NOT APPLYING THROUGH A SCHOOL OR COLLEGE

If you're not currently studying, you'll probably be applying as an independent applicant rather than through a school, college or other UCAS-registered centre. In this case you won't be able to provide a 'buzzword', but we'll ask you a few extra questions to check you are eligible to apply.

If you're not applying through a UCAS-registered centre, the procedure you use for obtaining a reference will depend on whether or not you want your reference to be provided through a registered centre. For information on the procedures for providing references, visit **www.ucas.com/students/applying/howtoapply/reference**.

APPLICATION CHECKLIST

We want this to run smoothly for you and we also want to process your application as quickly as possible. You can help us to do this by remembering to do the following:

✓ check the closing dates for applications – see pages 107 and 112
✓ check the student finance information at **www.ucas.com/students/studentfinance/** and course fees information in Course Search at **www.ucas.com** (Course Search will be live from May 2011, whilst fees information will be available in mid-July 2011)
✓ start early and allow plenty of time for completing your application – including enough time for your referee to complete the reference section
✓ read the online instructions carefully before you start
✓ consider what each question is actually asking for – use the 'help'
✓ pay special attention to your personal statement (see page 115) and start drafting it early
✓ ask a teacher, parent, friend or careers adviser to review your draft application – particularly the personal statement
✓ if you get stuck, watch our videos on YouTube, where we answer your frequently asked questions on completing a UCAS application at **www.youtube.com/ucasonline**
✓ if you have extra information that will not fit on your application, send it direct to your chosen universities or colleges after we have sent you your Welcome letter with your Personal ID – don't send it to us
✓ print a copy of the final version of your application, in case you are asked questions on it at an interview.

compose
your future

Find out about performing arts, music, dance, drama, broadcast, multimedia production courses and much more

Would you like the chance to talk to representatives from a wide range of colleges and universities, to pick up prospectuses and see live performances by undergraduates?

UCAS Compose your future exhibition is an annual event that offers the opportunity to find out more about higher education courses in performing arts, music, dance, drama, broadcast, multi-media production and related subjects, and the chance to meet organisations of a particular interest to prospective students.

The event will also feature:

- Workshops:
  Interactive sessions e.g. performance masterclasses
  Presentation sessions e.g. how to apply

- Live performances from current and past students from exhibiting institutions

TO FIND OUT MORE OR TO BOOK, PLEASE VISIT THE WEBSITE WWW.UCASEVENTS.COM/COMPOSE, OR CALL 01242 544979

Applying

2

How to apply through CUKAS

WHAT IS CUKAS?

The Conservatoires UK Admissions Service (CUKAS) is an admissions service operated by UCAS. CUKAS provides a central application service for practice-based music courses, and some drama and dance courses at seven conservatoires in the UK:

Birmingham Conservatoire
Leeds College of Music
Royal College of Music
Royal Northern College of Music
Royal Scottish Academy of Music and Drama
Royal Welsh College of Music and Drama
Trinity College of Music.

The Guildhall School of Music and Drama and the Royal Academy of Music do not recruit through CUKAS. Applicants should apply directly to these conservatoires. CUKAS processes applications for the following types of

full-time and part-time courses in music:

- undergraduate degree level courses
- postgraduate degree level courses
- postgraduate certificate and diploma courses
- courses with no award.

Applicants must apply through CUKAS for any courses listed on Course Search on the CUKAS website **www.cukas.ac.uk.**

WHEN TO APPLY

You can apply online through the CUKAS website **www.cukas.ac.uk** from early July, for courses that mostly start in September or October the following year. The online application system provides detailed help text to guide you through the application process. The closing date for 2012 entry on-time applications is 1 October 2011. Conservatoires must give equal consideration to all applications received by this date.

We will process all applications received from 2 October 2011 to 31 August 2012, but these are classed as late and will only be considered by the conservatoires if they still have vacancies after considering all the on-time applications. If you are applying after 1 February 2012, you should contact the conservatoires to check if they still have vacancies before making an application.

APPLICATION AND AUDITION FEES

You can apply for a maximum of six choices; the application fee is £16 regardless of how many choices you make.

All the conservatoires in the CUKAS application system, except Leeds College of Music, require you to pay your audition fees at the time of application. Leeds College of Music require you to pay once you have been invited to audition.

The amount of the audition fee varies depending on the type of course and whether:

- the audition is a live performance or a recording
- separate auditions are required for two study areas, for example, different instruments, singing or conducting
- the audition is held in the UK or abroad
- the application is 'on-time' or 'late' (received at CUKAS by 1 October 2011 or after 1 October 2011 respectively).

Some conservatoires will waive audition fees for applicants who are unable to pay if they are able to provide evidence of hardship.

REFERENCES

You must provide details of two referees - one to comment on your academic ability; and the other to comment on your music ability.

WHAT HAPPENS NEXT?

Once we have received your completed application, the following steps occur:

1. We process your application.
2. Your application is sent to your chosen conservatoire(s).
3. We send you a Welcome letter confirming your personal details and choices.
4. Invitations for auditions are sent by conservatoires.

THE AUDITION

The audition process will vary between conservatoires. If you are invited for audition, the conservatoire will provide advice on what the audition will include and what kind of pieces you should prepare. Further information to help you prepare for auditions is available in the Conservatoires UK (CUK) leaflet *Making the Most of Your Audition*, which you can download from the CUKAS website at **www.cukas.ac.uk**.

TRACK

After you have submitted your application to CUKAS, you can use the Track service to:

- follow the progress of your application to see details of auditions, decisions and any offers
- change your postal address, email address and/or telephone number
- make additional choices (if you have not already made six)
- reply to your offers.

Please note, CUKAS does not operate an Extra or Clearing service.

APPLYING THROUGH CUKAS AND UCAS

You can apply through CUKAS (maximum of six choices) and UCAS (maximum of five choices) simultaneously. However, if at any stage of the application cycle our records show that you have confirmed places through both CUKAS and UCAS, we will send you a letter asking you to accept one place and withdraw from the other.

Applying

The personal statement

Next to choosing your courses, this section of your application will be the most time-consuming. It is of immense importance as many institutions rely solely on the information in the application, rather than interviews and admissions tests, when selecting students. The personal statement can be the deciding factor in whether or not they offer you a place. If it is an institution that interviews, it could be the deciding factor in whether you get called for interview.

Keep a copy of your personal statement – if you are called for interview, you will almost certainly be asked questions based on it.

Tutors will look carefully at your exam results, actual and predicted, your reference and your own personal statement. Remember, they are looking for reasons to offer you a place – try to give them every opportunity to do so!

A SALES DOCUMENT

The personal statement is your opportunity to sell yourself, so do so. The university, college or conservatoire admissions tutor who reads your personal statement wants to get a rounded picture of you to decide whether you will make an interesting member of the institution, both academically and socially. They want to know more about you than the subjects you are studying at school.

HOW TO START

There are resources on **www.ucas.com** to help you, including a timeline, so that you start in good time, keep on track and give yourself a chance to get it all checked over and submitted on time. To help you with thinking about what should go in and how can it best represent your strengths, there is a mind map which will stretch your ideas and help you view things from all angles. Finally, you'll find a worksheet so that you're not starting off with just a blank sheet of paper, which can be very daunting indeed!

Include things like hobbies and work experience (see pages 97 and 117), and try to link the skills you have gained to the type of course you are applying for. Describe your career plans and goals. Have you belonged to theatre groups, dance groups or orchestras, or held positions of responsibility in the community? If you're applying for journalism, have you visited a news organisation? Try to give evidence of your ability to undertake higher level study successfully by showing your commitment and maturity. If you left full-time education a while ago, talk about the work you have done and the skills you have gathered or how you have juggled bringing up a family with other activities – that is solid evidence of time management skills. Whoever you are, make sure you explain what appeals to you about the course you are applying for.

Visit **www.ucas.tv** to view the video to help guide you through the process, and address the most common fears and concerns about writing a personal statement.

WHAT ADMISSIONS TUTORS LOOK FOR	WHAT TO TELL THEM
<ul><li>Your reasons for wanting to take this subject in general and this particular course.</li><li>Your communication skills – not only what you say but how you say it. Your grammar and spelling must be perfect.</li><li>Relevant experience – practical things you've done that are related to your choice of course.</li><li>Evidence of your teamworking ability, leadership capability, independence.</li><li>Evidence of your skills, for example: IT skills, empathy and people skills, debating and public speaking, research and analysis.</li><li>Other activities that show your dedication and ability to apply yourself and maintain your motivation.</li></ul>	<ul><li>Why you want to do this subject - how you know it is the subject for you.</li><li>What experience you already have in this field – for example work experience, school projects, hobbies, voluntary work.</li><li>The skills and qualities you have as a person that would make you a good student, for example anything that shows your dedication, communication ability, academic achievement, initiative.</li><li>Examples that show you can knuckle down and apply yourself, for example running a marathon or your Extended Project.</li><li>If you're taking a gap year, why you've chosen this and (if possible) what you're going to do during it.</li><li>About your other interests and activities away from studying – to show you're a rounded person. (But remember that it is mainly your suitability for the particular course that they're looking to judge.)</li></ul>

CUKAS applicants

You should make your personal statement truly convey your aspirations, personality, feelings about music and experience. Showing understanding of today's music profession, which is competitive and requires versatility, is helpful and indicates a suitable temperament. It is up to you how you write your statement, but we suggest you include some or all of the following points.

- Your reasons for choosing the courses you have listed. Remember that each conservatoire will be able to see which other conservatoires you have applied to.
- What interests you about your chosen study area (whether playing an instrument, singing, conducting or composing).
- Your experience of playing your chosen instrument(s), or in singing, conducting or composing, or in any other activity related to the course(s) to which you have applied.
- Membership of national and/or international orchestras, choirs or chamber groups, for example NYO, NYC, EUYO.

WORK EXPERIENCE

The real value of work experience is the skillset it will give you, which in turn will help you produce better work during your degree course. Your personal statement is where your work experience will help you stand out by allowing you to describe where you've worked, what it taught you and the skills it helped you develop.

Unfortunately there are no real systematic, formalised work experience schemes offered by employers in the media and performing arts fields. Some do offer work placements or ad hoc 'shadowing' schemes, where you shadow a professional for a week or a few days, but for these you'll have to apply direct to the company. There may, however, be the possibility of 'taster' days offered by careers organisations in conjunction with employers and, increasingly, the chance of work experience placements through your school. The rest is up to you.

If you only have **non**-performing arts or media work experience, it will still be useful to include it in any applications you make. The trick is to pull out the professional and personal skills you have developed that are relevant to the work or skills required in media and performing arts, such as interpersonal skills, working in teams, or practical hands-on work putting products together.

Offers

3

Step 3 – Offers

Once we have sent your UCAS application to your chosen universities and colleges, they will all consider it independently and tell us whether or not they can offer you a place. Some universities and colleges will take longer to make decisions than others. You may be asked to attend an interview, sit an additional test or provide a piece of work such as an essay or art portfolio before a decision can be made.

Many universities (particularly the more popular ones, running competitive courses) use interviews as part of their selection process. Universities will want to find out why you want to study your chosen course at their institution, and they can make sure the course is suitable for you and your future career plans. Interviews also give you an opportunity to ask the university any questions you may have about the course or their institution.

If you are called for interview, the key areas they are likely to cover will be:

- evidence of your academic ability
- your capacity to study hard
- your commitment to a career in media and performing arts.

CUKAS applicants will normally need to have auditions before the conservatoires can make their decisions. Please see page 113 for more information.

A lot of the interview will be based on information supplied on your application – especially your **personal statement** - see page 115 for tips about the personal statement.

Whenever a university, college or conservatoire makes a decision about your application, we record it and let you know. You can check the progress of your application using Track at **www.ucas.com** or **www.cukas.ac.uk**. These are secure online services which give you access to your application using the same username and password you used when you applied. You can use it to find out if you have been invited for audition or interview, or need to provide an additional piece of work, as well as check to see if you have received any offers.

Types of offer - UCAS

Universities can make two types of offer: conditional or unconditional.

Conditional offer

A conditional offer means the university or college is willing to offer you a place if you meet certain conditions – usually based on exam results. The conditions may be based on Tariff points (for example, 300 points from three A levels), or specify certain grades in named subjects (for example, A in economics, B in accounting, C in business studies).

Unconditional offer

If you've met all the academic requirements for the course and the university or college wants to accept you, they will make you an unconditional offer. If you accept this you'll have a definite place. However, there might be other requirements, like medical or financial conditions, that you need to meet before you can start your course.

Types of offer - CUKAS

Guaranteed unconditional - the conservatoire is satisfied, from the information you have given, that you have already met the conditions for entry.

Guaranteed conditional - the conservatoire has made the offer subject to you meeting certain conditions, usually examination results.

Reserve unconditional - the conservatoire is satisfied, from the information you have given, that you have already met the conditions for entry and have offered a place on their reserve list.

Reserve conditional - the conservatoire has offered a place on its reserve list subject to you meeting certain conditions, usually examination results.

For any type of offer, through UCAS or CUKAS, there may be some non-academic requirements:

- For courses that involve contact with children and vulnerable adults you may need to have criminal record checks before you can start the course.
- For students who are not resident in either the UK or the EU, there may be some financial conditions to meet.

When you have received decisions for all your choices, you must decide what you want to accept and you do this by using Track. You will be given a deadline by which to decide what to accept.

Replying to offers - UCAS

When you have received decisions for all your choices, you must decide what you want to accept. You will be given a deadline in Track by which you have to make your replies. Before replying, get advice from family, friends or advisers, but remember that you're the one taking the course so it's your decision.

Firm acceptance

- Your firm acceptance is your first choice - this is your preferred choice out of all the offers you have received. You can only have one firm acceptance.

- If you accept an unconditional offer, you are agreeing that you will attend the course, so you must decline any other offers.

- If you accept a conditional offer, you are agreeing that you will attend the course at that university or college if you meet the conditions of the offer. You can accept another offer as an insurance choice.

Insurance acceptance

- If your firm acceptance is a conditional offer, you can accept another offer as an insurance choice. Your insurance choice can be conditional or unconditional and acts as a back-up, so if you don't meet the conditions for your firm choice but meet the conditions for your insurance, you will be committed to the insurance choice. You can only have one insurance choice.

- The conditions for your insurance choice would usually be lower than your firm choice.

- You don't have to accept an insurance choice if you don't want one.

For more information watch our video guides *How to use Track*, *Making sense of your offers*, and *How to reply to your offers* at **www.ucas.tv**.

Replying to offers - CUKAS

You may only be able to accept one offer as your first choice, or you may be able to accept two offers and state your first and second choices. The number of offers you can accept will depend on the type of offers.

- If you accept a guaranteed unconditional offer you will be expected to take up this place. You cannot accept any other offer as a second choice.

- If you accept a guaranteed conditional offer as your first choice, you will also be expected to take up this place provided you meet the conditions. You cannot accept any other offer as a second choice.

- If you accept a reserve unconditional or a reserve conditional offer as your first choice, you may accept any type of offer as your second choice.

What if you have no offers?

If you have used all five choices on your application and either received no offers, or decided to turn down any offers you have received, you may be eligible to apply for another choice through Extra. Find out more about Extra on page 122.

If you are not eligible for Extra, in the summer you can contact universities and colleges with vacancies in Clearing. See page 136 for more information.

If you have applied through CUKAS and do not receive any offers, you can reapply in the next application cycle. CUKAS does not operate an Extra or Clearing service.

design

your future

Find out about art, design, media and other creative courses

The UCAS Design your future event is an excellent opportunity for students from Years 10,11,12 and foundation level to talk to representatives from a wide range of art colleges and universities, pick up prospectuses, and attend art and design study related workshops.

Some subjects covered include: Art; Design; Media; Architecture; Web Design; Fashion; Ceramics and many more...

Events are taking place in both London and Manchester and will include around one hundred exhibitors, from Universities and Colleges, to organisations of particular interest to prospective students.

TO FIND OUT MORE OR TO BOOK, PLEASE VISIT THE WEBSITE WWW.UCASEVENTS.COM/DESIGN OR CALL 01242 544979

UCAS

```
  ┌──────────────────────────────┐
  │         Offers               │
  │ ⌐                            │
  │ ⊃                            │
  └──────────────────────────────┘
```

Extra

Extra allows you to make additional choices through UCAS, one at a time, without having to wait for Clearing in July. It is completely optional and free, and is designed to encourage you to continue researching and choosing courses if you are holding no offers. The courses available through Extra will be highlighted on Course Search, at **www.ucas.com**.

From 24 February – early July
The Extra service is available to eligible applicants through Track at **www.ucas.com**.

CUKAS does not operate an Extra service.

Who is eligible?
You will be eligible for Extra if you have already made five choices and:

- you have had unsuccessful or withdrawal decisions from all five of your choices, or

- you have cancelled your outstanding choices and hold no offers, or
- you have received decisions from all five choices and have declined all offers made to you.

How does it work?
We contact you and explain what to do if you are eligible for Extra. If you are eligible a special Extra button will be available on your Track screen. If you want to use Extra you should:

- check on Course Search for courses that are available through Extra; they are shown by the symbol **X** after the course title
- choose one that you would like to apply for and enter the details on your Track screen.

When you have chosen a course, the university or college will be able to view your application and consider you for its course.

What happens next?

We give universities and colleges a maximum of 21 days to consider your Extra application. During this time, you cannot be considered by another university or college. If you have not heard after 21 days you can refer yourself to a different university or college if you wish, but it is a good idea to ring the one currently considering you before doing so. If you are made an offer, you can choose whether or not to accept it.

If you accept an offer, conditional or unconditional, you will not be able to take any further part in Extra.

If you are currently studying for examinations, any offer that you receive is likely to be an offer conditional on exam grades. If you already have your examination results, it is possible that a university or college may make an unconditional offer. If you accept an unconditional offer, you will be placed. If you decide to decline the offer, or the university or college decides they cannot make you an offer, you will be given another opportunity to use Extra, time permitting. Your Extra button on Track will be reactivated.

Once you have accepted an offer in Extra, you are committed to it in the same way as you would be with an offer through the main UCAS system. Conditional offers made through Extra will be treated in the same way as other conditional offers, when your examination results become available.

If your results do not meet the conditions and the university or college decides that they cannot confirm your Extra offer, you will automatically become eligible for Clearing if it is too late for you to be considered by another university or college in Extra.

If you are unsuccessful, decline an offer, or do not receive an offer, or 21 days has elapsed since choosing a course through Extra, you can use Extra to apply for another course, time permitting.

Advice

Do the same careful research and seek guidance on your Extra choice of university or college and course as you did for your initial choices. If you applied to high-demand courses and institutions in your original application and were unsuccessful, you could consider related or alternative subjects or perhaps apply for the subject you want in combination with another. Your teachers or careers advisers, or the universities and colleges themselves can provide useful guidance. Entry Profiles, which appear with most courses listed on Course Search, are another important source of information. Be flexible, that is the key to success. But you are the only one who knows how flexible you are prepared to be.

Visit **www.ucas.tv** to watch the video guide on how to use Extra.

Offers

3

The Tariff

Admission to higher education courses is generally dependent upon an individual's achievement in level 3 qualifications, such as GCE A levels. Did you know that there are currently over 3,000 level 3 qualifications available in the UK alone?

As if the number of qualifications available was not confusing enough, different qualifications can have different grading structures (alphabetical, numerical or a mixture of both). Finding out what qualifications are needed for different higher education courses can be very confusing.

The UCAS Tariff is the system for allocating points to qualifications used for entry to higher education. It allows students to use a range of different qualifications to help secure a place on an undergraduate course.

Universities, colleges and conservatoires use the UCAS Tariff to make comparisons between applicants with different qualifications. Tariff points are often used in entry requirements, although other factors are often taken into account. Entry Profiles provide a fuller picture of what admissions tutors are seeking.

The tables on the following pages show the qualifications covered by the UCAS Tariff. There may have been changes to these tables since this book was printed. You should visit **www.ucas.com** to view the most up-to-date tables.

FURTHER INFORMATION?

Although Tariff points can be accumulated in a variety of ways, not all of these will necessarily be acceptable for entry to a particular higher education course. The achievement of a points score therefore does not give an automatic entitlement to entry, and many other factors are taken into account in the admissions process.

The Course Search facility at **www.ucas.com** or **www.cukas.ac.uk** is the best source of reference to find out what qualifications are acceptable for entry to specific courses. Updates to the Tariff, including details on how new qualifications are added, can be found at **www.ucas.com/students/ucas_tariff/.**

HOW DOES THE TARIFF WORK?

- Students can collect Tariff points from a range of different qualifications, eg GCE A level with BTEC Nationals.
- There is no ceiling to the number of points that can be accumulated.
- There is no double counting. Certain qualifications within the Tariff build on qualifications in the same subject. In these cases only the qualification with the higher Tariff score will be counted. This principle applies to:
  - GCE Advanced Subsidiary level and GCE Advanced level
  - Scottish Highers and Advanced Highers
  - Speech, drama and music awards at grades 6, 7 and 8.
- Tariff points for the Advanced Diploma come from the Progression Diploma score plus the relevant Additional and Specialist Learning (ASL) Tariff points. Please see the appropriate qualification in the Tariff tables to calculate the ASL score.
- The Extended Project Tariff points are included within the Tariff points for Progression and Advanced Diplomas. Extended Project points represented in the Tariff only count when the qualification is taken outside of these Diplomas.
- Where the Tariff tables refer to specific awarding organisations, only qualifications from these awarding organisations attract Tariff points. Qualifications with a similar title, but from a different qualification awarding organisation do not attract Tariff points.

HOW DO UNIVERSITIES, COLLEGES AND CONSERVATOIRES USE THE TARIFF?

The Tariff provides a facility to help universities, colleges and conservatoires when expressing entrance requirements and when making conditional offers. Entry requirements and conditional offers expressed as Tariff points will often require a minimum level of achievement in a specified subject (for example, '300 points to include grade A at A level chemistry', or '260 points including SQA Higher grade B in mathematics').

Use of the Tariff may also vary from department to department at any one institution, and may in some cases be dependent on the programme being offered.

In July 2010, UCAS announced plans to renew the Tariff. This review will take between 18 months and two years. You can read more about the review at **www.ucas.com/qireview**.

WHAT QUALIFICATIONS ARE INCLUDED IN THE TARIFF?

The following qualifications are included in the UCAS Tariff. See the number on the qualification title to find the relevant section of the Tariff table.

1   AAT NVQ level 3 in Accounting
2   AAT level 3 Diploma in Accounting (QCF)
3   Advanced Diploma
4   Advanced Extension Awards
5   Advanced Placement Programme (US and Canada)
6   Arts Award (Gold)
7   ASDAN Community Volunteering qualification
8   Asset Languages Advanced Stage
9   British Horse Society (Stage 3 Horse Knowledge & Care, Stage 3 Riding and Preliminary Teacher's Certificate)
10 BTEC Awards (NQF)
11 BTEC Certificates and Extended Certificates (NQF)
12 BTEC Diplomas (NQF)
13 BTEC National in Early Years (NQF)
14 BTEC Nationals (NQF)
15 BTEC QCF Qualifications
16 CACHE Award, Certificate and Diploma in Child Care and Education
17 Cambridge ESOL Examinations
18 Cambridge Pre-U
19 CISI Introduction to Securities and Investment
20 Certificate of Personal Effectiveness (COPE)
21 Diploma in Fashion Retail
22 Diploma in Foundation Studies (Art & Design; Art, Design & Media)
23 EDI Level 3 Certificate in Accounting, Certificate in Accounting (IAS)
24 Essential Skills (Northern Ireland)
25 Essential Skills Wales
26 Extended Project (stand alone)
27 Free-standing Mathematics
28 Functional skills
29 GCE (AS, AS Double Award, A level, A level Double Award and A level (with additional AS))
30 Hong Kong Diploma of Secondary Education (from 2012 entry onwards)
31 ifs School of Finance (Certificate and Diploma in Financial Studies)
32 iMedia (OCR level Certificate/Diploma for iMedia Professionals)
33 International Baccalaureate (IB) Diploma
34 International Baccalaureate (IB) Certificate
35 Irish Leaving Certificate (Higher and Ordinary levels)
36 IT Professionals (iPRO) (Certificate and Diploma)
37 Key Skills (Levels 2, 3 and 4)
38 Music examinations (grades 6, 7 and 8)
39 NPTC Level 3 Land Based Qualifications
40 OCR Level 3 Certificate in Mathematics for Engineering
41 OCR Level 3 Certificate for Young Enterprise
42 OCR Nationals (National Certificate, National Diploma and National Extended Diploma)
43 Principal Learning Wales
44 Progression Diploma
45 Scottish Qualifications
46 Speech and Drama examinations (grades 6, 7 and 8 and Performance Studies)
47 Sports Leaders UK
48 Welsh Baccalaureate Advanced Diploma (Core)

Updates on the Tariff, including details on the incorporation of any new qualifications, are posted on **www.ucas.com**.

UCAS TARIFF TABLES

2

AAT NVQ LEVEL 3 IN ACCOUNTING	
GRADE	TARIFF POINTS
PASS	160

AAT LEVEL 3 DIPLOMA IN ACCOUNTING	
GRADE	TARIFF POINTS
PASS	160

3

ADVANCED DIPLOMA

Advanced Diploma = Progression Diploma plus Additional & Specialist Learning (ASL). Please see the appropriate qualification to calculate the ASL score. Please see the Progression Diploma (Table 44) for Tariff scores

4

ADVANCED EXTENSION AWARDS	
GRADE	TARIFF POINTS
DISTINCTION	40
MERIT	20

Points for Advanced Extension Awards are over and above those gained from the A level grade

6

ADVANCED PLACEMENT PROGRAMME (US & CANADA)	
GRADE	TARIFF POINTS
Group A	
5	120
4	90
3	60
Group B	
5	50
4	35
3	20

Details of the subjects covered by each group can be found at www.ucas.com/students/ucas_tariff/tarifftables

ARTS AWARD (GOLD)	
GRADE	TARIFF POINTS
PASS	35

7

ASDAN COMMUNITY VOLUNTEERING QUALIFICATION	
GRADE	TARIFF POINTS
CERTIFICATE	50
AWARD	30

8

ASSET LANGUAGES ADVANCED STAGE			
GRADE	TARIFF POINTS	GRADE	TARIFF POINTS
Speaking		Listening	
GRADE 12	28	GRADE 12	25
GRADE 11	20	GRADE 11	18
GRADE 10	12	GRADE 10	11
Reading		Writing	
GRADE 12	25	GRADE 12	25
GRADE 11	18	GRADE 11	18
GRADE 10	11	GRADE 10	11

9

BRITISH HORSE SOCIETY	
GRADE	TARIFF POINTS
Stage 3 Horse Knowledge & Care	
PASS	35
Stage 3 Riding	
PASS	35
Preliminary Teacher's Certificate	
PASS	35

Awarded by Equestrian Qualifications (GB) Ltd (EQL)

10

BTEC AWARDS (NQF) (EXCLUDING BTEC NATIONAL QUALIFICATIONS)			
GRADE	TARIFF POINTS		
	Group A	Group B	Group C
DISTINCTION	20	30	40
MERIT	13	20	26
PASS	7	10	13

Details of the subjects covered by each group can be found at www.ucas.com/students/ucas_tariff/tarifftables

11

BTEC CERTIFICATES AND EXTENDED CERTIFICATES (NQF) (EXCLUDING BTEC NATIONAL QUALIFICATIONS)					
GRADE	TARIFF POINTS				
	Group A	Group B	Group C	Group D	Extended Certificates
DISTINCTION	40	60	80	100	60
MERIT	26	40	52	65	40
PASS	13	20	26	35	20

Details of the subjects covered by each group can be found at www.ucas.com/students/ucas_tariff/tarifftables

12

BTEC DIPLOMAS (NQF) (EXCLUDING BTEC NATIONAL QUALIFICATIONS)			
GRADE	TARIFF POINTS		
	Group A	Group B	Group C
DISTINCTION	80	100	120
MERIT	52	65	80
PASS	26	35	40

Details of the subjects covered by each group can be found at www.ucas.com/students/ucas_tariff/tarifftables

13

BTEC NATIONAL IN EARLY YEARS (NQF)					
GRADE	TARIFF POINTS	GRADE	TARIFF POINTS	GRADE	TARIFF POINTS
Theory				Practical	
Diploma		Certificate		D	120
DDD	320	DD	200	M	80
DDM	280	DM	160	P	40
DMM	240	MM	120		
MMM	220	MP	80		
MMP	160	PP	40		
MPP	120				
PPP	80				

Points apply to the following qualifications only: BTEC National Diploma in Early Years (100/1279/5); BTEC National Certificate in Early Years (100/1280/1).

14

BTEC NATIONALS (NQF)					
GRADE	TARIFF POINTS	GRADE	TARIFF POINTS	GRADE	TARIFF POINTS
Diploma		Certificate		Award	
DDD	360	DD	240	D	120
DDM	320	DM	200	M	80
DMM	280	MM	160	P	40
MMM	240	MP	120		
MMP	200	PP	80		
MPP	160				
PPP	120				

15

BTEC QUALIFICATIONS (QCF) (SUITE OF QUALIFICATIONS KNOWN AS NATIONALS)				
EXTENDED DIPLOMA	DIPLOMA	SUBSIDIARY DIPLOMA	CERTIFICATE	TARIFF POINTS
D*D*D*				420
D*D*D				400
D*DD				380
DDD				360
DDM				320
DMM	D*D*			280
	D*D			260
MMM	DD			240
MMP	DM			200
MPP	MM			160
		D*		140
PPP	MP	D		120
	PP	M		80
			D*	70
			D	60
		P	M	40
			P	20

6

CACHE LEVEL 3 AWARD, CERTIFICATE AND DIPLOMA IN CHILD CARE & EDUCATION

AWARD		CERTIFICATE		DIPLOMA	
GRADE	TARIFF POINTS	GRADE	TARIFF POINTS	GRADE	TARIFF POINTS
A	30	A	110	A	360
B	25	B	90	B	300
C	20	C	70	C	240
D	15	D	55	D	180
E	10	E	35	E	120

17

CAMBRIDGE ESOL EXAMINATIONS

GRADE	TARIFF POINTS
Certificate of Proficiency in English	
A	140
B	110
C	70
Certificate in Advanced English	
A	70

18

CAMBRIDGE PRE-U

GRADE	TARIFF POINTS	GRADE	TARIFF POINTS	GRADE	TARIFF POINTS
Principal Subject		Global Perspectives and Research		Short Course	
D1	TBC	D1	TBC	D1	TBC
D2	145	D2	140	D2	TBC
D3	130	D3	126	D3	60
M1	115	M1	112	M1	53
M2	101	M2	98	M2	46
M3	87	M3	84	M3	39
P1	73	P1	70	P1	32
P2	59	P2	56	P2	26
P3	46	P3	42	P3	20

19

CISI INTRODUCTION TO SECURITIES AND INVESTMENT

GRADE	TARIFF POINTS
PASS WITH DISTINCTION	60
PASS WITH MERIT	40
PASS	20

20

CERTIFICATE OF PERSONAL EFFECTIVENESS (COPE)

GRADE	TARIFF POINTS
PASS	70

Points are awarded for the Certificate of Personal Effectiveness (CoPE) awarded by ASDAN and CCEA

21

DIPLOMA IN FASHION RETAIL

GRADE	TARIFF POINTS
DISTINCTION	160
MERIT	120
PASS	80

Awarded by ABC Awards

22

DIPLOMA IN FOUNDATION STUDIES (ART & DESIGN AND ART, DESIGN & MEDIA)

GRADE	TARIFF POINTS
DISTINCTION	285
MERIT	225
PASS	165

Awarded by ABC, Edexcel, UAL and WJEC

23

EDI LEVEL 3 CERTIFICATE IN ACCOUNTING, CERTIFICATE IN ACCOUNTING (IAS)

GRADE	TARIFF POINTS
DISTINCTION	120
MERIT	90
PASS	70

24

ESSENTIAL SKILLS (NORTHERN IRELAND)

GRADE	TARIFF POINTS
LEVEL 2	10

Details of the subjects covered by each group can be found at www.ucas.com/students/ucas_tariff/tarifftables

25

ESSENTIAL SKILLS WALES

GRADE	TARIFF POINTS
LEVEL 3	20
LEVEL 2	10

Only allocated at level 2 if studied as part of a wider composite qualification such as 14-19 Diploma or Welsh Baccalaureate

26

EXTENDED PROJECT (STAND ALONE)

GRADE	TARIFF POINTS
A*	70
A	60
B	50
C	40
D	30
E	20

Points for the Extended Project cannot be counted if taken as part of Progression/Advanced Diploma

27

FREE-STANDING MATHEMATICS

GRADE	TARIFF POINTS
A	20
B	17
C	13
D	10
E	7

Covers free-standing Mathematics - Additional Maths, Using and Applying Statistics, Working with Algebraic and Graphical Techniques, Modelling with Calculus

UCAS TARIFF TABLES

28

FUNCTIONAL SKILLS	
GRADE	TARIFF POINTS
LEVEL 2	10

Only allocated if studied as part of a wider composite qualification such as 14-19 Diploma or Welsh Baccalaureate

29

GCE AND VCE									
GRADE	TARIFF POINTS	GRADE	TARIFF POINTS	GRADE	TARIFF POINTS	GRADE	TARIFF POINTS	GRADE	TARIFF POINTS
GCE & AVCE Double Award		GCE A level with additional AS (9 units)		GCE A level & AVCE		GCE AS Double Award		GCE AS & AS VCE	
A*A*	280	A*A	200	A*	140	AA	120	A	60
A*A	260	AA	180	A	120	AB	110	B	50
AA	240	AB	170	B	100	BB	100	C	40
AB	220	BB	150	C	80	BC	90	D	30
BB	200	BC	140	D	60	CC	80	E	20
BC	180	CC	120	E	40	CD	70		
CC	160	CD	110			DD	60		
CD	140	DD	90			DE	50		
DD	120	DE	80			EE	40		
DE	100	EE	60						
EE	80								

30

HONG KONG DIPLOMA OF SECONDARY EDUCATION					
GRADE	TARIFF POINTS	GRADE	TARIFF POINTS	GRADE	TARIFF POINTS
All subjects except mathematics		Mathematics compulsory component		Mathematics optional components	
5**	No value	5**	No value	5**	No value
5*	130	5*	60	5*	70
5	120	5	45	5	60
4	80	4	35	4	50
3	40	3	25	3	40

Points come into effect for entry to higher education from 2012 onwards.
No value for 5** pending receipt of candidate evidence (post 2012)

31

IFS SCHOOL OF FINANCE (NQF & QCF)			
GRADE	TARIFF POINTS	GRADE	TARIFF POINTS
Certificate in Financial Studies (CeFS)		Diploma in Financial Studies (DipFS)	
A	60	A	60
B	50	B	50
C	40	C	40
D	30	D	30
E	20	E	20

Completion of both qualifications will result in a maximum of 120 UCAS Tariff points

32

LEVEL 3 CERTIFICATE / DIPLOMA FOR iMEDIA USERS (iMEDIA)	
GRADE	TARIFF POINTS
DIPLOMA	66
CERTIFICATE	40

Awarded by OCR

3

INTERNATIONAL BACCALAUREATE (IB) DIPLOMA

GRADE	TARIFF POINTS	GRADE	TARIFF POINTS
45	720	34	479
44	698	33	457
43	676	32	435
42	654	31	413
41	632	30	392
40	611	29	370
39	589	28	348
38	567	27	326
37	545	26	304
36	523	25	282
35	501	24	260

34

INTERNATIONAL BACCALAUREATE (IB) CERTIFICATE

GRADE	TARIFF POINTS	GRADE	TARIFF POINTS	GRADE	TARIFF POINTS
Higher Level		Standard Level		Core	
7	130	7	70	3	120
6	110	6	59	2	80
5	80	5	43	1	40
4	50	4	27	0	10
3	20	3	11		

5

IRISH LEAVING CERTIFICATE

GRADE	TARIFF POINTS	GRADE	TARIFF POINTS
Higher		Ordinary	
A1	90	A1	39
A2	77	A2	26
B1	71	B1	20
B2	64	B2	14
B3	58	B3	7
C1	52		
C2	45		
C3	39		
D1	33		
D2	26		
D3	20		

36

IT PROFESSIONALS (iPRO)

GRADE	TARIFF POINTS
DIPLOMA	100
CERTIFICATE	80

Awarded by OCR

37

KEY SKILLS

GRADE	TARIFF POINTS
LEVEL 4	30
LEVEL 3	20
LEVEL 2	10

Details of the subjects covered by each group can be found at www.ucas.com/students/ucas_tariff/tarifftables

38

MUSIC EXAMINATIONS

GRADE	TARIFF POINTS	GRADE	TARIFF POINTS	GRADE	TARIFF POINTS
Practical					
Grade 8		Grade 7		Grade 6	
DISTINCTION	75	DISTINCTION	60	DISTINCTION	45
MERIT	70	MERIT	55	MERIT	40
PASS	55	PASS	40	PASS	25
Theory					
Grade 8		Grade 7		Grade 6	
DISTINCTION	30	DISTINCTION	20	DISTINCTION	15
MERIT	25	MERIT	15	MERIT	10
PASS	20	PASS	10	PASS	5

Points shown are for the ABRSM, Guildhall, LCMM, Rockschool and Trinity College London Advanced level music examinations

UCAS TARIFF TABLES

39

	NPTC LEVEL 3 LAND BASED QUALIFICATIONS			
EXTENDED DIPLOMA	DIPLOMA	SUBSIDIARY DIPLOMA	CERTIFICATE	TARIFF POINTS
D				360
M	D			240
	M			160
P		D		120
	P	M		80
			D	60
		P	M	40
			P	20

Points come into effect for entry to higher education from 2011 onwards.

40

OCR LEVEL 3 CERTIFICATE IN MATHEMATICS FOR ENGINEERING	
GRADE	TARIFF POINTS
A*	TBC
A	90
B	75
C	60
D	45
E	30

41

OCR LEVEL 3 CERTIFICATE FOR YOUNG ENTERPRISE	
GRADE	TARIFF POINTS
DISTINCTION	40
MERIT	30
PASS	20

42

OCR NATIONALS					
GRADE	TARIFF POINTS	GRADE	TARIFF POINTS	GRADE	TARIFF POINTS
National Extended Diploma		National Diploma		National Certificate	
D1	360	D	240	D	120
D2/M1	320	M1	200	M	80
M2	280	M2/P1	160	P	40
M3	240	P2	120		
P1	200	P3	80		
P2	160				
P3	120				

43

PRINCIPAL LEARNING WALES	
GRADE	TARIFF POINTS
A*	210
A	180
B	150
C	120
D	90
E	60

Points for Principal Learning Wales come into effect for entry to higher education from 2011 onwards.

44

PROGRESSION DIPLOMA	
GRADE	TARIFF POINTS
A*	350
A	300
B	250
C	200
D	150
E	100

Advanced Diploma = Progression Diploma plus Additional & Specialist Learning (ASL). Please see the appropriate qualification to calculate the ASL score.

45

SCOTTISH QUALIFICATIONS							
GRADE	TARIFF POINTS	GRADE	TARIFF POINTS	GRADE	TARIFF POINTS	GROUP	TARIFF POINTS
Advanced Higher		Higher		Scottish Interdisciplinary Project		Scottish National Certificates	
A	130	A	80	A	65	C	125
B	110	B	65	B	55	B	100
C	90	C	50	C	45	A	75
D	72	D	36				
Ungraded Higher		NPA PC Passport					
PASS	45	PASS	45				
		Core Skills					
		HIGHER	20				

Details of the subjects covered by each Scottish National Certificate can be found at www.ucas.com/students/ucas_tariff/tarifftables

46

SPEECH AND DRAMA EXAMINATIONS							
GRADE	TARIFF POINTS	GRADE	TARIFF POINTS	GRADE	TARIFF POINTS	GRADE	TARIFF POINTS
PCertLAM		Grade 8		Grade 7		Grade 6	
DISTINCTION	90	DISTINCTION	65	DISTINCTION	55	DISTINCTION	40
MERIT	80	MERIT	60	MERIT	50	MERIT	35
PASS	60	PASS	45	PASS	35	PASS	20

Points shown are for ESB, LAMDA, LCMM and Trinity Guildhall Advanced level speech and drama examinations accredited in the National Qualifications Framework and LAMDA'S Certificates in Communication and Certificate in Performance accredited on the Qualifications and Credit framework (QCF). Tariff points are available for both the NQF and QCF PCertLAM.

47

SPORTS LEADERS UK	
GRADE	TARIFF POINTS
PASS	30

These points are awarded to Higher Sports Leader Award and Level 3 Certificate in Higher Sports Leadership (QCF)

48

WELSH BACCALAUREATE ADVANCED DIPLOMA (CORE)	
GRADE	TARIFF POINTS
PASS	120

These points are awarded only when a candidate achieves the Welsh Baccalaureate Advanced Diploma

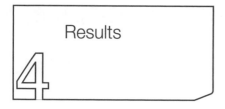

Results

4

Step 4 – Results

We receive many UK exam results direct from the exam boards – check the list at **www.ucas.com** or **www.cukas.ac.uk**. If your qualification is listed, you don't need to send your results to us or to the universities, colleges or conservatoires where you're holding offers. Check Track at **www.ucas.com** or **www.cukas.ac.uk** to see if you've got a place on your chosen course.

If your qualification is listed, we send your results to the universities, colleges or conservatoires that you have accepted as your firm and insurance choices through UCAS, or first and second choices if you applied through CUKAS. If your qualification is not listed, you must send your exam results to the universities, colleges or conservatoires where you are holding offers.

You should arrange your holidays so that you are at home when your exam results are published because, if there are any issues to discuss, admissions tutors will

want to speak to you in person.

After you have received your exam results check Track to find out if you have a place on your chosen course.

If you have met all the conditions for your firm or first choice, the university, college or conservatoire will confirm that you have a place. Sometimes, they may still confirm you have a place even if you have not quite met all the offer conditions; or they may offer you a place on a similar course.

If you have not met the conditions of your firm or first choice and the university, college or conservatoire has not confirmed your place, but you have met all the conditions of your insurance or second offer, the university, college or conservatoire will confirm that you have a place.

When a university, college or conservatoire tells us that you have a place, we send you confirmation by letter.

RE-MARKED EXAMS

If you ask for any of your exams to be re-marked, you must tell the universities, colleges or conservatoires where you're holding offers. If a university, college or conservatoire cannot confirm your place based on the initial results, you should ask them if they would be able to reconsider their decision after the re-mark. They don't have to reconsider their position even if your re-mark results in higher grades. Don't forget that re-marks may also result in lower grades.

The exam boards tell us about any re-marks that result in grade changes. We then send the revised grades to the universities, colleges or conservatoires where you're holding offers. As soon as you know about grade changes, you should also tell them.

'CASHING IN' A LEVEL RESULTS

If you have taken A levels, your school or college must certificate or 'cash in' all your unit scores before the exam board can award final grades. If when you collect your A level results you have to add up your unit scores to find out your final grades, it means your school or college has not 'cashed in' your results.

We only receive cashed in results from the exam boards, so if your school or college has not cashed in your results, you must ask them to send a 'cash in' request to the exam board. You also need to tell the universities, colleges or conservatoires where you're holding offers that there'll be a delay in receiving your results and call our Customer Service Unit to find out when your results have been received.

When we receive your 'cashed in' results from the exam board we'll send them to the universities, colleges or conservatoires where you're holding offers straight away.

WHAT IF YOU DON'T HAVE A PLACE?

UCAS only - If you have not met the conditions of either your firm or insurance choice, and your chosen universities or colleges have not confirmed your place, you are eligible for Clearing. In Clearing you can apply for courses that still have vacancies. Clearing operates from mid-July to late September 2012 (page136).

BETTER RESULTS THAN EXPECTED?

UCAS only - If you obtain exam results that meet and exceed the conditions of the offer for your firm choice, you can for a short period use a process called Adjustment to look for an alternative place, whilst still keeping your original firm choice. See page 137 for information about Adjustment.

Next steps

5

Step 5 – Next steps

You might find yourself with different exam results than you were expecting, or you may change your mind about what you want to do. If so, there may be other options open to you.

CLEARING

Clearing is a service that helps people without a place find suitable course vacancies. It runs from mid-July until the end of September, but most people use it after the exam results are published in August.

You could consider related or alternative subjects or perhaps combining your original choice of subject with another. Your teachers or careers adviser, or the universities and colleges themselves, can provide useful guidance.

Course vacancies are listed at **www.ucas.com** and in the national media following the publication of exam results in August. **Once you have your exam results**, if you're in Clearing you need to look at the vacancy listings and then contact any university or college you are interested in.

Talk to the institutions; don't be afraid to call them. Make sure you have your Personal ID and Clearing Number ready and prepare notes on what you will say to them about:

- why you want to study the course
- why you want to study at their university or college
- any relevant employment or activities you have done that relate to the course
- your grades.

Accepting an offer - you can contact as many universities and colleges as you like through Clearing, and you may informally be offered more than one place. If this happens, you will need to decide which offer you want to accept. If you're offered a place you want to be formally considered for, you enter the course details in Track, and the university or college will then let you know if they're accepting you.

ADJUSTMENT

If you receive better results than expected, and meet and exceed the conditions of your conditional firm choice, you have the opportunity to reconsider what and where you want to study. This process is called Adjustment.

Adjustment runs from A level results day on 16 August 2012 until the end of August. Your individual Adjustment period starts on A level results day or when your conditional firm choice changes to unconditional firm, whichever is the later. You then have a maximum of five calendar days to register and secure an alternative course, if you decide you want to do this. If you want to try to find an alternative course you must register in Track to use Adjustment, so universities and colleges can view your application.

There are no vacancy listings for Adjustment, so you'll need to talk to the institutions. When you contact a university or college make it clear that you are applying through Adjustment, not Clearing. If they want to consider you they will ask for your Personal ID, so they can view your application.

If you don't find an alternative place then you remain accepted at your original firm choice.

Adjustment is entirely optional; remember that nothing really beats the careful research you carried out to find the right courses before you made your UCAS application. Talk to a careers adviser at your school, college or local careers office, as they can help you decide if registering to use Adjustment is right for you.

More information about Adjustment and Clearing is available at **www.ucas.com**. You can also view UCAStv video guides on how to use Adjustment and Clearing at **www.ucas.tv**.

CUKAS does not operate a Clearing or Adjustment service.

IF YOU ARE STILL WITHOUT A PLACE TO STUDY:

If you haven't found a suitable place, or changed your mind about what you want to do, there are lots of other options. Ask for advice from your school, college or careers office. Here are some suggestions you might want to consider:

- studying a part-time course (there's a part-time course search at **www.ucas.com** from July until September)
- studying a foundation degree
- re-sit your exams
- getting some work experience
- studying in another country
- reapplying next year to university or college through UCAS
- taking a gap year
- doing an apprenticeship (you'll find a vacancy search on the National Apprenticeship Service (NAS) website at **www.apprenticeships.org.uk**)
- finding a job
- starting a business.

More advice and links to other organisations can be found on the UCAS website at **www.ucas.com/students/nextsteps/advice**.

Starting at a
university, college
or conservatoire

Step 6 – Starting at a university, college or conservatoire

Congratulations! Now you have your place at university, college or a conservatoire you will need to finalise your plans on how to get there, where to live and how to finance it. Make lists of things to do and people whose help you can call on. Will you have to travel independently or can your parents or relatives help with transport? If you are keeping a car, have you checked out parking facilities and told your insurance company?

Make sure you have everything organised, including travel arrangements, essential documents and paperwork, books and equipment required for the course. The university or conservatoire will send you joining information – contact the Admissions Office or the Students' Union if you have questions about anything to do with starting your course.

Where to live - unless you are planning to live at home, your university, college or conservatoire will usually provide you with guidance on how to find somewhere to live. The earlier you contact them the better your chance of finding a suitable range of options, from hall to private landlords, to choose from. Find out what facilities are available at the different accommodation options. Check what you need to bring with you and what is supplied. Don't leave it all to the last minute – especially things like arranging a bank account, checking what proof of identity you might need, gathering together a few essentials like supplies of coffee, insurance cover, TV licence etc.

Student finance - you will need to budget for living costs, accommodation, travel, books and tuition fees. Learn about budgeting by visiting **www.ucas.com** or **www.cukas.ac.uk**, where you will find further links to useful resources to help you manage your money. Remember that if you do get into financial difficulties the Welfare Office at the institution can help you change tack and manage better in future, but it is always better to live within your means from the outset.

www.yougofurther.co.uk - the UCAS student network allows you to make friends with other students who are going to the same university or college and could be on the same course. yougo allows you to talk to UCAS online as well as to the universities and colleges on their profile pages. yougo is your direct route to the information you need.

Useful contacts

CONNECTING WITH UCAS

You can follow UCAS on Twitter at **www.twitter.com/ucas_online**, and ask a question or see what others are asking on Facebook at **www.facebook.com/ucasonline**. You can also watch videos of UCAS advisers answering frequently asked questions on YouTube at **www.youtube.com/ucasonline**.

There are many UCAStv video guides to help with your journey into higher education, such as *How to choose your courses*, *Attending events*, and *How to apply*. These can all be viewed at **www.ucas.tv** or in the relevant section of **www.ucas.com**.

If you need to speak to UCAS, please contact the Customer Service Unit on 0871 468 0 468 or 0044 871 468 0 468 from outside the UK. Calls from BT landlines within the UK will cost no more than 9p per minute. The cost of calls from mobiles and other networks may vary.

If you have hearing difficulties, you can call the Text Relay service on 18001 0871 468 0 468 (outside the UK 0044 151 494 1260). Calls are charged at normal rates.

www.yougofurther.co.uk: 'yougo', as it is more commonly known, is the UCAS student network. On yougo you can make friends with other applicants who are going to the same university or college and/or who are going to be on the same course.

CONTACTING CUKAS

If you need help or advice on your individual application, you can contact the CUKAS Customer Service Unit on 0871 468 0 470 (or 0044 871 468 0 470 from outside the UK). UK BT landline calls will cost no more than 9p per minute. Calls from mobiles and other networks may vary.

If you have hearing difficulties, call the Text Relay service (text phone) on 18001 0871 468 0 470 from within the UK (or on 0044 151 494 1260 from outside the UK). You will need to ask the operator to dial 0871 468 0 470.

CAREERS ADVICE

Connexions Direct is for you if you live in England, are aged 13 to 19 and want advice on getting to where you want to be in life.

Connexions personal advisers can give you information, advice and practical help with all sorts of things, like choosing subjects at school or mapping out your future career options. They can help you with anything that might be affecting you at school, college, work or in your personal or family life.

www.direct.gov.uk/en/YoungPeople/index.htm.

Careers Scotland provides a starting point for anyone looking for careers information, advice or guidance. **www.careers-scotland.org.uk**.

Careers Wales – Wales' national all-age careers guidance service. **www.careerswales.com**.

Northern Ireland Careers Service website provides all-age careers guidance service in Northern Ireland. **www.careersserviceni.com**.

Learndirect – Not sure what job you want? Need help to decide which course to do? Give learndirect a call on 0800 101 901 or, for Scotland, 0808 100 9000. **www.learndirect.co.uk**
www.learndirectscotland.com.

GENERAL HIGHER EDUCATION ADVICE

Unistats at **www.direct.gov.uk/unistats** is the official website to help you make an informed choice when deciding which UK university or college to apply to. It includes the results of the latest National Student Survey.

National Union of Students (NUS) is the national voice of students, helping them to campaign, get cheap student discounts and provide advice on living student life to the full - **www.nus.org.uk**.

STUDENTS WITH DISABILITIES

If you have a disability or specific learning difficulty, you are strongly encouraged to make early direct contact with individual institutions before submitting your application. Most universities, colleges and conservatoires have disability coordinators or advisers. You can find their contact details and further advice at the Skill: National Bureau for Students with Disabilities' website – **www.skill.org.uk**.

There is financial help for students with disabilities known as Disabled Students' Allowances (DSAs). More information is available on the Directgov website at **www.direct.gov.uk/disabledstudents**

YEAR OUT

For useful information on taking a year out, see **www.gap-year.com**.

The Year Out Group website is packed with information and guidance for young people and their parents and advisers.
www.yearoutgroup.org.

Essential reading

UCAS has brought together the best books and resources you need to make the important decisions regarding entry to higher education. With guidance on choosing courses, finding the right institution, information about student finance, admissions tests, gap years and lots more, you can find the most trusted guides at **www.ucasbooks.com**.

The publications listed on the following pages and many others are available through **www.ucasbooks.com** or from UCAS Publication Services unless otherwise stated.

UCAS PUBLICATION SERVICES

UCAS Publication Services
PO Box 130
Cheltenham
Gloucestershire GL52 3ZF

f: 01242 544 806
e: publicationservices@ucas.ac.uk
// **www.ucasbooks.com**

ENTIRE RESEARCH AND APPLICATION PROCESS
EXPLAINED

The UCAS Guide to getting into University and College

This brand new guide contains advice and information about the entire research and application process, and brings together the expertise of UCAS staff, along with insights and tips from well known universities including Oxford and Cambridge, and students who are involved with or have experienced the process first-hand.

The book clearly sets out the information you need in an easy-to-read format, with myth busters, tips from students, checklists and much more; this book will be a companion for applicants throughout their entire journey into higher education.
Published by UCAS
Price: £11.99

NEED HELP COMPLETING YOUR APPLICATION?

How to Complete your UCAS Application 2012

A must for anyone applying through UCAS. Contains advice on the preparation needed, a step-by-step guide to filling out the UCAS application, information on the UCAS process and useful tips for completing the personal statement.
Published by Trotman
Price £12.99

Insider's Guide to Applying to University

Full of honest insights, this is a thorough guide to the application process. It reveals advice from careers advisers and current students, guidance on making sense of university information and choosing courses. Also includes tips for the personal statement, interviews, admissions tests, UCAS Extra and Clearing.
Published by Trotman
Price £12.99

How to Write a Winning UCAS Personal Statement

The personal statement is your chance to stand out from the crowd. Based on information from admissions tutors, this book will help you sell yourself. It includes specific guidance for over 30 popular subjects, common mistakes to avoid, information on what admissions tutors look for, and much more.
Published by Trotman
Price £12.99

CHOOSING COURSES

Progression Series 2012 entry

The 'Progression to…' titles are designed to help you access good quality, useful information on some of the most competitive subject areas. The books cover advice on applying through UCAS, routes to qualifications, course details, job prospects, case studies and career advice.

Progression to…
Art and Design
Economics, Finance and Accountancy
Engineering and Mathematics
Journalism, Broadcasting, Media Production and Performing Arts
Law
Medicine, Dentistry and Optometry
Nursing, Healthcare and Social Work
Psychology
Sports Science and Physiotherapy
Teaching and Education
Published by UCAS
Price £15.99 each

UCAS Parent Guide

Free of charge.

Order online at **www.ucas.com/parents**.

Open Days 2011

Attending open days, taster courses and higher education conventions is an important part of the application process. This publication makes planning attendance at these events quick and easy.

Published annually by UCAS.

Price £3.50

ESSENTIAL READING

'Getting into…' guides

Clear and concise guides to help applicants secure places. They include qualifications required, advice on applying, tests, interviews and case studies. The guides give an honest view and discuss current issues and careers.

Getting into Business and Economics

Getting into Oxford and Cambridge

Getting into Veterinary School

Published by Trotman

Price £12.99 each

Choosing Your Degree Course & University

With so many universities and courses to choose from, it is not an easy decision for students embarking on their journey to higher education. This guide will offer expert guidance on the questions students need to ask when considering the opportunities available.

Published by Trotman

Price £24.99

Degree Course Descriptions

Providing details of the nature of degree courses, the descriptions in this book are written by heads of departments and senior lecturers at major universities. Each description contains an overview of the course area, details of course structures, career opportunities and more.

Published by COA

Price £12.99

CHOOSING WHERE TO STUDY

The Virgin Guide to British Universities

An insider's guide to choosing a university or college. Written by students and using independent statistics, this guide evaluates what you get from a higher education institution.

Published by Virgin

Price £16.99

Times Good University Guide 2012

How do you find the best university for the subject you wish to study? You need a guide that evaluates the quality of what is available, giving facts, figures and comparative assessments of universities. The rankings provide hard data, analysed, interpreted and presented by a team of experts.

Published by Harper Collins

Price £16.99

Which Uni?

One person's perfect uni might be hell for someone else. Picking the right one will give you the best chance of future happiness, academic success and brighter job prospects. This guide is packed with tables from a variety of sources, rating universities on everything from the quality of teaching to the make-up of the student population and much more.

Published by Trotman

Price £14.99

Getting into the UK's Best Universities and Courses

This book is for those who set their goals high and dream of studying on a highly regarded course at a good university. It provides information on selecting the best courses for a subject, the application and personal statement, interviews, results day, timescales for applications and much more.
Published by Trotman
Price £12.99

FINANCIAL INFORMATION

Student Finance

All students need to know about tuition fees, loans, grants, bursaries and much more. Covering all forms of income and expenditure, this comprehensive guide is produced in association with UCAS and offers great value for money.
Published by Constable Robinson
Price: £7.99

The Essential Guide to Paying for University

Parents and students alike are increasingly concerned about the rising cost of university education. However, there are strategies that can help, and there are many bursaries that go unclaimed every year. This guide covers the cost of university, funding available to help, and how parents and students can plan and budget.
Published by Kogan Page
Price £9.99

University Scholarships, Awards & Bursaries

Students embarking on HE courses face an increasingly challenging financial situation. This book enables applicants and current students to find the support that may help them make ends meet. Packed with information on virtually all awards available.
Published by Trotman
Price £22.99

CAREERS PLANNING

A-Z of Careers and Jobs

It is vital to be well informed about career decisions and this guide will help you make the right choice. It provides full details of the wide range of opportunities on the market, the personal qualities and skills needed for each job, entry qualifications and training, realistic salary expectations and useful contact details.
Published by Kogan Page
Price £16.99

The Careers Directory

An indispensable resource for anyone seeking careers information, covering over 350 careers. It presents up-to-date information in an innovative double-page format. Ideal for students in years 10 to 13 who are considering their futures and for other careers professionals.
Published by COA
Price £14.99

Careers with a Science Degree

Over 100 jobs and areas of work for graduates of biological, chemical and physical sciences are described in this guide. Whether you have yet to choose your degree subject and want to know where the various choices could lead, or are struggling for ideas about what to do with your science degree, this book will guide and inspire you. The title includes: nature of the work and potential employers, qualifications required for entry, including personal qualities and skills; training routes and opportunities for career development and postgraduate study options.
Published by Lifetime Publishing
Price: £12.99

Careers with an Arts and Humanities Degree

Covers careers and graduate opportunities related to these degrees. The book describes over 100 jobs and areas of work suitable for graduates from a range of disciplines including: English and modern languages, history and geography, music and the fine arts. The guide highlights: graduate opportunities, training routes, postgraduate study options and entry requirements.
Published by Lifetime Publishing
Price: £12.99

DEFERRING ENTRY

Your Gap Year

The essential book for all young people planning a gap year before continuing with their education. This up-to-date guide provides essential information on specialist gap year programmes, as well as the vast range of jobs and voluntary opportunities available to young people around the world.
Published by Crimson Publishing
Price £12.99

Gap Year Guidebook 2011

This thorough and easy-to-use guide contains everything you need to know before taking a gap year. It includes real-life traveller tips, hundreds of contact details, realistic advice on everything from preparing, learning and working abroad, coping with coming home and much more.
Published by John Catt Education
Price £14.99

Summer Jobs Worldwide 2011

This unique and specialist guide contains over 40,000 jobs for all ages. No other book includes such a variety and wealth of summer work opportunities in Britain and aboard. Anything from horse trainer in Iceland, to a guide for nature walks in Peru, to a yoga centre helper in Greece, to an animal keeper for London Zoo, can be found.
Published by Crimson Publishing
Price £14.99

Please note all publications incur a postage and packing charge. All information was correct at the time of printing.

For a full list of publications, please visit **www.ucasbooks.com.**

Courses

Courses

Keen to get started on your career in journalism, media or performing arts career? This section contains details of the various degree courses available at UK institutions.

EXPLAINING THE LIST OF COURSES

The list of courses has been divided into subject categories (see page 150).

We list the universities and colleges by their UCAS institution codes. Within each institution, courses are listed first by award type (such as BA, BSc, FdA, HND, MA and many others), then alphabetically by course title.

All practice-based music, drama, and dance courses offered through CUKAS can be found between pages 324 – 331.

You might find some courses showing an award type '(Mod)', which indicates a combined degree that might be modular in design. A small number of courses have award type '(FYr)'. This indicates a 12-month foundation course, after which students can choose to apply for a degree course. In either case, you should contact the university or college for further details.

Generally speaking, when a course comprises two or more subjects, the word used to connect the subjects indicates the make-up of the award: 'Subject A and Subject B' is a joint award, where both subjects carry equal weight; 'Subject A with Subject B' is a major/minor award, where Subject A accounts for at least 60% of your study. If the title shows 'Subject A/Subject B', it may indicate that students can decide on the weighting of the subjects at the end of the first year. You should check with the university or college for full details.

Each entry shows the course code and the duration of the course. Where known, the entry contains details of the minimum qualification requirements for the course, as supplied to by the universities, colleges or conservatoires. Bear in mind that possessing the minimum qualifications does not guarantee acceptance to the course: there may be far more applicants than places. You may be asked to attend an interview or audition, present a portfolio or sit an admissions test.

Courses with entry requirements that require applicants to disclose information about spent and unspent convictions and may require a Criminal Records Bureau (---) check, are marked '**CRB Check:** Required'.

Before applying for any course, you are advised to contact the institution to check any changes in entry requirements and to see if any new courses have come on stream since the lists were approved for publication. To make this easy, each institution's entry starts with their address, email, phone and fax details, as well as their website address. You will also find it useful to check the Entry Profiles section of Course Search at **www.ucas.com** or **www.cukas.ac.uk**.

LIST OF SUBJECT CATEGORIES

The list of courses in this section has been divided into the following subject categories

PUBLICITY STUDIES

B22 UNIVERSITY OF BEDFORDSHIRE
PARK SQUARE
LUTON
BEDS LU1 3JU
t: 0844 8482234 f: 01582 489323
e: admissions@beds.ac.uk
// www.beds.ac.uk

PP25 BA Journalism and Public Relations
Duration: 3FT Hon
Entry Requirements: *Foundation:* Pass. *GCE:* 200. *SQAH:* BCC.
SQAAH: BCC. *IB:* 24. *BTEC NC:* MM. *BTEC ND:* MPP. *OCR ND:*
M1 *OCR NED:* P1 Interview required.

P3P2 BA Media Practices with Public Relations
Duration: 3FT Hon
Entry Requirements: *Foundation:* Pass. *GCE:* 200. *SQAH:* BCC.
SQAAH: BCC. *IB:* 24. *BTEC NC:* MM. *BTEC ND:* MPP. *OCR ND:*
M1 *OCR NED:* P1

P210 BA Public Relations
Duration: 3FT Hon
Entry Requirements: *Foundation:* Pass. *GCE:* 200. *SQAH:* BCC.
SQAAH: BCC. *IB:* 24. *BTEC NC:* MM. *BTEC ND:* MPP. *OCR ND:*
M1 *OCR NED:* P1

P211 BA Public Relations
Duration: 4SW Hon
Entry Requirements: *Foundation:* Pass. *GCE:* 200. *SQAH:* BCC.
SQAAH: BCC. *IB:* 24. *BTEC NC:* MM. *BTEC ND:* MPP. *OCR ND:*
M1 *OCR NED:* P1

B25 BIRMINGHAM CITY UNIVERSITY
PERRY BARR
BIRMINGHAM B42 2SU
t: 0121 331 5595 f: 0121 331 7994
e: choices@bcu.ac.uk
// www.bcu.ac.uk

NL12 BA Business and Public Relations
Duration: 3FT/4SW Hon
Entry Requirements: *GCE:* 280. *IB:* 32. *BTEC NC:* DD. *BTEC ND:*
DMM. *OCR ND:* D *OCR NED:* M2 Interview required. Portfolio
required.

P9P2 BA Media and Communication (Public Relations)
Duration: 3FT Hon
Entry Requirements: *Foundation:* Pass. *GCE:* BBC. *SQAH:* ABBB.
SQAAH: BBC. *IB:* 30. *BTEC ND:* DMM. Interview required. Portfolio
required.

B35 UNIVERSITY COLLEGE BIRMINGHAM
SUMMER ROW
BIRMINGHAM B3 1JB
t: 0121 604 1040 f: 0121 604 1166
e: admissions@ucb.ac.uk
// www.ucb.ac.uk

D6P2 BA Food, Media and Communications Management
Duration: 3FT Hon
Entry Requirements: *GCE:* 200. *IB:* 24. *BTEC NC:* DM. *BTEC ND:*
MMP.

D6PF FdA Food, Media and Communications Management
Duration: 2FT Fdg
Entry Requirements: *GCE:* 120.

B50 BOURNEMOUTH UNIVERSITY
TALBOT CAMPUS
FERN BARROW
POOLE
DORSET BH12 5BB
t: 01202 524111
// www.bournemouth.ac.uk

P210 BA Public Relations
Duration: 4SW Hon
Entry Requirements: *Foundation:* Distinction. *GCE:* 300. *IB:* 31.
BTEC NC: MM. *BTEC ND:* DMM. Interview required.

B94 BUCKINGHAMSHIRE NEW UNIVERSITY
QUEEN ALEXANDRA ROAD
HIGH WYCOMBE
BUCKINGHAMSHIRE HP11 2JZ
t: 0800 0565 660 f: 01494 605 023
e: admissions@bucks.ac.uk
// bucks.ac.uk

PN25 BA Public Relations and Marketing Communications
Duration: 3FT Hon
Entry Requirements: *GCE:* 200-240. *IB:* 24. *BTEC NC:* DM.
BTEC ND: MMM. *OCR ND:* M1 *OCR NED:* M3

C10 CANTERBURY CHRIST CHURCH UNIVERSITY
NORTH HOLMES ROAD
CANTERBURY
KENT CT1 1QU
t: 01227 782900 f: 01227 782888
e: admissions@canterbury.ac.uk
// www.canterbury.ac.uk

N1PJ BA Entrepreneurship with Film, Radio & Television Studies
Duration: 3FT Hon
Entry Requirements: *GCE:* 240. *IB:* 24.

C30 UNIVERSITY OF CENTRAL LANCASHIRE
PRESTON
LANCS PR1 2HE
t: 01772 201201 f: 01772 894954
e: uadmissions@uclan.ac.uk
// www.uclan.ac.uk

NPF2 BA Management and Public Relations
Duration: 3FT Hon
Entry Requirements: *GCE:* 240-280. *SQAH:* AABB-BBBC. *IB:* 28. *BTEC NC:* DD. *OCR ND:* D

NP52 BA Marketing and Public Relations
Duration: 3FT Hon
Entry Requirements: *GCE:* 240-280. *SQAH:* AABB-BBBC. *IB:* 28. *BTEC NC:* DD. *OCR ND:* D

P211 BA Public Relations
Duration: 3FT Hon
Entry Requirements: *GCE:* 240-280. *SQAH:* AABB-BBBC. *IB:* 28. *BTEC NC:* DD. *OCR ND:* D

P213 BA Public Relations (Business Communication)
Duration: 4SW Deg
Entry Requirements: Contact the institution for details.

P218 BA Public Relations (Business Communication)
Duration: 3FT Hon
Entry Requirements: Contact the institution for details.

P2L2 BA Public Relations (Business Communication) with International Study
Duration: 4SW Hon
Entry Requirements: Contact the institution for details.

P215 BA Public Relations (Entertainment)
Duration: 4SW Hon
Entry Requirements: Contact the institution for details.

P222 BA Public Relations (Entertainment)
Duration: 3FT Hon
Entry Requirements: Contact the institution for details.

L2P2 BA Public Relations (Entertainment) with International Study
Duration: 4SW Hon
Entry Requirements: Contact the institution for details.

P214 BA Public Relations (Political Communication)
Duration: 3FT Hon
Entry Requirements: Contact the institution for details.

P219 BA Public Relations (Political Communication)
Duration: 4SW Hon
Entry Requirements: Contact the institution for details.

P2LF BA Public Relations (Political Communication) with International Study
Duration: 4SW Hon
Entry Requirements: Contact the institution for details.

P210 BA Public Relations (Sandwich)
Duration: 4SW Hon
Entry Requirements: *GCE:* 240-280. *SQAH:* AABB-BBBC. *IB:* 28. *BTEC NC:* DD. *OCR ND:* D

P216 BA Public Relations (Sports)
Duration: 4SW Hon
Entry Requirements: Contact the institution for details.

P221 BA Public Relations (Sports)
Duration: 3FT Hon
Entry Requirements: Contact the institution for details.

L2PG BA Public Relations (Sports) with International Study
Duration: 4SW Hon
Entry Requirements: Contact the institution for details.

NP22 BA Public Relations and Management
Duration: 3FT Hon
Entry Requirements: *GCE:* 240-280. *SQAH:* AABB-BBBC. *IB:* 28. *BTEC NC:* DD. *OCR ND:* D

NPM2 BA Public Relations and Marketing
Duration: 3FT Hon
Entry Requirements: *GCE:* 240-280. *SQAH:* AABB-BBBC. *IB:* 28. *BTEC NC:* DD. *OCR ND:* D

P220 BA Public Relations with International Study
Duration: 4SW Hon
Entry Requirements: Contact the institution for details.

P212 BA Sport Public Relations
Duration: 3FT Hon
Entry Requirements: *GCE:* 240-280. *SQAH:* AABB-BBBC. *IB:* 28. *BTEC NC:* DD. *OCR ND:* D

C55 UNIVERSITY OF CHESTER
PARKGATE ROAD
CHESTER CH1 4BJ
t: 01244 511000 f: 01244 511300
e: enquiries@chester.ac.uk
// www.chester.ac.uk

PNF5 BA Marketing & Public Relations and Advertising
Duration: 3FT Hon
Entry Requirements: *GCE:* 240-280.

PW23 BA Marketing & Public Relations and Commercial Music Production
Duration: 3FT Hon
Entry Requirements: *Foundation:* Pass. *GCE:* 260-300. *SQAH:* BBBB. *IB:* 28. *BTEC NC:* DM. *BTEC ND:* DMM.

PW26 BA Marketing & Public Relations and Digital Photography
Duration: 3FT Hon
Entry Requirements: *GCE:* 240-280.

NP52 BA Marketing & Public Relations and Events Management
Duration: 3FT Hon
Entry Requirements: *GCE:* 240-280.

PPFH BA Marketing & Public Relations and Film Studies
Duration: 3FT Hon
Entry Requirements: *GCE:* 240-280.

PPF5 BA Marketing & Public Relations and Journalism
Duration: 3FT Hon
Entry Requirements: *GCE:* 240-280.

PPFJ BA Marketing & Public Relations and Media Studies
Duration: 3FT Hon
Entry Requirements: *GCE:* 240-280.

PN21 BA Marketing & Public Relations and Radio Production
Duration: 3FT Hon
Entry Requirements: *Foundation:* Pass. *GCE:* 260-300. *SQAH:* BBBB. *IB:* 28. *BTEC NC:* DM. *BTEC ND:* DMM.

PC2P BA Marketing & Public Relations and Sport Development
Duration: 3FT Hon
Entry Requirements: *GCE:* 240-280.

PP2I BA Marketing & Public Relations and Television Production
Duration: 3FT Hon
Entry Requirements: *Foundation:* Pass. *GCE:* 260-300. *SQAH:* BBBB. *IB:* 28. *BTEC NC:* DM. *BTEC ND:* DMM.

E42 EDGE HILL UNIVERSITY
ORMSKIRK
LANCASHIRE L39 4QP
t: 01695 657000 f: 01695 584355
e: study@edgehill.ac.uk
// www.edgehill.ac.uk

P210 BA Public Relations
Duration: 3FT Hon
Entry Requirements: *GCE:* 280. *IB:* 26. *BTEC NC:* DD. *BTEC ND:* DMM. *OCR ND:* D *OCR NED:* M2

NP52 BSc Marketing with Public Relations
Duration: 3FT Hon
Entry Requirements: *GCE:* 280. *IB:* 26. *BTEC NC:* DM. *BTEC ND:* MMP. *OCR ND:* D *OCR NED:* M2

G14 UNIVERSITY OF GLAMORGAN, CARDIFF AND PONTYPRIDD
ENQUIRIES AND ADMISSIONS UNIT
PONTYPRIDD CF37 1DL
t: 0800 716925 f: 01443 654050
e: enquiries@glam.ac.uk
// www.glam.ac.uk

JP92 BSc Live Event Technology
Duration: 3FT Hon
Entry Requirements: *GCE:* BBB. *IB:* 26.

H60 THE UNIVERSITY OF HUDDERSFIELD
QUEENSGATE
HUDDERSFIELD HD1 3DH
t: 01484 473969 f: 01484 472765
e: admissionsandrecords@hud.ac.uk
// www.hud.ac.uk

WP22 BA Fashion, Communication and Promotion
Duration: 3FT/4SW Hon
Entry Requirements: *GCE:* 300. *SQAH:* ABBB-BBBB. *IB:* 28. Interview required.

N5P2 BA Marketing with Public Relations
Duration: 4SW/3FT Hon
Entry Requirements: *GCE:* 300. *SQAH:* BBBC. *IB:* 26. *BTEC ND:* DDM. Interview required.

WP3F BA Music and Promotion
Duration: 3FT Hon
Entry Requirements: *GCE:* 200. *SQAH:* BBBC. *IB:* 25. Interview required.

N5PF BA Sports Marketing with Public Relations
Duration: 4SW/3FT Hon
Entry Requirements: *GCE:* 300. *SQAH:* BBBC. *IB:* 26. *BTEC ND:* DDM. Interview required.

K84 KINGSTON UNIVERSITY
STUDENT INFORMATION & ADVICE CENTRE
COOPER HOUSE
40-46 SURBITON ROAD
KINGSTON UPON THAMES KT1 2HX
t: 0844 8552177 f: 020 8547 7080
e: aps@kingston.ac.uk
// www.kingston.ac.uk

WP22 BA Design and Politics
Duration: 3FT Hon
Entry Requirements: *GCE:* 220-360. Interview required. Portfolio required.

L27 LEEDS METROPOLITAN UNIVERSITY
COURSE ENQUIRIES OFFICE
CITY SITE
LEEDS LS1 3HE
t: 0113 81 23113 f: 0113 81 23129
// www.leedsmet.ac.uk

RP12 BA French and Public Relations
Duration: 3FT/4SW Hon
Entry Requirements: *GCE:* 220. *IB:* 24.

RP22 BA German and Public Relations
Duration: 3FT/4SW Hon
Entry Requirements: *GCE:* 220. *IB:* 26.

P210 BA Public Relations
Duration: 3FT/4SW Hon
Entry Requirements: *GCE:* 260. *IB:* 24.

P2N5 BA Public Relations with Marketing
Duration: 3FT/4SW Hon
Entry Requirements: *GCE:* 260. *IB:* 24.

RP42 BA Spanish and Public Relations
Duration: 3FT/4SW Hon
Entry Requirements: *GCE:* 220. *IB:* 26.

NP52 BA Sports Marketing and Public Relations
Duration: 3FT Hon
Entry Requirements: *GCE:* 240. *IB:* 28.

L39 UNIVERSITY OF LINCOLN
ADMISSIONS
BRAYFORD POOL
LINCOLN LN6 7TS
t: 01522 886097 f: 01522 886146
e: admissions@lincoln.ac.uk
// www.lincoln.ac.uk

PN25 BA Advertising and Marketing
Duration: 3FT Hon
Entry Requirements: *GCE:* 260.

PP52 BA Journalism and Public Relations
Duration: 3FT Hon
Entry Requirements: *GCE:* 280.

L51 LIVERPOOL JOHN MOORES UNIVERSITY
KINGSWAY HOUSE
HATTON GARDEN
LIVERPOOL L3 2AJ
t: 0151 231 5090 f: 0151 231 3462
e: courses@ljmu.ac.uk
// www.ljmu.ac.uk

NP12 BA Business and Public Relations
Duration: 3FT/4SW Hon
Entry Requirements: *GCE:* 260.

L68 LONDON METROPOLITAN UNIVERSITY
166-220 HOLLOWAY ROAD
LONDON N7 8DB
t: 020 7133 4200
e: admissions@londonmet.ac.uk
// www.londonmet.ac.uk

NPM2 BA Advertising & Marketing Communication and Public Relations
Duration: 3FT Hon
Entry Requirements: *GCE:* 240. *IB:* 28.

NP82 BA Events Management and Public Relations
Duration: 3FT Hon
Entry Requirements: *GCE:* 240. *IB:* 28.

P210 BA Public Relations
Duration: 3FT Hon
Entry Requirements: *GCE:* 240. *IB:* 28.

M40 THE MANCHESTER METROPOLITAN UNIVERSITY
ADMISSIONS OFFICE
ALL SAINTS (GMS)
ALL SAINTS
MANCHESTER M15 6BH
t: 0161 247 2000
// www.mmu.ac.uk

NP52 BA Public Relations and Digital Communications Management
Duration: 3FT Hon
Entry Requirements: *GCE:* 240-280. *IB:* 29.

PP21 BA Public Relations and Digital Communications Management (Exchange)
Duration: 4FT Hon
Entry Requirements: Contact the institution for details.

NP5F BA Public Relations and Digital Communications Management (Sandwich)
Duration: 4SW Hon
Entry Requirements: *GCE:* 240-280. *IB:* 29.

NP5G BA Public Relations and Digital Communications Management (with Foundation Year)
Duration: 4FT/5SW Hon
Entry Requirements: *GCE:* 120. *IB:* 24.

N77 NORTHUMBRIA UNIVERSITY
TRINITY BUILDING
NORTHUMBERLAND ROAD
NEWCASTLE UPON TYNE NE1 8ST
t: 0191 243 7420 f: 0191 227 4561
e: er.admissions@northumbria.ac.uk
// www.northumbria.ac.uk

PP92 BSc Communication and Public Relations
Duration: 3FT Hon
Entry Requirements: *GCE:* 280. *SQAH:* BBCCC. *SQAAH:* BCC. *IB:* 25. *BTEC ND:* DMM. *OCR NED:* M2

Q25 QUEEN MARGARET UNIVERSITY, EDINBURGH
QUEEN MARGARET UNIVERSITY DRIVE
EDINBURGH EH21 6UU
t: 0131474 0000 f: 0131 474 0001
e: admissions@qmu.ac.uk
// www.qmu.ac.uk

PN25 BA Public Relations and Marketing
Duration: 4FT Hon
Entry Requirements: *GCE:* 260. *IB:* 28.

PP23 BA Public Relations and Media
Duration: 4FT Hon
Entry Requirements: *GCE:* 260. *IB:* 28.

R06 RAVENSBOURNE
6 PENROSE WAY
LONDON SE10 0EW
t: 020 3040 3500
e: info@rave.ac.uk
// www.rave.ac.uk

HP62 BSc Broadcast Audio Technology (Fast-Track)
Duration: 2FT Hon
Entry Requirements: Contact the institution for details.

R36 ROBERT GORDON UNIVERSITY
ROBERT GORDON UNIVERSITY
SCHOOLHILL
ABERDEEN
SCOTLAND AB10 1FR
t: 01224 26 27 28 f: 01224 26 21 47
e: UGOffice@rgu.ac.uk
// www.rgu.ac.uk

P9P2 BA Communication with Public Relations
Duration: 4FT Hon
Entry Requirements: *GCE:* CCC. *SQAH:* BBCC. *IB:* 26.

P210 BA (Hons) Public Relations
Duration: 4FT Hon
Entry Requirements: Contact the institution for details.

S21 SHEFFIELD HALLAM UNIVERSITY
CITY CAMPUS
HOWARD STREET
SHEFFIELD S1 1WB
t: 0114 225 5555 f: 0114 225 2167
e: admissions@shu.ac.uk
// www.shu.ac.uk

P210 BA Public Relations
Duration: 3FT Hon
Entry Requirements: *GCE:* 260.

PP23 BA Public Relations and Media
Duration: 3FT Hon
Entry Requirements: *GCE:* 260.

S28 SOMERSET COLLEGE OF ARTS AND TECHNOLOGY
WELLINGTON ROAD
TAUNTON
SOMERSET TA1 5AX
t: 01823 366331 f: 01823 366418
e: enquiries@somerset.ac.uk
// www.somerset.ac.uk/student-area/considering-a-degree.html

P240 BA Design: Advertising (Top-Up)
Duration: 1FT Hon
Entry Requirements: HND required.

S30 SOUTHAMPTON SOLENT UNIVERSITY
EAST PARK TERRACE
SOUTHAMPTON
HAMPSHIRE SO14 0RT
t: +44 (0) 23 8031 9039 f: + 44 (0)23 8022 2259
e: admissions@solent.ac.uk or ask@solent.ac.uk
// www.solent.ac.uk/

PN25 BA Advertising and Public Relations (Top-Up)
Duration: 1FT Hon
Entry Requirements: Interview required. HND required.

QP32 BA English and Public Relations
Duration: 3FT Hon
Entry Requirements: *Foundation:* Distinction. *GCE:* 240. *SQAAH:* AA-CCD. *IB:* 24. *BTEC NC:* DD. *BTEC ND:* MMM. *OCR ND:* D *OCR NED:* M3

QP3F BA English and Public Relations
Duration: 4SW Hon
Entry Requirements: *Foundation:* Distinction. *GCE:* 240. *SQAAH:* AA-CCD. *IB:* 24. *BTEC NC:* DD. *BTEC ND:* MMM. *OCR ND:* D *OCR NED:* M3

W2P2 BA Fashion with Public Relations
Duration: 3FT Hon
Entry Requirements: *GCE:* 160.

PH26 BA Public Relations and Communication
Duration: 3FT Hon
Entry Requirements: *Foundation:* Distinction. *GCE:* 240. *SQAAH:* AA-CCD. *IB:* 24. *BTEC NC:* DD. *BTEC ND:* MMM. *OCR ND:* D *OCR NED:* M3

P2Q3 BA Public Relations and Communications with International Foundation Year
Duration: 4FT Hon
Entry Requirements: *GCE:* 240.

S72 STAFFORDSHIRE UNIVERSITY
COLLEGE ROAD
STOKE ON TRENT ST4 2DE
t: 01782 292753 f: 01782 292740
e: admissions@staffs.ac.uk
// www.staffs.ac.uk

PP25 BA Sports PR and Journalism
Duration: 3FT Hon
Entry Requirements: *GCE:* 260.

S75 THE UNIVERSITY OF STIRLING
STIRLING FK9 4LA
t: 01786 467044 f: 01786 466800
e: admissions@stir.ac.uk
// www.stir.ac.uk

PP23 BA Film, Media and Communications Practice
Duration: 4FT Hon
Entry Requirements: *GCE:* BBC. *SQAH:* BBBB. *SQAAH:* AAA-CCC. *IB:* 32. *BTEC ND:* DDM.

PP52 BA Journalism Studies and Communications Practice
Duration: 4FT Hon
Entry Requirements: *GCE:* BBC. *SQAH:* BBBB. *SQAAH:* AAA-CCC. *IB:* 32. *BTEC ND:* DDM.

S84 UNIVERSITY OF SUNDERLAND
STUDENT HELPLINE
THE STUDENT GATEWAY
CHESTER ROAD
SUNDERLAND SR1 3SD
t: 0191 515 3000 f: 0191 515 3805
e: student.helpline@sunderland.ac.uk
// www.sunderland.ac.uk

T7P2 BA American Studies with Public Relations
Duration: 3FT Hon
Entry Requirements: *GCE:* 260-360. *BTEC NC:* DM. *BTEC ND:* MMM. *OCR ND:* D *OCR NED:* M3

NP12 BA Business Management and Public Relations
Duration: 3FT Hon
Entry Requirements: *GCE:* 260-360. *BTEC NC:* DM. *BTEC ND:* MMM. *OCR ND:* D *OCR NED:* M3

N1P2 BA Business Management with Public Relations
Duration: 3FT Hon
Entry Requirements: *GCE:* 260-360. *BTEC NC:* DM. *BTEC ND:* MMM. *OCR ND:* D *OCR NED:* M3

XPH2 BA Childhood Studies and Public Relations
Duration: 3FT Hon
Entry Requirements: *GCE:* 260-360.

X3P2 BA Childhood Studies with Public Relations
Duration: 3FT Hon
Entry Requirements: Contact the institution for details.

B9P2 BA Community Health with Public Relations
Duration: 3FT Hon
Entry Requirements: *GCE:* 260-360. *BTEC NC:* DM. *BTEC ND:* MMM. *OCR ND:* D *OCR NED:* M3

WP32 BA Community Music and Public Relations
Duration: 3FT Hon
Entry Requirements: *GCE:* 260-360.

WHP2 BA Community Music with Public Relations
Duration: 3FT Hon
Entry Requirements: *GCE:* 260-360.

MP92 BA Criminology and Public Relations
Duration: 3FT Hon
Entry Requirements: *GCE:* 260-360. *BTEC NC:* DM. *BTEC ND:* MMM. *OCR ND:* D *OCR NED:* M3

M9P2 BA Criminology with Public Relations
Duration: 3FT Hon
Entry Requirements: *GCE:* 260-360. *BTEC NC:* DM. *BTEC ND:* MMM. *OCR ND:* D *OCR NED:* M3

PW25 BA Dance and Public Relations
Duration: 3FT Hon
Entry Requirements: *GCE:* 260-360. *IB:* 31. *BTEC NC:* DM. *BTEC ND:* MMM. *OCR ND:* D *OCR NED:* M3

W5P2 BA Dance with Public Relations
Duration: 3FT Hon
Entry Requirements: *GCE:* 260-360. *IB:* 31. *BTEC NC:* DM. *BTEC ND:* MMM. *OCR ND:* D *OCR NED:* M3

W4P2 BA Drama with Public Relations
Duration: 3FT Hon
Entry Requirements: *GCE:* 260-360. *BTEC NC:* DM. *BTEC ND:* MMM. *OCR ND:* D *OCR NED:* M3

Q1P2 BA English Language & Linguistics with Public Relations
Duration: 3FT Hon
Entry Requirements: *GCE:* 260-360. *BTEC NC:* DM. *BTEC ND:* MMM. *OCR ND:* D *OCR NED:* M3

Q3P2 BA English Studies with Public Relations
Duration: 3FT Hon
Entry Requirements: *GCE:* 260-360. *BTEC NC:* DM. *BTEC ND:* MMM. *OCR ND:* D *OCR NED:* M3

NP32 BA Financial Management and Public Relations
Duration: 3FT Hon
Entry Requirements: *GCE:* 260-360. *BTEC NC:* DM. *BTEC ND:* MMM. *OCR ND:* D *OCR NED:* M3

N3P2 BA Financial Management with Public Relations
Duration: 3FT Hon
Entry Requirements: *GCE:* 260-360. *BTEC NC:* DM. *BTEC ND:* MMM. *OCR ND:* D *OCR NED:* M3

LP52 BA Health & Social Care and Public Relations
Duration: 3FT Hon
Entry Requirements: *GCE:* 260-360.

L5P2 BA Health & Social Care with Public Relations
Duration: 3FT Hon
Entry Requirements: Contact the institution for details.

PN26 BA Human Resource Management and Public Relations
Duration: 3FT Hon
Entry Requirements: *GCE:* 260-360. *BTEC NC:* DM. *BTEC ND:* MMM. *OCR ND:* D *OCR NED:* M3

N6P2 BA Human Resource Management with Public Relations
Duration: 3FT Hon
Entry Requirements: *GCE:* 260-360. *BTEC NC:* DM. *BTEC ND:* MMM. *OCR ND:* D *OCR NED:* M3

MP12 BA Law and Public Relations
Duration: 3FT Hon
Entry Requirements: *GCE:* 260-360. *BTEC NC:* DM. *BTEC ND:* MMM. *OCR ND:* D *OCR NED:* M3

NP52 BA Marketing Management and Public Relations (-)
Duration: 3FT Hon
Entry Requirements: *GCE:* 260-360. *BTEC NC:* DM. *BTEC ND:* MMM. *OCR ND:* D *OCR NED:* M3

N5P2 BA Marketing Management with Public Relations
Duration: 3FT Hon
Entry Requirements: *GCE:* 260-360. *BTEC NC:* DM. *BTEC ND:* MMM. *OCR ND:* D *OCR NED:* M3

RP12 BA Modern Foreign Languages (French) and Public Relations
Duration: 3FT Hon
Entry Requirements: *GCE:* 260-360. *IB:* 31. *BTEC NC:* DM. *BTEC ND:* MMM. *OCR ND:* D *OCR NED:* M3

PR22 BA Modern Foreign Languages (German) and Public Relations
Duration: 3FT Hon
Entry Requirements: *GCE:* 260-360. *IB:* 31. *BTEC NC:* DM. *BTEC ND:* MMM. *OCR ND:* D *OCR NED:* M3

PR24 BA Modern Foreign Languages (Spanish) and Public Relations
Duration: 3FT Hon
Entry Requirements: *GCE:* 260-360. *IB:* 31. *BTEC NC:* DM. *BTEC ND:* MMM. *OCR ND:* D *OCR NED:* M3

W3P2 BA Music with Public Relations
Duration: 3FT Hon
Entry Requirements: *GCE:* 260-360. *IB:* 31. *BTEC NC:* DM.
BTEC ND: MMM. *OCR ND:* D *OCR NED:* M3

L2P2 BA Politics with Public Relations
Duration: 3FT Hon
Entry Requirements: *GCE:* 260-360. *BTEC NC:* DM. *BTEC ND:* MMM. *OCR ND:* D *OCR NED:* M3

P210 BA Public Relations
Duration: 3FT Hon
Entry Requirements: *GCE:* 260-360. *IB:* 30. *BTEC ND:* DMM.

PT27 BA Public Relations and American Studies
Duration: 3FT Hon
Entry Requirements: *GCE:* 260-360. *BTEC NC:* DM. *BTEC ND:* MMM. *OCR ND:* D *OCR NED:* M3

PN21 BA Public Relations and Business Management
Duration: 3FT Hon
Entry Requirements: *GCE:* 260-360. *BTEC NC:* DM. *BTEC ND:* MMM. *OCR ND:* D *OCR NED:* M3

PB29 BA Public Relations and Community Health
Duration: 3FT Hon
Entry Requirements: *GCE:* 260-360. *BTEC NC:* DM. *BTEC ND:* MMM. *OCR ND:* D *OCR NED:* M3

PM29 BA Public Relations and Criminology
Duration: 3FT Hon
Entry Requirements: *GCE:* 260-360. *BTEC NC:* DM. *BTEC ND:* MMM. *OCR ND:* D *OCR NED:* M3

PW24 BA Public Relations and Drama
Duration: 3FT Hon
Entry Requirements: *GCE:* 260-360. *BTEC NC:* DM. *BTEC ND:* MMM. *OCR ND:* D *OCR NED:* M3

PX23 BA Public Relations and Education
Duration: 3FT Hon
Entry Requirements: *GCE:* 260-360. *BTEC NC:* DM. *BTEC ND:* MMM. *OCR ND:* D *OCR NED:* M3

PQ23 BA Public Relations and English
Duration: 3FT Hon
Entry Requirements: *GCE:* 260-360. *IB:* 31. *BTEC NC:* DM.
BTEC ND: MMM. *OCR ND:* D *OCR NED:* M3

PQ21 BA Public Relations and English Language/Linguistics
Duration: 3FT Hon
Entry Requirements: *GCE:* 260-360. *BTEC NC:* DM. *BTEC ND:* MMM. *OCR ND:* D *OCR NED:* M3

PV21 BA Public Relations and History
Duration: 3FT Hon
Entry Requirements: *GCE:* 260-360. *BTEC NC:* DM. *BTEC ND:* MMM. *OCR ND:* D *OCR NED:* M3

PP25 BA Public Relations and Journalism
Duration: 3FT Hon
Entry Requirements: *GCE:* 260-360. *BTEC NC:* DM. *BTEC ND:* MMM. *OCR ND:* D *OCR NED:* M3

PQ2H BA Public Relations and Modern Foreign Language (English)
Duration: 3FT Hon
Entry Requirements: *GCE:* 260-360. *BTEC NC:* DM. *BTEC ND:* MMM. *OCR ND:* D *OCR NED:* M3

PW23 BA Public Relations and Music
Duration: 3FT Hon
Entry Requirements: *GCE:* 260-360. *BTEC NC:* DM. *BTEC ND:* MMM. *OCR ND:* D *OCR NED:* M3

PW26 BA Public Relations and Photography
Duration: 3FT Hon
Entry Requirements: *GCE:* 260-360. *BTEC NC:* DM. *BTEC ND:* MMM. *OCR ND:* D *OCR NED:* M3

PL22 BA Public Relations and Politics
Duration: 3FT Hon
Entry Requirements: *GCE:* 260-360. *BTEC NC:* DM. *BTEC ND:* MMM. *OCR ND:* D *OCR NED:* M3

PC28 BA Public Relations and Psychology
Duration: 3FT Hon
Entry Requirements: *GCE:* 260-360. *IB:* 31. *BTEC NC:* DM.
BTEC ND: MMM. *OCR ND:* D *OCR NED:* M3

PL23 BA Public Relations and Sociology
Duration: 3FT Hon
Entry Requirements: *GCE:* 260-360. *BTEC NC:* DM. *BTEC ND:* MMM. *OCR ND:* D *OCR NED:* M3

PX21 BA Public Relations and TESOL
Duration: 3FT Hon
Entry Requirements: *GCE:* 260-360. *BTEC NC:* DM. *BTEC ND:* MMM. *OCR ND:* D *OCR NED:* M3

P2T7 BA Public Relations with American Studies
Duration: 3FT Hon
Entry Requirements: *GCE:* 260-360. *BTEC NC:* DM. *BTEC ND:* MMM. *OCR ND:* D *OCR NED:* M3

P2N1 BA Public Relations with Business Management
Duration: 3FT Hon
Entry Requirements: *GCE:* 260-360. *BTEC NC:* DM. *BTEC ND:* MMM. *OCR ND:* D *OCR NED:* M3

P2XH BA Public Relations with Childhood Studies
Duration: 3FT Hon
Entry Requirements: *GCE:* 260-360.

P2M9 BA Public Relations with Criminology
Duration: 3FT Hon
Entry Requirements: *GCE:* 260-360. *BTEC NC:* DM. *BTEC ND:* MMM. *OCR ND:* D *OCR NED:* M3

P2W5 BA Public Relations with Dance
Duration: 3FT Hon
Entry Requirements: *GCE:* 260-360. *IB:* 31. *BTEC NC:* DM. *BTEC ND:* MMM. *OCR ND:* D *OCR NED:* M3

P2W4 BA Public Relations with Drama
Duration: 3FT Hon
Entry Requirements: *GCE:* 260-360. *BTEC NC:* DM. *BTEC ND:* MMM. *OCR ND:* D *OCR NED:* M3

P2X3 BA Public Relations with Education
Duration: 3FT Hon
Entry Requirements: *GCE:* 260-360. *BTEC NC:* DM. *BTEC ND:* MMM. *OCR ND:* D *OCR NED:* M3

P2Q3 BA Public Relations with English
Duration: 3FT Hon
Entry Requirements: *GCE:* 260-360. *BTEC NC:* DM. *BTEC ND:* MMM. *OCR ND:* D *OCR NED:* M3

P2Q1 BA Public Relations with English Language/Linguistics
Duration: 3FT Hon
Entry Requirements: *GCE:* 260-360. *BTEC NC:* DM. *BTEC ND:* MMM. *OCR ND:* D *OCR NED:* M3

P2N3 BA Public Relations with Financial Management
Duration: 3FT Hon
Entry Requirements: *GCE:* 260-360. *BTEC NC:* DM. *BTEC ND:* MMM. *OCR ND:* D *OCR NED:* M3

P2L5 BA Public Relations with Health & Social Care
Duration: 3FT Hon
Entry Requirements: *GCE:* 260-360.

P2V1 BA Public Relations with History
Duration: 3FT Hon
Entry Requirements: *GCE:* 260-360. *BTEC NC:* DM. *BTEC ND:* MMM. *OCR ND:* D *OCR NED:* M3

P2P5 BA Public Relations with Journalism
Duration: 3FT Hon
Entry Requirements: *GCE:* 260-360. *BTEC NC:* DM. *BTEC ND:* MMM. *OCR ND:* D *OCR NED:* M3

P2N5 BA Public Relations with Marketing Management
Duration: 3FT Hon
Entry Requirements: *GCE:* 260-360. *BTEC NC:* DM. *BTEC ND:* MMM. *OCR ND:* D *OCR NED:* M3

P2QH BA Public Relations with Modern Foreign Languages (English)
Duration: 3FT Hon
Entry Requirements: *GCE:* 260-360. *BTEC NC:* DM. *BTEC ND:* MMM. *OCR ND:* D *OCR NED:* M3

P2R1 BA Public Relations with Modern Foreign Languages (French)
Duration: 3FT Hon
Entry Requirements: *GCE:* 260-360. *BTEC NC:* DM. *BTEC ND:* MMM. *OCR ND:* D *OCR NED:* M3

P2R2 BA Public Relations with Modern Foreign Languages (German)
Duration: 3FT Hon
Entry Requirements: *GCE:* 260-360. *BTEC NC:* DM. *BTEC ND:* MMM. *OCR ND:* D *OCR NED:* M3

P2W3 BA Public Relations with Music
Duration: 3FT Hon
Entry Requirements: *GCE:* 260-360. *IB:* 32. *BTEC NC:* DM. *BTEC ND:* MMM. *OCR ND:* D *OCR NED:* M3

P2W6 BA Public Relations with Photography
Duration: 3FT Hon
Entry Requirements: *GCE:* 260-360. *BTEC NC:* DM. *BTEC ND:* MMM. *OCR ND:* D *OCR NED:* M3

P2L2 BA Public Relations with Politics
Duration: 3FT Hon
Entry Requirements: *GCE:* 260-360. *BTEC NC:* DM. *BTEC ND:* MMM. *OCR ND:* D *OCR NED:* M3

P2L3 BA Public Relations with Sociology
Duration: 3FT Hon
Entry Requirements: *GCE:* 260-360. *BTEC NC:* DM. *BTEC ND:* MMM. *OCR ND:* D *OCR NED:* M3

P2C6 BA Public Relations with Sport
Duration: 3FT Hon
Entry Requirements: *GCE:* 260-360. *BTEC NC:* DM. *BTEC ND:* MMM. *OCR ND:* D *OCR NED:* M3

P2X1 BA Public Relations with TESOL
Duration: 3FT Hon
Entry Requirements: *GCE:* 260-360. *BTEC NC:* DM. *BTEC ND:* MMM. *OCR ND:* D *OCR NED:* M3

X1P2 BA TESOL with Public Relations
Duration: 3FT Hon
Entry Requirements: *GCE:* 260-360. *BTEC NC:* DM. *BTEC ND:* MMM. *OCR ND:* D *OCR NED:* M3

NP82 BA Tourism and Public Relations
Duration: 3FT Hon
Entry Requirements: *GCE:* 260-360. *IB:* 31. *BTEC NC:* DM.
BTEC ND: MMM. *OCR ND:* D *OCR NED:* M3

N8P2 BA Tourism with Public Relations
Duration: 3FT Hon
Entry Requirements: *GCE:* 220-360. *IB:* 31. *BTEC NC:* DM.
BTEC ND: MMM. *OCR ND:* D *OCR NED:* M3

P2B9 BA/BSc Public Relations with Community Health
Duration: 3FT Hon
Entry Requirements: *GCE:* 260-360. *BTEC NC:* DM. *BTEC ND:* MMM. *OCR ND:* D *OCR NED:* M3

P2C8 BA/BSc Public Relations with Psychology
Duration: 3FT Hon
Entry Requirements: *GCE:* 260-360. *BTEC NC:* DM. *BTEC ND:* MMM. *OCR ND:* D *OCR NED:* M3

CP62 BA/BSc Sport and Public Relations
Duration: 3FT Hon
Entry Requirements: *GCE:* 260-360. *BTEC NC:* DM. *BTEC ND:* MMM. *OCR ND:* D *OCR NED:* M3

C6P2 BSc Sport with Public Relations
Duration: 3FT Hon
Entry Requirements: *GCE:* 260-360. *BTEC NC:* DM. *BTEC ND:* MMM. *OCR ND:* D *OCR NED:* M3

S93 SWANSEA UNIVERSITY
SINGLETON PARK
SWANSEA SA2 8PP
t: 01792 295111 f: 01792 295110
e: admissions@swansea.ac.uk
// www.swansea.ac.uk

PP23 BA Public and Media Relations
Duration: 3FT Hon
Entry Requirements: *GCE:* BBB. *IB:* 32. *BTEC ND:* DDM.

U20 UNIVERSITY OF ULSTER
COLERAINE
CO. LONDONDERRY
NORTHERN IRELAND BT52 1SA
t: 028 7032 4221 f: 028 7032 4908
e: online@ulster.ac.uk
// www.ulster.ac.uk

P9P2 BSc Communication with Public Relations
Duration: 3FT Hon
Entry Requirements: *GCE:* 260. *IB:* 24. *BTEC ND:* DMM.

P2N5 BSc Communication, Advertising and Marketing
Duration: 4SW Hon
Entry Requirements: *GCE:* AAA. *SQAH:* AAAAA. *SQAAH:* AAA. *IB:* 39. *BTEC NC:* DD. *BTEC ND:* DDD.

Q9P2 BSc Language & Linguistics with Public Relations
Duration: 3FT Hon
Entry Requirements: *GCE:* 260. *IB:* 24. *BTEC ND:* DMM.

P210 BSc Public Relations (DPP)
Duration: 4SW Hon
Entry Requirements: *GCE:* 320. *IB:* 26. *BTEC ND:* DDM.

U65 UNIVERSITY OF THE ARTS LONDON
272 HIGH HOLBORN
LONDON WC1V 7EY
t: 020 7514 6000x6197 f: 020 7514 6198
e: c.anderson@arts.ac.uk
// www.arts.ac.uk

WP22 BA Fashion Public Relations
Duration: 3FT Hon
Entry Requirements: *IB:* 28. Interview required.

W2P2 BA Graphic and Media Design (Design for Information)
Duration: 3FT/4SW Hon
Entry Requirements: *IB:* 28. Foundation Course required. Interview required. Portfolio required.

P210 BA Public Relations
Duration: 3FT Hon
Entry Requirements: *IB:* 28. Foundation Course required. Interview required. Portfolio required.

W05 THE UNIVERSITY OF WEST LONDON
WALPOLE HOUSE
BOND STREET
EALING
LONDON W5 5AA
t: 0800 036 8888 f: 020 8566 1353
e: learning.advice@uwl.ac.uk
// www.uwl.ac.uk

P210 BA Public Relations
Duration: 3FT Hon
Entry Requirements: *GCE:* 200. *IB:* 28. Interview required.

W50 UNIVERSITY OF WESTMINSTER
2ND FLOOR
101 NEW CAVENDISH STREET,
LONDON W1W 6XH
t: 020 7911 5000 f: 020 7911 5788
e: course-enquiries@westminster.ac.uk
// www.westminster.ac.uk

P210 BA Public Relations
Duration: 3FT Hon
Entry Requirements: *GCE:* BBB. *SQAH:* AAAAA-BBBBB. *SQAAH:* AAA-BBB. *IB:* 30. *BTEC NC:* DD. *BTEC ND:* DDM. *OCR ND:* D *OCR NED:* D2 Interview required.

W80 UNIVERSITY OF WORCESTER
HENWICK GROVE
WORCESTER WR2 6AJ
t: 01905 855111 f: 01905 855377
e: admissions@worc.ac.uk
// www.worcester.ac.uk

NP12 BA Business, Accountancy & Public Relations
Duration: 3FT/4SW Hon
Entry Requirements: *GCE:* 280. *IB:* 25. *BTEC NC:* DD. *BTEC ND:* MMM. *OCR ND:* D *OCR NED:* M3

NP52 BA Business, Advertising & Public Relations
Duration: 3FT/4SW Hon
Entry Requirements: *GCE:* 280. *IB:* 25. *BTEC NC:* DD. *BTEC ND:* MMM. *OCR ND:* D *OCR NED:* M3

LP12 BA Business, Economics & Public Relations
Duration: 3FT/4SW Hon
Entry Requirements: *GCE:* 280. *IB:* 25. *BTEC NC:* DD. *BTEC ND:* MMM. *OCR ND:* D *OCR NED:* M3

NP21 BA Business, Entrepreneurship and Public Relations
Duration: 3FT/4SW Hon
Entry Requirements: *GCE:* 280. *IB:* 25. *BTEC NC:* DD. *BTEC ND:* MMM. *OCR ND:* D *OCR NED:* M3

NP62 BA Business, Human Resource Management & Public Relations
Duration: 3FT/4SW Hon
Entry Requirements: *GCE:* 280. *IB:* 25. *BTEC NC:* DD. *BTEC ND:* MMM. *OCR ND:* D *OCR NED:* M3

NP22 BA Business, Management & Public Relations
Duration: 3FT/4SW Hon
Entry Requirements: *GCE:* 280. *IB:* 25. *BTEC NC:* DD. *BTEC ND:* MMM. *OCR ND:* D *OCR NED:* M3

NP5F BA Marketing, Advertising & Public Relations
Duration: 3FT/4SW Hon
Entry Requirements: *GCE:* 280. *IB:* 25. *BTEC NC:* DD. *BTEC ND:* MMM. *OCR ND:* D *OCR NED:* M3

MEDIA STUDIES

A40 ABERYSTWYTH UNIVERSITY
WELCOME CENTRE, ABERYSTWYTH UNIVERSITY
PENGLAIS CAMPUS
ABERYSTWYTH
CEREDIGION SY23 3FB
t: 01970 622021 f: 01970 627410
e: ug-admissions@aber.ac.uk
// www.aber.ac.uk

VP1H BA Hanes a'r Cyfryngau
Duration: 3FT Hon
Entry Requirements: *GCE:* 300. *IB:* 29.

VP13 BA History and Media
Duration: 3FT Hon
Entry Requirements: *GCE:* 300. *IB:* 30.

QP5H BA Irish Language & Literature/Film & Television Studies
Duration: 4SW Hon
Entry Requirements: *GCE:* 300-320. *IB:* 32.

P300 BA Media and Communication Studies
Duration: 3FT Hon
Entry Requirements: *GCE:* 300-320. *IB:* 32.

A60 ANGLIA RUSKIN UNIVERSITY
BISHOP HALL LANE
CHELMSFORD
ESSEX CM1 1SQ
t: 0845 271 3333 f: 01245 251789
e: answers@anglia.ac.uk
// www.anglia.ac.uk

P391 BA Film Studies and Media Studies
Duration: 3FT Hon
Entry Requirements: *GCE:* 260. *SQAH:* BCCC. *SQAAH:* CC. *IB:* 24.

P300 BA Media Studies
Duration: 3FT Hon
Entry Requirements: *GCE:* 260. *SQAH:* BBCC. *SQAAH:* BC. *IB:* 24.

P310 BSc Media and Internet Technology
Duration: 3FT Hon
Entry Requirements: *GCE:* 150. *SQAH:* BBCC. *SQAAH:* BC. *IB:* 24.

B06 BANGOR UNIVERSITY
BANGOR UNIVERSITY
BANGOR
GWYNEDD LL57 2DG
t: 01248 388484 f: 01248 370451
e: admissions@bangor.ac.uk
// www.bangor.ac.uk

PH00 BA Astudiaethau'r Cyfryngau
Duration: 3FT Hon
Entry Requirements: Contact the institution for details.

W3P3 BA Astudiaethau'r Cyfryngau a Cherddoriaeth
Duration: 3FT Hon
Entry Requirements: *GCE:* 260-300. *IB:* 28.

WPQ0 BA Creative Studies
Duration: 3FT Hon
Entry Requirements: *GCE:* 240-260. *IB:* 28.

WQ93 BA Creative Studies and English Language
Duration: 3FT Hon
Entry Requirements: *GCE:* 240-260. *IB:* 28.

WR91 BA Creative Studies and French
Duration: 4FT Hon
Entry Requirements: *GCE:* 240-260. *IB:* 28.

WR92 BA Creative Studies and German
Duration: 4FT Hon
Entry Requirements: *GCE:* 240-260. *IB:* 28.

WR93 BA Creative Studies and Italian
Duration: 4FT Hon
Entry Requirements: *GCE:* 240-260. *IB:* 28.

WW93 BA Creative Studies and Music
Duration: 3FT Hon
Entry Requirements: *GCE:* 260-300. *IB:* 28.

WR94 BA Creative Studies and Spanish
Duration: 4FT Hon
Entry Requirements: *GCE:* 240-260. *IB:* 28.

WP83 BA Creative Writing and Media Studies
Duration: 3FT Hon
Entry Requirements: Contact the institution for details.

Q3P3 BA English Language with Media Studies
Duration: 3FT Hon
Entry Requirements: *GCE:* 240-300. *IB:* 28.

R1P3 BA French with Media Studies
Duration: 3FT Hon
Entry Requirements: *GCE:* 240-260. *IB:* 28.

R2P3 BA German with Media Studies
Duration: 4FT Hon
Entry Requirements: *GCE:* 240-260. *IB:* 28.

PP53 BA Journalism and Media Studies
Duration: 3FT Hon
Entry Requirements: *GCE:* 260-300. *IB:* 28.

P306 BA Media Studies
Duration: 3FT Hon
Entry Requirements: *GCE:* 260-300. *IB:* 28.

PQ3H BA Media Studies and English
Duration: 3FT Hon
Entry Requirements: *GCE:* 260-300. *IB:* 28.

PW33 BA Media Studies and Music
Duration: 3FT Hon
Entry Requirements: *GCE:* 260-300. *IB:* 28.

LP33 BA Media Studies and Sociology
Duration: 3FT Hon
Entry Requirements: *GCE:* 260-300. *IB:* 28.

P3R1 BA Media Studies with French
Duration: 3FT Hon
Entry Requirements: *GCE:* 260-300. *IB:* 28.

P3R2 BA Media Studies with German
Duration: 3FT Hon
Entry Requirements: *GCE:* 260-300. *IB:* 28.

P3R3 BA Media Studies with Italian
Duration: 3FT Hon
Entry Requirements: *GCE:* 260-300. *IB:* 28.

P3R4 BA Media Studies with Spanish
Duration: 3FT Hon
Entry Requirements: *GCE:* 260-300. *IB:* 28.

P3WK BA Media Studies with Theatre
Duration: 3FT Hon
Entry Requirements: *GCE:* 260-300. *IB:* 28.

R4P3 BA Spanish with Media Studies
Duration: 4FT Hon
Entry Requirements: *GCE:* 240-260. *IB:* 28.

B20 BATH SPA UNIVERSITY
NEWTON PARK
NEWTON ST LOE
BATH BA2 9BN
t: 01225 875875 f: 01225 875444
e: enquiries@bathspa.ac.uk
// www.bathspa.ac.uk/clearing

NP19 BA Business & Management/Media Communications
Duration: 3FT Hon
Entry Requirements: *GCE:* 220-280. *IB:* 24.

WP99 BA Creative Writing/Media Communications
Duration: 3FT Hon
Entry Requirements: *GCE:* 220-300. *IB:* 24.

WP49 BA Dance/Media Communication
Duration: 3FT Hon
Entry Requirements: *GCE:* 220-280. *IB:* 24. Interview required.

WP4H BA Drama Studies/Media Communications
Duration: 3FT Hon
Entry Requirements: *GCE:* 220-300. *IB:* 24.

XP13 BA Education/Media Communications
Duration: 3FT Hon   CRB Check: Required
Entry Requirements: *GCE:* 220-300. *IB:* 24.

XP39 BA Education/Media Communications
Duration: 3FT Hon   CRB Check: Required
Entry Requirements: *GCE:* 220-280. *IB:* 24.

QP39 BA English Literature/Media Communications
Duration: 3FT Hon
Entry Requirements: *GCE:* 220-300. *IB:* 24.

VP93 BA Heritage/Media Communications
Duration: 3FT Hon
Entry Requirements: Contact the institution for details.

VP19 BA History/Media Communications
Duration: 3FT Hon
Entry Requirements: *GCE:* 220-280. *IB:* 24.

P390 BA Media Communications
Duration: 3FT Hon
Entry Requirements: *GCE:* 220-280. *IB:* 24.

PW93 BA Media Communications/Music
Duration: 3FT Hon
Entry Requirements: *GCE:* 220-280. *IB:* 24.

WPQ3 BA Photography and Digital Media
Duration: 3FT Hon
Entry Requirements: *GCE:* 80-160. *IB:* 24. Portfolio required.

WP6H BA/BSc Film & Screen Studies/Media Communications
Duration: 3FT Hon
Entry Requirements: *GCE:* 220-280. *IB:* 24.

DP69 BA/BSc Food & Nutrition/Media Communications
Duration: 3FT Hon
Entry Requirements: *GCE:* 220-280. *IB:* 24.

PV3M BA/BSc Media Communications/Philosophy & Ethics
Duration: 3FT Hon
Entry Requirements: *GCE:* 220-280. *IB:* 24.

PC98 BA/BSc Media Communications/Psychology
Duration: 3FT Hon
Entry Requirements: *GCE:* 220-300. *IB:* 24.

PL93 BA/BSc Media Communications/Sociology
Duration: 3FT Hon
Entry Requirements: *GCE:* 220-280. *IB:* 24.

B22 UNIVERSITY OF BEDFORDSHIRE
PARK SQUARE
LUTON
BEDS LU1 3JU
t: 0844 8482234 f: 01582 489323
e: admissions@beds.ac.uk
// www.beds.ac.uk

P300 BA Media Practices (Mass Communications)
Duration: 3FT Hon
Entry Requirements: *Foundation:* Pass. *GCE:* 200. *SQAH:* BCC. *SQAAH:* BCC. *IB:* 24. *BTEC NC:* MM. *BTEC ND:* MPP. *OCR ND:* M1 *OCR NED:* P1

B25 BIRMINGHAM CITY UNIVERSITY
PERRY BARR
BIRMINGHAM B42 2SU
t: 0121 331 5595 f: 0121 331 7994
e: choices@bcu.ac.uk
// www.bcu.ac.uk

QP33 BA English and Media
Duration: 3FT Hon
Entry Requirements: *GCE:* 280. *IB:* 25. *BTEC ND:* DMM.

003P HND Media and Communication
Duration: 2FT HND
Entry Requirements: *GCE:* 120.

39PP HND Media, Communication and Production
Duration: 2FT HND
Entry Requirements: *GCE:* 120. *IB:* 24. *BTEC NC:* MP. *BTEC ND:* PPP.

B32 THE UNIVERSITY OF BIRMINGHAM
EDGBASTON
BIRMINGHAM B15 2TT
t: 0121 415 8900 f: 0121 414 7159
e: admissions@bham.ac.uk
// www.bham.ac.uk

RP83 BA Modern Languages and Film Studies
Duration: 4FT Hon
Entry Requirements: *GCE:* ABB. *SQAH:* ABBBB. *SQAAH:* AB. *IB:* 32.

B44 UNIVERSITY OF BOLTON
DEANE ROAD
BOLTON BL3 5AB
t: 01204 903903 f: 01204 399074
e: enquiries@bolton.ac.uk
// www.bolton.ac.uk

P300 BA Film & Media Studies
Duration: 3FT Hon
Entry Requirements: *GCE:* 240. Interview required.

B50 BOURNEMOUTH UNIVERSITY
TALBOT CAMPUS
FERN BARROW
POOLE
DORSET BH12 5BB
t: 01202 524111
// www.bournemouth.ac.uk

PP93 BA Interactive Media Production
Duration: 3FT Hon
Entry Requirements: *Foundation:* Distinction. *GCE:* 300. *IB:* 31. *BTEC NC:* DM. *BTEC ND:* DMM.

LP23 BA Politics and Media
Duration: 3FT Hon
Entry Requirements: Contact the institution for details.

P300 FdA Media Practice
Duration: 2FT Fdg
Entry Requirements: Contact the institution for details.

B56 THE UNIVERSITY OF BRADFORD
RICHMOND ROAD
BRADFORD
WEST YORKSHIRE BD7 1DP
t: 0800 073 1225 f: 01274 235585
e: course-enquiries@bradford.ac.uk
// www.bradford.ac.uk

GP43 BA Computing and Media with Foundation Year (International stream)
Duration: 4FT Hon
Entry Requirements: *GCE:* 120.

P300 BA Media Studies
Duration: 3FT Hon
Entry Requirements: *GCE:* 240. *IB:* 24.

P3W6 BA Media Studies with Cinematics
Duration: 3FT Hon
Entry Requirements: *GCE:* 240. *IB:* 24.

WP63 BA Photography for Digital Media
Duration: 3FT Hon
Entry Requirements: *GCE:* 240. *IB:* 24. Interview required.

LP23 BA War, Peace and Media Studies
Duration: 3FT Hon
Entry Requirements: *GCE:* 280. *IB:* 25. Interview required.

HP63 BSc Media Technology and Production
Duration: 3FT Hon
Entry Requirements: *GCE:* 260. *IB:* 24. Interview required.

B72 UNIVERSITY OF BRIGHTON
209 MITHRAS HOUSE
LEWES ROAD
BRIGHTON BN2 4AT
t: 01273 644644 f: 01273 642607
e: admissions@brighton.ac.uk
// www.brighton.ac.uk

QP33 BA English Language and Media
Duration: 3FT Hon
Entry Requirements: *GCE:* BBC. *IB:* 28. *BTEC ND:* DDM.

QP3H BA English Literature and Media Studies
Duration: 3FT Hon
Entry Requirements: *GCE:* CCC. *IB:* 28. *BTEC ND:* MMM.

DP43 BA Environment and Media Studies
Duration: 3FT/4SW Hon
Entry Requirements: *GCE:* BBB. *IB:* 30. *BTEC ND:* DMM.

P300 BA Media Studies
Duration: 3FT Hon
Entry Requirements: *GCE:* BBB. *IB:* 30.

PX33 BA Media Studies and Education
Duration: 3FT Hon
Entry Requirements: *GCE:* CCC. *IB:* 28. *BTEC ND:* MMM.

PL33 BA Media Studies and Sociology
Duration: 3FT Hon
Entry Requirements: *GCE:* CCC. *IB:* 28. *BTEC ND:* MMM.

PQ33 BA Media and English Literature
Duration: 3FT Hon
Entry Requirements: *GCE:* BBC. *IB:* 30. *BTEC ND:* DMM.

B80 UNIVERSITY OF THE WEST OF ENGLAND, BRISTOL
FRENCHAY CAMPUS
COLDHARBOUR LANE
BRISTOL BS16 1QY
t: +44 (0)117 32 83333 f: +44 (0)117 32 82810
e: admissions@uwe.ac.uk
// www.uwe.ac.uk

PP53 BA Journalism and Media & Cultural Studies
Duration: 3FT Hon
Entry Requirements: Contact the institution for details.

PL36 BA Media & Cultural Studies
Duration: 3FT Hon
Entry Requirements: Contact the institution for details.

B84 BRUNEL UNIVERSITY
UXBRIDGE
MIDDLESEX UB8 3PH
t: 01895 265265 f: 01895 269790
e: admissions@brunel.ac.uk
// www.brunel.ac.uk

PP93 BSc Communication and Media Studies
Duration: 3FT Hon
Entry Requirements: *GCE:* BCC. *SQAAH:* BCC. *IB:* 29. *BTEC ND:* DDM.

LP33 BSc Sociology and Media Studies
Duration: 3FT Hon
Entry Requirements: *GCE:* BCC. *SQAAH:* BCC. *IB:* 29. *BTEC ND:* DDM.

LP39 BSc Sociology and Media Studies (4 year Thin SW)
Duration: 4SW Hon
Entry Requirements: *GCE:* BCC. *SQAAH:* BCC. *IB:* 29. *BTEC ND:* DDM.

B90 THE UNIVERSITY OF BUCKINGHAM
YEOMANRY HOUSE
HUNTER STREET
BUCKINGHAM MK18 1EG
t: 01280 820313 f: 01280 822245
e: info@buckingham.ac.uk
// www.buckingham.ac.uk

Q3P0 BA Communication (EFL) and Media Studies
Duration: 2FT Hon
Entry Requirements: *GCE:* 200. *IB:* 24. *BTEC NC:* DD. *BTEC ND:* MMM.

Q3P3 BA English Studies with Media Communications
Duration: 2FT Hon
Entry Requirements: *GCE:* 240. *IB:* 24. *BTEC NC:* DD. *BTEC ND:* MMM.

N5P3 BSc Marketing with Media Communications
Duration: 2FT Hon
Entry Requirements: *GCE:* 280. *IB:* 26. *BTEC NC:* DD. *BTEC ND:* MMM.

C8P3 BSc Psychology with Media Communications
Duration: 2FT Hon
Entry Requirements: *GCE:* 280. *IB:* 26. *BTEC NC:* DD. *BTEC ND:* MMM.

B92 BROOKSBY MELTON COLLEGE
MELTON CAMPUS
ASFORDBY ROAD
MELTON MOWBRAY
LEICESTERSHIRE LE13 0HJ
t: 01664 850850 f: 01664 855355
// www.brooksbymelton.ac.uk

016W HND Media (Moving Image)
Duration: 2FT HND
Entry Requirements: Interview required. Portfolio required.

B94 BUCKINGHAMSHIRE NEW UNIVERSITY
QUEEN ALEXANDRA ROAD
HIGH WYCOMBE
BUCKINGHAMSHIRE HP11 2JZ
t: 0800 0565 660 f: 01494 605 023
e: admissions@bucks.ac.uk
// bucks.ac.uk

NP53 BA Advertising Management and Digital Communications
Duration: 3FT Hon
Entry Requirements: *GCE:* 200-240. *IB:* 24. *BTEC NC:* DM. *BTEC ND:* MMM. *OCR ND:* M1 *OCR NED:* M3

NP13 BA Business and Digital Media Communications
Duration: 3FT Hon
Entry Requirements: *GCE:* 200-240. *IB:* 24. *BTEC NC:* DM. *BTEC ND:* MMM. *OCR ND:* M1 *OCR NED:* M3

CP63 BA Football Business and Media
Duration: 3FT Hon
Entry Requirements: *GCE:* 200-240. *IB:* 24. *BTEC NC:* DM. *BTEC ND:* MMM. *OCR ND:* M1 *OCR NED:* M3

C10 CANTERBURY CHRIST CHURCH UNIVERSITY
NORTH HOLMES ROAD
CANTERBURY
KENT CT1 1QU
t: 01227 782900 f: 01227 782888
e: admissions@canterbury.ac.uk
// www.canterbury.ac.uk

MP9H BA Applied Criminology and Film, Radio & Television Studies
Duration: 3FT Hon
Entry Requirements: *GCE:* 240. *IB:* 24.

M9PH BA Applied Criminology with Film, Radio & Television Studies
Duration: 3FT Hon
Entry Requirements: *GCE:* 240. *IB:* 24.

GP5H BA Business Computing and Film, Radio & Television
Duration: 3FT Hon
Entry Requirements: *GCE:* 240. *IB:* 24.

G5PH BA Business Computing with Film, Radio & Television
Duration: 3FT Hon
Entry Requirements: *GCE:* 240. *IB:* 24.

P3G5 BA Film, Radio & Television Studies with Business Computing
Duration: 3FT Hon
Entry Requirements: *GCE:* 240. *IB:* 24.

LP23 BA Global Politics and Media and Communications
Duration: 3FT Hon
Entry Requirements: *GCE:* 240. *IB:* 24.

L2PA BA Global Politics with Media and Communications
Duration: 3FT Hon
Entry Requirements: *GCE:* 240. *IB:* 24.

L2P3 BA International Relations with Media and Communications
Duration: 3FT Hon
Entry Requirements: *GCE:* 240. *IB:* 24.

P9LG BA Media & Communications with Politics & Governance
Duration: 3FT Hon
Entry Requirements: *GCE:* 240. *IB:* 24.

P300 BA Media and Communications
Duration: 3FT Hon
Entry Requirements: *GCE:* 240. *IB:* 24.

PL36 BA Media and Communications 'International Only'
Duration: 4FT Hon
Entry Requirements: Interview required.

P3L2 BA Media and Communications with Global Politics
Duration: 3FT Hon
Entry Requirements: *GCE:* 240. *IB:* 24.

P3B9 BA Media and Communications with Health Studies
Duration: 3FT Hon
Entry Requirements: *GCE:* 240. *IB:* 24.

P3LG BA Media and Communications with International Relations
Duration: 3FT Hon
Entry Requirements: *GCE:* 240. *IB:* 24.

LP2H BA Politics & Governance and Media & Communications
Duration: 3FT Hon
Entry Requirements: *GCE:* 240. *IB:* 24.

L2PJ BA Politics & Governance with Media & Cultural Studies 'International Only'
Duration: 4FT Hon
Entry Requirements: Interview required.

L9P3 BA Politics and Governance with Media and Communications
Duration: 3FT Hon
Entry Requirements: *GCE:* 240. *IB:* 24.

TP73 BA/BSc American Studies and Media and Communications
Duration: 3FT Hon
Entry Requirements: *GCE:* 240. *IB:* 24.

TPR3 BA/BSc American Studies and Media and Communications (With a Year in USA)
Duration: 4FT Hon
Entry Requirements: Contact the institution for details.

TTP3 BA/BSc American Studies with Film, Radio & Television Studies (With a Year in USA)
Duration: 4FT Hon
Entry Requirements: Contact the institution for details.

T7P3 BA/BSc American Studies with Media and Communications
Duration: 3FT Hon
Entry Requirements: *GCE:* 240. *IB:* 24.

TRP3 BA/BSc American Studies with Media and Communications (With a Year in USA)
Duration: 4FT Hon
Entry Requirements: Contact the institution for details.

PN31 BA/BSc Business Studies and Media and Communications
Duration: 3FT Hon
Entry Requirements: *GCE:* 240. *IB:* 24.

GPK3 BA/BSc Computing and Film, Radio & Television
Duration: 3FT Hon
Entry Requirements: *GCE:* 240. *IB:* 24.

G4PH BA/BSc Computing with Film, Radio & Television Studies
Duration: 3FT Hon
Entry Requirements: *GCE:* 240. *IB:* 24.

X3P3 BA/BSc Education Studies with Media and Communications
Duration: 3FT Hon   CRB Check: Required
Entry Requirements: *GCE:* 240. *IB:* 24.

PQ33 BA/BSc English and Media and Communications
Duration: 3FT Hon
Entry Requirements: *GCE:* 240. *IB:* 24.

Q3P3 BA/BSc English with Media and Communications
Duration: 3FT Hon
Entry Requirements: *GCE:* 240. *IB:* 24.

W6P3 BA/BSc Film, Radio & Television Studies and Media and Communications
Duration: 3FT Hon
Entry Requirements: *GCE:* 240. *IB:* 24.

P3MX BA/BSc Film, Radio & Television Studies with Applied Criminology
Duration: 3FT Hon
Entry Requirements: *GCE:* 240. *IB:* 24.

PR31 BA/BSc French and Media and Communications
Duration: 3FT Hon
Entry Requirements: *GCE:* 240. *IB:* 24.

LP73 BA/BSc Geography and Media and Communications
Duration: 3FT Hon
Entry Requirements: *GCE:* 240. *IB:* 24.

BP93 BA/BSc Health Studies and Media and Communications
Duration: 3FT Hon
Entry Requirements: *GCE:* 240. *IB:* 24.

MP23 BA/BSc Legal Studies and Media and Communications
Duration: 3FT Hon
Entry Requirements: *GCE:* 240. *IB:* 24.

M2PH BA/BSc Legal Studies with Media and Communications
Duration: 3FT Hon
Entry Requirements: *GCE:* 240. *IB:* 24.

NP53 BA/BSc Marketing and Media and Communications
Duration: 3FT Hon
Entry Requirements: *GCE:* 240. *IB:* 24.

PW36 BA/BSc Media and Communications and Film, Radio and Television Studies
Duration: 3FT Hon
Entry Requirements: *GCE:* 240. *IB:* 24.

PW33 BA/BSc Media and Communications and Music
Duration: 3FT Hon
Entry Requirements: *GCE:* 240. *IB:* 24.

CP83 BA/BSc Media and Communications and Psychology
Duration: 3FT Hon
Entry Requirements: *GCE:* 240. *IB:* 24.

P3T7 BA/BSc Media and Communications with American Studies
Duration: 3FT Hon
Entry Requirements: *GCE:* 240. *IB:* 24.

PHT7 BA/BSc Media and Communications with American Studies (With a Year in USA)
Duration: 4FT Hon
Entry Requirements: Contact the institution for details.

P3N1 BA/BSc Media and Communications with Business Studies
Duration: 3FT Hon
Entry Requirements: *GCE:* 240. *IB:* 24.

P3GK BA/BSc Media and Communications with Digital Media
Duration: 3FT Hon
Entry Requirements: *GCE:* 240. *IB:* 24.

P3X3 BA/BSc Media and Communications with Education Studies
Duration: 3FT Hon   CRB Check: Required
Entry Requirements: *GCE:* 240. *IB:* 24.

PHQ3 BA/BSc Media and Communications with English
Duration: 3FT Hon
Entry Requirements: Contact the institution for details.

P3W6 BA/BSc Media and Communications with Film, Radio and Television Studies
Duration: 3FT Hon
Entry Requirements: *GCE:* 240. *IB:* 24.

P3R1 BA/BSc Media and Communications with French
Duration: 3FT Hon
Entry Requirements: *GCE:* 240. *IB:* 24.

P3L7 BA/BSc Media and Communications with Geography
Duration: 3FT Hon
Entry Requirements: *GCE:* 240. *IB:* 24.

P3NM BA/BSc Media and Communications with Marketing
Duration: 3FT Hon
Entry Requirements: *GCE:* 240. *IB:* 24.

P3W3 BA/BSc Media and Communications with Music
Duration: 3FT Hon
Entry Requirements: *GCE:* 240. *IB:* 24.

P3C8 BA/BSc Media and Communications with Psychology
Duration: 3FT Hon
Entry Requirements: *GCE:* 240. *IB:* 24.

P3L3 BA/BSc Media and Communications with Sociology and Social Science
Duration: 3FT Hon
Entry Requirements: *GCE:* 240. *IB:* 24.

LP33 BA/BSc Media and Cultural Studies and Sociology and Social Science
Duration: 3FT Hon
Entry Requirements: *GCE:* 240. *IB:* 24.

W3P3 BA/BSc Music with Media and Communications
Duration: 3FT Hon
Entry Requirements: *GCE:* 240. *IB:* 24.

C8P3 BA/BSc Psychology with Media and Communications
Duration: 3FT Hon
Entry Requirements: *GCE:* 240. *IB:* 24.

L3P3 BA/BSc Sociology & Social Science with Media & Communications
Duration: 3FT Hon
Entry Requirements: *GCE:* 240. *IB:* 24.

VP63 BA/BSc Theology and Media & Cultural Studies
Duration: 3FT Hon
Entry Requirements: *GCE:* 240. *IB:* 24.

V6PH BA/BSc Theology with Media & Cultural Studies
Duration: 3FT Hon
Entry Requirements: *GCE:* 240. *IB:* 24.

N1P3 BSc Business Studies with Media and Communications
Duration: 3FT Hon
Entry Requirements: *GCE:* 240. *IB:* 24.

N5P3 BSc Marketing with Media and Communications
Duration: 3FT Hon
Entry Requirements: *GCE:* 240. *IB:* 24.

GP43 BSc/BA Digital Media and Media and Communications
Duration: 3FT Hon
Entry Requirements: *GCE:* 240. *IB:* 24.

G4P3 BSc/BA Digital Media with Media and Communications
Duration: 3FT Hon
Entry Requirements: *GCE:* 240. *IB:* 24.

L7P3 BSc/BA Geography with Media and Communications
Duration: 3FT Hon
Entry Requirements: *GCE:* 240. *IB:* 24.

GP4J FdA Broadcast and Interactive TV
Duration: 2FT Fdg
Entry Requirements: *GCE:* 120. *IB:* 24.

C15 CARDIFF UNIVERSITY
PO BOX 927
30-36 NEWPORT ROAD
CARDIFF CF24 0DE
t: 029 2087 9999 f: 029 2087 6138
e: admissions@cardiff.ac.uk
// www.cardiff.ac.uk

PP53 BA Journalism, Media and Cultural Studies
Duration: 3FT Hon
Entry Requirements: *GCE:* ABB. *SQAAH:* AAABB. *IB:* 36. *BTEC ND:* DDD. Admissions Test required.

PQ53 BA Journalism, Media and English Literature
Duration: 3FT Hon
Entry Requirements: *GCE:* AAA. *SQAAH:* AAA. *IB:* 33. Interview required.

C20 UNIVERSITY OF WALES INSTITUTE, CARDIFF (UWIC)
ADMISSIONS UNIT
LLANDAFF CAMPUS
WESTERN AVENUE
CARDIFF CF5 2YB
t: 029 2041 6070 f: 029 2041 6286
e: admissions@uwic.ac.uk
// www.uwic.ac.uk

QP33 BA English and Contemporary Media
Duration: 3FT Hon
Entry Requirements: *GCE:* 260. *IB:* 24. Interview required.

C30 UNIVERSITY OF CENTRAL LANCASHIRE
PRESTON
LANCS PR1 2HE
t: 01772 201201 f: 01772 894954
e: uadmissions@uclan.ac.uk
// www.uclan.ac.uk

QP33 BA English for International Communication (Top-up)
Duration: 1FT Hon
Entry Requirements: Contact the institution for details.

PW36 BA Film and Media Studies
Duration: 3FT Hon
Entry Requirements: *GCE:* 240-260. *IB:* 28. *BTEC NC:* DD. *BTEC ND:* MMM. *OCR ND:* D *OCR NED:* M3

N5P3 BA Marketing Management with Digital Media
Duration: 4SW Hon
Entry Requirements: Contact the institution for details.

0951 BA Marketing Management with Digital Media
Duration: 3FT Hon
Entry Requirements: Contact the institution for details.

WP6H BA Photography
Duration: 3FT Hon
Entry Requirements: *GCE:* 240-260. *IB:* 28. *BTEC NC:* DD. *BTEC ND:* MMM. *OCR ND:* D *OCR NED:* M3

HP63 BSc Media Production & Technology
Duration: 3FT Hon
Entry Requirements: *GCE:* 300. *SQAH:* AAAB. *IB:* 30. *BTEC NC:* DD. *BTEC ND:* DDM. *OCR ND:* D *OCR NED:* D2

WP23 BSc News Graphics
Duration: 3FT Hon
Entry Requirements: *GCE:* 300. *SQAH:* AAAB. *IB:* 30. *BTEC NC:* DD. *BTEC ND:* DDM. *OCR ND:* D *OCR NED:* D2

C55 UNIVERSITY OF CHESTER
PARKGATE ROAD
CHESTER CH1 4BJ
t: 01244 511000 f: 01244 511300
e: enquiries@chester.ac.uk
// www.chester.ac.uk

PN35 BA Advertising and Media Studies
Duration: 3FT Hon
Entry Requirements: *GCE:* 240-280. *SQAH:* BBBB. *IB:* 26. *BTEC NC:* DM. *BTEC ND:* MMM.

NPDJ BA Business Management and Media Studies
Duration: 3FT Hon
Entry Requirements: *GCE:* 240-280. *SQAH:* BBBB. *IB:* 26. *BTEC NC:* DM. *BTEC ND:* MMM.

P399 BA Commercial Music Production and Media Studies
Duration: 3FT Hon
Entry Requirements: *Foundation:* Pass. *GCE:* 260-300. *SQAH:* BBBB. *IB:* 28. *BTEC NC:* DM. *BTEC ND:* DMM.

WP6H BA Digital Photography and Media Studies
Duration: 3FT Hon
Entry Requirements: *GCE:* 240-280. *SQAH:* BBBB. *IB:* 24. *BTEC NC:* DM. *BTEC ND:* MMM.

NP8J BA Events Management and Media Studies
Duration: 3FT Hon
Entry Requirements: *GCE:* 240-280. *SQAH:* BBBB. *IB:* 24. *BTEC NC:* DM. *BTEC ND:* MMM.

P398 BA Film Studies and Media Studies
Duration: 3FT Hon
Entry Requirements: *GCE:* 240-280. *SQAH:* BBBB. *IB:* 24. *BTEC NC:* DM. *BTEC ND:* MMM.

PP35 BA Journalism and Media Studies
Duration: 3FT Hon
Entry Requirements: *Foundation:* Pass. *GCE:* 240-280. *SQAH:* BBBB. *IB:* 24. *BTEC NC:* DM. *BTEC ND:* MMM.

CPP3 BA Sport Development and Commercial Music Production
Duration: 3FT Hon
Entry Requirements: *Foundation:* Pass. *GCE:* 260-300. *SQAH:* BBBB. *IB:* 28. *BTEC NC:* DM. *BTEC ND:* DMM.

CPPH BA Sport Development and Media Studies
Duration: 3FT Hon
Entry Requirements: *Foundation:* Pass. *GCE:* 240-280. *SQAH:* BBBB. *IB:* 24. *BTEC NC:* DM. *BTEC ND:* MMM.

CPQ3 BA Sport Development and Radio Production
Duration: 3FT Hon
Entry Requirements: *Foundation:* Pass. *GCE:* 260-300. *SQAH:* BBBB. *IB:* 28. *BTEC NC:* DM. *BTEC ND:* DMM.

CP6J BA Sport Development and TV Production
Duration: 3FT Hon
Entry Requirements: *Foundation:* Pass. *GCE:* 260-300. *SQAH:* BBBB. *IB:* 28. *BTEC NC:* DM. *BTEC ND:* DMM.

P3W2 BSc Multimedia Technologies
Duration: 3FT Hon
Entry Requirements: *GCE:* 240-280. *SQAH:* BBBB. *IB:* 24. *BTEC NC:* DM. *BTEC ND:* MMM.

C58 UNIVERSITY OF CHICHESTER
BISHOP OTTER CAMPUS
COLLEGE LANE
CHICHESTER
WEST SUSSEX PO19 6PE
t: 01243 816002 f: 01243 816161
e: admissions@chi.ac.uk
// www.chiuni.ac.uk

QP33 BA International English Studies and Media Studies
Duration: 3FT Hon
Entry Requirements: *GCE:* BCC. *SQAAH:* BCC. *IB:* 28. *BTEC NC:* DD. *BTEC ND:* DMM.

P390 BA Media Production
Duration: 3FT Hon
Entry Requirements: *GCE:* BCC. *SQAAH:* BCC. *IB:* 28. *BTEC NC:* DD. *BTEC ND:* DMM.

P300 BA Media Studies
Duration: 3FT Hon
Entry Requirements: *GCE:* BCC. *SQAAH:* BCC. *IB:* 28. *BTEC NC:* DD. *BTEC ND:* DMM.

P3Q3 BA Media Studies with English
Duration: 3FT Hon
Entry Requirements: Contact the institution for details.

P3V1 BA Media Studies with History
Duration: 3FT Hon
Entry Requirements: Contact the institution for details.

W3P3 BA Media Studies with Music
Duration: 3FT Hon
Entry Requirements: Contact the institution for details.

C60 CITY UNIVERSITY
NORTHAMPTON SQUARE
LONDON EC1V 0HB
t: 020 7040 5060 f: 020 7040 8995
e: ugadmissions@city.ac.uk
// www.city.ac.uk

PL33 BSc Media Studies and Sociology
Duration: 3FT Hon
Entry Requirements: *GCE:* BBB. *SQAH:* BBBBC. *IB:* 28. *BTEC ND:* DMM.

C78 CORNWALL COLLEGE
POOL
REDRUTH
CORNWALL TR15 3RD
t: 01209 616161 f: 01209 611612
e: he.admissions@cornwall.ac.uk
// www.cornwall.ac.uk

XP33 FdSc Wildlife Education & Media
Duration: 2FT Fdg
Entry Requirements: *BTEC ND:* MMP. Interview required.

C85 COVENTRY UNIVERSITY
THE STUDENT CENTRE
COVENTRY UNIVERSITY
1 GULSON RD
COVENTRY CV1 2JH
t: 024 7615 2222 f: 024 7615 2223
e: studentenquiries@coventry.ac.uk
// www.coventry.ac.uk

PP53 BA Journalism and Media
Duration: 3FT/4SW Hon
Entry Requirements: *GCE:* BCC. *SQAH:* BCCCC. *IB:* 28. *BTEC ND:* DMM. *OCR NED:* M2 Interview required. Portfolio required.

P300 BA Multimedia Computing
Duration: 3FT/4SW Hon
Entry Requirements: *GCE:* BCC. *SQAH:* BCCCC. *IB:* 28. *BTEC ND:* DMM. *OCR NED:* M2

C93 UNIVERSITY FOR THE CREATIVE ARTS
FALKNER ROAD
FARNHAM
SURREY GU9 7DS
t: 01252 722441 f: 01252 892624
e: admissions@ucreative.ac.uk
// www.ucreative.ac.uk

WP13 BA Arts & Media
Duration: 3FT Hon
Entry Requirements: *GCE:* 200. Interview required. Portfolio required.

C99 UNIVERSITY OF CUMBRIA
FUSEHILL STREET
CARLISLE
CUMBRIA CA1 2HH
t: 01228 616234 f: 01228 616235
// www.cumbria.ac.uk

NP83 BA Adventure and Media
Duration: 3FT Hon
Entry Requirements: *GCE:* 220. *SQAH:* BBBB. *BTEC ND:* MMM. Interview required.

D26 DE MONTFORT UNIVERSITY
THE GATEWAY
LEICESTER LE1 9BH
t: 0116 255 1551 f: 0116 250 6204
e: enquiries@dmu.ac.uk
// www.dmu.ac.uk

NP13 BA Business and Media & Communication
Duration: 3FT/4SW Hon
Entry Requirements: *GCE:* 280. *IB:* 28. *BTEC ND:* DMM. *OCR NED:* M2 Interview required.

PWH4 BA Drama Studies and Media & Communication
Duration: 3FT Hon
Entry Requirements: *GCE:* 260. *IB:* 28. *BTEC ND:* DMM.

QP33 BA English Language and Media & Communication
Duration: 3FT Hon
Entry Requirements: *GCE:* 260. *IB:* 28.

PQ33 BA English and Media & Communication
Duration: 3FT Hon
Entry Requirements: *GCE:* 260. *IB:* 28.

P390 BA Film Studies and Media & Communication
Duration: 3FT Hon
Entry Requirements: *GCE:* 260. *IB:* 28.

PPH5 BA Journalism and Media & Communication
Duration: 3FT Hon
Entry Requirements: *GCE:* 260. *IB:* 28. Interview required.

NP53 BA Marketing and Media & Communication
Duration: 3FT/4SW Hon
Entry Requirements: *GCE:* 280. *IB:* 28. *BTEC ND:* DMM. *OCR NED:* M2 Interview required.

P300 BA Media and Communication (with pathways)
Duration: 3FT Hon
Entry Requirements: *GCE:* 260. *IB:* 28.

HP63 BSc Media Technology
Duration: 3FT/4SW Hon
Entry Requirements: *GCE:* 260. *IB:* 28. *BTEC ND:* DMM. *OCR NED:* M2

D39 UNIVERSITY OF DERBY
KEDLESTON ROAD
DERBY DE22 1GB
t: 01332 591167 f: 01332 597724
e: askadmissions@derby.ac.uk
// www.derby.ac.uk

NPK3 BA Accounting and Broadcast Media
Duration: 3FT Hon
Entry Requirements: *Foundation:* Distinction. *GCE:* 260-300. *IB:* 28. *BTEC ND:* DMM. *OCR NED:* M2

PT37 BA American Studies and Film & Television Studies
Duration: 3FT Hon
Entry Requirements: *Foundation:* Distinction. *GCE:* 260-300. *IB:* 28. *BTEC ND:* DMM. *OCR NED:* M2

PQHJ BA Broadcast Media and English
Duration: 3FT Hon
Entry Requirements: *Foundation:* Distinction. *GCE:* 260-300. *IB:* 28. *BTEC ND:* DMM. *OCR NED:* M2

PVH1 BA Broadcast Media and History
Duration: 3FT Hon
Entry Requirements: *Foundation:* Distinction. *GCE:* 260-300. *IB:* 28. *BTEC ND:* DMM. *OCR NED:* M2

PMH1 BA Broadcast Media and Law
Duration: 3FT Hon
Entry Requirements: *Foundation:* Distinction. *GCE:* 260-300. *IB:* 28. *BTEC ND:* DMM. *OCR NED:* M2

PWJ3 BA Broadcast Media and Popular Music (Production)
Duration: 3FT Hon
Entry Requirements: *Foundation:* Distinction. *GCE:* 260-300. *IB:* 28. *BTEC ND:* DMM. *OCR NED:* M2

PLH3 BA Broadcast Media and Sociology
Duration: 3FT Hon
Entry Requirements: *Foundation:* Distinction. *GCE:* 260-300. *IB:* 28. *BTEC ND:* DMM. *OCR NED:* M2

PCJ6 BA Broadcast Media and Sport & Exercise Studies
Duration: 3FT Hon
Entry Requirements: *Foundation:* Distinction. *GCE:* 260-300. *IB:* 28. *BTEC ND:* DMM. *OCR NED:* M2

PWJ4 BA Broadcast Media and Theatre Arts
Duration: 3FT Hon
Entry Requirements: *Foundation:* Distinction. *GCE:* 260-300. *IB:* 28. *BTEC ND:* DMM. *OCR NED:* M2

NP23 BA Business Management and Film & Television Studies
Duration: 3FT Hon
Entry Requirements: *Foundation:* Distinction. *GCE:* 260-300. *IB:* 28. *BTEC ND:* DMM. *OCR NED:* M2

PW38 BA Creative Writing and Film & Television Studies
Duration: 3FT Hon
Entry Requirements: *Foundation:* Distinction. *GCE:* 260-300. *IB:* 28. *BTEC ND:* DMM. *OCR NED:* M2

MP93 BA Criminology and Broadcast Media
Duration: 3FT Hon
Entry Requirements: *Foundation:* Distinction. *GCE:* 260-300. *IB:* 28. *BTEC ND:* DMM. *OCR NED:* M2

PW35 BA Dance & Movement Studies and Film & Television Studies
Duration: 3FT Hon
Entry Requirements: *Foundation:* Distinction. *GCE:* 260-300. *IB:* 28. *BTEC ND:* DMM. *OCR NED:* M2

PQ33 BA English and Film & Television Studies
Duration: 3FT Hon
Entry Requirements: *Foundation:* Distinction. *GCE:* 260-300. *IB:* 28. *BTEC ND:* DMM. *OCR NED:* M2

MP13 BA Film & Television Studies and Law
Duration: 3FT Hon
Entry Requirements: *Foundation:* Distinction. *GCE:* 260-300. *IB:* 28. *BTEC ND:* DMM. *OCR NED:* M2

PW33 BA Film & Television Studies and Popular Music (Production)
Duration: 3FT Hon
Entry Requirements: *Foundation:* Distinction. *GCE:* 260-300. *IB:* 28. *BTEC ND:* DMM. *OCR NED:* M2

LP33 BA Film & Television Studies and Sociology
Duration: 3FT Hon
Entry Requirements: *Foundation:* Distinction. *GCE:* 260-300. *IB:* 28. *BTEC ND:* DMM. *OCR NED:* M2

PW3K BA Film & Television Studies and Theatre Arts
Duration: 3FT Hon
Entry Requirements: *Foundation:* Distinction. *GCE:* 260-300. *IB:* 28. *BTEC ND:* DMM. *OCR NED:* M2

P300 BA Media Studies
Duration: 3FT Hon
Entry Requirements: *Foundation:* Distinction. *GCE:* 260. *IB:* 28. *BTEC ND:* DMM. *OCR NED:* M2

PT3R BA Media Writing and American Studies
Duration: 3FT Hon
Entry Requirements: *Foundation:* Distinction. *GCE:* 260-300. *IB:* 28. *BTEC ND:* DMM. *OCR NED:* M2

PNJF BA Media Writing and Business Management
Duration: 3FT Hon
Entry Requirements: *Foundation:* Distinction. *GCE:* 260-300. *IB:* 28. *BTEC ND:* DMM. *OCR NED:* M2

PM39 BA Media Writing and Criminology
Duration: 3FT Hon
Entry Requirements: *Foundation:* Distinction. *GCE:* 260-300. *IB:* 28. *BTEC ND:* DMM. *OCR NED:* M2

PW3N BA Media Writing and Dance & Movement Studies
Duration: 3FT Hon
Entry Requirements: *Foundation:* Distinction. *GCE:* 260-300. *IB:* 28. *BTEC ND:* DMM. *OCR NED:* M2

PP43 BA Media Writing and Popular Culture & Media
Duration: 3FT Hon
Entry Requirements: *Foundation:* Distinction. *GCE:* 260-300. *IB:* 28. *BTEC ND:* DMM. *OCR NED:* M2

PQH3 BA Popular Culture & Media and English
Duration: 3FT Hon
Entry Requirements: *Foundation:* Distinction. *GCE:* 260-300. *IB:* 28. *BTEC ND:* DMM. *OCR NED:* M2

PL37 BA Popular Culture & Media and Geography
Duration: 3FT Hon
Entry Requirements: *Foundation:* Distinction. *GCE:* 260-300. *IB:* 28. *BTEC ND:* DMM. *OCR NED:* M2

PV3C BA Popular Culture & Media and History
Duration: 3FT Hon
Entry Requirements: *Foundation:* Distinction. *GCE:* 260-300. *IB:* 28. *BTEC ND:* DMM. *OCR NED:* M2

PM31 BA Popular Culture & Media and Law
Duration: 3FT Hon
Entry Requirements: *Foundation:* Distinction. *GCE:* 260-300. *IB:* 28. *BTEC ND:* DMM. *OCR NED:* M2

PN35 BA Popular Culture & Media and Marketing
Duration: 3FT Hon
Entry Requirements: *Foundation:* Distinction. *GCE:* 260-300. *IB:* 28. *BTEC ND:* DMM. *OCR NED:* M2

PWH3 BA Popular Culture & Media and Popular Music (Production)
Duration: 3FT Hon
Entry Requirements: *Foundation:* Distinction. *GCE:* 260-300. *IB:* 28. *BTEC ND:* DMM. *OCR NED:* M2

PC38 BA Popular Culture & Media and Psychology
Duration: 3FT Hon
Entry Requirements: *Foundation:* Distinction. *GCE:* 260-300. *IB:* 28. *BTEC ND:* DMM. *OCR NED:* M2

PL33 BA Popular Culture & Media and Sociology
Duration: 3FT Hon
Entry Requirements: *Foundation:* Distinction. *GCE:* 260-300. *IB:* 28. *BTEC ND:* DMM. *OCR NED:* M2

PW34 BA Popular Culture & Media and Theatre Arts
Duration: 3FT Hon
Entry Requirements: *Foundation:* Distinction. *GCE:* 260-300. *IB:* 28. *BTEC ND:* DMM. *OCR NED:* M2

PB39 BA/BSc Broadcast Media and Environmental Hazards
Duration: 3FT Hon
Entry Requirements: *Foundation:* Distinction. *GCE:* 260-300. *IB:* 28. *BTEC ND:* DMM. *OCR NED:* M2

PL3F BA/BSc Broadcast Media and International Relations & Global Development
Duration: 3FT Hon
Entry Requirements: *Foundation:* Distinction. *GCE:* 260-300. *IB:* 28. *BTEC ND:* DMM. *OCR NED:* M2

PC31 BA/BSc Media Writing and Biology
Duration: 3FT Hon
Entry Requirements: *Foundation:* Distinction. *GCE:* 260-300. *IB:* 28. *BTEC ND:* DMM. *OCR NED:* M2

PC33 BA/BSc Media Writing and Zoology
Duration: 3FT Hon
Entry Requirements: *Foundation:* Distinction. *GCE:* 260-300. *IB:* 28. *BTEC ND:* DMM. *OCR NED:* M2

KP13 BSc Architectural Design and Film & Television Studies
Duration: 3FT Hon
Entry Requirements: *Foundation:* Distinction. *GCE:* 260-300. *IB:* 28. *BTEC ND:* DMM. *OCR NED:* M2

E14 UNIVERSITY OF EAST ANGLIA
NORWICH NR4 7TJ
t: 01603 591515 f: 01603 458596
e: admissions@uea.ac.uk
// www.uea.ac.uk

P300 BA Media Studies
Duration: 3FT Hon   CRB Check: Required
Entry Requirements: *GCE:* ABB. *SQAAH:* ABB. *IB:* 32. *BTEC NC:* DM. *BTEC ND:* DDM.

PL32 BA Media and Politics
Duration: 3FT Hon   CRB Check: Required
Entry Requirements: Contact the institution for details.

LP33 BA Society, Culture and Media
Duration: 3FT Hon   CRB Check: Required
Entry Requirements: *GCE:* ABB. *SQAAH:* ABB. *IB:* 32.

RP13 BA Translation, Media and French
Duration: 4FT Hon   CRB Check: Required
Entry Requirements: *GCE:* BBC-BCC. *SQAAH:* BBC-BCC.

RP1H BA Translation, Media and French (3 years)
Duration: 3FT Hon   CRB Check: Required
Entry Requirements: *GCE:* ABC. *SQAAH:* ABC. *IB:* 32.

QP93 BA Translation, Media and Honours Language
Duration: 3FT Hon   CRB Check: Required
Entry Requirements: *GCE:* ABB. *SQAAH:* ABB. *IB:* 32.

QP9H BA Translation, Media and Honours Language(s)
Duration: 4FT Hon   CRB Check: Required
Entry Requirements: *GCE:* BBB. *SQAAH:* BBB. *IB:* 31.

QP9J BA Translation, Media and Japanese
Duration: 4FT Hon   CRB Check: Required
Entry Requirements: Contact the institution for details.

RP43 BA Translation, Media and Spanish
Duration: 4FT Hon   CRB Check: Required
Entry Requirements: *GCE:* BBC-BCC. *SQAAH:* BBC-BCC.

RP4H BA Translation, Media and Spanish (3 years)
Duration: 3FT Hon   CRB Check: Required
Entry Requirements: *GCE:* ABC. *SQAAH:* ABC. *IB:* 32.

Q9P3 BA Translation, Media with French and Japanese
Duration: 4FT Hon   CRB Check: Required
Entry Requirements: Contact the institution for details.

RP93 BA Translation, Media with French and Spanish
Duration: 4FT Hon   CRB Check: Required
Entry Requirements: *GCE:* BBC-BCC. *SQAAH:* BBC-BCC.

Q9PH BA Translation, Media with Spanish and Japanese
Duration: 4FT Hon   CRB Check: Required
Entry Requirements: Contact the institution for details.

E28 UNIVERSITY OF EAST LONDON
DOCKLANDS CAMPUS
UNIVERSITY WAY
LONDON E16 2RD
t: 020 8223 3333 f: 020 8223 2978
e: study@uel.ac.uk
// www.uel.ac.uk

PL31 BA Business Economics/Media Studies
Duration: 3FT Hon
Entry Requirements: *GCE:* 200. *IB:* 24. *BTEC NC:* DM. *BTEC ND:* MMP. *OCR ND:* M1 *OCR NED:* P1

NP23 BA Business Management/Media Studies
Duration: 3FT Hon
Entry Requirements: *GCE:* 200. *IB:* 24. *BTEC NC:* DM. *BTEC ND:* MMP. *OCR ND:* M1 *OCR NED:* P1

M9P3 BA Criminology with Media Studies
Duration: 3FT Hon
Entry Requirements: Contact the institution for details.

LP63 BA Cultural Studies/Media Studies
Duration: 3FT Hon
Entry Requirements: *GCE:* 200. *IB:* 24. *BTEC NC:* DM. *BTEC ND:* MMP.

XP33 BA Early Childhood Studies/Media Studies
Duration: 3FT Hon
Entry Requirements: *GCE:* 200. *IB:* 24. *BTEC NC:* DM. *BTEC ND:* MMP.

PQ33 BA English Literature/Media Studies
Duration: 3FT Hon
Entry Requirements: *GCE:* 200. *IB:* 24. *BTEC NC:* DM. *BTEC ND:* MMP.

N8P3 BA Events Management with Media Studies
Duration: 3FT Hon
Entry Requirements: *GCE:* 200. *IB:* 24. *BTEC NC:* DM. *BTEC ND:* MMP.

P390 BA Film Studies with Media Studies
Duration: 3FT Hon
Entry Requirements: *GCE:* 200. *IB:* 24. *BTEC NC:* DM. *BTEC ND:* MMP.

W2PJ BA Graphic Design with Media Studies
Duration: 3FT Hon
Entry Requirements: *GCE:* 200. *IB:* 24. *BTEC NC:* DM. *BTEC ND:* MMP. *OCR ND:* M1 *OCR NED:* P1

PV31 BA History/Media Studies
Duration: 3FT Hon
Entry Requirements: *GCE:* 200. *IB:* 24. *BTEC NC:* DM. *BTEC ND:* MMP.

NP63 BA Human Resource Management/Media Studies
Duration: 3FT Hon
Entry Requirements: *GCE:* 200. *IB:* 24. *BTEC NC:* DM. *BTEC ND:* MMP.

P5P3 BA Journalism Studies with Media Studies
Duration: 3FT Hon
Entry Requirements: *GCE:* 200. *IB:* 24. *BTEC NC:* DM. *BTEC ND:* MMP.

PP53 BA Journalism Studies/Media Studies
Duration: 3FT Hon
Entry Requirements: *GCE:* 200. *IB:* 24. *BTEC NC:* DM. *BTEC ND:* MMP.

NP53 BA Marketing/Media Studies
Duration: 3FT Hon
Entry Requirements: *GCE:* 200. *IB:* 24. *BTEC NC:* DM. *BTEC ND:* MMP.

V000 BA Media & Creative Industries option - Media Studies
Duration: 3FT Hon
Entry Requirements: *GCE:* 200. *IB:* 24.

V000 BA Media & Creative Industries
Duration: 3FT Hon
Entry Requirements: *GCE:* 200. *IB:* 24. *BTEC NC:* DM. *BTEC ND:* MMP. *OCR ND:* M1 *OCR NED:* P1

P300 BA Media Studies
Duration: 3FT Hon
Entry Requirements: *GCE:* 200. *IB:* 24. *BTEC NC:* DM. *BTEC ND:* MMP.

PW35 BA Media Studies / Dance: Urban Practice
Duration: 3FT Hon
Entry Requirements: *GCE:* 200. *IB:* 24. *BTEC NC:* DM. *BTEC ND:* MMP. *OCR ND:* M1 *OCR NED:* P1

P3W6 BA Media Studies with Animation
Duration: 3FT Hon
Entry Requirements: *GCE:* 200. *IB:* 24. *BTEC NC:* DM. *BTEC ND:* MMP. *OCR ND:* M1 *OCR NED:* P1

P3N2 BA Media Studies with Business Management
Duration: 3FT Hon
Entry Requirements: Contact the institution for details.

P3WL BA Media Studies with Community Arts Practice
Duration: 3FT Hon
Entry Requirements: *GCE:* 200. *IB:* 24. *BTEC NC:* DM. *BTEC ND:* MMP. *OCR ND:* M1 *OCR NED:* P1

P3Q3 BA Media Studies with English Language
Duration: 3FT Hon
Entry Requirements: *GCE:* 200. *IB:* 24. *BTEC NC:* DM. *BTEC ND:* MMP.

P3QJ BA Media Studies with English Literature
Duration: 3FT Hon
Entry Requirements: *GCE:* 200. *IB:* 24. *BTEC NC:* DM. *BTEC ND:* MMP.

P391 BA Media Studies with Film Studies
Duration: 3FT Hon
Entry Requirements: *GCE:* 200. *IB:* 24. *BTEC NC:* DM. *BTEC ND:* MMP.

P3P5 BA Media Studies with Journalism Studies
Duration: 3FT Hon
Entry Requirements: *GCE:* 200. *IB:* 24. *BTEC NC:* DM. *BTEC ND:* MMP.

P3WF BA Media Studies with Multimedia Design Technology
Duration: 3FT Hon
Entry Requirements: Contact the institution for details.

P3WH BA Media Studies with Music Culture
Duration: 3FT Hon
Entry Requirements: *GCE:* 200. *IB:* 24. *BTEC NC:* DM. *BTEC ND:* MMP. *OCR ND:* M1 *OCR NED:* P1

P3WA BA Media Studies with Theatre Studies
Duration: 3FT Hon
Entry Requirements: *GCE:* 200. *IB:* 24. *BTEC NC:* DM. *BTEC ND:* MMP. *OCR ND:* M1 *OCR NED:* P1

W2PH BA Multimedia Design Technology with Media Studies
Duration: 3FT Hon
Entry Requirements: Contact the institution for details.

WP33 BA Music Culture/Film Studies
Duration: 3FT Hon
Entry Requirements: *GCE:* 200. *IB:* 24. *BTEC NC:* DM. *BTEC ND:* MMP.

W6P3 BA Photography with Media Studies
Duration: 3FT Hon
Entry Requirements: *GCE:* 200. *IB:* 24. *BTEC NC:* DM. *BTEC ND:* MMP. *OCR ND:* M1 *OCR NED:* P1

PLH9 BA Third World Development/Media Studies
Duration: 3FT Hon
Entry Requirements: *GCE:* 200. *IB:* 24. *BTEC NC:* DM. *BTEC ND:* MMP.

L5P3 BA Youth & Community Work with Media Studies
Duration: 3FT Hon
Entry Requirements: *GCE:* 200. *IB:* 24. *BTEC NC:* DM. *BTEC ND:* MMP.

GP5J BA/BSc Business Information Systems/Media Studies
Duration: 3FT Hon
Entry Requirements: *GCE:* 200. *IB:* 24. *BTEC NC:* DM. *BTEC ND:* MMP. *OCR ND:* M1 *OCR NED:* P1

B1P3 BA/BSc Human Biology/Media Studies
Duration: 3FT Hon
Entry Requirements: *GCE:* 200. *IB:* 24. *BTEC NC:* DM. *BTEC ND:* MMP. *OCR ND:* M1 *OCR NED:* P1

GP53 BA/BSc Information Technology/Media Studies
Duration: 3FT Hon
Entry Requirements: *GCE:* 200. *IB:* 24. *BTEC NC:* DM. *BTEC ND:* MMP.

G6P3 BSc Software Engineering with Media Studies
Duration: 3FT Hon
Entry Requirements: *GCE:* 200. *IB:* 24. *BTEC NC:* DM. *BTEC ND:* MMP.

E29 EAST RIDING COLLEGE
LONGCROFT HALL
GALLOWS LANE
BEVERLEY
EAST YORKSHIRE HU17 7DT
t: 0845 120 0037
e: info@eastridingcollege.ac.uk
// www.eastridingcollege.ac.uk/

P304 FdA Applied Digital Media
Duration: 2FT Fdg
Entry Requirements: *GCE:* 120.

E42 EDGE HILL UNIVERSITY
ORMSKIRK
LANCASHIRE L39 4QP
t: 01695 657000 f: 01695 584355
e: study@edgehill.ac.uk
// www.edgehill.ac.uk

PW38 BA Creative Writing and Media
Duration: 3FT Hon
Entry Requirements: *GCE:* 280. *IB:* 26. *BTEC NC:* DD. *BTEC ND:* DMM. *OCR ND:* D *OCR NED:* M2

PW34 BA Drama and Media
Duration: 3FT Hon
Entry Requirements: *GCE:* 280. *IB:* 26. *BTEC NC:* DD. *BTEC ND:* DMM. *OCR ND:* D *OCR NED:* M2 Interview required.

PQ33 BA English and Media
Duration: 3FT Hon
Entry Requirements: *GCE:* 280. *IB:* 26. *BTEC NC:* DD. *BTEC ND:* DMM. *OCR ND:* M2 *OCR NED:* M2

P3W6 BA Film Studies with Film Production
Duration: 3FT Hon
Entry Requirements: *GCE:* 280. *IB:* 26. *BTEC NC:* DD. *BTEC ND:* DMM. *OCR ND:* D *OCR NED:* M2

P3V1 BA Film Studies with History
Duration: 3FT Hon
Entry Requirements: *GCE:* 280. *IB:* 26. *BTEC NC:* DD. *BTEC ND:* DMM. *OCR ND:* D *OCR NED:* M2

P307 BA Media (Film and Television)
Duration: 3FT Hon
Entry Requirements: *GCE:* 280. *IB:* 26. *BTEC NC:* DD. *BTEC ND:* DMM. *OCR ND:* D *OCR NED:* M2 Interview required.

PW33 BA Media, Music and Sound
Duration: 3FT Hon
Entry Requirements: *GCE:* 280. *IB:* 26. *BTEC NC:* DD. *BTEC ND:* DMM. *OCR ND:* D *OCR NED:* M2

E59 EDINBURGH NAPIER UNIVERSITY
CRAIGLOCKHART CAMPUS
EDINBURGH EH14 1DJ
t: +44 (0)8452 60 60 40 f: 0131 455 6464
e: info@napier.ac.uk
// www.napier.ac.uk

N5P3 BA Marketing with Digital Media
Duration: 3FT/4FT Ord/Hon
Entry Requirements: *GCE:* 230.

E70 THE UNIVERSITY OF ESSEX
WIVENHOE PARK
COLCHESTER
ESSEX CO4 3SQ
t: 01206 873666 f: 01206 874477
e: admit@essex.ac.uk
// www.essex.ac.uk

MP93 BA Criminology and the Media
Duration: 3FT Hon
Entry Requirements: *GCE:* ABB-BBB. *SQAH:* AAAB-AABB.

LP33 BA Media, Culture and Society
Duration: 3FT Hon
Entry Requirements: *GCE:* ABB-BBB. *SQAH:* AAAB-AABB.

PL33 BA Media, Culture and Society (Including Year Abroad)
Duration: 4FT Hon
Entry Requirements: *GCE:* ABB-BBB. *SQAH:* AAAB-AABB.

E78 EUROPEAN SCHOOL OF ECONOMICS
8/9 GROSVENOR PLACE
BELGRAVIA
LONDON SW1X 7SH
t: 020 7245 6148 f: 020 7245 6164
e: r.freitas@eselondon.ac.uk
// www.eselondon.ac.uk

P9P3 BA Organisational Communication with Media Management
Duration: 3FT Hon
Entry Requirements: Interview required. Portfolio required.

E81 EXETER COLLEGE
HELE ROAD
EXETER
DEVON EX4 4JS
t: 0845 111 6000
e: info@exe-coll.ac.uk
// www.exe-coll.ac.uk/he

WP23 FdA Graphic Communication
Duration: 2FT Fdg
Entry Requirements: *GCE:* 160.

PP35 FdA Journalism and Practical Media
Duration: 2FT Fdg
Entry Requirements: *GCE:* 160.

F66 FARNBOROUGH COLLEGE OF TECHNOLOGY
BOUNDARY ROAD
FARNBOROUGH
HAMPSHIRE GU14 6SB
t: 01252 407028 f: 01252 407041
e: admissions@farn-ct.ac.uk
// www.farn-ct.ac.uk

P394 BA Media Production (New Media)
Duration: 3FT Hon
Entry Requirements: *GCE:* 180-200. *BTEC NC:* MM. *BTEC ND:* MMM. *OCR ND:* M2 *OCR NED:* M3 Admissions Test required.

G14 UNIVERSITY OF GLAMORGAN, CARDIFF AND PONTYPRIDD
ENQUIRIES AND ADMISSIONS UNIT
PONTYPRIDD CF37 1DL
t: 0800 716925 f: 01443 654050
e: enquiries@glam.ac.uk
// www.glam.ac.uk

P300 BA Film and Video
Duration: 3FT Hon
Entry Requirements: *GCE:* ABB. *IB:* 24. *BTEC ND:* DMM. *OCR NED:* M2 Interview required.

PP35 BA (Hons) Media, Culture and Journalism
Duration: 3FT Hon
Entry Requirements: Contact the institution for details.

G28 UNIVERSITY OF GLASGOW
THE UNIVERSITY OF GLASGOW
THE FRASER BUILDING
65 HILLHEAD STREET
GLASGOW G12 8QF
t: 0141 330 6062 f: 0141 330 2961
e: student.recruitment@glasgow.ac.uk
// www.glasgow.ac.uk

PQ32 MA Comparative Literature/Film and Television Studies
Duration: 4FT Hon
Entry Requirements: *GCE:* AAA. *SQAH:* AAAA-AABB. *IB:* 36.

G42 GLASGOW CALEDONIAN UNIVERSITY
STUDENT RECRUITMENT & ADMISSIONS SERVICE
CITY CAMPUS
COWCADDENS ROAD
GLASGOW G4 0BA
t: 0141 331 3000 f: 0141 331 8676
e: undergraduate@gcu.ac.uk
// www.gcu.ac.uk

PP93 BA Media and Communication
Duration: 4FT Hon
Entry Requirements: *GCE:* BBC. *SQAH:* ABBB-BBBB. *IB:* 24.

G50 THE UNIVERSITY OF GLOUCESTERSHIRE
PARK CAMPUS
THE PARK
CHELTENHAM GL50 2RH
t: 01242 714503 f: 01242 714827
e: admissions@glos.ac.uk
// www.glos.ac.uk

P300 BA Creative Media
Duration: 3FT Hon
Entry Requirements: Contact the institution for details.

G56 GOLDSMITHS, UNIVERSITY OF LONDON
GOLDSMITHS, UNIVERSITY OF LONDON
NEW CROSS
LONDON SE14 6NW
t: 020 7048 5300 f: 020 7919 7509
e: admissions@gold.ac.uk
// www.gold.ac.uk

LP63 BA Anthropology and Media
Duration: 3FT Hon
Entry Requirements: *GCE:* ABB. *SQAH:* BBBBB. *SQAAH:* BBB. *BTEC ND:* DDM.

PP39 BA Media and Communication with Foundation Year (Integrated Degree)
Duration: 4FT Hon
Entry Requirements: Interview required.

P300 BA Media and Communications
Duration: 3FT Hon
Entry Requirements: *GCE:* AAB. *SQAH:* AAABB. *SQAAH:* AAB. *IB:* 34. *BTEC NC:* DD. *BTEC ND:* DDD. Interview required.

PQ33 BA Media and Modern Literature
Duration: 3FT Hon
Entry Requirements: *GCE:* ABB. *SQAH:* AABBB. *SQAAH:* ABB. *IB:* 32. *BTEC NC:* DD. *BTEC ND:* DDM. Interview required.

LP33 BA Media and Sociology
Duration: 3FT Hon
Entry Requirements: *GCE:* ABB. *SQAH:* BBBBB. *SQAAH:* BBB. *BTEC ND:* DDM.

G70 UNIVERSITY OF GREENWICH
GREENWICH CAMPUS
OLD ROYAL NAVAL COLLEGE
PARK ROW
LONDON SE10 9LS
t: 0800 005 006 f: 020 8331 8145
e: courseinfo@gre.ac.uk
// www.gre.ac.uk

P3V1 BA Film Studies with History
Duration: 3FT Hon
Entry Requirements: *GCE:* 240. *IB:* 24.

H36 UNIVERSITY OF HERTFORDSHIRE
UNIVERSITY ADMISSIONS SERVICE
COLLEGE LANE
HATFIELD
HERTS AL10 9AB
t: 01707 284800
// www.herts.ac.uk

Q1PH BA English Language & Communication with Film
Duration: 3FT Hon
Entry Requirements: *GCE:* 300.

Q1P3 BA English Language & Communication with Media Cultures
Duration: 3FT Hon
Entry Requirements: *GCE:* 300.

Q3PH BA English Literature with Film
Duration: 3FT Hon
Entry Requirements: *GCE:* 300.

Q3P3 BA English Literature with Media Cultures
Duration: 3FT Hon
Entry Requirements: *GCE:* 300.

V1PH BA History with Film
Duration: 3FT Hon
Entry Requirements: *GCE:* 300.

V1P3 BA History with Media Cultures
Duration: 3FT Hon
Entry Requirements: *GCE:* 300.

P300 BA Mass Communications
Duration: 3FT Hon
Entry Requirements: *GCE:* 300.

V5PH BA Philosophy with Film
Duration: 3FT Hon
Entry Requirements: *GCE:* 300.

V5P3 BA Philosophy with Media Cultures
Duration: 3FT Hon
Entry Requirements: *GCE:* 300.

P304 BSc Multimedia Technology (Extended)
Duration: 4FT/5SW Hon
Entry Requirements: Contact the institution for details.

H49 UNIVERSITY OF THE HIGHLANDS AND ISLANDS
UHI EXECUTIVE OFFICE
NESS WALK
INVERNESS
SCOTLAND IV3 5SQ
t: 01463 279000 f: 01463 279001
e: info@uhi.ac.uk
// www.uhi.ac.uk

QP53 BA Gaelic and Media Studies
Duration: 4FT Hon
Entry Requirements: *GCE:* C. *SQAH:* CCC. Interview required.

H60 THE UNIVERSITY OF HUDDERSFIELD
QUEENSGATE
HUDDERSFIELD HD1 3DH
t: 01484 473969 f: 01484 472765
e: admissionsandrecords@hud.ac.uk
// www.hud.ac.uk

G4P3 BA Interactive Multimedia
Duration: 3FT/4SW Hon
Entry Requirements: *GCE:* 240. *SQAH:* BBBB. *IB:* 28. *BTEC NC:* DD. *BTEC ND:* MMM.

P300 BA Media and Popular Culture
Duration: 3FT Hon
Entry Requirements: *GCE:* 280. *SQAH:* ABBB-BBBB. *IB:* 28.
Interview required.

H72 THE UNIVERSITY OF HULL
THE UNIVERSITY OF HULL
COTTINGHAM ROAD
HULL HU6 7RX
t: 01482 466100 f: 01482 442290
e: admissions@hull.ac.uk
// www.hull.ac.uk

TP73 BA American Studies and Film Studies
Duration: 3FT Hon
Entry Requirements: *GCE:* 280-300. *IB:* 28. *BTEC ND:* DMM.

WP83 BA Creative Writing and Media, Culture and Society
Duration: 3FT Hon
Entry Requirements: *GCE:* 280-300. *IB:* 28. *BTEC ND:* DMM.

QP33 BA English and Film Studies
Duration: 3FT Hon
Entry Requirements: *GCE:* 280-300. *IB:* 30. *BTEC ND:* DDM.

RP13 BA French and Film Studies
Duration: 4FT Hon
Entry Requirements: *GCE:* 280-300. *IB:* 28. *BTEC ND:* DMM.

RP23 BA German and Film Studies
Duration: 4FT Hon
Entry Requirements: *GCE:* 280-300. *IB:* 28. *BTEC ND:* DMM.

RP33 BA Italian and Film Studies
Duration: 4FT Hon
Entry Requirements: *GCE:* 280-300. *IB:* 28. *BTEC ND:* DMM.

VP53 BA Philosophy and Film Studies
Duration: 3FT Hon
Entry Requirements: *GCE:* 280-300. *IB:* 28. *BTEC ND:* DMM.

LP3H BA Sociology and Media Studies
Duration: 3FT Hon
Entry Requirements: *GCE:* 280-300. *IB:* 28. *BTEC ND:* DMM.

RP43 BA Spanish and Film Studies
Duration: 4FT Hon
Entry Requirements: *GCE:* 280-300. *IB:* 28. *BTEC ND:* DMM.

K12 KEELE UNIVERSITY
STAFFS ST5 5BG
t: 01782 734005 f: 01782 632343
e: undergraduate@keele.ac.uk
// www.keele.ac.uk

PN31 BA Business Management and Media, Communications and Culture
Duration: 3FT Hon
Entry Requirements: *GCE:* 300-320.

PM39 BA Criminology and Media, Communications & Culture
Duration: 3FT Hon
Entry Requirements: *GCE:* 300-320.

PQ33 BA English and Media, Communications & Culture
Duration: 3FT Hon
Entry Requirements: *GCE:* 300-320.

PN33 BA Finance and Media, Communications & Culture
Duration: 3FT Hon
Entry Requirements: *GCE:* 280-340.

PF38 BA Geography and Media, Communications & Culture
Duration: 3FT Hon
Entry Requirements: *GCE:* 300.

PV31 BA History and Media, Communications & Culture
Duration: 3FT Hon
Entry Requirements: *GCE:* 300.

PL37 BA Human Geography and Media, Communications & Culture
Duration: 3FT Hon
Entry Requirements: *GCE:* 300.

PN36 BA Human Resource Management and Media, Communications & Culture
Duration: 3FT Hon
Entry Requirements: *GCE:* 280-340.

PLH2 BA International Relations and Media, Communications & Culture
Duration: 3FT Hon
Entry Requirements: *GCE:* 260-300.

PM31 BA Law and Media, Communications & Culture
Duration: 3FT Hon
Entry Requirements: *GCE:* 300-320.

PN35 BA Marketing and Media, Communications & Culture
Duration: 3FT Hon
Entry Requirements: *GCE:* 300-320.

PW33 BA Media, Communications & Culture and Music
Duration: 3FT Hon
Entry Requirements: *GCE:* 260-320.

PJ39 BA Media, Communications & Culture and Music Technology
Duration: 3FT Hon
Entry Requirements: *GCE:* 260-280.

PV35 BA Media, Communications & Culture and Philosophy
Duration: 3FT Hon
Entry Requirements: *GCE:* 260-280.

PL32 BA Media, Communications & Culture and Politics
Duration: 3FT Hon
Entry Requirements: *GCE:* 260-280.

PL33 BA Media, Communications & Culture and Sociology
Duration: 3FT Hon
Entry Requirements: *GCE:* 300-320.

CP83 BSc Applied Psychology and Media, Communications and Culture
Duration: 4FT Deg
Entry Requirements: *GCE:* 320.

PF35 BSc Astrophysics and Media, Communications & Culture
Duration: 3FT Hon
Entry Requirements: *GCE:* 300-320.

PC37 BSc Biochemistry and Media, Communications & Culture
Duration: 3FT Hon
Entry Requirements: *GCE:* 300.

PC31 BSc Biology and Media, Communications & Culture
Duration: 3FT Hon
Entry Requirements: *GCE:* 300.

FP43 BSc Forensic Science and Media, Communications & Culture
Duration: 3FT Hon
Entry Requirements: *GCE:* 300.

PG31 BSc Mathematics and Media, Communications & Culture
Duration: 3FT Hon
Entry Requirements: *GCE:* 300.

PFH8 BSc Media, Communications & Culture and Physical Geography
Duration: 3FT Hon
Entry Requirements: *GCE:* 300.

PF33 BSc Media, Communications & Culture and Physics
Duration: 3FT Hon
Entry Requirements: *GCE:* 300-320.

PC38 BSc Media, Communications & Culture and Psychology
Duration: 3FT Hon
Entry Requirements: *GCE:* 300-320.

K60 KING'S COLLEGE LONDON (UNIVERSITY OF LONDON)
STRAND
LONDON WC2R 2LS
t: 020 7848 7070 f: 020 7848 7171
e: prospective@kcl.ac.uk
// www.kcl.ac.uk

Q3P3 BA English with Film
Duration: 3FT Hon
Entry Requirements: *GCE:* AAAb. *SQAH:* AAABB. *IB:* 38.

R1P3 BA French with Film (4 years)
Duration: 4FT Hon
Entry Requirements: *GCE:* ABBc. *SQAH:* AABBB. *IB:* 34.

R2P3 BA German with Film (4 years)
Duration: 4FT Hon
Entry Requirements: *GCE:* ABB-BBBc. *SQAH:* AABBC-ABBBB. *IB:* 32.

R4P3 BA Hispanic Studies with Film (4 years)
Duration: 4FT Hon
Entry Requirements: *GCE:* ABBc. *SQAH:* ABBBB. *IB:* 34.

K84 KINGSTON UNIVERSITY
STUDENT INFORMATION & ADVICE CENTRE
COOPER HOUSE
40-46 SURBITON ROAD
KINGSTON UPON THAMES KT1 2HX
t: 0844 8552177 f: 020 8547 7080
e: aps@kingston.ac.uk
// www.kingston.ac.uk

NP13 BA Business and Media & Cultural Studies
Duration: 3FT Hon
Entry Requirements: *GCE:* 280. *IB:* 30.

WPV3 BA Creative Writing and Media & Cultural Studies
Duration: 3FT Hon
Entry Requirements: *GCE:* 220-360. *IB:* 30.

W8P3 BA Creative Writing with Film Studies
Duration: 3FT Hon
Entry Requirements: *GCE:* 220-360. *IB:* 30.

W8PH BA Creative Writing with Media & Cultural Studies
Duration: 3FT Hon
Entry Requirements: *GCE:* 220-360. *IB:* 30.

LPH3 BA Criminology and Media & Cultural Studies
Duration: 3FT Hon
Entry Requirements: *GCE:* 220-320. *SQAH:* BBCCC. *SQAAH:* BBC.

M9P3 BA Criminology with Film Studies
Duration: 3FT Hon
Entry Requirements: *GCE:* 220-320. *SQAH:* BBCCC. *SQAAH:* BBC.

M9PH BA Criminology with Media & Cultural Studies
Duration: 3FT Hon
Entry Requirements: *GCE:* 220-320. *SQAH:* BBCCC. *SQAAH:* BBC.

WP5H BA Dance and Media & Cultural Studies
Duration: 3FT Hon
Entry Requirements: *GCE:* 300-360. *BTEC ND:* DDD. Interview required.

W5PJ BA Dance with Media & Cultural Studies
Duration: 3FT Hon
Entry Requirements: *GCE:* 300-360. *BTEC ND:* DDD. Interview required.

WP23 BA Design and Media & Cultural Studies
Duration: 3FT Hon
Entry Requirements: *GCE:* 280. *IB:* 28. Foundation Course required. Interview required. Portfolio required.

WPK3 BA Drama and Media & Cultural Studies
Duration: 3FT Hon
Entry Requirements: *GCE:* 300-360. *SQAH:* BBCCC. *SQAAH:* BBC.
BTEC ND: DDD.

W4P3 BA Drama with Film Studies
Duration: 3FT Hon
Entry Requirements: *GCE:* 300-360. *SQAH:* BBCCC. *SQAAH:* BBC.
BTEC ND: DDD.

W4PH BA Drama with Media & Cultural Studies
Duration: 3FT Hon
Entry Requirements: *GCE:* 300-360. *SQAH:* BBCCC. *SQAAH:* BBC.
BTEC ND: DDD.

LP13 BA Economics (Applied) and Media & Cultural Studies
Duration: 3FT Hon
Entry Requirements: *GCE:* 220-320. *IB:* 24.

L1P3 BA Economics (Applied) with Media & Cultural Studies
Duration: 3FT Hon
Entry Requirements: *GCE:* 220-320. *IB:* 24.

QP3H BA English Literature and Media & Cultural Studies
Duration: 3FT Hon
Entry Requirements: *GCE:* 240-360.

Q3P3 BA English Literature with Media & Cultural Studies
Duration: 3FT Hon
Entry Requirements: *GCE:* 240-360.

PH90 BA Film Studies and Media & Cultural Studies
Duration: 3FT Hon
Entry Requirements: *GCE:* 240-360. *IB:* 30.

P3W8 BA Film Studies with Creative Writing
Duration: 3FT Hon
Entry Requirements: *GCE:* 240-360.

P3M9 BA Film Studies with Criminology
Duration: 3FT Hon
Entry Requirements: *GCE:* 240-360. *IB:* 30.

P3W4 BA Film Studies with Drama
Duration: 3FT Hon
Entry Requirements: *GCE:* 300-360. *BTEC ND:* DDD.

P3P5 BA Film Studies with Journalism
Duration: 3FT Hon
Entry Requirements: *GCE:* 320. *BTEC ND:* DDM.

W6P3 BA Film Studies with Media & Cultural Studies
Duration: 3FT Hon
Entry Requirements: *GCE:* 240-360. *IB:* 30.

VPH3 BA History of Art, Des & Film and TV & New Broadcasting Media
Duration: 3FT Hon
Entry Requirements: *GCE:* 240.

VP33 BA History of Art, Design & Film and Media & Cultural Studies
Duration: 3FT Hon
Entry Requirements: *GCE:* 240.

V3P3 BA History of Art, Design & Film with Media & Cultural Studies
Duration: 3FT Hon
Entry Requirements: *GCE:* 240. *IB:* 30.

LPF3 BA Human Rights and Media & Cultural Studies
Duration: 3FT Hon
Entry Requirements: *GCE:* 220-360.

L2PJ BA Human Rights with Media & Cultural Studies
Duration: 3FT Hon
Entry Requirements: *GCE:* 220-360.

LP2H BA International Relations and Media & Cultural Studies
Duration: 3FT Hon
Entry Requirements: *GCE:* 220-360.

PP53 BA Journalism and Media & Cultural Studies
Duration: 3FT Hon
Entry Requirements: *GCE:* 320. *SQAH:* BBCCC. *SQAAH:* BBC. *IB:* 25. *BTEC ND:* DDM.

P5P3 BA Journalism with Film Studies
Duration: 3FT Hon
Entry Requirements: *GCE:* 320. *SQAH:* BBCCC. *SQAAH:* BBC. *IB:* 25. *BTEC ND:* DDM.

P5PH BA Journalism with Media & Cultural Studies
Duration: 3FT Hon
Entry Requirements: *GCE:* 320. *SQAH:* BBCCC. *SQAAH:* BBC. *IB:* 25. *BTEC ND:* DDM.

P300 BA Media & Cultural Studies
Duration: 3FT Hon
Entry Requirements: *GCE:* 280. *IB:* 30.

PLH2 BA Media & Cultural Studies and Politics
Duration: 3FT Hon
Entry Requirements: *GCE:* 240-360.

PC38 BA Media & Cultural Studies and Psychology
Duration: 3FT Hon
Entry Requirements: *GCE:* 240-360.

PLH3 BA Media & Cultural Studies and Sociology
Duration: 3FT Hon
Entry Requirements: *GCE:* 240-360. *IB:* 30.

PJ90 BA Media & Cultural Studies and Television & New Broadcasting Media
Duration: 3FT Hon
Entry Requirements: *GCE:* 240-360.

P3N1 BA Media & Cultural Studies with Business
Duration: 3FT Hon
Entry Requirements: *GCE:* 280. *IB:* 30.

P3WV BA Media & Cultural Studies with Creative Writing
Duration: 3FT Hon
Entry Requirements: *GCE:* 240-360.

P3MX BA Media & Cultural Studies with Criminology
Duration: 3FT Hon
Entry Requirements: *GCE:* 240-360.

P3WN BA Media & Cultural Studies with Dance
Duration: 3FT Hon
Entry Requirements: *GCE:* 300-360. *BTEC ND:* DDD. Interview required.

P3WK BA Media & Cultural Studies with Drama
Duration: 3FT Hon
Entry Requirements: *GCE:* 300-360. *BTEC ND:* DDD.

P3L1 BA Media & Cultural Studies with Economics (Applied)
Duration: 3FT Hon
Entry Requirements: *GCE:* 240-360.

P3Q3 BA Media & Cultural Studies with English Literature
Duration: 3FT Hon
Entry Requirements: *GCE:* 240-360.

P3W6 BA Media & Cultural Studies with Film
Duration: 3FT Hon
Entry Requirements: *GCE:* 240-360. *IB:* 30.

P3R1 BA Media & Cultural Studies with French
Duration: 3FT Hon
Entry Requirements: *GCE:* 240-360.

P3V3 BA Media & Cultural Studies with History of Art, Design & Film
Duration: 3FT Hon
Entry Requirements: *GCE:* 240-360. *IB:* 30.

P3LG BA Media & Cultural Studies with Human Rights
Duration: 3FT Hon
Entry Requirements: *GCE:* 240-360.

PL32 BA Media & Cultural Studies with International Relations
Duration: 3FT Hon
Entry Requirements: *GCE:* 240-360.

P3PM BA Media & Cultural Studies with Journalism
Duration: 3FT Hon
Entry Requirements: *GCE:* 320.

P3L2 BA Media & Cultural Studies with Politics
Duration: 3FT Hon
Entry Requirements: *GCE:* 240-360.

P3C8 BA Media & Cultural Studies with Psychology
Duration: 3FT Hon
Entry Requirements: *GCE:* 240-360.

P3L3 BA Media & Cultural Studies with Sociology
Duration: 3FT Hon
Entry Requirements: *GCE:* 240-360. *IB:* 30.

P3R4 BA Media & Cultural Studies with Spanish
Duration: 3FT Hon
Entry Requirements: *GCE:* 240-360.

P395 BA Media & Cultural Studies with Television & New Broadcasting Media
Duration: 3FT Hon
Entry Requirements: *GCE:* 240-360.

WP33 BA Music and Film Studies
Duration: 3FT Hon
Entry Requirements: *GCE:* 240-280. *BTEC ND:* MMM.

L2P3 BA Politics with Media & Cultural Studies
Duration: 3FT Hon
Entry Requirements: *GCE:* 220-360.

C8P3 BA Psychology with Media & Cultural Studies
Duration: 3FT Hon
Entry Requirements: *GCE:* 220-360.

L3P3 BA Sociology with Media & Cultural Studies
Duration: 3FT Hon
Entry Requirements: *GCE:* 220-360. *IB:* 30.

P393 BA Television & New Broadcasting Media with Media & Cultural Studies
Duration: 3FT Hon
Entry Requirements: *GCE:* 240-360.

PW32 BA Visual & Material Culture and Media & Cultural Studies
Duration: 3FT Hon
Entry Requirements: *GCE:* 240.

L2PB BSc International Relations with Media & Cultural Studies
Duration: 3FT Hon
Entry Requirements: *GCE:* 220-360.

PN31 BSc Media Technology and Business
Duration: 3FT Hon
Entry Requirements: *GCE:* 240-280. Interview required.

PN3C BSc Media Technology and Business
Duration: 4SW Hon
Entry Requirements: *GCE:* 240-280. Interview required.

PG34 BSc Media Technology and Computing
Duration: 3FT Hon
Entry Requirements: *GCE:* 240-280. Interview required.

PG3K BSc Media Technology and Computing
Duration: 4SW Hon
Entry Requirements: *GCE:* 240-280. Interview required.

PG35 BSc Media Technology and Web Development
Duration: 3FT Hon
Entry Requirements: *GCE:* 240-280. Interview required.

PGH5 BSc Media Technology and Web Development
Duration: 4SW Hon
Entry Requirements: *GCE:* 240-280. Interview required.

PGJ5 BSc Media Technology and Web Development (Foundation)
Duration: 4FT Hon
Entry Requirements: *GCE:* 60.

P3W2 BSc Media Technology with Design
Duration: 3FT Hon
Entry Requirements: *GCE:* 240-280. Interview required. Portfolio required.

L14 LANCASTER UNIVERSITY
THE UNIVERSITY
LANCASTER
LANCASHIRE LA1 4YW
t: 01524 592029 f: 01524 846243
e: ugadmissions@lancaster.ac.uk
// www.lancs.ac.uk

QP33 BA English Language in the Media
Duration: 3FT Hon
Entry Requirements: *GCE:* AAA-AAB. *SQAH:* ABBBB. *SQAAH:* AAB.

QP3H BA English Language in the Media (Study Abroad)
Duration: 3FT Hon
Entry Requirements: *GCE:* AAA-AAB. *SQAH:* ABBBB. *SQAAH:* AAB.

PV35 BA Film Studies and Philosophy
Duration: 3FT Hon
Entry Requirements: *GCE:* ABB. *SQAH:* BBBBB. *SQAAH:* ABB. *IB:* 32. *BTEC ND:* DDM.

PL33 BA Film Studies and Sociology
Duration: 3FT Hon
Entry Requirements: *GCE:* ABB. *SQAH:* BBBBC. *SQAAH:* BBB. *IB:* 32. *BTEC ND:* DDM.

LP63 BA Media and Cultural Studies
Duration: 3FT Hon
Entry Requirements: *GCE:* ABB. *SQAH:* BBBBC. *SQAAH:* BBB. *IB:* 32. *BTEC ND:* DDM.

L24 LEEDS TRINITY UNIVERSITY COLLEGE (FORMERLY LEEDS TRINITY AND ALL SAINTS)
BROWNBERRIE LANE
HORSFORTH
LEEDS LS18 5HD
t: 0113 283 7150 f: 0113 283 7222
e: enquiries@leedstrinity.ac.uk
// www.leedstrinity.ac.uk

QP33 BA English and Media
Duration: 3FT Hon
Entry Requirements: *GCE:* 220. *IB:* 24. *BTEC NC:* DD. *BTEC ND:* MMP.

P300 BA Media
Duration: 3FT Hon
Entry Requirements: *GCE:* 200. *IB:* 24. *BTEC NC:* DM. *BTEC ND:* MMP.

PN35 BA Media and Marketing
Duration: 3FT Hon
Entry Requirements: *GCE:* 200. *IB:* 24. *BTEC NC:* DM. *BTEC ND:* MMP.

L27 LEEDS METROPOLITAN UNIVERSITY
COURSE ENQUIRIES OFFICE
CITY SITE
LEEDS LS1 3HE
t: 0113 81 23113 f: 0113 81 23129
// www.leedsmet.ac.uk

P300 BA Media and Popular Culture
Duration: 3FT Hon
Entry Requirements: *GCE:* 220. *IB:* 24.

L34 UNIVERSITY OF LEICESTER
UNIVERSITY ROAD
LEICESTER LE1 7RH
t: 0116 252 5281 f: 0116 252 2447
e: admissions@le.ac.uk
// www.le.ac.uk

PV33 BA Film Studies and the Visual Arts
Duration: 3FT Hon
Entry Requirements: *GCE:* BBB. *SQAH:* BBBBB. *SQAAH:* BBB. *IB:* 30. *BTEC ND:* DDM.

PL33 BA Media and Sociology
Duration: 3FT Hon
Entry Requirements: *GCE:* BBB. *SQAH:* BBBBB. *SQAAH:* BBB. *IB:* 30. *BTEC ND:* DDM.

L46 LIVERPOOL HOPE UNIVERSITY
HOPE PARK
LIVERPOOL L16 9JD
t: 0151 291 3295 f: 0151 291 3444
e: admission@hope.ac.uk
// www.hope.ac.uk

NP43 BA Accounting and Media & Communication
Duration: 3FT Hon
Entry Requirements: *GCE:* 260-320. *IB:* 25.

VP33 BA Art & Design History and Media & Communication
Duration: 3FT Hon
Entry Requirements: *GCE:* 260-320. *IB:* 25.

VP63 BA Biblical Studies and Media & Communication
Duration: 3FT Hon
Entry Requirements: *GCE:* 260-320. *IB:* 25.

NP23 BA Business Management and Media & Communication
Duration: 3FT Hon
Entry Requirements: *GCE:* 260-320. *IB:* 25.

VP6H BA Christian Theology and Media & Communication
Duration: 3FT Hon
Entry Requirements: *GCE:* 260-320. *IB:* 25.

LP3H BA Criminology and Media & Communication
Duration: 3FT Hon
Entry Requirements: *GCE:* 260-320. *IB:* 25.

WP53 BA Dance and Media & Communication
Duration: 3FT Hon
Entry Requirements: *GCE:* 260-320. *IB:* 25.

XP33 BA Education and Media & Communication
Duration: 3FT Hon   CRB Check: Required
Entry Requirements: *GCE:* 260-320. *IB:* 25.

QP3H BA English Language and Media & Communication
Duration: 3FT Hon
Entry Requirements: *GCE:* 260-320. *IB:* 25.

QP33 BA English Literature and Media & Communication
Duration: 3FT Hon
Entry Requirements: *GCE:* 260-320. *IB:* 25.

WP1H BA Fine Art and Media & Communication
Duration: 3FT Hon
Entry Requirements: *GCE:* 260-320. *IB:* 25.

VPD3 BA History and Media & Communication
Duration: 3FT Hon
Entry Requirements: *GCE:* 260-320. *IB:* 25.

LP23 BA International Relations and Media & Communication
Duration: 3FT Hon
Entry Requirements: *GCE:* 260-320. *IB:* 25.

MP13 BA Law and Media & Communication
Duration: 3FT Hon
Entry Requirements: *GCE:* 260-320. *IB:* 25.

NP53 BA Marketing and Media & Communication
Duration: 3FT Hon
Entry Requirements: *GCE:* 260-320. *IB:* 25.

P300 BA Media & Communication
Duration: 3FT Hon
Entry Requirements: *GCE:* 260-320. *IB:* 25.

PW33 BA Media & Communication and Music
Duration: 3FT Hon
Entry Requirements: *GCE:* 260-320. *IB:* 25.

PN38 BA Media & Communication and Tourism
Duration: 3FT Hon
Entry Requirements: *GCE:* 260. *IB:* 25.

PV63 BA Media & Communication and World Religions
Duration: 3FT Hon
Entry Requirements: *GCE:* 260-320. *IB:* 25.

L51 LIVERPOOL JOHN MOORES UNIVERSITY
KINGSWAY HOUSE
HATTON GARDEN
LIVERPOOL L3 2AJ
t: 0151 231 5090 f: 0151 231 3462
e: courses@ljmu.ac.uk
// www.ljmu.ac.uk

PQ33 BA English and Media & Cultural Studies
Duration: 3FT Hon
Entry Requirements: *GCE:* 260.

P300 BA Media Professional Studies
Duration: 3FT Hon
Entry Requirements: *GCE:* 280. *IB:* 25. *BTEC ND:* DMM.

LP63 BA Media, Culture, Communication
Duration: 3FT Hon
Entry Requirements: *GCE:* 260. *IB:* 24.

HP63 BSc Broadcast and Media Production
Duration: 3FT/4SW Hon
Entry Requirements: *GCE:* 280. *BTEC NC:* MM. *BTEC ND:* DMM. *OCR ND:* M2 *OCR NED:* M2 Interview required.

L62 THE LONDON COLLEGE, UCK
VICTORIA GARDENS
NOTTING HILL GATE
LONDON W11 3PE
t: 020 7243 4000 f: 020 7243 1484
e: admissions@lcuck.ac.uk
// www.lcuck.ac.uk

103P Dip Media and Humanities
Duration: 1FT Oth
Entry Requirements: Contact the institution for details.

L68 LONDON METROPOLITAN UNIVERSITY
166-220 HOLLOWAY ROAD
LONDON N7 8DB
t: 020 7133 4200
e: admissions@londonmet.ac.uk
// www.londonmet.ac.uk

WP83 BA Creative Writing and Film & Television Studies
Duration: 3FT Hon
Entry Requirements: *GCE:* 260. *IB:* 28. Portfolio required.

QPH3 BA English Literature and Film & Television Studies
Duration: 3FT Hon
Entry Requirements: *GCE:* 260. *IB:* 28.

P3J9 BA Media Technology with Audio Systems
Duration: 3FT Hon
Entry Requirements: Contact the institution for details.

NP83 BA Music Industry and Events Management
Duration: 3FT Hon
Entry Requirements: *GCE:* 240. *IB:* 28.

PPH9 BSc Media & Communications
Duration: 3FT Hon
Entry Requirements: Contact the institution for details.

PP35 BSc Media & Communications and Journalism
Duration: 3FT Hon
Entry Requirements: Contact the institution for details.

L75 LONDON SOUTH BANK UNIVERSITY
103 BOROUGH ROAD
LONDON SE1 0AA
t: 020 7815 7815 f: 020 7815 8273
e: enquiry@lsbu.ac.uk
// www.lsbu.ac.uk

QP33 BA English and Media Studies
Duration: 3FT Hon
Entry Requirements: *GCE:* 240. *IB:* 24. *BTEC NC:* DD. *BTEC ND:* MMM.

PQ3H BA Media Studies and English
Duration: 3FT Hon
Entry Requirements: *GCE:* 240. *IB:* 24. *BTEC NC:* DD. *BTEC ND:* MMM.

P390 BA Media and Film Studies
Duration: 3FT Hon
Entry Requirements: *GCE:* 240. *IB:* 24. *BTEC NC:* DD. *BTEC ND:* MMM.

PQH3 BA (Hons) Film Studies and English
Duration: 3FT Hon
Entry Requirements: *GCE:* 240. *IB:* 24. *BTEC NC:* DD. *BTEC ND:* MMM.

PP39 BA (Hons) Film Studies and Media Studies
Duration: 3FT Hon
Entry Requirements: *GCE:* 240. *IB:* 24. *BTEC NC:* DD. *BTEC ND:* MMM.

PL33 BSc Media and Cultural Studies
Duration: 3FT Hon
Entry Requirements: *GCE:* 240. *IB:* 24. *BTEC NC:* DD. *BTEC ND:* MMM.

M10 THE MANCHESTER COLLEGE
OPENSHAW CAMPUS
ASHTON OLD ROAD
OPENSHAW
MANCHESTER M11 2WH
t: 0800 068 8585 f: 0161 920 4103
e: enquiries@themanchestercollege.ac.uk
// www.themanchestercollege.ac.uk

PN31 BSc Media and Creative Business
Duration: 1FT Hon
Entry Requirements: Portfolio required. HND required.

M40 THE MANCHESTER METROPOLITAN UNIVERSITY
ADMISSIONS OFFICE
ALL SAINTS (GMS)
ALL SAINTS
MANCHESTER M15 6BH
t: 0161 247 2000
// www.mmu.ac.uk

CP6H BA Coaching Studies/Film & Television Studies
Duration: 3FT Hon
Entry Requirements: *GCE:* 240-280. *BTEC ND:* MMM.

PW32 BA Contemporary Film and Video
Duration: 3FT Hon
Entry Requirements: *GCE:* 240-280. *IB:* 27. *BTEC ND:* MMM.
Interview required. Portfolio required.

PV32 BA Digital Media/Social History
Duration: 3FT Hon
Entry Requirements: *GCE:* 240-280. *IB:* 29.

P306 BA Film, TV and Cultural Studies
Duration: 3FT Hon
Entry Requirements: *GCE:* 240-280.

P307 BA Film, TV and Cultural Studies (Foundation)
Duration: 4FT Hon
Entry Requirements: *GCE:* 80.

PF31 BA/BSc Chemistry/Digital Media
Duration: 3FT Hon
Entry Requirements: *GCE:* 240-280. *IB:* 29.

MG9K BA/BSc Criminology/Digital Media
Duration: 3FT Hon
Entry Requirements: *GCE:* 240-280. *IB:* 29. *BTEC ND:* DMM.

PG53 BA/BSc Digital Media/Information & Communications
Duration: 3FT Hon
Entry Requirements: *GCE:* 240-280. *IB:* 29.

P304 BSc Digital Media and Communications
Duration: 3FT Hon
Entry Requirements: *GCE:* 240-280. *BTEC ND:* MMM.

HP63 BSc Media Technology
Duration: 3FT/4SW Hon
Entry Requirements: **GCE:** 240-280. **IB:** 27. **BTEC NC:** DD. **BTEC ND:** MMM. **OCR ND:** M2 **OCR NED:** P2

HPP3 BSc Media Technology (Foundation)
Duration: 4FT/5SW Hon
Entry Requirements: **GCE:** 80. **IB:** 24.

M80 MIDDLESEX UNIVERSITY
MIDDLESEX UNIVERSITY
THE BURROUGHS
LONDON NW4 4BT
t: 020 8411 5555 f: 020 8411 5649
e: enquiries@mdx.ac.uk
// www.mdx.ac.uk

NP53 BA Advertising, Public Relations and Media
Duration: 3FT Hon
Entry Requirements: **GCE:** 200-300. **IB:** 28.

WP83 BA Creative and Media Writing
Duration: 3FT Hon
Entry Requirements: **GCE:** 200-300. **IB:** 28.

QP33 BA English Literature and Media
Duration: 3FT Hon
Entry Requirements: **GCE:** 200-300. **IB:** 28.

P5PJ BA Journalism with Media & Cultural Studies
Duration: 3FT Hon
Entry Requirements: **GCE:** 200-300. **IB:** 28.

LP63 BA Media and Cultural Studies
Duration: 3FT Hon
Entry Requirements: **GCE:** 200-300. **IB:** 28.

PP43 BA Publishing, Media and Cultural Studies
Duration: 3FT Hon
Entry Requirements: **GCE:** 200-300. **IB:** 28.

N23 NEWCASTLE COLLEGE
STUDENT SERVICES
RYE HILL CAMPUS
SCOTSWOOD ROAD
NEWCASTLE UPON TYNE NE4 7SA
t: 0191 200 4110 f: 0191 200 4349
e: enquiries@ncl-coll.ac.uk
// www.newcastlecollege.co.uk

W6P3 FdA Television and Media Practice
Duration: 2FT Fdg   CRB Check: Required
Entry Requirements: **GCE:** 120. **BTEC NC:** MP. **BTEC ND:** PPP. **OCR ND:** P2 **OCR NED:** P3 Interview required.

N28 NEW COLLEGE DURHAM
FRAMWELLGATE MOOR CENTRE
DURHAM DH1 5ES
t: 0191 375 4210/4211 f: 0191 375 4222
e: admissions@newdur.ac.uk
// www.newdur.ac.uk

WP33 FdA Music Management
Duration: 2FT Fdg
Entry Requirements: **GCE:** 40. **BTEC NC:** PP. **BTEC ND:** PPP.

N36 NEWMAN UNIVERSITY COLLEGE, BIRMINGHAM
GENNERS LANE
BARTLEY GREEN
BIRMINGHAM B32 3NT
t: 0121 476 1181 f: 0121 476 1196
e: Admissions@newman.ac.uk
// www.newman.ac.uk

BP93 BA Counselling Studies and Media & Communication
Duration: 3FT Hon
Entry Requirements: **Foundation:** Distinction. **GCE:** 260. **IB:** 24. **BTEC NC:** MM. **BTEC ND:** DMM. **OCR ND:** M2 **OCR NED:** M2

W4P3 BA Drama with Media & Communication
Duration: 3FT Hon
Entry Requirements: **Foundation:** Distinction. **GCE:** 260. **IB:** 24. **BTEC NC:** MM. **BTEC ND:** DMM. **OCR ND:** M2 **OCR NED:** M2

XP33 BA Education Studies and Media & Communication
Duration: 3FT Hon
Entry Requirements: **Foundation:** Distinction. **GCE:** 260. **IB:** 24. **BTEC NC:** MM. **BTEC ND:** DMM. **OCR ND:** M2 **OCR NED:** M2

X3P3 BA Education Studies with Media & Communication
Duration: 3FT Hon
Entry Requirements: **Foundation:** Distinction. **GCE:** 260. **IB:** 24. **BTEC NC:** MM. **BTEC ND:** DMM. **OCR ND:** M2 **OCR NED:** M2

Q3P3 BA English with Media & Communication
Duration: 3FT Hon
Entry Requirements: **Foundation:** Distinction. **GCE:** 260. **IB:** 24. **BTEC NC:** MM. **BTEC ND:** DMM. **OCR ND:** M2 **OCR NED:** M2

GP53 BA IT and Media & Communication
Duration: 3FT Hon
Entry Requirements: **Foundation:** Distinction. **GCE:** 260. **IB:** 24. **BTEC NC:** MM. **BTEC ND:** DMM. **OCR ND:** M2 **OCR NED:** M2

G5P3 BA IT with Media & Communication
Duration: 3FT Hon
Entry Requirements: **Foundation:** Distinction. **GCE:** 260. **IB:** 24. **BTEC NC:** MM. **BTEC ND:** DMM. **OCR ND:** M2 **OCR NED:** M2

NP23 BA Management & Business and Media & Communication
Duration: 3FT Hon
Entry Requirements: *Foundation:* Distinction. *GCE:* 260. *IB:* 24. *BTEC NC:* MM. *BTEC ND:* DMM. *OCR ND:* M2 *OCR NED:* M2

N2PH BA Management & Business with Media & Communication
Duration: 3FT Hon
Entry Requirements: *Foundation:* Distinction. *GCE:* 260. *IB:* 24. *BTEC NC:* MM. *BTEC ND:* DMM. *OCR ND:* M2 *OCR NED:* M2

PC38 BA Media & Communication and Applied Psychology
Duration: 3FT Hon
Entry Requirements: *Foundation:* Distinction. *GCE:* 260. *IB:* 24. *BTEC NC:* MM. *BTEC ND:* DMM. *OCR ND:* M2 *OCR NED:* M2

PW31 BA Media & Communication and Art & Design
Duration: 3FT Hon
Entry Requirements: *Foundation:* Distinction. *GCE:* 260. *IB:* 24. *BTEC NC:* MM. *BTEC ND:* DMM. *OCR ND:* M2 *OCR NED:* M2

PW34 BA Media & Communication and Drama
Duration: 3FT Hon
Entry Requirements: *Foundation:* Distinction. *GCE:* 260. *IB:* 24. *BTEC NC:* MM. *BTEC ND:* DMM. *OCR ND:* M2 *OCR NED:* M2

PQ33 BA Media & Communication and English
Duration: 3FT Hon
Entry Requirements: *Foundation:* Distinction. *GCE:* 260. *IB:* 24. *BTEC NC:* MM. *BTEC ND:* DMM. *OCR ND:* M2 *OCR NED:* M2

PV35 BA Media & Communication and Philosophy, Religion & Ethics
Duration: 3FT Hon
Entry Requirements: *Foundation:* Distinction. *GCE:* 260. *IB:* 24. *BTEC NC:* MM. *BTEC ND:* DMM. *OCR ND:* M2 *OCR NED:* M2

PV36 BA Media & Communication and Theology
Duration: 3FT Hon
Entry Requirements: *Foundation:* Distinction. *GCE:* 260. *IB:* 24. *BTEC NC:* MM. *BTEC ND:* DMM. *OCR ND:* M2 *OCR NED:* M2

PL35 BA Media & Communication and Working with Children, Young People & Families
Duration: 3FT Hon
Entry Requirements: *Foundation:* Distinction. *GCE:* 260. *IB:* 24. *BTEC NC:* MM. *BTEC ND:* DMM. *OCR ND:* M2 *OCR NED:* M2

C8P3 BA Psychology with Media & Communication
Duration: 3FT Hon
Entry Requirements: *Foundation:* Distinction. *GCE:* 280. *IB:* 25. *BTEC NC:* MM. *BTEC ND:* DDM. *OCR ND:* M2 *OCR NED:* M2

V6P3 BA Theology with Media & Communication
Duration: 3FT Hon
Entry Requirements: *Foundation:* Distinction. *GCE:* 260. *IB:* 24. *BTEC NC:* MM. *BTEC ND:* DMM. *OCR ND:* M2 *OCR NED:* M2

LMP3 BA Working with Children Young People and Families with Media and Communication
Duration: 3FT Hon
Entry Requirements: *Foundation:* Distinction. *GCE:* 260. *IB:* 24. *BTEC NC:* MM. *BTEC ND:* DMM. *OCR ND:* M2 *OCR NED:* M2

N38 UNIVERSITY OF NORTHAMPTON
PARK CAMPUS
BOUGHTON GREEN ROAD
NORTHAMPTON NN2 7AL
t: 0800 358 2232 f: 01604 722083
e: admissions@northampton.ac.uk
// www.northampton.ac.uk

N5PH BA Advertising/Media Studies
Duration: 3FT Hon
Entry Requirements: *GCE:* 260-280. *SQAH:* AAA-BBBB. *IB:* 24. *BTEC NC:* DD. *BTEC ND:* DMM. *OCR ND:* D *OCR NED:* M2

N1P3 BA Business/Media Studies
Duration: 3FT Hon
Entry Requirements: *GCE:* 260-280. *SQAH:* AAA-BBBB. *IB:* 24. *BTEC NC:* DD. *BTEC ND:* DMM. *OCR ND:* D *OCR NED:* M2

W8P3 BA Creative Writing/Media Studies
Duration: 3FT Hon
Entry Requirements: *GCE:* 260-280. *SQAH:* AAA-BBBB. *IB:* 24. *BTEC NC:* DD. *BTEC ND:* DMM. *OCR ND:* D *OCR NED:* M2

W4P3 BA Drama/Media Studies
Duration: 3FT Hon
Entry Requirements: *GCE:* 260-280. *SQAH:* AAA-BBBB. *IB:* 24. *BTEC NC:* DD. *BTEC ND:* DMM. *OCR ND:* D *OCR NED:* M2
Interview required.

L1P3 BA Economics/Media Studies
Duration: 3FT Hon
Entry Requirements: *GCE:* 260-280. *SQAH:* AAA-BBBB. *IB:* 24. *BTEC NC:* DD. *BTEC ND:* DMM. *OCR ND:* D *OCR NED:* M2

X3P3 BA Education Studies/Media Studies
Duration: 3FT Hon
Entry Requirements: *GCE:* 260-280. *SQAH:* AAA-BBBB. *IB:* 24. *BTEC NC:* DD. *BTEC ND:* DMM. *OCR ND:* D *OCR NED:* M2

Q3P3 BA English/Media Studies
Duration: 3FT Hon
Entry Requirements: *GCE:* 260-280. *SQAH:* AAA-BBBB. *IB:* 24. *BTEC NC:* DD. *BTEC ND:* DMM. *OCR ND:* D *OCR NED:* M2

N8PH BA Events Management/Media Studies
Duration: 3FT Hon
Entry Requirements: *GCE:* 260-280. *SQAH:* AAA-BBBB. *IB:* 24.
BTEC NC: DD. *BTEC ND:* DMM. *OCR ND:* D *OCR NED:* M2

W6P3 BA Film & Television Studies/Media Studies
Duration: 3FT Hon
Entry Requirements: *GCE:* 260-280. *SQAH:* AAA-BBBB. *IB:* 24.
BTEC NC: DD. *BTEC ND:* DMM. *OCR ND:* D *OCR NED:* M2

L4P3 BA Health Studies/Media Studies
Duration: 3FT Hon
Entry Requirements: *GCE:* 260-280. *SQAH:* AAA-BBBB. *IB:* 24.
BTEC NC: DD. *BTEC ND:* DMM. *OCR ND:* D *OCR NED:* M2

D4P3 BA Heritage Management/Media Studies
Duration: 3FT Hon
Entry Requirements: *GCE:* 260-280. *SQAH:* AAA-BBBB. *IB:* 24.
BTEC NC: DD. *BTEC ND:* DMM. *OCR ND:* D *OCR NED:* M2

L9PH BA International Development/Media Studies
Duration: 3FT Hon
Entry Requirements: *GCE:* 260-280. *SQAH:* AAA-BBBB. *IB:* 24.
BTEC NC: DD. *BTEC ND:* DMM. *OCR ND:* D *OCR NED:* M2

M1P3 BA Law/Media Studies
Duration: 3FT Hon
Entry Requirements: *GCE:* 260-280. *SQAH:* AAA-BBBB. *IB:* 24.
BTEC NC: DD. *BTEC ND:* DMM. *OCR ND:* D *OCR NED:* M2

NP8J BA Leisure & Lifestyle Management/Media Production
Duration: 3FT Hon
Entry Requirements: *GCE:* 260-280. *SQAH:* AAA-BBBB. *IB:* 24.
BTEC NC: DD. *BTEC ND:* DMM. *OCR ND:* D *OCR NED:* M2

NP83 BA Leisure & Lifestyle Management/Media Studies
Duration: 3FT Hon
Entry Requirements: *GCE:* 260-280. *SQAH:* AAA-BBBB. *IB:* 24.
BTEC NC: DD. *BTEC ND:* DMM. *OCR ND:* D *OCR NED:* M2

N2P3 BA Management/Media Studies
Duration: 3FT Hon
Entry Requirements: *GCE:* 260-280. *SQAH:* AAA-BBBB. *IB:* 24.
BTEC NC: DD. *BTEC ND:* DMM. *OCR ND:* D *OCR NED:* M2

N5P3 BA Marketing/Media Studies
Duration: 3FT Hon
Entry Requirements: *GCE:* 260-280. *SQAH:* AAA-BBBB. *IB:* 24.
BTEC NC: DD. *BTEC ND:* DMM. *OCR ND:* D *OCR NED:* M2

P391 BA Media Production/Media Studies
Duration: 3FT Hon
Entry Requirements: *GCE:* 260-280. *SQAH:* AAA-BBBB. *IB:* 24.
BTEC NC: DD. *BTEC ND:* DMM. *OCR ND:* D *OCR NED:* M2

P301 BA Media Studies (top-up)
Duration: 1FT Hon
Entry Requirements: Contact the institution for details.

P3NX BA Media Studies with Applied Management
Duration: 3FT Hon
Entry Requirements: *GCE:* 260-280. *SQAH:* AAA-BBBB. *IB:* 24.
BTEC NC: DD. *BTEC ND:* DMM. *OCR ND:* D *OCR NED:* M2

P3D4 BA Media Studies with Equine Studies
Duration: 3FT Hon
Entry Requirements: *GCE:* 260-280. *SQAH:* AAA-BBBB. *IB:* 24.
BTEC NC: DD. *BTEC ND:* DMM. *OCR ND:* D *OCR NED:* M2

P3NM BA Media Studies/Advertising
Duration: 3FT Hon
Entry Requirements: *GCE:* 260-280. *SQAH:* AAA-BBBB. *IB:* 24.
BTEC NC: DD. *BTEC ND:* DMM. *OCR ND:* D *OCR NED:* M2

P3C1 BA Media Studies/Biological Conservation
Duration: 3FT Hon
Entry Requirements: *GCE:* 260-280. *SQAH:* AAA-BBBB. *IB:* 24.
BTEC NC: DD. *BTEC ND:* DMM. *OCR ND:* D *OCR NED:* M2

P3N1 BA Media Studies/Business
Duration: 3FT Hon
Entry Requirements: *GCE:* 260-280. *SQAH:* AAA-BBBB. *IB:* 24.
BTEC NC: DD. *BTEC ND:* DMM. *OCR ND:* D *OCR NED:* M2

P3G5 BA Media Studies/Business Computing Systems
Duration: 3FT Hon
Entry Requirements: *GCE:* 260-280. *SQAH:* AAA-BBBB. *IB:* 24.
BTEC NC: DD. *BTEC ND:* DMM. *OCR ND:* D *OCR NED:* M2

P3G4 BA Media Studies/Computing
Duration: 3FT Hon
Entry Requirements: *GCE:* 260-280. *SQAH:* AAA-BBBB. *IB:* 24.
BTEC NC: DD. *BTEC ND:* DMM. *OCR ND:* D *OCR NED:* M2

P3W8 BA Media Studies/Creative Writing
Duration: 3FT Hon
Entry Requirements: *GCE:* 260-280. *SQAH:* AAA-BBBB. *IB:* 24.
BTEC NC: DD. *BTEC ND:* DMM. *OCR ND:* D *OCR NED:* M2

P3W4 BA Media Studies/Drama
Duration: 3FT Hon
Entry Requirements: *GCE:* 260-280. *SQAH:* AAA-BBBB. *IB:* 24.
BTEC NC: DD. *BTEC ND:* DMM. *OCR ND:* D *OCR NED:* M2
Interview required.

P3L1 BA Media Studies/Economics
Duration: 3FT Hon
Entry Requirements: *GCE:* 260-280. *SQAH:* AAA-BBBB. *IB:* 24.
BTEC NC: DD. *BTEC ND:* DMM. *OCR ND:* D *OCR NED:* M2

P3X3 BA Media Studies/Education Studies
Duration: 3FT Hon
Entry Requirements: *GCE:* 260-280. *SQAH:* AAA-BBBB. *IB:* 24.
BTEC NC: DD. *BTEC ND:* DMM. *OCR ND:* D *OCR NED:* M2

P3Q3 BA Media Studies/English
Duration: 3FT Hon
Entry Requirements: *GCE:* 260-280. *SQAH:* AAA-BBBB. *IB:* 24.
BTEC NC: DD. *BTEC ND:* DMM. *OCR ND:* D *OCR NED:* M2

P3NV BA Media Studies/Events Management
Duration: 3FT Hon
Entry Requirements: *GCE:* 260-280. *SQAH:* AAA-BBBB. *IB:* 24.
BTEC NC: DD. *BTEC ND:* DMM. *OCR ND:* D *OCR NED:* M2

P3W6 BA Media Studies/Film & Television Studies
Duration: 3FT Hon
Entry Requirements: *GCE:* 260-280. *SQAH:* AAA-BBBB. *IB:* 24.
BTEC NC: DD. *BTEC ND:* DMM. *OCR ND:* D *OCR NED:* M2

P3L4 BA Media Studies/Health Studies
Duration: 3FT Hon
Entry Requirements: *GCE:* 260-280. *SQAH:* AAA-BBBB. *IB:* 24.
BTEC NC: DD. *BTEC ND:* DMM. *OCR ND:* D *OCR NED:* M2

PD3K BA Media Studies/Heritage Management
Duration: 3FT Hon
Entry Requirements: *GCE:* 260-280. *SQAH:* AAA-BBBB. *IB:* 24.
BTEC NC: DD. *BTEC ND:* DMM. *OCR ND:* D *OCR NED:* M2

P3M1 BA Media Studies/Law
Duration: 3FT Hon
Entry Requirements: *GCE:* 260-280. *SQAH:* AAA-BBBB. *IB:* 24.
BTEC NC: DD. *BTEC ND:* DMM. *OCR ND:* D *OCR NED:* M2

PN3W BA Media Studies/Leisure & Lifestyle Management
Duration: 3FT Hon
Entry Requirements: *GCE:* 260-280. *SQAH:* AAA-BBBB. *IB:* 24.
BTEC NC: DD. *BTEC ND:* DMM. *OCR ND:* D *OCR NED:* M2

P3N2 BA Media Studies/Management
Duration: 3FT Hon
Entry Requirements: *GCE:* 260-280. *SQAH:* AAA-BBBB. *IB:* 24.
BTEC NC: DD. *BTEC ND:* DMM. *OCR ND:* D *OCR NED:* M2

P3N5 BA Media Studies/Marketing
Duration: 3FT Hon
Entry Requirements: *GCE:* 260-280. *SQAH:* AAA-BBBB. *IB:* 24.
BTEC NC: DD. *BTEC ND:* DMM. *OCR ND:* D *OCR NED:* M2

P392 BA Media Studies/Media Production
Duration: 3FT Hon
Entry Requirements: *GCE:* 260-280. *SQAH:* AAA-BBBB. *IB:* 24.
BTEC NC: DD. *BTEC ND:* DMM. *OCR ND:* D *OCR NED:* M2

P3F8 BA Media Studies/Physical Geography
Duration: 3FT Hon
Entry Requirements: *GCE:* 260-280. *SQAH:* AAA-BBBB. *IB:* 24.
BTEC NC: DD. *BTEC ND:* DMM. *OCR ND:* D *OCR NED:* M2

P3L2 BA Media Studies/Politics
Duration: 3FT Hon
Entry Requirements: *GCE:* 260-280. *SQAH:* AAA-BBBB. *IB:* 24.
BTEC NC: DD. *BTEC ND:* DMM. *OCR ND:* D *OCR NED:* M2

P3W3 BA Media Studies/Popular Music
Duration: 3FT Hon
Entry Requirements: *GCE:* 260-280. *SQAH:* AAA-BBBB. *IB:* 24.
BTEC NC: DD. *BTEC ND:* DMM. *OCR ND:* D *OCR NED:* M2

P3C8 BA Media Studies/Psychology
Duration: 3FT Hon
Entry Requirements: *GCE:* 260-280. *SQAH:* AAA-BBBB. *IB:* 24.
BTEC NC: DD. *BTEC ND:* DMM. *OCR ND:* D *OCR NED:* M2

PN32 BA Media Studies/Social Enterprise Development
Duration: 3FT Hon
Entry Requirements: *GCE:* 260-280. *SQAH:* AAA-BBBB. *IB:* 24.
BTEC NC: DD. *BTEC ND:* DMM. *OCR ND:* D *OCR NED:* M2

P3L3 BA Media Studies/Sociology
Duration: 3FT Hon
Entry Requirements: *GCE:* 260-280. *SQAH:* AAA-BBBB. *IB:* 24.
BTEC NC: DD. *BTEC ND:* DMM. *OCR ND:* D *OCR NED:* M2

P3C6 BA Media Studies/Sport Studies
Duration: 3FT Hon
Entry Requirements: *GCE:* 260-280. *SQAH:* AAA-BBBB. *IB:* 24.
BTEC NC: DD. *BTEC ND:* DMM. *OCR ND:* D *OCR NED:* M2

P3N8 BA Media Studies/Tourism
Duration: 3FT Hon
Entry Requirements: *GCE:* 260-280. *SQAH:* AAA-BBBB. *IB:* 24.
BTEC NC: DD. *BTEC ND:* DMM. *OCR ND:* D *OCR NED:* M2

PG34 BA Media Studies/Web Design
Duration: 3FT Hon
Entry Requirements: *GCE:* 260-280. *SQAH:* AAA-BBBB. *IB:* 24.
BTEC NC: DD. *BTEC ND:* DMM. *OCR ND:* D *OCR NED:* M2

L2P3 BA Politics/Media Studies
Duration: 3FT Hon
Entry Requirements: *GCE:* 260-280. *SQAH:* AAA-BBBB. *IB:* 24.
BTEC NC: DD. *BTEC ND:* DMM. *OCR ND:* D *OCR NED:* M2

W3P3 BA Popular Music/Media Studies
Duration: 3FT Hon
Entry Requirements: *GCE:* 260-280. *SQAH:* AAA-BBBB. *IB:* 24.
BTEC NC: DD. *BTEC ND:* DMM. *OCR ND:* D *OCR NED:* M2

C8P3 BA Psychology/Media Studies
Duration: 3FT Hon
Entry Requirements: *GCE:* 260-280. *SQAH:* AAA-BBBB. *IB:* 24.
BTEC NC: DD. *BTEC ND:* DMM. *OCR ND:* D *OCR NED:* M2

N2PB BA Social Enterprise Development/Media Studies
Duration: 3FT Hon
Entry Requirements: *GCE:* 260-280. *SQAH:* AAA-BBBB. *IB:* 24.
BTEC NC: DD. *BTEC ND:* DMM. *OCR ND:* D *OCR NED:* M2

L3P3 BA Sociology/Media Studies
Duration: 3FT Hon
Entry Requirements: *GCE:* 260-280. *SQAH:* AAA-BBBB. *IB:* 24.
BTEC NC: DD. *BTEC ND:* DMM. *OCR ND:* D *OCR NED:* M2

C6P3 BA Sport Studies/Media Studies
Duration: 3FT Hon
Entry Requirements: *GCE:* 260-280. *SQAH:* AAA-BBBB. *IB:* 24.
BTEC NC: DD. *BTEC ND:* DMM. *OCR ND:* D *OCR NED:* M2

C1P3 BSc Biological Conservation/Media Studies
Duration: 3FT Hon
Entry Requirements: *GCE:* 260-280. *SQAH:* AAA-BBBB. *IB:* 24.
BTEC NC: DD. *BTEC ND:* DMM. *OCR ND:* D *OCR NED:* M2

G5P3 BSc Business Computing Systems/Media Studies
Duration: 3FT Hon
Entry Requirements: *GCE:* 260-280. *SQAH:* AAA-BBBB. *IB:* 24.
BTEC NC: DD. *BTEC ND:* DMM. *OCR ND:* D *OCR NED:* M2

G4P3 BSc Computing/Media Studies
Duration: 3FT Hon
Entry Requirements: *GCE:* 260-280. *SQAH:* AAA-BBBB. *IB:* 24.
BTEC NC: DD. *BTEC ND:* DMM. *OCR ND:* D *OCR NED:* M2

F8PH BSc Physical Geography/Media Studies
Duration: 3FT Hon
Entry Requirements: *GCE:* 260-280. *SQAH:* AAA-BBBB. *IB:* 24.
BTEC NC: DD. *BTEC ND:* DMM. *OCR ND:* D *OCR NED:* M2

G4PH BSc Web Design/Media Production
Duration: 3FT Hon
Entry Requirements: *GCE:* 260-280. *SQAH:* AAA-BBBB. *IB:* 24.
BTEC NC: DD. *BTEC ND:* DMM. *OCR ND:* D *OCR NED:* M2

G4PJ BSc Web Design/Media Studies
Duration: 3FT Hon
Entry Requirements: *GCE:* 260-280. *SQAH:* AAA-BBBB. *IB:* 24.
BTEC NC: DD. *BTEC ND:* DMM. *OCR ND:* D *OCR NED:* M2

N77 NORTHUMBRIA UNIVERSITY
TRINITY BUILDING
NORTHUMBERLAND ROAD
NEWCASTLE UPON TYNE NE1 8ST
t: 0191 243 7420 f: 0191 227 4561
e: er.admissions@northumbria.ac.uk
// www.northumbria.ac.uk

NP53 BA Advertising and Media
Duration: 3FT Hon
Entry Requirements: *GCE:* 300. *SQAH:* BBBBC. *SQAAH:* BBC. *IB:* 26. *BTEC ND:* DDM.

PP35 BA Media and Journalism
Duration: 3FT Hon
Entry Requirements: *GCE:* 300. *SQAH:* BBBBC. *SQAAH:* BBC. *IB:* 26. *BTEC ND:* DDM.

LP33 BA Media, Culture and Society
Duration: 3FT Hon
Entry Requirements: *GCE:* 300. *SQAH:* BBBBC. *SQAAH:* BBC. *IB:* 26. *BTEC ND:* DDM.

P300 BA (Hons) Media
Duration: 3FT Hon
Entry Requirements: *GCE:* 300. *SQAH:* BBBBC. *SQAAH:* BBC. *IB:* 26. *BTEC ND:* DDM.

N91 NOTTINGHAM TRENT UNIVERSITY
DRYDEN BUILDINGG
BURTON STREET
NOTTINGHAM NG1 4BU
t: +44 (0) 115 848 4200 f: +44 (0) 115 848 8869
e: applications@ntu.ac.uk
// www.ntu.ac.uk/

PQ33 BA English and Media
Duration: 3FT Hon
Entry Requirements: *GCE:* 260. *IB:* 29. *BTEC NC:* DM. *BTEC ND:* DDM.

PR32 BA Film & TV and German
Duration: 3FT Hon
Entry Requirements: *GCE:* 260. *IB:* 29. *BTEC NC:* DM. *BTEC ND:* DDM.

RP13 BA French and Film & TV
Duration: 3FT Hon
Entry Requirements: *GCE:* 260. *IB:* 29. *BTEC NC:* DM. *BTEC ND:* DDM.

RP23 BA German and Media
Duration: 4FT Hon
Entry Requirements: *GCE:* 260. *IB:* 29. *BTEC NC:* DM. *BTEC ND:* DDM.

LP93 BA Global Studies and Media
Duration: 3FT Hon
Entry Requirements: *GCE:* 260. *IB:* 29. *BTEC NC:* DM. *BTEC ND:* DDM.

RP33 BA Italian and Media
Duration: 4FT Hon
Entry Requirements: *GCE:* 260. *IB:* 29. *BTEC NC:* DM. *BTEC ND:* DDM.

PQ31 BA Linguistics and Media
Duration: 3FT Hon
Entry Requirements: *GCE:* 260. *IB:* 29. *BTEC NC:* DM. *BTEC ND:* DDM.

P300 BA Media (with specialist pathways)
Duration: 3FT Hon
Entry Requirements: *GCE:* 280. *IB:* 30. *BTEC ND:* DMM.

LP33 BA Media and Communication & Society
Duration: 3FT Hon
Entry Requirements: *GCE:* 260. *IB:* 29. *BTEC NC:* DM. *BTEC ND:* DDM.

PR39 BA Media and European Studies
Duration: 3FT Hon
Entry Requirements: *GCE:* 260. *IB:* 29. *BTEC NC:* DM. *BTEC ND:* DDM.

PV31 BA Media and History
Duration: 3FT Hon
Entry Requirements: *GCE:* 260. *IB:* 29. *BTEC NC:* DM. *BTEC ND:* DDM.

LP23 BA Media and International Relations
Duration: 3FT Hon
Entry Requirements: *GCE:* 260. *IB:* 29. *BTEC NC:* DM. *BTEC ND:* DDM.

VP53 BA Philosophy and Media
Duration: 3FT Hon
Entry Requirements: *GCE:* 260. *IB:* 29. *BTEC NC:* DM. *BTEC ND:* DDM.

RP43 BA Spanish and Media
Duration: 4FT Hon
Entry Requirements: *GCE:* 260. *IB:* 29. *BTEC NC:* DM. *BTEC ND:* DDM.

O66 OXFORD BROOKES UNIVERSITY
ADMISSIONS OFFICE
HEADINGTON CAMPUS
GIPSY LANE
OXFORD OX3 0BP
t: 01865 483040 f: 01865 483983
e: admissions@brookes.ac.uk
// www.brookes.ac.uk

QP93 BA English Language and Communication/Communication,Media and Culture
Duration: 3FT Hon
Entry Requirements: Contact the institution for details.

PP43 BA Publishing Media/Film Studies
Duration: 3FT Hon
Entry Requirements: Contact the institution for details.

PL32 BA/BSc Communications, Media and Culture/International Relations
Duration: 3FT Hon
Entry Requirements: *GCE:* BBC.

PR31 BA/BSc Film Studies/French Studies
Duration: 4SW Hon
Entry Requirements: *GCE:* BBC. *IB:* 31.

P304 BSc Media Technology
Duration: 3FT Hon
Entry Requirements: *GCE:* BBC. *IB:* 30. *BTEC ND:* DDM.

P56 UNIVERSITY CENTRE PETERBOROUGH
PARK CRESCENT
PETERBOROUGH PE1 4DZ
t: 0845 1965750 f: 01733 767986
e: UCPenquiries@anglia.ac.uk
// www.anglia.ac.uk/ucp

P300 BA Media
Duration: 3FT Hon
Entry Requirements: *GCE:* 120. Interview required.

P60 UNIVERSITY OF PLYMOUTH
DRAKE CIRCUS
PLYMOUTH PL4 8AA
t: 01752 588037 f: 01752 588050
e: admissions@plymouth.ac.uk
// www.plymouth.ac.uk

C1P3 BSc Science and the Media
Duration: 1FT Hon
Entry Requirements: Contact the institution for details.

P63 UCP MARJON - UNIVERSITY COLLEGE PLYMOUTH ST MARK & ST JOHN
DERRIFORD ROAD
PLYMOUTH PL6 8BH
t: 01752 636890 f: 01752 636819
e: admissions@marjon.ac.uk
// www.ucpmarjon.ac.uk

W8P3 BA Creative Writing with Media Studies
Duration: 3FT Hon
Entry Requirements: *GCE:* 220.

W4P3 BA Drama with Media Studies
Duration: 3FT Hon
Entry Requirements: *GCE:* 220.

X3P3 BA Education Studies with Media Studies
Duration: 3FT Hon
Entry Requirements: *GCE:* 180.

Q1P3 BA English Language & Linguistics with Media Studies
Duration: 3FT Hon
Entry Requirements: *GCE:* 220.

Q3P3 BA English Literature with Media Studies
Duration: 3FT Hon
Entry Requirements: *GCE:* 220.

P300 BA Media Studies
Duration: 3FT Hon
Entry Requirements: *GCE:* 220.

P3W8 BA Media Studies with Creative Writing
Duration: 3FT Hon
Entry Requirements: *GCE:* 220.

P3W4 BA Media Studies with Drama
Duration: 3FT Hon
Entry Requirements: *GCE:* 220.

P3X3 BA Media Studies with Education Studies
Duration: 3FT Hon
Entry Requirements: *GCE:* 220.

P3Q1 BA Media Studies with English Language & Linguistics
Duration: 3FT Hon
Entry Requirements: *GCE:* 220.

P3Q3 BA Media Studies with English Literature
Duration: 3FT Hon
Entry Requirements: *GCE:* 220.

P80 UNIVERSITY OF PORTSMOUTH
ACADEMIC REGISTRY
UNIVERSITY HOUSE
WINSTON CHURCHILL AVENUE
PORTSMOUTH PO1 2UP
t: 023 9284 8484 f: 023 9284 3082
e: admissions@port.ac.uk
// www.port.ac.uk

QP33 BA English and Media Studies
Duration: 3FT Hon
Entry Requirements: *GCE:* 240-300. *IB:* 28. *BTEC NC:* DD. *BTEC ND:* DMM.

P5P3 BA Journalism with Media Studies
Duration: 3FT Hon
Entry Requirements: *GCE:* 240-300. *IB:* 28. *BTEC NC:* DD. *BTEC ND:* DMM.

NP53 BA Marketing (Digital Media)
Duration: 3FT/4SW Hon
Entry Requirements: *GCE:* 280. *IB:* 30. *BTEC ND:* DMM.

P300 BA Media Studies
Duration: 3FT Hon
Entry Requirements: *GCE:* 240-300. *IB:* 25. *BTEC NC:* DD. *BTEC ND:* DMM.

PW36 BA Media Studies and Entertainment Technology
Duration: 3FT Hon
Entry Requirements: *GCE:* 240-300. *IB:* 25. *BTEC NC:* DD. *BTEC ND:* DMM.

LP33 BA Sociology and Media Studies
Duration: 3FT Hon
Entry Requirements: *GCE:* 240-300. *IB:* 28. *BTEC NC:* DD. *BTEC ND:* DMM.

Q25 QUEEN MARGARET UNIVERSITY, EDINBURGH
QUEEN MARGARET UNIVERSITY DRIVE
EDINBURGH EH21 6UU
t: 0131474 0000 f: 0131 474 0001
e: admissions@qmu.ac.uk
// www.qmu.ac.uk

P303 BA Film and Media
Duration: 4FT Hon
Entry Requirements: *GCE:* 260. *IB:* 28.

P301 BA Media
Duration: 4FT Hon
Entry Requirements: *GCE:* 260. *IB:* 28.

Q75 QUEEN'S UNIVERSITY BELFAST
UNIVERSITY ROAD
BELFAST BT7 1NN
t: 028 9097 3838 f: 028 9097 5151
e: admissions@qub.ac.uk
// www.qub.ac.uk

PV35 BA Film Studies and Philosophy
Duration: 3FT Hon
Entry Requirements: *GCE:* BBB-BBCb. *SQAH:* BBBBB. *SQAAH:* BBB. *IB:* 32.

R06 RAVENSBOURNE
6 PENROSE WAY
LONDON SE10 0EW
t: 020 3040 3500
e: info@rave.ac.uk
// www.rave.ac.uk

NP53 BA Fashion Promotion
Duration: 3FT Hon
Entry Requirements: *Foundation:* Pass. *GCE:* AA-CC. *IB:* 28. *BTEC NC:* PP. *BTEC ND:* PPP. Interview required. Portfolio required.

WP3H BA Music Production for Media (4 Year Route)
Duration: 4FT Hon
Entry Requirements: Contact the institution for details.

PN32 BA Web Media
Duration: 3FT Hon
Entry Requirements: *Foundation:* Pass. *GCE:* AA-CC. *IB:* 28.
BTEC NC: PP. *BTEC ND:* PPP. Interview required. Portfolio required.

PP53 BA Web Media (Fast-Track)
Duration: 2FT Hon
Entry Requirements: Contact the institution for details.

P304 BA Web Media (with Level 0)
Duration: 4FT Hon
Entry Requirements: Contact the institution for details.

R18 REGENTS BUSINESS SCHOOL, LONDON (REGENTS COLLEGE)
INNER CIRCLE, REGENT'S COLLEGE
REGENT'S PARK
LONDON NW1 4NS
t: +44(0)20 7487 7505 f: +44(0)20 7487 7425
e: exrel@regents.ac.uk
// www.regents.ac.uk/

W6P3 BA Film, Television and Digital Media Production
Duration: 3FT Hon
Entry Requirements: Contact the institution for details.

R20 RICHMOND, THE AMERICAN INTERNATIONAL UNIVERSITY IN LONDON
QUEENS ROAD
RICHMOND
SURREY TW10 6JP
t: 020 8332 9000 f: 020 8332 1596
e: enroll@richmond.ac.uk
// www.richmond.ac.uk

PP53 BA International Journalism and Media
Duration: 4FT Hon
Entry Requirements: Contact the institution for details.

R36 ROBERT GORDON UNIVERSITY
ROBERT GORDON UNIVERSITY
SCHOOLHILL
ABERDEEN
SCOTLAND AB10 1FR
t: 01224 26 27 28 f: 01224 26 21 47
e: UGOffice@rgu.ac.uk
// www.rgu.ac.uk

P300 BA Media
Duration: 4FT Hon
Entry Requirements: *GCE:* CCC. *SQAH:* BBCC. *IB:* 26.

R48 ROEHAMPTON UNIVERSITY
ERASMUS HOUSE
ROEHAMPTON LANE
LONDON SW15 5PU
t: 020 8392 3232 f: 020 8392 3470
e: enquiries@roehampton.ac.uk
// www.roehampton.ac.uk

PL33 BA Media & Culture
Duration: 3FT Hon
Entry Requirements: *Foundation:* Distinction. *GCE:* 240-320. *IB:* 24. *BTEC NC:* DD. *BTEC ND:* MMM. *OCR ND:* D *OCR NED:* M3 Interview required.

RP93 BA/BSc Modern Languages and Media & Culture Studies
Duration: 4FT Hon
Entry Requirements: *Foundation:* Distinction. *GCE:* 280-320. *IB:* 25. *BTEC ND:* DMM. *OCR NED:* M2 Interview required.

R72 ROYAL HOLLOWAY, UNIVERSITY OF LONDON
ROYAL HOLLOWAY, UNIVERSITY OF LONDON
EGHAM
SURREY TW20 0EX
t: 01784 434455 f: 01784 473662
e: Admissions@rhul.ac.uk
// www.rhul.ac.uk

R1P3 BA French with Film Studies
Duration: 4FT Hon
Entry Requirements: *GCE:* ABB-BBB. *SQAH:* AABBB-BBBBB. *SQAAH:* ABB-BBB. *IB:* 32. *BTEC ND:* DDM.

R2P3 BA German with Film Studies
Duration: 4FT Hon
Entry Requirements: *GCE:* ABB-BBB. *SQAH:* AABBB-BBBBB. *SQAAH:* ABB-BBB. *IB:* 32. *BTEC ND:* DDM.

R3P3 BA Italian with Film Studies
Duration: 4FT Hon
Entry Requirements: *GCE:* ABB-BBB. *SQAH:* AABBB-BBBBB. *SQAAH:* ABB-BBB. *IB:* 32. *BTEC ND:* DDM.

R4P3 BA Spanish with Film Studies
Duration: 4FT Hon
Entry Requirements: *GCE:* ABB-BBB. *SQAH:* AABBB-BBBBB. *SQAAH:* ABB-BBB. *IB:* 32. *BTEC ND:* DDM.

S03 THE UNIVERSITY OF SALFORD
SALFORD M5 4WT
t: 0161 295 4545 f: 0161 295 4646
e: ug-admissions@salford.ac.uk
// www.salford.ac.uk

PP53 BA Journalism and Broadcasting
Duration: 3FT Hon
Entry Requirements: *GCE:* 280. *IB:* 31. *BTEC ND:* DMM. *OCR NED:* M2 Interview required.

S21 SHEFFIELD HALLAM UNIVERSITY
CITY CAMPUS
HOWARD STREET
SHEFFIELD S1 1WB
t: 0114 225 5555 f: 0114 225 2167
e: admissions@shu.ac.uk
// www.shu.ac.uk

P300 BA Media
Duration: 3FT Hon
Entry Requirements: *GCE:* 280.

S30 SOUTHAMPTON SOLENT UNIVERSITY
EAST PARK TERRACE
SOUTHAMPTON
HAMPSHIRE SO14 0RT
t: +44 (0) 23 8031 9039 f: + 44 (0)23 8022 2259
e: admissions@solent.ac.uk or ask@solent.ac.uk
// www.solent.ac.uk/

QP33 BA English and Film
Duration: 3FT Hon
Entry Requirements: *Foundation:* Distinction. *GCE:* 240. *SQAAH:* AA-CCD. *IB:* 24. *BTEC NC:* DD. *BTEC ND:* MMM. *OCR ND:* D *OCR NED:* M3

QP3H BA English and Media
Duration: 3FT Hon
Entry Requirements: *Foundation:* Distinction. *GCE:* 240. *SQAAH:* AA-CCD. *IB:* 24. *BTEC NC:* DD. *BTEC ND:* MMM. *OCR ND:* D *OCR NED:* M3

QPH3 BA English and Media
Duration: 4SW Hon
Entry Requirements: *Foundation:* Distinction. *GCE:* 240. *SQAAH:* AA-CCD. *IB:* 24. *BTEC NC:* DD. *BTEC ND:* MMM. *OCR ND:* D *OCR NED:* M3

PP35 BA Media Writing (Top-Up)
Duration: 1FT Hon
Entry Requirements: Interview required. HND required.

P902 BA Media, Communications and Culture (Top-Up)
Duration: 1FT Hon
Entry Requirements: Interview required. HND required.

HP63 BSc Media Technology
Duration: 3FT Hon
Entry Requirements: *GCE:* 160.

HP6H BSc Media Technology (with foundation)
Duration: 4FT Hon
Entry Requirements: *GCE:* 40.

S43 SOUTH ESSEX COLLEGE OF FURTHER & HIGHER EDUCATION (PARTNER OF THE UNIVERSITY OF ESSEX)
LUKER ROAD
SOUTHEND-ON-SEA
ESSEX SS1 1ND
t: 0845 52 12345 f: 01702 432320
e: Admissions@southessex.ac.uk
// www.southessex.ac.uk

WP83 BA Creative Writing for Media
Duration: 3FT Hon
Entry Requirements: *GCE:* 160. *IB:* 24. Interview required.

S64 ST MARY'S UNIVERSITY COLLEGE, TWICKENHAM
WALDEGRAVE ROAD
STRAWBERRY HILL
MIDDLESEX TW1 4SX
t: 020 8240 4029 f: 020 8240 2361
e: admit@smuc.ac.uk
// www.smuc.ac.uk

PQ33 BA English and Media Arts
Duration: 3FT Hon
Entry Requirements: *GCE:* 240. *SQAH:* BBBC. *IB:* 28. *BTEC NC:* DM. *BTEC ND:* MMM. *OCR ND:* D *OCR NED:* M3 Interview required.

VP13 BA History and Media Arts
Duration: 3FT Hon
Entry Requirements: *GCE:* 240. *SQAH:* BBBC. *IB:* 28. *BTEC NC:* DM. *BTEC ND:* MMM. *OCR ND:* D *OCR NED:* M3 Interview required.

PQ35 BA Irish Studies and Media Arts
Duration: 3FT Hon
Entry Requirements: *GCE:* 240. *SQAH:* BBBC. *IB:* 28. *BTEC NC:* DM. *BTEC ND:* MMM. *OCR ND:* D *OCR NED:* M3 Interview required.

NP23 BA Management Studies and Media Arts
Duration: 3FT Hon
Entry Requirements: *GCE:* 240. *SQAH:* BBBC. *IB:* 28. *BTEC NC:* DM. *BTEC ND:* MMM. *OCR ND:* D *OCR NED:* M3 Interview required.

P300 BA Media Arts
Duration: 3FT Hon
Entry Requirements: *GCE:* 240. *SQAH:* BBBC. *IB:* 28. *BTEC NC:* DM. *BTEC ND:* MMM. *OCR ND:* D *OCR NED:* M3 Interview required.

PW38 BA Media Arts and Creative & Professional Writing
Duration: 3FT Hon
Entry Requirements: *GCE:* 240. *SQAH:* BBBC. *IB:* 28. *BTEC NC:* DM. *BTEC ND:* MMM. *OCR ND:* D *OCR NED:* M3 Interview required.

LP33 BA Media Arts and Sociology
Duration: 3FT Hon
Entry Requirements: *GCE:* 240. *SQAH:* BBBC. *IB:* 28. *BTEC NC:* DM. *BTEC ND:* MMM. *OCR ND:* D *OCR NED:* M3 Interview required.

PN38 BA Media Arts and Tourism
Duration: 3FT Hon
Entry Requirements: *GCE:* 240. *SQAH:* BBBC. *IB:* 28. *BTEC NC:* DM. *BTEC ND:* MMM. *OCR ND:* D *OCR NED:* M3 Interview required.

BPY3 BA/BSc Health, Exercise & Physical Activity and Media Arts
Duration: 3FT Hon
Entry Requirements: *GCE:* 240. *SQAH:* BBBC. *IB:* 28. *BTEC NC:* DM. *BTEC ND:* MMM. *OCR ND:* D *OCR NED:* M3 Interview required.

CP63 BA/BSc Media Arts and Sport Science
Duration: 3FT Hon
Entry Requirements: *GCE:* 240. *SQAH:* BBBC. *IB:* 28. *BTEC NC:* DM. *BTEC ND:* MMM. *OCR ND:* D *OCR NED:* M3 Interview required.

S72 STAFFORDSHIRE UNIVERSITY
COLLEGE ROAD
STOKE ON TRENT ST4 2DE
t: 01782 292753 f: 01782 292740
e: admissions@staffs.ac.uk
// www.staffs.ac.uk

PQ33 BA English Literature and Media Studies
Duration: 3FT Hon
Entry Requirements: *GCE:* 200-240. *IB:* 24.

PQH3 BA Film Studies and English Literature
Duration: 3FT Hon
Entry Requirements: *GCE:* 180-220. *IB:* 24.

PV35 BA Film Studies and Philosophy
Duration: 3FT Hon
Entry Requirements: *GCE:* 180-220. *IB:* 24.

PL3H BA Film Studies and Sociology
Duration: 3FT Hon
Entry Requirements: *GCE:* 180-220. *IB:* 24.

PV3J BA History, Film and Media Practice
Duration: 3FT Hon
Entry Requirements: *GCE:* 200-240. *IB:* 24.

VP23 BA International History and Media Studies
Duration: 3FT Hon
Entry Requirements: *GCE:* 200-240. *IB:* 24.

LP2H BA International Relations and Media Studies
Duration: 3FT Hon
Entry Requirements: *GCE:* 180-220. *IB:* 24.

PWH8 BA Media Studies and Scriptwriting
Duration: 3FT Hon
Entry Requirements: *GCE:* 200-240. *IB:* 24.

LP33 BA Media Studies and Sociology
Duration: 3FT Hon
Entry Requirements: *GCE:* 200-240. *IB:* 24.

PN32 BA Media and Leisure Industries
Duration: 3FT Hon
Entry Requirements: *GCE:* 180-220. *IB:* 24.

VP13 BA Modern History and Media Studies
Duration: 3FT Hon
Entry Requirements: *GCE:* 200-240. *IB:* 24.

W8P3 BA Screenwriting with Film Studies
Duration: 3FT Hon
Entry Requirements: *GCE:* 200-240. *IB:* 24.

WP43 BA Theatre Studies and Media Studies
Duration: 3FT Hon
Entry Requirements: *GCE:* 180-220. *IB:* 24.

LPH3 BA/BSc Crime, Deviance & Society and Media Studies
Duration: 3FT Hon
Entry Requirements: *GCE:* 200-240. *IB:* 24.

PP53 BA/BSc Journalism and Media Studies
Duration: 3FT Hon
Entry Requirements: *GCE:* 220-260. *IB:* 24.

P3N2 BSc Film Production Technology with Management
Duration: 3FT Hon
Entry Requirements: *GCE:* 240-280. *IB:* 24.

PJ39 BSc Film Production and Music Technology
Duration: 3FT/4SW Hon
Entry Requirements: *GCE:* 240-280. *IB:* 24.

GP53 BSc Media Studies and Multimedia Systems
Duration: 3FT Hon
Entry Requirements: *GCE:* 200-240. *IB:* 24.

P390 FdA Creative and Cultural Industries (Digital Media Production)
Duration: 2FT Hon
Entry Requirements: Interview required.

S74 STRATFORD UPON AVON COLLEGE
THE WILLOWS NORTH
ALCESTER ROAD
STRATFORD-UPON-AVON
WARWICKSHIRE CV37 9QR
t: 01789 266245 f: 01789 267524
e: college@stratford.ac.uk
// www.stratford.ac.uk

003P HND Media (Moving Image, Audio or Journalism)
Duration: 2FT HND
Entry Requirements: *GCE:* 200. Interview required. Portfolio required.

S75 THE UNIVERSITY OF STIRLING
STIRLING FK9 4LA
t: 01786 467044 f: 01786 466800
e: admissions@stir.ac.uk
// www.stir.ac.uk

NP13 BA Business Studies and Film & Media
Duration: 4FT Hon
Entry Requirements: *GCE:* BBC. *SQAH:* BBBB. *SQAAH:* AAA-CCC.
IB: 32. *BTEC ND:* DDM.

QP33 BA English Studies and Film & Media
Duration: 4FT Hon
Entry Requirements: *GCE:* BBC. *SQAH:* BBBB. *SQAAH:* AAA-CCC.
IB: 32. *BTEC ND:* DDM.

P3R1 BA European Film and Media
Duration: 4FT Hon
Entry Requirements: *GCE:* BBC. *SQAH:* BBBB. *SQAAH:* AAA-CCC.
IB: 32. *BTEC ND:* DDM.

P300 BA Film & Media
Duration: 4FT Hon
Entry Requirements: *GCE:* BBC. *SQAH:* BBBB. *SQAAH:* AAA-CCC.
IB: 32. *BTEC ND:* DDM.

RP13 BA Film & Media and French
Duration: 4FT Hon
Entry Requirements: *GCE:* BBC. *SQAH:* BBBB. *SQAAH:* AAA-CCC.
IB: 32. *BTEC ND:* DDM.

PV31 BA Film & Media and History
Duration: 4FT Hon
Entry Requirements: *GCE:* BBC. *SQAH:* BBBB. *SQAAH:* AAA-CCC.
IB: 32. *BTEC ND:* DDM.

PP35 BA Film & Media and Journalism Studies
Duration: 4FT Hon
Entry Requirements: *GCE:* BBC. *SQAH:* BBBB. *SQAAH:* AAA-CCC.
IB: 32. *BTEC ND:* DDM.

PN35 BA Film & Media and Marketing
Duration: 4FT Hon
Entry Requirements: *GCE:* BBC. *SQAH:* BBBB. *SQAAH:* AAA-CCC.
IB: 32. *BTEC ND:* DDM.

VP53 BA Film & Media and Philosophy
Duration: 4FT Hon
Entry Requirements: *GCE:* BBC. *SQAH:* BBBB. *SQAAH:* AAA-CCC.
IB: 32. *BTEC ND:* DDM.

PL32 BA Film & Media and Politics
Duration: 4FT Hon
Entry Requirements: *GCE:* BBC. *SQAH:* BBBB. *SQAAH:* AAA-CCC.
IB: 32. *BTEC ND:* DDM.

CP83 BA Film & Media and Psychology
Duration: 4FT Hon
Entry Requirements: *GCE:* BBC. *SQAH:* BBBB. *SQAAH:* AAA-CCC.
IB: 32. *BTEC ND:* DDM.

VP63 BA Film & Media and Religion
Duration: 4FT Hon
Entry Requirements: *GCE:* BBC. *SQAH:* BBBB. *SQAAH:* AAA-CCC.
IB: 32. *BTEC ND:* DDM.

LP33 BA Film & Media and Sociology
Duration: 4FT Hon
Entry Requirements: *GCE:* BBC. *SQAH:* BBBB. *SQAAH:* AAA-CCC.
IB: 32. *BTEC ND:* DDM.

RP43 BA Film & Media and Spanish
Duration: 4FT Hon
Entry Requirements: *GCE:* BBC. *SQAH:* BBBB. *SQAAH:* AAA-CCC.
IB: 32. *BTEC ND:* DDM.

CP63 BA Film & Media and Sports Studies
Duration: 4FT Hon
Entry Requirements: *GCE:* BBC. *SQAH:* BBBB. *SQAAH:* AAA-CCC.
IB: 32. *BTEC ND:* DDM.

S82 UNIVERSITY CAMPUS SUFFOLK (UCS)
WATERFRONT BUILDING
NEPTUNE QUAY
IPSWICH
SUFFOLK IP4 1QJ
t: 01473 338833 f: 01473 339900
e: info@ucs.ac.uk
// www.ucs.ac.uk

P300 BA Film
Duration: 3FT Hon
Entry Requirements: *GCE:* 280. *IB:* 28. Admissions Test required.

P391 FdA Visual Media Production
Duration: 2FT Fdg
Entry Requirements: *GCE:* 200. *IB:* 28. Interview required.

S84 UNIVERSITY OF SUNDERLAND
STUDENT HELPLINE
THE STUDENT GATEWAY
CHESTER ROAD
SUNDERLAND SR1 3SD
t: 0191 515 3000 f: 0191 515 3805
e: student.helpline@sunderland.ac.uk
// www.sunderland.ac.uk

TP73 BA American Studies and Media Studies
Duration: 3FT Hon
Entry Requirements: *GCE:* 260-360. *IB:* 31. *BTEC NC:* DM.
BTEC ND: MMM. *OCR ND:* D *OCR NED:* M3

T7P3 BA American Studies with Media Studies
Duration: 3FT Hon
Entry Requirements: *GCE:* 260-360. *BTEC NC:* DM. *BTEC ND:*
MMM. *OCR ND:* D *OCR NED:* M3

NP13 BA Business Management and Media Studies
Duration: 3FT Hon
Entry Requirements: *GCE:* 260-360. *IB:* 31. *BTEC NC:* DM.
BTEC ND: MMM. *OCR ND:* D *OCR NED:* M3

N1P3 BA Business Management with Media Studies
Duration: 3FT Hon
Entry Requirements: *GCE:* 260-360. *IB:* 31. *BTEC NC:* DM.
BTEC ND: MMM. *OCR ND:* D *OCR NED:* M3

XPH3 BA Childhood Studies and Media Studies
Duration: 3FT Hon
Entry Requirements: *GCE:* 260-360.

X3P3 BA Childhood Studies with Media Studies
Duration: 3FT Hon
Entry Requirements: *GCE:* 260-360.

BP93 BA Community Health and Media Studies
Duration: 3FT Hon
Entry Requirements: *GCE:* 260-360. *IB:* 32. *BTEC NC:* DM.
BTEC ND: MMM. *OCR ND:* D *OCR NED:* M3

WP33 BA Community Music and Media Studies
Duration: 3FT Hon
Entry Requirements: *GCE:* 260-360.

WHP3 BA Community Music with Media Studies
Duration: 3FT Hon
Entry Requirements: *GCE:* 260-360.

MP9H BA Criminology and Media Studies
Duration: 3FT Hon
Entry Requirements: *GCE:* 260-360. *BTEC NC:* DM. *BTEC ND:*
MMM. *OCR ND:* D *OCR NED:* M3

M9P3 BA Criminology with Media Studies
Duration: 3FT Hon
Entry Requirements: *GCE:* 260-360. *BTEC NC:* DM. *BTEC ND:*
MMM. *OCR ND:* D *OCR NED:* M3

PW35 BA Dance and Media Studies
Duration: 3FT Hon
Entry Requirements: *GCE:* 260-360. *IB:* 31. *BTEC NC:* DM.
BTEC ND: MMM. *OCR ND:* D *OCR NED:* M3

W5P3 BA Dance with Media Studies
Duration: 3FT Hon
Entry Requirements: *GCE:* 260-360. *IB:* 31. *BTEC NC:* DM.
BTEC ND: MMM. *OCR ND:* D *OCR NED:* M3

W4P3 BA Drama with Media Studies
Duration: 3FT Hon
Entry Requirements: *GCE:* 260-360. *BTEC NC:* DM. *BTEC ND:*
MMM. *OCR ND:* D *OCR NED:* M3

Q1P3 BA English Language & Linguistics with Media Studies
Duration: 3FT Hon
Entry Requirements: *GCE:* 260-360. *BTEC NC:* DM. *BTEC ND:*
MMM. *OCR ND:* D *OCR NED:* M3

QP33 BA English Studies and Media Studies
Duration: 3FT Hon
Entry Requirements: *GCE:* 260-360. *IB:* 31. *BTEC NC:* DM.
BTEC ND: MMM. *OCR ND:* D *OCR NED:* M3

Q3P3 BA English Studies with Media Studies
Duration: 3FT Hon
Entry Requirements: *GCE:* 260-360. *IB:* 31. *BTEC NC:* DM.
BTEC ND: MMM. *OCR ND:* D *OCR NED:* M3

PW36 BA Film and Media
Duration: 3FT Hon
Entry Requirements: *GCE:* 260-360. *IB:* 30. *BTEC ND:* DMM.

NP33 BA Financial Management and Media Studies
Duration: 3FT Hon
Entry Requirements: *GCE:* 260-360. *BTEC NC:* DM. *BTEC ND:*
MMM. *OCR ND:* D *OCR NED:* M3

N3P3 BA Financial Management with Media Studies
Duration: 3FT Hon
Entry Requirements: *GCE:* 260-360. *BTEC NC:* DM. *BTEC ND:*
MMM. *OCR ND:* D *OCR NED:* M3

LP53 BA Health & Social Care and Media Studies
Duration: 3FT Hon
Entry Requirements: *GCE:* 260-360.

L5P3 BA Health & Social Care with Media Studies
Duration: 3FT Hon
Entry Requirements: *GCE:* 260-360.

VP13 BA History and Media Studies
Duration: 3FT Hon
Entry Requirements: *GCE:* 260-360. *IB:* 31. *BTEC NC:* DM.
BTEC ND: MMM. *OCR ND:* D *OCR NED:* M3

V1P3 BA History with Media Studies
Duration: 3FT Hon
Entry Requirements: *GCE:* 260-360. *IB:* 31. *BTEC NC:* DM.
BTEC ND: MMM. *OCR ND:* D *OCR NED:* M3

NP63 BA Human Resource Management and Media Studies
Duration: 3FT Hon
Entry Requirements: *GCE:* 260-360. *BTEC NC:* DM. *BTEC ND:*
MMM. *OCR ND:* D *OCR NED:* M3

N6P3 BA Human Resource Management with Media
Duration: 3FT Hon
Entry Requirements: *GCE:* 260-360. *BTEC NC:* DM. *BTEC ND:*
MMM. *OCR ND:* D *OCR NED:* M3

MP13 BA Law and Media Studies
Duration: 3FT Hon
Entry Requirements: *GCE:* 260-360. *BTEC NC:* DM. *BTEC ND:*
MMM. *OCR ND:* D *OCR NED:* M3

NP53 BA Marketing Management and Media Studies
Duration: 3FT Hon
Entry Requirements: *GCE:* 260-360. *BTEC NC:* DM. *BTEC ND:*
MMM. *OCR ND:* D *OCR NED:* M3

N5P3 BA Marketing Management with Media Studies
Duration: 3FT Hon
Entry Requirements: *GCE:* 260-360. *BTEC NC:* DM. *BTEC ND:*
MMM. *OCR ND:* D *OCR NED:* M3

HP63 BA Media Production (Television and Radio)
Duration: 3FT Hon
Entry Requirements: *GCE:* 260-360. *IB:* 30. *BTEC ND:* DMM.
Interview required.

PH36 BA Media Production (Video and New Media)
Duration: 3FT Hon
Entry Requirements: *GCE:* 260-360. *IB:* 30. *BTEC ND:* DMM.
Interview required.

PW34 BA Media Studies and Drama
Duration: 3FT Hon
Entry Requirements: *GCE:* 260-360. *BTEC NC:* DM. *BTEC ND:*
MMM. *OCR ND:* D *OCR NED:* M3

PX33 BA Media Studies and Education
Duration: 3FT Hon
Entry Requirements: *GCE:* 220-360. *IB:* 32. *BTEC NC:* DM.
BTEC ND: MMM. *OCR ND:* D *OCR NED:* M3

PQ31 BA Media Studies and English Language/Linguistics
Duration: 3FT Hon
Entry Requirements: *GCE:* 260-360. *IB:* 32. *BTEC NC:* DM.
BTEC ND: MMM. *OCR ND:* D *OCR NED:* M3

PQ33 BA Media Studies and Modern Foreign Language (English)
Duration: 3FT Hon
Entry Requirements: *GCE:* 260-360. *BTEC NC:* DM. *BTEC ND:*
MMM. *OCR ND:* D *OCR NED:* M3

PW33 BA Media Studies and Music
Duration: 3FT Hon
Entry Requirements: *GCE:* 260-360. *IB:* 32. *BTEC NC:* DM.
BTEC ND: MMM. *OCR ND:* D *OCR NED:* M3

WP63 BA Media Studies and Photography
Duration: 3FT Hon
Entry Requirements: *GCE:* 260-360. *IB:* 32. *BTEC NC:* DM.
BTEC ND: MMM. *OCR ND:* D *OCR NED:* M3

PL32 BA Media Studies and Politics
Duration: 3FT Hon
Entry Requirements: *GCE:* 260-360. *IB:* 32. *BTEC NC:* DM.
BTEC ND: MMM. *OCR ND:* D *OCR NED:* M3

PL33 BA Media Studies and Sociology
Duration: 3FT Hon
Entry Requirements: *GCE:* 260-360. *IB:* 32. *BTEC NC:* DM.
BTEC ND: MMM. *OCR ND:* D *OCR NED:* M3

PX31 BA Media Studies and TESOL
Duration: 3FT Hon
Entry Requirements: *GCE:* 260-360. *BTEC NC:* DM. *BTEC ND:*
MMM. *OCR ND:* D *OCR NED:* M3

P3T7 BA Media Studies with American Studies
Duration: 3FT Hon
Entry Requirements: *GCE:* 260-360. *IB:* 32. *BTEC NC:* DM.
BTEC ND: MMM. *OCR ND:* D *OCR NED:* M3

P3N1 BA Media Studies with Business Management
Duration: 3FT Hon
Entry Requirements: *GCE:* 260-360. *IB:* 32. *BTEC NC:* DM.
BTEC ND: MMM. *OCR ND:* D *OCR NED:* M3

P3XH BA Media Studies with Childhood Studies
Duration: 3FT Hon
Entry Requirements: *GCE:* 260-360.

P3B9 BA Media Studies with Community Health
Duration: 3FT Hon
Entry Requirements: *GCE:* 260-360. *IB:* 32. *BTEC NC:* DM. *BTEC ND:* MMM. *OCR ND:* D *OCR NED:* M3

P3M9 BA Media Studies with Criminology
Duration: 3FT Hon
Entry Requirements: *GCE:* 260-360. *IB:* 32. *BTEC NC:* DM. *BTEC ND:* MMM. *OCR ND:* D *OCR NED:* M3

P3W5 BA Media Studies with Dance
Duration: 3FT Hon
Entry Requirements: *GCE:* 260-360. *IB:* 31. *BTEC NC:* DM. *BTEC ND:* MMM. *OCR ND:* D *OCR NED:* M3

P3W4 BA Media Studies with Drama
Duration: 3FT Hon
Entry Requirements: *GCE:* 260-360. *BTEC NC:* DM. *BTEC ND:* MMM. *OCR ND:* D *OCR NED:* M3

P3X3 BA Media Studies with Education
Duration: 3FT Hon
Entry Requirements: *GCE:* 260-360. *IB:* 32. *BTEC NC:* DM. *BTEC ND:* MMM. *OCR ND:* D *OCR NED:* M3

P3Q1 BA Media Studies with English Language/Linguistics
Duration: 3FT Hon
Entry Requirements: *GCE:* 260-360. *IB:* 32. *BTEC NC:* DM. *BTEC ND:* MMM. *OCR ND:* D *OCR NED:* M3

P3Q3 BA Media Studies with English Studies
Duration: 3FT Hon
Entry Requirements: *GCE:* 260-360. *IB:* 32. *BTEC NC:* DM. *BTEC ND:* MMM. *OCR ND:* D *OCR NED:* M3

P3L5 BA Media Studies with Health & Social Care
Duration: 3FT Hon
Entry Requirements: *GCE:* 260-360.

P3V1 BA Media Studies with History
Duration: 3FT Hon
Entry Requirements: *GCE:* 260-360. *IB:* 32. *BTEC NC:* DM. *BTEC ND:* MMM. *OCR ND:* D *OCR NED:* M3

P3R2 BA Media Studies with MFL (German)
Duration: 3FT Hon
Entry Requirements: *GCE:* 260-360. *BTEC NC:* DM. *BTEC ND:* MMM. *OCR ND:* D *OCR NED:* M3

P3R1 BA Media Studies with Modern Foreign Language (French)
Duration: 3FT Hon
Entry Requirements: *GCE:* 260-360. *BTEC NC:* DM. *BTEC ND:* MMM. *OCR ND:* D *OCR NED:* M3

P3R4 BA Media Studies with Modern Foreign Language (Spanish)
Duration: 3FT Hon
Entry Requirements: *GCE:* 260-360. *BTEC NC:* DM. *BTEC ND:* MMM. *OCR ND:* D *OCR NED:* M3

P3QH BA Media Studies with Modern Foreign Languages (English)
Duration: 3FT Hon
Entry Requirements: *GCE:* 260-360. *BTEC NC:* DM. *BTEC ND:* MMM. *OCR ND:* D *OCR NED:* M3

P3W3 BA Media Studies with Music
Duration: 3FT Hon
Entry Requirements: *GCE:* 260-360. *IB:* 32. *BTEC NC:* DM. *BTEC ND:* MMM. *OCR ND:* D *OCR NED:* M3

P3W6 BA Media Studies with Photography
Duration: 3FT Hon
Entry Requirements: *GCE:* 260-360. *IB:* 32. *BTEC NC:* DM. *BTEC ND:* MMM. *OCR ND:* D *OCR NED:* M3

P3L2 BA Media Studies with Politics
Duration: 3FT Hon
Entry Requirements: *GCE:* 260-360. *IB:* 32. *BTEC NC:* DM. *BTEC ND:* MMM. *OCR ND:* D *OCR NED:* M3

P3C8 BA Media Studies with Psychology
Duration: 3FT Hon
Entry Requirements: *GCE:* 260-360. *IB:* 32. *BTEC NC:* DM. *BTEC ND:* MMM. *OCR ND:* D *OCR NED:* M3

P3L3 BA Media Studies with Sociology
Duration: 3FT Hon
Entry Requirements: *GCE:* 260-360. *IB:* 32. *BTEC NC:* DM. *BTEC ND:* MMM. *OCR ND:* D *OCR NED:* M3

P3C6 BA Media Studies with Sport
Duration: 3FT Hon
Entry Requirements: *GCE:* 260-360. *BTEC NC:* DM. *BTEC ND:* MMM. *OCR ND:* D *OCR NED:* M3

P3X1 BA Media Studies with TESOL
Duration: 3FT Hon
Entry Requirements: *GCE:* 260-360. *BTEC NC:* DM. *BTEC ND:* MMM. *OCR ND:* D *OCR NED:* M3

P3N8 BA Media Studies with Tourism
Duration: 3FT Hon
Entry Requirements: *GCE:* 260-360. *BTEC NC:* DM. *BTEC ND:* MMM. *OCR ND:* D *OCR NED:* M3

P3N3 BA Media with Financial Management
Duration: 3FT Hon
Entry Requirements: *GCE:* 260-360. *BTEC NC:* DM. *BTEC ND:* MMM. *OCR ND:* D *OCR NED:* M3

P3N6 BA Media with Human Resource Management
Duration: 3FT Hon
Entry Requirements: *GCE:* 260-360. *BTEC NC:* DM. *BTEC ND:* MMM. *OCR ND:* D *OCR NED:* M3

P3N5 BA Media with Marketing Management
Duration: 3FT Hon
Entry Requirements: *GCE:* 260-360. *BTEC NC:* DM. *BTEC ND:* MMM. *OCR ND:* D *OCR NED:* M3

PP39 BA Media, Culture and Communication
Duration: 3FT Hon
Entry Requirements: *GCE:* 260-360. *IB:* 30. *BTEC ND:* DMM.

RP13 BA Modern Foreign Languages (French) and Media
Duration: 3FT Hon
Entry Requirements: *GCE:* 260-360. *IB:* 31. *BTEC NC:* DM. *BTEC ND:* MMM. *OCR ND:* D *OCR NED:* M3

PR32 BA Modern Foreign Languages (German) and Media Studies
Duration: 3FT Hon
Entry Requirements: *GCE:* 260-360. *IB:* 31. *BTEC NC:* DM. *BTEC ND:* MMM. *OCR ND:* D *OCR NED:* M3

PR34 BA Modern Foreign Languages (Spanish) and Media Studies
Duration: 3FT Hon
Entry Requirements: *GCE:* 260-360. *IB:* 31. *BTEC NC:* DM. *BTEC ND:* MMM. *OCR ND:* D *OCR NED:* M3

W3P3 BA Music with Media Studies
Duration: 3FT Hon
Entry Requirements: *GCE:* 260-360. *IB:* 31. *BTEC NC:* DM. *BTEC ND:* MMM. *OCR ND:* D *OCR NED:* M3

L2P3 BA Politics with Media Studies
Duration: 3FT Hon
Entry Requirements: *GCE:* 260-360. *IB:* 31. *BTEC NC:* DM. *BTEC ND:* MMM. *OCR ND:* D *OCR NED:* M3

L3P3 BA Sociology with Media Studies
Duration: 3FT Hon
Entry Requirements: *GCE:* 260-360. *IB:* 31. *BTEC NC:* DM. *BTEC ND:* MMM. *OCR ND:* D *OCR NED:* M3

X1P3 BA TESOL with Media Studies
Duration: 3FT Hon
Entry Requirements: *GCE:* 260-360. *BTEC NC:* DM. *BTEC ND:* MMM. *OCR ND:* D *OCR NED:* M3

NP83 BA Tourism and Media Studies
Duration: 3FT Hon
Entry Requirements: *GCE:* 260-360. *IB:* 31. *BTEC NC:* DM. *BTEC ND:* MMM. *OCR ND:* D *OCR NED:* M3

N8P3 BA Tourism with Media Studies
Duration: 3FT Hon
Entry Requirements: *GCE:* 220-360. *IB:* 31. *BTEC NC:* DM. *BTEC ND:* MMM. *OCR ND:* D *OCR NED:* M3

PC38 BA/BSc Media Studies and Psychology
Duration: 3FT Hon
Entry Requirements: *GCE:* 260-360. *IB:* 32. *BTEC NC:* DM. *BTEC ND:* MMM. *OCR ND:* D *OCR NED:* M3

CP63 BA/BSc Sport and Media Studies
Duration: 3FT Hon
Entry Requirements: *GCE:* 260-360. *BTEC NC:* DM. *BTEC ND:* MMM. *OCR ND:* D *OCR NED:* M3

B9P3 BSc Community Health with Media Studies
Duration: 3FT Hon
Entry Requirements: *GCE:* 220-360. *IB:* 31. *BTEC NC:* DM. *BTEC ND:* MMM. *OCR ND:* D *OCR NED:* M3

C8P3 BSc Psychology with Media Studies
Duration: 3FT Hon
Entry Requirements: *GCE:* 260-360. *IB:* 32. *BTEC NC:* DM. *BTEC ND:* MMM. *OCR ND:* D *OCR NED:* M3

C6P3 BSc Sport with Media Studies
Duration: 3FT Hon
Entry Requirements: *GCE:* 260-360. *BTEC NC:* DM. *BTEC ND:* MMM. *OCR ND:* D *OCR NED:* M3

S85 UNIVERSITY OF SURREY
STAG HILL
GUILDFORD
SURREY GU2 7XH
t: +44(0)1483 689305 f: +44(0)1483 689388
e: ugteam@surrey.ac.uk
// www.surrey.ac.uk

P306 BA Media Studies (3 or 4 years)
Duration: 3FT/4SW Hon
Entry Requirements: *GCE:* 300-320.

LP33 BSc Sociology, Culture and Media (3 years)
Duration: 3FT Hon
Entry Requirements: *GCE:* ABB. *BTEC ND:* DDM.

LP3H BSc Sociology, Culture and Media (4 years)
Duration: 4SW Hon
Entry Requirements: *GCE:* 300-320.

S90 UNIVERSITY OF SUSSEX
UNDERGRADUATE ADMISSIONS
SUSSEX HOUSE
UNIVERSITY OF SUSSEX
BRIGHTON BN1 9RH
t: 01273 678416 f: 01273 678545
e: ug.applicants@sussex.ac.uk
// www.sussex.ac.uk

TP73 BA American Studies and Film Studies
Duration: 4FT Hon
Entry Requirements: *GCE:* AAB-ABB. *SQAH:* AAABB-AABBB. *IB:* 34. *BTEC NC:* DM. *BTEC ND:* DDM. *OCR ND:* M1 *OCR NED:* D2

QP33 BA English and Media Studies
Duration: 3FT Hon
Entry Requirements: *GCE:* AAA-AAB. *SQAH:* AAAAA-AAABB. *SQAAH:* AAA-AAB. *IB:* 36. *BTEC NC:* DD. *BTEC ND:* DDD. *OCR ND:* D *OCR NED:* D2

P300 BA Film Studies
Duration: 3FT Hon
Entry Requirements: *GCE:* AAB-ABB. *SQAH:* AAABB-AABBB. *IB:* 34. *BTEC NC:* DM. *BTEC ND:* DDM. *OCR ND:* M1 *OCR NED:* D2

P306 BA Media Studies
Duration: 3FT Hon
Entry Requirements: *GCE:* ABB. *SQAH:* AABBB. *IB:* 34. *BTEC NC:* DM. *BTEC ND:* DDM. *OCR ND:* M1 *OCR NED:* D2

PRH9 BA Media Studies and a Language (French/Italian/Spanish)
Duration: 4FT Hon
Entry Requirements: *GCE:* ABB. *SQAH:* AABBB. *IB:* 34. *BTEC NC:* DM. *BTEC ND:* DDM. *OCR ND:* M1 *OCR NED:* D2

PR39 BA Media and Cultural Studies
Duration: 3FT Hon
Entry Requirements: *GCE:* ABB. *SQAH:* AABBB. *IB:* 34. *BTEC NC:* DM. *BTEC ND:* DDM. *OCR ND:* M1 *OCR NED:* D2

LP33 BA Sociology and Media Studies
Duration: 3FT Hon
Entry Requirements: *GCE:* ABB-BBB. *SQAH:* AABBB-ABBBB. *IB:* 32. *BTEC NC:* DM. *BTEC ND:* DDM. *OCR ND:* M1 *OCR NED:* D2

S93 SWANSEA UNIVERSITY
SINGLETON PARK
SWANSEA SA2 8PP
t: 01792 295111 f: 01792 295110
e: admissions@swansea.ac.uk
// www.swansea.ac.uk

P300 BA Media Studies
Duration: 3FT Hon
Entry Requirements: *GCE:* BBB. *IB:* 32. *BTEC ND:* DDM.

QP33 BA Media Studies and English
Duration: 3FT Hon
Entry Requirements: *GCE:* ABB-BBB. *BTEC ND:* DDM.

PR31 BA Media Studies and French
Duration: 4FT Hon
Entry Requirements: *GCE:* BBB. *IB:* 32. *BTEC ND:* DDM.

PR32 BA Media Studies and German
Duration: 4FT Hon
Entry Requirements: *GCE:* BBB. *IB:* 32. *BTEC ND:* DDM.

PR33 BA Media Studies and Italian
Duration: 4FT Hon
Entry Requirements: *GCE:* BBB. *IB:* 32. *BTEC ND:* DDM.

PR34 BA Media Studies and Spanish
Duration: 4FT Hon
Entry Requirements: *GCE:* BBB. *IB:* 32. *BTEC ND:* DDM.

PQ35 BA Media Studies and Welsh
Duration: 3FT Hon
Entry Requirements: *GCE:* BBB. *IB:* 32. *BTEC ND:* DDM.

PQ3M BA Screen Studies and Welsh
Duration: 3FT/4FT Hon
Entry Requirements: *GCE:* BBB. *IB:* 32. *BTEC ND:* DDM.

T20 TEESSIDE UNIVERSITY
MIDDLESBROUGH TS1 3BA
t: 01642 218121 f: 01642 384201
e: registry@tees.ac.uk
// www.tees.ac.uk

P300 BA Media Studies
Duration: 3FT Hon
Entry Requirements: *GCE:* 240-280. *IB:* 24.

T80 UNIVERSITY OF WALES TRINITY SAINT DAVID
COLLEGE ROAD
CARMARTHEN SA31 3EP
t: 01267 676767 f: 01267 676766
e: registrylc@trinitysaintdavid.ac.uk
// www.trinitysaintdavid.ac.uk/

PW33 BA Cerdd a'r Cyfryngau
Duration: 3FT Hon
Entry Requirements: *GCE:* 160-360. *IB:* 26. *BTEC NC:* MP. *BTEC ND:* PPP. Interview required.

P306 BA Y Cyfryngau Creadigol
Duration: 3FT Hon
Entry Requirements: *GCE:* 160-360. *IB:* 26. *BTEC NC:* MP. *BTEC ND:* PPP. Interview required.

U20 UNIVERSITY OF ULSTER
COLERAINE
CO. LONDONDERRY
NORTHERN IRELAND BT52 1SA
t: 028 7032 4221 f: 028 7032 4908
e: online@ulster.ac.uk
// www.ulster.ac.uk

PQ33 BA English and Media Studies
Duration: 3FT Hon
Entry Requirements: *GCE:* BCC. *IB:* 24. *BTEC NC:* DM. *BTEC ND:* DMM.

Q3PH BA English with Media Studies
Duration: 3FT Hon
Entry Requirements: *GCE:* BCC. *IB:* 24. *BTEC NC:* DM. *BTEC ND:* DMM.

PR39 BA European Studies and Media Studies
Duration: 3FT Hon
Entry Requirements: *GCE:* CCC. *IB:* 24. *BTEC NC:* MM. *BTEC ND:* MMM. Interview required.

R9PH BA European Studies with Media Studies
Duration: 3FT Hon
Entry Requirements: *GCE:* CCC. *IB:* 24. *BTEC NC:* MM. *BTEC ND:* MMM. Interview required.

P391 BA Film Studies and Media Studies
Duration: 3FT Hon
Entry Requirements: *GCE:* BCC. *IB:* 24. *BTEC NC:* DM. *BTEC ND:* DMM.

P392 BA Film Studies with Media Studies
Duration: 3FT Hon
Entry Requirements: *GCE:* BCC. *IB:* 24. *BTEC NC:* DM. *BTEC ND:* DMM.

RP13 BA French and Media Studies
Duration: 3FT Hon
Entry Requirements: *GCE:* CCC. *IB:* 24. *BTEC NC:* MM. *BTEC ND:* MMM. Interview required.

R1PH BA French with Media Studies
Duration: 4FT Hon
Entry Requirements: *GCE:* CCC. *IB:* 24. *BTEC NC:* MM. *BTEC ND:* MMM. Interview required.

RP23 BA German and Media Studies
Duration: 3FT Hon
Entry Requirements: *GCE:* CCC. *IB:* 24. *BTEC NC:* MM. *BTEC ND:* MMM. Interview required.

R2PH BA German with Media Studies
Duration: 4FT Hon
Entry Requirements: *GCE:* CCC. *IB:* 24. *BTEC NC:* MM. *BTEC ND:* MMM. Interview required.

VP13 BA History and Media Studies
Duration: 3FT Hon
Entry Requirements: *GCE:* BCC. *IB:* 24. *BTEC NC:* DM. *BTEC ND:* DMM.

V1PH BA History with Media Studies
Duration: 3FT Hon
Entry Requirements: *GCE:* BCC. *IB:* 24. *BTEC NC:* DM. *BTEC ND:* DMM.

QP53 BA Irish and Media Studies
Duration: 3FT Hon
Entry Requirements: *GCE:* BCD. *IB:* 24. Interview required.

Q5PH BA Irish with Media Studies
Duration: 3FT Hon
Entry Requirements: *GCE:* BCD. *IB:* 24. Interview required.

P300 BA Media Studies and Production
Duration: 3FT Hon
Entry Requirements: *GCE:* BCC. *IB:* 24. *BTEC NC:* DM. *BTEC ND:* DMM.

PRH4 BA Media Studies and Spanish
Duration: 3FT Hon
Entry Requirements: *GCE:* CCC. *IB:* 24. *BTEC NC:* MM. *BTEC ND:* MMM. Interview required.

P3N1 BA Media Studies with Business
Duration: 3FT Hon
Entry Requirements: *GCE:* BCC. *IB:* 24. *BTEC NC:* DM. *BTEC ND:* DMM.

P3G4 BA Media Studies with Computing
Duration: 3FT Hon
Entry Requirements: *GCE:* BCC. *IB:* 24. *BTEC NC:* DM. *BTEC ND:* DMM.

P3Q3 BA Media Studies with English
Duration: 3FT Hon
Entry Requirements: *GCE:* BCC. *IB:* 24. *BTEC NC:* DM. *BTEC ND:* DMM.

P3FV BA Media Studies with Environmental Science
Duration: 3FT Hon
Entry Requirements: *GCE:* BCC. *IB:* 24. *BTEC NC:* DM. *BTEC ND:* DMM.

P3R9 BA Media Studies with European Studies
Duration: 3FT Hon
Entry Requirements: *GCE:* BCC. *IB:* 24. *BTEC NC:* DM. *BTEC ND:* DMM.

P390 BA Media Studies with Film Studies
Duration: 3FT Hon
Entry Requirements: *GCE:* BCC. *IB:* 24. *BTEC NC:* DM. *BTEC ND:* DMM.

P3R1 BA Media Studies with French
Duration: 3FT Hon
Entry Requirements: *GCE:* BCC. *IB:* 24. *BTEC NC:* DM. *BTEC ND:* DMM.

P3F8 BA Media Studies with Geography
Duration: 3FT Hon
Entry Requirements: *GCE:* BCC. *IB:* 24. *BTEC NC:* DM. *BTEC ND:* DMM.

P3R2 BA Media Studies with German
Duration: 3FT Hon
Entry Requirements: *GCE:* BCC. *IB:* 24. *BTEC NC:* DM. *BTEC ND:* DMM.

P3V1 BA Media Studies with History
Duration: 3FT Hon
Entry Requirements: *GCE:* BCC. *IB:* 24. *BTEC NC:* DM. *BTEC ND:* DMM.

P3LX BA Media Studies with International Development
Duration: 4SW Hon
Entry Requirements: *GCE:* BCC. *IB:* 24. *BTEC NC:* DM. *BTEC ND:* DMM.

P3Q5 BA Media Studies with Irish
Duration: 3FT Hon
Entry Requirements: *GCE:* BCC. *IB:* 24. *BTEC NC:* DM. *BTEC ND:* DMM.

P3N5 BA Media Studies with Marketing
Duration: 4SW Hon
Entry Requirements: *GCE:* BCC. *IB:* 24. *BTEC NC:* DM. *BTEC ND:* DMM.

P3WP BA Media Studies with Photo-Imaging
Duration: 3FT Hon
Entry Requirements: *GCE:* BCC. *IB:* 24. *BTEC NC:* DM. *BTEC ND:* DMM.

P3C8 BA Media Studies with Psychology
Duration: 3FT Hon
Entry Requirements: *GCE:* BCC. *IB:* 24. *BTEC NC:* DM. *BTEC ND:* DMM.

P3N2 BA Media Studies with Retail Studies
Duration: 4SW Hon
Entry Requirements: *GCE:* BCC. *IB:* 24. *BTEC NC:* DM. *BTEC ND:* DMM.

P3R4 BA Media Studies with Spanish
Duration: 3FT Hon
Entry Requirements: *GCE:* BCC. *IB:* 24. *BTEC NC:* DM. *BTEC ND:* DMM.

R4PH BA Spanish with Media Studies
Duration: 4SW Hon
Entry Requirements: *GCE:* CCC. *IB:* 24. *BTEC NC:* MM. *BTEC ND:* MMM. Interview required.

N1PH BSc Business with Media Studies
Duration: 4SW Hon
Entry Requirements: *GCE:* 240. *IB:* 24. *BTEC NC:* MM. *BTEC ND:* MMM.

U40 UNIVERSITY OF THE WEST OF SCOTLAND
PAISLEY
RENFREWSHIRE
SCOTLAND PA1 2BE
t: 0141 848 3727 f: 0141 848 3623
e: admissions@uws.ac.uk
// www.uws.ac.uk

GP43 BSc Multimedia Technology
Duration: 3FT/4FT Ord/Hon
Entry Requirements: *GCE:* CC. *SQAH:* BBC.

U65 UNIVERSITY OF THE ARTS LONDON
272 HIGH HOLBORN
LONDON WC1V 7EY
t: 020 7514 6000x6197 f: 020 7514 6198
e: c.anderson@arts.ac.uk
// www.arts.ac.uk

WPF3 BA Illustration and Visual Media
Duration: 3FT Hon
Entry Requirements: Contact the institution for details.

P302 BA Media Communications
Duration: 3FT Hon
Entry Requirements: Contact the institution for details.

P306 BA Media Practice (Top-Up)
Duration: 1FT Hon
Entry Requirements: Contact the institution for details.

P300 BA Media and Cultural Studies
Duration: 3FT Hon
Entry Requirements: *IB:* 28. Foundation Course required. Interview required. Portfolio required.

P305 BA Print Media Management (Top-Up)
Duration: 1FT Hon
Entry Requirements: Contact the institution for details.

WP93 FdA Production for Live Events and Television
Duration: 2FT Fdg
Entry Requirements: *IB:* 28. Foundation Course required. Interview required. Portfolio required.

W05 THE UNIVERSITY OF WEST LONDON
WALPOLE HOUSE
BOND STREET
EALING
LONDON W5 5AA
t: 0800 036 8888 f: 020 8566 1353
e: learning.advice@uwl.ac.uk
// www.uwl.ac.uk

P306 BA Media Studies
Duration: 3FT Hon
Entry Requirements: *GCE:* 200. *IB:* 28. Interview required.

W50 UNIVERSITY OF WESTMINSTER
2ND FLOOR
101 NEW CAVENDISH STREET,
LONDON W1W 6XH
t: 020 7911 5000 f: 020 7911 5788
e: course-enquiries@westminster.ac.uk
// www.westminster.ac.uk

WP23 BA Mixed Media Fine Art
Duration: 3FT Hon
Entry Requirements: *GCE:* CC. *IB:* 28. *BTEC NC:* MM. *BTEC ND:* MPP. Interview required. Portfolio required.

GP43 BSc Multimedia Computing
Duration: 3FT/4SW Hon
Entry Requirements: *GCE:* AA-CCC. *SQAH:* BCCC-CCCCC. *IB:* 28. *BTEC NC:* DD. *BTEC ND:* MMM. *OCR ND:* M1 *OCR NED:* M1 Interview required.

W73 WIRRAL METROPOLITAN COLLEGE
CONWAY PARK CAMPUS
EUROPA BOULEVARD
BIRKENHEAD, WIRRAL
MERSEYSIDE CH41 4NT
t: 0151 551 7777 f: 0151 551 7001
// www.wmc.ac.uk

P300 BA Media Studies
Duration: 3FT Hon
Entry Requirements: *GCE:* DD. Interview required.

W75 UNIVERSITY OF WOLVERHAMPTON
ADMISSIONS UNIT
MX207, CAMP STREET
WOLVERHAMPTON
WEST MIDLANDS WV1 1AD
t: 01902 321000 f: 01902 321896
e: admissions@wlv.ac.uk
// www.wlv.ac.uk

WP8H BA Creative & Professional Writing and Media & Communication Studies
Duration: 3FT Hon
Entry Requirements: *GCE:* 160-220.

QP3H BA English Language and Media & Communication Studies
Duration: 3FT Hon
Entry Requirements: *GCE:* 160-220.

QPH3 BA English and Media & Cultural Studies
Duration: 3FT Hon
Entry Requirements: *GCE:* 160-220. *IB:* 24.

WPQ3 BA Film Studies and Media & Cultural Studies
Duration: 3FT Hon
Entry Requirements: *GCE:* 160-220. *IB:* 24.

PWH6 BA Media & Communication Studies and Film Studies
Duration: 3FT Hon
Entry Requirements: *GCE:* 160-220. *IB:* 28.

PQ33 BA Media & Cultural Studies and English Language
Duration: 3FT Hon
Entry Requirements: *GCE:* 160-220.

PL33 BA Media & Cultural Studies and Sociology
Duration: 3FT Hon
Entry Requirements: *GCE:* 160-220. *IB:* 24.

PP93 BA Media and Communication Studies
Duration: 3FT Hon
Entry Requirements: *GCE:* 160-220. *IB:* 28.

PL36 BA Media and Cultural Studies
Duration: 3FT Hon
Entry Requirements: *GCE:* 160-220. *IB:* 24.

LP23 BA Politics and Media & Communication Studies
Duration: 3FT Hon
Entry Requirements: *GCE:* 160-220. *IB:* 28.

W76 UNIVERSITY OF WINCHESTER
WINCHESTER
HANTS SO22 4NR
t: 01962 827234 f: 01962 827288
e: course.enquiries@winchester.ac.uk
// www.winchester.ac.uk

PT37 BA American Studies and Media Studies
Duration: 3FT Hon
Entry Requirements: *Foundation:* Distinction. *GCE:* 260-300. *IB:* 25. *BTEC NC:* DD. *BTEC ND:* DMM. *OCR ND:* D *OCR NED:* M2

FP43 BA Archaeology and Media Studies
Duration: 3FT Hon
Entry Requirements: *Foundation:* Distinction. *GCE:* 260-300. *IB:* 25. *BTEC NC:* DD. *BTEC ND:* DMM. *OCR ND:* D *OCR NED:* M2

NP13 BA Business Management and Media Studies
Duration: 3FT Hon
Entry Requirements: *Foundation:* Distinction. *GCE:* 260-300. *IB:* 25. *BTEC NC:* DD. *BTEC ND:* DMM. *OCR ND:* D *OCR NED:* M2

LPMH BA Childhood,Youth & Community Studies and Media Studies
Duration: 3FT Hon
Entry Requirements: *Foundation:* Distinction. *GCE:* 260-300. *IB:* 25. *BTEC NC:* DD. *BTEC ND:* DMM. *OCR ND:* D *OCR NED:* M2

PWJ5 BA Choreography & Dance and Media Studies
Duration: 3FT Hon
Entry Requirements: *Foundation:* Distinction. *GCE:* 260-300. *IB:* 25. *BTEC NC:* DD. *BTEC ND:* DMM. *OCR ND:* D *OCR NED:* M2

WPV3 BA Creative Writing and Media Studies
Duration: 3FT Hon
Entry Requirements: *Foundation:* Distinction. *GCE:* 260-300. *IB:* 25. *BTEC NC:* DD. *BTEC ND:* DMM. *OCR ND:* D *OCR NED:* M2

LP3H BA Criminology and Media Studies
Duration: 3FT Hon
Entry Requirements: *Foundation:* Distinction. *GCE:* 260-300. *IB:* 24. *BTEC NC:* DD. *BTEC ND:* DMM. *OCR ND:* D *OCR NED:* M2

PW34 BA Drama and Media Studies
Duration: 3FT Hon
Entry Requirements: *Foundation:* Distinction. *GCE:* 260-300. *IB:* 25. *BTEC NC:* DD. *BTEC ND:* DMM. *OCR ND:* D *OCR NED:* M2

QPJ3 BA English Language Studies and Media Studies
Duration: 3FT Hon
Entry Requirements: *Foundation:* Distinction. *GCE:* 260-300. *IB:* 25. *BTEC NC:* DD. *BTEC ND:* DMM. *OCR ND:* D *OCR NED:* M2

PQ33 BA English and Media Studies
Duration: 3FT Hon
Entry Requirements: *Foundation:* Distinction. *GCE:* 260-300. *IB:* 25. *BTEC NC:* DD. *BTEC ND:* DMM. *OCR ND:* D *OCR NED:* M2

NP8J BA Event Management and Media Studies
Duration: 3FT Hon
Entry Requirements: *Foundation:* Distinction. *GCE:* 260-300. *IB:* 25. *BTEC NC:* DD. *BTEC ND:* DMM. *OCR ND:* D *OCR NED:* M2

WP63 BA Film & Cinema Technologies and Media Studies
Duration: 3FT Hon
Entry Requirements: *Foundation:* Distinction. *GCE:* 260-300. *IB:* 25. *BTEC NC:* DD. *BTEC ND:* DMM. *OCR ND:* D *OCR NED:* M2

WPQ3 BA Film and Cinema Technologies
Duration: 3FT Hon
Entry Requirements: *Foundation:* Distinction. *GCE:* 260-300. *IB:* 24. *BTEC NC:* DD. *BTEC ND:* DMM. *OCR ND:* D *OCR NED:* M2

PL3N BA Health, Community & Social Care Studies and Media Studies
Duration: 3FT Hon   CRB Check: Required
Entry Requirements: Contact the institution for details.

VP13 BA History and Media Studies
Duration: 3FT Hon
Entry Requirements: *Foundation:* Distinction. *GCE:* 260-300. *IB:* 25. *BTEC NC:* DD. *BTEC ND:* DMM. *OCR ND:* D *OCR NED:* M2

PPM3 BA Journalism Studies and Media Studies
Duration: 3FT Hon
Entry Requirements: *Foundation:* Distinction. *GCE:* 260-300. *IB:* 25. *BTEC NC:* DD. *BTEC ND:* DMM. *OCR ND:* D *OCR NED:* M2

MPC3 BA Law and Media Studies
Duration: 3FT Hon
Entry Requirements: *Foundation:* Distinction. *GCE:* 260-300. *IB:* 25. *BTEC NC:* DD. *BTEC ND:* DMM. *OCR ND:* D *OCR NED:* M2

P3W6 BA Media Studies
Duration: 3FT Hon
Entry Requirements: *Foundation:* Distinction. *GCE:* 260-300. *IB:* 25. *BTEC NC:* DD. *BTEC ND:* DMM. *OCR ND:* D *OCR NED:* M2

PW39 BA Media Studies and Modern Liberal Arts
Duration: 3FT Hon
Entry Requirements: *Foundation:* Distinction. *GCE:* 260-300. *IB:* 25. *BTEC NC:* DD. *BTEC ND:* DMM. *OCR ND:* D *OCR NED:* M2

CP83 BA Media Studies and Psychology
Duration: 3FT Hon
Entry Requirements: *Foundation:* Distinction. *GCE:* 260-300. *IB:* 25. *BTEC NC:* DD. *BTEC ND:* DMM. *OCR ND:* D *OCR NED:* M2

PL3J BA Media Studies and Sociology
Duration: 3FT Hon
Entry Requirements: *Foundation:* Distinction. *GCE:* 260-300. *IB:* 25. *BTEC NC:* DD. *BTEC ND:* DMM. *OCR ND:* D *OCR NED:* M2

PNH8 BA Media Studies and Sports Management
Duration: 3FT Hon
Entry Requirements: *Foundation:* Distinction. *GCE:* 260-300. *IB:* 25. *BTEC NC:* DD. *BTEC ND:* MMM. *OCR ND:* D

CP63 BA Media Studies and Sports Studies
Duration: 3FT Hon
Entry Requirements: *Foundation:* Merit. *GCE:* 260-300. *IB:* 25. *BTEC NC:* DM. *BTEC ND:* MMP.

PVH6 BA Media Studies and Theology & Religious Studies
Duration: 3FT Hon
Entry Requirements: *Foundation:* Distinction. *GCE:* 260-300. *IB:* 25. *BTEC NC:* DD. *BTEC ND:* DMM. *OCR ND:* D *OCR NED:* M2

PWH3 BA Media Studies and Vocal & Choral Studies
Duration: 3FT Hon
Entry Requirements: *Foundation:* Distinction. *GCE:* 260-300. *IB:* 25. *BTEC NC:* DD. *BTEC ND:* DMM. *OCR ND:* D *OCR NED:* M2

LPF3 BA Politics & Global Studies and Media Studies
Duration: 3FT Hon
Entry Requirements: *Foundation:* Distinction. *GCE:* 260-300. *IB:* 25. *BTEC NC:* DD. *BTEC ND:* DMM. *OCR ND:* D *OCR NED:* M2

W80 UNIVERSITY OF WORCESTER
HENWICK GROVE
WORCESTER WR2 6AJ
t: 01905 855111 f: 01905 855377
e: admissions@worc.ac.uk
// www.worcester.ac.uk

WP13 BA Art & Design and Media & Cultural Studies
Duration: 3FT Hon
Entry Requirements: *GCE:* 240-260. *IB:* 24. *OCR ND:* D Interview required. Portfolio required.

NP23 BA Business Management and Media & Cultural Studies
Duration: 3FT Hon
Entry Requirements: *GCE:* 280-300. *IB:* 25. *BTEC NC:* DD. *BTEC ND:* MMM. *OCR ND:* D *OCR NED:* M3

WPF3 BA Creative Digital Media and Media & Cultural Studies
Duration: 3FT Hon
Entry Requirements: *GCE:* 240-260. *IB:* 24. *OCR ND:* D Interview required. Portfolio required.

WP63 BA Digital Film Production and Media & Cultural Studies
Duration: 3FT Hon
Entry Requirements: *GCE:* 240-260. *IB:* 24. *OCR ND:* D Interview required. Portfolio required.

PQ33 BA English Language Studies and Media & Cultural Studies
Duration: 3FT Hon
Entry Requirements: *GCE:* 240-260. *IB:* 24. *BTEC NC:* DD. *BTEC ND:* MMM. *OCR ND:* D *OCR NED:* M3

QP33 BA English Literary Studies and Media & Cultural Studies
Duration: 3FT Hon
Entry Requirements: *GCE:* 240-300. *IB:* 24. *BTEC NC:* DD. *BTEC ND:* MMM. *OCR ND:* D *OCR NED:* M3

VP13 BA History and Media & Cultural Studies
Duration: 3FT Hon
Entry Requirements: *GCE:* 240-300. *IB:* 24. *BTEC NC:* DD. *BTEC ND:* MMM. *OCR ND:* D *OCR NED:* M3

PW3V BA Media & Cultural Studies and Screen Writing
Duration: 3FT Hon
Entry Requirements: *GCE:* 240-300. *IB:* 24. *BTEC NC:* DD. *BTEC ND:* MMM. *OCR ND:* D *OCR NED:* M3

LP33 BA Media & Cultural Studies and Sociology
Duration: 3FT Hon
Entry Requirements: *GCE:* 240-300. *IB:* 24. *BTEC NC:* DD. *BTEC ND:* MMM. *OCR ND:* D *OCR NED:* M3

PCH6 BA/BSc Media & Cultural Studies and Sports Coaching Science
Duration: 3FT Hon
Entry Requirements: *GCE:* 280-300. *IB:* 25. *BTEC NC:* DD. *BTEC ND:* MMM. *OCR ND:* D *OCR NED:* M3

Y75 YORK ST JOHN UNIVERSITY
LORD MAYOR'S WALK
YORK YO31 7EX
t: 01904 876598 f: 01904 876940/876921
e: admissions@yorksj.ac.uk
// w3.yorksj.ac.uk

WP83 BA Creative Writing and Media
Duration: 3FT Hon
Entry Requirements: *GCE:* 200-240. *IB:* 24.

P391 BA Film Studies and Media
Duration: 3FT Hon
Entry Requirements: *GCE:* 200-240. *IB:* 24.

P305 BA Media
Duration: 3FT Hon
Entry Requirements: *Foundation:* Pass. *GCE:* 200-240. *IB:* 24.

P301 BA Media (for international applicants only)
Duration: 4FT Hon
Entry Requirements: *Foundation:* Pass. *GCE:* 200-240. *IB:* 24.

PQH3 BA Media and English Literature
Duration: 3FT Hon
Entry Requirements: *GCE:* 200-240. *IB:* 24.

QP33 BA Media and English Literature (for international applicants only)
Duration: 4FT Hon
Entry Requirements: *Foundation:* Pass. *GCE:* 200-240. *IB:* 24.

TELEVISION, FILM AND RADIO

A40 ABERYSTWYTH UNIVERSITY
WELCOME CENTRE, ABERYSTWYTH UNIVERSITY
PENGLAIS CAMPUS
ABERYSTWYTH
CEREDIGION SY23 3FB
t: 01970 622021 f: 01970 627410
e: ug-admissions@aber.ac.uk
// www.aber.ac.uk

P3P9 BA Astudiaethau Ffilm a Theledu gyda Cyfryngau a Chyfathrebu
Duration: 3FT Hon
Entry Requirements: *GCE:* 300-320. *IB:* 32.

WP4H BA Astudiaethau Perfformio/Astudiaethau Ffilm a Theledu
Duration: 3FT Hon
Entry Requirements: *GCE:* 300-320. *IB:* 32.

A60 ANGLIA RUSKIN UNIVERSITY
BISHOP HALL LANE
CHELMSFORD
ESSEX CM1 1SQ
t: 0845 271 3333 f: 01245 251789
e: answers@anglia.ac.uk
// www.anglia.ac.uk

WP4H BA Drama and Film Studies
Duration: 3FT Hon
Entry Requirements: *GCE:* 260. *SQAH:* BBCC. *SQAAH:* BB. *IB:* 24.

P303 BA Film Studies
Duration: 3FT Hon
Entry Requirements: *GCE:* 260. *SQAH:* BBCC. *SQAAH:* BC. *IB:* 24.

WP83 BA Writing and Film Studies
Duration: 3FT Hon
Entry Requirements: *GCE:* 260. *SQAH:* BBBC. *SQAAH:* BC. *IB:* 28.

B06 BANGOR UNIVERSITY
BANGOR UNIVERSITY
BANGOR
GWYNEDD LL57 2DG
t: 01248 388484 f: 01248 370451
e: admissions@bangor.ac.uk
// www.bangor.ac.uk

P301 BA Astudiaethau Ffilm a'r Cyfryngau
Duration: 3FT Hon
Entry Requirements: *GCE:* 220-260. *IB:* 28.

QP33 BA English and Film Studies
Duration: 3FT Hon
Entry Requirements: Contact the institution for details.

PR31 BA Film Studies and French
Duration: 4FT Hon
Entry Requirements: *GCE:* 260-300. *IB:* 28.

PR32 BA Film Studies and German
Duration: 4FT Hon
Entry Requirements: *GCE:* 260-300. *IB:* 28.

PR34 BA Film Studies and Spanish
Duration: 4FT Hon
Entry Requirements: *GCE:* 260-300. *IB:* 28.

P3W4 BA Film Studies with Theatre
Duration: 3FT Hon
Entry Requirements: *GCE:* 260-300. *IB:* 28.

VP23 BA Welsh History and Film Studies
Duration: 3FT Hon
Entry Requirements: *GCE:* 240-280. *IB:* 28.

V2P3 BA Welsh History with Film Studies
Duration: 3FT Hon
Entry Requirements: *GCE:* 240-280. *IB:* 28.

B20 BATH SPA UNIVERSITY
NEWTON PARK
NEWTON ST LOE
BATH BA2 9BN
t: 01225 875875 f: 01225 875444
e: enquiries@bathspa.ac.uk
// www.bathspa.ac.uk/clearing

P3V1 BA Film & Screen Studies/History
Duration: 3FT Hon
Entry Requirements: Contact the institution for details.

B32 THE UNIVERSITY OF BIRMINGHAM
EDGBASTON
BIRMINGHAM B15 2TT
t: 0121 415 8900 f: 0121 414 7159
e: admissions@bham.ac.uk
// www.bham.ac.uk

TP73 BA American & Canadian Studies and Film Studies
Duration: 3FT Hon
Entry Requirements: *GCE:* ABB. *SQAH:* ABBBB. *SQAAH:* AB. *IB:* 34.

R9P3 BA Modern Languages with Film Studies
Duration: 4FT Hon
Entry Requirements: *GCE:* ABB. *SQAH:* ABBBB. *SQAAH:* AB. *IB:* 32.

B44 UNIVERSITY OF BOLTON
DEANE ROAD
BOLTON BL3 5AB
t: 01204 903903 f: 01204 399074
e: enquiries@bolton.ac.uk
// www.bolton.ac.uk

WPV3 BA Creative Writing and Film & Media Studies
Duration: 3FT Hon
Entry Requirements: *GCE:* 240. Interview required.

QP33 BA English and Film & Media Studies
Duration: 3FT Hon
Entry Requirements: *GCE:* 240. Interview required.

WP2H BA Film & Media Studies and Graphic Design
Duration: 3FT Hon
Entry Requirements: *GCE:* 240. Interview required. Portfolio required.

WP6H BA Film & Media Studies and Photography
Duration: 3FT Hon
Entry Requirements: *GCE:* 240. Interview required. Portfolio required.

B56 THE UNIVERSITY OF BRADFORD
RICHMOND ROAD
BRADFORD
WEST YORKSHIRE BD7 1DP
t: 0800 073 1225 f: 01274 235585
e: course-enquiries@bradford.ac.uk
// www.bradford.ac.uk

P303 BA Film Studies
Duration: 3FT Hon
Entry Requirements: *GCE:* 240. *IB:* 24.

P301 BA Media Studies with Television
Duration: 3FT Hon
Entry Requirements: *GCE:* 240. *IB:* 24.

B80 UNIVERSITY OF THE WEST OF ENGLAND, BRISTOL
FRENCHAY CAMPUS
COLDHARBOUR LANE
BRISTOL BS16 1QY
t: +44 (0)117 32 83333 f: +44 (0)117 32 82810
e: admissions@uwe.ac.uk
// www.uwe.ac.uk

P303 BA Film Studies
Duration: 3FT Hon
Entry Requirements: Contact the institution for details.

QW36 BA Film Studies and English
Duration: 3FT Hon
Entry Requirements: Contact the institution for details.

PW38 BA Film Studies and Screen Writing
Duration: 3FT/4SW Hon
Entry Requirements: Contact the institution for details.

C10 CANTERBURY CHRIST CHURCH UNIVERSITY
NORTH HOLMES ROAD
CANTERBURY
KENT CT1 1QU
t: 01227 782900 f: 01227 782888
e: admissions@canterbury.ac.uk
// www.canterbury.ac.uk

NP13 BA Entrepreneurship and Film, Radio & Television Studies
Duration: 3FT Hon
Entry Requirements: *GCE:* 240. *IB:* 24.

P3NC BA Film, Radio & Television Studies with Entrepreneurship
Duration: 3FT Hon
Entry Requirements: *GCE:* 240. *IB:* 24.

P3GA BA Film, Radio & Television Studies with Internet Computing
Duration: 3FT Hon
Entry Requirements: *GCE:* 240. *IB:* 24.

GP4H BA Internet Computing and Film, Radio & Television
Duration: 3FT Hon
Entry Requirements: *GCE:* 240. *IB:* 24.

G4PJ BA Internet Computing with Film, Radio & Television
Duration: 3FT Hon
Entry Requirements: *GCE:* 240. *IB:* 24.

C55 UNIVERSITY OF CHESTER
PARKGATE ROAD
CHESTER CH1 4BJ
t: 01244 511000 f: 01244 511300
e: enquiries@chester.ac.uk
// www.chester.ac.uk

NPFJ BA Business Management and Film Studies
Duration: 3FT Hon
Entry Requirements: *GCE:* 240-280. *SQAH:* BBBB. *IB:* 26. *BTEC NC:* DM. *BTEC ND:* MMM.

WP63 BA Digital Photography and Film Studies
Duration: 3FT Hon
Entry Requirements: *GCE:* 240-280. *SQAH:* BBBB. *IB:* 24. *BTEC NC:* DM. *BTEC ND:* MMM.

NP8H BA Events Management and Film Studies
Duration: 3FT Hon
Entry Requirements: *GCE:* 240-280. *SQAH:* BBBB. *IB:* 24. *BTEC NC:* DM. *BTEC ND:* MMM.

PNH5 BA Film Studies and Advertising
Duration: 3FT Hon
Entry Requirements: *GCE:* 240-280. *SQAH:* BBBB. *IB:* 24. *BTEC NC:* DM. *BTEC ND:* MMM.

P392 BA Film Studies and Commercial Music Production
Duration: 3FT Hon
Entry Requirements: *Foundation:* Pass. *GCE:* 260-300. *SQAH:* BBBB. *IB:* 28. *BTEC NC:* DM. *BTEC ND:* DMM.

PPH5 BA Film Studies and Journalism
Duration: 3FT Hon
Entry Requirements: *GCE:* 240-280. *SQAH:* BBBB. *IB:* 24. *BTEC NC:* DM. *BTEC ND:* MMM.

P393 BA Film Studies and Radio Production
Duration: 3FT Hon
Entry Requirements: *Foundation:* Pass. *GCE:* 260-300. *SQAH:* BBBB. *IB:* 28. *BTEC NC:* DM. *BTEC ND:* DMM.

PC3Q BA Film Studies and Sport Development
Duration: 3FT Hon
Entry Requirements: *GCE:* 240-280. *SQAH:* BBBB. *IB:* 24. *BTEC NC:* DM. *BTEC ND:* MMM.

P394 BA Film Studies and TV Production
Duration: 3FT Hon
Entry Requirements: *GCE:* 260-300. *SQAH:* BBBB. *IB:* 24. *BTEC NC:* DM. *BTEC ND:* MMM.

P330 BA Radio Production and Media Studies
Duration: 3FT Hon
Entry Requirements: *Foundation:* Pass. *GCE:* 260-300. *SQAH:* BBBB. *IB:* 28. *BTEC NC:* DM. *BTEC ND:* DMM.

D26 DE MONTFORT UNIVERSITY
THE GATEWAY
LEICESTER LE1 9BH
t: 0116 255 1551 f: 0116 250 6204
e: enquiries@dmu.ac.uk
// www.dmu.ac.uk

WP83 BA Creative Writing and Film Studies
Duration: 3FT Hon
Entry Requirements: *GCE:* 260. *IB:* 28.

PP35 BA Film Studies and Journalism
Duration: 3FT Hon
Entry Requirements: *GCE:* 260. *IB:* 28. Interview required.

D39 UNIVERSITY OF DERBY
KEDLESTON ROAD
DERBY DE22 1GB
t: 01332 591167 f: 01332 597724
e: askadmissions@derby.ac.uk
// www.derby.ac.uk

NP43 BA Accounting and Film & Television Studies
Duration: 3FT Hon
Entry Requirements: *Foundation:* Distinction. *GCE:* 260-300. *IB:* 28. *BTEC ND:* DMM. *OCR NED:* M2

MP2H BA Criminology and Film & Television Studies
Duration: 3FT Hon
Entry Requirements: *Foundation:* Distinction. *GCE:* 260-300. *IB:* 28. *BTEC ND:* DMM. *OCR NED:* M2

PV31 BA Film & Television Studies and History
Duration: 3FT Hon
Entry Requirements: *Foundation:* Distinction. *GCE:* 260-300. *IB:* 28. *BTEC ND:* DMM. *OCR NED:* M2

PN3P BA Film & Television Studies and Human Resources Management
Duration: 3FT Hon
Entry Requirements: *Foundation:* Distinction. *GCE:* 260-300. *IB:* 28. *BTEC ND:* DMM. *OCR NED:* M2

PW3V BA Film & Television Studies and Media Writing
Duration: 3FT Hon
Entry Requirements: *Foundation:* Distinction. *GCE:* 260-300. *IB:* 28. *BTEC ND:* DMM. *OCR NED:* M2

PK32 BA Film & Television Studies and Property Development
Duration: 3FT Hon
Entry Requirements: *Foundation:* Distinction. *GCE:* 260-300. *IB:* 28. *BTEC ND:* DMM. *OCR NED:* M2

PC36 BA Film & Television Studies and Sport & Exercise Studies
Duration: 3FT Hon
Entry Requirements: *Foundation:* Distinction. *GCE:* 260-300. *IB:* 28. *BTEC ND:* DMM. *OCR NED:* M2

CP1H BA/BSc Biology and Film & Television Studies
Duration: 3FT Hon
Entry Requirements: *Foundation:* Distinction. *GCE:* 260-300. *IB:* 28. *BTEC ND:* DMM. *OCR NED:* M2

PL32 BA/BSc Film & TV Studies and International Relations & Global Development
Duration: 3FT Hon
Entry Requirements: *Foundation:* Distinction. *GCE:* 260-300. *IB:* 28. *BTEC ND:* DMM. *OCR NED:* M2

PF37 BA/BSc Film & Television Studies and Environmental Hazards
Duration: 3FT Hon
Entry Requirements: *Foundation:* Distinction. *GCE:* 260-300. *IB:* 28. *BTEC ND:* DMM. *OCR NED:* M2

PF3P BA/BSc Film & Television Studies and Geology
Duration: 3FT Hon
Entry Requirements: *Foundation:* Distinction. *GCE:* 260-300. *IB:* 28. *BTEC ND:* DMM. *OCR NED:* M2

PL39 BA/BSc Film & Television Studies and Third World Development
Duration: 3FT Hon
Entry Requirements: *Foundation:* Distinction. *GCE:* 260-300. *IB:* 28. *BTEC ND:* DMM. *OCR NED:* M2

CP3H BA/BSc Zoology and Film & Television Studies
Duration: 3FT Hon
Entry Requirements: *Foundation:* Distinction. *GCE:* 260-300. *IB:* 28. *BTEC ND:* DMM. *OCR NED:* M2

D65 UNIVERSITY OF DUNDEE
NETHERGATE
DUNDEE DD1 4HN
t: 01382 383838 f: 01382 388150
e: contactus@dundee.ac.uk
// www.dundee.ac.uk/admissions/undergraduate/

VP53 MA Philosophy and Film
Duration: 4FT Hon
Entry Requirements: *GCE:* BCC. *SQAH:* ABBB. *IB:* 30. *BTEC ND:* DMM.

E14 UNIVERSITY OF EAST ANGLIA
NORWICH NR4 7TJ
t: 01603 591515 f: 01603 458596
e: admissions@uea.ac.uk
// www.uea.ac.uk

RP1J BA French and Film & Television
Duration: 4FT Hon   CRB Check: Required
Entry Requirements: *GCE:* AAB-BBB. *SQAAH:* AAB-BBB.

VP53 BA Philosophy and Film Studies
Duration: 3FT Hon   CRB Check: Required
Entry Requirements: *GCE:* ABB. *SQAAH:* ABB. *IB:* 32. *BTEC NC:* DD. *BTEC ND:* DDM.

RP4J BA Spanish and Film & Television
Duration: 4FT Hon   CRB Check: Required
Entry Requirements: Contact the institution for details.

E28 UNIVERSITY OF EAST LONDON
DOCKLANDS CAMPUS
UNIVERSITY WAY
LONDON E16 2RD
t: 020 8223 3333 f: 020 8223 2978
e: study@uel.ac.uk
// www.uel.ac.uk

LP13 BA Business Economics/Film Studies
Duration: 3FT Hon
Entry Requirements: *GCE:* 200. *IB:* 24. *BTEC NC:* DM. *BTEC ND:* MMP. *OCR ND:* M1 *OCR NED:* P1

W4P3 BA Community Arts Practice with Film Studies
Duration: 3FT Hon
Entry Requirements: *GCE:* 200. *IB:* 24. *BTEC NC:* DM. *BTEC ND:* MMP. *OCR ND:* M1 *OCR NED:* P1 Interview required.

W8P3 BA Creative & Professional Writing with Film Studies
Duration: 3FT Hon
Entry Requirements: *GCE:* 200. *IB:* 24. *BTEC NC:* DM. *BTEC ND:* MMP.

Q3P3 BA English Literature with Film Studies
Duration: 3FT Hon
Entry Requirements: *GCE:* 200. *IB:* 24. *BTEC NC:* DM. *BTEC ND:* MMP.

P3P9 BA Film Studies with Communication Studies
Duration: 3FT Hon
Entry Requirements: *GCE:* 200. *IB:* 24. *BTEC NC:* DM. *BTEC ND:* MMP.

P3W4 BA Film Studies with Community Arts Practice
Duration: 3FT Hon
Entry Requirements: *GCE:* 200. *IB:* 24. *BTEC NC:* DM. *BTEC ND:* MMP. *OCR ND:* M1 *OCR NED:* P1

P3W8 BA Film Studies with Creative & Professional Writing
Duration: 3FT Hon
Entry Requirements: *GCE:* 200. *IB:* 24. *BTEC NC:* DM. *BTEC ND:* MMP.

P3L6 BA Film Studies with Cultural Studies
Duration: 3FT Hon
Entry Requirements: *GCE:* 200. *IB:* 24. *BTEC NC:* DM. *BTEC ND:* MMP.

P3QH BA Film Studies with English Literature
Duration: 3FT Hon
Entry Requirements: *GCE:* 200. *IB:* 24. *BTEC NC:* DM. *BTEC ND:* MMP.

P3G5 BA Film Studies with Information Technology
Duration: 3FT Hon
Entry Requirements: *GCE:* 200. *IB:* 24. *BTEC NC:* DM. *BTEC ND:* MMP.

P3N5 BA Film Studies with Marketing
Duration: 3FT Hon
Entry Requirements: *GCE:* 200. *IB:* 24. *BTEC NC:* DM. *BTEC ND:* MMP.

P3W3 BA Film Studies with Music Culture
Duration: 3FT Hon
Entry Requirements: *GCE:* 200. *IB:* 24. *BTEC NC:* DM. *BTEC ND:* MMP. *OCR ND:* M1 *OCR NED:* P1

P3WP BA Film Studies with Photography
Duration: 3FT Hon
Entry Requirements: *GCE:* 200. *IB:* 24. *BTEC NC:* DM. *BTEC ND:* MMP. *OCR ND:* M1 *OCR NED:* P1

P3WK BA Film Studies with Theatre Studies
Duration: 3FT Hon
Entry Requirements: *GCE:* 200. *IB:* 24. *BTEC NC:* DM. *BTEC ND:* MMP. *OCR ND:* M1 *OCR NED:* P1

PW38 BA Film Studies/Creative & Professional Writing
Duration: 3FT Hon
Entry Requirements: *GCE:* 200. *IB:* 24. *BTEC NC:* DM. *BTEC ND:* MMP.

PL36 BA Film Studies/Cultural Studies
Duration: 3FT Hon
Entry Requirements: *GCE:* 200. *IB:* 24. *BTEC NC:* DM. *BTEC ND:* MMP.

V000 BA Media & Creative Industries option - Film Studies
Duration: 3FT Hon
Entry Requirements: *GCE:* 200. *IB:* 24.

P301 BA Media Studies (Extended)
Duration: 4FT Hon
Entry Requirements: *GCE:* 40. *IB:* 24.

GP5H BA/BSc Business Information Systems/Film Studies
Duration: 3FT Hon
Entry Requirements: *GCE:* 200. *IB:* 24. *BTEC NC:* DM. *BTEC ND:* MMP. *OCR ND:* M1 *OCR NED:* P1

QP33 BA/BSc Film Studies/English Literature
Duration: 3FT Hon
Entry Requirements: *GCE:* 200. *IB:* 24. *BTEC NC:* DM. *BTEC ND:* MMP.

G4P3 BSc Computer Networks with Film Studies
Duration: 3FT Hon
Entry Requirements: *GCE:* 200. *IB:* 24. *BTEC NC:* DM. *BTEC ND:* MMP. *OCR ND:* M1 *OCR NED:* P1

WP23 BSc/BA Multimedia Design Technology/Film Studies
Duration: 3FT Hon
Entry Requirements: Contact the institution for details.

E42 EDGE HILL UNIVERSITY
ORMSKIRK
LANCASHIRE L39 4QP
t: 01695 657000 f: 01695 584355
e: study@edgehill.ac.uk
// www.edgehill.ac.uk

QP33 BA English Language and Film Studies
Duration: 3FT Hon
Entry Requirements: *GCE:* 280. *IB:* 26. *BTEC NC:* DD. *BTEC ND:* DMM. *OCR ND:* M2 *OCR NED:* M2

QP3J BA English Literature and Film Studies
Duration: 3FT Hon
Entry Requirements: *GCE:* 280. *IB:* 26. *BTEC NC:* DD. *BTEC ND:* DMM. *OCR ND:* M2 *OCR NED:* M2

P303 BA Film Studies
Duration: 3FT Hon
Entry Requirements: *GCE:* 280. *IB:* 26. *BTEC NC:* DD. *BTEC ND:* DMM. *OCR ND:* D *OCR NED:* M2

P3W9 BA Film Studies with Creative Writing
Duration: 3FT Hon
Entry Requirements: *GCE:* 280. *IB:* 26. *BTEC NC:* DD. *BTEC ND:* DMM. *OCR ND:* D *OCR NED:* M2

E59 EDINBURGH NAPIER UNIVERSITY
CRAIGLOCKHART CAMPUS
EDINBURGH EH14 1DJ
t: +44 (0)8452 60 60 40 f: 0131 455 6464
e: info@napier.ac.uk
// www.napier.ac.uk

QP33 BA English and Film
Duration: 3FT/4FT Ord/Hon
Entry Requirements: *GCE:* 220.

P301 BA Television
Duration: 2FT Hon
Entry Requirements: Contact the institution for details.

E70 THE UNIVERSITY OF ESSEX
WIVENHOE PARK
COLCHESTER
ESSEX CO4 3SQ
t: 01206 873666 f: 01206 874477
e: admit@essex.ac.uk
// www.essex.ac.uk

T7P3 BA American (United States) Studies with Film (term abroad)
Duration: 3FT Hon
Entry Requirements: *GCE:* ABB-BBB. *SQAH:* AAAB-AABB. Interview required.

P303 BA Film Studies (Including Year Abroad)
Duration: 4FT Hon
Entry Requirements: Contact the institution for details.

PQ32 BA Film Studies and Literature (Including Year Abroad)
Duration: 4FT Hon
Entry Requirements: Contact the institution for details.

PW38 BA Film and Creative Writing
Duration: 3FT Hon
Entry Requirements: *GCE:* ABB-BBB. *SQAH:* AAAB-AABB. *BTEC NC:* DD. *BTEC ND:* DDM.

PWH8 BA Film and Creative Writing (Including Year Abroad)
Duration: 4FT Hon
Entry Requirements: Contact the institution for details.

VP53 BA Philosophy and Film
Duration: 3FT Hon
Entry Requirements: *GCE:* ABB-BBB. *SQAH:* AAAB-AABB. *BTEC ND:* DDM.

E84 UNIVERSITY OF EXETER
LAVER BUILDING
NORTH PARK ROAD
EXETER
DEVON EX4 4QE
t: 01392 723044 f: 01392 722479
e: admissions@exeter.ac.uk
// www.exeter.ac.uk/admissions

W600 BA Film Studies
Duration: 3FT Hon
Entry Requirements: *GCE:* AAB-ABB. *SQAH:* AAABB-AABBB. *SQAAH:* ABB-BBB.

F66 FARNBOROUGH COLLEGE OF TECHNOLOGY
BOUNDARY ROAD
FARNBOROUGH
HAMPSHIRE GU14 6SB
t: 01252 407028 f: 01252 407041
e: admissions@farn-ct.ac.uk
// www.farn-ct.ac.uk

P396 BA Media Production (Film and Television)
Duration: 3FT Hon
Entry Requirements: *GCE:* 180-200. *BTEC NC:* MM. *BTEC ND:* MMM. *OCR ND:* M2 *OCR NED:* M3 Admissions Test required.

P395 BA Media Production (Radio)
Duration: 3FT Hon
Entry Requirements: *GCE:* 180-200. *BTEC NC:* MM. *BTEC ND:* MMM. *OCR ND:* M2 *OCR NED:* M3 Admissions Test required.

P302 BA Media Production (Radio) (Top Up)
Duration: 1FT Hon
Entry Requirements: Contact the institution for details.

P392 BA Media Production (Television and Film) (Top Up)
Duration: 1FT Hon
Entry Requirements: Contact the institution for details.

P390 FdSc Film and Television Production
Duration: 2FT Fdg
Entry Requirements: *GCE:* 160. *BTEC NC:* MM. *BTEC ND:* MMM.

P393 FdSc Radio & Television Production
Duration: 2FT Fdg
Entry Requirements: *GCE:* 160. *BTEC NC:* MM. *BTEC ND:* MMM.

G14 UNIVERSITY OF GLAMORGAN, CARDIFF AND PONTYPRIDD
ENQUIRIES AND ADMISSIONS UNIT
PONTYPRIDD CF37 1DL
t: 0800 716925 f: 01443 654050
e: enquiries@glam.ac.uk
// www.glam.ac.uk

PH03 BA Creative Industries (Film and Video Top-Up)
Duration: 1FT Hon
Entry Requirements: Contact the institution for details.

P301 BA Media Production (Photography/Radio/New Media)
Duration: 3FT Hon
Entry Requirements: *GCE:* ABB. *IB:* 24. *BTEC ND:* DMM. *OCR NED:* M2

G28 UNIVERSITY OF GLASGOW
THE UNIVERSITY OF GLASGOW
THE FRASER BUILDING
65 HILLHEAD STREET
GLASGOW G12 8QF
t: 0141 330 6062 f: 0141 330 2961
e: student.recruitment@glasgow.ac.uk
// www.glasgow.ac.uk

GP53 MA Arts & Media Informatics/Film & Television Studies
Duration: 4FT Hon
Entry Requirements: *GCE:* AAA. *SQAH:* AAAA-AABB. *IB:* 36.

QP83 MA Classics/Film & Television Studies
Duration: 4FT Hon
Entry Requirements: *GCE:* AAA. *SQAH:* AAAA-AABB. *IB:* 36.

G50 THE UNIVERSITY OF GLOUCESTERSHIRE
PARK CAMPUS
THE PARK
CHELTENHAM GL50 2RH
t: 01242 714503 f: 01242 714827
e: admissions@glos.ac.uk
// www.glos.ac.uk

P30H BA Film
Duration: 3FT Hon
Entry Requirements: Contact the institution for details.

G53 GLYNDWR UNIVERSITY
PLAS COCH
MOLD ROAD
WREXHAM LL11 2AW
t: 01978 293439 f: 01978 290008
e: sid@glyndwr.ac.uk
// www.glyndwr.ac.uk

PQ33 BA English and Screen Studies
Duration: 3FT Hon
Entry Requirements: *GCE:* 240.

PV31 BA History and Screen Studies
Duration: 3FT Hon
Entry Requirements: *GCE:* 200.

PP93 BA Media Communications and Screen Studies
Duration: 3FT Hon
Entry Requirements: *GCE:* 240.

WP43 BA Theatre, Television and Performance
Duration: 3FT Hon
Entry Requirements: *GCE:* 240. Interview required.

G70 UNIVERSITY OF GREENWICH
GREENWICH CAMPUS
OLD ROYAL NAVAL COLLEGE
PARK ROW
LONDON SE10 9LS
t: 0800 005 006 f: 020 8331 8145
e: courseinfo@gre.ac.uk
// www.gre.ac.uk

P303 BA Film Studies
Duration: 3FT Hon
Entry Requirements: *GCE:* 240. *IB:* 24.

PW38 BA Film Studies and Media Writing
Duration: 3FT Hon
Entry Requirements: *GCE:* 240. *IB:* 24.

P3V5 BA Film Studies with Philosophy
Duration: 3FT Hon
Entry Requirements: *GCE:* 240. *IB:* 24.

P3L2 BA Film Studies with Politics
Duration: 3FT Hon
Entry Requirements: *GCE:* 240. *IB:* 24.

P3LH BA Film Studies with Sociology
Duration: 3FT Hon
Entry Requirements: *GCE:* 240. *IB:* 24.

H72 THE UNIVERSITY OF HULL
THE UNIVERSITY OF HULL
COTTINGHAM ROAD
HULL HU6 7RX
t: 01482 466100 f: 01482 442290
e: admissions@hull.ac.uk
// www.hull.ac.uk

WP43 BA Drama and Film Studies
Duration: 3FT Hon
Entry Requirements: *GCE:* 300. *IB:* 28. *BTEC ND:* DDM.

VP13 BA History and Film Studies
Duration: 3FT Hon
Entry Requirements: *GCE:* 280-300. *IB:* 30. *BTEC ND:* DMM.

WP33 BA Music and Film Studies
Duration: 3FT Hon
Entry Requirements: *GCE:* 280-300. *IB:* 28. *BTEC ND:* DDM.
Interview required.

VP63 BA Religion and Film Studies
Duration: 3FT Hon
Entry Requirements: *GCE:* 280-300. *IB:* 28. *BTEC ND:* DMM.

LP33 BA Sociology and Film Studies
Duration: 3FT Hon
Entry Requirements: *GCE:* 260-300. *IB:* 28. *BTEC ND:* DMM.

K12 KEELE UNIVERSITY
STAFFS ST5 5BG
t: 01782 734005 f: 01782 632343
e: undergraduate@keele.ac.uk
// www.keele.ac.uk

NP43 BA Accounting and Film Studies
Duration: 3FT Hon
Entry Requirements: *GCE:* 300-320.

TP73 BA American Studies and Film Studies
Duration: 3FT Hon
Entry Requirements: *GCE:* 280-320.

NP23 BA Business Management and Film Studies
Duration: 3FT Hon
Entry Requirements: *GCE:* 300-320.

MP93 BA Criminology and Film Studies
Duration: 3FT Hon
Entry Requirements: *GCE:* 300-320.

LP13 BA Economics and Film Studies
Duration: 3FT Hon
Entry Requirements: *GCE:* 300.

XP33 BA Educational Studies and Film Studies
Duration: 3FT Hon
Entry Requirements: *GCE:* 280-300.

QP33 BA English and Film Studies
Duration: 3FT Hon
Entry Requirements: *GCE:* 300-320.

PV3C BA Film Studies and History
Duration: 3FT Hon
Entry Requirements: *GCE:* 280-300.

PN3P BA Film Studies and Human Resource Management
Duration: 3FT Hon
Entry Requirements: *GCE:* 300-320.

PN3C BA Film Studies and International Business
Duration: 3FT Hon
Entry Requirements: *GCE:* 300-320.

PN3M BA Film Studies and Marketing
Duration: 3FT Hon
Entry Requirements: *GCE:* 300-320.

PP39 BA Film Studies and Media, Communications & Culture
Duration: 3FT Hon
Entry Requirements: *GCE:* 280-300.

PW3H BA Film Studies and Music
Duration: 3FT Hon
Entry Requirements: *GCE:* 260-320.

PJ3X BA Film Studies and Music Technology
Duration: 3FT Hon
Entry Requirements: *GCE:* 260-320.

PV3M BA Film Studies and Philosophy
Duration: 3FT Hon
Entry Requirements: *GCE:* 260-320.

PL3F BA Film Studies and Politics
Duration: 3FT Hon
Entry Requirements: *GCE:* 260-320.

PL3H BA Film Studies and Sociology
Duration: 3FT Hon
Entry Requirements: *GCE:* 260-320.

P3V0 BA Film Studies with Humanities Foundation Year
Duration: 4FT Hon
Entry Requirements: Contact the institution for details.

FP73 BSc Applied Environmental Science and Film Studies
Duration: 3FT Hon
Entry Requirements: *GCE:* 300.

CP73 BSc Biochemistry and Film Studies
Duration: 3FT Hon
Entry Requirements: *GCE:* 300.

CP13 BSc Biology and Film Studies
Duration: 3FT Hon
Entry Requirements: *GCE:* 300.

FP13 BSc Chemistry and Film Studies
Duration: 3FT Hon
Entry Requirements: *GCE:* 300.

GP43 BSc Computer Science and Film Studies
Duration: 3FT Hon
Entry Requirements: *GCE:* 300.

GP4H BSc Creative Computing and Film Studies
Duration: 3FT Hon
Entry Requirements: *GCE:* 300.

PF3P BSc Film Studies and Geology
Duration: 3FT Hon
Entry Requirements: *GCE:* 300.

PB3C BSc Film Studies and Human Biology
Duration: 3FT Hon
Entry Requirements: *GCE:* 300.

PG35 BSc Film Studies and Information Systems
Duration: 3FT Hon
Entry Requirements: *GCE:* 300.

PG3C BSc Film Studies and Mathematics
Duration: 3FT Hon
Entry Requirements: *GCE:* 300.

PF31 BSc Film Studies and Medicinal Chemistry
Duration: 3FT Hon
Entry Requirements: *GCE:* 300.

PB3D BSc Film Studies and Neuroscience
Duration: 3FT Hon
Entry Requirements: *GCE:* 300.

PG37 BSc Film Studies and Smart Systems
Duration: 3FT Hon
Entry Requirements: *GCE:* 300.

K24 THE UNIVERSITY OF KENT
INFORMATION, RECRUITMENT & ADMISSIONS
REGISTRY
UNIVERSITY OF KENT
CANTERBURY, KENT CT2 7NZ
t: 01227 827272 f: 01227 827077
e: information@kent.ac.uk
// www.kent.ac.uk

W611 BA Film Studies with a Placement Year
Duration: 4FT Hon
Entry Requirements: Contact the institution for details.

K60 KING'S COLLEGE LONDON (UNIVERSITY OF LONDON)
STRAND
LONDON WC2R 2LS
t: 020 7848 7070 f: 020 7848 7171
e: prospective@kcl.ac.uk
// www.kcl.ac.uk

Q2P3 BA Comparative Literature with Film Studies
Duration: 3FT Hon
Entry Requirements: *GCE:* AAAc. *SQAH:* AAABB. *IB:* 38.

P303 BA Film Studies
Duration: 3FT Hon
Entry Requirements: *GCE:* AABc. *SQAH:* ABBBB. *IB:* 36.

K84 KINGSTON UNIVERSITY
STUDENT INFORMATION & ADVICE CENTRE
COOPER HOUSE
40-46 SURBITON ROAD
KINGSTON UPON THAMES KT1 2HX
t: 0844 8552177 f: 020 8547 7080
e: aps@kingston.ac.uk
// www.kingston.ac.uk

WPH3 BA Creative Music Technologies and Film Studies
Duration: 3FT Hon
Entry Requirements: *GCE:* 240-280. *BTEC ND:* MMM.

WPG3 BA Creative Music Technologies and TV & New Broadcasting Media
Duration: 3FT Hon
Entry Requirements: *GCE:* 240-280. *BTEC ND:* MMM.

WP83 BA Creative Writing and Film Studies
Duration: 3FT Hon
Entry Requirements: *GCE:* 220-360. *IB:* 30.

WPW3 BA Creative Writing and Television & New Broadcasting Media
Duration: 3FT Hon
Entry Requirements: *GCE:* 220-360.

W8PJ BA Creative Writing with Television & New Broadcasting Media
Duration: 3FT Hon
Entry Requirements: *GCE:* 220-360.

LP33 BA Criminology and Film Studies
Duration: 3FT Hon
Entry Requirements: *GCE:* 220-320. *SQAH:* BBCCC. *SQAAH:* BBC.

PW35 BA Dance and Film Studies
Duration: 3FT Hon
Entry Requirements: *GCE:* 300-360. *BTEC ND:* DDD. Interview required.

WPM3 BA Dance and Television & New Broadcasting Media
Duration: 3FT Hon
Entry Requirements: *GCE:* 300-360. *BTEC ND:* DDD. Interview required.

W5PH BA Dance with Film Studies
Duration: 3FT Hon
Entry Requirements: *GCE:* 300-360. *BTEC ND:* DDD. Interview required.

W5P3 BA Dance with Television & New Broadcasting Media
Duration: 3FT Hon
Entry Requirements: *GCE:* 300-360. *BTEC ND:* DDD. Interview required.

WP43 BA Drama and Film Studies
Duration: 3FT Hon
Entry Requirements: *GCE:* 300-360. *SQAH:* BBCCC. *SQAAH:* BBC.
BTEC ND: DDD.

LPC3 BA Economics (Applied) and Television & New Broadcasting Media
Duration: 3FT Hon
Entry Requirements: *GCE:* 220-320. *IB:* 24.

L1PH BA Economics (Applied) with Television & New Broadcasting Media
Duration: 3FT Hon
Entry Requirements: *GCE:* 220-320. *IB:* 24.

Q3PJ BA English Language & Communication with Television & New Broadcasting Media
Duration: 3FT Hon
Entry Requirements: *GCE:* 240-360.

QP33 BA English Language & Communications and Film Studies
Duration: 3FT Hon
Entry Requirements: *GCE:* 240-360.

QPH3 BA English Language & Communications and Television & New Broadcasting Media
Duration: 3FT Hon
Entry Requirements: *GCE:* 240-360.

QPJ3 BA English Literature and Film Studies
Duration: 3FT Hon
Entry Requirements: *GCE:* 240-360.

QP3J BA English Literature and Television & New Broadcasting Media
Duration: 3FT Hon
Entry Requirements: *GCE:* 240-360.

Q3PH BA English Literature with Television & New Broadcasting Media
Duration: 3FT Hon
Entry Requirements: *GCE:* 240-360.

PV31 BA Film Studies and History
Duration: 3FT Hon
Entry Requirements: *GCE:* 240-360. *IB:* 30.

PV33 BA Film Studies and History of Art, Design & Film
Duration: 3FT Hon
Entry Requirements: *GCE:* 240-360. *IB:* 30.

PP35 BA Film Studies and Journalism
Duration: 3FT Hon
Entry Requirements: *GCE:* 320. *BTEC ND:* DDM.

PM31 BA Film Studies and Law
Duration: 3FT Hon
Entry Requirements: *GCE:* 280.

PW33 BA Film Studies and Music
Duration: 3FT Hon
Entry Requirements: *GCE:* 240-360.

PL33 BA Film Studies and Sociology
Duration: 3FT Hon
Entry Requirements: *GCE:* 240-360. *IB:* 30.

PWH2 BA Film Studies and Visual & Material Culture
Duration: 3FT Hon
Entry Requirements: *GCE:* 240-360. *IB:* 30.

P396 BA Film Studies andTelevision & New Broadcasting Media
Duration: 3FT Hon
Entry Requirements: *GCE:* 220-360.

P3WM BA Film Studies with Dance
Duration: 3FT Hon
Entry Requirements: *GCE:* 300-360. *BTEC ND:* DDD. Interview required.

P3M1 BA Film Studies with Law
Duration: 3FT Hon
Entry Requirements: *GCE:* 280.

VP13 BA History and Television & New Broadcasting Media
Duration: 3FT Hon
Entry Requirements: *GCE:* 220-360.

V1P3 BA History with Television & New Broadcasting Media
Duration: 3FT Hon
Entry Requirements: *GCE:* 220-360.

LPG3 BA Human Rights and Television & New Broadcasting Media
Duration: 3FT Hon
Entry Requirements: *GCE:* 220-360.

L2P9 BA Human Rights with Television & New Broadcasting Media
Duration: 3FT Hon
Entry Requirements: *GCE:* 220-360.

MP13 BA Law and Film Studies
Duration: 3FT Hon
Entry Requirements: *GCE:* 280.

MPC3 BA Law and Television & New Broadcasting Media
Duration: 3FT Hon
Entry Requirements: *GCE:* 280.

WP3H BA Music Technology and Film Studies
Duration: 3FT Hon
Entry Requirements: *GCE:* 240-280. *BTEC ND:* MMM.

WP3J BA Music Technology and Television & New Broadcasting Media
Duration: 3FT Hon
Entry Requirements: *GCE:* 240-280. *BTEC ND:* MMM.

LPFH BA Politics and Television & New Broadcasting Media
Duration: 3FT Hon
Entry Requirements: *GCE:* 220-360.

L2PA BA Politics with Television & New Broadcasting Media
Duration: 3FT Hon
Entry Requirements: *GCE:* 220-360.

CP83 BA Psychology and Television & New Broadcasting Media
Duration: 3FT Hon
Entry Requirements: *GCE:* 220-360.

C8PH BA Psychology with Television & New Broadcasting Media
Duration: 3FT Hon
Entry Requirements: *GCE:* 220-360.

LPJ3 BA Sociology and Television & New Broadcasting Media
Duration: 3FT Hon
Entry Requirements: *GCE:* 220-360.

L3PH BA Sociology with Television and New Broadcasting Media
Duration: 3FT Hon
Entry Requirements: *GCE:* 220-360.

P3LC BA Television & New Broadcasting Media with Applied Economics
Duration: 3FT Hon
Entry Requirements: *GCE:* 240-360.

P3WW BA Television & New Broadcasting Media with Creative Writing
Duration: 3FT Hon
Entry Requirements: *GCE:* 240-360.

P3W5 BA Television & New Broadcasting Media with Dance
Duration: 3FT Hon
Entry Requirements: *GCE:* 300-360. *BTEC ND:* DDD. Interview required.

P3QH BA Television & New Broadcasting Media with English Language & Communication
Duration: 3FT Hon
Entry Requirements: *GCE:* 240-360.

P3QJ BA Television & New Broadcasting Media with English Literature
Duration: 3FT Hon
Entry Requirements: *GCE:* 240-360.

P394 BA Television & New Broadcasting Media with Film Studies
Duration: 3FT Hon
Entry Requirements: *GCE:* 240-360.

P3RC BA Television & New Broadcasting Media with French
Duration: 3FT Hon
Entry Requirements: *GCE:* 240-360.

P3V1 BA Television & New Broadcasting Media with History
Duration: 3FT Hon
Entry Requirements: *GCE:* 240-360.

P3LA BA Television & New Broadcasting Media with Human Rights
Duration: 3FT Hon
Entry Requirements: *GCE:* 240-360.

P3MC BA Television & New Broadcasting Media with Law
Duration: 3FT Hon
Entry Requirements: *GCE:* 280.

P3LB BA Television & New Broadcasting Media with Politics
Duration: 3FT Hon
Entry Requirements: *GCE:* 240-360.

P3CV BA Television & New Broadcasting Media with Psychology
Duration: 3FT Hon
Entry Requirements: *GCE:* 240-360.

P3LH BA Television & New Broadcasting Media with Sociology
Duration: 3FT Hon
Entry Requirements: *GCE:* 240-360.

LP2J BSc International Relations and Television & New Broadcasting Media
Duration: 3FT Hon
Entry Requirements: *GCE:* 220-360.

PP43 BSc Media Technology and Television & New Broadcasting Media
Duration: 3FT Hon
Entry Requirements: *GCE:* 240-280.

H6P3 BSc Television & Video Technology and Film Studies
Duration: 4SW Hon
Entry Requirements: *GCE:* 240-280.

H6PH BSc Television & Video Technology and Film Studies
Duration: 3FT Hon
Entry Requirements: *GCE:* 240-280.

P301 BSc Television and Video Technology (including Foundation Year)
Duration: 4FT Hon
Entry Requirements: Contact the institution for details.

L14 LANCASTER UNIVERSITY
THE UNIVERSITY
LANCASTER
LANCASHIRE LA1 4YW
t: 01524 592029 f: 01524 846243
e: ugadmissions@lancaster.ac.uk
// www.lancs.ac.uk

RP93 BA European Languages and Film Studies (4 years)
Duration: 4FT Hon
Entry Requirements: *GCE:* ABB. *SQAH:* BBBBC. *SQAAH:* BBB. *IB:* 32. *BTEC ND:* DDM.

P303 BA Film Studies
Duration: 3FT Hon
Entry Requirements: *GCE:* ABB. *SQAH:* BBBBB. *SQAAH:* BBB. *IB:* 32. *BTEC ND:* DDM.

PQ33 BA Film Studies and English Literature
Duration: 3FT Hon
Entry Requirements: *GCE:* AAB. *SQAH:* BBBBB. *SQAAH:* ABB. *IB:* 34.

L24 LEEDS TRINITY UNIVERSITY COLLEGE (FORMERLY LEEDS TRINITY AND ALL SAINTS)
BROWNBERRIE LANE
HORSFORTH
LEEDS LS18 5HD
t: 0113 283 7150 f: 0113 283 7222
e: enquiries@leedstrinity.ac.uk
// www.leedstrinity.ac.uk

QP3H BA English and Film Studies
Duration: 3FT Hon
Entry Requirements: *GCE:* 220. *IB:* 24. *BTEC NC:* DD. *BTEC ND:* MMP.

QP3J BA English and Television
Duration: 3FT Hon
Entry Requirements: *GCE:* 220. *IB:* 24. *BTEC NC:* PP. *BTEC ND:* PPP.

P303 BA Film Studies
Duration: 3FT Hon
Entry Requirements: *GCE:* 220. *IB:* 24. *BTEC NC:* DD. *BTEC ND:* MMP.

P391 BA Film and Television Studies
Duration: 3FT Hon
Entry Requirements: *GCE:* 220. *IB:* 24. *BTEC NC:* DD. *BTEC ND:* MMP.

P301 BA Television
Duration: 3FT Hon
Entry Requirements: *GCE:* 220. *IB:* 24. *BTEC NC:* DD. *BTEC ND:* MMP.

L34 UNIVERSITY OF LEICESTER
UNIVERSITY ROAD
LEICESTER LE1 7RH
t: 0116 252 5281 f: 0116 252 2447
e: admissions@le.ac.uk
// www.le.ac.uk

PQ33 BA Film Studies and English
Duration: 3FT Hon
Entry Requirements: *GCE:* BBB. *SQAH:* BBBBB. *SQAAH:* BBB. *IB:* 30. *BTEC ND:* DDM.

R8P3 BA Modern Languages with Film Studies
Duration: 4FT Hon
Entry Requirements: *GCE:* ABB. *SQAH:* AABBB. *SQAAH:* ABB. *IB:* 32. *BTEC ND:* DDM.

L39 UNIVERSITY OF LINCOLN
ADMISSIONS
BRAYFORD POOL
LINCOLN LN6 7TS
t: 01522 886097 f: 01522 886146
e: admissions@lincoln.ac.uk
// www.lincoln.ac.uk

PP3M BA Film & TV and Journalism
Duration: 3FT Hon
Entry Requirements: *GCE:* 280.

PW36 BA Film & Television
Duration: 3FT Hon
Entry Requirements: *GCE:* 280.

PQ3H BA Film & Television and English
Duration: 3FT Hon
Entry Requirements: *GCE:* 280.

P301 BA Media Production
Duration: 3FT Hon
Entry Requirements: *GCE:* 300.

L41 THE UNIVERSITY OF LIVERPOOL
THE FOUNDATION BUILDING
BROWNLOW HILL
LIVERPOOL L69 7ZX
t: 0151 794 2000 f: 0151 708 6502
e: ugrecruitment@liv.ac.uk
// www.liv.ac.uk

PR39 BA Film Studies (European) and a Modern Language
Duration: 4FT Hon
Entry Requirements: *GCE:* BBB. *SQAH:* BBBBB. *SQAAH:* BBB. *IB:* 30.

L51 LIVERPOOL JOHN MOORES UNIVERSITY
KINGSWAY HOUSE
HATTON GARDEN
LIVERPOOL L3 2AJ
t: 0151 231 5090 f: 0151 231 3462
e: courses@ljmu.ac.uk
// www.ljmu.ac.uk

P303 BA Film Studies
Duration: 3FT Hon
Entry Requirements: *GCE:* 280.

L68 LONDON METROPOLITAN UNIVERSITY
166-220 HOLLOWAY ROAD
LONDON N7 8DB
t: 020 7133 4200
e: admissions@londonmet.ac.uk
// www.londonmet.ac.uk

P303 BA Film and Television Studies
Duration: 3FT Hon
Entry Requirements: *GCE:* 260. *IB:* 28.

PPM3 BA Journalism and Film
Duration: 3FT Hon
Entry Requirements: Contact the institution for details.

L75 LONDON SOUTH BANK UNIVERSITY
103 BOROUGH ROAD
LONDON SE1 0AA
t: 020 7815 7815 f: 020 7815 8273
e: enquiry@lsbu.ac.uk
// www.lsbu.ac.uk

QP3H BA English with Film Studies
Duration: 3FT Hon
Entry Requirements: *GCE:* 240. *IB:* 24. *BTEC NC:* DD. *BTEC ND:* MMM.

M40 THE MANCHESTER METROPOLITAN UNIVERSITY
ADMISSIONS OFFICE
ALL SAINTS (GMS)
ALL SAINTS
MANCHESTER M15 6BH
t: 0161 247 2000
// www.mmu.ac.uk

P303 BA Studies in Film (Top-up)
Duration: 1FT Hon
Entry Requirements: Contact the institution for details.

M80 MIDDLESEX UNIVERSITY
MIDDLESEX UNIVERSITY
THE BURROUGHS
LONDON NW4 4BT
t: 020 8411 5555 f: 020 8411 5649
e: enquiries@mdx.ac.uk
// www.mdx.ac.uk

P303 BA Film
Duration: 3FT Hon
Entry Requirements: Contact the institution for details.

N77 NORTHUMBRIA UNIVERSITY
TRINITY BUILDING
NORTHUMBERLAND ROAD
NEWCASTLE UPON TYNE NE1 8ST
t: 0191 243 7420 f: 0191 227 4561
e: er.admissions@northumbria.ac.uk
// www.northumbria.ac.uk

P391 BA Film and Television Studies
Duration: 3FT Hon
Entry Requirements: *GCE:* 300. *SQAH:* BBBBC. *SQAAH:* BBC. *IB:* 26. *BTEC ND:* DMM. Portfolio required.

N84 THE UNIVERSITY OF NOTTINGHAM
THE ADMISSIONS OFFICE
THE UNIVERSITY OF NOTTINGHAM
UNIVERSITY PARK
NOTTINGHAM NG7 2RD
t: 0115 951 5151 f: 0115 951 4668
// www.nottingham.ac.uk

PL33 BA Film & Television Studies and Cultural Sociology
Duration: 3FT Hon
Entry Requirements: *GCE:* ABC-BBB. *SQAAH:* ABC-BBB. *IB:* 30.

RP23 BA Film & Television Studies and German (Beginners)
Duration: 4FT Hon
Entry Requirements: *GCE:* ABC-BBB. *SQAAH:* ABC-BBB. *IB:* 30.

P3T1 BA Film & Television Studies with Chinese Studies
Duration: 3FT Hon
Entry Requirements: *GCE:* ABC-BBB. *SQAAH:* ABC-BBB. *IB:* 30.

PR3K BA Film/Television Studies and Beginners' Spanish
Duration: 4FT Hon
Entry Requirements: *GCE:* ABC-BBB. *SQAAH:* ABC-BBB. *IB:* 30.

PR31 BA Film/Television Studies and French
Duration: 4FT Hon
Entry Requirements: *GCE:* ABB. *SQAAH:* ABB. *IB:* 32.

PR32 BA Film/Television Studies and German
Duration: 4FT Hon
Entry Requirements: *GCE:* ABC-BBB. *SQAAH:* ABC-BBB. *IB:* 30.

PR34 BA Film/Television Studies and Hispanic Studies
Duration: 4FT Hon
Entry Requirements: *GCE:* ABC-BBB. *SQAAH:* ABC-BBB. *IB:* 30.

PR37 BA Film/Television Studies and Russian
Duration: 4FT Hon
Entry Requirements: *GCE:* ABB. *SQAAH:* ABB. *IB:* 32.

PRH7 BA Film/Television Studies and Russian Beginners
Duration: 4FT Hon
Entry Requirements: *GCE:* ABB. *SQAAH:* ABB. *IB:* 32.

N91 NOTTINGHAM TRENT UNIVERSITY
DRYDEN BUILDINGG
BURTON STREET
NOTTINGHAM NG1 4BU
t: +44 (0) 115 848 4200 f: +44 (0) 115 848 8869
e: applications@ntu.ac.uk
// www.ntu.ac.uk/

PP93 BA Communication & Society and Film &TV
Duration: 3FT Hon
Entry Requirements: *GCE:* 260. *IB:* 29. *BTEC NC:* DM. *BTEC ND:* DDM.

QP33 BA English and Film & TV
Duration: 3FT Hon
Entry Requirements: *GCE:* 260. *IB:* 29. *BTEC NC:* DM. *BTEC ND:* DDM.

RP83 BA European Studies and Film & TV
Duration: 3FT Hon
Entry Requirements: *GCE:* 260. *IB:* 29. *BTEC NC:* DM. *BTEC ND:* DDM.

PL39 BA Film & TV and Global Studies
Duration: 3FT Hon
Entry Requirements: *GCE:* 260. *IB:* 29. *BTEC NC:* DM. *BTEC ND:* DDM.

PV3C BA Film & TV and History
Duration: 3FT Hon
Entry Requirements: *GCE:* 260. *IB:* 29. *BTEC NC:* DM. *BTEC ND:* DDM.

PL32 BA Film & TV and International Relations
Duration: 3FT Hon
Entry Requirements: *GCE:* 260. *IB:* 29. *BTEC NC:* DM. *BTEC ND:* DDM.

PR33 BA Film & TV and Italian
Duration: 3FT Hon
Entry Requirements: *GCE:* 260. *IB:* 29. *BTEC NC:* DM. *BTEC ND:* DDM.

PQ3C BA Film & TV and Linguistics
Duration: 3FT Hon
Entry Requirements: *GCE:* 260. *IB:* 29. *BTEC NC:* DM. *BTEC ND:* DDM.

PV35 BA Film & TV and Philosophy
Duration: 3FT Hon
Entry Requirements: *GCE:* 260. *IB:* 29. *BTEC NC:* DM. *BTEC ND:* DDM.

PR34 BA Film & TV and Spanish
Duration: 3FT Hon
Entry Requirements: *GCE:* 260. *IB:* 29. *BTEC NC:* DM. *BTEC ND:* DDM.

TP13 BA Mandarin Chinese and Film and TV
Duration: 3FT Hon
Entry Requirements: *GCE:* 260. *IB:* 29. *BTEC NC:* DM. *BTEC ND:* DDM.

O66 OXFORD BROOKES UNIVERSITY
ADMISSIONS OFFICE
HEADINGTON CAMPUS
GIPSY LANE
OXFORD OX3 0BP
t: 01865 483040 f: 01865 483983
e: admissions@brookes.ac.uk
// www.brookes.ac.uk

QP33 BA English/Film Studies
Duration: 3FT Hon
Entry Requirements: *GCE:* BBB.

P303 BA Film Studies
Duration: 3FT Hon
Entry Requirements: *GCE:* BBC.

NP23 BA/BSc Business Management/Film Studies
Duration: 3FT Hon
Entry Requirements: *GCE:* BBB.

PP39 BA/BSc Communications, Media and Culture/Film Studies
Duration: 3FT Hon
Entry Requirements: *GCE:* BBC.

WP43 BA/BSc Drama/Film Studies
Duration: 3FT Hon
Entry Requirements: *GCE:* BBC.

QP9H BA/BSc English Language and Communication/Film Studies
Duration: 3FT Hon
Entry Requirements: Contact the institution for details.

P3R4 BA/BSc Film Studies with Spanish (Minor)
Duration: 4SW Hon
Entry Requirements: *GCE:* BBC. *IB:* 31.

PV31 BA/BSc Film Studies/History
Duration: 3FT Hon
Entry Requirements: *GCE:* BBC.

PV33 BA/BSc Film Studies/History of Art
Duration: 3FT Hon
Entry Requirements: *GCE:* BBC.

PW33 BA/BSc Film Studies/Music
Duration: 3FT Hon
Entry Requirements: *GCE:* BCC.

PV35 BA/BSc Film Studies/Philosophy
Duration: 3FT Hon
Entry Requirements: *GCE:* BBC.

W1P3 BA/BSc Fine Art/Film Studies
Duration: 3FT Hon
Entry Requirements: Contact the institution for details.

TP23 BA/BSc Japanese Studies/Film Studies
Duration: 4SW Hon
Entry Requirements: *GCE:* BBB.

P80 UNIVERSITY OF PORTSMOUTH
ACADEMIC REGISTRY
UNIVERSITY HOUSE
WINSTON CHURCHILL AVENUE
PORTSMOUTH PO1 2UP
t: 023 9284 8484 f: 023 9284 3082
e: admissions@port.ac.uk
// www.port.ac.uk

PW38 BA Film Studies and Creative Writing
Duration: 3FT Hon
Entry Requirements: *GCE:* 240-300. *IB:* 26. *BTEC NC:* DD. *BTEC ND:* DMM.

P391 BA Film and Television Studies
Duration: 3FT Hon
Entry Requirements: *GCE:* 240-300. *IB:* 25. *BTEC NC:* DD. *BTEC ND:* DMM.

P301 BSc Digital Media
Duration: 3FT/4SW Hon
Entry Requirements: *GCE:* 240-300. *IB:* 28. *BTEC NC:* DD. *BTEC ND:* DMM.

P30C BSc Television and Broadcasting
Duration: 3FT/4SW Hon
Entry Requirements: *GCE:* 240-300. *IB:* 28. *BTEC NC:* DD. *BTEC ND:* DMM.

Q50 QUEEN MARY, UNIVERSITY OF LONDON
QUEEN MARY, UNIVERSITY OF LONDON
MILE END ROAD
LONDON E1 4NS
t: 020 7882 5555 f: 020 7882 5500
e: admissions@qmul.ac.uk
// www.qmul.ac.uk

QP23 BA Comparative Literature and Film Studies
Duration: 3FT Hon
Entry Requirements: *GCE:* 340. *IB:* 32. *BTEC NC:* DD. *BTEC ND:* DDM.

P303 BA Film Studies
Duration: 3FT Hon
Entry Requirements: *GCE:* 340. *IB:* 32. *BTEC NC:* DD. *BTEC ND:* DDM.

R48 ROEHAMPTON UNIVERSITY
ERASMUS HOUSE
ROEHAMPTON LANE
LONDON SW15 5PU
t: 020 8392 3232 f: 020 8392 3470
e: enquiries@roehampton.ac.uk
// www.roehampton.ac.uk

PW38 BA Film and Creative Writing
Duration: 3FT Hon
Entry Requirements: *GCE:* 300-340. *IB:* 26. *BTEC ND:* DDM.
OCR NED: D2 Interview required.

PWH4 BA Film and Drama, Theatre & Performance Studies
Duration: 3FT Hon
Entry Requirements: *Foundation:* Distinction. *GCE:* 280-340. *IB:* 25. *BTEC ND:* DMM. *OCR NED:* M2 Interview required.

QP3H BA Film and English Literature
Duration: 3FT Hon
Entry Requirements: *GCE:* 300-340. *IB:* 26. *BTEC ND:* DDM.
OCR NED: D2 Interview required.

RP43 BA Film and Spanish
Duration: 4FT Hon
Entry Requirements: *Foundation:* Distinction. *GCE:* 280-340. *IB:* 25. *BTEC ND:* DMM. *OCR NED:* M2 Interview required.

WP63 BA Photography and Film
Duration: 3FT Hon
Entry Requirements: *Foundation:* Distinction. *GCE:* 280-340. *IB:* 25. *BTEC ND:* DMM. *OCR NED:* M2 Interview required.

PR39 BA/BSc Film and Modern Languages
Duration: 4FT Hon
Entry Requirements: *Foundation:* Distinction. *GCE:* 280-340. *IB:* 25. *BTEC ND:* DMM. *OCR NED:* M2 Interview required.

PP53 BA/BSc Journalism & News Media and Film
Duration: 3FT Hon
Entry Requirements: *GCE:* 300-340. *IB:* 26. *BTEC ND:* DDM. *OCR NED:* D2 Interview required.

P391 BA/BSc Media & Culture and Film
Duration: 3FT Hon
Entry Requirements: *Foundation:* Distinction. *GCE:* 280-340. *IB:* 25. *BTEC ND:* DMM. *OCR NED:* M2 Interview required.

R72 ROYAL HOLLOWAY, UNIVERSITY OF LONDON
ROYAL HOLLOWAY, UNIVERSITY OF LONDON
EGHAM
SURREY TW20 0EX
t: 01784 434455 f: 01784 473662
e: Admissions@rhul.ac.uk
// www.rhul.ac.uk

Q2P3 BA Comparative Literature & Culture with Film Studies
Duration: 3FT Hon
Entry Requirements: *GCE:* ABB-BBB. *SQAH:* AAABB-BBBBB. *SQAAH:* ABB-BBB. *IB:* 34. *BTEC ND:* DDM.

S03 THE UNIVERSITY OF SALFORD
SALFORD M5 4WT
t: 0161 295 4545 f: 0161 295 4646
e: ug-admissions@salford.ac.uk
// www.salford.ac.uk

QP33 BA English and Film Studies
Duration: 3FT Hon
Entry Requirements: *GCE:* 280. *IB:* 31.

P303 BA Film Studies
Duration: 3FT Hon
Entry Requirements: *GCE:* 280. *IB:* 31. *BTEC ND:* DMM. *OCR NED:* M2

S21 SHEFFIELD HALLAM UNIVERSITY
CITY CAMPUS
HOWARD STREET
SHEFFIELD S1 1WB
t: 0114 225 5555 f: 0114 225 2167
e: admissions@shu.ac.uk
// www.shu.ac.uk

QP33 BA English and Screen Studies
Duration: 3FT Hon
Entry Requirements: *GCE:* 240.

P303 BA Screen Studies
Duration: 3FT Hon
Entry Requirements: *GCE:* 240.

W8P3 BA Scriptwriting with Screen Studies
Duration: 3FT Hon
Entry Requirements: *GCE:* 240.

S27 UNIVERSITY OF SOUTHAMPTON
HIGHFIELD
SOUTHAMPTON SO17 1BJ
t: 023 8059 4732 f: 023 8059 3037
e: admissions@soton.ac.uk
// www.southampton.ac.uk

P303 BA Film
Duration: 3FT Hon
Entry Requirements: *GCE:* AAB. *IB:* 34.

S30 SOUTHAMPTON SOLENT UNIVERSITY
EAST PARK TERRACE
SOUTHAMPTON
HAMPSHIRE SO14 0RT
t: +44 (0) 23 8031 9039 f: + 44 (0)23 8022 2259
e: admissions@solent.ac.uk or ask@solent.ac.uk
// www.solent.ac.uk/

QP3J BA English and Film
Duration: 4SW Hon
Entry Requirements: *Foundation:* Distinction. *GCE:* 240. *SQAAH:* AA-CCD. *IB:* 24. *BTEC NC:* DD. *BTEC ND:* MMM. *OCR ND:* D *OCR NED:* M3

P901 BA Film and Television (Top-Up)
Duration: 1FT Hon
Entry Requirements: Interview required. HND required.

P303 BA Film and Television Studies
Duration: 3FT Hon
Entry Requirements: *Foundation:* Distinction. *GCE:* 240. *SQAAH:* AA-CCD. *IB:* 24. *BTEC NC:* DD. *BTEC ND:* MMM. *OCR ND:* D *OCR NED:* M3

P301 BA Media Culture and Production
Duration: 3FT Hon
Entry Requirements: *Foundation:* Distinction. *GCE:* 240. *SQAAH:* AA-CCD. *IB:* 24. *BTEC NC:* DD. *BTEC ND:* MMM. *OCR ND:* D *OCR NED:* M3

PP34 BA Television and Video Production with IFY
Duration: 4FT Hon
Entry Requirements: Contact the institution for details.

S36 UNIVERSITY OF ST ANDREWS
ST KATHARINE'S WEST
16 THE SCORES
ST ANDREWS
FIFE KY16 9AX
t: 01334 462150 f: 01334 463330
e: admissions@st-andrews.ac.uk
// www.st-andrews.ac.uk

VP13 MA Ancient History-Film Studies
Duration: 4FT Hon
Entry Requirements: *GCE:* AAB. *SQAH:* AABB. *IB:* 35.

TPP3 MA Arabic and Film Studies with Integrated Year Abroad
Duration: 5FT Hon
Entry Requirements: *GCE:* AAB. *SQAH:* AABB. *IB:* 35.

TP63 MA Arabic-Film Studies
Duration: 4FT Hon
Entry Requirements: *GCE:* AAB. *SQAH:* AABB. *IB:* 35.

VP33 MA Art History-Film Studies
Duration: 4FT Hon
Entry Requirements: *GCE:* AAB. *SQAH:* AABB. *IB:* 35.

VP63 MA Biblical Studies-Film Studies
Duration: 4FT Hon
Entry Requirements: *GCE:* AAA. *SQAH:* AAAB. *IB:* 36.

QP83 MA Classical Studies-Film Studies
Duration: 4FT Hon
Entry Requirements: *GCE:* AAB. *SQAH:* AABB. *IB:* 35.

LP13 MA Economics-Film Studies
Duration: 4FT Hon
Entry Requirements: *GCE:* AAA. *SQAH:* AAAB. *IB:* 38.

PQ33 MA English-Film Studies
Duration: 4FT Hon
Entry Requirements: *GCE:* AAA. *SQAH:* AAAB. *IB:* 36.

PR31 MA Film Studies-French
Duration: 4FT Hon
Entry Requirements: *GCE:* AAB. *SQAH:* AABB. *IB:* 35.

PR3C MA Film Studies-French (with Integrated Year Abroad)
Duration: 5FT Hon
Entry Requirements: *GCE:* AAB. *SQAH:* AABB. *IB:* 35.

LP73 MA Film Studies-Geography
Duration: 4FT Hon
Entry Requirements: *GCE:* AAA. *SQAH:* AAAB. *IB:* 36.

PR32 MA Film Studies-German
Duration: 4FT Hon
Entry Requirements: *GCE:* AAB. *SQAH:* AABB. *IB:* 35.

PR3F MA Film Studies-German (with Integrated Year Abroad)
Duration: 5FT Hon
Entry Requirements: *GCE:* AAB. *SQAH:* AABB. *IB:* 35.

LP23 MA Film Studies-International Relations
Duration: 4FT Hon
Entry Requirements: *GCE:* AAA. *SQAH:* AAAA. *IB:* 38.

PR33 MA Film Studies-Italian
Duration: 4FT Hon
Entry Requirements: *GCE:* AAB. *SQAH:* AABB. *IB:* 35.

PR3H MA Film Studies-Italian (with Integrated Year Abroad)
Duration: 5FT Hon
Entry Requirements: *GCE:* AAB. *SQAH:* AABB. *IB:* 35.

PV31 MA Film Studies-Modern History
Duration: 4FT Hon
Entry Requirements: *GCE:* AAA. *SQAH:* AABB. *IB:* 36.

PV35 MA Film Studies-Philosophy
Duration: 4FT Hon
Entry Requirements: *GCE:* AAB. *SQAH:* AABB. *IB:* 35.

CP83 MA Film Studies-Psychology
Duration: 4FT Hon
Entry Requirements: *GCE:* AAA. *SQAH:* AAAB. *IB:* 36.

PR37 MA Film Studies-Russian
Duration: 4FT Hon
Entry Requirements: *GCE:* AAB. *SQAH:* AABB. *IB:* 35.

PRH7 MA Film Studies-Russian (with Integrated Year Abroad)
Duration: 5FT Hon
Entry Requirements: *GCE:* AAB. *SQAH:* AABB. *IB:* 35.

PV32 MA Film Studies-Scottish History
Duration: 4FT Hon
Entry Requirements: *GCE:* AAA. *SQAH:* AABB. *IB:* 36.

PL36 MA Film Studies-Social Anthropology
Duration: 4FT Hon
Entry Requirements: *GCE:* AAB. *SQAH:* AABB. *IB:* 35.

PR34 MA Film Studies-Spanish
Duration: 4FT Hon
Entry Requirements: *GCE:* AAB. *SQAH:* AABB. *IB:* 35.

PR3K MA Film Studies-Spanish (with Integrated Year Abroad)
Duration: 5FT Hon
Entry Requirements: *GCE:* AAB. *SQAH:* AABB. *IB:* 35.

PV36 MA Film Studies-Theological Studies
Duration: 4FT Hon
Entry Requirements: *GCE:* AAA. *SQAH:* AAAB. *IB:* 36.

C8P3 MA Psychology with Film Studies
Duration: 4FT Hon
Entry Requirements: *GCE:* AAA. *SQAH:* AAAB. *IB:* 36.

QP23 MA Hons Comparative Literature and Film Studies
Duration: 4FT Hon
Entry Requirements: *GCE:* AAB. *SQAH:* AABB. *IB:* 35.

S43 SOUTH ESSEX COLLEGE OF FURTHER & HIGHER EDUCATION (PARTNER OF THE UNIVERSITY OF ESSEX)
LUKER ROAD
SOUTHEND-ON-SEA
ESSEX SS1 1ND
t: 0845 52 12345 f: 01702 432320
e: Admissions@southessex.ac.uk
// www.southessex.ac.uk

P320 BA Television Production and Screen Media
Duration: 3FT Hon
Entry Requirements: *GCE:* 160. *IB:* 24. Interview required.

S64 ST MARY'S UNIVERSITY COLLEGE, TWICKENHAM
WALDEGRAVE ROAD
STRAWBERRY HILL
MIDDLESEX TW1 4SX
t: 020 8240 4029 f: 020 8240 2361
e: admit@smuc.ac.uk
// www.smuc.ac.uk

XP93 BA Education & Social Science and Film & Popular Culture
Duration: 3FT Hon
Entry Requirements: *GCE:* 240. *SQAH:* BBBC. *IB:* 28. *BTEC NC:* DM. *BTEC ND:* MMM. *OCR ND:* D *OCR NED:* M3 Interview required.

QP33 BA English and Film & Popular Culture
Duration: 3FT Hon
Entry Requirements: *GCE:* 240. *SQAH:* BBBC. *IB:* 28. *BTEC NC:* DM. *BTEC ND:* MMM. *OCR ND:* D *OCR NED:* M3 Interview required.

P303 BA Film & Popular Culture
Duration: 3FT Hon
Entry Requirements: *GCE:* 240. *SQAH:* BBBC. *IB:* 28. *BTEC NC:* DM. *BTEC ND:* MMM. *OCR ND:* D *OCR NED:* M3 Interview required.

PM32 BA Film & Popular Culture and Business Law
Duration: 3FT Hon
Entry Requirements: *GCE:* 240. *SQAH:* BBBC. *IB:* 28. *BTEC NC:* DM. *BTEC ND:* MMM. *OCR ND:* D *OCR NED:* M3 Interview required.

PW3V BA Film & Popular Culture and Creative & Professional Writing
Duration: 3FT Hon
Entry Requirements: *GCE:* 240. *SQAH:* BBBC. *IB:* 28. *BTEC NC:* DM. *BTEC ND:* MMM. *OCR ND:* D *OCR NED:* M3 Interview required.

PQ3M BA Film & Popular Culture and Irish Studies
Duration: 3FT Hon
Entry Requirements: *GCE:* 240. *SQAH:* BBBC. *IB:* 28. *BTEC NC:* DM. *BTEC ND:* MMM. *OCR ND:* D *OCR NED:* M3 Interview required.

PW3P BA Film & Popular Culture and Media Arts
Duration: 3FT Hon
Entry Requirements: *GCE:* 240. *SQAH:* BBBC. *IB:* 28. *BTEC NC:* DM. *BTEC ND:* MMM. *OCR ND:* D *OCR NED:* M3 Interview required.

PV35 BA Film & Popular Culture and Philosophy
Duration: 3FT Hon
Entry Requirements: *GCE:* 240. *SQAH:* BBBC. *IB:* 28. *BTEC NC:* DM. *BTEC ND:* MMM. *OCR ND:* D *OCR NED:* M3 Interview required.

PL33 BA Film & Popular Culture and Sociology
Duration: 3FT Hon
Entry Requirements: *GCE:* 240. *SQAH:* BBBC. *IB:* 28. *BTEC NC:* DM. *BTEC ND:* MMM. *OCR ND:* D *OCR NED:* M3 Interview required.

PN3V BA Film & Popular Culture and Tourism
Duration: 3FT Hon
Entry Requirements: *GCE:* 240. *SQAH:* BBBC. *IB:* 28. *BTEC NC:* DM. *BTEC ND:* MMM. *OCR ND:* D *OCR NED:* M3 Interview required.

CP83 BA/BSc Film & Popular Culture and Psychology
Duration: 3FT Hon
Entry Requirements: *GCE:* 240. *SQAH:* BBBC. *IB:* 28. *BTEC NC:* DM. *BTEC ND:* MMM. *OCR ND:* D *OCR NED:* M3 Interview required.

FP83 BA/BSc Geography and Film & Popular Culture
Duration: 3FT Hon
Entry Requirements: *GCE:* 240. *SQAH:* BBBC. *IB:* 28. *BTEC NC:* DM. *BTEC ND:* MMM. *OCR ND:* D *OCR NED:* M3 Interview required.

S72 STAFFORDSHIRE UNIVERSITY
COLLEGE ROAD
STOKE ON TRENT ST4 2DE
t: 01782 292753 f: 01782 292740
e: admissions@staffs.ac.uk
// www.staffs.ac.uk

LP3H BA Ethics and Film Studies
Duration: 3FT Hon
Entry Requirements: *GCE:* 180-220. *IB:* 24.

P303 BA Film Studies
Duration: 3FT Hon
Entry Requirements: *GCE:* 180-220. *IB:* 24.

PV32 BA Film Studies and International History
Duration: 3FT Hon
Entry Requirements: *GCE:* 180-220. *IB:* 24.

PV31 BA Film Studies and Modern History
Duration: 3FT Hon
Entry Requirements: *GCE:* 180-220. *IB:* 24.

LP23 BA International Relations and Film Studies
Duration: 3FT Hon
Entry Requirements: *GCE:* 180-220. *IB:* 24.

QP23 BA Modern Literature and Film
Duration: 3FT Hon
Entry Requirements: *GCE:* 180-220. *IB:* 24.

P301 BSc Television Production Technology
Duration: 3FT/4SW Hon
Entry Requirements: Contact the institution for details.

S75 THE UNIVERSITY OF STIRLING
STIRLING FK9 4LA
t: 01786 467044 f: 01786 466800
e: admissions@stir.ac.uk
// www.stir.ac.uk

P390 BA Global Cinema
Duration: 4FT Hon
Entry Requirements: *GCE:* BBC. *SQAH:* BBBB. *SQAAH:* AAA-CCC.
IB: 32. *BTEC ND:* DDM.

S84 UNIVERSITY OF SUNDERLAND
STUDENT HELPLINE
THE STUDENT GATEWAY
CHESTER ROAD
SUNDERLAND SR1 3SD
t: 0191 515 3000 f: 0191 515 3805
e: student.helpline@sunderland.ac.uk
// www.sunderland.ac.uk

QP3H BA English and Film
Duration: 3FT Hon
Entry Requirements: *GCE:* 260-360. *BTEC NC:* DM. *BTEC ND:* MMM. *OCR ND:* D *OCR NED:* M3

P301 BA Television Studies
Duration: 3FT Hon
Entry Requirements: *GCE:* 260-360. *IB:* 30. *BTEC ND:* DMM.

P302 FdA Community Radio
Duration: 2FT Fdg
Entry Requirements: *GCE:* 80-360. *IB:* 22. Interview required.

S90 UNIVERSITY OF SUSSEX
UNDERGRADUATE ADMISSIONS
SUSSEX HOUSE
UNIVERSITY OF SUSSEX
BRIGHTON BN1 9RH
t: 01273 678416 f: 01273 678545
e: ug.applicants@sussex.ac.uk
// www.sussex.ac.uk

VP33 BA Art History and Film Studies
Duration: 3FT Hon
Entry Requirements: *GCE:* ABB. *SQAH:* AABBB. *IB:* 34. *BTEC NC:* DM. *BTEC ND:* DDM. *OCR NED:* D2

WP43 BA Drama Studies and Film Studies
Duration: 3FT Hon
Entry Requirements: *GCE:* AAB-ABB. *SQAH:* AAABB-AABBB. *BTEC NC:* DM. *BTEC ND:* DDM. *OCR ND:* M1 *OCR NED:* D2

QP3H BA English and Film Studies
Duration: 3FT Hon
Entry Requirements: *GCE:* AAA-AAB. *SQAH:* AAAAA-AAABB. *SQAAH:* AAA-AAB. *IB:* 36. *BTEC NC:* DD. *BTEC ND:* DDD. *OCR ND:* D *OCR NED:* D2

PRJ9 BA Film Studies and a Language (French/Italian/Spanish)
Duration: 4FT Hon
Entry Requirements: *GCE:* AAB-ABB. *SQAH:* AAABB-AABBB. *IB:* 34. *BTEC NC:* DM. *BTEC ND:* DDM. *OCR ND:* M1 *OCR NED:* D2

VP13 BA History and Film Studies
Duration: 3FT Hon
Entry Requirements: *GCE:* AAB. *SQAH:* AAABB. *IB:* 36. *BTEC NC:* DM. *BTEC ND:* DDD. *OCR ND:* D *OCR NED:* D1

S93 SWANSEA UNIVERSITY
SINGLETON PARK
SWANSEA SA2 8PP
t: 01792 295111 f: 01792 295110
e: admissions@swansea.ac.uk
// www.swansea.ac.uk

PR3C BA Screen Studies and French
Duration: 4FT Hon
Entry Requirements: *GCE:* BBB. *IB:* 32. *BTEC ND:* DDM.

PR3F BA Screen Studies and German
Duration: 4FT Hon
Entry Requirements: *GCE:* BBB. *IB:* 32. *BTEC ND:* DDM.

PR3H BA Screen Studies and Italian
Duration: 4FT Hon
Entry Requirements: *GCE:* BBB. *IB:* 32. *BTEC ND:* DDM.

PR3K BA Screen Studies and Spanish
Duration: 4FT Hon
Entry Requirements: *GCE:* BBB. *IB:* 32. *BTEC ND:* DDM.

U20 UNIVERSITY OF ULSTER
COLERAINE
CO. LONDONDERRY
NORTHERN IRELAND BT52 1SA
t: 028 7032 4221 f: 028 7032 4908
e: online@ulster.ac.uk
// www.ulster.ac.uk

QP33 BA English and Film Studies
Duration: 3FT Hon
Entry Requirements: *GCE:* BCC. *IB:* 24. *BTEC NC:* DM. *BTEC ND:* DMM.

Q3P3 BA English with Film Studies
Duration: 3FT Hon
Entry Requirements: *GCE:* BCC. *IB:* 24. *BTEC NC:* DM. *BTEC ND:* DMM.

RP93 BA European Studies and Film Studies
Duration: 3FT Hon
Entry Requirements: *GCE:* CCC. *IB:* 24. *BTEC NC:* MM. *BTEC ND:* MMM. Interview required.

R9P3 BA European Studies with Film Studies
Duration: 3FT Hon
Entry Requirements: *GCE:* CCC. *IB:* 24. *BTEC NC:* MM. *BTEC ND:* MMM. Interview required.

PR31 BA Film Studies and French
Duration: 3FT Hon
Entry Requirements: *GCE:* CCC. *IB:* 24. *BTEC NC:* MM. *BTEC ND:* MMM. Interview required.

PF38 BA Film Studies and Geography
Duration: 3FT Hon
Entry Requirements: *GCE:* BCC. *IB:* 24. *BTEC NC:* DM. *BTEC ND:* DMM.

PR32 BA Film Studies and German
Duration: 3FT Hon
Entry Requirements: *GCE:* CCC. *IB:* 24. *BTEC NC:* MM. *BTEC ND:* MMM. Interview required.

PV31 BA Film Studies and History
Duration: 3FT Hon
Entry Requirements: *GCE:* BCC. *IB:* 24. *BTEC NC:* DM. *BTEC ND:* DMM.

PQ35 BA Film Studies and Irish
Duration: 3FT Hon
Entry Requirements: *GCE:* BCC. *IB:* 24. *BTEC NC:* DM. *BTEC ND:* DMM.

PR34 BA Film Studies and Spanish
Duration: 3FT Hon
Entry Requirements: *GCE:* CCC. *IB:* 24. *BTEC NC:* MM. *BTEC ND:* MMM. Interview required.

P3QH BA Film Studies with English
Duration: 3FT Hon
Entry Requirements: *GCE:* BCC. *IB:* 24. *BTEC NC:* DM. *BTEC ND:* DMM.

P3R8 BA Film Studies with European Studies
Duration: 3FT Hon
Entry Requirements: *GCE:* BCC. *IB:* 24. *BTEC NC:* DM. *BTEC ND:* DMM.

P3RC BA Film Studies with French
Duration: 3FT Hon
Entry Requirements: *GCE:* BCC. *IB:* 24. *BTEC NC:* DM. *BTEC ND:* DMM.

P3RF BA Film Studies with German
Duration: 3FT Hon
Entry Requirements: *GCE:* BCC. *IB:* 24. *BTEC NC:* DM. *BTEC ND:* DMM.

P3VC BA Film Studies with History
Duration: 3FT Hon
Entry Requirements: *GCE:* BCC. *IB:* 24. *BTEC NC:* DM. *BTEC ND:* DMM.

P3L9 BA Film Studies with International Development
Duration: 3FT Hon
Entry Requirements: *GCE:* BCC. *IB:* 24. *BTEC NC:* DM. *BTEC ND:* DMM.

P3QM BA Film Studies with Irish
Duration: 3FT Hon
Entry Requirements: *GCE:* BCC. *IB:* 24. *BTEC NC:* DM. *BTEC ND:* DMM.

P3W6 BA Film Studies with Photo-Imaging
Duration: 3FT Hon
Entry Requirements: *GCE:* BCC. *IB:* 24. *BTEC NC:* DM. *BTEC ND:* DMM.

P3RK BA Film Studies with Spanish
Duration: 3FT Hon
Entry Requirements: *GCE:* BCC. *IB:* 24. *BTEC NC:* DM. *BTEC ND:* DMM.

R1P3 BA French with Film Studies
Duration: 4FT Hon
Entry Requirements: *GCE:* CCC. *IB:* 24. *BTEC NC:* MM. *BTEC ND:* MMM. Interview required.

R2P3 BA German with Film Studies
Duration: 4FT Hon
Entry Requirements: *GCE:* CCC. *IB:* 24. *BTEC NC:* MM. *BTEC ND:* MMM. Interview required.

V1P3 BA History with Film Studies
Duration: 3FT Hon
Entry Requirements: *GCE:* BCC. *IB:* 24. *BTEC NC:* DM. *BTEC ND:* DMM.

Q5P3 BA Irish with Film Studies
Duration: 3FT Hon
Entry Requirements: *GCE:* BCD. *IB:* 24. Interview required.

P5P3 BA Journalism with Film Studies
Duration: 3FT Hon
Entry Requirements: *GCE:* BCC. *IB:* 24. *BTEC NC:* DM. *BTEC ND:* DMM.

R4P3 BA Spanish with Film Studies
Duration: 4SW Hon
Entry Requirements: *GCE:* CCC. *IB:* 24. *BTEC NC:* MM. *BTEC ND:* MMM. Interview required.

U65 UNIVERSITY OF THE ARTS LONDON
272 HIGH HOLBORN
LONDON WC1V 7EY
t: 020 7514 6000x6197 f: 020 7514 6198
e: c.anderson@arts.ac.uk
// www.arts.ac.uk

P301 FdA Media Practice
Duration: 2FT Fdg
Entry Requirements: *GCE:* 40. *IB:* 28. Foundation Course required. Interview required. Portfolio required.

W05 THE UNIVERSITY OF WEST LONDON
WALPOLE HOUSE
BOND STREET
EALING
LONDON W5 5AA
t: 0800 036 8888 f: 020 8566 1353
e: learning.advice@uwl.ac.uk
// www.uwl.ac.uk

P303 BA (Hons) Film
Duration: 3FT Hon
Entry Requirements: *GCE:* 200. *IB:* 28. Interview required.

W75 UNIVERSITY OF WOLVERHAMPTON
ADMISSIONS UNIT
MX207, CAMP STREET
WOLVERHAMPTON
WEST MIDLANDS WV1 1AD
t: 01902 321000 f: 01902 321896
e: admissions@wlv.ac.uk
// www.wlv.ac.uk

WP83 BA Creative & Professional Writing and Film Studies
Duration: 3FT Hon
Entry Requirements: *GCE:* 160-220.

WP4H BA Drama and Film Studies
Duration: 3FT Hon CRB Check: Required
Entry Requirements: *GCE:* 180. Interview required.

WP6H BA Film Production and Studies
Duration: 3FT Hon
Entry Requirements: *GCE:* 240. Interview required. Portfolio required.

P303 BA Film Studies
Duration: 3FT Hon
Entry Requirements: *GCE:* 160-220. *IB:* 24.

PV35 BA Film Studies and Philosophy
Duration: 3FT Hon
Entry Requirements: Contact the institution for details.

W76 UNIVERSITY OF WINCHESTER
WINCHESTER
HANTS SO22 4NR
t: 01962 827234 f: 01962 827288
e: course.enquiries@winchester.ac.uk
// www.winchester.ac.uk

TP73 BA American Studies and Film Studies
Duration: 3FT Hon
Entry Requirements: *Foundation:* Distinction. *GCE:* 260-300. *IB:* 24. *BTEC NC:* DD. *BTEC ND:* DMM. *OCR ND:* D *OCR NED:* M2

NPC3 BA Business Management and Film Studies
Duration: 3FT Hon
Entry Requirements: *Foundation:* Distinction. *GCE:* 260-300. *IB:* 24. *BTEC NC:* DD. *BTEC ND:* DMM. *OCR ND:* D *OCR NED:* M2

LP5H BA Childhood,Youth & Community Studies and Film Studies
Duration: 3FT Hon
Entry Requirements: *GCE:* 260-300. *IB:* 24.

PW35 BA Choreography & Dance and Film Studies
Duration: 3FT Hon
Entry Requirements: *Foundation:* Distinction. *GCE:* 260-300. *IB:* 25. *BTEC NC:* DD. *BTEC ND:* DMM. *OCR ND:* D *OCR NED:* M2

PW3K BA Contemporary Performance and Film Studies
Duration: 3FT Hon
Entry Requirements: *Foundation:* Distinction. *GCE:* 260-300. *IB:* 24. *BTEC NC:* DD. *BTEC ND:* DMM. *OCR ND:* D *OCR NED:* M2

PWH8 BA Creative Writing and Film Studies
Duration: 3FT Hon
Entry Requirements: *Foundation:* Distinction. *GCE:* 260-300. *IB:* 25. *BTEC NC:* DD. *BTEC ND:* DMM. *OCR ND:* D *OCR NED:* M2

XP33 BA Education Studies (Early Childhood) and Film Studies
Duration: 3FT Hon
Entry Requirements: *Foundation:* Distinction. *GCE:* 260-300. *IB:* 24. *BTEC NC:* DD. *BTEC ND:* DMM. *OCR ND:* D *OCR NED:* M2

XPH3 BA Education Studies and Film Studies
Duration: 3FT Hon
Entry Requirements: *Foundation:* Distinction. *GCE:* 260-300. *IB:* 24. *BTEC NC:* DD. *BTEC ND:* DMM. *OCR ND:* D *OCR NED:* M2

QPH3 BA English and Film Studies
Duration: 3FT Hon
Entry Requirements: *Foundation:* Distinction. *GCE:* 260-300. *IB:* 25. *BTEC NC:* DD. *BTEC ND:* DMM. *OCR ND:* D *OCR NED:* M2

NP8H BA Event Management and Film Studies
Duration: 3FT Hon
Entry Requirements: *Foundation:* Distinction. *GCE:* 260-300. *IB:* 24. *BTEC NC:* DD. *BTEC ND:* DMM. *OCR ND:* D *OCR NED:* M2

PL53 BA Film & Cinema Technologies and Health, Community & Social Care Studies
Duration: 3FT Hon   CRB Check: Required
Entry Requirements: Contact the institution for details.

P303 BA Film Studies
Duration: 3FT Hon
Entry Requirements: *Foundation:* Distinction. *GCE:* 260-300. *IB:* 25. *BTEC NC:* DD. *BTEC ND:* DMM. *OCR ND:* D *OCR NED:* M2

PW36 BA Film Studies and Film & Cinema Technologies
Duration: 3FT Hon
Entry Requirements: *Foundation:* Distinction. *GCE:* 260-300. *IB:* 24. *BTEC NC:* DD. *BTEC ND:* DMM. *OCR ND:* D *OCR NED:* M2

PL5H BA Film Studies and Health, Community & Social Care Studies
Duration: 3FT Hon   CRB Check: Required
Entry Requirements: Contact the institution for details.

PV31 BA Film Studies and History
Duration: 3FT Hon
Entry Requirements: *Foundation:* Distinction. *GCE:* 260-300. *IB:* 24. *BTEC NC:* DD. *BTEC ND:* DMM. *OCR ND:* D *OCR NED:* M2

PP35 BA Film Studies and Journalism Studies
Duration: 3FT Hon
Entry Requirements: *Foundation:* Distinction. *GCE:* 260-300. *IB:* 24. *BTEC NC:* DD. *BTEC ND:* DMM. *OCR ND:* D *OCR NED:* M2

P392 BA Film Studies and Media Production
Duration: 3FT Hon
Entry Requirements: *Foundation:* Distinction. *GCE:* 260-300. *IB:* 24. *BTEC NC:* DD. *BTEC ND:* DMM. *OCR ND:* D *OCR NED:* M2

CPX3 BA Film Studies and Psychology
Duration: 3FT Hon
Entry Requirements: *Foundation:* Distinction. *GCE:* 260-300. *IB:* 25. *BTEC NC:* DD. *BTEC ND:* DMM. *OCR ND:* D *OCR NED:* M2

PLJ3 BA Film Studies and Sociology
Duration: 3FT Hon
Entry Requirements: *Foundation:* Distinction. *GCE:* 260-300. *IB:* 24. *BTEC NC:* DD. *BTEC ND:* DMM. *OCR ND:* D *OCR NED:* M2

PV36 BA Film Studies and Theology & Religious Studies
Duration: 3FT Hon
Entry Requirements: *Foundation:* Distinction. *GCE:* 260-300. *IB:* 25. *BTEC NC:* DD. *BTEC ND:* DMM. *OCR ND:* D *OCR NED:* M2

PW33 BA Film Studies and Vocal & Choral Studies
Duration: 3FT Hon
Entry Requirements: *Foundation:* Distinction. *GCE:* 260-300. *IB:* 24. *BTEC NC:* DD. *BTEC ND:* DMM. *OCR ND:* D *OCR NED:* M2

MP13 BA Law and Film Studies
Duration: 3FT Hon
Entry Requirements: *Foundation:* Distinction. *GCE:* 260-300. *IB:* 25. *BTEC NC:* DD. *BTEC ND:* DMM. *OCR ND:* D *OCR NED:* M2

LP23 BA Politics & Global Studies and Film Studies
Duration: 3FT Hon
Entry Requirements: *Foundation:* Distinction. *GCE:* 260-300. *IB:* 24. *BTEC NC:* DD. *BTEC ND:* MMM. *OCR ND:* D

W80 UNIVERSITY OF WORCESTER
HENWICK GROVE
WORCESTER WR2 6AJ
t: 01905 855111 f: 01905 855377
e: admissions@worc.ac.uk
// www.worcester.ac.uk

WP2H BA Creative Digital Media and Film Studies
Duration: 3FT Hon
Entry Requirements: *GCE:* 240-260. *IB:* 24. *OCR ND:* D Interview required. Portfolio required.

PW36 BA Digital Film Production and Film Studies
Duration: 3FT Hon
Entry Requirements: *GCE:* 240-260. *IB:* 24. *OCR ND:* D Interview required. Portfolio required.

WP4H BA Drama & Performance and Film Studies
Duration: 3FT Hon
Entry Requirements: *GCE:* 240-260. *IB:* 24. *BTEC NC:* DD. *BTEC ND:* MMM. *OCR ND:* D *OCR NED:* M3

QP3J BA English Language Studies and Film Studies
Duration: 3FT Hon
Entry Requirements: *GCE:* 240-260. *IB:* 24. *BTEC NC:* DD. *BTEC ND:* MMM. *OCR ND:* D *OCR NED:* M3

QP3H BA English Literary Studies and Film Studies
Duration: 3FT Hon
Entry Requirements: *GCE:* 240-260. *IB:* 24. *BTEC NC:* DD. *BTEC ND:* MMM. *OCR ND:* D *OCR NED:* M3

PW3F BA Film Studies and Graphic Design & Multimedia
Duration: 3FT Hon
Entry Requirements: *GCE:* 240-300. *IB:* 24. *BTEC NC:* DD. *BTEC ND:* MMM. *OCR ND:* D *OCR NED:* M3

PV31 BA Film Studies and History
Duration: 3FT Hon
Entry Requirements: *GCE:* 240-300. *IB:* 24. *BTEC NC:* DD. *BTEC ND:* MMM. *OCR ND:* D *OCR NED:* M3

P390 BA Film Studies and Media & Cultural Studies
Duration: 3FT Hon
Entry Requirements: *GCE:* 240-300. *IB:* 24. *BTEC NC:* DD. *BTEC ND:* MMM. *OCR ND:* D *OCR NED:* M3

PW38 BA Film Studies and Screen Writing
Duration: 3FT Hon
Entry Requirements: *GCE:* 240-300. *IB:* 24. *BTEC NC:* DD. *BTEC ND:* MMM. *OCR ND:* D *OCR NED:* M3

PL33 BA Film Studies and Sociology
Duration: 3FT Hon
Entry Requirements: *GCE:* 240-300. *IB:* 24. *BTEC NC:* DD. *BTEC ND:* MMM. *OCR ND:* D *OCR NED:* M3

Y75 YORK ST JOHN UNIVERSITY
LORD MAYOR'S WALK
YORK YO31 7EX
t: 01904 876598 f: 01904 876940/876921
e: admissions@yorksj.ac.uk
// w3.yorksj.ac.uk

TP7H BA American Studies and Film Studies
Duration: 3FT Hon
Entry Requirements: *GCE:* 200-240. *IB:* 24.

TPR3 BA American Studies and Film Studies (international only)
Duration: 4FT Hon
Entry Requirements: *GCE:* 200-240. *IB:* 24.

QP3H BA English Literature and Film Studies
Duration: 3FT Hon
Entry Requirements: *GCE:* 200-240. *IB:* 24.

MEDIA PRODUCTION

A40 ABERYSTWYTH UNIVERSITY
WELCOME CENTRE, ABERYSTWYTH UNIVERSITY
PENGLAIS CAMPUS
ABERYSTWYTH
CEREDIGION SY23 3FB
t: 01970 622021 f: 01970 627410
e: ug-admissions@aber.ac.uk
// www.aber.ac.uk

W620 BA Film & Television Studies
Duration: 3FT Hon
Entry Requirements: *GCE:* 300-320. *IB:* 32.

WW64 BA Film & Television Studies/Drama & Theatre Studies
Duration: 3FT Hon
Entry Requirements: *GCE:* 300-320. *IB:* 32.

WX63 BA Film & Television Studies/Education
Duration: 3FT Hon
Entry Requirements: *GCE:* 300-320. *IB:* 32.

QW36 BA Film & Television Studies/English Literature
Duration: 3FT Hon
Entry Requirements: *GCE:* 300-320. *IB:* 32.

WW16 BA Film & Television Studies/Fine Art
Duration: 3FT Hon
Entry Requirements: *GCE:* 300-320. *IB:* 32. Portfolio required.

RW16 BA French/Film & Television Studies (4 years)
Duration: 4FT Hon
Entry Requirements: *GCE:* 300-320. *IB:* 32.

QP53 BA Gwyddeleg: Iaith a Lln/Astudiaethau Ffilm a Theledu
Duration: 4FT Hon
Entry Requirements: *GCE:* 300-320. *IB:* 32.

VW26 BA Hanes Cymru ac Astudiaethau Ffilm a Theledu
Duration: 3FT Hon
Entry Requirements: *GCE:* 300-320. *IB:* 32.

VW16 BA History/Film & Television Studies
Duration: 3FT Hon
Entry Requirements: *GCE:* 300-320. *IB:* 32.

LW26 BA International Politics/Film & Television Studies
Duration: 3FT Hon
Entry Requirements: *GCE:* 300-320. *IB:* 32.

GW16 BA Mathematics/Film & Television Studies
Duration: 3FT Hon
Entry Requirements: *GCE:* 300-320. *IB:* 32.

WW46 BA Performance Studies/Film & Television Studies
Duration: 3FT Hon
Entry Requirements: *GCE:* 300-320. *IB:* 32.

LWF6 BA Politics/Film & Television Studies
Duration: 3FT Hon
Entry Requirements: *GCE:* 300-320. *IB:* 32.

WP43 BA Scenography & Theatre Design/Film & Television Studies
Duration: 3FT Hon
Entry Requirements: *GCE:* 300-320. *IB:* 32.

RW46 BA Spanish/Film & Television Studies (4 years)
Duration: 4FT Hon
Entry Requirements: *GCE:* 300-320. *IB:* 30.

VWF6 BA Welsh History/Film & Television Studies
Duration: 3FT Hon
Entry Requirements: *GCE:* 300-320. *IB:* 32.

A44 ACCRINGTON & ROSSENDALE COLLEGE
BROAD OAK ROAD,
ACCRINGTON,
LANCASHIRE, BB5 2AW.
t: 01254 389933 f: 01254 354001
e: info@accross.ac.uk
// www.accrosshighereducation.co.uk/

WP63 BA (Hons) Film and Digital Media
Duration: 3FT Hon
Entry Requirements: *BTEC ND:* MMM. Interview required.

A66 THE ARTS UNIVERSITY COLLEGE AT BOURNEMOUTH (FORMERLY ARTS INSTITUTE AT BOURNEMOUTH)
WALLISDOWN
POOLE
DORSET BH12 5HH
t: 01202 363228 f: 01202 537729
e: admissions@aucb.ac.uk
// www.aucb.ac.uk

P310 BA Digital Media Production
Duration: 3FT Hon
Entry Requirements: Contact the institution for details.

B20 BATH SPA UNIVERSITY
NEWTON PARK
NEWTON ST LOE
BATH BA2 9BN
t: 01225 875875 f: 01225 875444
e: enquiries@bathspa.ac.uk
// www.bathspa.ac.uk/clearing

WP93 BA Creative Media Practice
Duration: 3FT Hon
Entry Requirements: *GCE:* 220-300. *IB:* 24. Interview required. Portfolio required.

PW36 FdA Broadcast Media: Process and Production
Duration: 2FT Fdg
Entry Requirements: *GCE:* 160-200. *IB:* 24.

B22 UNIVERSITY OF BEDFORDSHIRE
PARK SQUARE
LUTON
BEDS LU1 3JU
t: 0844 8482234 f: 01582 489323
e: admissions@beds.ac.uk
// www.beds.ac.uk

P310 BA Media Production
Duration: 3FT Hon
Entry Requirements: *Foundation:* Pass. *GCE:* 200. *SQAH:* BCC. *SQAAH:* BCC. *IB:* 24. *BTEC NC:* MM. *BTEC ND:* MPP. *OCR ND:* M1 *OCR NED:* P1

PW36 BA Media Production (Moving Image)
Duration: 3FT Hon
Entry Requirements: *Foundation:* Pass. *GCE:* 200. *SQAH:* BCC.
SQAAH: BCC. *IB:* 24. *BTEC NC:* MM. *BTEC ND:* MPP. *OCR ND:*
M1 *OCR NED:* P1

PW3G BA Media Production (New Media)
Duration: 3FT Hon
Entry Requirements: *Foundation:* Pass. *GCE:* 200. *SQAH:* BCC.
SQAAH: BCC. *IB:* 24. *BTEC NC:* MM. *BTEC ND:* MPP. *OCR ND:*
M1 *OCR NED:* P1

P312 BA Media Production (Radio)
Duration: 3FT Hon
Entry Requirements: *Foundation:* Pass. *GCE:* 200. *SQAH:* BCC.
SQAAH: BCC. *IB:* 24. *BTEC NC:* MM. *BTEC ND:* MPP. *OCR ND:*
M1 *OCR NED:* P1

P314 FdA Media Production
Duration: 2FT Fdg
Entry Requirements: Contact the institution for details.

B25 BIRMINGHAM CITY UNIVERSITY
PERRY BARR
BIRMINGHAM B42 2SU
t: 0121 331 5595 f: 0121 331 7994
e: choices@bcu.ac.uk
// www.bcu.ac.uk

PN38 BA Media and Communication (Event and Exhibition Industries)
Duration: 3FT Hon
Entry Requirements: Contact the institution for details.

PJ39 BA Media and Communication (Music Industries)
Duration: 3FT Hon
Entry Requirements: *Foundation:* Pass. *GCE:* BBC. *SQAH:* ABBB.
SQAAH: BBC. *IB:* 30. *BTEC ND:* DMM. Interview required. Portfolio
required.

P9P3 BA Media and Communication (Radio)
Duration: 3FT Hon
Entry Requirements: *Foundation:* Pass. *GCE:* BBC. *SQAH:* ABBB.
SQAAH: BBC. *IB:* 30. *BTEC ND:* DMM. Interview required. Portfolio
required.

W614 BSc Film Technology and Special Effects
Duration: 3FT/4SW Hon
Entry Requirements: *GCE:* 280. Interview required.

WP63 BSc Film, Production and Technology
Duration: 3FT/4SW Hon
Entry Requirements: *GCE:* 300. *IB:* 30. *BTEC ND:* DMM.
Interview required.

P310 BSc Multimedia Technology
Duration: 3FT/4SW Hon
Entry Requirements: *GCE:* 280. *IB:* 30. *BTEC NC:* DM. *BTEC ND:*
MMP. Interview required.

B41 BLACKPOOL AND THE FYLDE COLLEGE AN ASSOCIATE COLLEGE OF LANCASTER UNIVERSITY
ASHFIELD ROAD
BISPHAM
BLACKPOOL
LANCS FY2 0HB
t: 01253 504346 f: 01253 504198
e: admissions@blackpool.ac.uk
// www.blackpool.ac.uk

P310 BA Hons Media Writing and Production (Top-Up)
Duration: 1FT Hon
Entry Requirements: Contact the institution for details.

WP83 FdA Media Writing with Production
Duration: 2FT Fdg
Entry Requirements: Contact the institution for details.

B44 UNIVERSITY OF BOLTON
DEANE ROAD
BOLTON BL3 5AB
t: 01204 903903 f: 01204 399074
e: enquiries@bolton.ac.uk
// www.bolton.ac.uk

P3C0 BA Media Production
Duration: 1FT Hon
Entry Requirements: Interview required. Portfolio required.

PWH8 BA Media, Writing & Production
Duration: 3FT Hon
Entry Requirements: *GCE:* 240. Interview required. Portfolio
required.

P310 FdA Media Production
Duration: 2FT Fdg
Entry Requirements: *GCE:* 120. Interview required. Portfolio
required.

B50 BOURNEMOUTH UNIVERSITY
TALBOT CAMPUS
FERN BARROW
POOLE
DORSET BH12 5BB
t: 01202 524111
// www.bournemouth.ac.uk

PW36 BA Film Production and Cinematography
Duration: 3FT Hon
Entry Requirements: *GCE:* 240. *IB:* 26. Interview required.

P31F BA Radio
Duration: 3FT Hon
Entry Requirements: Contact the institution for details.

P312 BA Radio Production (Top-Up)
Duration: 1FT Hon
Entry Requirements: Interview required. Portfolio required.

P314 FdA Commercial Video with Multimedia
Duration: 2FT Fdg
Entry Requirements: Contact the institution for details.

P391 FdA Digital Media Practice
Duration: 2FT Fdg
Entry Requirements: Contact the institution for details.

JP93 FdA Radio Production
Duration: 2FT Fdg
Entry Requirements: *GCE:* 80. *IB:* 24. Interview required.

B56 THE UNIVERSITY OF BRADFORD
RICHMOND ROAD
BRADFORD
WEST YORKSHIRE BD7 1DP
t: 0800 073 1225 f: 01274 235585
e: course-enquiries@bradford.ac.uk
// www.bradford.ac.uk

P311 BA Television Production
Duration: 3FT Hon
Entry Requirements: *GCE:* 240. *IB:* 24. Interview required.

B72 UNIVERSITY OF BRIGHTON
209 MITHRAS HOUSE
LEWES ROAD
BRIGHTON BN2 4AT
t: 01273 644644 f: 01273 642607
e: admissions@brighton.ac.uk
// www.brighton.ac.uk

P314 BA Broadcast Media (top-up)
Duration: 1FT Hon
Entry Requirements: Contact the Institution for details.

P310 FdA Broadcast Media
Duration: 2FT Fdg
Entry Requirements: *GCE:* 160. *IB:* 24.

P312 FdA Radio Production (at UCH)
Duration: 2FT Fdg
Entry Requirements: *GCE:* 160. *IB:* 24.

P311 FdA Television Production (at UCH)
Duration: 2FT Fdg
Entry Requirements: *GCE:* 160. *IB:* 24.

B77 BRISTOL, CITY OF BRISTOL COLLEGE
ASHLEY DOWN CENTRE
ASHLEY DOWN ROAD
BRISTOL BS7 9BU
t: 0117 312 5211 f: 0117 312 5050
e: admissions@cityofbristol.ac.uk
// www.cityofbristol.ac.uk

P310 FdA Digital Media Production
Duration: 2FT Fdg
Entry Requirements: *GCE:* 140.

B94 BUCKINGHAMSHIRE NEW UNIVERSITY
QUEEN ALEXANDRA ROAD
HIGH WYCOMBE
BUCKINGHAMSHIRE HP11 2JZ
t: 0800 0565 660 f: 01494 605 023
e: admissions@bucks.ac.uk
// bucks.ac.uk

PW36 BA Film and TV Production
Duration: 3FT Hon
Entry Requirements: *GCE:* 200-240. *IB:* 24. *BTEC NC:* DM. *BTEC ND:* MMM. *OCR ND:* M1 *OCR NED:* M3

P312 FdA Radio Production
Duration: 2FT Fdg
Entry Requirements: *GCE:* 100-140. *IB:* 24. *BTEC NC:* MP. *BTEC ND:* PPP. *OCR ND:* P2 *OCR NED:* P3 Interview required.

P311 FdA Television Production
Duration: 2FT Fdg
Entry Requirements: *GCE:* 100-140. *IB:* 24. *BTEC NC:* MP. *BTEC ND:* PPP. *OCR ND:* P2 *OCR NED:* P3 Interview required.

C10 CANTERBURY CHRIST CHURCH UNIVERSITY
NORTH HOLMES ROAD
CANTERBURY
KENT CT1 1QU
t: 01227 782900 f: 01227 782888
e: admissions@canterbury.ac.uk
// www.canterbury.ac.uk

P310 BA Film, Radio & Television Studies (Broadcasting)
Duration: 3FT Hon
Entry Requirements: *GCE:* 260. *IB:* 24.

P314 BA Film, Radio & Television Studies (Film)
Duration: 3FT Hon
Entry Requirements: *GCE:* 260. *IB:* 24.

P312 BA Film, Radio & Television Studies (Radio)
Duration: 3FT Hon
Entry Requirements: *GCE:* 260. *IB:* 24.

P311 BA Film, Radio & Television Studies (Television)
Duration: 3FT Hon
Entry Requirements: *GCE:* 260. *IB:* 24.

N1PH BSc Business Studies with Film, Radio & Television 'International Only'
Duration: 4FT FYr
Entry Requirements: Interview required.

C30 UNIVERSITY OF CENTRAL LANCASHIRE
PRESTON
LANCS PR1 2HE
t: 01772 201201 f: 01772 894954
e: uadmissions@uclan.ac.uk
// www.uclan.ac.uk

WP6J BA Film Production
Duration: 3FT Hon
Entry Requirements: *GCE:* 240-260. *IB:* 28. *BTEC NC:* DD. *BTEC ND:* MMM. *OCR ND:* D *OCR NED:* M3 Portfolio required.

PW3P BA Film Production & Film & Media
Duration: 3FT Hon
Entry Requirements: *GCE:* 260-300. *IB:* 28. *BTEC NC:* DM. *BTEC ND:* DMM. *OCR ND:* D *OCR NED:* M2

PW38 BA Film Production and Film & TV Screenwriting
Duration: 3FT Hon
Entry Requirements: *GCE:* 260-300. *IB:* 28. *BTEC NC:* DM. *BTEC ND:* DMM. *OCR ND:* D *OCR NED:* M2 Interview required.

PWH6 BA Film Production and Media Production & Technology
Duration: 3FT Hon
Entry Requirements: *GCE:* 260-300. *IB:* 28. *BTEC NC:* DM. *BTEC ND:* DMM. *OCR ND:* D *OCR NED:* M2

P311 BSc TV Production
Duration: 3FT Hon
Entry Requirements: *GCE:* 300. *SQAH:* AAAB. *IB:* 30. *BTEC NC:* DD. *BTEC ND:* DDM. *OCR ND:* D *OCR NED:* D2

C55 UNIVERSITY OF CHESTER
PARKGATE ROAD
CHESTER CH1 4BJ
t: 01244 511000 f: 01244 511300
e: enquiries@chester.ac.uk
// www.chester.ac.uk

NP5H BA Advertising and Commercial Music Production
Duration: 3FT Hon
Entry Requirements: *GCE:* 240-280. *SQAH:* BBBB. *IB:* 26. *BTEC NC:* DM. *BTEC ND:* MMM.

NP5J BA Advertising and Radio Production
Duration: 3FT Hon
Entry Requirements: *Foundation:* Pass. *GCE:* 260-300. *SQAH:* BBBB. *IB:* 28. *BTEC NC:* DM. *BTEC ND:* DMM.

NPMH BA Advertising and TV Production
Duration: 3FT Hon
Entry Requirements: *Foundation:* Pass. *GCE:* 260-300. *SQAH:* BBBB. *IB:* 28. *BTEC NC:* DM. *BTEC ND:* DMM.

NPC3 BA Business Management and Commercial Music Production
Duration: 3FT Hon
Entry Requirements: *Foundation:* Pass. *GCE:* 260-300. *SQAH:* BBBB. *IB:* 28. *BTEC NC:* DM. *BTEC ND:* DMM.

NPD3 BA Business Management and Radio Production
Duration: 3FT Hon
Entry Requirements: *Foundation:* Pass. *GCE:* 260-300. *SQAH:* BBBB. *IB:* 28. *BTEC NC:* DM. *BTEC ND:* DMM.

NPCH BA Business Management and TV Production
Duration: 3FT Hon
Entry Requirements: *Foundation:* Pass. *GCE:* 260-300. *SQAH:* BBBB. *IB:* 28. *BTEC NC:* DM. *BTEC ND:* DMM.

WP6J BA Digital Photography and Radio Production
Duration: 3FT Hon
Entry Requirements: *Foundation:* Pass. *GCE:* 260-300. *SQAH:* BBBB. *IB:* 28. *BTEC NC:* DM. *BTEC ND:* DMM.

WPP3 BA Digital Photography and TV Production
Duration: 3FT Hon
Entry Requirements: *Foundation:* Pass. *GCE:* 260-300. *SQAH:* BBBB. *IB:* 28. *BTEC NC:* DM. *BTEC ND:* DMM.

NPV3 BA Events Management and Radio Production
Duration: 3FT Hon
Entry Requirements: *Foundation:* Pass. *GCE:* 260-300. *SQAH:* BBBB. *IB:* 28. *BTEC NC:* DM. *BTEC ND:* DMM.

NPVH BA Events Management and TV Production
Duration: 3FT Hon
Entry Requirements: *Foundation:* Pass. *GCE:* 260-300. *SQAH:* BBBB. *IB:* 28. *BTEC NC:* DM. *BTEC ND:* DMM.

PPM3 BA Journalism and Commercial Music Production
Duration: 3FT Hon
Entry Requirements: *Foundation:* Pass. *GCE:* 260-300. *SQAH:* BBBB. *IB:* 28. *BTEC NC:* DM. *BTEC ND:* DMM.

PPN3 BA Journalism and Radio Production
Duration: 3FT Hon
Entry Requirements: *Foundation:* Pass. *GCE:* 260-300. *SQAH:* BBBB. *IB:* 28. *BTEC NC:* DM. *BTEC ND:* DMM.

PPMJ BA Journalism and TV Production
Duration: 3FT Hon
Entry Requirements: *Foundation:* Pass. *GCE:* 260-300. *SQAH:* BBBB. *IB:* 28. *BTEC NC:* DM. *BTEC ND:* DMM.

P314 BA Radio Production and Commercial Music Production
Duration: 3FT Hon
Entry Requirements: *Foundation:* Pass. *GCE:* 260-300. *SQAH:* BBBB. *IB:* 28. *BTEC NC:* DM. *BTEC ND:* DMM.

P317 BA TV Production and Commercial Music Production
Duration: 3FT Hon
Entry Requirements: *Foundation:* Pass. *GCE:* 260-300. *SQAH:* BBBB. *IB:* 28. *BTEC NC:* DM. *BTEC ND:* DMM.

P310 BA TV Production and Media Studies
Duration: 3FT Hon
Entry Requirements: *Foundation:* Pass. *GCE:* 260-300. *SQAH:* BBBB. *IB:* 28. *BTEC NC:* DM. *BTEC ND:* DMM.

P318 BA TV Production and Radio Production
Duration: 3FT Hon
Entry Requirements: *Foundation:* Pass. *GCE:* 260-300. *SQAH:* BBBB. *IB:* 28. *BTEC NC:* DM. *BTEC ND:* DMM.

C58 UNIVERSITY OF CHICHESTER
BISHOP OTTER CAMPUS
COLLEGE LANE
CHICHESTER
WEST SUSSEX PO19 6PE
t: 01243 816002 f: 01243 816161
e: admissions@chi.ac.uk
// www.chiuni.ac.uk

P3W3 BA Media Production with Music
Duration: 3FT Hon
Entry Requirements: Contact the institution for details.

C85 COVENTRY UNIVERSITY
THE STUDENT CENTRE
COVENTRY UNIVERSITY
1 GULSON RD
COVENTRY CV1 2JH
t: 024 7615 2222 f: 024 7615 2223
e: studentenquiries@coventry.ac.uk
// www.coventry.ac.uk

P310 BA Media Production
Duration: 3FT/4SW Hon
Entry Requirements: *GCE:* BCC. *SQAH:* BCCCC. *IB:* 27. *BTEC ND:* DMM. *OCR NED:* M2 Interview required. Portfolio required.

C92 CROYDON COLLEGE
COLLEGE ROAD
CROYDON CR9 1DX
t: 020 8760 5914 f: 020 8760 5880
e: info@croydon.ac.uk
// www.croydon.ac.uk

P313 BA Digital Film Production
Duration: 1FT Hon
Entry Requirements: Contact the institution for details.

PWJ4 BA Digital Film Production Design
Duration: 1FT Hon
Entry Requirements: Contact the institution for details.

PW34 FdA Digital Film Production Design
Duration: 2FT Fdg
Entry Requirements: Contact the institution for details.

C99 UNIVERSITY OF CUMBRIA
FUSEHILL STREET
CARLISLE
CUMBRIA CA1 2HH
t: 01228 616234 f: 01228 616235
// www.cumbria.ac.uk

P311 BA Film & Television Production
Duration: 3FT Hon
Entry Requirements: *Foundation:* Pass. *GCE:* 240. *SQAH:* BBC. *SQAAH:* CC. *IB:* 30. *BTEC NC:* DD. *BTEC ND:* MMM. *OCR ND:* D Interview required. Portfolio required.

P314 BA Film and Television Production (with Year 0)
Duration: 4FT Hon
Entry Requirements: *Foundation:* Pass. *GCE:* C-cccc. *SQAH:* CC. *SQAAH:* C. *IB:* 25. *BTEC NC:* MP. *BTEC ND:* PPP. Interview required. Portfolio required.

P3C0 BA Mass Communication (Top-up)
Duration: 1FT Hon
Entry Requirements: Contact the institution for details.

D26 DE MONTFORT UNIVERSITY
THE GATEWAY
LEICESTER LE1 9BH
t: 0116 255 1551 f: 0116 250 6204
e: enquiries@dmu.ac.uk
// www.dmu.ac.uk

P310 BSc Media Production
Duration: 3FT/4SW Hon
Entry Requirements: *IB:* 30. *BTEC ND:* DDM. *OCR NED:* D2

WP63 FdSc Digital Video and Broadcast Production
Duration: 2FT Fdg
Entry Requirements: *GCE:* 120. *IB:* 28.

D39 UNIVERSITY OF DERBY
KEDLESTON ROAD
DERBY DE22 1GB
t: 01332 591167 f: 01332 597724
e: askadmissions@derby.ac.uk
// www.derby.ac.uk

P310 BA Media Production
Duration: 3FT Hon
Entry Requirements: *Foundation:* Merit. *GCE:* 240. *IB:* 26. *BTEC NC:* DD. *BTEC ND:* MMM. *OCR ND:* D *OCR NED:* M3

LP9H BA/BSc Third World Development and Broadcast Media
Duration: 3FT Hon
Entry Requirements: *Foundation:* Distinction. *GCE:* 260-300. *IB:* 28. *BTEC ND:* DMM. *OCR NED:* M2

E14 UNIVERSITY OF EAST ANGLIA
NORWICH NR4 7TJ
t: 01603 591515 f: 01603 458596
e: admissions@uea.ac.uk
// www.uea.ac.uk

RP9H BA Honours Language and Film & Television
Duration: 4FT Hon   CRB Check: Required
Entry Requirements: *GCE:* ABB. *SQAAH:* ABB. *IB:* 32.

TP23 BA Japanese and Film & Television
Duration: 4FT Hon
Entry Requirements: Contact the institution for details.

E42 EDGE HILL UNIVERSITY
ORMSKIRK
LANCASHIRE L39 4QP
t: 01695 657000 f: 01695 584355
e: study@edgehill.ac.uk
// www.edgehill.ac.uk

P311 BA Television Production Management
Duration: 3FT Hon
Entry Requirements: *GCE:* 280. *IB:* 26. *BTEC NC:* DD. *BTEC ND:* DMM. *OCR ND:* D *OCR NED:* M2 Interview required. Portfolio required.

E81 EXETER COLLEGE
HELE ROAD
EXETER
DEVON EX4 4JS
t: 0845 111 6000
e: info@exe-coll.ac.uk
// www.exe-coll.ac.uk/he

P310 FdA Creative Digital Video
Duration: 2FT Fdg
Entry Requirements: *GCE:* 160.

P311 FdA Television Production
Duration: 2FT Fdg
Entry Requirements: *GCE:* 160.

F33 UNIVERSITY COLLEGE FALMOUTH
WOODLANE
FALMOUTH
CORNWALL TR11 4RH
t: 01326213730
e: admissions@falmouth.ac.uk
// www.falmouth.ac.uk

P312 FdA Radio Production
Duration: 2FT Fdg
Entry Requirements: *GCE:* 220. *IB:* 24. Interview required.

F66 FARNBOROUGH COLLEGE OF TECHNOLOGY
BOUNDARY ROAD
FARNBOROUGH
HAMPSHIRE GU14 6SB
t: 01252 407028 f: 01252 407041
e: admissions@farn-ct.ac.uk
// www.farn-ct.ac.uk

HP63 BA Media Production
Duration: 3FT Hon
Entry Requirements: *GCE:* 180-200. *BTEC NC:* MM. *BTEC ND:* MMM. *OCR ND:* M2 *OCR NED:* M3 Admissions Test required.

WP33 BA Media Production (Music)
Duration: 3FT Hon
Entry Requirements: *GCE:* 180-200. *BTEC NC:* MM. *BTEC ND:* MMM. *OCR ND:* M2 *OCR NED:* M3 Admissions Test required.

PW33 BA Media Production (Music, Top-Up)
Duration: 1FT Hon
Entry Requirements: Contact the institution for details.

PW3J BA Media Production (Performance)
Duration: 3FT Hon
Entry Requirements: *GCE:* 180-200. *BTEC NC:* MM. *BTEC ND:* MMM. *OCR ND:* M2 *OCR NED:* M3 Admissions Test required.

PW34 BA Media Production (Performance) (Top Up)
Duration: 1FT Hon
Entry Requirements: Contact the institution for details.

PW36 BA Media Production (Photography)
Duration: 3FT Hon
Entry Requirements: *GCE:* 180-200. *BTEC NC:* MM. *BTEC ND:* MMM. *OCR ND:* M2 *OCR NED:* M3 Admissions Test required.

P311 BA Media Production (Top-Up)
Duration: 1FT Hon
Entry Requirements: Contact the institution for details.

P314 FdSc Television Production and Studio Engineering
Duration: 2FT Fdg
Entry Requirements: *GCE:* 160. *BTEC NC:* MM. *BTEC ND:* MMM.

G14 UNIVERSITY OF GLAMORGAN, CARDIFF AND PONTYPRIDD
ENQUIRIES AND ADMISSIONS UNIT
PONTYPRIDD CF37 1DL
t: 0800 716925 f: 01443 654050
e: enquiries@glam.ac.uk
// www.glam.ac.uk

P310 BA Cynhyrchu yn y Cyfryngau - Cwrs Dwyieithog
Duration: 3FT Hon
Entry Requirements: *GCE:* ABB. *OCR NED:* M2

PW36 BA Photography
Duration: 3FT Hon
Entry Requirements: *GCE:* BBB. *IB:* 24. *BTEC ND:* DMM. *OCR NED:* M2 Interview required. Portfolio required.

P312 BA Radio
Duration: 3FT Hon
Entry Requirements: *GCE:* BBC. *IB:* 24. *BTEC ND:* DMM. *OCR NED:* M2

PH10 BSc Creative Industries (Popular Music Technology) (Top-Up)
Duration: 1FT Hon
Entry Requirements: Contact the institution for details.

G50 THE UNIVERSITY OF GLOUCESTERSHIRE
PARK CAMPUS
THE PARK
CHELTENHAM GL50 2RH
t: 01242 714503 f: 01242 714827
e: admissions@glos.ac.uk
// www.glos.ac.uk

P310 BA Media Production
Duration: 1FT Hon
Entry Requirements: Contact the institution for details.

P312 BA Radio Production
Duration: 3FT Hon
Entry Requirements: *GCE:* 280-300. Interview required.

P311 BA Television Production
Duration: 3FT Hon
Entry Requirements: *GCE:* 280-300. Interview required.

G70 UNIVERSITY OF GREENWICH
GREENWICH CAMPUS
OLD ROYAL NAVAL COLLEGE
PARK ROW
LONDON SE10 9LS
t: 0800 005 006 f: 020 8331 8145
e: courseinfo@gre.ac.uk
// www.gre.ac.uk

P315 BA Media Arts Production
Duration: 3FT Hon
Entry Requirements: *GCE:* 200. *IB:* 24.

PG34 BSc Digital Television and Interactive Media
Duration: 3FT Hon
Entry Requirements: *GCE:* 240. *IB:* 24.

P311 BSc Film & TV Production
Duration: 3FT Hon
Entry Requirements: *GCE:* 240. *IB:* 24.

P314 BSc Media Arts Production
Duration: 3FT Hon
Entry Requirements: *GCE:* 200. *IB:* 24.

P310 FdA Moving Image Production
Duration: 2FT Fdg
Entry Requirements: *IB:* 24.

G80 GRIMSBY INSTITUTE OF FURTHER AND HIGHER EDUCATION
NUNS CORNER
GRIMSBY
NE LINCOLNSHIRE DN34 5BQ
t: 0800 328 3631 f: 01472 315506/879924
e: headmissions@grimsby.ac.uk
// www.grimsby.ac.uk

P314 BA Digital Film and Television Production
Duration: 3FT Hon
Entry Requirements: Interview required.

H14 HAVERING COLLEGE OF FURTHER AND HIGHER EDUCATION
ARDLEIGH GREEN ROAD
HORNCHURCH
ESSEX RM11 2LL
t: 01708 462793 f: 01708 462736
e: HE@havering-college.ac.uk
// www.havering-college.ac.uk

013P HNC Media Production
Duration: 1FT HNC
Entry Requirements: Interview required. Portfolio required.

H18 HEREFORD COLLEGE OF ARTS
FOLLY LANE
HEREFORD HR1 1LT
t: 01432 273359 f: 01432 341099
e: undergrad@hca.ac.uk
// www.hca.ac.uk

WP63 BA Film and Screen Media (Top-Up)
Duration: 1FT Hon   CRB Check: Required
Entry Requirements: Interview required. Portfolio required. HND required.

H36 UNIVERSITY OF HERTFORDSHIRE
UNIVERSITY ADMISSIONS SERVICE
COLLEGE LANE
HATFIELD
HERTS AL10 9AB
t: 01707 284800
// www.herts.ac.uk

WP63 BA Film and Television Entertainment
Duration: 3FT Hon
Entry Requirements: *GCE:* 300. Interview required. Portfolio required.

P310 BSc Multimedia Technology
Duration: 3FT/4SW Hon
Entry Requirements: *GCE:* 240.

H39 HIGHBURY COLLEGE
DOVERCOURT ROAD
COSHAM
PORTSMOUTH PO6 2SA
t: 023 9231 3373 f: 023 9232 5551
e: info@highbury.ac.uk
// www.highbury.ac.uk

P390 FdA Professional Media Practice
Duration: 2FT Fdg
Entry Requirements: Contact the institution for details.

H73 HULL COLLEGE
QUEEN'S GARDENS
HULL HU1 3DG
t: 01482 329943 f: 01482 598733
e: info@hull-college.ac.uk
// www.hull-college.ac.uk/HE

P314 BA Broadcast Media (Top-Up)
Duration: 1FT Hon
Entry Requirements: Contact the institution for details.

P310 FdA Broadcast Media
Duration: 2FT Fdg
Entry Requirements: *GCE:* 200. *BTEC NC:* MM. *BTEC ND:* MMP. *OCR NED:* P2 Interview required. Portfolio required.

K84 KINGSTON UNIVERSITY
STUDENT INFORMATION & ADVICE CENTRE
COOPER HOUSE
40-46 SURBITON ROAD
KINGSTON UPON THAMES KT1 2HX
t: 0844 8552177 f: 020 8547 7080
e: aps@kingston.ac.uk
// www.kingston.ac.uk

WP63 BA Film Making, Design & Production
Duration: 3FT Hon
Entry Requirements: *Foundation:* Pass. *GCE:* 240. Foundation Course required. Interview required. Portfolio required.

LP23 BSc International Relations with Television & New Broadcasting Media
Duration: 3FT Hon
Entry Requirements: *GCE:* 220-360.

P310 BSc Media Technology
Duration: 3FT Hon
Entry Requirements: *GCE:* 240-280.

P314 BSc Media Technology
Duration: 4SW Hon
Entry Requirements: *GCE:* 240-280.

P318 BSc Media Technology (Foundation)
Duration: 4FT Hon
Entry Requirements: *GCE:* 60.

L27 LEEDS METROPOLITAN UNIVERSITY
COURSE ENQUIRIES OFFICE
CITY SITE
LEEDS LS1 3HE
t: 0113 81 23113 f: 0113 81 23129
// www.leedsmet.ac.uk

P314 BA Film & Moving Image Production
Duration: 3FT Hon
Entry Requirements: *GCE:* 240. *IB:* 24. *BTEC NC:* DM. *BTEC ND:* MMP. Interview required. Portfolio required.

WP33 BA Music Performance
Duration: 3FT/4SW Hon
Entry Requirements: *GCE:* 240. *IB:* 24. Interview required.

HP63 BSc Broadcast Media Technologies
Duration: 3FT Hon
Entry Requirements: *GCE:* 200. *IB:* 24. Interview required.

P313 FdA Film and Television Production
Duration: 2FT Fdg
Entry Requirements: *GCE:* 80. *IB:* 24. Interview required.

L53 COLEG LLANDRILLO CYMRU
LLANDUDNO ROAD
RHOS-ON-SEA
COLWYN BAY
NORTH WALES LL28 4HZ
t: 01492 542338/339 f: 01492 543052
e: degrees@llandrillo.ac.uk
// www.llandrillo.ac.uk

WP63 FdA Digital Media and Television Production
Duration: 2FT Fdg
Entry Requirements: *GCE:* 120.

L62 THE LONDON COLLEGE, UCK
VICTORIA GARDENS
NOTTING HILL GATE
LONDON W11 3PE
t: 020 7243 4000 f: 020 7243 1484
e: admissions@lcuck.ac.uk
// www.lcuck.ac.uk

013P HNC Creative Media Production
Duration: 1FT HNC
Entry Requirements: Contact the institution for details.

113P HND Creative Media Production
Duration: 2FT HND
Entry Requirements: Contact the institution for details.

L68 LONDON METROPOLITAN UNIVERSITY
166-220 HOLLOWAY ROAD
LONDON N7 8DB
t: 020 7133 4200
e: admissions@londonmet.ac.uk
// www.londonmet.ac.uk

P313 BA Media Practice with Honours in Film and Broadcast Production
Duration: 3FT Hon
Entry Requirements: Contact the institution for details.

M10 THE MANCHESTER COLLEGE
OPENSHAW CAMPUS
ASHTON OLD ROAD
OPENSHAW
MANCHESTER M11 2WH
t: 0800 068 8585 f: 0161 920 4103
e: enquiries@themanchestercollege.ac.uk
// www.themanchestercollege.ac.uk

P300 FdA Digital Technologies - Video and Post Production
Duration: 2FT Fdg
Entry Requirements: *GCE:* 120. Portfolio required.

P312 FdA Radio Production
Duration: 2FT Fdg
Entry Requirements: *GCE:* 120.

P301 FdSc Broadcast Television
Duration: 2FT Fdg
Entry Requirements: *GCE:* 120.

M40 THE MANCHESTER METROPOLITAN UNIVERSITY
ADMISSIONS OFFICE
ALL SAINTS (GMS)
ALL SAINTS
MANCHESTER M15 6BH
t: 0161 247 2000
// www.mmu.ac.uk

PV3H BA European Film/Social History
Duration: 3FT Hon
Entry Requirements: *GCE:* 240-280. *IB:* 29.

PG3M BA/BSc European Film/Information & Communications
Duration: 3FT Hon
Entry Requirements: *GCE:* 240-280. *IB:* 29.

M80 MIDDLESEX UNIVERSITY
MIDDLESEX UNIVERSITY
THE BURROUGHS
LONDON NW4 4BT
t: 020 8411 5555 f: 020 8411 5649
e: enquiries@mdx.ac.uk
// www.mdx.ac.uk

P311 BA Television Production
Duration: 3FT Hon
Entry Requirements: *GCE:* 200-300. *IB:* 28.

P314 BA Television Production - Technical Arts
Duration: 3FT Hon
Entry Requirements: *GCE:* 200-300. *IB:* 28.

N13 NEATH PORT TALBOT COLLEGE
NEATH CAMPUS
DWR-Y-FELIN ROAD
NEATH
NEATH PORT TALBOT BOROUGH SA10 7RF
t: 01639 648033 f: 01639 648077
e: admissions@nptc.ac.uk
// www.nptc.ac.uk

WP93 FdA Creative Industries (Media Production)
Duration: 2FT Fdg
Entry Requirements: Contact the institution for details.

N23 NEWCASTLE COLLEGE
STUDENT SERVICES
RYE HILL CAMPUS
SCOTSWOOD ROAD
NEWCASTLE UPON TYNE NE4 7SA
t: 0191 200 4110 f: 0191 200 4349
e: enquiries@ncl-coll.ac.uk
// www.newcastlecollege.co.uk

WP63 BA Television & Media Practice (Top-up)
Duration: 1FT Hon
Entry Requirements: Interview required. HND required.

N30 NEW COLLEGE NOTTINGHAM
ADAMS BUILDING
STONEY STREET
THE LACE MARKET
NOTTINGHAM NG1 1NG
t: 0115 910 0100 f: 0115 953 4349
e: enquiries@ncn.ac.uk
// www.ncn.ac.uk

PP35 FdA Broadcast Media
Duration: 2FT Fdg
Entry Requirements: *GCE:* 100. Interview required.

N36 NEWMAN UNIVERSITY COLLEGE, BIRMINGHAM
GENNERS LANE
BARTLEY GREEN
BIRMINGHAM B32 3NT
t: 0121 476 1181 f: 0121 476 1196
e: Admissions@newman.ac.uk
// www.newman.ac.uk

NP13 FdA Business and Media Production
Duration: 2FT Fdg
Entry Requirements: Contact the institution for details.

N38 UNIVERSITY OF NORTHAMPTON
PARK CAMPUS
BOUGHTON GREEN ROAD
NORTHAMPTON NN2 7AL
t: 0800 358 2232 f: 01604 722083
e: admissions@northampton.ac.uk
// www.northampton.ac.uk

N4P3 BA Accounting/Media Production
Duration: 3FT Hon
Entry Requirements: *GCE:* 260-280. *SQAH:* AAA-BBBB. *IB:* 24.
BTEC NC: DD. *BTEC ND:* DMM. *OCR ND:* D *OCR NED:* M2

C1PH BA Biological Conservation/Media Production
Duration: 3FT Hon
Entry Requirements: *GCE:* 260-280. *SQAH:* AAA-BBBB. *IB:* 24.
BTEC NC: DD. *BTEC ND:* DMM. *OCR ND:* D *OCR NED:* M2

N1PH BA Business Entrepreneurship/Media Production
Duration: 3FT Hon
Entry Requirements: *GCE:* 260-280. *SQAH:* AAA-BBBB. *IB:* 24.
BTEC NC: DD. *BTEC ND:* DMM. *OCR ND:* D *OCR NED:* M2

N1PJ BA Business/Media Production
Duration: 3FT Hon
Entry Requirements: *GCE:* 260-280. *SQAH:* AAA-BBBB. *IB:* 24.
BTEC NC: DD. *BTEC ND:* DMM. *OCR ND:* D *OCR NED:* M2

W8PH BA Creative Writing/Media Production
Duration: 3FT Hon
Entry Requirements: *GCE:* 260-280. *SQAH:* AAA-BBBB. *IB:* 24.
BTEC NC: DD. *BTEC ND:* DMM. *OCR ND:* D *OCR NED:* M2

M9PH BA Criminology/Media Production
Duration: 3FT Hon
Entry Requirements: *GCE:* 260-280. *SQAH:* AAA-BBBB. *IB:* 24.
BTEC NC: DD. *BTEC ND:* DMM. *OCR ND:* D *OCR NED:* M2

W5PH BA Dance/Media Production
Duration: 3FT Hon
Entry Requirements: *GCE:* 260-280. *SQAH:* AAA-BBBB. *IB:* 24.
BTEC NC: DD. *BTEC ND:* DMM. *OCR ND:* D *OCR NED:* M2
Interview required.

W4PJ BA Drama/Media Production
Duration: 3FT Hon
Entry Requirements: *GCE:* 260-280. *SQAH:* AAA-BBBB. *IB:* 24.
BTEC NC: DD. *BTEC ND:* DMM. *OCR ND:* D *OCR NED:* M2
Interview required.

L1PH BA Economics/Media Production
Duration: 3FT Hon
Entry Requirements: *GCE:* 260-280. *SQAH:* AAA-BBBB. *IB:* 24.
BTEC NC: DD. *BTEC ND:* DMM. *OCR ND:* D *OCR NED:* M2

X3PH BA Education Studies/Media Production
Duration: 3FT Hon
Entry Requirements: *GCE:* 260-280. *SQAH:* AAA-BBBB. *IB:* 24.
BTEC NC: DD. *BTEC ND:* DMM. *OCR ND:* D *OCR NED:* M2

N8PJ BA Events Management/Media Production
Duration: 3FT Hon
Entry Requirements: *GCE:* 260-280. *SQAH:* AAA-BBBB. *IB:* 24.
BTEC NC: DD. *BTEC ND:* DMM. *OCR ND:* D *OCR NED:* M2

W6PH BA Film & Television Studies/Media Production
Duration: 3FT Hon
Entry Requirements: *GCE:* 260-280. *SQAH:* AAA-BBBB. *IB:* 24.
BTEC NC: DD. *BTEC ND:* DMM. *OCR ND:* D *OCR NED:* M2

W1PH BA Fine Art Painting & Drawing/Media Production
Duration: 3FT Hon
Entry Requirements: *GCE:* 260-280. *SQAH:* AAA-BBBB. *IB:* 24.
BTEC NC: DD. *BTEC ND:* DMM. *OCR ND:* D *OCR NED:* M2

R1PH BA French/Media Production
Duration: 3FT Hon
Entry Requirements: *GCE:* 260-280. *SQAH:* AAA-BBBB. *IB:* 24. *BTEC NC:* DD. *BTEC ND:* DMM. *OCR ND:* D *OCR NED:* M2

L4PH BA Health Studies/Media Production
Duration: 3FT Hon
Entry Requirements: *GCE:* 260-280. *SQAH:* AAA-BBBB. *IB:* 24. *BTEC NC:* DD. *BTEC ND:* DMM. *OCR ND:* D *OCR NED:* M2

D4PH BA Heritage Management/Media Production
Duration: 3FT Hon
Entry Requirements: *GCE:* 260-280. *SQAH:* AAA-BBBB. *IB:* 24. *BTEC NC:* DD. *BTEC ND:* DMM. *OCR ND:* D *OCR NED:* M2

V1PH BA History/Media Production
Duration: 3FT Hon
Entry Requirements: *GCE:* 260-280. *SQAH:* AAA-BBBB. *IB:* 24. *BTEC NC:* DD. *BTEC ND:* DMM. *OCR ND:* D *OCR NED:* M2

L7P3 BA Human Geography/Media Production
Duration: 3FT Hon
Entry Requirements: *GCE:* 260-280. *SQAH:* AAA-BBBB. *IB:* 24. *BTEC NC:* DD. *BTEC ND:* DMM. *OCR ND:* D *OCR NED:* M2

N6PH BA Human Resource Management/Media Production
Duration: 3FT Hon
Entry Requirements: *GCE:* 260-280. *SQAH:* AAA-BBBB. *IB:* 24. *BTEC NC:* DD. *BTEC ND:* DMM. *OCR ND:* D *OCR NED:* M2

P5P3 BA Journalism/Media Production
Duration: 3FT Hon
Entry Requirements: *GCE:* 260-280. *SQAH:* AAA-BBBB. *IB:* 24. *BTEC NC:* DD. *BTEC ND:* DMM. *OCR ND:* D *OCR NED:* M2

N2PJ BA Management/Media Production
Duration: 3FT Hon
Entry Requirements: *GCE:* 260-280. *SQAH:* AAA-BBBB. *IB:* 24. *BTEC NC:* DD. *BTEC ND:* DMM. *OCR ND:* D *OCR NED:* M2

P390 BA Media Production
Duration: 3FT Hon
Entry Requirements: *GCE:* 260-280. *SQAH:* AAA-BBBB. *IB:* 24. *BTEC NC:* DD. *BTEC ND:* DMM. *OCR ND:* D *OCR NED:* M2

P3NB BA Media Production with Applied Management
Duration: 3FT Hon
Entry Requirements: *GCE:* 260-280. *SQAH:* AAA-BBBB. *IB:* 24. *BTEC NC:* DD. *BTEC ND:* DMM. *OCR ND:* D *OCR NED:* M2

P3DK BA Media Production with Equine Studies
Duration: 3FT Hon
Entry Requirements: *GCE:* 260-280. *SQAH:* AAA-BBBB. *IB:* 24. *BTEC NC:* DD. *BTEC ND:* DMM. *OCR ND:* D *OCR NED:* M2

P3NK BA Media Production/Accounting
Duration: 3FT Hon
Entry Requirements: *GCE:* 260-280. *SQAH:* AAA-BBBB. *IB:* 24. *BTEC NC:* DD. *BTEC ND:* DMM. *OCR ND:* D *OCR NED:* M2

P3CC BA Media Production/Biological Conservation
Duration: 3FT Hon
Entry Requirements: *GCE:* 260-280. *SQAH:* AAA-BBBB. *IB:* 24. *BTEC NC:* DD. *BTEC ND:* DMM. *OCR ND:* D *OCR NED:* M2

P3ND BA Media Production/Business
Duration: 3FT Hon
Entry Requirements: *GCE:* 260-280. *SQAH:* AAA-BBBB. *IB:* 24. *BTEC NC:* DD. *BTEC ND:* DMM. *OCR ND:* D *OCR NED:* M2

P3GM BA Media Production/Business Computing Systems
Duration: 3FT Hon
Entry Requirements: *GCE:* 260-280. *SQAH:* AAA-BBBB. *IB:* 24. *BTEC NC:* DD. *BTEC ND:* DMM. *OCR ND:* D *OCR NED:* M2

P3NC BA Media Production/Business Entrepreneurship
Duration: 3FT Hon
Entry Requirements: *GCE:* 260-280. *SQAH:* AAA-BBBB. *IB:* 24. *BTEC NC:* DD. *BTEC ND:* DMM. *OCR ND:* D *OCR NED:* M2

P3WV BA Media Production/Creative Writing
Duration: 3FT Hon
Entry Requirements: *GCE:* 260-280. *SQAH:* AAA-BBBB. *IB:* 24. *BTEC NC:* DD. *BTEC ND:* DMM. *OCR ND:* D *OCR NED:* M2

P3MX BA Media Production/Criminology
Duration: 3FT Hon
Entry Requirements: *GCE:* 260-280. *SQAH:* AAA-BBBB. *IB:* 24. *BTEC NC:* DD. *BTEC ND:* DMM. *OCR ND:* D *OCR NED:* M2

P3WM BA Media Production/Dance
Duration: 3FT Hon
Entry Requirements: *GCE:* 260-280. *SQAH:* AAA-BBBB. *IB:* 24. *BTEC NC:* DD. *BTEC ND:* DMM. *OCR ND:* D *OCR NED:* M2
Interview required.

P3WL BA Media Production/Drama
Duration: 3FT Hon
Entry Requirements: *GCE:* 260-280. *SQAH:* AAA-BBBB. *IB:* 24. *BTEC NC:* DD. *BTEC ND:* DMM. *OCR ND:* D *OCR NED:* M2
Interview required.

P3LC BA Media Production/Economics
Duration: 3FT Hon
Entry Requirements: *GCE:* 260-280. *SQAH:* AAA-BBBB. *IB:* 24. *BTEC NC:* DD. *BTEC ND:* DMM. *OCR ND:* D *OCR NED:* M2

P3XJ BA Media Production/Education Studies
Duration: 3FT Hon
Entry Requirements: *GCE:* 260-280. *SQAH:* AAA-BBBB. *IB:* 24. *BTEC NC:* DD. *BTEC ND:* DMM. *OCR ND:* D *OCR NED:* M2

P3NW BA Media Production/Events Management
Duration: 3FT Hon
Entry Requirements: *GCE:* 260-280. *SQAH:* AAA-BBBB. *IB:* 24.
BTEC NC: DD. *BTEC ND:* DMM. *OCR ND:* D *OCR NED:* M2

P3WP BA Media Production/Film & Television Studies
Duration: 3FT Hon
Entry Requirements: *GCE:* 260-280. *SQAH:* AAA-BBBB. *IB:* 24.
BTEC NC: DD. *BTEC ND:* DMM. *OCR ND:* D *OCR NED:* M2

P3WC BA Media Production/Fine Art Painting & Drawing
Duration: 3FT Hon
Entry Requirements: *GCE:* 260-280. *SQAH:* AAA-BBBB. *IB:* 24.
BTEC NC: DD. *BTEC ND:* DMM. *OCR ND:* D *OCR NED:* M2

P3RC BA Media Production/French
Duration: 3FT Hon
Entry Requirements: *GCE:* 260-280. *SQAH:* AAA-BBBB. *IB:* 24.
BTEC NC: DD. *BTEC ND:* DMM. *OCR ND:* D *OCR NED:* M2

P3LL BA Media Production/Health Studies
Duration: 3FT Hon
Entry Requirements: *GCE:* 260-280. *SQAH:* AAA-BBBB. *IB:* 24.
BTEC NC: DD. *BTEC ND:* DMM. *OCR ND:* D *OCR NED:* M2

PD34 BA Media Production/Heritage Management
Duration: 3FT Hon
Entry Requirements: *GCE:* 260-280. *SQAH:* AAA-BBBB. *IB:* 24.
BTEC NC: DD. *BTEC ND:* DMM. *OCR ND:* D *OCR NED:* M2

P3VC BA Media Production/History
Duration: 3FT Hon
Entry Requirements: *GCE:* 260-280. *SQAH:* AAA-BBBB. *IB:* 24.
BTEC NC: DD. *BTEC ND:* DMM. *OCR ND:* D *OCR NED:* M2

P3B1 BA Media Production/Human Bioscience
Duration: 3FT Hon
Entry Requirements: *GCE:* 260-280. *SQAH:* AAA-BBBB. *IB:* 24.
BTEC NC: DD. *BTEC ND:* DMM. *OCR ND:* D *OCR NED:* M2

P3L7 BA Media Production/Human Geography
Duration: 3FT Hon
Entry Requirements: *GCE:* 260-280. *SQAH:* AAA-BBBB. *IB:* 24.
BTEC NC: DD. *BTEC ND:* DMM. *OCR ND:* D *OCR NED:* M2

P3NP BA Media Production/Human Resource Management
Duration: 3FT Hon
Entry Requirements: *GCE:* 260-280. *SQAH:* AAA-BBBB. *IB:* 24.
BTEC NC: DD. *BTEC ND:* DMM. *OCR ND:* D *OCR NED:* M2

P3P5 BA Media Production/Journalism
Duration: 3FT Hon
Entry Requirements: *GCE:* 260-280. *SQAH:* AAA-BBBB. *IB:* 24.
BTEC NC: DD. *BTEC ND:* DMM. *OCR ND:* D *OCR NED:* M2

PN3V BA Media Production/Leisure & Lifestyle Management
Duration: 3FT Hon
Entry Requirements: *GCE:* 260-280. *SQAH:* AAA-BBBB. *IB:* 24.
BTEC NC: DD. *BTEC ND:* DMM. *OCR ND:* D *OCR NED:* M2

P3NA BA Media Production/Management
Duration: 3FT Hon
Entry Requirements: *GCE:* 260-280. *SQAH:* AAA-BBBB. *IB:* 24.
BTEC NC: DD. *BTEC ND:* DMM. *OCR ND:* D *OCR NED:* M2

P3FW BA Media Production/Physical Geography
Duration: 3FT Hon
Entry Requirements: *GCE:* 260-280. *SQAH:* AAA-BBBB. *IB:* 24.
BTEC NC: DD. *BTEC ND:* DMM. *OCR ND:* D *OCR NED:* M2

P3LF BA Media Production/Politics
Duration: 3FT Hon
Entry Requirements: *GCE:* 260-280. *SQAH:* AAA-BBBB. *IB:* 24.
BTEC NC: DD. *BTEC ND:* DMM. *OCR ND:* D *OCR NED:* M2

P3WH BA Media Production/Popular Music
Duration: 3FT Hon
Entry Requirements: *GCE:* 260-280. *SQAH:* AAA-BBBB. *IB:* 24.
BTEC NC: DD. *BTEC ND:* DMM. *OCR ND:* D *OCR NED:* M2
Interview required.

P3CV BA Media Production/Psychology
Duration: 3FT Hon
Entry Requirements: *GCE:* 260-280. *SQAH:* AAA-BBBB. *IB:* 24.
BTEC NC: DD. *BTEC ND:* DMM. *OCR ND:* D *OCR NED:* M2

P3L5 BA Media Production/Social Care
Duration: 3FT Hon
Entry Requirements: *GCE:* 260-280. *SQAH:* AAA-BBBB. *IB:* 24.
BTEC NC: DD. *BTEC ND:* DMM. *OCR ND:* D *OCR NED:* M2

P3N9 BA Media Production/Social Enterprise Development
Duration: 3FT Hon
Entry Requirements: *GCE:* 260-280. *SQAH:* AAA-BBBB. *IB:* 24.
BTEC NC: DD. *BTEC ND:* DMM. *OCR ND:* D *OCR NED:* M2

P3LH BA Media Production/Sociology
Duration: 3FT Hon
Entry Requirements: *GCE:* 260-280. *SQAH:* AAA-BBBB. *IB:* 24.
BTEC NC: DD. *BTEC ND:* DMM. *OCR ND:* D *OCR NED:* M2

P3GL BA Media Production/Web Design
Duration: 3FT Hon
Entry Requirements: *GCE:* 260-280. *SQAH:* AAA-BBBB. *IB:* 24.
BTEC NC: DD. *BTEC ND:* DMM. *OCR ND:* D *OCR NED:* M2

L2PH BA Politics/Media Production
Duration: 3FT Hon
Entry Requirements: *GCE:* 260-280. *SQAH:* AAA-BBBB. *IB:* 24.
BTEC NC: DD. *BTEC ND:* DMM. *OCR ND:* D *OCR NED:* M2

W3PH BA Popular Music/Media Production
Duration: 3FT Hon
Entry Requirements: *GCE:* 260-280. *SQAH:* AAA-BBBB. *IB:* 24.
BTEC NC: DD. *BTEC ND:* DMM. *OCR ND:* D *OCR NED:* M2

C8PH BA Psychology/Media Production
Duration: 3FT Hon
Entry Requirements: *GCE:* 260-280. *SQAH:* AAA-BBBB. *IB:* 24.
BTEC NC: DD. *BTEC ND:* DMM. *OCR ND:* D *OCR NED:* M2

L5P3 BA Social Care/Media Production
Duration: 3FT Hon
Entry Requirements: *GCE:* 260-280. *SQAH:* AAA-BBBB. *IB:* 24.
BTEC NC: DD. *BTEC ND:* DMM. *OCR ND:* D *OCR NED:* M2

N2PA BA Social Enterprise Development/Media Production
Duration: 3FT Hon
Entry Requirements: *GCE:* 260-280. *SQAH:* AAA-BBBB. *IB:* 24.
BTEC NC: DD. *BTEC ND:* DMM. *OCR ND:* D *OCR NED:* M2

L3PH BA Sociology/Media Production
Duration: 3FT Hon
Entry Requirements: *GCE:* 260-280. *SQAH:* AAA-BBBB. *IB:* 24.
BTEC NC: DD. *BTEC ND:* DMM. *OCR ND:* D *OCR NED:* M2

G5PH BSc Business Computing Systems/Media Production
Duration: 3FT Hon
Entry Requirements: *GCE:* 260-280. *SQAH:* AAA-BBBB. *IB:* 24.
BTEC NC: DD. *BTEC ND:* DMM. *OCR ND:* D *OCR NED:* M2

B1P3 BSc Human Bioscience/Media Production
Duration: 3FT Hon
Entry Requirements: *GCE:* 260-280. *SQAH:* AAA-BBBB. *IB:* 24.
BTEC NC: DD. *BTEC ND:* DMM. *OCR ND:* D *OCR NED:* M2

F8PJ BSc Physical Geography/Media Production
Duration: 3FT Hon
Entry Requirements: *GCE:* 260-280. *SQAH:* AAA-BBBB. *IB:* 24.
BTEC NC: DD. *BTEC ND:* DMM. *OCR ND:* D *OCR NED:* M2

N77 NORTHUMBRIA UNIVERSITY
TRINITY BUILDING
NORTHUMBERLAND ROAD
NEWCASTLE UPON TYNE NE1 8ST
t: 0191 243 7420 f: 0191 227 4561
e: er.admissions@northumbria.ac.uk
// www.northumbria.ac.uk

P310 BA Media Production
Duration: 3FT Hon
Entry Requirements: *GCE:* 300. *SQAH:* BBBBC. *SQAAH:* BBC. *IB:* 26. *BTEC ND:* DDM.

N82 NORWICH CITY COLLEGE OF FURTHER AND HIGHER EDUCATION (AN ASSOCIATE COLLEGE OF UEA)
IPSWICH ROAD
NORWICH
NORFOLK NR2 2LJ
t: 01603 773005 f: 01603 773301
e: admissions@ccn.ac.uk
// www.ccn.ac.uk

P310 FdA Media Practice
Duration: 2FT Fdg
Entry Requirements: Contact the institution for details.

O25 OXFORD & CHERWELL VALLEY COLLEGE
BANBURY CAMPUS
BROUGHTON ROAD
BANBURY
OXON OX16 9QA
t: 01865 551691 f: 01865 551777
e: uni@ocvc.ac.uk
// www.ocvc.ac.uk

013P HND Creative Media Production
Duration: 2FT HND
Entry Requirements: Contact the institution for details.

P63 UCP MARJON - UNIVERSITY COLLEGE PLYMOUTH ST MARK & ST JOHN
DERRIFORD ROAD
PLYMOUTH PL6 8BH
t: 01752 636890 f: 01752 636819
e: admissions@marjon.ac.uk
// www.ucpmarjon.ac.uk

P310 BA Media Production
Duration: 3FT Hon
Entry Requirements: *GCE:* 220.

P314 BA Sports Media and Journalism
Duration: 3FT Hon CRB Check: Required
Entry Requirements: *GCE:* 220.

R06 RAVENSBOURNE
6 PENROSE WAY
LONDON SE10 0EW
t: 020 3040 3500
e: info@rave.ac.uk
// www.rave.ac.uk

WP23 BA Content Development and Production (Fast-Track)
Duration: 2FT Hon
Entry Requirements: *Foundation:* Pass. *GCE:* AA-CC. *IB:* 28. *BTEC NC:* PP. *BTEC ND:* PPP. Interview required. Portfolio required.

P313 BA Digital Film Production
Duration: 3FT Hon
Entry Requirements: Contact the institution for details.

PH13 BA Digital Film Production (Fast-Track)
Duration: 2FT Hon
Entry Requirements: Contact the institution for details.

WP33 BA Music Production for Media
Duration: 3FT Hon
Entry Requirements: *Foundation:* Pass. *GCE:* AA-CC. *IB:* 28. *BTEC NC:* PP. *BTEC ND:* PPP.

S21 SHEFFIELD HALLAM UNIVERSITY
CITY CAMPUS
HOWARD STREET
SHEFFIELD S1 1WB
t: 0114 225 5555 f: 0114 225 2167
e: admissions@shu.ac.uk
// www.shu.ac.uk

P391 MArt Film and Media Production
Duration: 4FT Hon
Entry Requirements: Contact the institution for details.

S22 SHEFFIELD COLLEGE
THE SHEFFIELD COLLEGE
HE UNIT
HILLSBOROUGH COLLEGE AT THE BARRACKS
SHEFFIELD S6 2LR
t: 0114 260 2597
e: heunit@sheffcol.ac.uk
// www.sheffcol.ac.uk

P310 FdA Media Production
Duration: 2FT Fdg
Entry Requirements: *GCE:* 120.

S30 SOUTHAMPTON SOLENT UNIVERSITY
EAST PARK TERRACE
SOUTHAMPTON
HAMPSHIRE SO14 0RT
t: +44 (0) 23 8031 9039 f: + 44 (0)23 8022 2259
e: admissions@solent.ac.uk or ask@solent.ac.uk
// www.solent.ac.uk/

P319 BA Media Production (Top-Up)
Duration: 1FT Hon
Entry Requirements: Interview required. HND required.

P390 BA Television & Video Production
Duration: 3FT Hon
Entry Requirements: *Foundation:* Distinction. *GCE:* 240. *SQAAH:* AA-CCD. *IB:* 24. *BTEC NC:* DD. *BTEC ND:* MMM. *OCR ND:* D *OCR NED:* M3 Interview required.

P318 BA Television Post-Production
Duration: 3FT Hon
Entry Requirements: *Foundation:* Distinction. *GCE:* 240. *SQAAH:* AA-CCD. *IB:* 24. *BTEC NC:* DD. *BTEC ND:* MMM. *OCR ND:* D *OCR NED:* M3 Interview required.

P311 BA Television Studio Production
Duration: 3FT Hon
Entry Requirements: *Foundation:* Distinction. *GCE:* 240. *SQAAH:* AA-CCD. *IB:* 24. *BTEC NC:* DD. *BTEC ND:* MMM. *OCR ND:* D *OCR NED:* M3 Interview required.

P310 BSc Outside Broadcast (Production Operations)
Duration: 3FT Hon
Entry Requirements: *GCE:* 160.

P316 BSc Outside Broadcast (Production Operations) with fdn
Duration: 4FT Hon
Entry Requirements: *GCE:* 40.

S32 SOUTH DEVON COLLEGE
LONG ROAD
PAIGNTON
DEVON TQ4 7EJ
t: 08000 380123 f: 01803 540541
e: highereducation@southdevon.ac.uk
// www.southdevon.ac.uk

WP33 FdA Creative Digital Media
Duration: 2FT Fdg
Entry Requirements: Contact the institution for details.

S41 SOUTH CHESHIRE COLLEGE
DANE BANK AVENUE
CREWE CW2 8AB
t: 01270 654654 f: 01270 651515
e: admissions@s-cheshire.ac.uk
// www.s-cheshire.ac.uk

WP63 FdA Film Production and Management
Duration: 2FT Fdg
Entry Requirements: *GCE:* 200. Interview required.

S72 STAFFORDSHIRE UNIVERSITY
COLLEGE ROAD
STOKE ON TRENT ST4 2DE
t: 01782 292753 f: 01782 292740
e: admissions@staffs.ac.uk
// www.staffs.ac.uk

P310 BA Music Broadcasting
Duration: 3FT Hon
Entry Requirements: *GCE:* 200-240. *IB:* 24.

P312 BA Radio Production
Duration: 3FT Hon
Entry Requirements: *GCE:* 200-240. *IB:* 24.

P391 FdA Film and Television Production Technology and Management
Duration: 2FT Hon
Entry Requirements: Interview required.

P392 FdSc Film and Television Production Technology
Duration: 2FT Fdg
Entry Requirements: Contact the institution for details.

N2P3 FdSc Film and Television Production Technology with Management
Duration: 2FT Fdg
Entry Requirements: Interview required.

P3W6 FdSc Film and Television Production Technology with Sound
Duration: 2FT Fdg
Entry Requirements: Contact the institution for details.

S76 STOCKPORT COLLEGE
WELLINGTON ROAD SOUTH
STOCKPORT SK1 3UQ
t: 0161 958 3143 f: 0161 958 3663
e: susan.kelly@stockport.ac.uk
// www.stockport.ac.uk

P311 FdA Television Production
Duration: 2FT Fdg
Entry Requirements: Contact the institution for details.

S84 UNIVERSITY OF SUNDERLAND
STUDENT HELPLINE
THE STUDENT GATEWAY
CHESTER ROAD
SUNDERLAND SR1 3SD
t: 0191 515 3000 f: 0191 515 3805
e: student.helpline@sunderland.ac.uk
// www.sunderland.ac.uk

P391 BA Mass Communications
Duration: 3FT Hon
Entry Requirements: Contact the institution for details.

P312 BA Radio (Top-up)
Duration: 1FT Hon
Entry Requirements: Interview required. HND required.

P310 BA Television and Video (Top-up)
Duration: 1FT Hon
Entry Requirements: Interview required. HND required.

S90 UNIVERSITY OF SUSSEX
UNDERGRADUATE ADMISSIONS
SUSSEX HOUSE
UNIVERSITY OF SUSSEX
BRIGHTON BN1 9RH
t: 01273 678416 f: 01273 678545
e: ug.applicants@sussex.ac.uk
// www.sussex.ac.uk

P310 BA Media Practice
Duration: 3FT Hon
Entry Requirements: *GCE:* ABB. *SQAH:* AABBB. *IB:* 34. *BTEC NC:* DM. *BTEC ND:* DDM. *OCR ND:* M1 *OCR NED:* D2

S96 SWANSEA METROPOLITAN UNIVERSITY
MOUNT PLEASANT CAMPUS
SWANSEA SA1 6ED
t: 01792 481000 f: 01792 481061
e: gemma.garbutt@smu.ac.uk
// www.smu.ac.uk

013P HND Technical Theatre
Duration: 2FT HND
Entry Requirements: *GCE:* 60-360. *IB:* 24. Interview required. Portfolio required.

T20 TEESSIDE UNIVERSITY
MIDDLESBROUGH TS1 3BA
t: 01642 218121 f: 01642 384201
e: registry@tees.ac.uk
// www.tees.ac.uk

P314 BA Broadcast Media Production
Duration: 3FT Hon
Entry Requirements: *GCE:* 280. *IB:* 25. Interview required. Portfolio required.

WP43 BA Performance for Live & Recorded Media
Duration: 3FT Hon
Entry Requirements: *GCE:* 280. *IB:* 25. Interview required.

P331 BA Television and Film Production
Duration: 3FT Hon
Entry Requirements: *GCE:* 280. *IB:* 25. Interview required.
Portfolio required.

WP4H FdA Stage and Media Production
Duration: 2FT Fdg
Entry Requirements: *GCE:* 80-100. *IB:* 24. Interview required.

U20 UNIVERSITY OF ULSTER
COLERAINE
CO. LONDONDERRY
NORTHERN IRELAND BT52 1SA
t: 028 7032 4221 f: 028 7032 4908
e: online@ulster.ac.uk
// www.ulster.ac.uk

P310 BA Interactive Media Arts
Duration: 3FT Hon
Entry Requirements: *GCE:* 240. *IB:* 24. *BTEC NC:* MM. *BTEC ND:* MMM.

U65 UNIVERSITY OF THE ARTS LONDON
272 HIGH HOLBORN
LONDON WC1V 7EY
t: 020 7514 6000x6197 f: 020 7514 6198
e: c.anderson@arts.ac.uk
// www.arts.ac.uk

WP23 BA Digital Media Design
Duration: 3FT Hon
Entry Requirements: *GCE:* 80. *IB:* 28. Foundation Course required. Interview required. Portfolio required.

P311 BA Production for Live Events and Television (Top-Up)
Duration: 1FT Hon
Entry Requirements: Contact the institution for details.

P315 FdA Digital Media Design
Duration: 2FT Fdg
Entry Requirements: *GCE:* 40. *IB:* 28. Foundation Course required. Interview required. Portfolio required.

W05 THE UNIVERSITY OF WEST LONDON
WALPOLE HOUSE
BOND STREET
EALING
LONDON W5 5AA
t: 0800 036 8888 f: 020 8566 1353
e: learning.advice@uwl.ac.uk
// www.uwl.ac.uk

P315 BA Broadcasting
Duration: 3FT Hon
Entry Requirements: *GCE:* 200. *IB:* 28. Interview required.

P310 BA Digital Media Production
Duration: 3FT Hon
Entry Requirements: *GCE:* 200. *IB:* 28. Interview required.
Portfolio required.

W50 UNIVERSITY OF WESTMINSTER
2ND FLOOR
101 NEW CAVENDISH STREET,
LONDON W1W 6XH
t: 020 7911 5000 f: 020 7911 5788
e: course-enquiries@westminster.ac.uk
// www.westminster.ac.uk

P312 BA Radio Production
Duration: 3FT Hon
Entry Requirements: *GCE:* BBB. *SQAH:* AAAAA-BBBBB. *SQAAH:* AAA-BBB. *IB:* 30. *BTEC NC:* DD. *BTEC ND:* DDM. *OCR ND:* D *OCR NED:* D2 Interview required.

P311 BA Television
Duration: 3FT Hon
Entry Requirements: *GCE:* BBB. *SQAH:* AAAAA-BBBBB. *SQAAH:* AAA-BBB. *IB:* 30. *BTEC NC:* DD. *BTEC ND:* DDM. *OCR ND:* D *OCR NED:* D2 Interview required.

W65 WEST THAMES COLLEGE
LONDON ROAD
ISLEWORTH
MIDDLESEX TW7 4HS
t: 020 8326 2000 f: 020 8326 2001
e: info@west-thames.ac.uk
// www.west-thames.ac.uk/en/
higher-education/

JP93 HND Media and Sound Production
Duration: 2FT HND
Entry Requirements: Contact the institution for details.

W75 UNIVERSITY OF WOLVERHAMPTON
ADMISSIONS UNIT
MX207, CAMP STREET
WOLVERHAMPTON
WEST MIDLANDS WV1 1AD
t: 01902 321000 f: 01902 321896
e: admissions@wlv.ac.uk
// www.wlv.ac.uk

PP35 BA Broadcasting and Journalism
Duration: 3FT Hon
Entry Requirements: Contact the institution for details.

W76 UNIVERSITY OF WINCHESTER
WINCHESTER
HANTS SO22 4NR
t: 01962 827234 f: 01962 827288
e: course.enquiries@winchester.ac.uk
// www.winchester.ac.uk

TP7H BA American Studies and Media Production
Duration: 3FT Hon
Entry Requirements: *Foundation:* Distinction. *GCE:* 260-300. *IB:* 24. *BTEC NC:* DD. *BTEC ND:* DMM. *OCR ND:* D *OCR NED:* M2

VP4H BA Archaeology and Media Production
Duration: 3FT Hon
Entry Requirements: *Foundation:* Distinction. *GCE:* 260-300. *IB:* 24. *BTEC NC:* DD. *BTEC ND:* DMM. *OCR ND:* D *OCR NED:* M2

NPFJ BA Business Management and Media Production
Duration: 3FT Hon
Entry Requirements: *Foundation:* Distinction. *GCE:* 260-300. *IB:* 24. *BTEC NC:* DD. *BTEC ND:* DMM. *OCR ND:* D *OCR NED:* M2

LP5J BA Childhood,Youth & Community Studies and Media Production
Duration: 3FT Hon
Entry Requirements: *GCE:* 260-300. *IB:* 24.

WP53 BA Choreography & Dance and Media Production
Duration: 3FT Hon
Entry Requirements: *Foundation:* Distinction. *GCE:* 260-300. *IB:* 25. *BTEC NC:* DD. *BTEC ND:* DMM. *OCR ND:* D *OCR NED:* M2

WP8H BA Creative Writing and Media Production
Duration: 3FT Hon
Entry Requirements: *Foundation:* Distinction. *GCE:* 260-300. *IB:* 25. *BTEC NC:* DD. *BTEC ND:* DMM. *OCR ND:* D *OCR NED:* M2

LP33 BA Criminology and Media Production
Duration: 3FT Hon
Entry Requirements: *Foundation:* Distinction. *GCE:* 260-300. *IB:* 24. *BTEC NC:* DD. *BTEC ND:* DMM. *OCR ND:* D *OCR NED:* M2

WP43 BA Drama and Media Production
Duration: 3FT Hon
Entry Requirements: *Foundation:* Distinction. *GCE:* 260-300. *IB:* 25. *BTEC NC:* DD. *BTEC ND:* DMM. *OCR ND:* D *OCR NED:* M2

QP3J BA English Language Studies and Media Production
Duration: 3FT Hon
Entry Requirements: *Foundation:* Distinction. *GCE:* 260-300. *IB:* 25. *BTEC NC:* DD. *BTEC ND:* DMM. *OCR ND:* D *OCR NED:* M2

QP3H BA English and Media Production
Duration: 3FT Hon
Entry Requirements: *Foundation:* Distinction. *GCE:* 260-300. *IB:* 25. *BTEC NC:* DD. *BTEC ND:* DMM. *OCR ND:* D *OCR NED:* M2

NPV3 BA Event Management and Media Production
Duration: 3FT Hon
Entry Requirements: *Foundation:* Distinction. *GCE:* 260-300. *IB:* 24. *BTEC NC:* DD. *BTEC ND:* DMM. *OCR ND:* D *OCR NED:* M2

WP6H BA Film & Cinema Technologies and Media Production
Duration: 3FT Hon
Entry Requirements: *Foundation:* Distinction. *GCE:* 260-300. *IB:* 24. *BTEC NC:* DD. *BTEC ND:* DMM. *OCR ND:* D *OCR NED:* M2

PL5J BA Health, Community & Social Care Studies and Media Production
Duration: 3FT Hon CRB Check: Required
Entry Requirements: Contact the institution for details.

VPC3 BA History and Media Production
Duration: 3FT Hon
Entry Requirements: *Foundation:* Distinction. *GCE:* 260-300. *IB:* 24. *BTEC NC:* DD. *BTEC ND:* DMM. *OCR ND:* D *OCR NED:* M2

PP53 BA Journalism Studies and Media Production
Duration: 3FT Hon
Entry Requirements: *Foundation:* Distinction. *GCE:* 260-300. *IB:* 24. *BTEC NC:* DD. *BTEC ND:* DMM. *OCR ND:* D *OCR NED:* M2

MP1H BA Law and Media Production
Duration: 3FT Hon
Entry Requirements: *Foundation:* Distinction. *GCE:* 260-300. *IB:* 25. *BTEC NC:* DD. *BTEC ND:* DMM. *OCR ND:* D *OCR NED:* M2

P310 BA Media Production
Duration: 3FT Hon
Entry Requirements: *Foundation:* Distinction. *GCE:* 260-300. *IB:* 25. *BTEC NC:* DD. *BTEC ND:* DMM. *OCR ND:* D *OCR NED:* M2

PW3Y BA Media Production and Modern Liberal Arts
Duration: 3FT Hon
Entry Requirements: *Foundation:* Distinction. *GCE:* 260-300. *IB:* 25. *BTEC NC:* DD. *BTEC ND:* DMM. *OCR ND:* D *OCR NED:* M2

PC38 BA Media Production and Psychology
Duration: 3FT Hon
Entry Requirements: *Foundation:* Distinction. *GCE:* 260-300. *IB:* 25. *BTEC NC:* DD. *BTEC ND:* DMM. *OCR ND:* D *OCR NED:* M2

PLHJ BA Media Production and Sociology
Duration: 3FT Hon
Entry Requirements: *Foundation:* Distinction. *GCE:* 260-300. *IB:* 24. *BTEC NC:* DD. *BTEC ND:* DMM. *OCR ND:* D *OCR NED:* M2

PN3V BA Media Production and Sports Management
Duration: 3FT Hon
Entry Requirements: *Foundation:* Pass. *GCE:* 260-300. *IB:* 24. *BTEC NC:* DD. *BTEC ND:* MMP. *OCR ND:* D

PC36 BA Media Production and Sports Studies
Duration: 3FT Hon
Entry Requirements: *Foundation:* Merit. *GCE:* 260-300. *IB:* 24. *BTEC NC:* DM. *BTEC ND:* MMP.

PV3P BA Media Production and Theology & Religious Studies
Duration: 3FT Hon
Entry Requirements: *Foundation:* Distinction. *GCE:* 260-300. *IB:* 25. *BTEC NC:* DD. *BTEC ND:* DMM. *OCR ND:* D *OCR NED:* M2

PWHH BA Media Production and Vocal & Choral Studies
Duration: 3FT Hon
Entry Requirements: *Foundation:* Distinction. *GCE:* 260-300. *IB:* 24. *BTEC NC:* DD. *BTEC ND:* DMM. *OCR ND:* D *OCR NED:* M2

PWJ4 BA Performance Management
Duration: 3FT Hon
Entry Requirements: *Foundation:* Distinction. *GCE:* 260-300. *IB:* 26. *BTEC NC:* DD. *BTEC ND:* DDM. *OCR ND:* D Interview required.

LP2H BA Politics & Global Studies and Media Production
Duration: 3FT Hon
Entry Requirements: *Foundation:* Distinction. *GCE:* 260-300. *IB:* 24. *BTEC NC:* DD. *BTEC ND:* MMM. *OCR ND:* D

JOURNALISM

A60 ANGLIA RUSKIN UNIVERSITY
BISHOP HALL LANE
CHELMSFORD
ESSEX CM1 1SQ
t: 0845 271 3333 f: 01245 251789
e: answers@anglia.ac.uk
// www.anglia.ac.uk

P500 BA Journalism
Duration: 3FT Hon
Entry Requirements: *GCE:* 180. *SQAH:* CCCC. *SQAAH:* BC. *IB:* 24.

P501 FdA Sports Journalism
Duration: 2FT Fdg
Entry Requirements: *GCE:* 80.

B06 BANGOR UNIVERSITY
BANGOR UNIVERSITY
BANGOR
GWYNEDD LL57 2DG
t: 01248 388484 f: 01248 370451
e: admissions@bangor.ac.uk
// www.bangor.ac.uk

Q5P5 BA Cymraeg gyda Newyddiaduraeth
Duration: 3FT Hon
Entry Requirements: *GCE:* 220-260. *IB:* 28.

Q5PM BA Cymraeg gyda Newyddiaduraeth
Duration: 4FT Hon
Entry Requirements: Contact the institution for details.

PQ53 BA English Language and Journalism
Duration: 3FT Hon
Entry Requirements: *GCE:* 260-300. *IB:* 28.

Q3P5 BA English with Journalism
Duration: 3FT Hon
Entry Requirements: *GCE:* 240-300. *IB:* 28.

R1P5 BA French with Journalism
Duration: 4FT Hon
Entry Requirements: *GCE:* 240-260. *IB:* 28.

R2P5 BA German with Journalism
Duration: 4FT Hon
Entry Requirements: *GCE:* 240-260. *IB:* 28.

V1PM BA Hanes gyda Newyddiaduraeth
Duration: 3FT Hon
Entry Requirements: *GCE:* 240-280. *IB:* 28.

V1P5 BA History with Journalism
Duration: 3FT Hon
Entry Requirements: *GCE:* 240-280. *IB:* 28.

R4P5 BA Spanish with Journalism
Duration: 4FT Hon
Entry Requirements: *GCE:* 240-260. *IB:* 28.

B22 UNIVERSITY OF BEDFORDSHIRE
PARK SQUARE
LUTON
BEDS LU1 3JU
t: 0844 8482234 f: 01582 489323
e: admissions@beds.ac.uk
// www.beds.ac.uk

P503 BA Broadcast Journalism
Duration: 3FT Hon
Entry Requirements: *Foundation:* Pass. *GCE:* 240. *SQAH:* BBBB-BBBC. *SQAAH:* BCC. *IB:* 24. *BTEC NC:* DD. *BTEC ND:* MMM. *OCR ND:* D *OCR NED:* M3 Interview required.

WP85 BA Creative Writing and Journalism
Duration: 3FT Hon
Entry Requirements: Contact the institution for details.

P500 BA Journalism
Duration: 3FT Hon
Entry Requirements: *Foundation:* Pass. *GCE:* 200. *SQAH:* BCC. *SQAAH:* BCC. *IB:* 24. *BTEC NC:* MM. *BTEC ND:* MPP. *OCR ND:* M1 *OCR NED:* P1 Interview required.

P501 BA Magazine Journalism
Duration: 3FT Hon
Entry Requirements: *Foundation:* Pass. *GCE:* 200. *SQAH:* BCC. *SQAAH:* BCC. *IB:* 24. *BTEC NC:* MM. *BTEC ND:* MPP. *OCR ND:* M1 *OCR NED:* P1 Interview required.

P504 BA Multiplatform Journalism
Duration: 3FT Hon
Entry Requirements: *Foundation:* Pass. *GCE:* 240. *SQAH:* BBBB-BBBC. *SQAAH:* BCC. *IB:* 24. *BTEC NC:* DD. *BTEC ND:* MMM. *OCR ND:* D *OCR NED:* M3 Interview required.

P590 BA Sport Journalism
Duration: 3FT Hon
Entry Requirements: *Foundation:* Pass. *GCE:* 200. *SQAH:* BCC. *SQAAH:* BCC. *IB:* 24. *BTEC NC:* MM. *BTEC ND:* MPP. *OCR ND:* M1 *OCR NED:* P1

P502 FdA Journalism
Duration: 2FT Fdg
Entry Requirements: Contact the institution for details.

B25 BIRMINGHAM CITY UNIVERSITY
PERRY BARR
BIRMINGHAM B42 2SU
t: 0121 331 5595 f: 0121 331 7994
e: choices@bcu.ac.uk
// www.bcu.ac.uk

P9P5 BA Media and Communication (Journalism)
Duration: 3FT Hon
Entry Requirements: *Foundation:* Pass. *GCE:* BBC. *SQAH:* ABBB. *SQAAH:* BBC. *IB:* 30. *BTEC ND:* DMM. Interview required. Portfolio required.

B40 BLACKBURN COLLEGE
FEILDEN STREET
BLACKBURN BB2 1LH
t: 01254 292594 f: 01254 679647
e: he-admissions@blackburn.ac.uk
// www.blackburn.ac.uk

P501 BA Journalism (Top-Up)
Duration: 1FT Hon
Entry Requirements: Contact the institution for details.

P500 FdA Journalism
Duration: 2FT Fdg
Entry Requirements: Contact the institution for details.

B50 BOURNEMOUTH UNIVERSITY
TALBOT CAMPUS
FERN BARROW
POOLE
DORSET BH12 5BB
t: 01202 524111
// www.bournemouth.ac.uk

P500 BA Multimedia Journalism
Duration: 3FT Hon
Entry Requirements: *Foundation:* Distinction. *GCE:* 340. *IB:* 33. *BTEC NC:* DD. *BTEC ND:* DDM. Interview required.

B72 UNIVERSITY OF BRIGHTON
209 MITHRAS HOUSE
LEWES ROAD
BRIGHTON BN2 4AT
t: 01273 644644 f: 01273 642607
e: admissions@brighton.ac.uk
// www.brighton.ac.uk

P501 BA Broadcast Journalism (at UCH)
Duration: 3FT/4SW Hon
Entry Requirements: *GCE:* BBB. *IB:* 24. *BTEC NC:* DD. *BTEC ND:* MMM.

P500 BA Sport Journalism
Duration: 3FT Hon
Entry Requirements: *GCE:* ABB. *IB:* 32. *BTEC ND:* DDM.

B80 UNIVERSITY OF THE WEST OF ENGLAND, BRISTOL
FRENCHAY CAMPUS
COLDHARBOUR LANE
BRISTOL BS16 1QY
t: +44 (0)117 32 83333 f: +44 (0)117 32 82810
e: admissions@uwe.ac.uk
// www.uwe.ac.uk

QP3M BA English and Journalism
Duration: 3FT Hon
Entry Requirements: Contact the institution for details.

P500 BA (Hons) Journalism
Duration: 3FT Hon
Entry Requirements: *GCE:* 280-320.

B84 BRUNEL UNIVERSITY
UXBRIDGE
MIDDLESEX UB8 3PH
t: 01895 265265 f: 01895 269790
e: admissions@brunel.ac.uk
// www.brunel.ac.uk

P500 BA Journalism
Duration: 3FT Hon
Entry Requirements: *GCE:* BBB. *SQAAH:* BBB. *IB:* 32. *BTEC NC:* DD. *BTEC ND:* DDD. Admissions Test required.

B90 THE UNIVERSITY OF BUCKINGHAM
YEOMANRY HOUSE
HUNTER STREET
BUCKINGHAM MK18 1EG
t: 01280 820313 f: 01280 822245
e: info@buckingham.ac.uk
// www.buckingham.ac.uk

QP35 BA Communication, Media and Journalism
Duration: 2FT Hon
Entry Requirements: *GCE:* 200. *IB:* 24. *BTEC NC:* DD. *BTEC ND:* MMM.

Q3P5 BA English Literature with Journalism
Duration: 2FT Hon
Entry Requirements: *GCE:* 260. *IB:* 27. *BTEC NC:* DD. *BTEC ND:* DMM. *OCR NED:* M2

Q3PM BA English Studies with Journalism
Duration: 2FT Hon
Entry Requirements: *GCE:* 240. *IB:* 24. *BTEC NC:* DD. *BTEC ND:* MMM.

V2P5 BA History with Journalism
Duration: 2FT Hon
Entry Requirements: *GCE:* 240. *IB:* 26. *BTEC NC:* DD. *BTEC ND:* MMM. *OCR NED:* M2

L9P5 BA International Studies with Journalism
Duration: 2FT Hon
Entry Requirements: *GCE:* 240. *IB:* 26. *BTEC NC:* DD. *BTEC ND:* MMM.

P5P9 BA Journalism with Communication Studies
Duration: 2FT Hon
Entry Requirements: *GCE:* 240. *IB:* 24. *BTEC NC:* DD. *BTEC ND:* MMM.

P5Q3 BA Journalism with English Literature
Duration: 2FT Hon
Entry Requirements: *GCE:* 240. *IB:* 24. *BTEC NC:* DD. *BTEC ND:* MMM.

P5L2 BA Journalism with International Studies
Duration: 2FT Hon
Entry Requirements: *GCE:* 240. *IB:* 24. *BTEC NC:* DD. *BTEC ND:* MMM.

L1P5 BSc Economics with Journalism
Duration: 2FT Hon
Entry Requirements: *GCE:* 300. *IB:* 26. *BTEC NC:* DD. *BTEC ND:* MMM.

C10 CANTERBURY CHRIST CHURCH UNIVERSITY
NORTH HOLMES ROAD
CANTERBURY
KENT CT1 1QU
t: 01227 782900 f: 01227 782888
e: admissions@canterbury.ac.uk
// www.canterbury.ac.uk

P501 BA Journalism: Multimedia Journalism
Duration: 3FT Hon
Entry Requirements: *GCE:* 260. *IB:* 24.

C15 CARDIFF UNIVERSITY
PO BOX 927
30-36 NEWPORT ROAD
CARDIFF CF24 0DE
t: 029 2087 9999 f: 029 2087 6138
e: admissions@cardiff.ac.uk
// www.cardiff.ac.uk

LP35 BA Journalism, Media and Sociology
Duration: 3FT Hon
Entry Requirements: *GCE:* ABB. *SQAAH:* AAABB. *IB:* 36. *BTEC ND:* DDD. Admissions Test required.

C30 UNIVERSITY OF CENTRAL LANCASHIRE
PRESTON
LANCS PR1 2HE
t: 01772 201201 f: 01772 894954
e: uadmissions@uclan.ac.uk
// www.uclan.ac.uk

QP35 BA English Language and Journalism
Duration: 3FT Hon
Entry Requirements: *GCE:* 240-260. *IB:* 28. *BTEC NC:* DD. *BTEC ND:* MMM. *OCR ND:* D *OCR NED:* M3

P502 BA International Journalism
Duration: 3FT Hon
Entry Requirements: *GCE:* BCC. *IB:* 28. *BTEC NC:* DD. *BTEC ND:* DMM. *OCR ND:* D *OCR NED:* M2

P500 BA Journalism
Duration: 3FT Hon
Entry Requirements: *GCE:* ABB. *IB:* 32. *BTEC NC:* DD. *BTEC ND:* DDM. *OCR ND:* D *OCR NED:* D2

P503 BA Journalism (Foundation Entry)
Duration: 4FT Hon
Entry Requirements: Contact the institution for details.

PQ53 BA Journalism and English Literature
Duration: 3FT Hon
Entry Requirements: *GCE:* BCC. *IB:* 28. *BTEC NC:* DD. *BTEC ND:* DMM. *OCR ND:* D *OCR NED:* M2

P501 BA Sports Journalism
Duration: 3FT Hon
Entry Requirements: *GCE:* ABB. *SQAH:* AAAB. *IB:* 30. *BTEC NC:* DD. *BTEC ND:* DDM. *OCR ND:* D *OCR NED:* D2

C55 UNIVERSITY OF CHESTER
PARKGATE ROAD
CHESTER CH1 4BJ
t: 01244 511000 f: 01244 511300
e: enquiries@chester.ac.uk
// www.chester.ac.uk

NPM5 BA Advertising and Journalism
Duration: 3FT Hon
Entry Requirements: *GCE:* 240-280. *SQAH:* BBBB. *IB:* 26. *BTEC NC:* DM. *BTEC ND:* MMM.

NP2M BA Business Management and Journalism
Duration: 3FT Hon
Entry Requirements: *GCE:* 240-280. *SQAH:* BBBB. *IB:* 26. *BTEC NC:* DM. *BTEC ND:* MMM.

WP85 BA Creative Writing and Journalism
Duration: 3FT Hon
Entry Requirements: *Foundation:* Merit. *GCE:* 260-300. *SQAH:* BBBB. *IB:* 28. *BTEC NC:* DM. *BTEC ND:* DMM.

WP6M BA Digital Photography and Journalism
Duration: 3FT Hon
Entry Requirements: *GCE:* 240-280. *SQAH:* BBBB. *IB:* 24. *BTEC NC:* DM. *BTEC ND:* MMM.

QP35 BA English Language and Journalism
Duration: 3FT Hon
Entry Requirements: *GCE:* 260-300. *SQAH:* BBBB. *IB:* 24. *BTEC NC:* DM. *BTEC ND:* MPP.

NP8M BA Events Management and Journalism
Duration: 3FT Hon
Entry Requirements: *GCE:* 240-280. *SQAH:* BBBB. *IB:* 24. *BTEC NC:* DM. *BTEC ND:* MMM.

P500 BA Journalism
Duration: 3FT Hon
Entry Requirements: *GCE:* 260-300. *SQAH:* BBBB. *IB:* 24. *BTEC NC:* DM. *BTEC ND:* MMM.

MP95 BA Journalism and Criminology
Duration: 3FT Hon
Entry Requirements: *GCE:* 240-280. *SQAH:* BBBB. *IB:* 24. *BTEC NC:* DM. *BTEC ND:* MMM.

PW54 BA Journalism and Drama & Theatre Studies
Duration: 3FT Hon
Entry Requirements: *Foundation:* Pass. *GCE:* 260-300. *SQAH:* BBBB. *IB:* 28. *BTEC NC:* DM. *BTEC ND:* DMM.

PQ53 BA Journalism and English
Duration: 3FT Hon
Entry Requirements: *GCE:* 260-300. *SQAH:* BBBB. *IB:* 24. *BTEC NC:* DM. *BTEC ND:* MPP.

PR51 BA Journalism and French
Duration: 4FT Hon
Entry Requirements: *GCE:* 240-280. *SQAH:* BBBB. *IB:* 24. *BTEC NC:* DM. *BTEC ND:* MMM.

PV51 BA Journalism and History
Duration: 3FT Hon
Entry Requirements: *GCE:* 260-300. *SQAH:* BBBB. *IB:* 28. *BTEC NC:* DM. *BTEC ND:* MMP.

PR54 BA Journalism and Spanish
Duration: 4FT Hon
Entry Requirements: *GCE:* 240-280. *SQAH:* BBBB. *IB:* 26. *BTEC NC:* DM. *BTEC ND:* MMM.

PC56 BA Journalism and Sport Development
Duration: 3FT Hon
Entry Requirements: *Foundation:* Pass. *GCE:* 240-280. *SQAH:* BBBB. *IB:* 24. *BTEC NC:* DM. *BTEC ND:* MMM.

MP15 BA Law and Journalism
Duration: 3FT Hon
Entry Requirements: *GCE:* 240-280. *SQAH:* BBBB. *IB:* 24. *BTEC NC:* DM. *BTEC ND:* MMM.

FP75 BA Natural Hazard Management and Journalism
Duration: 3FT Hon
Entry Requirements: *GCE:* 240-280. *SQAH:* BBBB. *IB:* 24. *BTEC NC:* DM. *BTEC ND:* MMM.

PW5P BA Photography and Journalism
Duration: 3FT Hon
Entry Requirements: *GCE:* 240-280. *SQAH:* BBBB. *IB:* 24. *BTEC NC:* DM. *BTEC ND:* MMM.

P590 BA Sports Journalism
Duration: 3FT Hon
Entry Requirements: *GCE:* 260-300. *SQAH:* BBBB. *IB:* 24. *BTEC NC:* DM. *BTEC ND:* MMM.

C60 CITY UNIVERSITY
NORTHAMPTON SQUARE
LONDON EC1V 0HB
t: 020 7040 5060 f: 020 7040 8995
e: ugadmissions@city.ac.uk
// www.city.ac.uk

P500 BA Journalism (3 years or 4 year SW)
Duration: 3FT Hon
Entry Requirements: *GCE:* ABB. *IB:* 32.

LP15 BA Journalism and Economics (3 years or 4 year SW)
Duration: 3FT Hon
Entry Requirements: *GCE:* ABB. *IB:* 32.

CP85 BA Journalism and Psychology (3 years or 4 year SW)
Duration: 3FT Hon
Entry Requirements: *GCE:* ABB. *IB:* 32.

LP35 BA Journalism and Sociology (3 years or 4 year SW)
Duration: 3FT Hon
Entry Requirements: *GCE:* ABB. *IB:* 32.

C78 CORNWALL COLLEGE
POOL
REDRUTH
CORNWALL TR15 3RD
t: 01209 616161 f: 01209 611612
e: he.admissions@cornwall.ac.uk
// www.cornwall.ac.uk

P500 FdA Newspaper & Magazine Journalism
Duration: 2FT Fdg   CRB Check: Required
Entry Requirements: *GCE:* 80-120. *BTEC ND:* MMP. Interview required.

C85 COVENTRY UNIVERSITY
THE STUDENT CENTRE
COVENTRY UNIVERSITY
1 GULSON RD
COVENTRY CV1 2JH
t: 024 7615 2222 f: 024 7615 2223
e: studentenquiries@coventry.ac.uk
// www.coventry.ac.uk

QP35 BA English and Journalism
Duration: 3FT/4SW Hon
Entry Requirements: *GCE:* BCC. *SQAH:* BCCCC. *IB:* 28. *BTEC ND:* DMM. *OCR NED:* M2

C93 UNIVERSITY FOR THE CREATIVE ARTS
FALKNER ROAD
FARNHAM
SURREY GU9 7DS
t: 01252 722441 f: 01252 892624
e: admissions@ucreative.ac.uk
// www.ucreative.ac.uk

WP25 BA Fashion Journalism
Duration: 3FT Hon
Entry Requirements: *GCE:* 220. Interview required. Portfolio required.

WP35 BA Music Journalism
Duration: 3FT Hon
Entry Requirements: *GCE:* 220. Interview required. Portfolio required.

C99 UNIVERSITY OF CUMBRIA
FUSEHILL STREET
CARLISLE
CUMBRIA CA1 2HH
t: 01228 616234 f: 01228 616235
// www.cumbria.ac.uk

P500 BA Journalism
Duration: 3FT Hon
Entry Requirements: *Foundation:* Merit. *GCE:* 240. *SQAH:* BBC. *SQAAH:* CC. *IB:* 30. *BTEC NC:* DD. *BTEC ND:* MMM. *OCR ND:* D Interview required. Portfolio required.

P502 BA Journalism (with Year 0)
Duration: 4FT Hon
Entry Requirements: *Foundation:* Pass. *GCE:* C-cccc. *SQAH:* CC. *SQAAH:* C. *IB:* 25. *BTEC NC:* MP. *BTEC ND:* PPP. Interview required. Portfolio required.

PW58 BA Journalism and Creative Writing
Duration: 3FT Hon
Entry Requirements: *GCE:* 200. *IB:* 33. *BTEC NC:* DM. *BTEC ND:* MMM.

D26 DE MONTFORT UNIVERSITY
THE GATEWAY
LEICESTER LE1 9BH
t: 0116 255 1551 f: 0116 250 6204
e: enquiries@dmu.ac.uk
// www.dmu.ac.uk

WP85 BA Creative Writing and Journalism
Duration: 3FT Hon
Entry Requirements: *GCE:* 260. *IB:* 28. Interview required.

QP35 BA English Language and Journalism
Duration: 3FT Hon
Entry Requirements: *GCE:* 260. *IB:* 28. Interview required.

PQ53 BA English and Journalism
Duration: 3FT Hon
Entry Requirements: *GCE:* 260. *IB:* 28. Interview required.

PV51 BA History and Journalism
Duration: 3FT Hon
Entry Requirements: *GCE:* 260. *IB:* 28. Interview required.

LP25 BA International Relations and Journalism
Duration: 3FT Hon
Entry Requirements: *GCE:* 260. *IB:* 28. Interview required.

P500 BA Journalism
Duration: 3FT Hon
Entry Requirements: *GCE:* 260. *IB:* 28. Interview required.
Admissions Test required.

LPF5 BA Journalism and Politics
Duration: 3FT Hon
Entry Requirements: *GCE:* 260. *IB:* 28. Interview required.

D39 UNIVERSITY OF DERBY
KEDLESTON ROAD
DERBY DE22 1GB
t: 01332 591167 f: 01332 597724
e: askadmissions@derby.ac.uk
// www.derby.ac.uk

P500 BA Journalism
Duration: 3FT Hon
Entry Requirements: *Foundation:* Merit. *GCE:* 240. *IB:* 26. *BTEC NC:* DD. *BTEC ND:* MMM. *OCR ND:* D *OCR NED:* M3

E28 UNIVERSITY OF EAST LONDON
DOCKLANDS CAMPUS
UNIVERSITY WAY
LONDON E16 2RD
t: 020 8223 3333 f: 020 8223 2978
e: study@uel.ac.uk
// www.uel.ac.uk

W8P5 BA Creative & Professional Writing with Journalism Studies
Duration: 3FT Hon
Entry Requirements: *GCE:* 200. *IB:* 24. *BTEC NC:* DM. *BTEC ND:* MMP.

NP65 BA Human Resource Management/Journalism Studies
Duration: 3FT Hon
Entry Requirements: *GCE:* 200. *IB:* 24. *BTEC NC:* DM. *BTEC ND:* MMP.

NP15 BA International Business/Journalism Studies
Duration: 3FT Hon
Entry Requirements: *GCE:* 200. *IB:* 24. *BTEC NC:* DM. *BTEC ND:* MMP. *OCR ND:* M1 *OCR NED:* P1

P500 BA Journalism
Duration: 3FT Hon
Entry Requirements: *GCE:* 200. *IB:* 24. *BTEC NC:* DM. *BTEC ND:* MMP.

P501 BA Journalism (Extended)
Duration: 4FT Hon
Entry Requirements: *GCE:* 40. *IB:* 24.

P5W6 BA Journalism Studies with Animation
Duration: 3FT Hon
Entry Requirements: *GCE:* 200. *IB:* 24. *BTEC NC:* DM. *BTEC ND:* MMP. *OCR ND:* M1 *OCR NED:* P1

P5P9 BA Journalism Studies with Communication Studies
Duration: 3FT Hon
Entry Requirements: *GCE:* 200. *IB:* 24. *BTEC NC:* DM. *BTEC ND:* MMP.

P5W8 BA Journalism Studies with Creative & Professional Writing
Duration: 3FT Hon
Entry Requirements: *GCE:* 200. *IB:* 24. *BTEC NC:* DM. *BTEC ND:* MMP.

P5Q3 BA Journalism Studies with English Literature
Duration: 3FT Hon
Entry Requirements: *GCE:* 200. *IB:* 24. *BTEC NC:* DM. *BTEC ND:* MMP.

P5G5 BA Journalism Studies with Information Technology
Duration: 3FT Hon
Entry Requirements: *GCE:* 200. *IB:* 24. *BTEC NC:* DM. *BTEC ND:* MMP.

PW58 BA Journalism Studies/Creative & Professional Writing
Duration: 3FT Hon
Entry Requirements: *GCE:* 200. *IB:* 24. *BTEC NC:* DM. *BTEC ND:* MMP.

PL52 BA Journalism Studies/International Politics
Duration: 3FT Hon
Entry Requirements: *GCE:* 200. *IB:* 24. *BTEC NC:* DM. *BTEC ND:* MMP.

LP35 BA Journalism Studies/Sociology
Duration: 3FT Hon
Entry Requirements: *GCE:* 200. *IB:* 24. *BTEC NC:* DM. *BTEC ND:* MMP.

V000 BA Media & Creative Industries option - Journalism Studies
Duration: 3FT Hon
Entry Requirements: *GCE:* 200. *IB:* 24.

N2P5 BA Music Industry Management with Journalism Studies
Duration: 3FT Hon
Entry Requirements: *GCE:* 200. *IB:* 24. *BTEC NC:* DM. *BTEC ND:* MMP.

P502 BA Sports Journalism
Duration: 3FT Hon
Entry Requirements: *GCE:* 280. *IB:* 24. *BTEC NC:* DM. *BTEC ND:* MMP.

P503 BA Sports Journalism (Extended)
Duration: 4FT Hon
Entry Requirements: Contact the institution for details.

GP55 BA/BSc Business Information Systems/Journalism Studies
Duration: 3FT Hon
Entry Requirements: *GCE:* 200. *IB:* 24. *BTEC NC:* DM. *BTEC ND:* MMP. *OCR ND:* M1 *OCR NED:* P1

CP65 BA/BSc Sports Coaching/Journalism Studies
Duration: 3FT Hon
Entry Requirements: *GCE:* 200. *IB:* 24. *BTEC NC:* DM. *BTEC ND:* MMP.

CP6M BSc Fitness & Health and Sport Journalism
Duration: 3FT Hon
Entry Requirements: Contact the institution for details.

C6P5 BSc Fitness & Health with Sport Journalism
Duration: 3FT Hon
Entry Requirements: Contact the institution for details.

CP6N BSc Sports & Exercise Science and Sport Journalism
Duration: 3FT Hon
Entry Requirements: Contact the institution for details.

C6PM BSc Sports & Exercise Science with Sport Journalism
Duration: 3FT Hon
Entry Requirements: Contact the institution for details.

CPP5 BSc Sports Development and Sport Journalism
Duration: 3FT Hon
Entry Requirements: Contact the institution for details.

C6PN BSc Sports Development with Sport Journalism
Duration: 3FT Hon
Entry Requirements: Contact the institution for details.

E59 EDINBURGH NAPIER UNIVERSITY
CRAIGLOCKHART CAMPUS
EDINBURGH EH14 1DJ
t: +44 (0)8452 60 60 40 f: 0131 455 6464
e: info@napier.ac.uk
// www.napier.ac.uk

P500 BA Journalism
Duration: 3FT/4FT Ord/Hon
Entry Requirements: *GCE:* 240. Interview required.

F33 UNIVERSITY COLLEGE FALMOUTH
WOODLANE
FALMOUTH
CORNWALL TR11 4RH
t: 01326213730
e: admissions@falmouth.ac.uk
// www.falmouth.ac.uk

P500 BA(Hons) Journalism
Duration: 3FT Hon
Entry Requirements: *GCE:* 220. *IB:* 24. Interview required. Portfolio required.

WP65 BA(Hons) Press & Editorial Photography
Duration: 3FT Hon
Entry Requirements: *GCE:* 220. *IB:* 24. Interview required. Portfolio required.

G14 UNIVERSITY OF GLAMORGAN, CARDIFF AND PONTYPRIDD
ENQUIRIES AND ADMISSIONS UNIT
PONTYPRIDD CF37 1DL
t: 0800 716925 f: 01443 654050
e: enquiries@glam.ac.uk
// www.glam.ac.uk

P500 BA Journalism
Duration: 3FT Hon
Entry Requirements: *GCE:* BBB. *IB:* 24. *BTEC ND:* DMM. *OCR NED:* M2 Interview required. Admissions Test required.

G42 GLASGOW CALEDONIAN UNIVERSITY
STUDENT RECRUITMENT & ADMISSIONS SERVICE
CITY CAMPUS
COWCADDENS ROAD
GLASGOW G4 0BA
t: 0141 331 3000 f: 0141 331 8676
e: undergraduate@gcu.ac.uk
// www.gcu.ac.uk

P500 BA Multimedia Journalism
Duration: 4FT Hon
Entry Requirements: *GCE:* BBC. *SQAH:* ABBB-BBBB. *IB:* 25. Interview required. Admissions Test required.

G50 THE UNIVERSITY OF GLOUCESTERSHIRE
PARK CAMPUS
THE PARK
CHELTENHAM GL50 2RH
t: 01242 714503 f: 01242 714827
e: admissions@glos.ac.uk
// www.glos.ac.uk

P502 BA Journalism
Duration: 3FT Hon
Entry Requirements: *GCE:* 280-300. Interview required.

WP65 BA Photojournalism & Documentary Photography
Duration: 3FT Hon
Entry Requirements: *GCE:* 280-300. Interview required. Portfolio required.

G53 GLYNDWR UNIVERSITY
PLAS COCH
MOLD ROAD
WREXHAM LL11 2AW
t: 01978 293439 f: 01978 290008
e: sid@glyndwr.ac.uk
// www.glyndwr.ac.uk

PP35 BA Broadcasting, Journalism and Media Communications
Duration: 3FT Hon
Entry Requirements: *GCE:* 240.

QP35 BA English, Broadcasting and Journalism
Duration: 3FT Hon
Entry Requirements: *GCE:* 240.

HP65 BSc Radio Production and Communication
Duration: 3FT Hon
Entry Requirements: *GCE:* 240.

G70 UNIVERSITY OF GREENWICH
GREENWICH CAMPUS
OLD ROYAL NAVAL COLLEGE
PARK ROW
LONDON SE10 9LS
t: 0800 005 006 f: 020 8331 8145
e: courseinfo@gre.ac.uk
// www.gre.ac.uk

Q3P5 BA English Literature with Media Writing
Duration: 3FT Hon
Entry Requirements: *GCE:* 280. *IB:* 24.

V1P5 BA History with Media Writing
Duration: 3FT Hon
Entry Requirements: *GCE:* 200. *IB:* 24.

P590 BA Media Writing
Duration: 3FT Hon
Entry Requirements: *GCE:* 280. *IB:* 24.

P5V1 BA Media Writing with History
Duration: 3FT Hon
Entry Requirements: *GCE:* 280. *IB:* 24.

P5L2 BA Media Writing with Politics
Duration: 3FT Hon
Entry Requirements: *GCE:* 280. *IB:* 24.

G80 GRIMSBY INSTITUTE OF FURTHER AND HIGHER EDUCATION
NUNS CORNER
GRIMSBY
NE LINCOLNSHIRE DN34 5BQ
t: 0800 328 3631 f: 01472 315506/879924
e: headmissions@grimsby.ac.uk
// www.grimsby.ac.uk

P502 BA Multi-Platform Journalism
Duration: 3FT Hon
Entry Requirements: Interview required.

H36 UNIVERSITY OF HERTFORDSHIRE
UNIVERSITY ADMISSIONS SERVICE
COLLEGE LANE
HATFIELD
HERTS AL10 9AB
t: 01707 284800
// www.herts.ac.uk

Q1P5 BA English Language & Communication with Journalism
Duration: 3FT Hon
Entry Requirements: *GCE:* 300.

Q3P5 BA English Literature with Journalism
Duration: 3FT Hon
Entry Requirements: *GCE:* 300.

NP15 BA Entrepreneurship/Journalism and Media Cultures
Duration: 3FT/4SW Hon
Entry Requirements: Contact the institution for details.

V1P5 BA History with Journalism
Duration: 3FT Hon
Entry Requirements: *GCE:* 300.

V5P5 BA Philosophy with Journalism
Duration: 3FT Hon
Entry Requirements: *GCE:* 300.

N1P5 BSc Business/Journalism & Media Cultures
Duration: 3FT/4SW Hon
Entry Requirements: Contact the institution for details.

H6P5 BSc Digital Media Technology/Journalism & Media Cultures
Duration: 3FT/4SW Hon
Entry Requirements: Contact the institution for details.

Q1PM BSc English Language & Communication/Journalism & Media Cultures
Duration: 3FT/4SW Hon
Entry Requirements: *GCE:* 220.

G9P5 BSc Financial Mathematics/Journalism & Media Cultures
Duration: 3FT/3.5SW Hon
Entry Requirements: *GCE:* 220-260.

B9P5 BSc Health Studies/Journalism & Media Cultures
Duration: 3FT/4SW Hon
Entry Requirements: Contact the institution for details.

B1P5 BSc Human Biology/Journalism & Media Cultures
Duration: 3FT/4SW Hon
Entry Requirements: Contact the institution for details.

L7P5 BSc Human Geography/Journalism & Media Cultures
Duration: 3FT/4SW Hon
Entry Requirements: Contact the institution for details.

P5N1 BSc Journalism & Media Cultures/Business
Duration: 3FT/4SW Hon
Entry Requirements: Contact the institution for details.

P5H6 BSc Journalism & Media Cultures/Digital Media Technology
Duration: 3FT/4SW Hon
Entry Requirements: Contact the institution for details.

P5Q1 BSc Journalism & Media Cultures/English Language & Communication
Duration: 3FT/4SW Hon
Entry Requirements: *GCE:* 260.

P5G9 BSc Journalism & Media Cultures/Financial Mathematics
Duration: 3FT/4SW Hon
Entry Requirements: *GCE:* 260.

P5B9 BSc Journalism & Media Cultures/Health Studies
Duration: 3FT/4SW Hon
Entry Requirements: Contact the institution for details.

P5B1 BSc Journalism & Media Cultures/Human Biology
Duration: 3FT/4SW Hon
Entry Requirements: Contact the institution for details.

P5L7 BSc Journalism & Media Cultures/Human Geography
Duration: 3FT/4SW Hon
Entry Requirements: Contact the institution for details.

P5M1 BSc Journalism & Media Cultures/Law
Duration: 3FT/4SW Hon
Entry Requirements: Contact the institution for details.

P5G1 BSc Journalism & Media Cultures/Mathematics
Duration: 3FT/4SW Hon
Entry Requirements: Contact the institution for details.

P5V5 BSc Journalism & Media Cultures/Philosophy
Duration: 3FT/4SW Hon
Entry Requirements: *GCE:* 260.

P5C6 BSc Journalism & Media Cultures/Sports Studies
Duration: 3FT/4SW Hon
Entry Requirements: Contact the institution for details.

P5N8 BSc Journalism & Media Cultures/Tourism
Duration: 3FT/4SW Hon
Entry Requirements: Contact the institution for details.

M1P5 BSc Law/Journalism & Media Cultures
Duration: 3FT/4SW Hon
Entry Requirements: Contact the institution for details.

G1P5 BSc Mathematics/Journalism & Media Cultures
Duration: 3FT/4SW Hon
Entry Requirements: Contact the institution for details.

V5PM BSc Philosophy/Journalism & Media Cultures
Duration: 3FT/4SW Hon
Entry Requirements: *GCE:* 220.

C6P5 BSc Sports Studies/Journalism & Media Cultures
Duration: 3FT/4SW Hon
Entry Requirements: Contact the institution for details.

N8P5 BSc Tourism/Journalism & Media Cultures
Duration: 3FT/4SW Hon
Entry Requirements: Contact the institution for details.

H60 THE UNIVERSITY OF HUDDERSFIELD
QUEENSGATE
HUDDERSFIELD HD1 3DH
t: 01484 473969 f: 01484 472765
e: admissionsandrecords@hud.ac.uk
// www.hud.ac.uk

P501 BA Broadcast Journalism
Duration: 3FT Hon
Entry Requirements: *GCE:* 280. *SQAH:* ABBB-BBBB. *IB:* 28.
Interview required.

NP15 BA Business and Journalism
Duration: 3FT/4SW Hon
Entry Requirements: *GCE:* 300. *SQAH:* BBBB. *IB:* 26. *BTEC ND:*
DDM.

P500 BA Journalism
Duration: 3FT Hon
Entry Requirements: *GCE:* 280. *SQAH:* ABBB-BBBB. *IB:* 28.
Interview required.

P502 BA Music Journalism
Duration: 3FT Hon
Entry Requirements: *GCE:* 280. *SQAH:* ABBB-BBBB. *IB:* 28.
Interview required.

P503 BA Sports Journalism
Duration: 3FT Hon
Entry Requirements: *GCE:* 280. *SQAH:* ABBB-BBBB. *IB:* 28.
Interview required.

H73 HULL COLLEGE
QUEEN'S GARDENS
HULL HU1 3DG
t: 01482 329943 f: 01482 598733
e: info@hull-college.ac.uk
// www.hull-college.ac.uk/HE

P500 FdA Digital Media Journalism
Duration: 2FT Fdg
Entry Requirements: *GCE:* 200. Foundation Course required.
Interview required. Portfolio required.

K24 THE UNIVERSITY OF KENT
INFORMATION, RECRUITMENT & ADMISSIONS
REGISTRY
UNIVERSITY OF KENT
CANTERBURY, KENT CT2 7NZ
t: 01227 827272 f: 01227 827077
e: information@kent.ac.uk
// www.kent.ac.uk

P500 BA Journalism
Duration: 3FT Hon
Entry Requirements: *GCE:* ABB. *IB:* 33. *BTEC NC:* DD. *BTEC ND:*
DMM. *OCR ND:* M1 *OCR NED:* M2 Interview required. Admissions
Test required.

K84 KINGSTON UNIVERSITY
STUDENT INFORMATION & ADVICE CENTRE
COOPER HOUSE
40-46 SURBITON ROAD
KINGSTON UPON THAMES KT1 2HX
t: 0844 8552177 f: 020 8547 7080
e: aps@kingston.ac.uk
// www.kingston.ac.uk

WP85 BA Creative Writing and Journalism
Duration: 3FT Hon
Entry Requirements: *GCE:* 320. *BTEC ND:* DDM.

W8P5 BA Creative Writing with Journalism
Duration: 3FT Hon
Entry Requirements: *GCE:* 320. *BTEC ND:* DDM.

LP15 BA Economics (Applied) and Journalism
Duration: 3FT Hon
Entry Requirements: *GCE:* 320. *BTEC ND:* DDM.

L1P5 BA Economics (Applied) with Journalism
Duration: 3FT Hon
Entry Requirements: *GCE:* 320. *BTEC ND:* DDM.

Q3PM BA English Language & Communication with Journalism
Duration: 3FT Hon
Entry Requirements: *GCE:* 320. *BTEC ND:* DDM.

QP35 BA English Language & Communications and Journalism
Duration: 3FT Hon
Entry Requirements: *GCE:* 320. *BTEC ND:* DDM.

QPH5 BA English Literature and Journalism
Duration: 3FT Hon
Entry Requirements: *GCE:* 320. *BTEC ND:* DDM.

Q3P5 BA English Literature with Journalism
Duration: 3FT Hon
Entry Requirements: *GCE:* 320. *BTEC ND:* DDM.

VP15 BA History and Journalism
Duration: 3FT Hon
Entry Requirements: *GCE:* 320. *BTEC ND:* DDM.

VP35 BA History of Art, Design & Film and Journalism
Duration: 3FT Hon
Entry Requirements: *GCE:* 320.

V3P5 BA History of Art, Design & Film with Journalism
Duration: 3FT Hon
Entry Requirements: *GCE:* 320. *BTEC ND:* DDM.

V1P5 BA History with Journalism
Duration: 3FT Hon
Entry Requirements: *GCE:* 320. *BTEC ND:* DDM.

LP25 BA Human Rights and Journalism
Duration: 3FT Hon
Entry Requirements: *GCE:* 320. *BTEC ND:* DDM.

L2PM BA Human Rights with Journalism
Duration: 3FT Hon
Entry Requirements: *GCE:* 320. *BTEC ND:* DDM.

LPF5 BA International Relations and Journalism
Duration: 3FT Hon
Entry Requirements: *GCE:* 320. *BTEC ND:* DDD.

P500 BA Journalism
Duration: 3FT Hon
Entry Requirements: *GCE:* 320. *SQAH:* BBCCC. *SQAAH:* BBC. *IB:* 25. *BTEC ND:* DDM.

PL52 BA Journalism and Politics
Duration: 3FT Hon
Entry Requirements: *GCE:* 320. *SQAH:* BBCCC. *SQAAH:* BBC. *IB:* 25. *BTEC ND:* DDM.

PC58 BA Journalism and Psychology
Duration: 3FT Hon
Entry Requirements: *GCE:* 320. *SQAH:* BBCCC. *SQAAH:* BBC. *IB:* 25. *BTEC ND:* DDM.

PL53 BA Journalism and Sociology
Duration: 3FT Hon
Entry Requirements: *GCE:* 320. *SQAH:* BBCCC. *SQAAH:* BBC. *IB:* 25. *BTEC ND:* DDM.

P5W8 BA Journalism with Creative Writing
Duration: 3FT Hon
Entry Requirements: *GCE:* 320. *SQAH:* BBCCC. *SQAAH:* BBC. *IB:* 25. *BTEC ND:* DDM.

P5L1 BA Journalism with Economics (Applied)
Duration: 3FT Hon
Entry Requirements: *GCE:* 300-320. *SQAH:* BBCCC. *SQAAH:* BBC. *IB:* 25. *BTEC ND:* DDM.

P5Q1 BA Journalism with English Language & Communication
Duration: 3FT Hon
Entry Requirements: *GCE:* 320. *SQAH:* BBCCC. *SQAAH:* BBC. *IB:* 25. *BTEC ND:* DDM.

P5Q3 BA Journalism with English Literature
Duration: 3FT Hon
Entry Requirements: *GCE:* 320. *SQAH:* BBCCC. *SQAAH:* BBC. *IB:* 25. *BTEC ND:* DDM.

P5R1 BA Journalism with French
Duration: 3FT Hon
Entry Requirements: *GCE:* 320. *SQAH:* BBCCC. *SQAAH:* BBC. *IB:* 25. *BTEC ND:* DDM.

P5V1 BA Journalism with History
Duration: 3FT Hon
Entry Requirements: *GCE:* 320. *SQAH:* BBCCC. *SQAAH:* BBC. *IB:* 25. *BTEC ND:* DDM.

P5V3 BA Journalism with History of Art, Design & Film
Duration: 3FT Hon
Entry Requirements: *GCE:* 320. *SQAH:* BBCCC. *SQAAH:* BBC. *IB:* 25. *BTEC ND:* DDM.

P5LF BA Journalism with Human Rights
Duration: 3FT Hon
Entry Requirements: *GCE:* 320. *SQAH:* BBCCC. *SQAAH:* BBC. *IB:* 25. *BTEC ND:* DDM.

P5LG BA Journalism with International Relations
Duration: 3FT Hon
Entry Requirements: *GCE:* 320. *SQAH:* BBCCC. *SQAAH:* BBC. *IB:* 25. *BTEC ND:* DDM.

P5L2 BA Journalism with Politics
Duration: 3FT Hon
Entry Requirements: *GCE:* 320. *SQAH:* BBCCC. *SQAAH:* BBC. *IB:* 25. *BTEC ND:* DDM.

P5C8 BA Journalism with Psychology
Duration: 3FT Hon
Entry Requirements: *GCE:* 320. *SQAH:* BBCCC. *SQAAH:* BBC. *IB:* 25. *BTEC ND:* DDM.

P5L3 BA Journalism with Sociology
Duration: 3FT Hon
Entry Requirements: *GCE:* 320. *SQAH:* BBCCC. *SQAAH:* BBC. *IB:* 25. *BTEC ND:* DDM.

L2P5 BA Politics with Journalism
Duration: 3FT Hon
Entry Requirements: *GCE:* 320. *BTEC ND:* DDD.

C8P5 BA Psychology with Journalism
Duration: 3FT Hon
Entry Requirements: *GCE:* 320. *BTEC ND:* DDD.

L3P5 BA Sociology with Journalism
Duration: 3FT Hon
Entry Requirements: *GCE:* BBB.

P5R4 BA (Hons) Journalism with Spanish
Duration: 3FT Hon
Entry Requirements: *GCE:* 320. *SQAH:* BBCCC. *SQAAH:* BBC. *IB:* 25. *BTEC ND:* DDM.

L2PN BSc International Relations with Journalism
Duration: 3FT Hon
Entry Requirements: *GCE:* 320. *BTEC ND:* DDD.

L23 UNIVERSITY OF LEEDS
THE UNIVERSITY OF LEEDS
WOODHOUSE LANE
LEEDS LS2 9JT
t: 0113 343 3999
e: admissions@leeds.ac.uk
// www.leeds.ac.uk

PJ59 BA Broadcast Journalism
Duration: 3FT Hon
Entry Requirements: *GCE:* ABB. *SQAH:* AAABB. *SQAAH:* ABB. *IB:* 34.

L24 LEEDS TRINITY UNIVERSITY COLLEGE (FORMERLY LEEDS TRINITY AND ALL SAINTS)
BROWNBERRIE LANE
HORSFORTH
LEEDS LS18 5HD
t: 0113 283 7150 f: 0113 283 7222
e: enquiries@leedstrinity.ac.uk
// www.leedstrinity.ac.uk

P501 BA Journalism
Duration: 3FT Hon
Entry Requirements: *GCE:* 240. *IB:* 24. *BTEC NC:* DD. *BTEC ND:* MMM.

P591 BA Sports Journalism
Duration: 3FT Hon
Entry Requirements: *GCE:* 240. *IB:* 24. *BTEC NC:* PP. *BTEC ND:* MMM.

L27 LEEDS METROPOLITAN UNIVERSITY
COURSE ENQUIRIES OFFICE
CITY SITE
LEEDS LS1 3HE
t: 0113 81 23113 f: 0113 81 23129
// www.leedsmet.ac.uk

P500 BA Journalism
Duration: 3FT Hon
Entry Requirements: *GCE:* 260.

WP65 BSc Photographic Journalism
Duration: 3FT Hon
Entry Requirements: *GCE:* 200. *IB:* 24. Interview required.

L39 UNIVERSITY OF LINCOLN
ADMISSIONS
BRAYFORD POOL
LINCOLN LN6 7TS
t: 01522 886097 f: 01522 886146
e: admissions@lincoln.ac.uk
// www.lincoln.ac.uk

PQ53 BA English and Journalism
Duration: 3FT Hon
Entry Requirements: *GCE:* 280.

PV51 BA History and Journalism
Duration: 3FT Hon
Entry Requirements: *GCE:* 280.

P590 BA Investigative Journalism and Research
Duration: 3FT Hon
Entry Requirements: *GCE:* 280.

P500 BA Journalism
Duration: 3FT Hon
Entry Requirements: *GCE:* 280.

LP25 BA/BSc Journalism and Politics
Duration: 3FT Hon
Entry Requirements: *GCE:* 280.

P591 FdA Community Journalism
Duration: 2FT Hon
Entry Requirements: *GCE:* 120.

L51 LIVERPOOL JOHN MOORES UNIVERSITY
KINGSWAY HOUSE
HATTON GARDEN
LIVERPOOL L3 2AJ
t: 0151 231 5090 f: 0151 231 3462
e: courses@ljmu.ac.uk
// www.ljmu.ac.uk

P510 BA International Journalism
Duration: 3FT Hon
Entry Requirements: *GCE:* 280.

P500 BA Journalism
Duration: 3FT Hon
Entry Requirements: *GCE:* 280. *IB:* 25. *BTEC ND:* DMM.

L62 THE LONDON COLLEGE, UCK
VICTORIA GARDENS
NOTTING HILL GATE
LONDON W11 3PE
t: 020 7243 4000 f: 020 7243 1484
e: admissions@lcuck.ac.uk
// www.lcuck.ac.uk

105P HNC Creative Media Production (Journalism)
Duration: 1FT HNC
Entry Requirements: Contact the institution for details.

205P HND Creative Media Production (Journalism)
Duration: 2FT HND
Entry Requirements: Contact the institution for details.

L68 LONDON METROPOLITAN UNIVERSITY
166-220 HOLLOWAY ROAD
LONDON N7 8DB
t: 020 7133 4200
e: admissions@londonmet.ac.uk
// www.londonmet.ac.uk

WP85 BA Creative Writing and Journalism
Duration: 3FT Hon
Entry Requirements: *GCE:* 280. *IB:* 28. Portfolio required.

P503 BA Digital Journalism
Duration: 3FT Hon
Entry Requirements: Contact the institution for details.

NP5M BA Fashion Marketing and Journalism
Duration: 3FT Hon
Entry Requirements: *GCE:* 280. *IB:* 28.

P502 BA Journalism
Duration: 3FT Hon
Entry Requirements: *GCE:* 280. *IB:* 28.

PX53 BA Journalism and Education Studies
Duration: 3FT Hon
Entry Requirements: Contact the institution for details.

PQ53 BA Journalism and English
Duration: 3FT Hon
Entry Requirements: Contact the institution for details.

L75 LONDON SOUTH BANK UNIVERSITY
103 BOROUGH ROAD
LONDON SE1 0AA
t: 020 7815 7815 f: 020 7815 8273
e: enquiry@lsbu.ac.uk
// www.lsbu.ac.uk

P501 BA Multimedia Journalism
Duration: 3FT Hon
Entry Requirements: *GCE:* 240. *IB:* 24. *BTEC NC:* DD. *BTEC ND:* MMM.

M80 MIDDLESEX UNIVERSITY
MIDDLESEX UNIVERSITY
THE BURROUGHS
LONDON NW4 4BT
t: 020 8411 5555 f: 020 8411 5649
e: enquiries@mdx.ac.uk
// www.mdx.ac.uk

WP85 BA Creative Writing and Journalism Studies
Duration: 3FT Hon
Entry Requirements: *GCE:* 200-300. *IB:* 28.

PP59 BA Journalism and Communication Studies
Duration: 3FT Hon
Entry Requirements: *GCE:* 200-300. *IB:* 28.

PP54 BA Journalism and Publishing Studies
Duration: 3FT Hon
Entry Requirements: *GCE:* 200-300. *IB:* 28.

PP45 BA Publishing, Journalism and Media
Duration: 3FT Hon
Entry Requirements: *GCE:* 200-300. *IB:* 28.

P590 BA Television Journalism
Duration: 3FT Hon
Entry Requirements: *GCE:* 200-300. *IB:* 28.

N38 UNIVERSITY OF NORTHAMPTON
PARK CAMPUS
BOUGHTON GREEN ROAD
NORTHAMPTON NN2 7AL
t: 0800 358 2232 f: 01604 722083
e: admissions@northampton.ac.uk
// www.northampton.ac.uk

N5PM BA Advertising/Journalism
Duration: 3FT Hon
Entry Requirements: *GCE:* 260-280. *SQAH:* AAA-BBBB. *IB:* 24. *BTEC NC:* DD. *BTEC ND:* DMM. *OCR ND:* D *OCR NED:* M2

N1P5 BA Business/Journalism
Duration: 3FT Hon
Entry Requirements: *GCE:* 260-280. *SQAH:* AAA-BBBB. *IB:* 24. *BTEC NC:* DD. *BTEC ND:* DMM. *OCR ND:* D *OCR NED:* M2

W8P5 BA Creative Writing/Journalism
Duration: 3FT Hon
Entry Requirements: *GCE:* 260-280. *SQAH:* AAA-BBBB. *IB:* 24.
BTEC NC: DD. *BTEC ND:* DMM. *OCR ND:* D *OCR NED:* M2

W4P5 BA Drama/Journalism
Duration: 3FT Hon
Entry Requirements: *GCE:* 260-280. *SQAH:* AAA-BBBB. *IB:* 24.
BTEC NC: DD. *BTEC ND:* DMM. *OCR ND:* D *OCR NED:* M2
Interview required.

L1P5 BA Economics/Journalism
Duration: 3FT Hon
Entry Requirements: *GCE:* 260-280. *SQAH:* AAA-BBBB. *IB:* 24.
BTEC NC: DD. *BTEC ND:* DMM. *OCR ND:* D *OCR NED:* M2

X3P5 BA Education Studies/Journalism
Duration: 3FT Hon
Entry Requirements: *GCE:* 260-280. *SQAH:* AAA-BBBB. *IB:* 24.
BTEC NC: DD. *BTEC ND:* DMM. *OCR ND:* D *OCR NED:* M2

Q3P5 BA English/Journalism
Duration: 3FT Hon
Entry Requirements: *GCE:* 260-280. *SQAH:* AAA-BBBB. *IB:* 24.
BTEC NC: DD. *BTEC ND:* DMM. *OCR ND:* D *OCR NED:* M2

N8PN BA Events Management/Journalism
Duration: 3FT Hon
Entry Requirements: *GCE:* 260-280. *SQAH:* AAA-BBBB. *IB:* 24.
BTEC NC: DD. *BTEC ND:* DMM. *OCR ND:* D *OCR NED:* M2

W6P5 BA Film & Television Studies/Journalism
Duration: 3FT Hon
Entry Requirements: *GCE:* 260-280. *SQAH:* AAA-BBBB. *IB:* 24.
BTEC NC: DD. *BTEC ND:* DMM. *OCR ND:* D *OCR NED:* M2

L4P5 BA Health Studies/Journalism
Duration: 3FT Hon
Entry Requirements: *GCE:* 260-280. *SQAH:* AAA-BBBB. *IB:* 24.
BTEC NC: DD. *BTEC ND:* DMM. *OCR ND:* D *OCR NED:* M2

D4P5 BA Heritage Management/Journalism
Duration: 3FT Hon
Entry Requirements: *GCE:* 260-280. *SQAH:* AAA-BBBB. *IB:* 24.
BTEC NC: DD. *BTEC ND:* DMM. *OCR ND:* D *OCR NED:* M2

L9P5 BA International Development/Journalism
Duration: 3FT Hon
Entry Requirements: *GCE:* 260-280. *SQAH:* AAA-BBBB. *IB:* 24.
BTEC NC: DD. *BTEC ND:* DMM. *OCR ND:* D *OCR NED:* M2

P500 BA Journalism
Duration: 3FT Hon
Entry Requirements: *GCE:* 260-280. *SQAH:* AAA-BBBB. *IB:* 24.
BTEC NC: DD. *BTEC ND:* DMM. *OCR ND:* D *OCR NED:* M2

P501 BA Journalism (top-up)
Duration: 1FT Hon
Entry Requirements: Contact the institution for details.

P5NF BA Journalism with Applied Management
Duration: 3FT Hon
Entry Requirements: *GCE:* 260-280. *SQAH:* AAA-BBBB. *IB:* 24.
BTEC NC: DD. *BTEC ND:* DMM. *OCR ND:* D *OCR NED:* M2

P5D4 BA Journalism with Equine Studies
Duration: 3FT Hon
Entry Requirements: *GCE:* 260-280. *SQAH:* AAA-BBBB. *IB:* 24.
BTEC NC: DD. *BTEC ND:* DMM. *OCR ND:* D *OCR NED:* M2

P5NM BA Journalism/Advertising
Duration: 3FT Hon
Entry Requirements: *GCE:* 260-280. *SQAH:* AAA-BBBB. *IB:* 24.
BTEC NC: DD. *BTEC ND:* DMM. *OCR ND:* D *OCR NED:* M2

P5C1 BA Journalism/Biological Conservation
Duration: 3FT Hon
Entry Requirements: *GCE:* 260-280. *SQAH:* AAA-BBBB. *IB:* 24.
BTEC NC: DD. *BTEC ND:* DMM. *OCR ND:* D *OCR NED:* M2

P5N1 BA Journalism/Business
Duration: 3FT Hon
Entry Requirements: *GCE:* 260-280. *SQAH:* AAA-BBBB. *IB:* 24.
BTEC NC: DD. *BTEC ND:* DMM. *OCR ND:* D *OCR NED:* M2

P5G5 BA Journalism/Business Computing Systems
Duration: 3FT Hon
Entry Requirements: *GCE:* 260-280. *SQAH:* AAA-BBBB. *IB:* 24.
BTEC NC: DD. *BTEC ND:* DMM. *OCR ND:* D *OCR NED:* M2

P5G4 BA Journalism/Computing
Duration: 3FT Hon
Entry Requirements: *GCE:* 260-280. *SQAH:* AAA-BBBB. *IB:* 24.
BTEC NC: DD. *BTEC ND:* DMM. *OCR ND:* D *OCR NED:* M2

P5W8 BA Journalism/Creative Writing
Duration: 3FT Hon
Entry Requirements: *GCE:* 260-280. *SQAH:* AAA-BBBB. *IB:* 24.
BTEC NC: DD. *BTEC ND:* DMM. *OCR ND:* D *OCR NED:* M2

P5W4 BA Journalism/Drama
Duration: 3FT Hon
Entry Requirements: *GCE:* 260-280. *SQAH:* AAA-BBBB. *IB:* 24.
BTEC NC: DD. *BTEC ND:* DMM. *OCR ND:* D *OCR NED:* M2

P5L1 BA Journalism/Economics
Duration: 3FT Hon
Entry Requirements: *GCE:* 260-280. *SQAH:* AAA-BBBB. *IB:* 24.
BTEC NC: DD. *BTEC ND:* DMM. *OCR ND:* D *OCR NED:* M2

P5X3 BA Journalism/Education Studies
Duration: 3FT Hon
Entry Requirements: *GCE:* 260-280. *SQAH:* AAA-BBBB. *IB:* 24.
BTEC NC: DD. *BTEC ND:* DMM. *OCR ND:* D *OCR NED:* M2

P5Q3 BA Journalism/English
Duration: 3FT Hon
Entry Requirements: *GCE:* 260-280. *SQAH:* AAA-BBBB. *IB:* 24.
BTEC NC: DD. *BTEC ND:* DMM. *OCR ND:* D *OCR NED:* M2

P5NV BA Journalism/Events Management
Duration: 3FT Hon
Entry Requirements: *GCE:* 260-280. *SQAH:* AAA-BBBB. *IB:* 24.
BTEC NC: DD. *BTEC ND:* DMM. *OCR ND:* D *OCR NED:* M2

P5W6 BA Journalism/Film & Television Studies
Duration: 3FT Hon
Entry Requirements: *GCE:* 260-280. *SQAH:* AAA-BBBB. *IB:* 24.
BTEC NC: DD. *BTEC ND:* DMM. *OCR ND:* D *OCR NED:* M2

P5L4 BA Journalism/Health Studies
Duration: 3FT Hon
Entry Requirements: *GCE:* 260-280. *SQAH:* AAA-BBBB. *IB:* 24.
BTEC NC: DD. *BTEC ND:* DMM. *OCR ND:* D *OCR NED:* M2

P5DK BA Journalism/Heritage Management
Duration: 3FT Hon
Entry Requirements: *GCE:* 260-280. *SQAH:* AAA-BBBB. *IB:* 24.
BTEC NC: DD. *BTEC ND:* DMM. *OCR ND:* D *OCR NED:* M2

P5L9 BA Journalism/International Development
Duration: 3FT Hon
Entry Requirements: *GCE:* 260-280. *SQAH:* AAA-BBBB. *IB:* 24.
BTEC NC: DD. *BTEC ND:* DMM. *OCR ND:* D *OCR NED:* M2

P5M1 BA Journalism/Law
Duration: 3FT Hon
Entry Requirements: *GCE:* 260-280. *SQAH:* AAA-BBBB. *IB:* 24.
BTEC NC: DD. *BTEC ND:* DMM. *OCR ND:* D *OCR NED:* M2

P5NW BA Journalism/Leisure & Lifestyle Management
Duration: 3FT Hon
Entry Requirements: *GCE:* 260-280. *SQAH:* AAA-BBBB. *IB:* 24.
BTEC NC: DD. *BTEC ND:* DMM. *OCR ND:* D *OCR NED:* M2

P5N2 BA Journalism/Management
Duration: 3FT Hon
Entry Requirements: *GCE:* 260-280. *SQAH:* AAA-BBBB. *IB:* 24.
BTEC NC: DD. *BTEC ND:* DMM. *OCR ND:* D *OCR NED:* M2

P5N5 BA Journalism/Marketing
Duration: 3FT Hon
Entry Requirements: *GCE:* 260-280. *SQAH:* AAA-BBBB. *IB:* 24.
BTEC NC: DD. *BTEC ND:* DMM. *OCR ND:* D *OCR NED:* M2

P5F8 BA Journalism/Physical Geography
Duration: 3FT Hon
Entry Requirements: *GCE:* 260-280. *SQAH:* AAA-BBBB. *IB:* 24.
BTEC NC: DD. *BTEC ND:* DMM. *OCR ND:* D *OCR NED:* M2

P5L2 BA Journalism/Politics
Duration: 3FT Hon
Entry Requirements: *GCE:* 260-280. *SQAH:* AAA-BBBB. *IB:* 24.
BTEC NC: DD. *BTEC ND:* DMM. *OCR ND:* D *OCR NED:* M2

P5W3 BA Journalism/Popular Music
Duration: 3FT Hon
Entry Requirements: *GCE:* 260-280. *SQAH:* AAA-BBBB. *IB:* 24.
BTEC NC: DD. *BTEC ND:* DMM. *OCR ND:* D *OCR NED:* M2

P5C8 BA Journalism/Psychology
Duration: 3FT Hon
Entry Requirements: *GCE:* 260-280. *SQAH:* AAA-BBBB. *IB:* 24.
BTEC NC: DD. *BTEC ND:* DMM. *OCR ND:* D *OCR NED:* M2

P5NA BA Journalism/Social Enterprise Development
Duration: 3FT Hon
Entry Requirements: *GCE:* 260-280. *SQAH:* AAA-BBBB. *IB:* 24.
BTEC NC: DD. *BTEC ND:* DMM. *OCR ND:* D *OCR NED:* M2

P5L3 BA Journalism/Sociology
Duration: 3FT Hon
Entry Requirements: *GCE:* 260-280. *SQAH:* AAA-BBBB. *IB:* 24.
BTEC NC: DD. *BTEC ND:* DMM. *OCR ND:* D *OCR NED:* M2

P5C6 BA Journalism/Sport Studies
Duration: 3FT Hon
Entry Requirements: *GCE:* 260-280. *SQAH:* AAA-BBBB. *IB:* 24.
BTEC NC: DD. *BTEC ND:* DMM. *OCR ND:* D *OCR NED:* M2

P5N8 BA Journalism/Tourism
Duration: 3FT Hon
Entry Requirements: *GCE:* 260-280. *SQAH:* AAA-BBBB. *IB:* 24.
BTEC NC: DD. *BTEC ND:* DMM. *OCR ND:* D *OCR NED:* M2

P5FV BA Journalism/Wastes Management
Duration: 3FT Hon
Entry Requirements: *GCE:* 260-280. *SQAH:* AAA-BBBB. *IB:* 24.
BTEC NC: DD. *BTEC ND:* DMM. *OCR ND:* D *OCR NED:* M2

P5GK BA Journalism/Web Design
Duration: 3FT Hon
Entry Requirements: *GCE:* 260-280. *SQAH:* AAA-BBBB. *IB:* 24.
BTEC NC: DD. *BTEC ND:* DMM. *OCR ND:* D *OCR NED:* M2

M1P5 BA Law/Journalism
Duration: 3FT Hon
Entry Requirements: *GCE:* 260-280. *SQAH:* AAA-BBBB. *IB:* 24.
BTEC NC: DD. *BTEC ND:* DMM. *OCR ND:* D *OCR NED:* M2

NP85 BA Leisure & Lifestyle Management/Journalism
Duration: 3FT Hon
Entry Requirements: *GCE:* 260-280. *SQAH:* AAA-BBBB. *IB:* 24.
BTEC NC: DD. *BTEC ND:* DMM. *OCR ND:* D *OCR NED:* M2

N2P5 BA Management/Journalism
Duration: 3FT Hon
Entry Requirements: *GCE:* 260-280. *SQAH:* AAA-BBBB. *IB:* 24.
BTEC NC: DD. *BTEC ND:* DMM. *OCR ND:* D *OCR NED:* M2

N5P5 BA Marketing/Journalism
Duration: 3FT Hon
Entry Requirements: *GCE:* 260-280. *SQAH:* AAA-BBBB. *IB:* 24.
BTEC NC: DD. *BTEC ND:* DMM. *OCR ND:* D *OCR NED:* M2

L2P5 BA Politics/Journalism
Duration: 3FT Hon
Entry Requirements: *GCE:* 260-280. *SQAH:* AAA-BBBB. *IB:* 24.
BTEC NC: DD. *BTEC ND:* DMM. *OCR ND:* D *OCR NED:* M2

W3P5 BA Popular Music/Journalism
Duration: 3FT Hon
Entry Requirements: *GCE:* 260-280. *SQAH:* AAA-BBBB. *IB:* 24.
BTEC NC: DD. *BTEC ND:* DMM. *OCR ND:* D *OCR NED:* M2
Interview required.

C8P5 BA Psychology/Journalism
Duration: 3FT Hon
Entry Requirements: *GCE:* 260-280. *SQAH:* AAA-BBBB. *IB:* 24.
BTEC NC: DD. *BTEC ND:* DMM. *OCR ND:* D *OCR NED:* M2

N2PN BA Social Enterprise Development/Journalism
Duration: 3FT Hon
Entry Requirements: *GCE:* 260-280. *SQAH:* AAA-BBBB. *IB:* 24.
BTEC NC: DD. *BTEC ND:* DMM. *OCR ND:* D *OCR NED:* M2

L3P5 BA Sociology/Journalism
Duration: 3FT Hon
Entry Requirements: *GCE:* 260-280. *SQAH:* AAA-BBBB. *IB:* 24.
BTEC NC: DD. *BTEC ND:* DMM. *OCR ND:* D *OCR NED:* M2

C6P5 BA Sport Studies/Journalism
Duration: 3FT Hon
Entry Requirements: *GCE:* 260-280. *SQAH:* AAA-BBBB. *IB:* 24.
BTEC NC: DD. *BTEC ND:* DMM. *OCR ND:* D *OCR NED:* M2

N8P5 BA Tourism/Journalism
Duration: 3FT Hon
Entry Requirements: *GCE:* 260-280. *SQAH:* AAA-BBBB. *IB:* 24.
BTEC NC: DD. *BTEC ND:* DMM. *OCR ND:* D *OCR NED:* M2

C1P5 BSc Biological Conservation/Journalism
Duration: 3FT Hon
Entry Requirements: *GCE:* 260-280. *SQAH:* AAA-BBBB. *IB:* 24.
BTEC NC: DD. *BTEC ND:* DMM. *OCR ND:* D *OCR NED:* M2

G5P5 BSc Business Computing Systems/Journalism
Duration: 3FT Hon
Entry Requirements: *GCE:* 260-280. *SQAH:* AAA-BBBB. *IB:* 24.
BTEC NC: DD. *BTEC ND:* DMM. *OCR ND:* D *OCR NED:* M2

G4P5 BSc Computing/Journalism
Duration: 3FT Hon
Entry Requirements: *GCE:* 260-280. *SQAH:* AAA-BBBB. *IB:* 24.
BTEC NC: DD. *BTEC ND:* DMM. *OCR ND:* D *OCR NED:* M2

F8P5 BSc Physical Geography/Journalism
Duration: 3FT Hon
Entry Requirements: *GCE:* 260-280. *SQAH:* AAA-BBBB. *IB:* 24.
BTEC NC: DD. *BTEC ND:* DMM. *OCR ND:* D *OCR NED:* M2

F8PM BSc Wastes Management/Journalism
Duration: 3FT Hon
Entry Requirements: *GCE:* 260-280. *SQAH:* AAA-BBBB. *IB:* 24.
BTEC NC: DD. *BTEC ND:* DMM. *OCR ND:* D *OCR NED:* M2

G4PM BSc Web Design/Journalism
Duration: 3FT Hon
Entry Requirements: *GCE:* 260-280. *SQAH:* AAA-BBBB. *IB:* 24.
BTEC NC: DD. *BTEC ND:* DMM. *OCR ND:* D *OCR NED:* M2

N41 NORTHBROOK COLLEGE SUSSEX
LITTLEHAMPTON ROAD
WORTHING
WEST SUSSEX BN12 6NU
t: 0845 155 6060 f: 01903 606073
e: enquiries@nbcol.ac.uk
// www.northbrook.ac.uk

P501 FdA Journalism
Duration: 2FT Fdg
Entry Requirements: Interview required. Portfolio required.

N77 NORTHUMBRIA UNIVERSITY
TRINITY BUILDING
NORTHUMBERLAND ROAD
NEWCASTLE UPON TYNE NE1 8ST
t: 0191 243 7420 f: 0191 227 4561
e: er.admissions@northumbria.ac.uk
// www.northumbria.ac.uk

P500 BA Journalism
Duration: 3FT Hon
Entry Requirements: *GCE:* 300. *SQAH:* BBBBC. *SQAAH:* BBC. *IB:* 26. *BTEC ND:* DDM.

PQ53 BA Journalism and English Literature
Duration: 3FT Hon
Entry Requirements: *GCE:* 320. *SQAH:* BBBBB. *SQAAH:* BBB. *IB:* 27.

N82 NORWICH CITY COLLEGE OF FURTHER AND HIGHER EDUCATION (AN ASSOCIATE COLLEGE OF UEA)
IPSWICH ROAD
NORWICH
NORFOLK NR2 2LJ
t: 01603 773005 f: 01603 773301
e: admissions@ccn.ac.uk
// www.ccn.ac.uk

P500 FdA Journalism
Duration: 2FT Fdg
Entry Requirements: Contact the institution for details.

N91 NOTTINGHAM TRENT UNIVERSITY
DRYDEN BUILDINGG
BURTON STREET
NOTTINGHAM NG1 4BU
t: +44 (0) 115 848 4200 f: +44 (0) 115 848 8869
e: applications@ntu.ac.uk
// www.ntu.ac.uk/

P500 BA Broadcast Journalism
Duration: 3FT Hon
Entry Requirements: *GCE:* 300. *IB:* 32. *BTEC ND:* DDM. Interview required. Admissions Test required.

P501 BA Print Journalism
Duration: 3FT Hon
Entry Requirements: *GCE:* 300. *IB:* 32. *BTEC ND:* DDM. Interview required. Admissions Test required.

P56 UNIVERSITY CENTRE PETERBOROUGH
PARK CRESCENT
PETERBOROUGH PE1 4DZ
t: 0845 1965750 f: 01733 767986
e: UCPenquiries@anglia.ac.uk
// www.anglia.ac.uk/ucp

P500 BA Journalism
Duration: 3FT Hon
Entry Requirements: *GCE:* 120. Interview required.

P63 UCP MARJON - UNIVERSITY COLLEGE PLYMOUTH ST MARK & ST JOHN
DERRIFORD ROAD
PLYMOUTH PL6 8BH
t: 01752 636890 f: 01752 636819
e: admissions@marjon.ac.uk
// www.ucpmarjon.ac.uk

P590 BA Media Writing and Journalism
Duration: 3FT Hon
Entry Requirements: *GCE:* 220.

P80 UNIVERSITY OF PORTSMOUTH
ACADEMIC REGISTRY
UNIVERSITY HOUSE
WINSTON CHURCHILL AVENUE
PORTSMOUTH PO1 2UP
t: 023 9284 8484 f: 023 9284 3082
e: admissions@port.ac.uk
// www.port.ac.uk

P500 BA Journalism
Duration: 3FT Hon
Entry Requirements: *GCE:* 240-300. *IB:* 28. *BTEC NC:* DD. *BTEC ND:* DMM.

P5Q3 BA Journalism with English Language
Duration: 3FT Hon
Entry Requirements: *GCE:* 240-300. *IB:* 28. *BTEC NC:* DD. *BTEC ND:* DMM.

P5QJ BA Journalism with English Literature
Duration: 3FT Hon
Entry Requirements: *GCE:* 240-300. *IB:* 28. *BTEC NC:* DD. *BTEC ND:* DMM.

R36 ROBERT GORDON UNIVERSITY
ROBERT GORDON UNIVERSITY
SCHOOLHILL
ABERDEEN
SCOTLAND AB10 1FR
t: 01224 26 27 28 f: 01224 26 21 47
e: UGOffice@rgu.ac.uk
// www.rgu.ac.uk

P500 BA Journalism
Duration: 4FT Hon
Entry Requirements: *GCE:* CCC. *SQAH:* BBCC. *IB:* 26. Interview required.

R48 ROEHAMPTON UNIVERSITY
ERASMUS HOUSE
ROEHAMPTON LANE
LONDON SW15 5PU
t: 020 8392 3232 f: 020 8392 3470
e: enquiries@roehampton.ac.uk
// www.roehampton.ac.uk

PR54 BA Journalism & News Media and Spanish
Duration: 4FT Hon
Entry Requirements: *GCE:* 300-340. *IB:* 26. *BTEC ND:* DDM. *OCR NED:* D2 Interview required.

WP65 BA Photography and Journalism & News Media
Duration: 3FT Hon
Entry Requirements: *GCE:* 300-340. *IB:* 26. *BTEC ND:* DDM. *OCR NED:* D2 Interview required.

PP3M BA,BSc Media & Culture and Journalism & News Media
Duration: 3FT Hon
Entry Requirements: *GCE:* 300-340. *IB:* 26. *BTEC ND:* DDM. *OCR NED:* D2 Interview required.

PW58 BA/BSc Journalism & News Media and Creative Writing
Duration: 3FT Hon
Entry Requirements: *GCE:* 300-340. *IB:* 26. *BTEC ND:* DDM. *OCR NED:* D2 Interview required.

PM52 BA/BSc Journalism & News Media and Criminology
Duration: 3FT Hon
Entry Requirements: *GCE:* 300-340. *IB:* 26. *BTEC ND:* DDM. *OCR NED:* D2 Interview required.

PW54 BA/BSc Journalism & News Media and Drama,Theatre & Performance Studies
Duration: 3FT Hon
Entry Requirements: *GCE:* 300-340. *IB:* 26. *BTEC ND:* DDM.
OCR NED: D2 Interview required.

PQ5J BA/BSc Journalism & News Media and English Language & Linguistics
Duration: 3FT Hon
Entry Requirements: *GCE:* 300-340. *IB:* 26. *BTEC ND:* DDM.
OCR NED: D2 Interview required.

PQM3 BA/BSc Journalism & News Media and English Literature
Duration: 3FT Hon
Entry Requirements: *GCE:* 300-340. *IB:* 26. *BTEC ND:* DDM.
OCR NED: D2 Interview required.

PL5H BA/BSc Journalism & News Media and Sociology
Duration: 3FT Hon
Entry Requirements: *GCE:* 300-340. *IB:* 26. *BTEC ND:* DDM.
OCR NED: D2 Interview required.

RP95 BA/BSc Modern Languages and Journalism & News Media
Duration: 4FT Hon
Entry Requirements: *GCE:* 300-340. *IB:* 26. *BTEC ND:* DDM.
OCR NED: D2 Interview required.

S03 THE UNIVERSITY OF SALFORD
SALFORD M5 4WT
t: 0161 295 4545 f: 0161 295 4646
e: ug-admissions@salford.ac.uk
// www.salford.ac.uk

Q3P5 BA English Literature with Journalism
Duration: 3FT Hon
Entry Requirements: *GCE:* 280. *IB:* 31. *BTEC ND:* DMM. *OCR NED:* M2 Interview required.

P500 BA Journalism
Duration: 3FT Hon
Entry Requirements: *GCE:* 280. *IB:* 31. *BTEC ND:* DMM. *OCR NED:* M2 Interview required.

PQ53 BA Journalism and English Literature
Duration: 3FT Hon
Entry Requirements: *GCE:* 280. *IB:* 31. *BTEC ND:* DMM. *OCR NED:* M2 Interview required.

S18 THE UNIVERSITY OF SHEFFIELD
THE UNIVERSITY OF SHEFFIELD
9 NORTHUMBERLAND ROAD
SHEFFIELD S10 2TT
t: 0114 222 8030 f: 0114 222 8032
// www.sheffield.ac.uk

P500 BA Journalism Studies
Duration: 3FT Hon
Entry Requirements: *GCE:* ABB. *SQAH:* AABBB. *SQAAH:* B. *IB:* 33. *BTEC ND:* DDM.

PR51 BA Journalism and French
Duration: 4FT Hon
Entry Requirements: *GCE:* ABB. *SQAH:* AABBB. *SQAAH:* B. *IB:* 33. *BTEC ND:* DDM.

PR52 BA Journalism and Germanic Studies
Duration: 4FT Hon
Entry Requirements: *GCE:* ABB. *SQAH:* AABBB. *SQAAH:* B. *IB:* 33. *BTEC ND:* DDM.

PR54 BA Journalism and Hispanic Studies
Duration: 4FT Hon
Entry Requirements: *GCE:* ABB. *SQAH:* AABBB. *SQAAH:* B. *IB:* 33. *BTEC ND:* DDM.

PR57 BA Journalism and Russian
Duration: 4FT Hon
Entry Requirements: *GCE:* ABB. *SQAH:* AABBB. *SQAAH:* B. *IB:* 33. *BTEC ND:* DDM.

S21 SHEFFIELD HALLAM UNIVERSITY
CITY CAMPUS
HOWARD STREET
SHEFFIELD S1 1WB
t: 0114 225 5555 f: 0114 225 2167
e: admissions@shu.ac.uk
// www.shu.ac.uk

P500 BA Journalism
Duration: 3FT Hon
Entry Requirements: *GCE:* 280.

S30 SOUTHAMPTON SOLENT UNIVERSITY
EAST PARK TERRACE
SOUTHAMPTON
HAMPSHIRE SO14 0RT
t: +44 (0) 23 8031 9039 f: + 44 (0)23 8022 2259
e: admissions@solent.ac.uk or ask@solent.ac.uk
// www.solent.ac.uk/

QP35 BA English and Magazine Journalism
Duration: 3FT Hon
Entry Requirements: *Foundation:* Distinction. *GCE:* 240. *SQAAH:* AA-CCD. *IB:* 24. *BTEC NC:* DD. *BTEC ND:* MMM. *OCR ND:* D *OCR NED:* M3

QP3M BA English and Magazine Journalism
Duration: 4SW Hon
Entry Requirements: *Foundation:* Distinction. *GCE:* 240. *SQAAH:* AA-CCD. *IB:* 24. *BTEC NC:* DD. *BTEC ND:* MMM. *OCR ND:* D *OCR NED:* M3

P500 BA Journalism
Duration: 3FT Hon
Entry Requirements: *Foundation:* Distinction. *GCE:* 260. *SQAAH:* AA-CCC. *IB:* 24. *BTEC ND:* DMM. *OCR NED:* M2 Interview required.

P501 BA Journalism
Duration: 4SW Hon
Entry Requirements: *Foundation:* Distinction. *GCE:* 260. *SQAAH:* AA-CCC. *IB:* 24. *BTEC ND:* DMM. *OCR NED:* M2 Interview required.

P502 BA Journalism (Top-Up)
Duration: 1FT Hon
Entry Requirements: Interview required. HND required.

PW58 BA Magazine Journalism and Feature Writing
Duration: 3FT Hon
Entry Requirements: *Foundation:* Distinction. *GCE:* 260. *SQAAH:* AA-CCC. *IB:* 24. *BTEC ND:* DMM. *OCR NED:* M2 Interview required.

P5Q3 BA Magazine Journalism and Feature Writing with International Foundation Year
Duration: 4FT Hon
Entry Requirements: *GCE:* 240. Interview required.

P593 BA Multimedia Journalism
Duration: 3FT Hon
Entry Requirements: *Foundation:* Distinction. *GCE:* 240. *SQAAH:* AA-CCD. *IB:* 24. *BTEC NC:* DD. *BTEC ND:* MMM. *OCR ND:* D *OCR NED:* M3 Interview required.

P592 BA Popular Music Journalism
Duration: 3FT Hon
Entry Requirements: *Foundation:* Distinction. *GCE:* 240. *SQAAH:* AA-CCD. *IB:* 24. *BTEC NC:* DD. *BTEC ND:* MMM. *OCR ND:* D *OCR NED:* M3 Interview required.

P590 BA Sport Journalism
Duration: 3FT Hon
Entry Requirements: *Foundation:* Distinction. *GCE:* 240. *SQAAH:* AA-CCD. *IB:* 24. *BTEC NC:* DD. *BTEC ND:* MMM. *OCR ND:* D *OCR NED:* M3 Interview required.

P5QH BA Sport Journalism with International Foundation Year
Duration: 4FT Hon
Entry Requirements: *GCE:* 240. Interview required.

P509 BA Writing Fashion and Culture
Duration: 3FT Hon
Entry Requirements: *Foundation:* Distinction. *GCE:* 260. *SQAAH:* AA-CCC. *IB:* 24. *BTEC ND:* DMM. *OCR NED:* M2 Interview required.

S43 SOUTH ESSEX COLLEGE OF FURTHER & HIGHER EDUCATION (PARTNER OF THE UNIVERSITY OF ESSEX)
LUKER ROAD
SOUTHEND-ON-SEA
ESSEX SS1 1ND
t: 0845 52 12345 f: 01702 432320
e: Admissions@southessex.ac.uk
// www.southessex.ac.uk

P500 BA Journalism
Duration: 3FT Hon
Entry Requirements: *GCE:* 160. *IB:* 24. Interview required.

S72 STAFFORDSHIRE UNIVERSITY
COLLEGE ROAD
STOKE ON TRENT ST4 2DE
t: 01782 292753 f: 01782 292740
e: admissions@staffs.ac.uk
// www.staffs.ac.uk

PL52 BA Broadcast Journalism
Duration: 3FT Hon
Entry Requirements: *GCE:* 240-300. *IB:* 24. Interview required.

P590 BA Celebrity Journalism
Duration: 3FT Hon
Entry Requirements: *GCE:* 220-260. *IB:* 24.

WP85 BA Creative Writing and Journalism
Duration: 3FT Hon
Entry Requirements: *GCE:* 220-260. *IB:* 24.

PQ53 BA English Literature and Journalism
Duration: 3FT Hon
Entry Requirements: *GCE:* 220-260. *IB:* 24.

PV5M BA Ethical World Journalism
Duration: 3FT Hon
Entry Requirements: *GCE:* 220-260. *IB:* 24.

LP3M BA Ethics and Journalism
Duration: 3FT Hon
Entry Requirements: *GCE:* 220-260. *IB:* 24.

VP25 BA International History and Journalism
Duration: 3FT Hon
Entry Requirements: *GCE:* 220-260. *IB:* 24.

LP25 BA International Relations and Journalism
Duration: 3FT Hon
Entry Requirements: *GCE:* 240-300. *IB:* 24.

P500 BA Journalism
Duration: 3FT Hon
Entry Requirements: *GCE:* 240-300. *IB:* 24. Interview required.

PV55 BA Journalism and Philosophy
Duration: 3FT Hon
Entry Requirements: *GCE:* 220-260. *IB:* 24.

PW58 BA Journalism and Scriptwriting
Duration: 3FT Hon
Entry Requirements: *GCE:* 220-260. *IB:* 24.

LP35 BA Journalism and Sociology
Duration: 3FT Hon
Entry Requirements: *GCE:* 220-260. *IB:* 24.

PV51 BA Modern History and Journalism
Duration: 3FT Hon
Entry Requirements: *GCE:* 220-260. *IB:* 24.

PJ59 BA Music Journalism and Broadcasting
Duration: 3FT Hon
Entry Requirements: *GCE:* 220-260. *IB:* 24.

WP65 BA Photojournalism
Duration: 3FT Hon
Entry Requirements: *Foundation:* Merit. *GCE:* 200-240. *IB:* 24.
Interview required. Portfolio required.

P501 BA Sports Journalism
Duration: 3FT Hon
Entry Requirements: *GCE:* 240-300. *IB:* 24.

CP65 BA Sports Studies and Journalism
Duration: 3FT Hon
Entry Requirements: *GCE:* 180-240. *IB:* 24. *BTEC NC:* DM.
BTEC ND: MMM.

P510 BA Television and Radio Documentary
Duration: 3FT Hon
Entry Requirements: *GCE:* 200-240. *IB:* 24.

WP45 BA Theatre Studies and Journalism
Duration: 3FT Hon
Entry Requirements: *GCE:* 220-260. *IB:* 24.

PL53 BA/BSc Crime, Deviance & Society and Journalism
Duration: 3FT Hon
Entry Requirements: *GCE:* 220-260. *IB:* 24.

M1P5 LLB Law with Journalism
Duration: 3FT Hon
Entry Requirements: *GCE:* ABB-BB. *SQAAH:* ABB-BB. *IB:* 26.
BTEC NC: DM. *BTEC ND:* DDM. *OCR ND:* D

S75 THE UNIVERSITY OF STIRLING
STIRLING FK9 4LA
t: 01786 467044 f: 01786 466800
e: admissions@stir.ac.uk
// www.stir.ac.uk

QP35 BA English Studies and Journalism Studies
Duration: 4FT Hon
Entry Requirements: *GCE:* BBC. *SQAH:* BBBB. *SQAAH:* AAA-CCC.
IB: 32. *BTEC ND:* DDM.

RP15 BA French and Journalism Studies
Duration: 4FT Hon
Entry Requirements: *GCE:* BBC. *SQAH:* BBBB. *SQAAH:* AAA-CCC.
IB: 32. *BTEC ND:* DDM.

VP15 BA History and Journalism Studies
Duration: 4FT Hon
Entry Requirements: *GCE:* BBC. *SQAH:* BBBB. *SQAAH:* AAA-CCC.
IB: 32. *BTEC ND:* DDM.

P500 BA Journalism Studies
Duration: 4FT Hon
Entry Requirements: *GCE:* BBC. *SQAH:* BBBB. *SQAAH:* AAA-CCC.
IB: 32. *BTEC ND:* DDM.

PL52 BA Journalism Studies and Politics
Duration: 4FT Hon
Entry Requirements: *GCE:* BBC. *SQAH:* BBBB. *SQAAH:* AAA-CCC.
IB: 32. *BTEC ND:* DDM.

PR54 BA Journalism Studies and Spanish
Duration: 4FT Hon
Entry Requirements: *GCE:* BBC. *SQAH:* BBBB. *SQAAH:* AAA-CCC.
IB: 32. *BTEC ND:* DDM.

PC56 BA Journalism Studies and Sports Studies
Duration: 4FT Hon
Entry Requirements: *GCE:* BBC. *SQAH:* BBBB. *SQAAH:* AAA-CCC.
IB: 32. *BTEC ND:* DDM.

S78 THE UNIVERSITY OF STRATHCLYDE
GLASGOW G1 1XQ
t: 0141 552 4400 f: 0141 552 0775
// www.strath.ac.uk

LP15 BA Economics and Journalism & Creative Writing
Duration: 4FT Hon
Entry Requirements: *GCE:* AAB. *SQAH:* AAAA-AAAAB. *IB:* 36.
Portfolio required.

QP35 BA English and Journalism & Creative Writing
Duration: 4FT Hon
Entry Requirements: *GCE:* AAB. *SQAH:* AAAA-AAAAB. *IB:* 36.
Portfolio required.

RP15 BA French and Journalism & Creative Writing
Duration: 5FT Hon
Entry Requirements: *GCE:* AAB. *SQAH:* AAAA-AAAAB. *IB:* 36.
Portfolio required.

LP75 BA Geography and Journalism & Creative Writing
Duration: 4FT Hon
Entry Requirements: *GCE:* AAB. *SQAH:* AAAA-AAAAB. *IB:* 36.
Portfolio required.

VP15 BA History and Journalism & Creative Writing
Duration: 4FT Hon
Entry Requirements: *GCE:* AAB. *SQAH:* AAAA-AAAAB. *IB:* 36.
Portfolio required.

NP65 BA Human Resource Management and Journalism & Creative Writing
Duration: 4FT Hon
Entry Requirements: *GCE:* AAB. *SQAH:* AAAA-AAAAB. *IB:* 36.
Portfolio required.

RP35 BA Italian and Journalism & Creative Writing
Duration: 5FT Hon
Entry Requirements: *GCE:* AAB. *SQAH:* AAAA-AAAAB. *IB:* 36.
Portfolio required.

PM51 BA Journalism & Creative Writing and Law
Duration: 4FT Hon
Entry Requirements: *GCE:* AAB. *SQAH:* AAAA-AAAAB. *IB:* 36.
Portfolio required.

PR54 BA Journalism & Creative Writing and Spanish
Duration: 5FT Hon
Entry Requirements: *GCE:* AAB. *SQAH:* AAAA-AAAAB. *IB:* 36.
Portfolio required.

LP25 BA Politics and Journalism & Creative Writing
Duration: 4FT Hon
Entry Requirements: *GCE:* AAB. *SQAH:* AAAA-AAAAB. *IB:* 36.
Portfolio required.

LP35 BA Sociology and Journalism & Creative Writing
Duration: 4FT Hon
Entry Requirements: *GCE:* AAB. *SQAH:* AAAA-AAAAB. *IB:* 36.
Portfolio required.

S84 UNIVERSITY OF SUNDERLAND
STUDENT HELPLINE
THE STUDENT GATEWAY
CHESTER ROAD
SUNDERLAND SR1 3SD
t: 0191 515 3000 f: 0191 515 3805
e: student.helpline@sunderland.ac.uk
// www.sunderland.ac.uk

PT57 BA American Studies and Journalism
Duration: 3FT Hon
Entry Requirements: *GCE:* 260-360. *IB:* 31. *BTEC NC:* DM. *BTEC ND:* MMM. *OCR ND:* D *OCR NED:* M3

T7P5 BA American Studies with Journalism
Duration: 3FT Hon
Entry Requirements: *GCE:* 260-360. *BTEC NC:* DM. *BTEC ND:* MMM. *OCR ND:* D *OCR NED:* M3

P501 BA Broadcast Journalism
Duration: 3FT Hon
Entry Requirements: *GCE:* 260-360. *IB:* 30. *BTEC ND:* DMM.
Interview required.

NP15 BA Business Management and Journalism
Duration: 3FT Hon
Entry Requirements: *GCE:* 260-360. *IB:* 31. *BTEC NC:* DM. *BTEC ND:* MMM. *OCR ND:* D *OCR NED:* M3

N2P5 BA Business Management with Journalism
Duration: 3FT Hon
Entry Requirements: *GCE:* 220-360. *IB:* 31. *BTEC NC:* DM. *BTEC ND:* MMM. *OCR ND:* D *OCR NED:* M3

XPH5 BA Childhood Studies and Journalism
Duration: 3FT Hon
Entry Requirements: *GCE:* 260-360.

X3P5 BA Childhood Studies with Journalism
Duration: 3FT Hon
Entry Requirements: *GCE:* 260-360.

WP35 BA Community Music and Journalism
Duration: 3FT Hon
Entry Requirements: Contact the institution for details.

WHP5 BA Community Music with Journalism
Duration: 3FT Hon
Entry Requirements: *GCE:* 260-360.

MP95 BA Criminology and Journalism
Duration: 3FT Hon
Entry Requirements: *GCE:* 260-360. *BTEC NC:* DM. *BTEC ND:* MMM. *OCR ND:* D *OCR NED:* M3

M9P5 BA Criminology with Journalism
Duration: 3FT Hon
Entry Requirements: *GCE:* 260-360. *BTEC NC:* DM. *BTEC ND:* MMM. *OCR ND:* D *OCR NED:* M3

PW55 BA Dance and Journalism
Duration: 3FT Hon
Entry Requirements: *GCE:* 260-360. *IB:* 31. *BTEC NC:* DM.
BTEC ND: MMM. *OCR ND:* D *OCR NED:* M3

W5P5 BA Dance with Journalism
Duration: 3FT Hon
Entry Requirements: *GCE:* 260-360. *IB:* 31. *BTEC NC:* DM.
BTEC ND: MMM. *OCR ND:* D *OCR NED:* M3

W4P5 BA Drama with Journalisim
Duration: 3FT Hon
Entry Requirements: *GCE:* 260-360. *BTEC NC:* DM. *BTEC ND:*
MMM. *OCR ND:* D *OCR NED:* M3

Q1P5 BA English Language & Linguistics with Journalism
Duration: 3FT Hon
Entry Requirements: *GCE:* 260-360. *BTEC NC:* DM. *BTEC ND:*
MMM. *OCR ND:* D *OCR NED:* M3

PQ53 BA English Studies and Journalism
Duration: 3FT Hon
Entry Requirements: *GCE:* 260-360. *IB:* 31. *BTEC NC:* DM.
BTEC ND: MMM. *OCR ND:* D *OCR NED:* M3

Q3P5 BA English Studies with Journalism
Duration: 3FT Hon
Entry Requirements: *GCE:* 260-360. *IB:* 31. *BTEC NC:* DM.
BTEC ND: MMM. *OCR ND:* D *OCR NED:* M3

P507 BA Fashion Journalism
Duration: 3FT Hon
Entry Requirements: *GCE:* 260-360. *IB:* 30. *BTEC ND:* DMM.

NP35 BA Financial Management and Journalism
Duration: 3FT Hon
Entry Requirements: *GCE:* 260-360. *BTEC NC:* DM. *BTEC ND:*
MMM. *OCR ND:* D *OCR NED:* M3

N3P5 BA Financial Management with Journalism
Duration: 3FT Hon
Entry Requirements: *GCE:* 260-360. *BTEC NC:* DM. *BTEC ND:*
MMM. *OCR ND:* D *OCR NED:* M3

L5P5 BA Health & Social Care with Journalism
Duration: 3FT Hon
Entry Requirements: *GCE:* 260-360.

PV51 BA History and Journalism
Duration: 3FT Hon
Entry Requirements: *GCE:* 260-360. *IB:* 31. *BTEC NC:* DM.
BTEC ND: MMM. *OCR ND:* D *OCR NED:* M3

V1P5 BA History with Journalism
Duration: 3FT Hon
Entry Requirements: *GCE:* 260-360. *IB:* 31. *BTEC NC:* DM.
BTEC ND: MMM. *OCR ND:* D *OCR NED:* M3

NP65 BA Human Resource Management and Journalism
Duration: 3FT Hon
Entry Requirements: *GCE:* 260-360. *BTEC NC:* DM. *BTEC ND:*
MMM. *OCR ND:* D *OCR NED:* M3

N6P5 BA Human Resource Management with Journalism
Duration: 3FT Hon
Entry Requirements: *GCE:* 260-360. *BTEC NC:* DM. *BTEC ND:*
MMM. *OCR ND:* D *OCR NED:* M3

P508 BA International Journalism
Duration: 3FT Hon
Entry Requirements: *GCE:* 260-360. *IB:* 30. *BTEC ND:* DMM.

P5B9 BA Journalisim with Community Health
Duration: 3FT Hon
Entry Requirements: *GCE:* 260-360. *IB:* 32. *BTEC NC:* DM.
BTEC ND: MMM. *OCR ND:* D *OCR NED:* M3

P500 BA Journalism
Duration: 3FT Hon
Entry Requirements: *GCE:* 260-360. *IB:* 30. *BTEC ND:* DMM.

PW54 BA Journalism and Drama
Duration: 3FT Hon
Entry Requirements: *GCE:* 260-360. *BTEC NC:* DM. *BTEC ND:*
MMM. *OCR ND:* D *OCR NED:* M3

PX53 BA Journalism and Education
Duration: 3FT Hon
Entry Requirements: *GCE:* 260-360. *IB:* 32. *BTEC NC:* DM.
BTEC ND: MMM. *OCR ND:* D *OCR NED:* M3

PQ51 BA Journalism and English Language/Linguistics
Duration: 3FT Hon
Entry Requirements: *GCE:* 260-360. *IB:* 32. *BTEC NC:* DM.
BTEC ND: MMM. *OCR ND:* D *OCR NED:* M3

PQ5H BA Journalism and Modern Foreign Language (English)
Duration: 3FT Hon
Entry Requirements: *GCE:* 260-360. *BTEC NC:* DM. *BTEC ND:*
MMM. *OCR ND:* D *OCR NED:* M3

PW53 BA Journalism and Music
Duration: 3FT Hon
Entry Requirements: *GCE:* 260-360. *IB:* 32. *BTEC NC:* DM.
BTEC ND: MMM. *OCR ND:* D *OCR NED:* M3

PW56 BA Journalism and Photography
Duration: 3FT Hon
Entry Requirements: *GCE:* 260-360. *IB:* 32. *BTEC NC:* DM.
BTEC ND: MMM. *OCR ND:* D *OCR NED:* M3

LP25 BA Journalism and Politics
Duration: 3FT Hon
Entry Requirements: *GCE:* 260-360. *IB:* 32. *BTEC NC:* DM.
BTEC ND: MMM. *OCR ND:* D *OCR NED:* M3

CP85 BA Journalism and Psychology
Duration: 3FT Hon
Entry Requirements: *GCE:* 260-360. *IB:* 32. *BTEC NC:* DM.
BTEC ND: MMM. *OCR ND:* D *OCR NED:* M3

LP35 BA Journalism and Sociology
Duration: 3FT Hon
Entry Requirements: *GCE:* 260-360. *IB:* 32. *BTEC NC:* DM.
BTEC ND: MMM. *OCR ND:* D *OCR NED:* M3

PX51 BA Journalism and TESOL
Duration: 3FT Hon
Entry Requirements: *GCE:* 260-360. *BTEC NC:* DM. *BTEC ND:*
MMM. *OCR ND:* D *OCR NED:* M3

P5T7 BA Journalism with American Studies
Duration: 3FT Hon
Entry Requirements: *GCE:* 260-360. *IB:* 32. *BTEC NC:* DM.
BTEC ND: MMM. *OCR ND:* D *OCR NED:* M3

P5N1 BA Journalism with Business Management
Duration: 3FT Hon
Entry Requirements: *GCE:* 260-360. *IB:* 32. *BTEC NC:* DM.
BTEC ND: MMM. *OCR ND:* D *OCR NED:* M3

P5XH BA Journalism with Childhood Studies
Duration: 3FT Hon
Entry Requirements: *GCE:* 260-360.

P5M9 BA Journalism with Criminology
Duration: 3FT Hon
Entry Requirements: *GCE:* 260-360. *IB:* 32. *BTEC NC:* DM.
BTEC ND: MMM. *OCR ND:* D *OCR NED:* M3

P5W5 BA Journalism with Dance
Duration: 3FT Hon
Entry Requirements: *GCE:* 260-360. *IB:* 31. *BTEC NC:* DM.
BTEC ND: MMM. *OCR ND:* D *OCR NED:* M3

P5W4 BA Journalism with Drama
Duration: 3FT Hon
Entry Requirements: *GCE:* 260-360. *BTEC NC:* DM. *BTEC ND:*
MMM. *OCR ND:* D *OCR NED:* M3

P5X3 BA Journalism with Education
Duration: 3FT Hon
Entry Requirements: *GCE:* 260-360. *IB:* 32. *BTEC NC:* DM.
BTEC ND: MMM. *OCR ND:* D *OCR NED:* M3

P5Q1 BA Journalism with English Language/Linguistics
Duration: 3FT Hon
Entry Requirements: *GCE:* 260-360. *IB:* 32. *BTEC NC:* DM.
BTEC ND: MMM. *OCR ND:* D *OCR NED:* M3

P5Q3 BA Journalism with English Studies
Duration: 3FT Hon
Entry Requirements: *GCE:* 260-360. *IB:* 32. *BTEC NC:* DM.
BTEC ND: MMM. *OCR ND:* D *OCR NED:* M3

P5N3 BA Journalism with Financial Management
Duration: 3FT Hon
Entry Requirements: *GCE:* 260-360. *BTEC NC:* DM. *BTEC ND:*
MMM. *OCR ND:* D *OCR NED:* M3

P5L5 BA Journalism with Health & Social Care
Duration: 3FT Hon
Entry Requirements: *GCE:* 260-360.

P5V1 BA Journalism with History
Duration: 3FT Hon
Entry Requirements: *GCE:* 260-360. *IB:* 32. *BTEC NC:* DM.
BTEC ND: MMM. *OCR ND:* D *OCR NED:* M3

P5M1 BA Journalism with Law
Duration: 3FT Hon
Entry Requirements: *GCE:* 260-360. *BTEC NC:* DM. *BTEC ND:*
MMM. *OCR ND:* D *OCR NED:* M3

P5R1 BA Journalism with MFL (French)
Duration: 3FT Hon
Entry Requirements: *GCE:* 260-360. *BTEC NC:* DM. *BTEC ND:*
MMM. *OCR ND:* D *OCR NED:* M3

P5R2 BA Journalism with MFL (German)
Duration: 3FT Hon
Entry Requirements: *GCE:* 260-360. *BTEC NC:* DM. *BTEC ND:*
MMM. *OCR ND:* D *OCR NED:* M3

P5R4 BA Journalism with MFL (Spanish)
Duration: 3FT Hon
Entry Requirements: *GCE:* 260-360. *BTEC NC:* DM. *BTEC ND:*
MMM. *OCR ND:* D *OCR NED:* M3

P5N5 BA Journalism with Marketing Management
Duration: 3FT Hon
Entry Requirements: *GCE:* 260-360. *BTEC NC:* DM. *BTEC ND:*
MMM. *OCR ND:* D *OCR NED:* M3

P5QH BA Journalism with Modern Foreign Languages (English)
Duration: 3FT Hon
Entry Requirements: *GCE:* 260-360. *BTEC NC:* DM. *BTEC ND:*
MMM. *OCR ND:* D *OCR NED:* M3

P5W3 BA Journalism with Music
Duration: 3FT Hon
Entry Requirements: *GCE:* 260-360. *IB:* 32. *BTEC NC:* DM.
BTEC ND: MMM. *OCR ND:* D *OCR NED:* M3

P5W6 BA Journalism with Photography
Duration: 3FT Hon
Entry Requirements: *GCE:* 260-360. *IB:* 32. *BTEC NC:* DM.
BTEC ND: MMM. *OCR ND:* D *OCR NED:* M3

P5L2 BA Journalism with Politics
Duration: 3FT Hon
Entry Requirements: *GCE:* 260-360. *IB:* 32. *BTEC NC:* DM.
BTEC ND: MMM. *OCR ND:* D *OCR NED:* M3

P5C8 BA Journalism with Psychology
Duration: 3FT Hon
Entry Requirements: *GCE:* 260-360. *IB:* 32. *BTEC NC:* DM.
BTEC ND: MMM. *OCR ND:* D *OCR NED:* M3

P5L3 BA Journalism with Sociology
Duration: 3FT Hon
Entry Requirements: *GCE:* 260-360. *IB:* 32. *BTEC NC:* DM.
BTEC ND: MMM. *OCR ND:* D *OCR NED:* M3

P5C6 BA Journalism with Sport
Duration: 3FT Hon
Entry Requirements: *GCE:* 260-360. *BTEC NC:* DM. *BTEC ND:*
MMM. *OCR ND:* D *OCR NED:* M3

P5X1 BA Journalism with TESOL
Duration: 3FT Hon
Entry Requirements: *GCE:* 260-360. *BTEC NC:* DM. *BTEC ND:*
MMM. *OCR ND:* D *OCR NED:* M3

MP15 BA Law and Journalism
Duration: 3FT Hon
Entry Requirements: *GCE:* 260-360. *BTEC NC:* DM. *BTEC ND:*
MMM. *OCR ND:* D *OCR NED:* M3

P503 BA Magazine Journalism
Duration: 3FT Hon
Entry Requirements: *GCE:* 260-360. *IB:* 30. *BTEC ND:* DMM.

NP55 BA Marketing Management and Journalism
Duration: 3FT Hon
Entry Requirements: *GCE:* 260-360. *BTEC NC:* DM. *BTEC ND:*
MMM. *OCR ND:* D *OCR NED:* M3

N5P5 BA Marketing Management with Journalism
Duration: 3FT Hon
Entry Requirements: *GCE:* 260-360. *BTEC NC:* DM. *BTEC ND:*
MMM. *OCR ND:* D *OCR NED:* M3

RP15 BA Modern Foreign Languages (French) and Journalism
Duration: 3FT Hon
Entry Requirements: *GCE:* 260-360. *IB:* 31. *BTEC NC:* DM.
BTEC ND: MMM. *OCR ND:* D *OCR NED:* M3

PR52 BA Modern Foreign Languages (German) and Journalism
Duration: 3FT Hon
Entry Requirements: *GCE:* 260-360. *IB:* 31. *BTEC NC:* DM.
BTEC ND: MMM. *OCR ND:* D *OCR NED:* M3

PR54 BA Modern Foreign Languages (Spanish) and Journalism
Duration: 3FT Hon
Entry Requirements: *GCE:* 260-360. *IB:* 31. *BTEC NC:* DM.
BTEC ND: MMM. *OCR ND:* D *OCR NED:* M3

W3P5 BA Music with Journalism
Duration: 3FT Hon
Entry Requirements: *GCE:* 260-360. *IB:* 31. *BTEC NC:* DM.
BTEC ND: MMM. *OCR ND:* D *OCR NED:* M3

P504 BA News Journalism
Duration: 3FT Hon
Entry Requirements: *GCE:* 260-360. *IB:* 30. *BTEC ND:* DMM.

L2P5 BA Politics with Journalism
Duration: 3FT Hon
Entry Requirements: *GCE:* 260-360. *IB:* 31. *BTEC NC:* DM.
BTEC ND: MMM. *OCR ND:* D *OCR NED:* M3

L3P5 BA Sociology with Journalism
Duration: 3FT Hon
Entry Requirements: *GCE:* 260-360. *IB:* 31. *BTEC NC:* DM.
BTEC ND: MMM. *OCR ND:* D *OCR NED:* M3

P505 BA Sports Journalism
Duration: 3FT Hon
Entry Requirements: *GCE:* 260-360. *IB:* 30. *BTEC ND:* DMM.

X1P5 BA TESOL with Journalism
Duration: 3FT Hon
Entry Requirements: *GCE:* 260-360. *BTEC NC:* DM. *BTEC ND:*
MMM. *OCR ND:* D *OCR NED:* M3

NP85 BA Tourism and Journalism
Duration: 3FT Hon
Entry Requirements: *GCE:* 260-360. *IB:* 31. *BTEC NC:* DM.
BTEC ND: MMM. *OCR ND:* D *OCR NED:* M3

N8P5 BA Tourism with Journalism
Duration: 3FT Hon
Entry Requirements: *GCE:* 260-360. *IB:* 31. *BTEC NC:* DM.
BTEC ND: MMM. *OCR ND:* D *OCR NED:* M3

B9P5 BSc Community Health with Journalism
Duration: 3FT Hon
Entry Requirements: *GCE:* 260-360. *IB:* 31. *BTEC NC:* DM.
BTEC ND: MMM. *OCR ND:* D *OCR NED:* M3

C8P5 BSc Psychology with Journalism
Duration: 3FT Hon
Entry Requirements: *GCE:* 260-360. *BTEC NC:* DM. *BTEC ND:*
MMM. *OCR ND:* D *OCR NED:* M3

CP65 BSc Sport and Journalism
Duration: 3FT Hon
Entry Requirements: *GCE:* 260-360. *BTEC NC:* DM. *BTEC ND:*
MMM. *OCR ND:* D *OCR NED:* M3

S96 SWANSEA METROPOLITAN UNIVERSITY
MOUNT PLEASANT CAMPUS
SWANSEA SA1 6ED
t: 01792 481000 f: 01792 481061
e: gemma.garbutt@smu.ac.uk
// www.smu.ac.uk

W6P5 BA Photojournalism
Duration: 3FT Hon
Entry Requirements: *Foundation:* Pass. *GCE:* 200-360. *IB:* 24.
Interview required. Portfolio required.

WP65 BA Photojournalism (4 Year Programme)
Duration: 4FT Hon
Entry Requirements: *Foundation:* Pass. *GCE:* 200-360. *IB:* 24.
Interview required. Portfolio required.

T20 TEESSIDE UNIVERSITY
MIDDLESBROUGH TS1 3BA
t: 01642 218121 f: 01642 384201
e: registry@tees.ac.uk
// www.tees.ac.uk

P590 BA Journalism and News Practice
Duration: 1FT Hon
Entry Requirements: Contact the institution for details.

P502 BA Multimedia Journalism Professional Practice
Duration: 3FT Hon
Entry Requirements: *GCE:* 280. *IB:* 25.

P500 FdA Journalism
Duration: 2FT Fdg
Entry Requirements: *GCE:* 80-100. *IB:* 24.

U20 UNIVERSITY OF ULSTER
COLERAINE
CO. LONDONDERRY
NORTHERN IRELAND BT52 1SA
t: 028 7032 4221 f: 028 7032 4908
e: online@ulster.ac.uk
// www.ulster.ac.uk

P5N4 BA Journalism with Accounting
Duration: 3FT Hon
Entry Requirements: *GCE:* BCC. *IB:* 24. *BTEC NC:* DM. *BTEC ND:* DMM.

P5N1 BA Journalism with Business
Duration: 3FT Hon
Entry Requirements: *GCE:* BCC. *IB:* 24. *BTEC NC:* DM. *BTEC ND:* DMM.

P5G4 BA Journalism with Computing
Duration: 3FT Hon
Entry Requirements: *GCE:* BCC. *IB:* 24. *BTEC NC:* DM. *BTEC ND:* DMM.

P5X3 BA Journalism with Education
Duration: 3FT Hon
Entry Requirements: *GCE:* BCC. *IB:* 24. *BTEC NC:* DM. *BTEC ND:* DMM.

P5Q3 BA Journalism with English
Duration: 3FT Hon
Entry Requirements: *GCE:* BCC. *IB:* 24. *BTEC NC:* DM. *BTEC ND:* DMM.

P5F8 BA Journalism with Environmental Science
Duration: 3FT Hon
Entry Requirements: *GCE:* BCC. *IB:* 24. *BTEC NC:* DM. *BTEC ND:* DMM.

P5R9 BA Journalism with European Studies
Duration: 3FT Hon
Entry Requirements: *GCE:* BCC. *IB:* 24. *BTEC NC:* DM. *BTEC ND:* DMM.

P5R1 BA Journalism with French
Duration: 3FT Hon
Entry Requirements: *GCE:* BCC. *IB:* 24. *BTEC NC:* DM. *BTEC ND:* DMM.

P5FV BA Journalism with Geography
Duration: 3FT Hon
Entry Requirements: *GCE:* BCC. *IB:* 24. *BTEC NC:* DM. *BTEC ND:* DMM.

P5R2 BA Journalism with German
Duration: 3FT Hon
Entry Requirements: *GCE:* BCC. *IB:* 24. *BTEC NC:* DM. *BTEC ND:* DMM.

P5V1 BA Journalism with History
Duration: 3FT Hon
Entry Requirements: *GCE:* BCC. *IB:* 24. *BTEC NC:* DM. *BTEC ND:* DMM.

P5L9 BA Journalism with International Development
Duration: 3FT Hon
Entry Requirements: *GCE:* BCC. *IB:* 24. *BTEC NC:* DM. *BTEC ND:* DMM.

P5Q5 BA Journalism with Irish
Duration: 3FT Hon
Entry Requirements: *GCE:* BCC. *IB:* 24. *BTEC NC:* DM. *BTEC ND:* DMM.

P5N5 BA Journalism with Marketing
Duration: 3FT Hon
Entry Requirements: *GCE:* BCC. *IB:* 24. *BTEC NC:* DM. *BTEC ND:* DMM.

P5W6 BA Journalism with Photo Imaging
Duration: 3FT Hon
Entry Requirements: *GCE:* BCC. *IB:* 24. *BTEC NC:* DM. *BTEC ND:* DMM.

P5C8 BA Journalism with Psychology
Duration: 3FT Hon
Entry Requirements: *GCE:* BCC. *IB:* 24. *BTEC NC:* DM. *BTEC ND:* DMM.

P5N2 BA Journalism with Retail Studies
Duration: 3FT Hon
Entry Requirements: *GCE:* BCC. *IB:* 24. *BTEC NC:* DM. *BTEC ND:* DMM.

P5R4 BA Journalism with Spanish
Duration: 3FT Hon
Entry Requirements: *GCE:* BCC. *IB:* 24. *BTEC NC:* DM. *BTEC ND:* DMM.

U40 UNIVERSITY OF THE WEST OF SCOTLAND
PAISLEY
RENFREWSHIRE
SCOTLAND PA1 2BE
t: 0141 848 3727 f: 0141 848 3623
e: admissions@uws.ac.uk
// www.uws.ac.uk

P500 BA Journalism
Duration: 3FT/4FT Ord/Hon
Entry Requirements: *GCE:* BC. *SQAH:* BBC. Interview required. Portfolio required.

P501 BA Sports Journalism
Duration: 3FT/4FT Ord/Hon
Entry Requirements: *GCE:* CC. *SQAH:* BBC. Interview required.

U65 UNIVERSITY OF THE ARTS LONDON
272 HIGH HOLBORN
LONDON WC1V 7EY
t: 020 7514 6000x6197 f: 020 7514 6198
e: c.anderson@arts.ac.uk
// www.arts.ac.uk

P507 BA Fashion Journalism (Print, Broadcast)
Duration: 3FT Hon
Entry Requirements: Interview required.

P500 BA Journalism
Duration: 3FT Hon
Entry Requirements: *GCE:* 80. *IB:* 28. Foundation Course required. Interview required. Portfolio required.

P503 BA Photojournalism
Duration: 3FT Hon
Entry Requirements: *GCE:* 80. *IB:* 28. Foundation Course required. Interview required. Portfolio required.

P506 BA Sports Journalism (Top-Up)
Duration: 1FT Hon
Entry Requirements: Contact the institution for details.

P504 FdA Sports Journalism
Duration: 2FT Fdg
Entry Requirements: *GCE:* 40. *IB:* 28. Foundation Course required. Interview required. Portfolio required.

W05 THE UNIVERSITY OF WEST LONDON
WALPOLE HOUSE
BOND STREET
EALING
LONDON W5 5AA
t: 0800 036 8888 f: 020 8566 1353
e: learning.advice@uwl.ac.uk
// www.uwl.ac.uk

P500 BA Broadcast Journalism
Duration: 3FT Hon
Entry Requirements: *GCE:* 200. *IB:* 28. Interview required.

W50 UNIVERSITY OF WESTMINSTER
2ND FLOOR
101 NEW CAVENDISH STREET,
LONDON W1W 6XH
t: 020 7911 5000 f: 020 7911 5788
e: course-enquiries@westminster.ac.uk
// www.westminster.ac.uk

P500 BA Journalism
Duration: 3FT Hon
Entry Requirements: *GCE:* BBB. *SQAH:* AAAAA-BBBBB. *SQAAH:* AAA-BBB. *IB:* 30. *BTEC NC:* DD. *BTEC ND:* DDM. *OCR ND:* D *OCR NED:* D2 Interview required.

W75 UNIVERSITY OF WOLVERHAMPTON
ADMISSIONS UNIT
MX207, CAMP STREET
WOLVERHAMPTON
WEST MIDLANDS WV1 1AD
t: 01902 321000 f: 01902 321896
e: admissions@wlv.ac.uk
// www.wlv.ac.uk

P500 FdA Broadcast Journalism
Duration: 2FT Fdg
Entry Requirements: *GCE:* 80-140.

W76 UNIVERSITY OF WINCHESTER
WINCHESTER
HANTS SO22 4NR
t: 01962 827234 f: 01962 827288
e: course.enquiries@winchester.ac.uk
// www.winchester.ac.uk

TP7M BA American Studies and Journalism Studies
Duration: 3FT Hon
Entry Requirements: *Foundation:* Distinction. *GCE:* 260-300. *IB:* 24. *BTEC NC:* DD. *BTEC ND:* DMM. *OCR ND:* D *OCR NED:* M2

VP45 BA Archaeology and Journalism Studies
Duration: 3FT Hon

Entry Requirements: *Foundation:* Distinction. *GCE:* 260-300. *IB:* 24. *BTEC NC:* DD. *BTEC ND:* DMM. *OCR ND:* D *OCR NED:* M2

WP55 BA Choreography & Dance and Journalism Studies
Duration: 3FT Hon

Entry Requirements: *Foundation:* Distinction. *GCE:* 260-300. *IB:* 25. *BTEC NC:* DD. *BTEC ND:* DMM. *OCR ND:* D *OCR NED:* M2

PW54 BA Contemporary Performance and Journalism Studies
Duration: 3FT Hon

Entry Requirements: *Foundation:* Distinction. *GCE:* 260-300. *IB:* 24. *BTEC NC:* DD. *BTEC ND:* DMM. *OCR ND:* D *OCR NED:* M2

WP85 BA Creative Writing and Journalism Studies
Duration: 3FT Hon

Entry Requirements: *Foundation:* Distinction. *GCE:* 260-300. *IB:* 25. *BTEC NC:* DD. *BTEC ND:* DMM. *OCR ND:* D *OCR NED:* M2

LP35 BA Criminology and Journalism Studies
Duration: 3FT Hon

Entry Requirements: *Foundation:* Distinction. *GCE:* 260-300. *IB:* 24. *BTEC NC:* DD. *BTEC ND:* DMM. *OCR ND:* D *OCR NED:* M2

WP45 BA Drama and Journalism Studies
Duration: 3FT Hon

Entry Requirements: *Foundation:* Distinction. *GCE:* 260-300. *IB:* 25. *BTEC NC:* DD. *BTEC ND:* DMM. *OCR ND:* D *OCR NED:* M2

XP35 BA Education Studies (Early Childhood) and Journalism Studies
Duration: 3FT Hon

Entry Requirements: *Foundation:* Distinction. *GCE:* 260-300. *IB:* 24. *BTEC NC:* DD. *BTEC ND:* DMM. *OCR ND:* D *OCR NED:* M2

XP3N BA Education Studies (Modern Liberal Arts) and Journalism
Duration: 3FT Hon

Entry Requirements: *Foundation:* Distinction. *GCE:* 260-300. *IB:* 24. *BTEC NC:* DD. *BTEC ND:* DMM. *OCR ND:* D *OCR NED:* M2

XPH5 BA Education Studies and Journalism Studies
Duration: 3FT Hon

Entry Requirements: *Foundation:* Distinction. *GCE:* 260-300. *IB:* 24. *BTEC NC:* DD. *BTEC ND:* DMM. *OCR ND:* D *OCR NED:* M2

QP3N BA English Language Studies and Journalism
Duration: 3FT Hon

Entry Requirements: *Foundation:* Distinction. *GCE:* 260-300. *IB:* 25. *BTEC NC:* DD. *BTEC ND:* DMM. *OCR ND:* D *OCR NED:* M2

QP35 BA English and Journalism Studies
Duration: 3FT Hon

Entry Requirements: *Foundation:* Distinction. *GCE:* 260-300. *IB:* 25. *BTEC NC:* DD. *BTEC ND:* DMM. *OCR ND:* D *OCR NED:* M2

NP85 BA Event Management and Journalism Studies
Duration: 3FT Hon

Entry Requirements: *Foundation:* Distinction. *GCE:* 260-300. *IB:* 24. *BTEC NC:* DD. *BTEC ND:* DMM. *OCR ND:* D *OCR NED:* M2

LP55 BA Health, Community & Social Care Studies and Journalism Studies
Duration: 3FT Hon   CRB Check: Required

Entry Requirements: Contact the institution for details.

P500 BA Journalism
Duration: 3FT Hon

Entry Requirements: *Foundation:* Distinction. *GCE:* 260-300. *IB:* 26. *BTEC NC:* DD. *BTEC ND:* DDM. *OCR ND:* D Interview required.

PW5X BA Journalism Studies and Modern Liberal Arts
Duration: 3FT Hon

Entry Requirements: *Foundation:* Distinction. *GCE:* 260-300. *IB:* 25. *BTEC NC:* DD. *BTEC ND:* DMM. *OCR ND:* D *OCR NED:* M2

PC58 BA Journalism Studies and Psychology
Duration: 3FT Hon

Entry Requirements: *Foundation:* Distinction. *GCE:* 260-300. *IB:* 25. *BTEC NC:* DD. *BTEC ND:* DMM. *OCR ND:* D *OCR NED:* M2

PNM8 BA Journalism Studies and Sports Management
Duration: 3FT Hon

Entry Requirements: *Foundation:* Pass. *GCE:* 260-300. *IB:* 24. *BTEC NC:* DD. *BTEC ND:* MMP. *OCR ND:* D

PCM6 BA Journalism Studies and Sports Studies
Duration: 3FT Hon

Entry Requirements: *Foundation:* Merit. *GCE:* 260-300. *IB:* 24. *BTEC NC:* DM. *BTEC ND:* MMP.

PV56 BA Journalism Studies and Theology & Religious Studies
Duration: 3FT Hon

Entry Requirements: *Foundation:* Distinction. *GCE:* 260-300. *IB:* 25. *BTEC NC:* DD. *BTEC ND:* DMM. *OCR ND:* D *OCR NED:* M2

PW5H BA Journalism Studies and Vocal & Choral Studies
Duration: 3FT Hon

Entry Requirements: *Foundation:* Distinction. *GCE:* 260-300. *IB:* 24. *BTEC NC:* DD. *BTEC ND:* DMM. *OCR ND:* D *OCR NED:* M2

MP15 BA Law and Journalism Studies
Duration: 3FT Hon

Entry Requirements: *Foundation:* Distinction. *GCE:* 260-300. *IB:* 25. *BTEC NC:* DD. *BTEC ND:* DMM. *OCR ND:* D *OCR NED:* M2

LP25 BA Politics & Global Studies and Journalism Studies
Duration: 3FT Hon
Entry Requirements: *Foundation:* Distinction. *GCE:* 260-300. *IB:* 24. *BTEC NC:* DD. *BTEC ND:* MMM. *OCR ND:* D

W80 UNIVERSITY OF WORCESTER
HENWICK GROVE
WORCESTER WR2 6AJ
t: 01905 855111 f: 01905 855377
e: admissions@worc.ac.uk
// www.worcester.ac.uk

GP45 BA Creative Digital Media and Journalism
Duration: 3FT Hon
Entry Requirements: *GCE:* 240-260. *IB:* 24. *OCR ND:* D Interview required. Portfolio required.

PQ53 BA English Language Studies and Journalism
Duration: 3FT Hon
Entry Requirements: *GCE:* 240-260. *IB:* 24. *BTEC NC:* DD. *BTEC ND:* MMM. *OCR ND:* D *OCR NED:* M3

QP35 BA English Literary Studies and Journalism
Duration: 3FT Hon
Entry Requirements: *GCE:* 240-300. *IB:* 24. *BTEC NC:* DD. *BTEC ND:* MMM. *OCR ND:* D *OCR NED:* M3

WP65 BA Film Studies and Journalism
Duration: 3FT Hon
Entry Requirements: *GCE:* 240-300. *IB:* 24. *BTEC NC:* DD. *BTEC ND:* MMM. *OCR ND:* D *OCR NED:* M3

P500 BA Journalism
Duration: 3FT Hon
Entry Requirements: *GCE:* 280-300. *IB:* 25. *BTEC NC:* DD. *BTEC ND:* MMM. *OCR ND:* D *OCR NED:* M3

PP53 BA Journalism and Media & Cultural Studies
Duration: 3FT Hon
Entry Requirements: *GCE:* 240-300. *IB:* 24. *BTEC NC:* DD. *BTEC ND:* MMM. *OCR ND:* D *OCR NED:* M3

PL52 BA Journalism and Politics: People and Power
Duration: 3FT Hon
Entry Requirements: *GCE:* 240-300. *IB:* 24. *BTEC NC:* DD. *BTEC ND:* MMM. *OCR ND:* D *OCR NED:* M3

PW58 BA Journalism and Screen Writing
Duration: 3FT Hon
Entry Requirements: *GCE:* 240-300. *IB:* 24. *BTEC NC:* DD. *BTEC ND:* MMM. *OCR ND:* D *OCR NED:* M3

PC5P BA/BSc Journalism and Sports Studies
Duration: 3FT Hon
Entry Requirements: *GCE:* 240-300. *IB:* 24. *OCR ND:* D Interview required. Portfolio required.

MUSIC

A20 THE UNIVERSITY OF ABERDEEN
UNIVERSITY OFFICE
KING'S COLLEGE
ABERDEEN AB24 3FX
t: +44 (0) 1224 273504 f: +44 (0) 1224 272034
e: sras@abdn.ac.uk
// www.abdn.ac.uk/sras

W300 BMus Music
Duration: 4FT Hon
Entry Requirements: *SQAH:* BBB. *SQAAH:* B. *IB:* 30. Interview required.

XW13 BMus Music Education
Duration: 4FT Hon   CRB Check: Required
Entry Requirements: *SQAH:* BBB. *SQAAH:* B. *IB:* 30. Interview required.

M1W3 LLB Law with options in Music
Duration: 4FT Hon
Entry Requirements: *GCE:* BBB. *SQAH:* AABB-ABBBB. *SQAAH:* BBB. *IB:* 34.

V6W3 MA Divinity with Music Studies
Duration: 4FT Hon
Entry Requirements: *GCE:* BBB. *SQAH:* BBBB. *IB:* 30. *BTEC ND:* MMM.

Q3W3 MA English with Music Studies
Duration: 4FT Hon
Entry Requirements: *GCE:* BBB. *SQAH:* BBBB. *IB:* 30. *BTEC ND:* MMM.

R1W3 MA French with Music Studies
Duration: 5FT Hon
Entry Requirements: *GCE:* BBB. *SQAH:* BBBB. *IB:* 30. *BTEC ND:* MMM.

R1WH MA French with Music Studies
Duration: 4FT Hon
Entry Requirements: *GCE:* BBB. *SQAH:* BBBB. *IB:* 30. *BTEC ND:* MMM.

R2W3 MA German with Music Studies
Duration: 5FT Hon
Entry Requirements: *GCE:* BBB. *SQAH:* BBBB. *IB:* 30. *BTEC ND:* MMM.

R2WH MA German with Music Studies
Duration: 4FT Hon
Entry Requirements: *GCE:* BBB. *SQAH:* BBBB. *IB:* 30. *BTEC ND:* MMM.

R4W3 MA Hispanic Studies with Music Studies
Duration: 5FT Hon
Entry Requirements: *GCE:* BBB. *SQAH:* BBBB. *IB:* 30. *BTEC ND:* MMM.

R4WH MA Hispanic Studies with Music Studies
Duration: 4FT Hon
Entry Requirements: *GCE:* BBB. *SQAH:* BBBB. *IB:* 30. *BTEC ND:* MMM.

V3W3 MA History of Art with Music Studies
Duration: 4FT Hon
Entry Requirements: *GCE:* BBB. *SQAH:* BBBB. *IB:* 30. *BTEC ND:* MMM.

V1W3 MA History with Music Studies
Duration: 4FT Hon
Entry Requirements: *GCE:* BBB. *SQAH:* BBBB. *IB:* 30. *BTEC ND:* MMM.

V5W3 MA Philosophy with Music Studies
Duration: 4FT Hon
Entry Requirements: *GCE:* BBB. *SQAH:* BBBB. *IB:* 30. *BTEC ND:* MMM.

V6WH MA Religious Studies with Music Studies
Duration: 4FT Hon
Entry Requirements: *GCE:* BBB. *SQAH:* BBBB. *IB:* 30. *BTEC ND:* MMM.

A30 UNIVERSITY OF ABERTAY DUNDEE
BELL STREET
DUNDEE DD1 1HG
t: 01382 308080 f: 01382 308081
e: sro@abertay.ac.uk
// www.abertay.ac.uk

JG94 BA Creative Sound Production (Top-Up)
Duration: 2FT Hon
Entry Requirements: Interview required. HND required.

A44 ACCRINGTON & ROSSENDALE COLLEGE
BROAD OAK ROAD,
ACCRINGTON,
LANCASHIRE, BB5 2AW.
t: 01254 389933 f: 01254 354001
e: info@accross.ac.uk
// www.accrosshighereducation.co.uk/

J930 FdA Music Production
Duration: 2FT Fdg
Entry Requirements: *BTEC ND:* MMM. Interview required.

A60 ANGLIA RUSKIN UNIVERSITY
BISHOP HALL LANE
CHELMSFORD
ESSEX CM1 1SQ
t: 0845 271 3333 f: 01245 251789
e: answers@anglia.ac.uk
// www.anglia.ac.uk

WJ39 BA Creative Music Technology
Duration: 3FT Hon
Entry Requirements: *GCE:* 260. *SQAH:* BBCC. *SQAAH:* BB. *IB:* 26.

JW93 BA Creative Music Technology and Music
Duration: 3FT Hon
Entry Requirements: *GCE:* 260. *SQAH:* BBCC. *SQAAH:* BB. *IB:* 26.

W300 BA Music
Duration: 3FT Hon
Entry Requirements: *GCE:* 260. *SQAH:* BBCC. *SQAAH:* BB. *IB:* 26.

W341 BA Popular Music (Top-Up)
Duration: 1FT Hon
Entry Requirements: Interview required.

W340 FdA Popular Music
Duration: 2FT Fdg
Entry Requirements: *GCE:* 160. Interview required.

B06 BANGOR UNIVERSITY
BANGOR UNIVERSITY
BANGOR
GWYNEDD LL57 2DG
t: 01248 388484 f: 01248 370451
e: admissions@bangor.ac.uk
// www.bangor.ac.uk

QW5H BA Cymraeg Creadigol gyda Cherddoriaeth Boblogaidd
Duration: 3FT Hon
Entry Requirements: *GCE:* 260-300. *IB:* 28.

QW53 BA Cymraeg/Music
Duration: 3FT Hon
Entry Requirements: *GCE:* 260-300. *IB:* 28.

QW33 BA English and Music
Duration: 3FT Hon
Entry Requirements: *GCE:* 260-300. *IB:* 28.

Q3W8 BA English with Songwriting
Duration: 3FT Hon
Entry Requirements: *GCE:* 240-300. *IB:* 28.

VW23 BA Hanes Cymru a Cherddoriaeth
Duration: 3FT Hon
Entry Requirements: *GCE:* 260-300. *IB:* 28.

VW13 BA History and Music
Duration: 3FT Hon
Entry Requirements: *GCE:* 260-300. *IB:* 28.

WQ35 BA Llenyddiaeth Gymraeg a Llenyddiaeth y Cyfryngau a Cherdd
Duration: 3FT Hon
Entry Requirements: *GCE:* 260-300. *IB:* 28.

W300 BA Music
Duration: 3FT Hon
Entry Requirements: *GCE:* 260-300. *IB:* 28.

JH9P BA Music Technology and Electronics
Duration: 3FT Hon
Entry Requirements: *GCE:* 280. *IB:* 28.

WW38 BA Music and Creative Writing
Duration: 3FT Hon
Entry Requirements: *GCE:* 260-300. *IB:* 28.

WW36 BA Music and Film Studies
Duration: 3FT Hon
Entry Requirements: *GCE:* 260-300. *IB:* 28.

WV32 BA Music and History & Welsh History
Duration: 3FT Hon
Entry Requirements: *GCE:* 260-300. *IB:* 28.

RW13 BA Music/French
Duration: 4FT Hon
Entry Requirements: *GCE:* 260-300. *IB:* 28.

WR32 BA Music/German
Duration: 4FT Hon
Entry Requirements: *GCE:* 260-300. *IB:* 28.

WR33 BA Music/Italian
Duration: 4FT Hon
Entry Requirements: *GCE:* 260-300. *IB:* 28.

WR34 BA Music/Spanish
Duration: 4FT Hon
Entry Requirements: *GCE:* 260-300. *IB:* 28.

VW2H BA Welsh History and Music
Duration: 3FT Hon
Entry Requirements: *GCE:* 260-300. *IB:* 28.

W302 BMus Music
Duration: 3FT Hon
Entry Requirements: *GCE:* 260-300. *IB:* 28.

JH96 BSc Music Technology and Electronics
Duration: 3FT Hon
Entry Requirements: *GCE:* 280. *IB:* 28.

B20 BATH SPA UNIVERSITY
NEWTON PARK
NEWTON ST LOE
BATH BA2 9BN
t: 01225 875875 f: 01225 875444
e: enquiries@bathspa.ac.uk
// www.bathspa.ac.uk/clearing

WW13 BA Art/Music
Duration: 3FT Hon
Entry Requirements: *Foundation:* Pass. *GCE:* 220-300. *IB:* 24.
Interview required.

NW13 BA Business & Management/Music
Duration: 3FT Hon
Entry Requirements: *GCE:* 220-280. *IB:* 24.

WW2H BA Ceramics/Music
Duration: 3FT Hon
Entry Requirements: *Foundation:* Pass. *GCE:* 220-300. *IB:* 24.
Interview required.

W304 BA Commercial Music
Duration: 3FT Hon
Entry Requirements: *GCE:* 220-300. *IB:* 24. Interview required.

J931 BA Creative Music Technology
Duration: 3FT Hon
Entry Requirements: *GCE:* 220-300. *IB:* 24. Interview required.
Portfolio required.

WW93 BA Creative Writing/Music
Duration: 3FT Hon
Entry Requirements: *GCE:* 220-300. *IB:* 24.

WW53 BA Dance/Music
Duration: 3FT Hon
Entry Requirements: *GCE:* 220-300. *IB:* 24. Interview required.

WW3K BA Drama Studies/Music
Duration: 3FT Hon
Entry Requirements: *GCE:* 220-300. *IB:* 24.

XW13 BA Education/Music
Duration: 3FT Hon   CRB Check: Required
Entry Requirements: *GCE:* 220-300. *IB:* 24. Interview required.

XW33 BA Education/Music
Duration: 3FT Hon   CRB Check: Required
Entry Requirements: *GCE:* 220-280. *IB:* 24. Interview required.

QW33 BA English Literature/Music
Duration: 3FT Hon
Entry Requirements: *GCE:* 220-300. *IB:* 24.

VW13 BA History/Music
Duration: 3FT Hon
Entry Requirements: *GCE:* 220-280. *IB:* 24.

W300 BA Music
Duration: 3FT Hon
Entry Requirements: *GCE:* 220-280. *IB:* 24. Interview required.

WV36 BA Music/Study of Religions
Duration: 3FT Hon
Entry Requirements: *GCE:* 220-280. *IB:* 24.

WWH2 BA Music/Textile Design Studies
Duration: 3FT Hon
Entry Requirements: *GCE:* 220-300. *IB:* 24. Interview required.
Portfolio required.

WW32 BA Music/Visual Design
Duration: 3FT Hon
Entry Requirements: *Foundation:* Pass. *GCE:* 220-300. *IB:* 24.
Interview required.

WW3L BA Musical Theatre
Duration: 1FT Hon
Entry Requirements: Interview required.

CW13 BA/BSc Biology/Music
Duration: 3FT Hon
Entry Requirements: *GCE:* 220-280. *IB:* 24.

WW63 BA/BSc Film & Screen Studies/Music
Duration: 3FT Hon
Entry Requirements: *GCE:* 220-280. *IB:* 24.

DW63 BA/BSc Food & Nutrition/Music
Duration: 3FT Hon
Entry Requirements: *GCE:* 220-280. *IB:* 24.

FW83 BA/BSc Geography/Music
Duration: 3FT Hon
Entry Requirements: *GCE:* 220-280. *IB:* 24.

WV3M BA/BSc Music/Philosophy & Ethics
Duration: 3FT Hon
Entry Requirements: *GCE:* 220-280. *IB:* 24.

WC38 BA/BSc Music/Psychology
Duration: 3FT Hon
Entry Requirements: *GCE:* 220-300. *IB:* 24.

WL33 BA/BSc Music/Sociology
Duration: 3FT Hon
Entry Requirements: *GCE:* 220-280. *IB:* 24.

WW34 FdA Musical Theatre
Duration: 2FT Fdg
Entry Requirements: *GCE:* 160-200. *IB:* 24.

J930 FdMus Music Production
Duration: 2FT Fdg
Entry Requirements: *GCE:* 160-200. *IB:* 24.

W340 FdMus Popular Music
Duration: 2FT Fdg
Entry Requirements: *GCE:* 160-200. *IB:* 24. Portfolio required.

W310 FdMus Professional Musicianship
Duration: 2FT Fdg
Entry Requirements: *GCE:* 160-200. *IB:* 24.

B25 BIRMINGHAM CITY UNIVERSITY
PERRY BARR
BIRMINGHAM B42 2SU
t: 0121 331 5595 f: 0121 331 7994
e: choices@bcu.ac.uk
// www.bcu.ac.uk

W350 BSc Music Technology
Duration: 3FT/4SW Hon
Entry Requirements: *GCE:* 300. *IB:* 30. *BTEC NC:* DM. *BTEC ND:*
MMP. Interview required.

143W HND Popular Music Practice
Duration: 2FT HND
Entry Requirements: Contact the institution for details.

B32 THE UNIVERSITY OF BIRMINGHAM
EDGBASTON
BIRMINGHAM B15 2TT
t: 0121 415 8900 f: 0121 414 7159
e: admissions@bham.ac.uk
// www.bham.ac.uk

WW34 BA Drama and Music
Duration: 3FT Hon
Entry Requirements: *GCE:* AAB. *SQAH:* AABBB. *SQAAH:* AA. *IB:*
36.

QW33 BA English Language and Music
Duration: 3FT Hon
Entry Requirements: *GCE:* AAB. *SQAH:* AABBB. *SQAAH:* AA. *IB:*
36.

QW3H BA English Literature and Music
Duration: 3FT Hon
Entry Requirements: *GCE:* AAB. *SQAH:* AABBB. *SQAAH:* AA. *IB:*
36.

RW13 BA French Studies and Music (4 years)
Duration: 4FT Hon
Entry Requirements: *GCE:* ABB. *SQAH:* ABBBB. *SQAAH:* AB. *IB:*
32.

RW23 BA German Studies and Music (4 years)
Duration: 4FT Hon
Entry Requirements: *GCE:* ABB. *SQAH:* ABBBB. *SQAAH:* AB. *IB:*
32.

RW33 BA Italian Studies and Music (4 years)
Duration: 4FT Hon
Entry Requirements: *GCE:* ABB. *SQAH:* ABBBB. *SQAAH:* AB. *IB:*
34.

GW13 BA Mathematics and Music
Duration: 3FT Hon
Entry Requirements: *GCE:* AAB. *SQAH:* AAAAA-AABBB. *SQAAH:* AA-AB. *IB:* 34.

RW73 BA Music and Russian Studies (4 years)
Duration: 4FT Hon
Entry Requirements: *GCE:* ABB. *SQAH:* ABBBB. *SQAAH:* AB. *IB:* 34.

W302 BMus Music
Duration: 3FT Hon
Entry Requirements: *GCE:* AAA-AAB. *SQAH:* AAABB-AABBB. *SQAAH:* AA.

B38 BISHOP GROSSETESTE UNIVERSITY COLLEGE LINCOLN
BISHOP GROSSETESTE UNIVERSITY COLLEGE
LINCOLN LN1 3DY
t: 01522 583658 f: 01522 530243
e: admissions@bishopg.ac.uk
// www.bishopg.ac.uk/courses

WW43 BA Applied Drama and Music
Duration: 3FT Hon **CRB Check:** Required
Entry Requirements: Contact the institution for details.

W4W3 BA Applied Drama with Music
Duration: 3FT Hon **CRB Check:** Required
Entry Requirements: Contact the institution for details.

XW33 BA Early Childhood Studies and Music
Duration: 3FT Hon **CRB Check:** Required
Entry Requirements: *GCE:* 220. *IB:* 24.

X3W3 BA Early Childhood Studies with Music
Duration: 3FT Hon **CRB Check:** Required
Entry Requirements: *GCE:* 220. *IB:* 24.

X1W3 BA Education Studies and Music
Duration: 3FT Hon **CRB Check:** Required
Entry Requirements: *GCE:* 220.

X3WC BA Education Studies with Music
Duration: 3FT Hon **CRB Check:** Required
Entry Requirements: Contact the institution for details.

QW33 BA English and Music
Duration: 3FT Hon **CRB Check:** Required
Entry Requirements: Contact the institution for details.

Q3W3 BA English with Music
Duration: 3FT Hon **CRB Check:** Required
Entry Requirements: Contact the institution for details.

VW13 BA History and Music
Duration: 3FT Hon **CRB Check:** Required
Entry Requirements: Contact the institution for details.

XW3H BA Special Educational Needs & Inclusion and Music
Duration: 3FT Hon **CRB Check:** Required
Entry Requirements: Contact the institution for details.

B41 BLACKPOOL AND THE FYLDE COLLEGE AN ASSOCIATE COLLEGE OF LANCASTER UNIVERSITY
ASHFIELD ROAD
BISPHAM
BLACKPOOL
LANCS FY2 0HB
t: 01253 504346 f: 01253 504198
e: admissions@blackpool.ac.uk
// www.blackpool.ac.uk

WW34 BA Musical Theatre
Duration: 3FT Hon
Entry Requirements: *GCE:* 120-360. *IB:* 24. *BTEC NC:* MP. *BTEC ND:* PPP. *OCR ND:* P2 *OCR NED:* P3 Interview required.

B44 UNIVERSITY OF BOLTON
DEANE ROAD
BOLTON BL3 5AB
t: 01204 903903 f: 01204 399074
e: enquiries@bolton.ac.uk
// www.bolton.ac.uk

WN35 BSc Music & Creative Industries Business
Duration: 3FT Hon
Entry Requirements: *GCE:* 260. Interview required.

B50 BOURNEMOUTH UNIVERSITY
TALBOT CAMPUS
FERN BARROW
POOLE
DORSET BH12 5BB
t: 01202 524111
// www.bournemouth.ac.uk

WW34 FdA Performing Arts: Music Theatre
Duration: 2FT Fdg
Entry Requirements: *IB:* 24. Interview required.

W340 FdA Popular Music
Duration: 2FT Fdg
Entry Requirements: *GCE:* 120. *IB:* 24. Interview required.

B72 UNIVERSITY OF BRIGHTON
209 MITHRAS HOUSE
LEWES ROAD
BRIGHTON BN2 4AT
t: 01273 644644 f: 01273 642607
e: admissions@brighton.ac.uk
// www.brighton.ac.uk

WJ39 BA Creative Music Production (top-up)
Duration: 1FT Hon
Entry Requirements: Interview required. Portfolio required. HND required.

W390 BA Digital Music and Sound Arts
Duration: 3FT Hon
Entry Requirements: *GCE:* BBC. Interview required. Portfolio required.

W301 BA Music Production and Creative Recording (Top-Up)
Duration: 1FT Hon
Entry Requirements: Interview required. Portfolio required. HND required.

WW31 BA Music and Visual Art
Duration: 3FT Hon
Entry Requirements: *GCE:* BBC. Foundation Course required. Interview required. Portfolio required.

W302 FdA Music Production (City College Brighton & Hove)
Duration: 2FT Fdg
Entry Requirements: *GCE:* 160. *IB:* 24. Interview required.

W300 FdA Music Production and Creative Recording
Duration: 2FT Fdg
Entry Requirements: *GCE:* 120. Interview required. Portfolio required.

W391 MFA Digital Music and Sound Arts
Duration: 4FT Hon
Entry Requirements: *GCE:* BBC. *BTEC ND:* MMM. Interview required. Portfolio required.

B78 UNIVERSITY OF BRISTOL
UNDERGRADUATE ADMISSIONS OFFICE
SENATE HOUSE
TYNDALL AVENUE
BRISTOL BS8 1TH
t: 0117 928 9000 f: 0117 925 1424
e: ug-admissions@bristol.ac.uk
// www.bristol.ac.uk

W300 BA Music
Duration: 3FT Hon
Entry Requirements: *GCE:* AAB-BBB. *SQAH:* AAAAB-BBBBC. *SQAAH:* BB. *BTEC ND:* DDM.

WR31 BA Music and French (4 years)
Duration: 4FT Hon
Entry Requirements: *GCE:* AAB-BBB. *SQAH:* AAAAB-BBBBC. *SQAAH:* BB. *BTEC ND:* DDM.

WR32 BA Music and German (4 years)
Duration: 4FT Hon
Entry Requirements: *GCE:* AAB-BBB. *SQAH:* AAAAB-BBBBC. *SQAAH:* BB. *BTEC ND:* DDM.

WR33 BA Music and Italian (4 years)
Duration: 4FT Hon
Entry Requirements: *GCE:* AAB-BBB. *SQAH:* AAAAB-BBBBC. *SQAAH:* BB. *BTEC ND:* DDM.

B79 BRISTOL FILTON COLLEGE
FILTON AVENUE
BRISTOL BS34 7AT
t: 0117 909 2255 f: 0117 931 2233
e: info@filton.ac.uk
// www.filton.ac.uk

34WW HND Performing Arts (Musical Theatre)
Duration: 2FT HND
Entry Requirements: Contact the institution for details.

43WW HND Performing Arts (Performance)
Duration: 2FT HND
Entry Requirements: *BTEC ND:* MMM. Interview required. Portfolio required.

B80 UNIVERSITY OF THE WEST OF ENGLAND, BRISTOL
FRENCHAY CAMPUS
COLDHARBOUR LANE
BRISTOL BS16 1QY
t: +44 (0)117 32 83333 f: +44 (0)117 32 82810
e: admissions@uwe.ac.uk
// www.uwe.ac.uk

WJ39 BSc Creative Music Technology
Duration: 3FT/4SW Hon
Entry Requirements: Contact the institution for details.

B84 BRUNEL UNIVERSITY
UXBRIDGE
MIDDLESEX UB8 3PH
t: 01895 265265 f: 01895 269790
e: admissions@brunel.ac.uk
// www.brunel.ac.uk

QW33 BA English and Music
Duration: 3FT Hon
Entry Requirements: *GCE:* BBC. *SQAH:* BBC. *IB:* 30. *BTEC ND:* DDM. Admissions Test required.

W3W6 BA Film & Television Studies and Music
Duration: 3FT Hon
Entry Requirements: *GCE:* BCC. *SQAAH:* BCC. *IB:* 29. *BTEC NC:* DM. *BTEC ND:* DDM. Admissions Test required.

WW23 BA Games Design and Music
Duration: 3FT Hon
Entry Requirements: *GCE:* BCC. *SQAAH:* BCC. *IB:* 29. *BTEC NC:* DM. *BTEC ND:* DDM. Admissions Test required.

WW2H BA Games Design and Sonic Arts
Duration: 3FT Hon
Entry Requirements: *GCE:* BCC. *SQAAH:* BCC. *IB:* 29. *BTEC ND:* DDM.

W300 BA Music
Duration: 3FT Hon
Entry Requirements: *GCE:* BCC. *SQAAH:* BCC. *IB:* 29. *BTEC NC:* DM. *BTEC ND:* DDM. Admissions Test required.

WJ39 BA Sonic Arts
Duration: 3FT Hon
Entry Requirements: *GCE:* BCC. *SQAAH:* BCC. *IB:* 29. *BTEC NC:* DM. *BTEC ND:* DDM.

WW43 BA Theatre and Music
Duration: 3FT Hon
Entry Requirements: *GCE:* BCC. *SQAAH:* BCC. *IB:* 29. *BTEC NC:* DM. *BTEC ND:* DDM. Admissions Test required.

W302 BMus Musical Composition
Duration: 3FT Hon
Entry Requirements: *GCE:* BCC. *SQAAH:* BCC. *IB:* 29. *BTEC NC:* DM. *BTEC ND:* DDM. Admissions Test required.

W312 BMus Musical Performance
Duration: 3FT Hon
Entry Requirements: *GCE:* BCC. *SQAAH:* BCC. *IB:* 29. *BTEC NC:* DM. *BTEC ND:* DDM. Admissions Test required.

B92 BROOKSBY MELTON COLLEGE
MELTON CAMPUS
ASFORDBY ROAD
MELTON MOWBRAY
LEICESTERSHIRE LE13 0HJ
t: 01664 850850 f: 01664 855355
// www.brooksbymelton.ac.uk

W345 BA Performing Arts
Duration: 3FT Hon
Entry Requirements: Contact the institution for details.

W310 HND Contemporary Performance
Duration: 2FT HND
Entry Requirements: Contact the institution for details.

B94 BUCKINGHAMSHIRE NEW UNIVERSITY
QUEEN ALEXANDRA ROAD
HIGH WYCOMBE
BUCKINGHAMSHIRE HP11 2JZ
t: 0800 0565 660 f: 01494 605 023
e: admissions@bucks.ac.uk
// bucks.ac.uk

NW23 BA Music Management and Artist Development
Duration: 3FT Hon
Entry Requirements: *GCE:* 200-240. *IB:* 24. *BTEC NC:* DM. *BTEC ND:* MMM. *OCR ND:* M1 *OCR NED:* M3

WW43 BA Musical Theatre (Top-Up)
Duration: 1FT Hon
Entry Requirements: Contact the institution for details.

W391 FdA Commercial Music Performance & Production
Duration: 2FT Fdg
Entry Requirements: *GCE:* 100-140. *IB:* 24. *BTEC NC:* MP. *BTEC ND:* PPP. *OCR ND:* P2 *OCR NED:* P3 Interview required.

WW4H FdA Musical Theatre
Duration: 2FT Fdg
Entry Requirements: *GCE:* 100-140. *IB:* 24. *BTEC NC:* MP. *BTEC ND:* PPP. *OCR ND:* P2 *OCR NED:* P3 Interview required.

C05 UNIVERSITY OF CAMBRIDGE
CAMBRIDGE ADMISSIONS OFFICE
FITZWILLIAM HOUSE
32 TRUMPINGTON STREET
CAMBRIDGE CB2 1QY
t: 01223 333 308 f: 01223 746 868
e: admissions@cam.ac.uk
// www.cam.ac.uk/admissions/undergraduate/

X3W3 BA Education with Music
Duration: 3FT Hon
Entry Requirements: *GCE:* A*AA. *SQAAH:* AAA-AAB. Interview required.

W300 BA Music
Duration: 3FT Hon
Entry Requirements: *GCE:* A*AA. *SQAAH:* AAA-AAB. Interview required.

C10 CANTERBURY CHRIST CHURCH
UNIVERSITY
NORTH HOLMES ROAD
CANTERBURY
KENT CT1 1QU
t: 01227 782900 f: 01227 782888
e: admissions@canterbury.ac.uk
// www.canterbury.ac.uk

GW53 BA Business Computing and Music
Duration: 3FT Hon
Entry Requirements: *GCE:* 240. *IB:* 24.

G5WH BA Business Computing with Music
Duration: 3FT Hon
Entry Requirements: *GCE:* 240. *IB:* 24.

W340 BA Commercial Music
Duration: 3FT Hon
Entry Requirements: *GCE:* 200. *IB:* 24. Interview required.

W341 BA Commercial Music 'International only'
Duration: 4FT Hon
Entry Requirements: Interview required.

QW33 BA English Language & Communication and Music
Duration: 3FT Hon
Entry Requirements: *GCE:* 240. *IB:* 24. Interview required.

Q3WH BA English Language & Communication with Music
Duration: 3FT Hon
Entry Requirements: *GCE:* 240. *IB:* 24. Interview required.

BW93 BA Health Studies and Music
Duration: 3FT Hon
Entry Requirements: *GCE:* 240. *IB:* 24.

GW4J BA Internet Computing and Music
Duration: 3FT Hon
Entry Requirements: *GCE:* 240. *IB:* 24.

W3GM BA Music with Business Computing
Duration: 3FT Hon
Entry Requirements: *GCE:* 240. *IB:* 24.

W3QH BA Music with English Language & Communication
Duration: 3FT Hon
Entry Requirements: *GCE:* 240. *IB:* 24.

W3W1 BA Music with Fine & Applied Arts
Duration: 3FT Hon
Entry Requirements: *GCE:* 240. *IB:* 24.

W3B9 BA Music with Health Studies
Duration: 3FT Hon
Entry Requirements: *GCE:* 240. *IB:* 24.

W3GL BA Music with Internet Computing
Duration: 3FT Hon
Entry Requirements: *GCE:* 240. *IB:* 24.

W310 BA Performing Arts (Vocal Studies)
Duration: 3FT Hon
Entry Requirements: *GCE:* 200. *IB:* 24. Interview required.

WN31 BA/BSc Business Studies and Music
Duration: 3FT Hon
Entry Requirements: *GCE:* 240. *IB:* 24. Interview required.

WG35 BA/BSc Computing and Music
Duration: 3FT Hon
Entry Requirements: *GCE:* 240. *IB:* 24.

XW3H BA/BSc Education Studies and Music
Duration: 3FT Hon   CRB Check: Required
Entry Requirements: *GCE:* 240. *IB:* 24. Interview required.

X3WH BA/BSc Education Studies with Music
Duration: 3FT Hon   CRB Check: Required
Entry Requirements: *GCE:* 240. *IB:* 24.

WQ33 BA/BSc English and Music
Duration: 3FT Hon
Entry Requirements: *GCE:* 240. *IB:* 24. Interview required.

Q3W3 BA/BSc English with Music
Duration: 3FT Hon
Entry Requirements: *GCE:* 240. *IB:* 24. Interview required.

W6W3 BA/BSc Film, Radio & Television Studies with Music
Duration: 3FT Hon
Entry Requirements: *GCE:* 240. *IB:* 24. Interview required.

WW13 BA/BSc Fine & Applied Arts and Music
Duration: 3FT Hon
Entry Requirements: *GCE:* 240. *IB:* 24.

W1W3 BA/BSc Fine & Applied Arts with Music
Duration: 3FT Hon
Entry Requirements: *GCE:* 240. *IB:* 24. Interview required.

RW13 BA/BSc French and Music
Duration: 3FT Hon
Entry Requirements: *GCE:* 240. *IB:* 24.

B9W3 BA/BSc Health Studies with Music
Duration: 3FT Hon
Entry Requirements: *GCE:* 240. *IB:* 24.

VW13 BA/BSc History and Music
Duration: 3FT Hon
Entry Requirements: *GCE:* 240. *IB:* 24. Interview required.

L2WJ BA/BSc International Relations with Music
Duration: 3FT Hon
Entry Requirements: *GCE:* 240. *IB:* 24.

MW23 BA/BSc Legal Studies and Music
Duration: 3FT Hon
Entry Requirements: *GCE:* 240. *IB:* 24. Interview required.

M2W3 BA/BSc Legal Studies with Music
Duration: 3FT Hon
Entry Requirements: *GCE:* 240. *IB:* 24.

GWK3 BA/BSc Multimedia Design and Music Production
Duration: 3FT Hon
Entry Requirements: *GCE:* 240. *IB:* 24.

WW63 BA/BSc Music and Film, Radio & Television Studies
Duration: 3FT Hon
Entry Requirements: *GCE:* 240. *IB:* 24.

CW83 BA/BSc Music and Psychology
Duration: 3FT Hon
Entry Requirements: *GCE:* 240. *IB:* 24.

VW63 BA/BSc Music and Religious Studies
Duration: 3FT Hon
Entry Requirements: *GCE:* 240. *IB:* 24. Interview required.

LW33 BA/BSc Music and Sociology & Social Science
Duration: 3FT Hon
Entry Requirements: *GCE:* 240. *IB:* 24.

NW83 BA/BSc Music and Tourism & Leisure Studies
Duration: 3FT Hon
Entry Requirements: *GCE:* 240. *IB:* 24.

W3C1 BA/BSc Music with Biosciences
Duration: 3FT Hon
Entry Requirements: *GCE:* 240. *IB:* 24.

W3N1 BA/BSc Music with Business Studies
Duration: 3FT Hon
Entry Requirements: *GCE:* 240. *IB:* 24.

W3G5 BA/BSc Music with Computing
Duration: 3FT Hon
Entry Requirements: *GCE:* 240. *IB:* 24.

W3XJ BA/BSc Music with Education Studies
Duration: 3FT Hon   CRB Check: Required
Entry Requirements: *GCE:* 240. *IB:* 24.

W3Q3 BA/BSc Music with English
Duration: 3FT Hon
Entry Requirements: *GCE:* 240. *IB:* 24.

W3W6 BA/BSc Music with Film, Radio & Television Studies
Duration: 3FT Hon
Entry Requirements: *GCE:* 240. *IB:* 24.

W3R1 BA/BSc Music with French
Duration: 3FT Hon
Entry Requirements: *GCE:* 240. *IB:* 24.

W3V1 BA/BSc Music with History
Duration: 3FT Hon
Entry Requirements: *GCE:* 240. *IB:* 24.

W3M2 BA/BSc Music with Legal Studies
Duration: 3FT Hon
Entry Requirements: *GCE:* 240. *IB:* 24.

W3C8 BA/BSc Music with Psychology
Duration: 3FT Hon
Entry Requirements: *GCE:* 240. *IB:* 24.

W3V6 BA/BSc Music with Religious Studies
Duration: 3FT Hon
Entry Requirements: *GCE:* 240. *IB:* 24.

W3L3 BA/BSc Music with Sociology & Social Science
Duration: 3FT Hon
Entry Requirements: *GCE:* 240. *IB:* 24.

W3VP BA/BSc Music with Theology
Duration: 3FT Hon
Entry Requirements: *GCE:* 240. *IB:* 24.

W3N8 BA/BSc Music with Tourism & Leisure Studies
Duration: 3FT Hon
Entry Requirements: *GCE:* 240. *IB:* 24.

C8W3 BA/BSc Psychology with Music
Duration: 3FT Hon
Entry Requirements: *GCE:* 240. *IB:* 24.

V6W3 BA/BSc Religious Studies with Music
Duration: 3FT Hon
Entry Requirements: *GCE:* 240. *IB:* 24.

L3W3 BA/BSc Sociology & Social Science with Music
Duration: 3FT Hon
Entry Requirements: *GCE:* 240. *IB:* 24.

VW6H BA/BSc Theology and Music
Duration: 3FT Hon
Entry Requirements: *GCE:* 240. *IB:* 24.

V6WH BA/BSc Theology with Music
Duration: 3FT Hon
Entry Requirements: *GCE:* 240. *IB:* 24.

N8W3 BA/BSc Tourism & Leisure Studies with Music
Duration: 3FT Hon
Entry Requirements: *GCE:* 240. *IB:* 24.

W300 BMus Music
Duration: 3FT Hon
Entry Requirements: *GCE:* 240. *IB:* 24. Interview required.

N1W3 BSc Business Studies with Music
Duration: 3FT Hon
Entry Requirements: *GCE:* 240. *IB:* 24.

CW13 BSc/BA Biosciences and Music
Duration: 3FT Hon
Entry Requirements: *GCE:* 240. *IB:* 24.

C1W3 BSc/BA Biosciences with Music
Duration: 3FT Hon
Entry Requirements: *GCE:* 240. *IB:* 24.

G5W3 BSc/BA Computing with Music
Duration: 3FT Hon
Entry Requirements: *GCE:* 240. *IB:* 24.

V1W3 BSc/BA History with Music
Duration: 3FT Hon
Entry Requirements: *GCE:* 240. *IB:* 24.

W302 FYr International Foundation Music
Duration: 4FT FYr
Entry Requirements: Interview required.

W342 FdA Church Music
Duration: 2FT Fdg
Entry Requirements: Contact the institution for details.

013W HND Music Performance
Duration: 2FT HND
Entry Requirements: *GCE:* 100. Interview required.

C15 CARDIFF UNIVERSITY
PO BOX 927
30-36 NEWPORT ROAD
CARDIFF CF24 0DE
t: 029 2087 9999 f: 029 2087 6138
e: admissions@cardiff.ac.uk
// www.cardiff.ac.uk

LW93 BA Cultural Criticism/Music
Duration: 3FT Hon
Entry Requirements: *GCE:* AAA. *IB:* 34.

WQ33 BA English Literature/Music
Duration: 3FT Hon
Entry Requirements: *GCE:* AAA. *SQAAH:* AAA. *IB:* 36. Interview required.

WR31 BA French/Music (4 years)
Duration: 4FT Hon
Entry Requirements: *GCE:* ABB. *SQAAH:* ABB. *IB:* 34.

WR32 BA German/Music (4 years)
Duration: 4FT Hon
Entry Requirements: *GCE:* BBB. *IB:* 32.

WV31 BA History/Music
Duration: 3FT Hon
Entry Requirements: *GCE:* ABB. *SQAH:* ABB-BBB. *SQAAH:* AA-BBB. *IB:* 34. Interview required.

WR33 BA Italian/Music (4 years)
Duration: 4FT Hon
Entry Requirements: *GCE:* BBB. *IB:* 32.

GW13 BA Mathematics/Music
Duration: 3FT Hon
Entry Requirements: *GCE:* AAB. *SQAAH:* AAB. *IB:* 36.

W300 BA Music
Duration: 3FT Hon
Entry Requirements: *GCE:* AAB-BBB. *IB:* 32.

VW53 BA Music/Philosophy
Duration: 3FT Hon
Entry Requirements: *GCE:* AAB. *IB:* 34.

VW63 BA Music/Religious Studies
Duration: 3FT Hon
Entry Requirements: *GCE:* BBB. *IB:* 32.

QW53 BA Music/Welsh
Duration: 3FT Hon
Entry Requirements: *GCE:* ABB-BBB. *IB:* 32.

W302 BMus Music
Duration: 3FT Hon
Entry Requirements: *GCE:* AAB-BBB. *IB:* 32.

FW33 BSc Physics and Music
Duration: 3FT Hon
Entry Requirements: *GCE:* BBB. *SQAAH:* BBB. *IB:* 30. Interview required. Admissions Test required.

C20 UNIVERSITY OF WALES INSTITUTE, CARDIFF (UWIC)
ADMISSIONS UNIT
LLANDAFF CAMPUS
WESTERN AVENUE
CARDIFF CF5 2YB
t: 029 2041 6070 f: 029 2041 6286
e: admissions@uwic.ac.uk
// www.uwic.ac.uk

XW33 BA Secondary Education Music leading to QTS (3 years or 2 year Fast-track)
Duration: 2FT/3FT Hon   CRB Check: Required
Entry Requirements: *GCE:* 260. *IB:* 24. Interview required.

C30 UNIVERSITY OF CENTRAL LANCASHIRE
PRESTON
LANCS PR1 2HE
t: 01772 201201 f: 01772 894954
e: uadmissions@uclan.ac.uk
// www.uclan.ac.uk

W300 BA Music Practice
Duration: 3FT Hon
Entry Requirements: *GCE:* 260-300. *IB:* 26. Interview required.

WJ39 BA Music Production
Duration: 3FT Hon
Entry Requirements: *GCE:* 260-300. *IB:* 26. Interview required.

W310 BA Music Theatre
Duration: 3FT Hon
Entry Requirements: *GCE:* 260-300. *IB:* 26. Interview required.

W301 FdA Music
Duration: 2FT Fdg
Entry Requirements: *GCE:* 160.

C35 CENTRAL SCHOOL OF SPEECH AND DRAMA, UNIVERSITY OF LONDON
EMBASSY THEATRE
64 ETON AVENUE
LONDON NW3 3HY
t: 0207 722 8183 f: 0207 722 4132
e: enquiries@cssd.ac.uk
// www.cssd.ac.uk

WW34 BA Theatre Practice: Theatre Sound
Duration: 3FT Hon
Entry Requirements: *GCE:* BBC. Interview required. Portfolio required.

C55 UNIVERSITY OF CHESTER
PARKGATE ROAD
CHESTER CH1 4BJ
t: 01244 511000 f: 01244 511300
e: enquiries@chester.ac.uk
// www.chester.ac.uk

W340 BA Popular Music Performance
Duration: 3FT Hon
Entry Requirements: *GCE:* 260-300. *SQAH:* BBBB. *IB:* 24. *BTEC NC:* DM. *BTEC ND:* MMM. Interview required.

C58 UNIVERSITY OF CHICHESTER
BISHOP OTTER CAMPUS
COLLEGE LANE
CHICHESTER
WEST SUSSEX PO19 6PE
t: 01243 816002 f: 01243 816161
e: admissions@chi.ac.uk
// www.chiuni.ac.uk

W341 BA Commercial Music
Duration: 1FT Hon
Entry Requirements: Interview required.

WW83 BA English & Creative Writing and Music
Duration: 3FT Hon
Entry Requirements: *GCE:* BCC. *SQAH:* BBBB-BBBC. *SQAAH:* BCC. *IB:* 30. *BTEC ND:* DMM.

W8WH BA English & Creative Writing with Music
Duration: 3FT Hon
Entry Requirements: *GCE:* BCC. *SQAH:* BBBB-BBBC. *SQAAH:* BCC. *IB:* 30. *BTEC ND:* DMM.

QW33 BA English and Music
Duration: 3FT Hon
Entry Requirements: *GCE:* BCC. *SQAH:* BBBB-BBBC. *SQAAH:* BCC. *IB:* 30. *BTEC ND:* DMM.

Q3W3 BA English with Music
Duration: 3FT Hon
Entry Requirements: *GCE:* BCC. *SQAH:* BBBB-BBBC. *SQAAH:* BCC. *IB:* 30. *BTEC ND:* DMM.

VW13 BA History and Music
Duration: 3FT Hon
Entry Requirements: *GCE:* BCC. *IB:* 28. *BTEC ND:* MMM.

QW3H BA International English Studies and Music
Duration: 3FT Hon
Entry Requirements: *GCE:* 160-200. *IB:* 28. *BTEC NC:* MM. *BTEC ND:* MPP. Interview required.

W300 BA Music
Duration: 3FT Hon
Entry Requirements: *GCE:* CCD. *SQAAH:* CCC-CCD. *IB:* 28. *BTEC NC:* DM. *BTEC ND:* MMM. *OCR ND:* D *OCR NED:* M1 Interview required.

W311 BA Music (Performance)
Duration: 3FT Hon
Entry Requirements: *GCE:* CCD. *SQAAH:* CCC-CCD. *IB:* 28. *BTEC NC:* DM. *BTEC ND:* MMM. *OCR ND:* D *OCR NED:* M1 Interview required.

W390 BA Music with Community Music
Duration: 3FT Hon
Entry Requirements: *GCE:* CCD. *SQAAH:* CCC-CCD. *IB:* 28. *BTEC NC:* DM. *BTEC ND:* MMM. *OCR ND:* D *OCR NED:* M1 Interview required.

W3Q3 BA Music with English
Duration: 3FT Hon
Entry Requirements: *GCE:* CCD. *SQAAH:* CCC-CCD. *IB:* 28. *BTEC NC:* DM. *BTEC ND:* MMM. *OCR ND:* D *OCR NED:* M1 Interview required.

W3V1 BA Music with History
Duration: 3FT Hon
Entry Requirements: *GCE:* CCD. *SQAAH:* CCC-CCD. *IB:* 28. *BTEC NC:* DM. *BTEC ND:* MMM. *OCR ND:* D *OCR NED:* M1 Interview required.

W3XD BA Music with Instrumental/Vocal Teaching
Duration: 3FT Hon
Entry Requirements: *GCE:* CCD. *SQAAH:* CCC-CCD. *IB:* 28. *BTEC NC:* DM. *BTEC ND:* MMM. *OCR ND:* D *OCR NED:* M1 Interview required.

W3QH BA Music with International English Studies
Duration: 3FT Hon
Entry Requirements: *GCE:* CCD. *SQAAH:* CCC-CCD. *IB:* 28. *BTEC NC:* DM. *BTEC ND:* MMM. *OCR ND:* D *OCR NED:* M1 Interview required.

W3N5 BA Music with Music, Marketing & Administration
Duration: 3FT Hon
Entry Requirements: *GCE:* CCD. *SQAAH:* CCC-CCD. *IB:* 28. *BTEC NC:* DM. *BTEC ND:* MMM. *OCR ND:* D *OCR NED:* M1 Interview required.

W391 BA Music with Musical Theatre
Duration: 3FT Hon
Entry Requirements: *GCE:* CCD. *SQAAH:* CCC-CCD. *IB:* 28. *BTEC NC:* DM. *BTEC ND:* MMM. *OCR ND:* D *OCR NED:* M1 Interview required.

W3V6 BA Music with Theology & Religion
Duration: 3FT Hon
Entry Requirements: *GCE:* CCD. *SQAAH:* CCC-CCD. *IB:* 28. *BTEC NC:* DM. *BTEC ND:* MMM. *OCR ND:* D *OCR NED:* M1 Interview required.

WW3K BA Musical Theatre
Duration: 1FT Hon   CRB Check: Required
Entry Requirements: Interview required.

WW4J BA Performing Arts (Theatre Performance and Music)
Duration: 3FT Hon
Entry Requirements: *GCE:* BBC-BCC. *SQAAH:* BBC-BCC. *IB:* 28. *BTEC NC:* DD. *BTEC ND:* DMM. Interview required.

W340 FdA Commercial Music
Duration: 2FT Fdg
Entry Requirements: *GCE:* 240-280. *IB:* 28. *BTEC NC:* DD. *BTEC ND:* DMM. Interview required.

XW13 FdA Instrumental & Vocal Music Teaching
Duration: 2FT Fdg   CRB Check: Required
Entry Requirements: *GCE:* 80. *IB:* 28. Interview required.

WW34 FdA Musical Theatre
Duration: 2FT Fdg   CRB Check: Required
Entry Requirements: *GCE:* CCD. *SQAAH:* CCC-CCD. *IB:* 28. *BTEC NC:* DM. *BTEC ND:* MMM. *OCR ND:* D *OCR NED:* M1 Interview required.

C60 CITY UNIVERSITY
NORTHAMPTON SQUARE
LONDON EC1V 0HB
t: 020 7040 5060 f: 020 7040 8995
e: ugadmissions@city.ac.uk
// www.city.ac.uk

W300 BMus Music
Duration: 3FT Hon
Entry Requirements: *GCE:* 260-300. *SQAH:* AABB. *SQAAH:* BBC-BCC. *IB:* 32. *BTEC ND:* DMM.

C69 CITY OF SUNDERLAND COLLEGE
HYLTON CENTRE
NORTH HYLTON ROAD
SUNDERLAND SR5 5DB
t: 0191 511 6260
e: highered.admissions@citysun.ac.uk
// www.citysun.ac.uk

W390 FdA Music Practice
Duration: 2FT Fdg
Entry Requirements: Contact the institution for details.

C75 COLCHESTER INSTITUTE
SHEEPEN ROAD
COLCHESTER
ESSEX CO3 3LL
t: 01206 712777 f: 01206 712800
e: info@colchester.ac.uk
// www.colchester.ac.uk

W301 BA Film Music and Soundtrack Production
Duration: 3FT Hon
Entry Requirements: Contact the institution for details.

W300 BA Music
Duration: 3FT Hon
Entry Requirements: *GCE:* 160. *SQAH:* CCCC. Interview required.

W300 BA Music option - Arts Business
Duration: 3FT Hon
Entry Requirements: *GCE:* 160. Interview required.

W300 BA Music option - Composition
Duration: 3FT Hon
Entry Requirements: *GCE:* 160. Interview required.

W300 BA Music option - Education
Duration: 3FT Hon
Entry Requirements: *GCE:* 160. Interview required.

W300 BA Music option - Performance Studies
Duration: 3FT Hon
Entry Requirements: *GCE:* 160. Interview required.

WW34 BA Musical Theatre
Duration: 3FT Hon
Entry Requirements: *GCE:* 160. Interview required.

W341 BA Popular Music
Duration: 3FT Hon
Entry Requirements: *GCE:* 160. Interview required.

W390 FdA Musical Theatre
Duration: 2FT Fdg
Entry Requirements: *GCE:* 80. Interview required.

W340 FdA Popular Music
Duration: 2FT Fdg
Entry Requirements: *GCE:* 80. Interview required.

C85 COVENTRY UNIVERSITY
THE STUDENT CENTRE
COVENTRY UNIVERSITY
1 GULSON RD
COVENTRY CV1 2JH
t: 024 7615 2222 f: 024 7615 2223
e: studentenquiries@coventry.ac.uk
// www.coventry.ac.uk

W303 BA Music Composition
Duration: 3FT/4SW Hon
Entry Requirements: *GCE:* CCC. *SQAH:* CCCCC. *IB:* 27. *BTEC ND:* MMM. *OCR NED:* M3 Interview required.

W304 BA Music Performance
Duration: 3FT/4SW Hon
Entry Requirements: *GCE:* CCC. *SQAH:* CCCCC. *IB:* 27. *BTEC ND:* MMM. *OCR NED:* M3 Interview required.

C99 UNIVERSITY OF CUMBRIA
FUSEHILL STREET
CARLISLE
CUMBRIA CA1 2HH
t: 01228 616234 f: 01228 616235
// www.cumbria.ac.uk

WW53 BA Dance Performance and Musical Theatre Performance
Duration: 3FT Hon
Entry Requirements: *GCE:* 280. *IB:* 30. *BTEC NC:* DD. *BTEC ND:* DMM. *OCR ND:* D Interview required.

WW43 BA Drama Performance and Musical Theatre Performance
Duration: 3FT Hon
Entry Requirements: *GCE:* 280. *IB:* 30. *BTEC NC:* DD. *BTEC ND:* DMM. *OCR ND:* D Interview required.

D26 DE MONTFORT UNIVERSITY
THE GATEWAY
LEICESTER LE1 9BH
t: 0116 255 1551 f: 0116 250 6204
e: enquiries@dmu.ac.uk
// www.dmu.ac.uk

JW93 BA Music, Technology and Performance
Duration: 3FT Hon
Entry Requirements: *GCE:* 260. *IB:* 28. *BTEC ND:* DMM. Interview required.

JW9H BSc Music Technology
Duration: 3FT Hon
Entry Requirements: *GCE:* 260. *IB:* 28. *BTEC ND:* DMM. *OCR NED:* M2

D39 UNIVERSITY OF DERBY
KEDLESTON ROAD
DERBY DE22 1GB
t: 01332 591167 f: 01332 597724
e: askadmissions@derby.ac.uk
// www.derby.ac.uk

NW43 BA Accounting and Popular Music Production
Duration: 3FT Hon
Entry Requirements: *Foundation:* Distinction. *GCE:* 260-300. *IB:* 28. *BTEC ND:* DMM. *OCR NED:* M2

TW73 BA American Studies and Popular Music (Production)
Duration: 3FT Hon
Entry Requirements: *Foundation:* Distinction. *GCE:* 260-300. *IB:* 28. *BTEC ND:* DMM. *OCR NED:* M2

W391 BA Creative Expressive Therapies (Music)
Duration: 3FT Hon   CRB Check: Required
Entry Requirements: *Foundation:* Merit. *GCE:* 180-200. *IB:* 26. *BTEC NC:* DM. *BTEC ND:* MMP. Interview required.

MW23 BA Criminology and Popular Music Production
Duration: 3FT Hon
Entry Requirements: *Foundation:* Distinction. *GCE:* 260-300. *IB:* 28. *BTEC ND:* DMM. *OCR NED:* M2

WW35 BA Dance & Movement Studies and Popular Music (Production)
Duration: 3FT Hon
Entry Requirements: *Foundation:* Distinction. *GCE:* 260-300. *IB:* 28. *BTEC ND:* DMM. *OCR NED:* M2

WX33 BA Education Studies and Popular Music (Production)
Duration: 3FT Hon
Entry Requirements: *Foundation:* Distinction. *GCE:* 260-300. *IB:* 28. *BTEC ND:* DMM. *OCR NED:* M2

VW13 BA History and Popular Music (Production)
Duration: 3FT Hon
Entry Requirements: *Foundation:* Distinction. *GCE:* 260-300. *IB:* 28. *BTEC ND:* DMM. *OCR NED:* M2

NW53 BA Marketing and Popular Music (Production)
Duration: 3FT Hon
Entry Requirements: *Foundation:* Distinction. *GCE:* 260-300. *IB:* 28. *BTEC ND:* DMM. *OCR NED:* M2

WP33 BA Media Writing and Popular Music Production
Duration: 3FT Hon
Entry Requirements: *Foundation:* Distinction. *GCE:* 260-300. *IB:* 28. *BTEC ND:* DMM. *OCR NED:* M2

LW33 BA Popular Music (Production) and Sociology
Duration: 3FT Hon
Entry Requirements: *Foundation:* Distinction. *GCE:* 260-300. *IB:* 28. *BTEC ND:* DMM. *OCR NED:* M2

WW34 BA Popular Music (Production) and Theatre Arts
Duration: 3FT Hon
Entry Requirements: *Foundation:* Distinction. *GCE:* 260-300. *IB:* 28. *BTEC ND:* DMM. *OCR NED:* M2

WC36 BA Popular Music Production and Sport & Exercise Studies
Duration: 3FT Hon
Entry Requirements: *Foundation:* Distinction. *GCE:* 260-300. *IB:* 28. *BTEC ND:* DMM. *OCR NED:* M2

W340 BA Popular Music with Music Technology
Duration: 3FT Hon
Entry Requirements: *GCE:* 240. *IB:* 26. *BTEC NC:* DD. *BTEC ND:* MMM. *OCR ND:* D *OCR NED:* M3

LW73 BA/BSc Geography and Popular Music Production
Duration: 3FT Hon
Entry Requirements: *Foundation:* Distinction. *GCE:* 260-300. *IB:* 28. *BTEC ND:* DMM. *OCR NED:* M2

GW13 BA/BSc Mathematics and Popular Music Production
Duration: 3FT Hon
Entry Requirements: *Foundation:* Distinction. *GCE:* 260-300. *IB:* 28. *BTEC ND:* DMM. *OCR NED:* M2

CW13 BSc Biology and Popular Music (Production)
Duration: 3FT Hon
Entry Requirements: *Foundation:* Distinction. *GCE:* 260-300. *IB:* 28. *BTEC ND:* DMM. *OCR NED:* M2

GW43 BSc Interactive Media Production
Duration: 3FT Hon
Entry Requirements: *Foundation:* Merit. *GCE:* 240. *IB:* 26. *BTEC NC:* DD. *BTEC ND:* MMM. *OCR ND:* D *OCR NED:* M3

CW83 BSc Psychology and Popular Music (Production)
Duration: 3FT Hon
Entry Requirements: *Foundation:* Distinction. *GCE:* 260-300. *IB:* 28. *BTEC ND:* DMM. *OCR NED:* M2

GW4H FYr Interactive Media Production Foundation
Duration: 1FT FYr
Entry Requirements: *Foundation:* Pass. *GCE:* 180-240. *IB:* 26. *BTEC NC:* DM. *BTEC ND:* MMP. *OCR ND:* M1 *OCR NED:* P1

W3J9 FYr Popular Music with Music Technology Foundation
Duration: 1FT FYr
Entry Requirements: *Foundation:* Pass. *GCE:* 180-240. *IB:* 26. *BTEC NC:* DM. *BTEC ND:* MMP. *OCR ND:* M1 *OCR NED:* P1

D52 DONCASTER COLLEGE
THE HUB
CHAPPELL DRIVE
SOUTH YORKSHIRE DN1 2RF
t: 01302 553610
e: he@don.ac.uk
// www.don.ac.uk

W391 BA Creative Music Technology
Duration: 3FT Hon
Entry Requirements: *GCE:* 180-240.

D86 DURHAM UNIVERSITY
DURHAM UNIVERSITY
UNIVERSITY OFFICE
DURHAM DH1 3HP
t: 0191 334 2000 f: 0191 334 6055
e: admissions@durham.ac.uk
// www.durham.ac.uk

W300 BA Music
Duration: 3FT Hon
Entry Requirements: *GCE:* AAB. *SQAH:* AAABB. *SQAAH:* AAB. *IB:* 36.

E14 UNIVERSITY OF EAST ANGLIA
NORWICH NR4 7TJ
t: 01603 591515 f: 01603 458596
e: admissions@uea.ac.uk
// www.uea.ac.uk

W300 BA Music
Duration: 3FT Hon CRB Check: Required
Entry Requirements: *GCE:* BBB. *SQAAH:* ABB-BBC. *IB:* 31. *BTEC NC:* DD. *BTEC ND:* DDM. Interview required.

W350 BA Music and Technology
Duration: 3FT Hon   CRB Check: Required
Entry Requirements: *GCE:* BBC. *SQAAH:* BBC. *IB:* 30. *BTEC NC:*
DD. *BTEC ND:* DMM. Interview required.

E28 UNIVERSITY OF EAST LONDON
DOCKLANDS CAMPUS
UNIVERSITY WAY
LONDON E16 2RD
t: 020 8223 3333 f: 020 8223 2978
e: study@uel.ac.uk
// www.uel.ac.uk

WW43 BA Community Arts Practice/Music Cultures
Duration: 3FT Hon
Entry Requirements: *GCE:* 200. *IB:* 24. *BTEC NC:* DM. *BTEC ND:*
MMP. *OCR ND:* M1 *OCR NED:* P1 Interview required.

NW63 BA Human Resource Management/Music Cultures
Duration: 3FT Hon
Entry Requirements: *GCE:* 200. *IB:* 24. *BTEC NC:* DM. *BTEC ND:*
MMP. *OCR ND:* M1 *OCR NED:* P1

W3P9 BA Music Culture with Communication Studies
Duration: 3FT Hon
Entry Requirements: *GCE:* 200. *IB:* 24. *BTEC NC:* DM. *BTEC ND:*
MMP. *OCR ND:* M1 *OCR NED:* P1

W3W4 BA Music Culture with Community Arts Practice
Duration: 3FT Hon
Entry Requirements: *GCE:* 200. *IB:* 24. *BTEC NC:* DM. *BTEC ND:*
MMP. *OCR ND:* M1 *OCR NED:* P1

W3L6 BA Music Culture with Cultural Studies
Duration: 3FT Hon
Entry Requirements: *GCE:* 200. *IB:* 24. *BTEC NC:* DM. *BTEC ND:*
MMP. *OCR ND:* M1 *OCR NED:* P1

W3C6 BA Music Culture with Sports Development
Duration: 3FT Hon
Entry Requirements: *GCE:* 200. *IB:* 24. *BTEC NC:* DM. *BTEC ND:*
MMP. *OCR ND:* M1 *OCR NED:* P1

W3WK BA Music Culture with Theatre Studies
Duration: 3FT Hon
Entry Requirements: *GCE:* 200. *IB:* 24. *BTEC NC:* DM. *BTEC ND:*
MMP. *OCR ND:* M1 *OCR NED:* P1

WR39 BA Music Culture/Cultural Studies
Duration: 3FT Hon
Entry Requirements: *GCE:* 200. *IB:* 24. *BTEC NC:* DM. *BTEC ND:*
MMP. *OCR ND:* M1 *OCR NED:* P1

WJ39 BA Music Culture: Theory and Production
Duration: 3FT Hon
Entry Requirements: *GCE:* 200. *IB:* 24. *BTEC NC:* DM. *BTEC ND:*
MMP.

WJ3X BA Music Culture: Theory and Production (Extended)
Duration: 4FT Hon
Entry Requirements: *GCE:* 40. *IB:* 24.

N2W3 BA Music Industry Management with Music Culture
Duration: 3FT Hon
Entry Requirements: *GCE:* 200. *IB:* 24. *BTEC NC:* DM. *BTEC ND:*
MMP. *OCR ND:* M1 *OCR NED:* P1

W4W3 BA Theatre Studies with Music Culture
Duration: 3FT Hon
Entry Requirements: *GCE:* 200. *IB:* 24. *BTEC NC:* DM. *BTEC ND:*
MMP. *OCR ND:* M1 *OCR NED:* P1

GW53 BA/BSc Business Information Systems/Music Culture
Duration: 3FT Hon
Entry Requirements: *GCE:* 200. *IB:* 24. *BTEC NC:* DM. *BTEC ND:*
MMP. *OCR ND:* M1 *OCR NED:* P1 Interview required.

W310 BMus Popular Music Performance
Duration: 3FT Hon
Entry Requirements: *GCE:* 200. *IB:* 27. Interview required.

G4W3 BSc Computer Networks with Music Culture
Duration: 3FT Hon
Entry Requirements: *GCE:* 200. *IB:* 24. *BTEC NC:* DM. *BTEC ND:*
MMP. *OCR ND:* M1 *OCR NED:* P1 Interview required.

L3W3 BSc Sociology (Professional Development) with Music Culture
Duration: 3FT Hon
Entry Requirements: *GCE:* 200. *IB:* 24. *BTEC NC:* DM. *BTEC ND:*
MMP. *OCR ND:* M1 *OCR NED:* P1

W391 FdA Music and Production
Duration: 2FT Fdg
Entry Requirements: Contact the institution for details.

E42 EDGE HILL UNIVERSITY
ORMSKIRK
LANCASHIRE L39 4QP
t: 01695 657000 f: 01695 584355
e: study@edgehill.ac.uk
// www.edgehill.ac.uk

WJ39 BA Music and Sound with Drama
Duration: 3FT Hon
Entry Requirements: **GCE:** 280. **IB:** 26. **BTEC NC:** DD. **BTEC ND:** DMM. **OCR ND:** D **OCR NED:** M2 Interview required.

W390 BA Music, Sound and Enterprise
Duration: 3FT Hon
Entry Requirements: **GCE:** 280. **IB:** 26. **BTEC NC:** DD. **BTEC ND:** DMM. **OCR ND:** D **OCR NED:** M2 Interview required.

E56 THE UNIVERSITY OF EDINBURGH
STUDENT RECRUITMENT & ADMISSIONS
57 GEORGE SQUARE
EDINBURGH EH8 9JU
t: 0131 650 4360 f: 0131 651 1236
e: sra.enquiries@ed.ac.uk
// www.ed.ac.uk/studying/undergraduate/

W302 BMus Music
Duration: 4FT Hon
Entry Requirements: **GCE:** BBB. **SQAH:** ABBB-ABBC. **IB:** 34. Interview required.

W351 BMus Music Technology
Duration: 4FT Hon
Entry Requirements: **GCE:** BBB. **SQAH:** ABBB-ABBC. **IB:** 34. Interview required.

GW13 BSc Mathematics and Music
Duration: 4FT Hon
Entry Requirements: **GCE:** AAA-ABB. **SQAH:** AAAA-ABBB.

FW33 BSc Physics and Music
Duration: 4FT Hon
Entry Requirements: **GCE:** AAA-ABB. **SQAH:** AAAA-ABBB.

VW33 MA History of Art and History of Music
Duration: 4FT Hon
Entry Requirements: **GCE:** AAA-BBB. **SQAH:** AAAA-BBBB. **IB:** 34.

E59 EDINBURGH NAPIER UNIVERSITY
CRAIGLOCKHART CAMPUS
EDINBURGH EH14 1DJ
t: +44 (0)8452 60 60 40 f: 0131 455 6464
e: info@napier.ac.uk
// www.napier.ac.uk

W341 BA Popular Music
Duration: 3FT/4FT Ord/Hon
Entry Requirements: **GCE:** 240. Interview required.

W302 BMus Music
Duration: 3FT/4FT Ord/Hon
Entry Requirements: **GCE:** 240. Interview required.

E81 EXETER COLLEGE
HELE ROAD
EXETER
DEVON EX4 4JS
t: 0845 111 6000
e: info@exe-coll.ac.uk
// www.exe-coll.ac.uk/he

WW34 FdA Performance Production
Duration: 2FT Fdg
Entry Requirements: **GCE:** 160.

F33 UNIVERSITY COLLEGE FALMOUTH
WOODLANE
FALMOUTH
CORNWALL TR11 4RH
t: 01326213730
e: admissions@falmouth.ac.uk
// www.falmouth.ac.uk

W390 BA(Hons) Creative Music Technology
Duration: 3FT Hon
Entry Requirements: **GCE:** 220. **IB:** 24. Interview required. Portfolio required.

W300 BA(Hons) Music
Duration: 3FT Hon
Entry Requirements: **GCE:** 220. **IB:** 24. Interview required. Portfolio required.

WW34 BA(Hons) Music Theatre
Duration: 3FT Hon
Entry Requirements: **GCE:** 220. **IB:** 24. Interview required.

W340 BA(Hons) Popular Music
Duration: 3FT Hon
Entry Requirements: **GCE:** 220. **IB:** 24. Interview required. Portfolio required.

F66 FARNBOROUGH COLLEGE OF TECHNOLOGY
BOUNDARY ROAD
FARNBOROUGH
HAMPSHIRE GU14 6SB
t: 01252 407028 f: 01252 407041
e: admissions@farn-ct.ac.uk
// www.farn-ct.ac.uk

W300 FdSc Music Production
Duration: 2FT Fdg
Entry Requirements: **GCE:** 160. **BTEC NC:** MM. **BTEC ND:** MMM.

G14 UNIVERSITY OF GLAMORGAN, CARDIFF AND PONTYPRIDD
ENQUIRIES AND ADMISSIONS UNIT
PONTYPRIDD CF37 1DL
t: 0800 716925 f: 01443 654050
e: enquiries@glam.ac.uk
// www.glam.ac.uk

W340 BA Cerddoriaeth Boblogaidd - Cwrs Dwyieithog
Duration: 3FT Hon
Entry Requirements: *GCE:* BBB. *IB:* 24. *BTEC ND:* DMM. *OCR NED:* M2 Interview required.

W300 BA Popular Music
Duration: 3FT Hon
Entry Requirements: *GCE:* BBB. *IB:* 24. *BTEC ND:* DMM. *OCR NED:* M2 Interview required.

WJ39 FdA Creative Industries (Popular Music Technology)
Duration: 2FT Fdg
Entry Requirements: *GCE:* CCC.

G28 UNIVERSITY OF GLASGOW
THE UNIVERSITY OF GLASGOW
THE FRASER BUILDING
65 HILLHEAD STREET
GLASGOW G12 8QF
t: 0141 330 6062 f: 0141 330 2961
e: student.recruitment@glasgow.ac.uk
// www.glasgow.ac.uk

H6W3 BEng Electronics with Music
Duration: 4FT Hon
Entry Requirements: *GCE:* ABB. *SQAH:* AAAB-BBB. *IB:* 32.

W302 BMus Music
Duration: 4FT Hon
Entry Requirements: *GCE:* ABB. *SQAH:* ABBB. *IB:* 32.

VW43 MA Archaeology/Music
Duration: 4FT Hon
Entry Requirements: *GCE:* AAA. *SQAH:* AAAA-AABB. *IB:* 36.

GW5H MA Arts & Media Informatics/Music
Duration: 4FT Hon
Entry Requirements: *GCE:* AAA. *SQAH:* AAAA-AABB. *IB:* 36.

NW23 MA Business & Management/Music
Duration: 4FT Hon
Entry Requirements: *GCE:* AAA. *SQAH:* AAAA-AABB. *IB:* 36.

QW53 MA Celtic Studies/Music
Duration: 4FT Hon
Entry Requirements: *GCE:* AAA. *SQAH:* AAAA-AABB. *IB:* 36.

RWR3 MA Central & East European Studies/Music
Duration: 4FT Hon
Entry Requirements: *GCE:* AAA. *SQAH:* AAAA-AABB. *IB:* 36.

QW83 MA Classics/Music
Duration: 4FT Hon
Entry Requirements: *GCE:* AAA. *SQAH:* AAAA-AABB. *IB:* 36.

QWF3 MA Comparative Literature/Music
Duration: 4FT Hon
Entry Requirements: *GCE:* AAA. *SQAH:* AAAA-AABB. *IB:* 36.

GW43 MA Computing/Music
Duration: 4FT Hon
Entry Requirements: *GCE:* AAA. *SQAH:* AAAA-AABB. *IB:* 36.

VW33 MA Economic & Social History/Music
Duration: 4FT Hon
Entry Requirements: *GCE:* AAA. *SQAH:* AAAA-AABB. *IB:* 36.

LW13 MA Economics/Music
Duration: 4FT Hon
Entry Requirements: *GCE:* AAA. *SQAH:* AAAA-AABB. *IB:* 36.

QW3J MA English Language/Music
Duration: 4FT Hon
Entry Requirements: *GCE:* AAA. *SQAH:* AAAA-AABB. *IB:* 36.

QW3H MA English Literature/Music
Duration: 4FT Hon
Entry Requirements: *GCE:* AAA. *SQAH:* AAAA-AABB. *IB:* 36.

WW36 MA Film & Television Studies/Music
Duration: 4FT Hon
Entry Requirements: *GCE:* AAA. *SQAH:* AAAA-AABB. *IB:* 36.

RW13 MA French/Music
Duration: 5FT Hon
Entry Requirements: *GCE:* AAA. *SQAH:* AAAA-AABB. *IB:* 36.

LW73 MA Geography/Music
Duration: 4FT Hon
Entry Requirements: *GCE:* AAA. *SQAH:* AAAA-AABB. *IB:* 36.

RW23 MA German/Music
Duration: 5FT Hon
Entry Requirements: *GCE:* AAA. *SQAH:* AAAA-AABB. *IB:* 36.

QW73 MA Greek/Music
Duration: 4FT Hon
Entry Requirements: *GCE:* AAA. *SQAH:* AAAA-AABB. *IB:* 36.

VWH3 MA History of Art/Music
Duration: 4FT Hon
Entry Requirements: *GCE:* AAA. *SQAH:* AAAA-AABB. *IB:* 36.

VW13 MA History/Music
Duration: 4FT Hon
Entry Requirements: *GCE:* AAA. *SQAH:* AAAA-AABB. *IB:* 36.

RW33 MA Italian/Music
Duration: 5FT Hon
Entry Requirements: *GCE:* AAA. *SQAH:* AAAA-AABB. *IB:* 36.

QW63 MA Latin/Music
Duration: 4FT Hon
Entry Requirements: *GCE:* AAA. *SQAH:* AAAA-AABB. *IB:* 36.

GW13 MA Mathematics/Music
Duration: 4FT Hon
Entry Requirements: *GCE:* AAA. *SQAH:* AAAA-AABB. *IB:* 36.

W300 MA Music
Duration: 4FT Hon
Entry Requirements: *GCE:* AAA. *SQAH:* AAAA-AABB. *IB:* 36.

VW53 MA Music/Philosophy
Duration: 4FT Hon
Entry Requirements: *GCE:* AAA. *SQAH:* AAAA-AABB. *IB:* 36.

FW33 MA Music/Physics
Duration: 4FT Hon
Entry Requirements: *GCE:* AAA. *SQAH:* AAAA-AABB. *IB:* 36.

LW23 MA Music/Politics
Duration: 4FT Hon
Entry Requirements: *GCE:* AAA. *SQAH:* AAAA-AABB. *IB:* 36.

CW83 MA Music/Psychology
Duration: 4FT Hon
Entry Requirements: *GCE:* AAA. *SQAH:* AAAA-AABB. *IB:* 36.

LW43 MA Music/Public Policy
Duration: 4FT Hon
Entry Requirements: *GCE:* AAA. *SQAH:* AAAA-AABB. *IB:* 36.

RW73 MA Music/Russian
Duration: 5FT Hon
Entry Requirements: *GCE:* AAA. *SQAH:* AAAA-AABB. *IB:* 36.

VWF3 MA Music/Scottish History
Duration: 4FT Hon
Entry Requirements: *GCE:* AAA. *SQAH:* AAAA-AABB. *IB:* 36.

QW23 MA Music/Scottish Literature
Duration: 4FT Hon
Entry Requirements: *GCE:* AAA. *SQAH:* AAAA-AABB. *IB:* 36.

WR3T MA Music/Slavonic Studies
Duration: 4FT Hon
Entry Requirements: *GCE:* AAA. *SQAH:* AAAA-AABB. *IB:* 36.

WW34 MA Music/Theatre Studies
Duration: 4FT Hon
Entry Requirements: *GCE:* AAA. *SQAH:* AAAA-AABB. *IB:* 36.

WV36 MA Music/Theology & Religious Studies
Duration: 4FT Hon
Entry Requirements: *GCE:* AAA. *SQAH:* AAAA-AABB. *IB:* 36.

RW4H MA Spanish/Music
Duration: 5FT Hon
Entry Requirements: *GCE:* AAA. *SQAH:* AAAA-AABB. *IB:* 36.

H6WJ MEng Electronics with Music
Duration: 5FT Hon
Entry Requirements: *GCE:* AAB. *SQAH:* AAAA-AAABB. *IB:* 34.

G50 THE UNIVERSITY OF GLOUCESTERSHIRE
PARK CAMPUS
THE PARK
CHELTENHAM GL50 2RH
t: 01242 714503 f: 01242 714827
e: admissions@glos.ac.uk
// www.glos.ac.uk

W300 BA Popular Music
Duration: 3FT Hon
Entry Requirements: *GCE:* 280-300. Interview required. Portfolio required.

G53 GLYNDWR UNIVERSITY
PLAS COCH
MOLD ROAD
WREXHAM LL11 2AW
t: 01978 293439 f: 01978 290008
e: sid@glyndwr.ac.uk
// www.glyndwr.ac.uk

HWP3 BSc Studio Recording and Performance Technology
Duration: 3FT Hon
Entry Requirements: *GCE:* 240.

G56 GOLDSMITHS, UNIVERSITY OF LONDON
GOLDSMITHS, UNIVERSITY OF LONDON
NEW CROSS
LONDON SE14 6NW
t: 020 7048 5300 f: 020 7919 7509
e: admissions@gold.ac.uk
// www.gold.ac.uk

W302 BMus Music
Duration: 3FT Hon
Entry Requirements: *GCE:* ABB. *SQAH:* AABBB. *SQAAH:* ABB. *IB:* 32. *BTEC NC:* DM. *BTEC ND:* DDM. Interview required.

W303 BMus Music (4-year extension degree)
Duration: 4FT Hon
Entry Requirements: Contact the institution for details.

WG34 BMus Music Computing
Duration: 3FT Hon
Entry Requirements: *GCE:* BBB. *SQAH:* BBBBB. *SQAAH:* BBB. *IB:* 30. *BTEC NC:* DM. *BTEC ND:* DDM. Interview required.

W340 BMus Popular Music
Duration: 3FT Hon
Entry Requirements: *GCE:* BBB. *SQAH:* BBBBB. *SQAAH:* BBB. *IB:* 32. *BTEC NC:* DM. *BTEC ND:* DDM.

G80 GRIMSBY INSTITUTE OF FURTHER AND HIGHER EDUCATION
NUNS CORNER
GRIMSBY
NE LINCOLNSHIRE DN34 5BQ
t: 0800 328 3631 f: 01472 315506/879924
e: headmissions@grimsby.ac.uk
// www.grimsby.ac.uk

W390 BA Creative Music
Duration: 3FT Hon
Entry Requirements: *GCE:* 160. Interview required.

H14 HAVERING COLLEGE OF FURTHER AND HIGHER EDUCATION
ARDLEIGH GREEN ROAD
HORNCHURCH
ESSEX RM11 2LL
t: 01708 462793 f: 01708 462736
e: HE@havering-college.ac.uk
// www.havering-college.ac.uk

WJ3X BA Contemporary Music and Technology
Duration: 3FT Hon
Entry Requirements: Interview required. Portfolio required.

H36 UNIVERSITY OF HERTFORDSHIRE
UNIVERSITY ADMISSIONS SERVICE
COLLEGE LANE
HATFIELD
HERTS AL10 9AB
t: 01707 284800
// www.herts.ac.uk

W300 BSc Music Composition and Technology
Duration: 3FT Hon
Entry Requirements: *GCE:* 260.

W352 BSc Music Technology
Duration: 3FT Hon
Entry Requirements: *GCE:* 220.

W390 BSc Music: Commercial Composition and Technology
Duration: 3FT Hon
Entry Requirements: *GCE:* 240.

W391 BSc Sound Design Technology
Duration: 3FT Hon
Entry Requirements: *GCE:* 220.

WN32 BSc/BA Music and Entertainment Industry Management
Duration: 3FT Hon
Entry Requirements: *GCE:* 300.

H49 UNIVERSITY OF THE HIGHLANDS AND ISLANDS
UHI EXECUTIVE OFFICE
NESS WALK
INVERNESS
SCOTLAND IV3 5SQ
t: 01463 279000 f: 01463 279001
e: info@uhi.ac.uk
// www.uhi.ac.uk

QW53 BA Gaelic and Traditional Music
Duration: 4FT Hon
Entry Requirements: *GCE:* C. *SQAH:* CCC. Interview required.

W310 BA Popular Music
Duration: 3FT Hon
Entry Requirements: Interview required.

W3N1 BA Hons Music Business
Duration: 3FT Hon
Entry Requirements: Interview required.

103W HNC Music
Duration: 1FT HNC
Entry Requirements: *GCE:* D. *SQAH:* C. Interview required.

31WN HNC Music Business
Duration: 1FT HNC
Entry Requirements: *GCE:* D. *SQAH:* C. Interview required.

H60 THE UNIVERSITY OF HUDDERSFIELD
QUEENSGATE
HUDDERSFIELD HD1 3DH
t: 01484 473969 f: 01484 472765
e: admissionsandrecords@hud.ac.uk
// www.hud.ac.uk

WW63 BA Film, Animation, Music and Enterprise
Duration: 3FT/4SW Hon
Entry Requirements: *GCE:* 240. *SQAH:* BBB. *IB:* 25. *BTEC NC:* DD. *BTEC ND:* MMM. Interview required.

WJ3X BA Music Production and Sound Recording
Duration: 3FT Hon
Entry Requirements: *GCE:* 240. *SQAH:* BBBB. *IB:* 26.

HW63 BA Music Technology
Duration: 3FT/4SW Hon
Entry Requirements: *GCE:* 280. *SQAH:* AAAA-BBBB. *IB:* 28. *BTEC NC:* DD. *BTEC ND:* DMM.

JWX3 BA Music Technology and Popular Music
Duration: 3FT/4SW Hon
Entry Requirements: *GCE:* 280. *SQAH:* AAAA-BBBB. *IB:* 28. *BTEC NC:* DD. *BTEC ND:* DMM.

W3W4 BA Music with Drama
Duration: 3FT Hon
Entry Requirements: *GCE:* 300. *IB:* 26. Interview required.

W3Q3 BA Music with English
Duration: 3FT Hon
Entry Requirements: *GCE:* 300. *IB:* 26. Interview required.

W3R9 BA Music with a Modern Language
Duration: 4SW Hon
Entry Requirements: *GCE:* 300. *IB:* 26. Interview required.

W340 BA Popular Music
Duration: 3FT Hon
Entry Requirements: *GCE:* 200. *SQAH:* BBBC. *IB:* 25. Interview required.

WJ39 BA Popular Music Production
Duration: 3FT/4SW Hon
Entry Requirements: *GCE:* 300. *SQAH:* AAAA-AAAB. *IB:* 30. *BTEC ND:* DDM.

W300 BMus Music
Duration: 3FT Hon
Entry Requirements: *GCE:* 300. *IB:* 26. Interview required.

H6W3 BSc Music Technology and Audio Systems
Duration: 3FT/4SW Hon
Entry Requirements: *GCE:* 300. *SQAH:* AAAA-AAAB. *IB:* 30. *BTEC ND:* DDM.

JW93 BSc Popular Music Production
Duration: 3FT/4SW Hon
Entry Requirements: *GCE:* 300. *SQAH:* AAAA-AAAB. *IB:* 30. *BTEC ND:* DDM.

H72 THE UNIVERSITY OF HULL
THE UNIVERSITY OF HULL
COTTINGHAM ROAD
HULL HU6 7RX
t: 01482 466100 f: 01482 442290
e: admissions@hull.ac.uk
// www.hull.ac.uk

W3N2 BA Creative Music Technology with Business Management
Duration: 3FT Hon
Entry Requirements: *GCE:* 240. *IB:* 24. *BTEC ND:* DMM.

WW34 BA Drama and Music
Duration: 3FT Hon
Entry Requirements: *GCE:* 280-300. *IB:* 28. *BTEC ND:* DDM. Interview required.

QW33 BA English and Music
Duration: 3FT Hon
Entry Requirements: *GCE:* 280-300. *IB:* 30. *BTEC ND:* DDM. Interview required.

W340 BA Jazz and Popular Music
Duration: 3FT Hon
Entry Requirements: *GCE:* 280-300. *IB:* 28. *BTEC ND:* DDM. Interview required.

W300 BA Music
Duration: 3FT Hon
Entry Requirements: *GCE:* 280-300. *IB:* 28. *BTEC ND:* DDM. Interview required.

W3Q3 BA Music (including Foundation English Language)
Duration: 4FT Hon
Entry Requirements: *GCE:* 280-300. *IB:* 28. *BTEC ND:* DDM.

WR31 BA Music and French
Duration: 4FT Hon
Entry Requirements: *GCE:* 280-300. *IB:* 28. *BTEC ND:* DDM. Interview required.

WR32 BA Music and German
Duration: 4FT Hon
Entry Requirements: *GCE:* 280-300. *IB:* 28. *BTEC ND:* DDM. Interview required.

WR33 BA Music and Italian
Duration: 4FT Hon
Entry Requirements: *GCE:* 280-300. *IB:* 28. *BTEC ND:* DDM. Interview required.

WR34 BA Music and Spanish
Duration: 4FT Hon
Entry Requirements: *GCE:* 280-300. *IB:* 28. *BTEC ND:* DDM. Interview required.

WW3K BA Music and Theatre
Duration: 3FT Hon
Entry Requirements: *GCE:* 280-300. *IB:* 28. *BTEC ND:* DDM. Interview required.

W341 BA Popular Music
Duration: 3FT Hon
Entry Requirements: *GCE:* 240. *IB:* 24. *BTEC ND:* DMM.

W302 BMus Music
Duration: 3FT Hon
Entry Requirements: *GCE:* 280-300. *IB:* 28. *BTEC ND:* DDM. Interview required.

H73 HULL COLLEGE
QUEEN'S GARDENS
HULL HU1 3DG
t: 01482 329943 f: 01482 598733
e: info@hull-college.ac.uk
// www.hull-college.ac.uk/HE

W313 BA Music Performance
Duration: 1FT Hon
Entry Requirements: Interview required. Admissions Test required.
Portfolio required. HND required.

WJ39 BA Music Production (Top-Up)
Duration: 1FT Hon
Entry Requirements: Interview required. Admissions Test required.
Portfolio required. HND required.

WW3K BA Musical Theatre
Duration: 1FT Hon
Entry Requirements: Interview required. HND required.

W312 FdA Music Performance
Duration: 2FT Fdg
Entry Requirements: GCE: 180-200. Interview required.
Admissions Test required. Portfolio required.

WJ3X FdA Music Production
Duration: 2FT Fdg
Entry Requirements: GCE: 180-200. Interview required.
Admissions Test required. Portfolio required.

WW34 FdA Musical Theatre
Duration: 2FT Fdg
Entry Requirements: GCE: 240. Interview required. Admissions Test
required. Portfolio required.

I50 IMPERIAL COLLEGE LONDON
REGISTRY
SOUTH KENSINGTON CAMPUS
IMPERIAL COLLEGE LONDON
LONDON SW7 2AZ
t: 020 7589 5111 f: 020 7594 8004
// www.imperial.ac.uk

F3W3 BSc Physics and Musical Performance
Duration: 4FT Hon
Entry Requirements: GCE: A*AA. SQAAH: AAA. IB: 38. Interview
required.

K12 KEELE UNIVERSITY
STAFFS ST5 5BG
t: 01782 734005 f: 01782 632343
e: undergraduate@keele.ac.uk
// www.keele.ac.uk

NW43 BA Accounting and Music
Duration: 3FT Hon
Entry Requirements: GCE: 260-320.

TW73 BA American Studies and Music
Duration: 3FT Hon
Entry Requirements: GCE: 280-320.

TWR3 BA American Studies and Music Technology
Duration: 3FT Hon
Entry Requirements: GCE: 280.

NW23 BA Business Management and Music Technology
Duration: 3FT Hon
Entry Requirements: GCE: 280-340.

MWX3 BA Criminology and Music
Duration: 3FT Hon
Entry Requirements: GCE: 260-320.

LW13 BA Economics and Music
Duration: 3FT Hon
Entry Requirements: GCE: 260-320.

LWC3 BA Economics and Music Technology
Duration: 3FT Hon
Entry Requirements: GCE: 280-300.

WX33 BA Educational Studies and Music
Duration: 3FT Hon
Entry Requirements: GCE: 260-320.

WXH3 BA Educational Studies and Music Technology
Duration: 3FT Hon
Entry Requirements: GCE: 260-280.

QW33 BA English and Music
Duration: 3FT Hon
Entry Requirements: GCE: 300-320.

NW33 BA Finance and Music
Duration: 3FT Hon
Entry Requirements: GCE: 260-320.

NWH3 BA Finance and Music Technology
Duration: 3FT Hon
Entry Requirements: GCE: 280-300.

LW73 BA Geography and Music
Duration: 3FT Hon
Entry Requirements: GCE: 300.

LWT3 BA Geography and Music Technology
Duration: 3FT Hon
Entry Requirements: GCE: 300.

VW13 BA History and Music
Duration: 3FT Hon
Entry Requirements: GCE: 300-320.

WV31 BA History and Music Technology
Duration: 3FT Hon
Entry Requirements: GCE: 260-280.

LWR3 BA Human Geography and Music
Duration: 3FT Hon
Entry Requirements: *GCE:* 300.

WL37 BA Human Geography and Music Technology
Duration: 3FT Hon
Entry Requirements: *GCE:* 300-320.

NW63 BA Human Resource Management and Music
Duration: 3FT Hon
Entry Requirements: *GCE:* 260-320.

LWG3 BA International Relations and Music
Duration: 3FT Hon
Entry Requirements: *GCE:* 260-320.

LWF3 BA International Relations and Music Technology
Duration: 3FT Hon
Entry Requirements: *GCE:* 260-280.

MW13 BA Law and Music
Duration: 3FT Hon
Entry Requirements: *GCE:* 260-320.

MWD3 BA Law and Music Technology
Duration: 3FT Hon
Entry Requirements: *GCE:* 300-320.

NW53 BA Marketing and Music Technology
Duration: 3FT Hon
Entry Requirements: *GCE:* 280-340.

W301 BA Music
Duration: 3FT Hon
Entry Requirements: *GCE:* 260-320.

WJ39 BA Music Technology
Duration: 3FT Hon
Entry Requirements: *GCE:* 260-320.

WV35 BA Music Technology and Philosophy
Duration: 3FT Hon
Entry Requirements: *GCE:* 260-280.

LW33 BA Music Technology and Sociology
Duration: 3FT Hon
Entry Requirements: *GCE:* 260-280.

LW23 BA Music and Politics
Duration: 3FT Hon
Entry Requirements: *GCE:* 260-320.

W300 BA Music with Humanities foundation year
Duration: 4FT Hon
Entry Requirements: *GCE:* 160. Interview required.

FW73 BSc Applied Environmental Science and Music
Duration: 3FT Hon
Entry Requirements: *GCE:* 300.

CW8H BSc Applied Psychology and Music
Duration: 4FT Deg
Entry Requirements: *GCE:* 260-320.

FW53 BSc Astrophysics and Music
Duration: 3FT Hon
Entry Requirements: *GCE:* 300-320.

FWM3 BSc Astrophysics and Music Technology
Duration: 3FT Hon
Entry Requirements: *GCE:* 300-320.

CW73 BSc Biochemistry and Music
Duration: 3FT Hon
Entry Requirements: *GCE:* 280-300.

CW13 BSc Biology and Music Technology
Duration: 3FT Hon
Entry Requirements: *GCE:* 280-300.

FW13 BSc Chemistry and Music
Duration: 3FT Hon
Entry Requirements: *GCE:* 300.

FW1J BSc Chemistry and Music Technology
Duration: 3FT Hon
Entry Requirements: *GCE:* 300.

GW43 BSc Computer Science and Music
Duration: 3FT Hon
Entry Requirements: *GCE:* 260-320.

GWK3 BSc Computer Science and Music Technology
Duration: 3FT Hon
Entry Requirements: *GCE:* 280-300.

GW4H BSc Creative Computing and Music
Duration: 3FT Hon
Entry Requirements: *GCE:* 260-320.

FW43 BSc Forensic Science and Music
Duration: 3FT Hon
Entry Requirements: *GCE:* 300.

FW4H BSc Forensic Science and Music Technology
Duration: 3FT Hon
Entry Requirements: *GCE:* 300.

FW63 BSc Geology and Music
Duration: 3FT Hon
Entry Requirements: *GCE:* 300.

WG34 BSc Information Systems and Music
Duration: 3FT Hon
Entry Requirements: *GCE:* 260-320.

GW13 BSc Mathematics and Music
Duration: 3FT Hon
Entry Requirements: *GCE:* 280-300.

FWD3 BSc Medicinal Chemistry and Music
Duration: 3FT Hon
Entry Requirements: *GCE:* 300.

FWC3 BSc Medicinal Chemistry and Music Technology
Duration: 3FT Hon
Entry Requirements: *GCE:* 300.

BW13 BSc Music Technology and Neuroscience
Duration: 3FT Hon
Entry Requirements: *GCE:* 280-300.

WF38 BSc Music Technology and Physical Geography
Duration: 3FT Hon
Entry Requirements: *GCE:* 300.

FWH3 BSc Music Technology and Physics
Duration: 3FT Hon
Entry Requirements: *GCE:* 300-320.

CWV3 BSc Music Technology and Psychology
Duration: 3FT Hon
Entry Requirements: *GCE:* 300-320.

FW83 BSc Music and Physical Geography
Duration: 3FT Hon
Entry Requirements: *GCE:* 300.

FW33 BSc Music and Physics
Duration: 3FT Hon
Entry Requirements: *GCE:* 300-320.

CW83 BSc Music and Psychology
Duration: 3FT Hon
Entry Requirements: *GCE:* 260-320.

GW73 BSc Smart Systems and Music
Duration: 3FT Hon
Entry Requirements: *GCE:* 260-320.

K24 THE UNIVERSITY OF KENT
INFORMATION, RECRUITMENT & ADMISSIONS REGISTRY
UNIVERSITY OF KENT
CANTERBURY, KENT CT2 7NZ
t: 01227 827272 f: 01227 827077
e: information@kent.ac.uk
// www.kent.ac.uk

W311 BA Popular Music Performance (Top-up)
Duration: 1FT Hon
Entry Requirements: Interview required. Portfolio required.

W351 BSc Music Technology
Duration: 3FT Hon
Entry Requirements: *GCE:* 300. *IB:* 33. *BTEC NC:* DD. *BTEC ND:* DDM. *OCR ND:* D *OCR NED:* M1 Interview required.

W310 FdA Popular Music Performance
Duration: 2FT Fdg
Entry Requirements: *GCE:* 100. *BTEC ND:* MMM. *OCR NED:* M2 Interview required. Portfolio required.

K60 KING'S COLLEGE LONDON (UNIVERSITY OF LONDON)
STRAND
LONDON WC2R 2LS
t: 020 7848 7070 f: 020 7848 7171
e: prospective@kcl.ac.uk
// www.kcl.ac.uk

RW23 BA German and Music (4 years)
Duration: 4FT Hon
Entry Requirements: *GCE:* AAAc. *SQAH:* AAABB. *IB:* 38.

W302 BMus Music
Duration: 3FT Hon
Entry Requirements: *GCE:* AAAc. *SQAH:* AAAAB. *IB:* 36.

K84 KINGSTON UNIVERSITY
STUDENT INFORMATION & ADVICE CENTRE
COOPER HOUSE
40-46 SURBITON ROAD
KINGSTON UPON THAMES KT1 2HX
t: 0844 8552177 f: 020 8547 7080
e: aps@kingston.ac.uk
// www.kingston.ac.uk

WWH4 BA Creative Music Technologies and Dance
Duration: 3FT Hon
Entry Requirements: *GCE:* 300-360. *BTEC ND:* DDD. Interview required.

WWG4 BA Creative Music Technologies and Drama
Duration: 3FT Hon
Entry Requirements: *GCE:* 300-360.

WW53 BA Dance and Music
Duration: 3FT Hon
Entry Requirements: *GCE:* 300-360. *BTEC ND:* DDD. Interview required.

W5W3 BA Dance with Music
Duration: 3FT Hon
Entry Requirements: *GCE:* 300-360. *BTEC ND:* DDD. Interview required.

WW43 BA Drama and Music
Duration: 3FT Hon
Entry Requirements: *GCE:* 300-360.

VW33 BA History of Art, Design & Film and Music
Duration: 3FT Hon
Entry Requirements: *GCE:* 240.

WW35 BA Music Technology and Dance
Duration: 3FT Hon
Entry Requirements: *GCE:* 320-360. *BTEC ND:* DDD. Interview required.

WW3K BA Music Technology and Drama
Duration: 3FT Hon
Entry Requirements: *GCE:* 320-360. *BTEC ND:* DDD.

WW34 BA Music and Drama
Duration: 3FT Hon
Entry Requirements: *GCE:* 300-360. *BTEC ND:* DDD.

WV33 BA Music and History of Art, Design and Film
Duration: 3FT Hon
Entry Requirements: *GCE:* 240-280. *BTEC ND:* MMM.

W3W5 BA Music with Dance
Duration: 3FT Hon
Entry Requirements: *GCE:* 300-360. *BTEC ND:* DDD. Interview required.

W301 BMus Creative Music Technologies
Duration: 3FT Hon
Entry Requirements: *GCE:* 240-280. *BTEC ND:* MMM.

W300 BMus Music
Duration: 3FT Hon
Entry Requirements: *GCE:* 240-280. *BTEC ND:* MMM.

W393 BMus Music Technology
Duration: 3FT Hon
Entry Requirements: *GCE:* 240-280. *BTEC ND:* MMM.

L14 LANCASTER UNIVERSITY
THE UNIVERSITY
LANCASTER
LANCASHIRE LA1 4YW
t: 01524 592029 f: 01524 846243
e: ugadmissions@lancaster.ac.uk
// www.lancs.ac.uk

WQ33 BA English Literature and Music
Duration: 3FT Hon
Entry Requirements: *GCE:* ABB. *SQAH:* BBBBB. *SQAAH:* ABB. *IB:* 34.

WR31 BA French Studies and Music
Duration: 4SW Hon
Entry Requirements: *GCE:* ABB. *SQAH:* BBBBC. *SQAAH:* BBB-BBC. *IB:* 32. *BTEC ND:* DDM.

WR32 BA German Studies and Music
Duration: 4SW Hon
Entry Requirements: *GCE:* ABB. *SQAH:* BBBBC. *SQAAH:* BBB-BBC. *IB:* 32. *BTEC ND:* DDM.

WV31 BA History and Music
Duration: 3FT Hon
Entry Requirements: *GCE:* ABB. *SQAH:* BBBBB. *SQAAH:* ABB. *IB:* 32. *BTEC ND:* DDM.

W300 BA Music
Duration: 3FT Hon
Entry Requirements: *GCE:* ABB. *SQAH:* BBBBC. *SQAAH:* BBB. *IB:* 32. *BTEC ND:* DDM.

W390 BA Music Technology
Duration: 3FT Hon
Entry Requirements: *GCE:* ABB. *SQAH:* BBBBC. *SQAAH:* BBB-BBC. *IB:* 32. *BTEC ND:* DDM.

WR34 BA Spanish Studies and Music
Duration: 4SW Hon
Entry Requirements: *GCE:* ABB. *SQAH:* BBBBC. *SQAAH:* BBB-BBC. *IB:* 32. *BTEC ND:* DDM.

GW43 BSc Computer Science and Music
Duration: 3FT Hon
Entry Requirements: *GCE:* ABB. *SQAH:* BBBBC. *SQAAH:* BBB-BBC. *IB:* 32. *BTEC ND:* DDM.

L23 UNIVERSITY OF LEEDS
THE UNIVERSITY OF LEEDS
WOODHOUSE LANE
LEEDS LS2 9JT
t: 0113 343 3999
e: admissions@leeds.ac.uk
// www.leeds.ac.uk

QW33 BA English and Music
Duration: 3FT Hon
Entry Requirements: *GCE:* ABB. *SQAAH:* ABB. *IB:* 33.

RW13 BA French and Music
Duration: 4FT Hon
Entry Requirements: *GCE:* ABB. *SQAAH:* ABB.

RW23 BA German and Music
Duration: 4FT Hon
Entry Requirements: *GCE:* ABB. *SQAAH:* ABB.

VW13 BA History and Music
Duration: 3FT Hon
Entry Requirements: *GCE:* ABB. *SQAAH:* ABB. *IB:* 33.

RW33 BA Italian A and Music
Duration: 4FT Hon
Entry Requirements: *GCE:* ABB. *SQAAH:* ABB.

RWH3 BA Italian B and Music
Duration: 4FT Hon
Entry Requirements: *GCE:* ABB. *SQAAH:* ABB.

W300 BA Music
Duration: 3FT/4FT Hon
Entry Requirements: *GCE:* ABB. *SQAH:* AAABB. *SQAAH:* ABB. *IB:* 33.

VW53 BA Music and Philosophy
Duration: 3FT Hon
Entry Requirements: *GCE:* BBB. *SQAAH:* BBB. *IB:* 32.

WR34 BA Music and Spanish
Duration: 4FT Hon
Entry Requirements: Contact the institution for details.

VW63 BA Music and Theology & Religious Studies
Duration: 3FT Hon
Entry Requirements: *GCE:* BBB. *SQAAH:* BBB. *IB:* 32.

GW13 BSc Mathematics and Music
Duration: 3FT/4FT Hon
Entry Requirements: *GCE:* AAB. *SQAAH:* AAB.

WGH4 BSc Music, Multimedia & Electronics
Duration: 3FT Hon
Entry Requirements: *GCE:* AAB. *SQAAH:* AAB. *IB:* 36.

L27 LEEDS METROPOLITAN UNIVERSITY
COURSE ENQUIRIES OFFICE
CITY SITE
LEEDS LS1 3HE
t: 0113 81 23113 f: 0113 81 23129
// www.leedsmet.ac.uk

WJ3X BA Music Production
Duration: 3FT/4SW Hon
Entry Requirements: *GCE:* 240. *IB:* 24. Interview required.

JW9H BSc Music and New Media Technology
Duration: 3FT/4SW Hon
Entry Requirements: *GCE:* 160. *IB:* 24.

L30 LEEDS COLLEGE OF MUSIC
3 QUARRY HILL
LEEDS
WEST YORKSHIRE LS2 7PD
t: 0113 222 3416 f: 0113 243 8798
e: enquiries@lcm.ac.uk
// www.lcm.ac.uk

W300 BA Music (Classical Music)
Duration: 3FT Hon
Entry Requirements: *GCE:* 240. *BTEC NC:* DD. *BTEC ND:* MMM. Interview required. Portfolio required.

W341 BA Music (Jazz)
Duration: 3FT Hon
Entry Requirements: *GCE:* 240. *BTEC NC:* DD. *BTEC ND:* MMM. Interview required. Portfolio required.

W302 BA Music (Popular Music)
Duration: 3FT Hon
Entry Requirements: *GCE:* 240. *BTEC NC:* DD. *BTEC ND:* MMM. Interview required. Portfolio required.

W301 BA Music (Production)
Duration: 3FT Hon
Entry Requirements: *GCE:* 240. *BTEC NC:* DD. *BTEC ND:* MMM. Interview required. Portfolio required.

W303 BA Music (combined)
Duration: 3FT Hon
Entry Requirements: *GCE:* 240. *BTEC NC:* DD. *BTEC ND:* MMM. Interview required. Portfolio required.

W304 BA Music Production (Top-up)
Duration: 1FT Hon
Entry Requirements: Contact the institution for details.

W305 BA Popular Music (Top-Up)
Duration: 1FT Hon
Entry Requirements: Contact the institution for details.

W306 FdA Music Production
Duration: 2FT Fdg
Entry Requirements: Contact the institution for details.

L31 LEEDS COLLEGE OF MUSIC
3 QUARRY HILL
LEEDS
WEST YORKSHIRE LS2 7PD
t: 0113 222 3416 f: 0113 243 8798
e: enquiries.assistant@lcm.ac.uk
// www.lcm.ac.uk

720F MA MA Composition
Duration: 1FT PMD
Entry Requirements: Interview required.

L41 THE UNIVERSITY OF LIVERPOOL
THE FOUNDATION BUILDING
BROWNLOW HILL
LIVERPOOL L69 7ZX
t: 0151 794 2000 f: 0151 708 6502
e: ugrecruitment@liv.ac.uk
// www.liv.ac.uk

W300 BA Music/Popular Music
Duration: 3FT Hon
Entry Requirements: *GCE:* ABB. *SQAH:* ABBBB. *SQAAH:* ABB. *IB:* 33. *BTEC ND:* DDM. Interview required.

L43 LIVERPOOL COMMUNITY COLLEGE
LIVERPOOL COMMUNITY COLLEGE
CLARENCE STREET
LIVERPOOL L3 5TP
t: 0151 252 3352 f: 0151 252 3351
e: enquiry@liv-coll.ac.uk
// www.liv-coll.ac.uk

W340 FdA Popular Music
Duration: 2FT Fdg
Entry Requirements: *GCE:* AA-CC. *SQAH:* A-C. *BTEC ND:* DMM.
Interview required.

L46 LIVERPOOL HOPE UNIVERSITY
HOPE PARK
LIVERPOOL L16 9JD
t: 0151 291 3295 f: 0151 291 3444
e: admission@hope.ac.uk
// www.hope.ac.uk

WX33 BA Education and Music
Duration: 3FT Hon   CRB Check: Required
Entry Requirements: *GCE:* 260-320. *IB:* 25.

QW33 BA English Literature and Music
Duration: 3FT Hon
Entry Requirements: *GCE:* 260-320. *IB:* 25.

WW1H BA Fine Art and Music
Duration: 3FT Hon
Entry Requirements: *GCE:* 260-320. *IB:* 25.

VW13 BA History and Music
Duration: 3FT Hon
Entry Requirements: *GCE:* 260-320. *IB:* 25.

W300 BA Music
Duration: 3FT Hon
Entry Requirements: *GCE:* 260-320. *IB:* 25. Interview required.

X1WJ BA Primary Teaching with Music
Duration: 4FT Hon   CRB Check: Required
Entry Requirements: *GCE:* 300. *IB:* 25. Interview required.

L48 THE LIVERPOOL INSTITUTE FOR PERFORMING ARTS
MOUNT STREET
LIVERPOOL L1 9HF
t: 0151 330 3000 f: 0151 330 3131
e: admissions@lipa.ac.uk
// www.lipa.ac.uk

W300 BA Music
Duration: 3FT Hon
Entry Requirements: *GCE:* 280. Interview required.

HW63 BA Sound Technology
Duration: 3FT Hon
Entry Requirements: *GCE:* 260. Interview required.

L51 LIVERPOOL JOHN MOORES UNIVERSITY
KINGSWAY HOUSE
HATTON GARDEN
LIVERPOOL L3 2AJ
t: 0151 231 5090 f: 0151 231 3462
e: courses@ljmu.ac.uk
// www.ljmu.ac.uk

W340 BA Popular Music Studies
Duration: 3FT Hon
Entry Requirements: *GCE:* 260.

L68 LONDON METROPOLITAN UNIVERSITY
166-220 HOLLOWAY ROAD
LONDON N7 8DB
t: 020 7133 4200
e: admissions@londonmet.ac.uk
// www.londonmet.ac.uk

WN39 BA Music & Media Business Management
Duration: 3FT/4SW Hon
Entry Requirements: *GCE:* 240. *IB:* 28.

W300 BA Music Industry Management
Duration: 3FT Hon
Entry Requirements: Contact the institution for details.

W390 BA Music Technology with Music Production
Duration: 3FT Hon
Entry Requirements: Contact the institution for details.

L75 LONDON SOUTH BANK UNIVERSITY
103 BOROUGH ROAD
LONDON SE1 0AA
t: 020 7815 7815 f: 020 7815 8273
e: enquiry@lsbu.ac.uk
// www.lsbu.ac.uk

WW43 BA Drama and Performance Studies
Duration: 3FT Hon
Entry Requirements: *GCE:* 240. *IB:* 24. *BTEC NC:* DD. *BTEC ND:* MMM.

L77 LOUGHBOROUGH COLLEGE
RADMOOR ROAD
LOUGHBOROUGH LE11 3BT
t: 0845 166 2950 f: 0845 833 2840
e: info@loucoll.ac.uk
// www.loucoll.ac.uk

JW93 BA Music Production and Performance
Duration: 1FT Hon
Entry Requirements: Contact the institution for details.

WJ39 FdA Music Performance and Production
Duration: 2FT Fdg
Entry Requirements: *GCE:* 140.

M10 THE MANCHESTER COLLEGE
OPENSHAW CAMPUS
ASHTON OLD ROAD
OPENSHAW
MANCHESTER M11 2WH
t: 0800 068 8585 f: 0161 920 4103
e: enquiries@themanchestercollege.ac.uk
// www.themanchestercollege.ac.uk

WJ39 FdA Popular Music and Production
Duration: 2FT Fdg
Entry Requirements: *GCE:* 160. Interview required.

WN38 FdSc Music Industries Management
Duration: 2FT Fdg
Entry Requirements: *GCE:* 160. Interview required.

M20 THE UNIVERSITY OF MANCHESTER
OXFORD ROAD
MANCHESTER M13 9PL
t: 0161 275 2077 f: 0161 275 2106
e: ug-admissions@manchester.ac.uk
// www.manchester.ac.uk

WW34 BA Music and Drama
Duration: 3FT Hon
Entry Requirements: *GCE:* AAA-AAB. *SQAAH:* AAB. *BTEC ND:* MMM. Interview required.

W302 BMus Music
Duration: 3FT Hon
Entry Requirements: *GCE:* AAB. *SQAAH:* AAB. *BTEC ND:* MMM.

M40 THE MANCHESTER METROPOLITAN UNIVERSITY
ADMISSIONS OFFICE
ALL SAINTS (GMS)
ALL SAINTS
MANCHESTER M15 6BH
t: 0161 247 2000
// www.mmu.ac.uk

LWM3 BA Abuse Studies/Popular Music
Duration: 3FT Hon
Entry Requirements: *GCE:* 240-280. *BTEC ND:* DMM.

NW13 BA Business/Music
Duration: 3FT Hon
Entry Requirements: *GCE:* 240-280. *SQAH:* BBB. *SQAAH:* CC. *IB:* 28. Interview required.

CWQ3 BA Coaching Studies/Music
Duration: 3FT Hon
Entry Requirements: *GCE:* 240-280. *BTEC ND:* DMM. Interview required.

WC36 BA Coaching Studies/Popular Music
Duration: 3FT Hon
Entry Requirements: *GCE:* 240-280. *BTEC ND:* DMM.

W394 BA Creative Music Production
Duration: 3FT Hon
Entry Requirements: *GCE:* 240-280. Interview required.

WL35 BA Creative Music Production/Abuse Studies
Duration: 3FT Hon
Entry Requirements: *GCE:* 240-280. Interview required.

WW3W BA Creative Music Production/Creative Writing
Duration: 3FT Hon
Entry Requirements: *GCE:* 240-280.

WLHJ BA Creative Music Production/Crime Studies
Duration: 3FT Hon
Entry Requirements: *GCE:* 240-280.

WWH5 BA Creative Music Production/Dance
Duration: 3FT Hon
Entry Requirements: *GCE:* 240-280.

WXHH BA Creative Music Production/Education Studies
Duration: 3FT Hon
Entry Requirements: *GCE:* 240-280.

WW3Q BA Creative Music Production/Film & Television Studies
Duration: 3FT Hon
Entry Requirements: *GCE:* 240-280.

WN33 BA Creative Music Production/Financial Management
Duration: 3FT Hon
Entry Requirements: *GCE:* 240-280.

WN36 BA Creative Music Production/Human Resource Management
Duration: 3FT Hon
Entry Requirements: *GCE:* 240-280.

WM32 BA Creative Music Production/Legal Studies
Duration: 3FT Hon
Entry Requirements: *GCE:* 240-280. Interview required.

WN35 BA Creative Music Production/Marketing
Duration: 3FT Hon
Entry Requirements: *GCE:* 240-280. Interview required.

W395 BA Creative Music Production/Music
Duration: 3FT Hon
Entry Requirements: *GCE:* 240-280. Interview required.

W396 BA Creative Music Production/Popular Music
Duration: 3FT Hon
Entry Requirements: *GCE:* 240-280.

WLJH BA Creative Music Production/Sociology
Duration: 3FT Hon
Entry Requirements: *GCE:* 240-280.

WCHP BA Creative Music Production/Sport Development
Duration: 3FT Hon
Entry Requirements: *GCE:* 240-280.

WW34 BA Drama/Music
Duration: 3FT Hon
Entry Requirements: *GCE:* 240-280. *SQAH:* BBB. *SQAAH:* CC. *IB:* 28. Interview required.

WW3K BA Drama/Popular Music
Duration: 3FT Hon
Entry Requirements: *GCE:* 240-280. Interview required.

NW33 BA Financial Management/Music
Duration: 3FT Hon
Entry Requirements: *GCE:* 240-280. *BTEC ND:* DMM.

NW6H BA Human Resource Management/Popular Music
Duration: 3FT Hon
Entry Requirements: *GCE:* 240-280. *BTEC ND:* DMM.

W301 BA Music
Duration: 3FT Hon
Entry Requirements: *GCE:* 240-280. Interview required.

WW35 BA Music/Dance
Duration: 3FT Hon
Entry Requirements: *GCE:* 240-280. Interview required.

WX33 BA Music/Education Studies
Duration: 3FT Hon
Entry Requirements: *GCE:* 240-280. Interview required.

WW36 BA Music/Film & Television Studies
Duration: 3FT Hon
Entry Requirements: *GCE:* 240-280.

MWG3 BA Music/Legal Studies
Duration: 3FT Hon
Entry Requirements: *GCE:* 240-280.

VW53 BA Music/Philosophy
Duration: 3FT Hon
Entry Requirements: *GCE:* 240-280. *IB:* 28. *BTEC ND:* DMM.

WCJP BA Music/Sport Development
Duration: 3FT Hon
Entry Requirements: *GCE:* 240-280.

W340 BA Popular Music
Duration: 3FT Hon
Entry Requirements: *GCE:* 240-280. Interview required.

NW1H BA/BSc Business/Popular Music
Duration: 3FT Hon
Entry Requirements: *GCE:* 240-280. Interview required.

WXH3 BA/BSc Childhood & Youth Studies/Music
Duration: 3FT Hon
Entry Requirements: *GCE:* 240-280. *SQAH:* BBB. *SQAAH:* CC. *IB:* 28. Interview required.

WX3H BA/BSc Childhood & Youth Studies/Popular Music
Duration: 3FT Hon
Entry Requirements: *GCE:* 240-280. Interview required.

WC3Q BA/BSc Creative Music Production/Outdoor Studies
Duration: 3FT Hon
Entry Requirements: *GCE:* 240-280.

WC3V BA/BSc Creative Music Production/Psychology
Duration: 3FT Hon
Entry Requirements: *GCE:* 240-280.

LW3J BA/BSc Crime Studies/Popular Music
Duration: 3FT Hon
Entry Requirements: *GCE:* 240-280.

QW3H BA/BSc English/Popular Music
Duration: 3FT Hon
Entry Requirements: *GCE:* 240-280. *BTEC ND:* DMM.

NW5H BA/BSc Marketing/Popular Music
Duration: 3FT Hon
Entry Requirements: *GCE:* 240-280. *BTEC ND:* DMM.

WCHQ BA/BSc Music/Outdoor Studies
Duration: 3FT Hon
Entry Requirements: *GCE:* 240-280.

W391 BA/BSc Music/Popular Music
Duration: 3FT Hon
Entry Requirements: *GCE:* 240-280. *BTEC ND:* DMM. Interview required.

WC38 BA/BSc Music/Psychology
Duration: 3FT Hon
Entry Requirements: *GCE:* 240-280.

VW5H BA/BSc Philosophy/Popular Music
Duration: 3FT Hon
Entry Requirements: *GCE:* 240-280. *BTEC ND:* DMM.

WW38 BA/BSc Popular Music/Creative Writing
Duration: 3FT Hon
Entry Requirements: *GCE:* 240-280. *BTEC ND:* DMM.

LWHJ BA/BSc Popular Music/Sociology
Duration: 3FT Hon
Entry Requirements: *GCE:* 240-280. *BTEC ND:* DMM.

CW6H BA/BSc Popular Music/Sport
Duration: 3FT Hon
Entry Requirements: *GCE:* 240-280. *BTEC ND:* DMM.

M80 MIDDLESEX UNIVERSITY
MIDDLESEX UNIVERSITY
THE BURROUGHS
LONDON NW4 4BT
t: 020 8411 5555 f: 020 8411 5649
e: enquiries@mdx.ac.uk
// www.mdx.ac.uk

W340 BA Jazz
Duration: 3FT Hon
Entry Requirements: *GCE:* 200-300. *IB:* 28. Interview required.

W305 BA Music Composition
Duration: 3FT Hon
Entry Requirements: *GCE:* 200-300. *IB:* 28. Interview required.

W312 BA Music Performance
Duration: 3FT Hon
Entry Requirements: *GCE:* 200-300. *IB:* 28. Interview required.

W3N2 BA Music and Arts Management
Duration: 3FT Hon
Entry Requirements: *GCE:* 200-300. *IB:* 28. Interview required.

W341 BMUS Popular Music
Duration: 3FT Hon
Entry Requirements: *GCE:* 200-300. *IB:* 28. Interview required.

N13 NEATH PORT TALBOT COLLEGE
NEATH CAMPUS
DWR-Y-FELIN ROAD
NEATH
NEATH PORT TALBOT BOROUGH SA10 7RF
t: 01639 648033 f: 01639 648077
e: admissions@nptc.ac.uk
// www.nptc.ac.uk

W300 FdA Popular Music
Duration: 2FT Fdg
Entry Requirements: Contact the institution for details.

N21 NEWCASTLE UNIVERSITY
KING'S GATE
NEWCASTLE UPON TYNE NE1 7RU
t: 0191 208 3333 f: 0191 222 6143
// www.ncl.ac.uk

W300 BA Music
Duration: 3FT Hon
Entry Requirements: *GCE:* ABB. *SQAH:* AABBB. *IB:* 33. *BTEC ND:* DDM. Interview required.

W340 BMus Folk and Traditional Music
Duration: 4FT Hon
Entry Requirements: *GCE:* BBB. *SQAH:* AAAB. *IB:* 32. *BTEC ND:* DDM. Interview required.

W304 BMus Music
Duration: 4FT Hon
Entry Requirements: *GCE:* AAB. *SQAH:* AAABB. *IB:* 35. *BTEC ND:* DDD. Interview required.

W301 BMus Popular and Contemporary Music
Duration: 2FT Hon
Entry Requirements: Contact the institution for details.

N23 NEWCASTLE COLLEGE
STUDENT SERVICES
RYE HILL CAMPUS
SCOTSWOOD ROAD
NEWCASTLE UPON TYNE NE4 7SA
t: 0191 200 4110 f: 0191 200 4349
e: enquiries@ncl-coll.ac.uk
// www.newcastlecollege.co.uk

W392 BA Music Enterprise (Top-up)
Duration: 1FT Hon
Entry Requirements: Interview required. HND required.

WW34 FdA Live Music and Theatre Production
Duration: 2FT Fdg   CRB Check: Required
Entry Requirements: *GCE:* 120. *BTEC NC:* MP. *BTEC ND:* PPP. *OCR ND:* P2 *OCR NED:* P3 Interview required.

W300 FdA Music Production
Duration: 2FT Fdg   CRB Check: Required
Entry Requirements: *GCE:* 120. *BTEC NC:* MP. *BTEC ND:* PPP. *OCR ND:* P2 *OCR NED:* P3 Interview required.

W391 FdA Musical Theatre
Duration: 2FT Fdg   CRB Check: Required
Entry Requirements: *GCE:* 120. *BTEC NC:* MP. *BTEC ND:* PPP. *OCR ND:* P2 *OCR NED:* P3 Interview required.

W341 FdA Popular Music
Duration: 2FT Fdg   CRB Check: Required
Entry Requirements: *GCE:* 120. *BTEC NC:* MP. *BTEC ND:* PPP. *OCR ND:* P2 *OCR NED:* P3 Interview required.

N30 NEW COLLEGE NOTTINGHAM
ADAMS BUILDING
STONEY STREET
THE LACE MARKET
NOTTINGHAM NG1 1NG
t: 0115 910 0100 f: 0115 953 4349
e: enquiries@ncn.ac.uk
// www.ncn.ac.uk

W390 BA Sonic Arts (Top-up)
Duration: 1FT Hon
Entry Requirements: Interview required. Portfolio required.

WJ3X FdA Music and Sonic Arts (Music Performance)
Duration: 2FT Fdg
Entry Requirements: *GCE:* 120. Interview required. Portfolio required.

WJ39 FdA Music and Sonic Arts (Music Technology)
Duration: 2FT Fdg
Entry Requirements: *GCE:* 120. Interview required. Portfolio required.

N37 UNIVERSITY OF WALES, NEWPORT
ADMISSIONS
LODGE ROAD
CAERLEON
NEWPORT NP18 3QT
t: 01633 432030 f: 01633 432850
e: admissions@newport.ac.uk
// www.newport.ac.uk

W000 BA Performing Arts
Duration: 3FT Hon
Entry Requirements: *Foundation:* Merit. *GCE:* 240-260. *IB:* 24.
Interview required. Portfolio required.

N38 UNIVERSITY OF NORTHAMPTON
PARK CAMPUS
BOUGHTON GREEN ROAD
NORTHAMPTON NN2 7AL
t: 0800 358 2232 f: 01604 722083
e: admissions@northampton.ac.uk
// www.northampton.ac.uk

N4W3 BA Accounting/Popular Music
Duration: 3FT Hon
Entry Requirements: *GCE:* 260-280. *SQAH:* AAA-BBBB. *IB:* 24.
BTEC NC: DD. *BTEC ND:* DMM. *OCR ND:* D *OCR NED:* M2

N5WH BA Advertising/Popular Music
Duration: 3FT Hon
Entry Requirements: *GCE:* 260-280. *SQAH:* AAA-BBBB. *IB:* 24.
BTEC NC: DD. *BTEC ND:* DMM. *OCR ND:* D *OCR NED:* M2
Interview required.

N1WH BA Business Entrepreneurship/Popular Music
Duration: 3FT Hon
Entry Requirements: *GCE:* 260-280. *SQAH:* AAA-BBBB. *IB:* 24.
BTEC NC: DD. *BTEC ND:* DMM. *OCR ND:* D *OCR NED:* M2
Interview required.

N1W3 BA Business/Popular Music
Duration: 3FT Hon
Entry Requirements: *GCE:* 260-280. *SQAH:* AAA-BBBB. *IB:* 24.
BTEC NC: DD. *BTEC ND:* DMM. *OCR ND:* D *OCR NED:* M2

M9W3 BA Criminology/Popular Music
Duration: 3FT Hon
Entry Requirements: *GCE:* 260-280. *SQAH:* AAA-BBBB. *IB:* 24.
BTEC NC: DD. *BTEC ND:* DMM. *OCR ND:* D *OCR NED:* M2

W5W3 BA Dance/Popular Music
Duration: 3FT Hon
Entry Requirements: *GCE:* 260-280. *SQAH:* AAA-BBBB. *IB:* 24.
BTEC NC: DD. *BTEC ND:* DMM. *OCR ND:* D *OCR NED:* M2
Interview required.

W4W3 BA Drama/Popular Music
Duration: 3FT Hon
Entry Requirements: *GCE:* 260-280. *SQAH:* AAA-BBBB. *IB:* 24.
BTEC NC: DD. *BTEC ND:* DMM. *OCR ND:* D *OCR NED:* M2
Interview required.

X3W3 BA Education Studies/Popular Music
Duration: 3FT Hon
Entry Requirements: *GCE:* 260-280. *SQAH:* AAA-BBBB. *IB:* 24.
BTEC NC: DD. *BTEC ND:* DMM. *OCR ND:* D *OCR NED:* M2
Interview required.

Q3W3 BA English/Popular Music
Duration: 3FT Hon
Entry Requirements: *GCE:* 260-280. *SQAH:* AAA-BBBB. *IB:* 24.
BTEC NC: DD. *BTEC ND:* DMM. *OCR ND:* D *OCR NED:* M2
Interview required.

N8WH BA Events Management/Popular Music
Duration: 3FT Hon
Entry Requirements: *GCE:* 260-280. *SQAH:* AAA-BBBB. *IB:* 24.
BTEC NC: DD. *BTEC ND:* DMM. *OCR ND:* D *OCR NED:* M2
Interview required.

W6W3 BA Film & Television Studies/Popular Music
Duration: 3FT Hon
Entry Requirements: *GCE:* 260-280. *SQAH:* AAA-BBBB. *IB:* 24.
BTEC NC: DD. *BTEC ND:* DMM. *OCR ND:* D *OCR NED:* M2
Interview required.

W1W3 BA Fine Art Painting & Drawing/Popular Music
Duration: 3FT Hon
Entry Requirements: *GCE:* 260-280. *SQAH:* AAA-BBBB. *IB:* 24.
BTEC NC: DD. *BTEC ND:* DMM. *OCR ND:* D *OCR NED:* M2
Interview required.

R1W3 BA French/Popular Music
Duration: 3FT Hon
Entry Requirements: *GCE:* 260-280. *SQAH:* AAA-BBBB. *IB:* 24.
BTEC NC: DD. *BTEC ND:* DMM. *OCR ND:* D *OCR NED:* M2
Interview required.

L4W3 BA Health Studies/Popular Music
Duration: 3FT Hon
Entry Requirements: *GCE:* 260-280. *SQAH:* AAA-BBBB. *IB:* 24.
BTEC NC: DD. *BTEC ND:* DMM. *OCR ND:* D *OCR NED:* M2

V1W3 BA History/Popular Music
Duration: 3FT Hon
Entry Requirements: *GCE:* 260-280. *SQAH:* AAA-BBBB. *IB:* 24.
BTEC NC: DD. *BTEC ND:* DMM. *OCR ND:* D *OCR NED:* M2

L7W3 BA Human Geography/Popular Music
Duration: 3FT Hon
Entry Requirements: *GCE:* 260-280. *SQAH:* AAA-BBBB. *IB:* 24.
BTEC NC: DD. *BTEC ND:* DMM. *OCR ND:* D *OCR NED:* M2

N6W3 BA Human Resource Management/Popular Music
Duration: 3FT Hon
Entry Requirements: *GCE:* 260-280. *SQAH:* AAA-BBBB. *IB:* 24.
BTEC NC: DD. *BTEC ND:* DMM. *OCR ND:* D *OCR NED:* M2

L9WH BA International Development/Popular Music
Duration: 3FT Hon
Entry Requirements: *GCE:* 260-280. *SQAH:* AAA-BBBB. *IB:* 24.
BTEC NC: DD. *BTEC ND:* DMM. *OCR ND:* D *OCR NED:* M2

M1W3 BA Law/Popular Music
Duration: 3FT Hon
Entry Requirements: *GCE:* 260-280. *SQAH:* AAA-BBBB. *IB:* 24.
BTEC NC: DD. *BTEC ND:* DMM. *OCR ND:* D *OCR NED:* M2

N2W3 BA Management/Popular Music
Duration: 3FT Hon
Entry Requirements: *GCE:* 260-280. *SQAH:* AAA-BBBB. *IB:* 24.
BTEC NC: DD. *BTEC ND:* DMM. *OCR ND:* D *OCR NED:* M2

N5W3 BA Marketing/Popular Music
Duration: 3FT Hon
Entry Requirements: *GCE:* 260-280. *SQAH:* AAA-BBBB. *IB:* 24.
BTEC NC: DD. *BTEC ND:* DMM. *OCR ND:* D *OCR NED:* M2
Interview required.

W391 BA Music Production (top-up)
Duration: 1FT Hon
Entry Requirements: Interview required. HND required.

W340 BA Popular Music
Duration: 3FT Hon
Entry Requirements: *GCE:* 260-280. *SQAH:* AAA-BBBB. *IB:* 24.
BTEC NC: DD. *BTEC ND:* DMM. *OCR ND:* D *OCR NED:* M2
Interview required.

W3NA BA Popular Music with Applied Management
Duration: 3FT Hon
Entry Requirements: *GCE:* 260-280. *SQAH:* AAA-BBBB. *IB:* 24.
BTEC NC: DD. *BTEC ND:* DMM. *OCR ND:* D *OCR NED:* M2
Interview required.

W3N4 BA Popular Music/Accounting
Duration: 3FT Hon
Entry Requirements: *GCE:* 260-280. *SQAH:* AAA-BBBB. *IB:* 24.
BTEC NC: DD. *BTEC ND:* DMM. *OCR ND:* D *OCR NED:* M2

W3NM BA Popular Music/Advertising
Duration: 3FT Hon
Entry Requirements: *GCE:* 260-280. *SQAH:* AAA-BBBB. *IB:* 24.
BTEC NC: DD. *BTEC ND:* DMM. *OCR ND:* D *OCR NED:* M2
Interview required.

W3C1 BA Popular Music/Biological Conservation
Duration: 3FT Hon
Entry Requirements: *GCE:* 260-280. *SQAH:* AAA-BBBB. *IB:* 24.
BTEC NC: DD. *BTEC ND:* DMM. *OCR ND:* D *OCR NED:* M2

W3N1 BA Popular Music/Business
Duration: 3FT Hon
Entry Requirements: *GCE:* 260-280. *SQAH:* AAA-BBBB. *IB:* 24.
BTEC NC: DD. *BTEC ND:* DMM. *OCR ND:* D *OCR NED:* M2
Interview required.

W3NF BA Popular Music/Business Entrepreneurship
Duration: 3FT Hon
Entry Requirements: *GCE:* 260-280. *SQAH:* AAA-BBBB. *IB:* 24.
BTEC NC: DD. *BTEC ND:* DMM. *OCR ND:* D *OCR NED:* M2

W3G4 BA Popular Music/Computing
Duration: 3FT Hon
Entry Requirements: *GCE:* 260-280. *SQAH:* AAA-BBBB. *IB:* 24.
BTEC NC: DD. *BTEC ND:* DMM. *OCR ND:* D *OCR NED:* M2

W3M9 BA Popular Music/Criminology
Duration: 3FT Hon
Entry Requirements: *GCE:* 260-280. *SQAH:* AAA-BBBB. *IB:* 24.
BTEC NC: DD. *BTEC ND:* DMM. *OCR ND:* D *OCR NED:* M2

W3W5 BA Popular Music/Dance
Duration: 3FT Hon
Entry Requirements: *GCE:* 260-280. *SQAH:* AAA-BBBB. *IB:* 24.
BTEC NC: DD. *BTEC ND:* DMM. *OCR ND:* D *OCR NED:* M2
Interview required.

W3W4 BA Popular Music/Drama
Duration: 3FT Hon
Entry Requirements: *GCE:* 260-280. *SQAH:* AAA-BBBB. *IB:* 24.
BTEC NC: DD. *BTEC ND:* DMM. *OCR ND:* D *OCR NED:* M2
Interview required.

W3X3 BA Popular Music/Education Studies
Duration: 3FT Hon
Entry Requirements: *GCE:* 260-280. *SQAH:* AAA-BBBB. *IB:* 24.
BTEC NC: DD. *BTEC ND:* DMM. *OCR ND:* D *OCR NED:* M2

W3Q3 BA Popular Music/English
Duration: 3FT Hon
Entry Requirements: *GCE:* 260-280. *SQAH:* AAA-BBBB. *IB:* 24.
BTEC NC: DD. *BTEC ND:* DMM. *OCR ND:* D *OCR NED:* M2
Interview required.

W3NV BA Popular Music/Events Management
Duration: 3FT Hon
Entry Requirements: *GCE:* 260-280. *SQAH:* AAA-BBBB. *IB:* 24.
BTEC NC: DD. *BTEC ND:* DMM. *OCR ND:* D *OCR NED:* M2
Interview required.

W3W6 BA Popular Music/Film & Television Studies
Duration: 3FT Hon
Entry Requirements: *GCE:* 260-280. *SQAH:* AAA-BBBB. *IB:* 24. *BTEC NC:* DD. *BTEC ND:* DMM. *OCR ND:* D *OCR NED:* M2
Interview required.

W3W1 BA Popular Music/Fine Art Painting & Drawing
Duration: 3FT Hon
Entry Requirements: *GCE:* 260-280. *SQAH:* AAA-BBBB. *IB:* 24. *BTEC NC:* DD. *BTEC ND:* DMM. *OCR ND:* D *OCR NED:* M2
Interview required.

W3R1 BA Popular Music/French
Duration: 3FT Hon
Entry Requirements: *GCE:* 260-280. *SQAH:* AAA-BBBB. *IB:* 24. *BTEC NC:* DD. *BTEC ND:* DMM. *OCR ND:* D *OCR NED:* M2
Interview required.

W3L4 BA Popular Music/Health Studies
Duration: 3FT Hon
Entry Requirements: *GCE:* 260-280. *SQAH:* AAA-BBBB. *IB:* 24. *BTEC NC:* DD. *BTEC ND:* DMM. *OCR ND:* D *OCR NED:* M2

W3V1 BA Popular Music/History
Duration: 3FT Hon
Entry Requirements: *GCE:* 260-280. *SQAH:* AAA-BBBB. *IB:* 24. *BTEC NC:* DD. *BTEC ND:* DMM. *OCR ND:* D *OCR NED:* M2

W3B1 BA Popular Music/Human Biology
Duration: 3FT Hon
Entry Requirements: *GCE:* 260-280. *SQAH:* AAA-BBBB. *IB:* 24. *BTEC NC:* DD. *BTEC ND:* DMM. *OCR ND:* D *OCR NED:* M2
Interview required.

W3L7 BA Popular Music/Human Geography
Duration: 3FT Hon
Entry Requirements: *GCE:* 260-280. *SQAH:* AAA-BBBB. *IB:* 24. *BTEC NC:* DD. *BTEC ND:* DMM. *OCR ND:* D *OCR NED:* M2

W3N6 BA Popular Music/Human Resource Management
Duration: 3FT Hon
Entry Requirements: *GCE:* 260-280. *SQAH:* AAA-BBBB. *IB:* 24. *BTEC NC:* DD. *BTEC ND:* DMM. *OCR ND:* D *OCR NED:* M2

W3LX BA Popular Music/International Development
Duration: 3FT Hon
Entry Requirements: *GCE:* 260-280. *SQAH:* AAA-BBBB. *IB:* 24. *BTEC NC:* DD. *BTEC ND:* DMM. *OCR ND:* D *OCR NED:* M2

W3M1 BA Popular Music/Law
Duration: 3FT Hon
Entry Requirements: *GCE:* 260-280. *SQAH:* AAA-BBBB. *IB:* 24. *BTEC NC:* DD. *BTEC ND:* DMM. *OCR ND:* D *OCR NED:* M2

W3N2 BA Popular Music/Management
Duration: 3FT Hon
Entry Requirements: *GCE:* 260-280. *SQAH:* AAA-BBBB. *IB:* 24. *BTEC NC:* DD. *BTEC ND:* DMM. *OCR ND:* D *OCR NED:* M2

W3N5 BA Popular Music/Marketing
Duration: 3FT Hon
Entry Requirements: *GCE:* 260-280. *SQAH:* AAA-BBBB. *IB:* 24. *BTEC NC:* DD. *BTEC ND:* DMM. *OCR ND:* D *OCR NED:* M2

W3L5 BA Popular Music/Social Care
Duration: 3FT Hon
Entry Requirements: *GCE:* 260-280. *SQAH:* AAA-BBBB. *IB:* 24. *BTEC NC:* DD. *BTEC ND:* DMM. *OCR ND:* D *OCR NED:* M2

W3L3 BA Popular Music/Sociology
Duration: 3FT Hon
Entry Requirements: *GCE:* 260-280. *SQAH:* AAA-BBBB. *IB:* 24. *BTEC NC:* DD. *BTEC ND:* DMM. *OCR ND:* D *OCR NED:* M2

W3C6 BA Popular Music/Sport Studies
Duration: 3FT Hon
Entry Requirements: *GCE:* 260-280. *SQAH:* AAA-BBBB. *IB:* 24. *BTEC NC:* DD. *BTEC ND:* DMM. *OCR ND:* D *OCR NED:* M2

W3N8 BA Popular Music/Tourism
Duration: 3FT Hon
Entry Requirements: *GCE:* 260-280. *SQAH:* AAA-BBBB. *IB:* 24. *BTEC NC:* DD. *BTEC ND:* DMM. *OCR ND:* D *OCR NED:* M2

L5W3 BA Social Care/Popular Music
Duration: 3FT Hon
Entry Requirements: *GCE:* 260-280. *SQAH:* AAA-BBBB. *IB:* 24. *BTEC NC:* DD. *BTEC ND:* DMM. *OCR ND:* D *OCR NED:* M2

L3W3 BA Sociology/Popular Music
Duration: 3FT Hon
Entry Requirements: *GCE:* 260-280. *SQAH:* AAA-BBBB. *IB:* 24. *BTEC NC:* DD. *BTEC ND:* DMM. *OCR ND:* D *OCR NED:* M2

C6W3 BA Sport Studies/Popular Music
Duration: 3FT Hon
Entry Requirements: *GCE:* 260-280. *SQAH:* AAA-BBBB. *IB:* 24. *BTEC NC:* DD. *BTEC ND:* DMM. *OCR ND:* D *OCR NED:* M2

N8W3 BA Tourism/Popular Music
Duration: 3FT Hon
Entry Requirements: *GCE:* 260-280. *SQAH:* AAA-BBBB. *IB:* 24. *BTEC NC:* DD. *BTEC ND:* DMM. *OCR ND:* D *OCR NED:* M2

C1W3 BSc Biological Conservation/Popular Music
Duration: 3FT Hon
Entry Requirements: *GCE:* 260-280. *SQAH:* AAA-BBBB. *IB:* 24. *BTEC NC:* DD. *BTEC ND:* DMM. *OCR ND:* D *OCR NED:* M2

G4W3 BSc Computing/Popular Music
Duration: 3FT Hon
Entry Requirements: *GCE:* 260-280. *SQAH:* AAA-BBBB. *IB:* 24. *BTEC NC:* DD. *BTEC ND:* DMM. *OCR ND:* D *OCR NED:* M2

B1W3 BSc Human Bioscience/Popular Music
Duration: 3FT Hon
Entry Requirements: *GCE:* 260-280. *SQAH:* AAA-BBBB. *IB:* 24.
BTEC NC: DD. *BTEC ND:* DMM. *OCR ND:* D *OCR NED:* M2
Interview required.

003W HND Music Practice
Duration: 2FT HND
Entry Requirements: *GCE:* 60-100. *SQAH:* BC-CCC. *IB:* 24. *BTEC NC:* MP. *BTEC ND:* MPP. *OCR ND:* P1 *OCR NED:* P2 Interview required.

093W HND Music Production
Duration: 2FT HND
Entry Requirements: *GCE:* 60-100. *SQAH:* BC-CCC. *IB:* 24. *BTEC NC:* MP. *BTEC ND:* MPP. *OCR ND:* P1 *OCR NED:* P2 Interview required.

N41 NORTHBROOK COLLEGE SUSSEX
LITTLEHAMPTON ROAD
WORTHING
WEST SUSSEX BN12 6NU
t: 0845 155 6060 f: 01903 606073
e: enquiries@nbcol.ac.uk
// www.northbrook.ac.uk

JN91 BA Music Business and Management (Top-Up)
Duration: 1FT Hon
Entry Requirements: Interview required. Portfolio required. HND required.

W393 BA Music Composition for Film and Media (Top-Up)
Duration: 1FT Hon
Entry Requirements: Interview required. Portfolio required. HND required.

W310 BA Music Performance (Top-Up)
Duration: 1FT Hon
Entry Requirements: Interview required. Portfolio required. HND required.

W361 BA Music Production (Top-Up)
Duration: 1FT Hon
Entry Requirements: Interview required. Portfolio required. HND required.

WW24 FdA Lighting and Sound Design
Duration: 2FT Fdg
Entry Requirements: *BTEC ND:* MMP. Interview required. Portfolio required.

N190 FdA Music Business and Management
Duration: 2FT Fdg
Entry Requirements: Interview required. Portfolio required.

W300 FdA Music Composition for Film and Media
Duration: 2FT Fdg
Entry Requirements: *BTEC ND:* MMM. Interview required. Portfolio required.

W313 FdA Music Performance
Duration: 2FT Fdg
Entry Requirements: Interview required. Portfolio required.

J931 FdA Music Production
Duration: 2FT Fdg
Entry Requirements: *BTEC ND:* MMM. Interview required. Portfolio required.

W392 FdA Theatre Arts - Musical Theatre
Duration: 2FT Fdg
Entry Requirements: *BTEC ND:* MMP. Interview required.

N49 NESCOT, SURREY
REIGATE ROAD
EWELL
EPSOM
SURREY KT17 3DS
t: 020 8394 3038 f: 020 8394 3030
e: info@nescot.ac.uk
// www.nescot.ac.uk

34WW HND Performing Arts
Duration: 1FT/2FT HNC/HND
Entry Requirements: *GCE:* 160. *BTEC ND:* MPP.

N82 NORWICH CITY COLLEGE OF FURTHER AND HIGHER EDUCATION (AN ASSOCIATE COLLEGE OF UEA)
IPSWICH ROAD
NORWICH
NORFOLK NR2 2LJ
t: 01603 773005 f: 01603 773301
e: admissions@ccn.ac.uk
// www.ccn.ac.uk

W390 FdA Popular Music Performance and Production
Duration: 2FT Fdg
Entry Requirements: Interview required.

N84 THE UNIVERSITY OF NOTTINGHAM
THE ADMISSIONS OFFICE
THE UNIVERSITY OF NOTTINGHAM
UNIVERSITY PARK
NOTTINGHAM NG7 2RD
t: 0115 951 5151 f: 0115 951 4668
// www.nottingham.ac.uk

RW2H BA German (Beginners) and Music
Duration: 4FT Hon
Entry Requirements: *GCE:* ABC. *SQAAH:* ABC. *IB:* 30.

RW23 BA German and Music
Duration: 4FT Hon
Entry Requirements: *GCE:* ABC. *SQAAH:* ABC. *IB:* 30.

W300 BA Music
Duration: 3FT Hon
Entry Requirements: *GCE:* ABB. *SQAAH:* ABB. *IB:* 34.

WV35 BA Music and Philosophy
Duration: 3FT Hon
Entry Requirements: *GCE:* ABC. *SQAAH:* ABC. *IB:* 32.

O33 OXFORD UNIVERSITY
UNDERGRADUATE ADMISSIONS OFFICE
UNIVERSITY OF OXFORD
WELLINGTON SQUARE
OXFORD OX1 2JD
t: 01865 288000 f: 01865 270212
e: undergraduate.admissions@admin.ox.ac.uk
// www.admissions.ox.ac.uk

W300 BA Music
Duration: 3FT Hon
Entry Requirements: *GCE:* AAA. *SQAH:* AAAAA-AAAAB. *SQAAH:* AAB. Interview required. Admissions Test required.

O66 OXFORD BROOKES UNIVERSITY
ADMISSIONS OFFICE
HEADINGTON CAMPUS
GIPSY LANE
OXFORD OX3 0BP
t: 01865 483040 f: 01865 483983
e: admissions@brookes.ac.uk
// www.brookes.ac.uk

QW3H BA English/Music
Duration: 3FT Hon
Entry Requirements: *GCE:* BBC.

W300 BA Music
Duration: 3FT Hon
Entry Requirements: *GCE:* BBC.

GW4H BA/BSc Computer Science/Music
Duration: 3FT Hon
Entry Requirements: *GCE:* BCC.

WW43 BA/BSc Drama/Music
Duration: 3FT Hon
Entry Requirements: *GCE:* BBC.

XW33 BA/BSc Education Studies/Music
Duration: 3FT Hon
Entry Requirements: *GCE:* BCC.

QW93 BA/BSc English Language and Communication/Music
Duration: 3FT Hon
Entry Requirements: *GCE:* BCC.

W1W3 BA/BSc Fine Art/Music
Duration: 3FT Hon
Entry Requirements: *GCE:* BCC.

RW13 BA/BSc French Studies/Music
Duration: 4SW Hon
Entry Requirements: *GCE:* BBC.

VW33 BA/BSc History of Art/Music
Duration: 3FT Hon
Entry Requirements: *GCE:* BCC.

VW13 BA/BSc History/Music
Duration: 3FT Hon
Entry Requirements: *GCE:* BCC.

TW2H BA/BSc Japanese Studies/Music
Duration: 4SW Hon
Entry Requirements: *GCE:* BBC.

GW13 BA/BSc Mathematics/Music
Duration: 3FT Hon
Entry Requirements: *GCE:* BCC.

W3R4 BA/BSc Music with Spanish (Minor)
Duration: 4SW Hon
Entry Requirements: *GCE:* BBC. *IB:* 31.

VW53 BA/BSc Music/Philosophy
Duration: 3FT Hon
Entry Requirements: *GCE:* BCC.

CW83 BA/BSc Music/Psychology
Duration: 3FT Hon
Entry Requirements: *GCE:* BBB.

PW4H BA/BSc Publishing Media/Music
Duration: 3FT Hon
Entry Requirements: *GCE:* BCC.

P51 PETROC
OLD STICKLEPATH HILL
BARNSTAPLE
NORTH DEVON EX31 2BQ
t: 01271 338100 f: 01271 338121
e: he@petroc.ac.uk
// www.petroc.ac.uk

W310 FdA Music Performance
Duration: 2FT Fdg
Entry Requirements: Contact the institution for details.

P60 UNIVERSITY OF PLYMOUTH
DRAKE CIRCUS
PLYMOUTH PL4 8AA
t: 01752 588037 f: 01752 588050
e: admissions@plymouth.ac.uk
// www.plymouth.ac.uk

W300 BA Music
Duration: 3FT Hon
Entry Requirements: *GCE:* 220. *IB:* 25. *BTEC ND:* MMM.

X1W3 BEd Music and General Primary 5-11 years
Duration: 4FT Hon   CRB Check: Required
Entry Requirements: *GCE:* 240. *IB:* 26. *BTEC NC:* DD. *BTEC ND:* MMM. *OCR ND:* D *OCR NED:* M Interview required.

W391 FdA Community Music
Duration: 2FT Fdg
Entry Requirements: *GCE:* 80. *IB:* 24. *BTEC NC:* PP. *BTEC ND:* PPP. *OCR ND:* P3 *OCR NED:* P3

P63 UCP MARJON - UNIVERSITY COLLEGE PLYMOUTH ST MARK & ST JOHN
DERRIFORD ROAD
PLYMOUTH PL6 8BH
t: 01752 636890 f: 01752 636819
e: admissions@marjon.ac.uk
// www.ucpmarjon.ac.uk

W390 BA Live Music
Duration: 3FT Hon
Entry Requirements: *GCE:* 220. Portfolio required.

Q75 QUEEN'S UNIVERSITY BELFAST
UNIVERSITY ROAD
BELFAST BT7 1NN
t: 028 9097 3838 f: 028 9097 5151
e: admissions@qub.ac.uk
// www.qub.ac.uk

QW3H BA English and Ethnomusicology
Duration: 3FT Hon
Entry Requirements: *GCE:* BBB-BBCb. *SQAH:* BBBBB. *SQAAH:* BBB. *IB:* 32.

W341 BA Ethnomusicology
Duration: 3FT Hon
Entry Requirements: *GCE:* BBB-BBCb. *SQAH:* BBBBB. *SQAAH:* BBB. *IB:* 32.

WQ31 BA Ethnomusicology and Linguistics
Duration: 3FT Hon
Entry Requirements: *GCE:* BBB-BBCb. *SQAH:* BBBBB. *SQAAH:* BBB. *IB:* 32.

W350 BA Ethnomusicology and Music
Duration: 3FT Hon
Entry Requirements: *GCE:* BBB-BBCb. *SQAH:* BBBBB. *SQAAH:* BBB. *IB:* 32.

WLH2 BA Ethnomusicology and Politics
Duration: 3FT Hon
Entry Requirements: *GCE:* BBB-BBCb. *SQAH:* BBBBB. *SQAAH:* BBB. *IB:* 32.

WLH6 BA Ethnomusicology and Social Anthropology
Duration: 3FT Hon
Entry Requirements: *GCE:* BBB-BBCb. *SQAH:* BBBBB. *SQAAH:* BBB. *IB:* 32.

W302 BMus Music
Duration: 3FT Hon
Entry Requirements: *GCE:* BBB-BBCb. *SQAH:* ABBBC. *SQAAH:* BBB. *IB:* 32.

R06 RAVENSBOURNE
6 PENROSE WAY
LONDON SE10 0EW
t: 020 3040 3500
e: info@rave.ac.uk
// www.rave.ac.uk

WPH3 BA Music Production for Media (Fast-Track)
Duration: 2FT Hon
Entry Requirements: Contact the institution for details.

R12 THE UNIVERSITY OF READING
THE UNIVERSITY OF READING
PO BOX 217
READING RG6 6AH
t: 0118 378 8619 f: 0118 378 8924
e: student.recruitment@reading.ac.uk
// www.reading.ac.uk

X1W3 BA Educational Studies (Primary) with Music (4 years)
Duration: 4FT Hon   CRB Check: Required
Entry Requirements: *GCE:* 180. Interview required.

R48 ROEHAMPTON UNIVERSITY
ERASMUS HOUSE
ROEHAMPTON LANE
LONDON SW15 5PU
t: 020 8392 3232 f: 020 8392 3470
e: enquiries@roehampton.ac.uk
// www.roehampton.ac.uk

XWC3 BA Primary Education Foundation Stage & Key Stage 1 (Music)
Duration: 3FT Hon   CRB Check: Required
Entry Requirements: *GCE:* 300-360. *IB:* 26. *BTEC ND:* DDM. *OCR NED:* D2 Interview required.

XW1H BA Primary Education Key Stage 2 (Music Education)
Duration: 3FT Hon   **CRB Check:** Required
Entry Requirements: *GCE:* 300-360. *IB:* 26. *BTEC ND:* DDM.
OCR NED: D2 Interview required.

R51 ROSE BRUFORD COLLEGE
LAMORBEY PARK
BURNT OAK LANE
SIDCUP
KENT DA15 9DF
t: 0208 308 2600 f: 020 8308 0542
e: enquiries@bruford.ac.uk
// www.bruford.ac.uk

W4W3 BA Actor Musician
Duration: 3FT Hon
Entry Requirements: *GCE:* 160-280.

R52 ROTHERHAM COLLEGE OF ARTS AND TECHNOLOGY
EASTWOOD LANE
ROTHERHAM
SOUTH YORKSHIRE S65 1EG
t: 08080 722777 f: 01709 373053
e: info@rotherham.ac.uk
// www.rotherham.ac.uk

W300 FdA Music
Duration: 2FT Fdg
Entry Requirements: *GCE:* 120. *BTEC ND:* MMP. Interview required.

R72 ROYAL HOLLOWAY, UNIVERSITY OF LONDON
ROYAL HOLLOWAY, UNIVERSITY OF LONDON
EGHAM
SURREY TW20 0EX
t: 01784 434455 f: 01784 473662
e: Admissions@rhul.ac.uk
// www.rhul.ac.uk

WW43 BA Drama and Music
Duration: 3FT Hon
Entry Requirements: *GCE:* ABB. *SQAH:* AABBB. *SQAAH:* ABB. *IB:* 34. *BTEC ND:* DDM.

L1W3 BA Economics with Music
Duration: 3FT Hon
Entry Requirements: *GCE:* AAA-ABB. *SQAH:* AAAAA-AABBB. *SQAAH:* AAA-ABB. *IB:* 32. *BTEC NC:* DM. *BTEC ND:* DDM.

RW13 BA French and Music
Duration: 4FT Hon
Entry Requirements: *GCE:* ABB. *SQAH:* AABBB. *SQAAH:* ABB. *IB:* 33. *BTEC ND:* DDM.

R1W3 BA French with Music
Duration: 4FT Hon
Entry Requirements: *GCE:* ABB-BBB. *SQAH:* AABBB-BBBBB. *SQAAH:* ABB-BBB. *IB:* 32. *BTEC ND:* DDM.

RW23 BA German and Music
Duration: 4FT Hon
Entry Requirements: *GCE:* ABB. *SQAH:* AABBB. *SQAAH:* ABB. *IB:* 34. *BTEC ND:* DDM.

R2W3 BA German with Music
Duration: 4FT Hon
Entry Requirements: *GCE:* ABB-BBB. *SQAH:* AABBB-BBBBB. *SQAAH:* ABB-BBB. *IB:* 32. *BTEC ND:* DDM.

VW13 BA History and Music
Duration: 3FT Hon
Entry Requirements: *GCE:* ABB. *SQAH:* AABBB. *SQAAH:* ABB. *IB:* 34. *BTEC ND:* DDM.

RW33 BA Italian and Music
Duration: 4FT Hon
Entry Requirements: *GCE:* ABB. *SQAH:* AABBB. *SQAAH:* ABB. *IB:* 34. *BTEC ND:* DDM.

R3W3 BA Italian with Music
Duration: 4FT Hon
Entry Requirements: *GCE:* ABB-BBB. *SQAH:* AABBB-BBBBB. *SQAAH:* ABB-BBB. *IB:* 32. *BTEC ND:* DDM.

GW13 BA Mathematics and Music
Duration: 3FT Hon
Entry Requirements: *GCE:* 340. *SQAH:* AAAAB. *SQAAH:* A. *IB:* 35.

WV35 BA Music and Philosophy
Duration: 3FT Hon
Entry Requirements: *GCE:* ABB. *SQAH:* AABBB. *SQAAH:* ABB. *IB:* 34. *BTEC ND:* DDM.

W3R1 BA Music with French
Duration: 3FT Hon
Entry Requirements: *GCE:* ABB. *SQAH:* AABBB. *SQAAH:* ABB. *IB:* 34. *BTEC ND:* DDM.

W3R2 BA Music with German
Duration: 3FT Hon
Entry Requirements: *GCE:* ABB. *SQAH:* AABBB. *SQAAH:* ABB. *IB:* 34. *BTEC ND:* DDM.

W3R3 BA Music with Italian
Duration: 3FT Hon
Entry Requirements: *GCE:* ABB. *SQAH:* AABBB. *SQAAH:* ABB. *IB:* 34. *BTEC ND:* DDM.

W3V5 BA Music with Philosophy
Duration: 3FT Hon
Entry Requirements: *GCE:* ABB. *SQAH:* AABBB. *SQAAH:* ABB. *IB:* 34. *BTEC ND:* DDM.

W3L2 BA Music with Political Studies
Duration: 3FT Hon
Entry Requirements: *GCE:* ABB. *SQAH:* AABBB. *SQAAH:* ABB. *IB:* 34. *BTEC ND:* DDM.

W3C8 BA Music with Psychology
Duration: 3FT Hon
Entry Requirements: *GCE:* ABB. *SQAH:* AABBB. *SQAAH:* ABB. *IB:* 34. *BTEC ND:* DDM.

W3R4 BA Music with Spanish
Duration: 3FT Hon
Entry Requirements: *GCE:* ABB. *SQAH:* AABBB. *SQAAH:* ABB. *IB:* 34. *BTEC ND:* DDM.

R4W3 BA Spanish with Music
Duration: 4FT Hon
Entry Requirements: *GCE:* ABB-BBB. *SQAH:* AABBB-BBBBB. *SQAAH:* ABB-BBB. *IB:* 32. *BTEC ND:* DDM.

W302 BMus Music
Duration: 3FT Hon
Entry Requirements: *GCE:* ABB. *SQAH:* AABBB. *SQAAH:* ABB. *IB:* 34. *BTEC ND:* DDM.

F3W3 BSc Physics with Music
Duration: 3FT Hon
Entry Requirements: *GCE:* 320-340. *IB:* 34.

S03 THE UNIVERSITY OF SALFORD
SALFORD M5 4WT
t: 0161 295 4545 f: 0161 295 4646
e: ug-admissions@salford.ac.uk
// www.salford.ac.uk

W304 BA Music
Duration: 3FT Hon
Entry Requirements: *GCE:* 280. *IB:* 31. *BTEC NC:* DD. *BTEC ND:* DMM. *OCR ND:* D *OCR NED:* M2 Interview required.

W350 BA Popular Musicology
Duration: 3FT Hon
Entry Requirements: *GCE:* 280. *IB:* 31. *BTEC NC:* DD. *BTEC ND:* DMM. *OCR ND:* D *OCR NED:* M2 Interview required.

S09 SCHOOL OF ORIENTAL AND AFRICAN STUDIES (UNIVERSITY OF LONDON)
THORNHAUGH STREET
RUSSELL SQUARE
LONDON WC1H 0XG
t: 020 7898 4301 f: 020 7898 4039
e: undergradadmissions@soas.ac.uk
// www.soas.ac.uk

VW33 BA History of Art/Archaeology and Music
Duration: 3FT Hon
Entry Requirements: *GCE:* BCC. *SQAH:* BBCCC. *SQAAH:* BCC. *IB:* 30. *BTEC ND:* MMM.

TW2H BA Japanese Studies and Music
Duration: 3FT Hon
Entry Requirements: *GCE:* AAB.

QW33 BA Linguistics and Music
Duration: 3FT Hon
Entry Requirements: Contact the institution for details.

TW6H BA Middle Eastern Studies and Music
Duration: 3FT Hon
Entry Requirements: *GCE:* BBB. *SQAH:* BBBBB. *SQAAH:* BBB. *IB:* 34. *BTEC ND:* DMM.

W300 BA Music
Duration: 3FT Hon
Entry Requirements: *GCE:* BBB.

WT35 BA Music and African Studies
Duration: 3FT Hon
Entry Requirements: Contact the institution for details.

TW63 BA Music and Arabic
Duration: 4FT Hon
Entry Requirements: Contact the institution for details.

TWH3 BA Music and Burmese
Duration: 3FT Hon
Entry Requirements: Contact the institution for details.

TW13 BA Music and Chinese
Duration: 4FT Hon
Entry Requirements: Contact the institution for details.

LW93 BA Music and Development Studies
Duration: 3FT Hon
Entry Requirements: Contact the institution for details.

LW73 BA Music and Geography
Duration: 3FT Hon
Entry Requirements: Contact the institution for details.

TW93 BA Music and Georgian
Duration: 3FT Hon
Entry Requirements: Contact the institution for details.

TWM3 BA Music and Hausa
Duration: 4FT Hon
Entry Requirements: Contact the institution for details.

QW43 BA Music and Hebrew
Duration: 4FT Hon
Entry Requirements: Contact the institution for details.

VW13 BA Music and History
Duration: 3FT Hon
Entry Requirements: Contact the institution for details.

TWHH BA Music and Indonesian
Duration: 3FT Hon
Entry Requirements: Contact the institution for details.

TW23 BA Music and Japanese
Duration: 4FT Hon
Entry Requirements: Contact the institution for details.

TWLH BA Music and Korean
Duration: 4FT Hon
Entry Requirements: Contact the institution for details.

WTHH BA Music and South-East Asian Studies
Duration: 3FT Hon
Entry Requirements: *GCE:* ABB. *SQAH:* BBBBB. *SQAAH:* BBB. *IB:* 34. *BTEC ND:* DMM.

TWQ3 BA Persian and Music
Duration: 3FT Hon
Entry Requirements: Contact the institution for details.

LW63 BA Social Anthropology and Music
Duration: 3FT Hon
Entry Requirements: Contact the institution for details.

WTH3 BA South Asian Studies and Music
Duration: 3FT Hon
Entry Requirements: Contact the institution for details.

TW33 BA South Asian Studies and Music (including year abroad)
Duration: 4FT Hon
Entry Requirements: Contact the institution for details.

VW63 BA Study of Religions and Music
Duration: 3FT Hon
Entry Requirements: Contact the institution for details.

TWN3 BA Swahili and Music
Duration: 4FT Hon
Entry Requirements: Contact the institution for details.

WT33 BA Thai and Music
Duration: 3FT Hon
Entry Requirements: Contact the institution for details.

TWP3 BA Turkish and Music
Duration: 4FT Hon
Entry Requirements: Contact the institution for details.

WTJ3 BA Vietnamese and Music
Duration: 3FT Hon
Entry Requirements: Contact the institution for details.

S18 THE UNIVERSITY OF SHEFFIELD
THE UNIVERSITY OF SHEFFIELD
9 NORTHUMBERLAND ROAD
SHEFFIELD S10 2TT
t: 0114 222 8030 f: 0114 222 8032
// www.sheffield.ac.uk

QW33 BA English and Music
Duration: 3FT Hon
Entry Requirements: *GCE:* ABB. *SQAH:* AABBB. *SQAAH:* AB. *IB:* 33. *BTEC ND:* DDM.

RW13 BA French and Music
Duration: 4FT Hon
Entry Requirements: *GCE:* BBB. *SQAH:* BBBBB. *SQAAH:* B. *IB:* 32. *BTEC ND:* DDM.

RW23 BA German and Music
Duration: 4FT Hon
Entry Requirements: *GCE:* BBB. *SQAH:* BBBBB. *SQAAH:* B. *IB:* 32. *BTEC ND:* DDM.

WT31 BA Music and Chinese Studies
Duration: 4FT Hon
Entry Requirements: *GCE:* ABB. *SQAH:* AAABB. *IB:* 33. *BTEC ND:* DDM.

WT34 BA Music and East Asian Studies
Duration: 3FT Hon
Entry Requirements: *GCE:* ABB. *SQAH:* AAABB. *IB:* 33. *BTEC ND:* DDM.

RW43 BA Music and Hispanic Studies
Duration: 4FT Hon
Entry Requirements: *GCE:* BBB. *SQAH:* BBBBB. *SQAAH:* B. *IB:* 32. *BTEC ND:* DDM.

WTH4 BA Music and Korean Studies
Duration: 3FT Hon
Entry Requirements: *GCE:* ABB. *SQAH:* AAABB. *IB:* 33. *BTEC ND:* DDM.

VW53 BA Music and Philosophy
Duration: 3FT Hon
Entry Requirements: *GCE:* ABB. *SQAH:* AAABB. *IB:* 33. *BTEC ND:* DDM.

RW73 BA Russian and Music
Duration: 4FT Hon
Entry Requirements: *GCE:* BBB. *SQAH:* BBBBB. *SQAAH:* B. *IB:* 32. *BTEC ND:* DDM.

VW63 BA Theology and Music
Duration: 3FT Hon
Entry Requirements: *GCE:* ABB. *SQAH:* AAABB. *IB:* 33. *BTEC ND:* DDM.

W302 BMus Music
Duration: 3FT Hon
Entry Requirements: *GCE:* ABB. *SQAH:* AAABB. *IB:* 33. *BTEC ND:* DDM.

S27 UNIVERSITY OF SOUTHAMPTON
HIGHFIELD
SOUTHAMPTON SO17 1BJ
t: 023 8059 4732 f: 023 8059 3037
e: admissions@soton.ac.uk
// www.southampton.ac.uk

QW33 BA English and Music
Duration: 3FT Hon
Entry Requirements: *GCE:* ABB. *SQAH:* AABBB. *IB:* 32.

RW13 BA French and Music (4 years)
Duration: 4FT Hon
Entry Requirements: *GCE:* AAB. *IB:* 34.

RW23 BA German and Music (4 years)
Duration: 4FT Hon
Entry Requirements: *GCE:* AAB. *IB:* 34.

W300 BA Music
Duration: 3FT Hon
Entry Requirements: *GCE:* ABB. *IB:* 32.

WN32 BA Music and Management Sciences
Duration: 3FT Hon
Entry Requirements: *GCE:* ABB. *IB:* 32.

HW73 BSc Acoustics and Music
Duration: 3FT Hon
Entry Requirements: *GCE:* AAA-BBB. *IB:* 35. Interview required.

G1W3 BSc Mathematics with Music
Duration: 3FT Hon
Entry Requirements: *GCE:* AAA-AAB. *SQAH:* AAAAA. *SQAAH:* AA.
IB: 36.

S30 SOUTHAMPTON SOLENT UNIVERSITY
EAST PARK TERRACE
SOUTHAMPTON
HAMPSHIRE SO14 0RT
t: +44 (0) 23 8031 9039 f: + 44 (0)23 8022 2259
e: admissions@solent.ac.uk or ask@solent.ac.uk
// www.solent.ac.uk/

WJ39 BA Digital Music
Duration: 3FT Hon
Entry Requirements: *Foundation:* Merit. *GCE:* 200. *SQAAH:* AC-
DDD. *IB:* 24. *BTEC NC:* DM. *BTEC ND:* MMP. *OCR ND:* M1 *OCR*
NED: P1 Interview required. Portfolio required.

WN35 BA Music Promotion
Duration: 3FT Hon
Entry Requirements: *Foundation:* Distinction. *GCE:* 240. *SQAAH:*
AA-CCD. *IB:* 24. *BTEC NC:* DD. *BTEC ND:* MMM. *OCR ND:* D
OCR NED: M3 Interview required.

W310 BA Popular Music Performance
Duration: 3FT Hon
Entry Requirements: *Foundation:* Distinction. *GCE:* 240. *SQAAH:*
AA-CCD. *IB:* 24. *BTEC NC:* DD. *BTEC ND:* MMM. *OCR ND:* D
OCR NED: M3 Interview required.

W313 BA Popular Music Performance (Top-Up)
Duration: 1FT Hon
Entry Requirements: Interview required. HND required.

W390 BA Popular Music Production (Top-Up)
Duration: 1FT Hon
Entry Requirements: Interview required. HND required.

W300 BA Popular Music and Record Production
Duration: 3FT Hon
Entry Requirements: *Foundation:* Distinction. *GCE:* 240. *SQAAH:*
AA-CCD. *IB:* 24. *BTEC NC:* DD. *BTEC ND:* MMM. *OCR ND:* D
OCR NED: M3 Interview required.

JW93 BA Popular Music and Record Production with IFY
Duration: 4FT Hon
Entry Requirements: Contact the institution for details.

WH36 BSc Audio Technology
Duration: 3FT Hon
Entry Requirements: *GCE:* 160.

WHH6 BSc Audio Technology (with foundation)
Duration: 4FT Hon
Entry Requirements: *GCE:* 40.

S32 SOUTH DEVON COLLEGE
LONG ROAD
PAIGNTON
DEVON TQ4 7EJ
t: 08000 380123 f: 01803 540541
e: highereducation@southdevon.ac.uk
// www.southdevon.ac.uk

W310 FdA Modern Music Practice (Performance and Technology)
Duration: 2FT Fdg
Entry Requirements: Contact the institution for details.

S42 SOUTH DOWNS COLLEGE
COLLEGE ROAD
WATERLOOVILLE
HAMPSHIRE PO7 8AA
t: 023 9279 7979 f: 023 9279 4609
e: college@southdowns.ac.uk
// www.southdowns.ac.uk

503W HND Music Performance
Duration: 2FT HND
Entry Requirements: *GCE:* 80. Interview required.

S43 SOUTH ESSEX COLLEGE OF FURTHER & HIGHER EDUCATION (PARTNER OF THE UNIVERSITY OF ESSEX)
LUKER ROAD
SOUTHEND-ON-SEA
ESSEX SS1 1ND
t: 0845 52 12345 f: 01702 432320
e: Admissions@southessex.ac.uk
// www.southessex.ac.uk

W311 BA Music Performance & Practice
Duration: 1FT Hon
Entry Requirements: Interview required. Admissions Test required.

W312 BA Music Performance, Production and Composition
Duration: 3FT Hon
Entry Requirements: Contact the institution for details.

W310 BA Music Production
Duration: 3FT Hon
Entry Requirements: *GCE:* 160. *IB:* 24. Interview required.

213W CertHE Music Production
Duration: 1FT Cer
Entry Requirements: Contact the institution for details.

113W DipHE Music Performance, Production and Composition
Duration: 2FT Dip
Entry Requirements: Contact the institution for details.

313W DipHE Music Production
Duration: 2FT Dip
Entry Requirements: Contact the institution for details.

S51 ST HELENS COLLEGE
WATER STREET
ST HELENS
MERSEYSIDE WA10 1PP
t: 01744 733766 f: 01744 623400
e: enquiries@sthelens.ac.uk
// www.sthelens.ac.uk

HW63 FdA Music Production and Sound Design
Duration: 2FT Fdg
Entry Requirements: *GCE:* 40-80. *IB:* 18. *BTEC NC:* MM. *BTEC ND:* MMP. Interview required. Admissions Test required.

S52 SOUTH TYNESIDE COLLEGE
ST GEORGE'S AVENUE
SOUTH SHIELDS
TYNE & WEAR NE34 6ET
t: 0191 427 3500 f: 0191 427 3535
e: info@stc.ac.uk
// www.stc.ac.uk

W390 FdA Applied Music Practice
Duration: 2FT Fdg
Entry Requirements: *GCE:* 80-120. Interview required.

S72 STAFFORDSHIRE UNIVERSITY
COLLEGE ROAD
STOKE ON TRENT ST4 2DE
t: 01782 292753 f: 01782 292740
e: admissions@staffs.ac.uk
// www.staffs.ac.uk

JW93 BSc Creative Music Technology
Duration: 3FT/4SW Hon
Entry Requirements: *GCE:* 240-280. *IB:* 24.

W3N2 BSc Music Technology with Management
Duration: 3FT/4SW Hon
Entry Requirements: *GCE:* 240-280. *IB:* 24.

J9H0 FdA Music Technology
Duration: 2FT Fdg
Entry Requirements: Interview required.

193W HND Music Production
Duration: 2FT Hon
Entry Requirements: Interview required.

S82 UNIVERSITY CAMPUS SUFFOLK (UCS)
WATERFRONT BUILDING
NEPTUNE QUAY
IPSWICH
SUFFOLK IP4 1QJ
t: 01473 338833 f: 01473 339900
e: info@ucs.ac.uk
// www.ucs.ac.uk

JW93 BA Music Production (Level 3 entry only)
Duration: 1FT Hon
Entry Requirements: Interview required.

W300 FdA Creative Music
Duration: 2FT Fdg
Entry Requirements: *GCE:* 200. *IB:* 28. Interview required. Portfolio required.

S84 UNIVERSITY OF SUNDERLAND
STUDENT HELPLINE
THE STUDENT GATEWAY
CHESTER ROAD
SUNDERLAND SR1 3SD
t: 0191 515 3000 f: 0191 515 3805
e: student.helpline@sunderland.ac.uk
// www.sunderland.ac.uk

TW73 BA American Studies and Music
Duration: 3FT Hon
Entry Requirements: *GCE:* 260-360. *IB:* 31. *BTEC NC:* DM.
BTEC ND: MMM. *OCR ND:* D *OCR NED:* M3

T7W3 BA American Studies with Music
Duration: 3FT Hon
Entry Requirements: *GCE:* 260-360. *BTEC NC:* DM. *BTEC ND:*
MMM. *OCR ND:* D *OCR NED:* M3

NW13 BA Business Management and Music
Duration: 3FT Hon
Entry Requirements: *GCE:* 260-360. *IB:* 24. *BTEC NC:* DM.
BTEC ND: MMM. *OCR ND:* D *OCR NED:* M3

N1W3 BA Business Management with Music
Duration: 3FT Hon
Entry Requirements: *GCE:* 260-360. *IB:* 31. *BTEC NC:* DM.
BTEC ND: MMM. *OCR ND:* D *OCR NED:* M3

XWH3 BA Childhood Studies and Music
Duration: 3FT Hon
Entry Requirements: *GCE:* 260-360.

X3W3 BA Childhood Studies with Music
Duration: 3FT Hon
Entry Requirements: *GCE:* 260-360.

BW93 BA Community Health and Music
Duration: 3FT Hon
Entry Requirements: *GCE:* 260-360. *IB:* 31. *BTEC NC:* DM.
BTEC ND: MMM. *OCR ND:* D *OCR NED:* M3

WX39 BA Community Music
Duration: 3FT Hon   CRB Check: Required
Entry Requirements: *GCE:* 220. *BTEC NC:* DD. *BTEC ND:* MMM.
OCR ND: D *OCR NED:* M3 Interview required.

WT37 BA Community Music and American Studies
Duration: 3FT Hon
Entry Requirements: *GCE:* 260-360.

WN31 BA Community Music and Business Management
Duration: 3FT Hon
Entry Requirements: *GCE:* 260-360.

WX3H BA Community Music and Childhood Studies
Duration: 3FT Hon
Entry Requirements: *GCE:* 260-360.

WB39 BA Community Music and Community Health
Duration: 3FT Hon
Entry Requirements: *GCE:* 260-360.

WM39 BA Community Music and Criminology
Duration: 3FT Hon
Entry Requirements: *GCE:* 260-360.

WW3M BA Community Music and Dance
Duration: 3FT Hon
Entry Requirements: *GCE:* 260-360.

WWH4 BA Community Music and Drama
Duration: 3FT Hon
Entry Requirements: *GCE:* 260-360.

WXH3 BA Community Music and Education
Duration: 3FT Hon
Entry Requirements: *GCE:* 260-360.

WQH3 BA Community Music and English
Duration: 3FT Hon
Entry Requirements: *GCE:* 260-360.

WQ39 BA Community Music and English Language & Linguistics
Duration: 3FT Hon
Entry Requirements: *GCE:* 260-360.

WQJ3 BA Community Music and English as a Foreign Language
Duration: 3FT Hon
Entry Requirements: *GCE:* 260-360.

WR31 BA Community Music and French
Duration: 3FT Hon
Entry Requirements: *GCE:* 260-360.

WR32 BA Community Music and German
Duration: 3FT Hon
Entry Requirements: *GCE:* 260-360.

WL35 BA Community Music and Health & Social Care
Duration: 3FT Hon
Entry Requirements: *GCE:* 260-360.

WV31 BA Community Music and History
Duration: 3FT Hon
Entry Requirements: *GCE:* 260-360.

WM31 BA Community Music and Law
Duration: 3FT Hon
Entry Requirements: *GCE:* 260-360.

WW36 BA Community Music and Photography
Duration: 3FT Hon
Entry Requirements: Contact the institution for details.

WL32 BA Community Music and Politics
Duration: 3FT Hon
Entry Requirements: *GCE:* 260-360.

WHC8 BA Community Music and Psychology
Duration: 3FT Hon
Entry Requirements: *GCE:* 260-360.

WLH3 BA Community Music and Sociology
Duration: 3FT Hon
Entry Requirements: *GCE:* 260-360.

WR34 BA Community Music and Spanish
Duration: 3FT Hon
Entry Requirements: *GCE:* 260-360.

WC36 BA Community Music and Sport
Duration: 3FT Hon
Entry Requirements: *GCE:* 260-360.

WXH1 BA Community Music and Teaching English to Speakers of Other Languages
Duration: 3FT Hon
Entry Requirements: *GCE:* 260-360.

WN38 BA Community Music and Tourism
Duration: 3FT Hon
Entry Requirements: *GCE:* 260-360.

WHT7 BA Community Music with American Studies
Duration: 3FT Hon
Entry Requirements: *GCE:* 260-360.

WHN1 BA Community Music with Business Management
Duration: 3FT Hon
Entry Requirements: *GCE:* 260-360.

WHCV BA Community Music with Childhood Studies
Duration: 3FT Hon
Entry Requirements: *GCE:* 260-360.

W3L4 BA Community Music with Community Health
Duration: 3FT Hon
Entry Requirements: *GCE:* 260-360.

W3MX BA Community Music with Criminology
Duration: 3FT Hon
Entry Requirements: *GCE:* 260-360.

WHW5 BA Community Music with Dance
Duration: 3FT Hon
Entry Requirements: *GCE:* 260-360.

WHW4 BA Community Music with Drama
Duration: 3FT Hon
Entry Requirements: *GCE:* 260-360.

WHX3 BA Community Music with Education
Duration: 3FT Hon
Entry Requirements: *GCE:* 260-360.

WHQ3 BA Community Music with English
Duration: 3FT Hon
Entry Requirements: *GCE:* 260-360.

WHQH BA Community Music with English Language & Linguistics
Duration: 3FT Hon
Entry Requirements: *GCE:* 260-360.

WJQ3 BA Community Music with English as a Foreign Language
Duration: 3FT Hon
Entry Requirements: *GCE:* 260-360.

WHR1 BA Community Music with French
Duration: 3FT Hon
Entry Requirements: *GCE:* 260-360.

WHR2 BA Community Music with German
Duration: 3FT Hon
Entry Requirements: *GCE:* 260-360.

WHL5 BA Community Music with Health and Social Care
Duration: 3FT Hon
Entry Requirements: *GCE:* 260-360.

WHV2 BA Community Music with History
Duration: 3FT Hon
Entry Requirements: *GCE:* 260-360.

WHN6 BA Community Music with Human Resource Management
Duration: 3FT Hon
Entry Requirements: *GCE:* 260-360.

WHM1 BA Community Music with Law
Duration: 3FT Hon
Entry Requirements: *GCE:* 260-360.

WHW6 BA Community Music with Photography
Duration: 3FT Hon
Entry Requirements: *GCE:* 260-360.

WHL2 BA Community Music with Politics
Duration: 3FT Hon
Entry Requirements: *GCE:* 260-360.

WJCV BA Community Music with Psychology
Duration: 3FT Hon
Entry Requirements: *GCE:* 260-360.

WHL3 BA Community Music with Sociology
Duration: 3FT Hon
Entry Requirements: *GCE:* 260-360.

WHR4 BA Community Music with Spanish
Duration: 3FT Hon
Entry Requirements: *GCE:* 260-360.

WHC6 BA Community Music with Sport
Duration: 3FT Hon
Entry Requirements: *GCE:* 260-360.

WHX1 BA Community Music with Teaching English to Speakers of Other Languages
Duration: 3FT Hon
Entry Requirements: *GCE:* 260-360.

WHN8 BA Community Music with Tourism
Duration: 3FT Hon
Entry Requirements: *GCE:* 260-360.

MW9H BA Criminology and Music
Duration: 3FT Hon
Entry Requirements: *GCE:* 260-360. *IB:* 31. *BTEC NC:* DM. *BTEC ND:* MMM. *OCR ND:* D *OCR NED:* M3

M9W3 BA Criminology with Music
Duration: 3FT Hon
Entry Requirements: *GCE:* 260-360. *IB:* 31. *BTEC NC:* DM. *BTEC ND:* MMM. *OCR ND:* D *OCR NED:* M3

WW35 BA Dance and Music
Duration: 3FT Hon
Entry Requirements: *GCE:* 260-360. *IB:* 31. *BTEC NC:* DM. *BTEC ND:* MMM. *OCR ND:* D *OCR NED:* M3

W5W3 BA Dance with Music
Duration: 3FT Hon
Entry Requirements: *GCE:* 260-360. *IB:* 31. *BTEC NC:* DM. *BTEC ND:* MMM. *OCR ND:* D *OCR NED:* M3

W4W3 BA Drama with Music
Duration: 3FT Hon
Entry Requirements: *GCE:* 260-360. *BTEC NC:* DM. *BTEC ND:* MMM. *OCR ND:* D *OCR NED:* M3

Q1W3 BA English Language & Linguistics with Music
Duration: 3FT Hon
Entry Requirements: *GCE:* 260-360. *BTEC NC:* DM. *BTEC ND:* MMM. *OCR ND:* D *OCR NED:* M3

QW33 BA English Studies and Music
Duration: 3FT Hon
Entry Requirements: *GCE:* 260-360. *IB:* 31. *BTEC NC:* DM. *BTEC ND:* MMM. *OCR ND:* D *OCR NED:* M3

Q3W3 BA English Studies with Music
Duration: 3FT Hon
Entry Requirements: *GCE:* 260-360. *IB:* 31. *BTEC NC:* DM. *BTEC ND:* MMM. *OCR ND:* D *OCR NED:* M3

NW33 BA Financial Management and Music
Duration: 3FT Hon
Entry Requirements: *GCE:* 260-360. *BTEC NC:* DM. *BTEC ND:* MMM. *OCR ND:* D *OCR NED:* M3

N3W3 BA Financial Management with Music
Duration: 3FT Hon
Entry Requirements: *GCE:* 260-360. *BTEC NC:* DM. *BTEC ND:* MMM. *OCR ND:* D *OCR NED:* M3

LW53 BA Health & Social Care and Music
Duration: 3FT Hon
Entry Requirements: *GCE:* 260-360.

L5W3 BA Health and Social Care with Music
Duration: 3FT Hon
Entry Requirements: *GCE:* 260-360.

VW13 BA History and Music
Duration: 3FT Hon
Entry Requirements: *GCE:* 260-360. *IB:* 31. *BTEC NC:* DM. *BTEC ND:* MMM. *OCR ND:* D *OCR NED:* M3

V1W3 BA History with Music
Duration: 3FT Hon
Entry Requirements: *GCE:* 260-360. *IB:* 31. *BTEC NC:* DM. *BTEC ND:* MMM. *OCR ND:* D *OCR NED:* M3

NW63 BA Human Resource Management and Music
Duration: 3FT Hon
Entry Requirements: *GCE:* 260-360. *BTEC NC:* DM. *BTEC ND:* MMM. *OCR ND:* D *OCR NED:* M3

NW53 BA Marketing Management and Music
Duration: 3FT Hon
Entry Requirements: *GCE:* 260-360. *BTEC NC:* DM. *BTEC ND:* MMM. *OCR ND:* D *OCR NED:* M3

N5W3 BA Marketing Management with Music
Duration: 3FT Hon
Entry Requirements: *GCE:* 260-360. *BTEC NC:* DM. *BTEC ND:* MMM. *OCR ND:* D *OCR NED:* M3

RW13 BA Modern Foreign Languages (French) and Music
Duration: 3FT Hon
Entry Requirements: *GCE:* 260-360. *IB:* 31. *BTEC NC:* DM. *BTEC ND:* MMM. *OCR ND:* D *OCR NED:* M3

RW23 BA Modern Foreign Languages (German) and Music
Duration: 3FT Hon
Entry Requirements: *GCE:* 260-360. *IB:* 31. *BTEC NC:* DM. *BTEC ND:* MMM. *OCR ND:* D *OCR NED:* M3

RW43 BA Modern Foreign Languages (Spanish) and Music
Duration: 3FT Hon
Entry Requirements: *GCE:* 260-360. *IB:* 31. *BTEC NC:* DM. *BTEC ND:* MMM. *OCR ND:* D *OCR NED:* M3

W301 BA Music (Top-up)
Duration: 1FT Hon
Entry Requirements: Interview required. HND required.

WW34 BA Music and Drama
Duration: 3FT Hon
Entry Requirements: *GCE:* 260-360. *IB:* 31. *BTEC NC:* DM.
BTEC ND: MMM. *OCR ND:* D *OCR NED:* M3

WX33 BA Music and Education
Duration: 3FT Hon
Entry Requirements: *GCE:* 260-360. *IB:* 31. *BTEC NC:* DM.
BTEC ND: MMM. *OCR ND:* D *OCR NED:* M3

QW13 BA Music and English Language & Linguistics
Duration: 3FT Hon
Entry Requirements: *GCE:* 260-360. *IB:* 31. *BTEC NC:* DM.
BTEC ND: MMM. *OCR ND:* D *OCR NED:* M3

WQ33 BA Music and Modern Foreign Language (English)
Duration: 3FT Hon
Entry Requirements: *GCE:* 260-360. *IB:* 31. *BTEC NC:* DM.
BTEC ND: MMM. *OCR ND:* D *OCR NED:* M3

WW3P BA Music and Photography
Duration: 3FT Hon
Entry Requirements: *GCE:* 260-360.

WX31 BA Music and TESOL
Duration: 3FT Hon
Entry Requirements: *GCE:* 260-360. *IB:* 31. *BTEC NC:* DM.
BTEC ND: MMM. *OCR ND:* D *OCR NED:* M3

W3T7 BA Music with American Studies
Duration: 3FT Hon
Entry Requirements: *GCE:* 260-360. *IB:* 31. *BTEC NC:* DM.
BTEC ND: MMM. *OCR ND:* D *OCR NED:* M3

W3N1 BA Music with Business Management
Duration: 3FT Hon
Entry Requirements: *GCE:* 260-360. *IB:* 31. *BTEC NC:* DM.
BTEC ND: MMM. *OCR ND:* D *OCR NED:* M3

W3XH BA Music with Childhood Studies
Duration: 3FT Hon
Entry Requirements: *GCE:* 260-360.

W3B9 BA Music with Community Health
Duration: 3FT Hon
Entry Requirements: *GCE:* 260-360. *IB:* 31. *BTEC NC:* DM.
BTEC ND: MMM. *OCR ND:* D *OCR NED:* M3

W3M9 BA Music with Criminology
Duration: 3FT Hon
Entry Requirements: *GCE:* 260-360. *IB:* 31. *BTEC NC:* DM.
BTEC ND: MMM. *OCR ND:* D *OCR NED:* M3

W3W5 BA Music with Dance
Duration: 3FT Hon
Entry Requirements: *GCE:* 260-360. *IB:* 31. *BTEC NC:* DM.
BTEC ND: MMM. *OCR ND:* D *OCR NED:* M3

W3W4 BA Music with Drama
Duration: 3FT Hon
Entry Requirements: *GCE:* 260-360. *IB:* 31. *BTEC NC:* DM.
BTEC ND: MMM. *OCR ND:* D *OCR NED:* M3

W3X3 BA Music with Education
Duration: 3FT Hon
Entry Requirements: *GCE:* 260-360. *IB:* 31. *BTEC NC:* DM.
BTEC ND: MMM. *OCR ND:* D *OCR NED:* M3

W3Q3 BA Music with English
Duration: 3FT Hon
Entry Requirements: *GCE:* 260-360. *IB:* 31. *BTEC NC:* DM.
BTEC ND: MMM. *OCR ND:* D *OCR NED:* M3

W3Q1 BA Music with English Language & Linguistics
Duration: 3FT Hon
Entry Requirements: *GCE:* 260-360. *IB:* 31. *BTEC NC:* DM.
BTEC ND: MMM. *OCR ND:* D *OCR NED:* M3

W3N3 BA Music with Financial Management
Duration: 3FT Hon
Entry Requirements: *GCE:* 260-360. *IB:* 31. *BTEC NC:* DM.
BTEC ND: MMM. *OCR ND:* D *OCR NED:* M3

W3RF BA Music with German
Duration: 3FT Hon
Entry Requirements: *GCE:* 260-360.

W3L5 BA Music with Health & Social Care
Duration: 3FT Hon
Entry Requirements: *GCE:* 260-360.

W3N6 BA Music with Human Resource Management
Duration: 3FT Hon
Entry Requirements: *GCE:* 260-360. *IB:* 31. *BTEC NC:* DM.
BTEC ND: MMM. *OCR ND:* D *OCR NED:* M3

W3N5 BA Music with Marketing Management
Duration: 3FT Hon
Entry Requirements: *GCE:* 260-360. *IB:* 31. *BTEC NC:* DM.
BTEC ND: MMM. *OCR ND:* D *OCR NED:* M3

W3QH BA Music with Modern Foreign Languages (English)
Duration: 3FT Hon
Entry Requirements: *GCE:* 260-360. *IB:* 31. *BTEC NC:* DM.
BTEC ND: MMM. *OCR ND:* D *OCR NED:* M3

W3R1 BA Music with Modern Foreign Languages (French)
Duration: 3FT Hon
Entry Requirements: *GCE:* 260-360. *IB:* 31. *BTEC NC:* DM.
BTEC ND: MMM. *OCR ND:* D *OCR NED:* M3

W3R2 BA Music with Modern Foreign Languages (German)
Duration: 3FT Hon
Entry Requirements: *GCE:* 260-360. *IB:* 31. *BTEC NC:* DM. *BTEC ND:* MMM. *OCR ND:* D *OCR NED:* M3

W3R4 BA Music with Modern Foreign Languages (Spanish)
Duration: 3FT Hon
Entry Requirements: *GCE:* 260-360. *IB:* 31. *BTEC NC:* DM. *BTEC ND:* MMM. *OCR ND:* D *OCR NED:* M3

W3WP BA Music with Photography
Duration: 3FT Hon
Entry Requirements: *GCE:* 260-360.

W3L2 BA Music with Politics
Duration: 3FT Hon
Entry Requirements: *GCE:* 260-360. *IB:* 31. *BTEC NC:* DM. *BTEC ND:* MMM. *OCR ND:* D *OCR NED:* M3

W3C8 BA Music with Psychology
Duration: 3FT Hon
Entry Requirements: *GCE:* 260-360. *IB:* 31. *BTEC NC:* DM. *BTEC ND:* MMM. *OCR ND:* D *OCR NED:* M3

W3C6 BA Music with Sport
Duration: 3FT Hon
Entry Requirements: *GCE:* 260-360.

W3X1 BA Music with TESOL
Duration: 3FT Hon
Entry Requirements: *GCE:* 260-360. *IB:* 31. *BTEC NC:* DM. *BTEC ND:* MMM. *OCR ND:* D *OCR NED:* M3

W3N8 BA Music with Tourism
Duration: 3FT Hon
Entry Requirements: *GCE:* 260-360. *IB:* 31. *BTEC NC:* DM. *BTEC ND:* MMM. *OCR ND:* D *OCR NED:* M3

LW23 BA Politics and Music
Duration: 3FT Hon
Entry Requirements: *GCE:* 260-360. *IB:* 31. *BTEC NC:* DM. *BTEC ND:* MMM. *OCR ND:* D *OCR NED:* M3

L2W3 BA Politics with Music
Duration: 3FT Hon
Entry Requirements: *GCE:* 260-360. *IB:* 31. *BTEC NC:* DM. *BTEC ND:* MMM. *OCR ND:* D *OCR NED:* M3

WL33 BA Sociology and Music
Duration: 3FT Hon
Entry Requirements: *GCE:* 260-360. *IB:* 31. *BTEC NC:* DM. *BTEC ND:* MMM. *OCR ND:* D *OCR NED:* M3

L3W3 BA Sociology with Music
Duration: 3FT Hon
Entry Requirements: *GCE:* 260-360. *IB:* 31. *BTEC NC:* DM. *BTEC ND:* MMM. *OCR ND:* D *OCR NED:* M3

X1W3 BA TESOL with Music
Duration: 3FT Hon
Entry Requirements: *GCE:* 260-360. *BTEC NC:* DM. *BTEC ND:* MMM. *OCR ND:* D *OCR NED:* M3

NW83 BA Tourism and Music
Duration: 3FT Hon
Entry Requirements: *GCE:* 260-360. *IB:* 31. *BTEC NC:* DM. *BTEC ND:* MMM. *OCR ND:* D *OCR NED:* M3

N8W3 BA Tourism with Music
Duration: 3FT Hon
Entry Requirements: *GCE:* 220-360. *IB:* 31. *BTEC NC:* DM. *BTEC ND:* MMM. *OCR ND:* D *OCR NED:* M3

CW63 BA/BSc Sport and Music
Duration: 3FT Hon
Entry Requirements: *GCE:* 260-360. *BTEC NC:* DM. *BTEC ND:* MMM. *OCR ND:* D *OCR NED:* M3

W340 BMus Jazz, Popular and Commercial Music
Duration: 3FT Hon
Entry Requirements: Contact the institution for details.

B9W3 BSc Community Health with Music
Duration: 3FT Hon
Entry Requirements: *GCE:* 260-360. *IB:* 31. *BTEC NC:* DM. *BTEC ND:* MMM. *OCR ND:* D *OCR NED:* M3

CW83 BSc Music and Psychology
Duration: 3FT Hon
Entry Requirements: *GCE:* 260-360. *IB:* 31. *BTEC NC:* DM. *BTEC ND:* MMM. *OCR ND:* D *OCR NED:* M3

C8W3 BSc Psychology with Music
Duration: 3FT Hon
Entry Requirements: *GCE:* 260-360. *IB:* 31. *BTEC NC:* DM. *BTEC ND:* MMM. *OCR ND:* D *OCR NED:* M3

C6W3 BSc Sport with Music
Duration: 3FT Hon
Entry Requirements: *GCE:* 260-360. *BTEC NC:* DM. *BTEC ND:* MMM. *OCR ND:* D *OCR NED:* M3

W390 FdA Applied Music Practice
Duration: 2FT Fdg
Entry Requirements: *GCE:* 80-220. *SQAH:* CCCC. *IB:* 22. Interview required.

S85 UNIVERSITY OF SURREY
STAG HILL
GUILDFORD
SURREY GU2 7XH
t: +44(0)1483 689305 f: +44(0)1483 689388
e: ugteam@surrey.ac.uk
// www.surrey.ac.uk

W3G5 BMus Creative Music Technology (3 years)
Duration: 3FT Hon
Entry Requirements: *GCE:* ABB. *SQAH:* ABBB. *SQAAH:* ABB. *IB:* 34. *BTEC ND:* DDM. Interview required.

W300 BMus Music (3 years)
Duration: 3FT Hon
Entry Requirements: *GCE:* 320. *SQAH:* ABBB. *IB:* 32.

W301 BMus Music (4 years)
Duration: 4SW Hon
Entry Requirements: *GCE:* 320. *SQAH:* ABBB. *IB:* 32.

G1W3 BSc Mathematics with Music (3 years)
Duration: 3FT Hon
Entry Requirements: *GCE:* 340. Interview required.

G1WH BSc Mathematics with Music (4 years)
Duration: 4SW Hon
Entry Requirements: *GCE:* 340. Interview required.

S90 UNIVERSITY OF SUSSEX
UNDERGRADUATE ADMISSIONS
SUSSEX HOUSE
UNIVERSITY OF SUSSEX
BRIGHTON BN1 9RH
t: 01273 678416 f: 01273 678545
e: ug.applicants@sussex.ac.uk
// www.sussex.ac.uk

W300 BA Music
Duration: 3FT Hon
Entry Requirements: *GCE:* ABB. *SQAH:* AABBB. *IB:* 34. *BTEC NC:* DM. *BTEC ND:* DDM. *OCR ND:* M1 *OCR NED:* D2

WG34 BA Music Informatics
Duration: 3FT Hon
Entry Requirements: *GCE:* ABB. *SQAH:* AABBB. *IB:* 34. *BTEC NC:* DM. *BTEC ND:* DDM. *OCR ND:* M1 *OCR NED:* D2

VW53 BA Philosophy and Music
Duration: 3FT Hon
Entry Requirements: *GCE:* AAB. *SQAH:* AAABB. *IB:* 36. *BTEC NC:* DD. *BTEC ND:* DDD. *OCR ND:* D *OCR NED:* D1

WGH4 BSc Music Informatics
Duration: 3FT Hon
Entry Requirements: *GCE:* ABB. *SQAH:* AABBB. *IB:* 34. *BTEC NC:* DM. *BTEC ND:* DDM. *OCR ND:* M1 *OCR NED:* D2

W310 FdA Professional Musicianship
Duration: 2FT Fdg
Entry Requirements: *GCE:* CCC. *SQAH:* CCCCC. *IB:* 28. *BTEC ND:* MMM. Interview required.

T20 TEESSIDE UNIVERSITY
MIDDLESBROUGH TS1 3BA
t: 01642 218121 f: 01642 384201
e: registry@tees.ac.uk
// www.tees.ac.uk

WW4H BA Performing Arts (Music Performance)
Duration: 1FT Hon
Entry Requirements: Interview required.

WW43 FdA Creating Music Performance
Duration: 2FT Fdg
Entry Requirements: *GCE:* 80-100. *IB:* 24.

T80 UNIVERSITY OF WALES TRINITY SAINT DAVID
COLLEGE ROAD
CARMARTHEN SA31 3EP
t: 01267 676767 f: 01267 676766
e: registrylc@trinitysaintdavid.ac.uk
// www.trinitysaintdavid.ac.uk/

W390 BA Cerddoriaeth Broffesiynol
Duration: 3FT Hon
Entry Requirements: *GCE:* 160-360. *IB:* 26. *BTEC NC:* MP. *BTEC ND:* PPP. Interview required.

T85 TRURO AND PENWITH COLLEGE (FORMERLY TRURO COLLEGE)
TRURO COLLEGE
COLLEGE ROAD
TRURO
CORNWALL TR1 3XX
t: 01872 267122 f: 01872 267526
e: heinfo@trurocollege.ac.uk
// www.trurocollege.ac.uk

W341 BA (Hons) Contemporary World Jazz
Duration: 3FT Hon
Entry Requirements: *GCE:* 160. *IB:* 24. *BTEC NC:* PP. *BTEC ND:* PPP. Interview required.

W340 FdA Commercial Music Performance and Production
Duration: 2FT Fdg
Entry Requirements: *GCE:* 60. *IB:* 24. *BTEC NC:* PP. *BTEC ND:* PPP. Interview required.

W310 FdA Music Performance
Duration: 2FT Fdg
Entry Requirements: *GCE:* 60. *IB:* 24. *BTEC NC:* PP. *BTEC ND:* PPP. Interview required.

U20 UNIVERSITY OF ULSTER
COLERAINE
CO. LONDONDERRY
NORTHERN IRELAND BT52 1SA
t: 028 7032 4221 f: 028 7032 4908
e: online@ulster.ac.uk
// www.ulster.ac.uk

W5W3 BA Dance with Music
Duration: 3FT Hon
Entry Requirements: *GCE:* CCD. *IB:* 24. *BTEC NC:* MM. *BTEC ND:* MMM. Interview required.

W4W3 BA Drama with Music
Duration: 3FT Hon
Entry Requirements: *GCE:* BBC. *IB:* 24. *BTEC NC:* DM. *BTEC ND:* DMM. Interview required.

V2W3 BA Irish History with Music
Duration: 3FT Hon
Entry Requirements: *GCE:* CCC. *IB:* 24. Interview required.

QW53 BA Irish and Music
Duration: 3FT/4SW Hon
Entry Requirements: *GCE:* BCD. *IB:* 24. Interview required.

Q5W3 BA Irish with Music
Duration: 3FT/4SW Hon
Entry Requirements: *GCE:* BCD. *IB:* 24. Interview required.

W3W5 BA Music with Dance
Duration: 3FT Hon
Entry Requirements: *GCE:* CCC. *IB:* 24. *BTEC NC:* MM. *BTEC ND:* MMM. Interview required.

W3W4 BA Music with Drama
Duration: 3FT Hon
Entry Requirements: *GCE:* CCC. *IB:* 24. *BTEC NC:* MM. *BTEC ND:* MMM. Interview required.

W3Q5 BA Music with Irish
Duration: 3FT Hon
Entry Requirements: *GCE:* BCD. *IB:* 24. Interview required.

W3C8 BA Music with Psychology
Duration: 3FT Hon
Entry Requirements: *GCE:* CCC. *IB:* 24. *BTEC NC:* MM. *BTEC ND:* MMM. Interview required.

W302 BMus Music
Duration: 3FT Hon
Entry Requirements: *GCE:* BBC. *IB:* 24. *BTEC ND:* DMM. Interview required.

U40 UNIVERSITY OF THE WEST OF SCOTLAND
PAISLEY
RENFREWSHIRE
SCOTLAND PA1 2BE
t: 0141 848 3727 f: 0141 848 3623
e: admissions@uws.ac.uk
// www.uws.ac.uk

W340 BA Commercial Music
Duration: 3FT/4FT Ord/Hon
Entry Requirements: *GCE:* CC. *SQAH:* BBC. Interview required. Portfolio required.

W385 BA Commercial Music Performance
Duration: 1FT Ord
Entry Requirements: Contact the institution for details.

WW34 BA Musical Theatre
Duration: 1FT/2FT Ord/Hon
Entry Requirements: Interview required.

W350 BSc Music Technology
Duration: 3FT/4FT Ord/Hon
Entry Requirements: *GCE:* CC. *SQAH:* BBC. *BTEC NC:* PP.

U65 UNIVERSITY OF THE ARTS LONDON
272 HIGH HOLBORN
LONDON WC1V 7EY
t: 020 7514 6000x6197 f: 020 7514 6198
e: c.anderson@arts.ac.uk
// www.arts.ac.uk

W390 BA Sound Arts and Design
Duration: 3FT Hon
Entry Requirements: *GCE:* 80. *IB:* 28. Foundation Course required. Interview required. Portfolio required.

W05 THE UNIVERSITY OF WEST LONDON
WALPOLE HOUSE
BOND STREET
EALING
LONDON W5 5AA
t: 0800 036 8888 f: 020 8566 1353
e: learning.advice@uwl.ac.uk
// www.uwl.ac.uk

W312 BA Music Performance/Composition with Options
Duration: 3FT Hon
Entry Requirements: *GCE:* 200. *IB:* 28. Interview required.

W351 BA Music Technology Specialist
Duration: 3FT Hon
Entry Requirements: *GCE:* 200. *IB:* 28. Interview required. Portfolio required.

JW93 BA Music Technology and Music Performance/Composition
Duration: 3FT Hon
Entry Requirements: *GCE:* 200. *IB:* 28. Interview required. Portfolio required.

JW9J BA Music Technology and Pop Music Performance
Duration: 3FT Hon
Entry Requirements: *GCE:* 200. *IB:* 28. Interview required. Portfolio required.

W304 BMus Music (Performance/Composition)
Duration: 3FT Hon
Entry Requirements: *GCE:* 200. *IB:* 28. Interview required.

W311 BMus Music (Performance/Composition) (with foundation year)
Duration: 4FT Hon
Entry Requirements: *GCE:* 50. Interview required.

W300 BMus Music Performance and Recording
Duration: 3FT Hon
Entry Requirements: *GCE:* 200. *IB:* 28. Interview required.

W316 BMus Popular Music Performance and Recording
Duration: 3FT Hon
Entry Requirements: *GCE:* 200. *IB:* 28. Interview required.

W08 WAKEFIELD COLLEGE
MARGARET STREET
WAKEFIELD
WEST YORKSHIRE WF1 2DH
t: 01924 789111 f: 01924 789281
e: courseinfo@wakefield.ac.uk
// www.wakefield.ac.uk

113W HND Music Performance (Popular Music)
Duration: 2FT HND
Entry Requirements: *GCE:* 240. *BTEC ND:* MMM. Interview required.

W17 WARRINGTON COLLEGIATE
WINWICK ROAD CAMPUS
WINWICK ROAD
WARRINGTON
CHESHIRE WA2 8QA
t: 01925 494494 f: 01925 418328
e: admissions@warrington.ac.uk
// www.warrington.ac.uk

W370 FYr Music Technology (Year 0)
Duration: 1FT FYr
Entry Requirements: Contact the institution for details.

W50 UNIVERSITY OF WESTMINSTER
2ND FLOOR
101 NEW CAVENDISH STREET,
LONDON W1W 6XH
t: 020 7911 5000 f: 020 7911 5788
e: course-enquiries@westminster.ac.uk
// www.westminster.ac.uk

W304 BA Commercial Music
Duration: 3FT Hon
Entry Requirements: *GCE:* CC. *SQAH:* CCCC. *IB:* 26. *BTEC NC:* MM. *BTEC ND:* MPP. Interview required.

W310 BMus Commercial Music Performance
Duration: 3FT Hon
Entry Requirements: *GCE:* CC. *SQAH:* CCCC. *IB:* 26. *BTEC NC:* MM. *BTEC ND:* MPP. Interview required.

WN32 FdA Creative Music Production and Business
Duration: 2FT Fdg
Entry Requirements: *GCE:* 120-180. Interview required.

W311 FdA Popular Musician
Duration: 2FT Fdg
Entry Requirements: *GCE:* 120-180. Interview required.

W75 UNIVERSITY OF WOLVERHAMPTON
ADMISSIONS UNIT
MX207, CAMP STREET
WOLVERHAMPTON
WEST MIDLANDS WV1 1AD
t: 01902 321000 f: 01902 321896
e: admissions@wlv.ac.uk
// www.wlv.ac.uk

WJ3X BA Music Technology
Duration: 3FT Hon
Entry Requirements: *GCE:* 180. Interview required.

W391 BA Music Technology and Popular Music
Duration: 3FT Hon
Entry Requirements: *GCE:* 160-220. Interview required.

W300 BMus Music
Duration: 3FT Hon
Entry Requirements: *GCE:* 160-220. *IB:* 26. Interview required.

WW33 BMus Music and Popular Music
Duration: 3FT Hon
Entry Requirements: *GCE:* 160-220. *IB:* 26. Interview required.

W390 BMus Popular Music
Duration: 3FT Hon
Entry Requirements: *GCE:* 160-220. *IB:* 24. Interview required.

WJ39 FdA Creative Music Technology
Duration: 2FT Fdg
Entry Requirements: *GCE:* 100.

W310 FdA Music Performance
Duration: 2FT Fdg
Entry Requirements: *GCE:* 100.

W76 UNIVERSITY OF WINCHESTER
WINCHESTER
HANTS SO22 4NR
t: 01962 827234 f: 01962 827288
e: course.enquiries@winchester.ac.uk
// www.winchester.ac.uk

TW7J BA American Studies and Vocal & Choral Studies
Duration: 3FT Hon
Entry Requirements: *Foundation:* Distinction. *GCE:* 260-300. *IB:* 24. *BTEC NC:* DD. *BTEC ND:* DMM. *OCR ND:* D *OCR NED:* M2

VW4J BA Archaeology and Vocal & Choral Studies
Duration: 3FT Hon
Entry Requirements: *Foundation:* Distinction. *GCE:* 260-300. *IB:* 24. *BTEC NC:* DD. *BTEC ND:* DMM. *OCR ND:* D *OCR NED:* M2

NW23 BA Business Management and Vocal & Choral Studies
Duration: 3FT Hon
Entry Requirements: *Foundation:* Distinction. *GCE:* 260-300. *IB:* 24. *BTEC NC:* DD. *BTEC ND:* DMM. *OCR ND:* D *OCR NED:* M2

LW5H BA Childhood Youth & Community Studies and Vocal & Choral Studies
Duration: 3FT Hon
Entry Requirements: *Foundation:* Distinction. *GCE:* 260-300. *IB:* 24. *BTEC NC:* DD. *BTEC ND:* MMM. *OCR ND:* D

WW53 BA Choreography & Dance and Vocal & Choral Studies
Duration: 3FT Hon
Entry Requirements: *Foundation:* Distinction. *GCE:* 260-300. *IB:* 25. *BTEC NC:* DD. *BTEC ND:* DMM. *OCR ND:* D *OCR NED:* M2

WL35 BA Contemporary Performance and Health, Community & Social Care Studies
Duration: 3FT Hon   CRB Check: Required
Entry Requirements: Contact the institution for details.

WW4J BA Contemporary Performance and Vocal & Choral Studies
Duration: 3FT Hon
Entry Requirements: *Foundation:* Distinction. *GCE:* 260-300. *IB:* 24. *BTEC NC:* DD. *BTEC ND:* MMM. *OCR ND:* D

LW3J BA Criminology and Vocal & Choral Studies
Duration: 3FT Hon
Entry Requirements: *Foundation:* Distinction. *GCE:* 260-300. *IB:* 24. *BTEC NC:* DD. *BTEC ND:* DMM. *OCR ND:* D *OCR NED:* M2

WW43 BA Drama and Vocal & Choral Studies
Duration: 3FT Hon
Entry Requirements: *Foundation:* Distinction. *GCE:* 260-300. *IB:* 25. *BTEC NC:* DD. *BTEC ND:* DMM. *OCR ND:* D *OCR NED:* M2

XW3H BA Education Studies (Early Childhood) and Vocal & Choral Studies
Duration: 3FT Hon
Entry Requirements: *Foundation:* Distinction. *GCE:* 260-300. *IB:* 24. *BTEC NC:* DD. *BTEC ND:* DMM. *OCR ND:* D *OCR NED:* M2

XWJ3 BA Education Studies (Modern Liberal Arts) and Vocal & Choral Studies
Duration: 3FT Hon
Entry Requirements: *Foundation:* Distinction. *GCE:* 260-300. *IB:* 24. *BTEC NC:* DD. *BTEC ND:* DMM. *OCR ND:* D *OCR NED:* M2

XWH3 BA Education Studies and Vocal & Choral Studies
Duration: 3FT Hon
Entry Requirements: *Foundation:* Distinction. *GCE:* 260-300. *IB:* 24. *BTEC NC:* DD. *BTEC ND:* DMM. *OCR ND:* D *OCR NED:* M2

QW3J BA English Language Studies and Vocal & Choral Studies
Duration: 3FT Hon
Entry Requirements: *Foundation:* Distinction. *GCE:* 260-300. *IB:* 25. *BTEC NC:* DD. *BTEC ND:* DMM. *OCR ND:* D *OCR NED:* M2

QW33 BA English and Vocal & Choral Studies
Duration: 3FT Hon
Entry Requirements: *Foundation:* Distinction. *GCE:* 260-300. *IB:* 25. *BTEC NC:* DD. *BTEC ND:* DMM. *OCR ND:* D *OCR NED:* M2

WW6H BA Film & Cinema Technology and Vocal & Choral Studies
Duration: 3FT Hon
Entry Requirements: *Foundation:* Distinction. *GCE:* 260-300. *IB:* 24. *BTEC NC:* DD. *BTEC ND:* DMM. *OCR ND:* D *OCR NED:* M2

VW1H BA History and Vocal & Choral Studies
Duration: 3FT Hon
Entry Requirements: *Foundation:* Distinction. *GCE:* 260-300. *IB:* 24. *BTEC NC:* DD. *BTEC ND:* DMM. *OCR ND:* D *OCR NED:* M2

MW1H BA Law and Vocal & Choral Studies
Duration: 3FT Hon
Entry Requirements: *Foundation:* Distinction. *GCE:* 260-300. *IB:* 25. *BTEC NC:* DD. *BTEC ND:* DMM. *OCR ND:* D *OCR NED:* M2

WW93 BA Modern Liberal Arts and Vocal & Choral Studies
Duration: 3FT Hon
Entry Requirements: *Foundation:* Distinction. *GCE:* 260-300. *IB:* 25. *BTEC NC:* DD. *BTEC ND:* DMM. *OCR ND:* D *OCR NED:* M2

LW23 BA Politics & Global Studies and Vocal & Choral Studies
Duration: 3FT Hon
Entry Requirements: *Foundation:* Distinction. *GCE:* 260-300. *IB:* 24. *BTEC NC:* DD. *BTEC ND:* MMM. *OCR ND:* D

LW33 BA Sociology and Vocal & Choral Studies
Duration: 3FT Hon
Entry Requirements: *Foundation:* Distinction. *GCE:* 260-300. *IB:* 24. *BTEC NC:* DD. *BTEC ND:* DMM. *OCR ND:* D *OCR NED:* M2

NW83 BA Sports Management and Vocal & Choral Studies
Duration: 3FT Hon
Entry Requirements: *Foundation:* Pass. *GCE:* 260-300. *IB:* 24. *BTEC NC:* DD. *BTEC ND:* MMP. *OCR ND:* D

CW6H BA Sports Studies and Vocal & Choral Studies
Duration: 3FT Hon
Entry Requirements: *Foundation:* Pass. *GCE:* 260-300. *IB:* 24. *BTEC NC:* DD. *BTEC ND:* MMP. *OCR ND:* D

VW6J BA Theology & Religious Studies and Vocal & Choral Studies
Duration: 3FT Hon
Entry Requirements: *Foundation:* Distinction. *GCE:* 260-300. *IB:* 25. *BTEC NC:* DD. *BTEC ND:* DMM. *OCR ND:* D *OCR NED:* M2

W80 UNIVERSITY OF WORCESTER
HENWICK GROVE
WORCESTER WR2 6AJ
t: 01905 855111 f: 01905 855377
e: admissions@worc.ac.uk
// www.worcester.ac.uk

043W HND Urban & Electronic Music
Duration: 2FT HND
Entry Requirements: *GCE:* 60. *IB:* 24. *BTEC NC:* PP. *BTEC ND:* PPP.

W81 WORCESTER COLLEGE OF TECHNOLOGY
DEANSWAY
WORCESTER WR1 2JF
t: 01905 725555 f: 01905 28906
// www.wortech.ac.uk

WJ39 FdSc Popular Music Technology
Duration: 2FT Fdg
Entry Requirements: Contact the institution for details.

Y50 THE UNIVERSITY OF YORK
ADMISSIONS AND UK/EU STUDENT RECRUITMENT
UNIVERSITY OF YORK
HESLINGTON
YORK YO10 5DD
t: 01904 433539 f: 01904 433538
e: admissions@york.ac.uk
// www.york.ac.uk

W300 BA Music
Duration: 3FT Hon
Entry Requirements: *GCE:* ABB. *SQAH:* AABBB. *SQAAH:* AB. *IB:* 32. *BTEC ND:* DDM. Interview required.

Y75 YORK ST JOHN UNIVERSITY
LORD MAYOR'S WALK
YORK YO31 7EX
t: 01904 876598 f: 01904 876940/876921
e: admissions@yorksj.ac.uk
// w3.yorksj.ac.uk

W300 BA Music
Duration: 3FT Hon
Entry Requirements: *Foundation:* Pass. *GCE:* 200-240. *IB:* 24.

W301 BA Music (for international applicants only)
Duration: 4FT Hon
Entry Requirements: *Foundation:* Pass. *GCE:* 200-240. *IB:* 24.

PRACTICE-BASED MUSIC, DANCE AND DRAMA
COURSES - CUKAS

B34 BIRMINGHAM CONSERVATOIRE
BIRMINGHAM CONSERVATOIRE
PARADISE PLACE
BIRMINGHAM B3 3HG
t: +44 (0)121 331 5901 f: +44 (0)121 331 5906
e: conservatoire.admissions@bcu.ac.uk
// www.conservatoire.bcu.ac.uk

602F AdvPGDip AdvPgDip Music (Professional Performance)
Duration: 1FT PMD
Entry Requirements: Interview required.

602P AdvPgDip AdvPgDip Music (Professional Performance)
Duration: 2PT PMD
Entry Requirements: Interview required.

310F BMus BMus(Hons) Jazz
Duration: 4FT Hon
Entry Requirements: *IB:* 24. Interview required. Admissions Test required.

300F BMus BMus(Hons) Music
Duration: 4FT Hon
Entry Requirements: *IB:* 24. Interview required. Admissions Test required.

410F GradDip GradDip Jazz
Duration: 1FT PMD
Entry Requirements: Interview required.

410P GradDip GradDip Jazz
Duration: 2PT PMD
Entry Requirements: Interview required.

802F MMus Conducting
Duration: 2FT PMD
Entry Requirements: Interview required.

802P MMus Conducting
Duration: 3PT PMD
Entry Requirements: Interview required.

807F MMus Conducting
Duration: 1FT PMD
Entry Requirements: Contact the institution for details.

805F MMus Instrumental Performance/Composition/Music Technology/Musicology
Duration: 1FT PMD
Entry Requirements: Interview required.

803F MMus Jazz Perfomance/Composition
Duration: 2FT PMD
Entry Requirements: Interview required.

803P MMus Jazz Performance/Composition
Duration: 3PT PMD
Entry Requirements: Interview required.

808F MMus Jazz Performance/Composition
Duration: 1FT PMD
Entry Requirements: Interview required.

800F MMus MMus Music
Duration: 2FT PMD
Entry Requirements: Interview required.

800P MMus MMus Music
Duration: 3PT PMD
Entry Requirements: Interview required.

809F MMus Orchestral Performance (Strings)
Duration: 2FT PMD
Entry Requirements: Interview required.

810F MMus Orchestral Performance (Strings)
Duration: 1FT PMD
Entry Requirements: Interview required.

804F MMus Performance and Pedagogy
Duration: 2FT PMD
Entry Requirements: Interview required.

804P MMus Performance and Pedagogy
Duration: 3PT PMD
Entry Requirements: Interview required.

801F MMus Vocal Performance
Duration: 2FT PMD
Entry Requirements: Interview required.

801P MMus Vocal Performance
Duration: 3PT PMD
Entry Requirements: Interview required.

806F MMus Vocal Performance
Duration: 1FT PMD
Entry Requirements: Interview required.

501F PGCert PGCert Music (Specialist Performance)
Duration: 1FT PMD
Entry Requirements: Interview required.

500P PGCert PgCert Music
Duration: 1PT PMD
Entry Requirements: Interview required.

600F PGDip PgDip Music
Duration: 1FT PMD
Entry Requirements: Interview required.

503F PgCert Music Specialist Performance (Vocal)
Duration: 1FT PMD
Entry Requirements: Interview required.

502P PgCert Vocal Performance
Duration: 1PT PMD
Entry Requirements: Contact the institution for details.

604F PgDip Jazz (Performance/Composition)
Duration: 1FT PMD
Entry Requirements: Interview required.

604P PgDip Jazz (Performance/Composition)
Duration: 2PT PMD
Entry Requirements: Interview required.

603F PgDip Music (Conducting)
Duration: 1FT PMD
Entry Requirements: Interview required.

603P PgDip Music (Conducting)
Duration: 2PT PMD
Entry Requirements: Interview required.

601P PgDip Music (Vocal Performance)
Duration: 2PT PMD
Entry Requirements: Interview required.

605F PgDip Orchestral Performance (Strings)
Duration: 1FT PMD
Entry Requirements: Interview required.

605P PgDip Orchestral Performance (Strings)
Duration: 2PT PMD
Entry Requirements: Interview required.

600P PgDip PgDip Music
Duration: 2PT PMD
Entry Requirements: Interview required.

601F PgDip Vocal Performance
Duration: 1FT PMD
Entry Requirements: Interview required.

L31 LEEDS COLLEGE OF MUSIC
3 QUARRY HILL
LEEDS
WEST YORKSHIRE LS2 7PD
t: 0113 222 3416 f: 0113 243 8798
e: enquiries.assistant@lcm.ac.uk
// www.lcm.ac.uk

720F MA MA Composition
Duration: 1FT PMD
Entry Requirements: Interview required.

720P MA MA Composition
Duration: 2.5PT PMD
Entry Requirements: Interview required.

790F MA MA Music Production
Duration: 1FT PMD
Entry Requirements: Interview required.

790P MA MA Music Production
Duration: 2PT PMD
Entry Requirements: Interview required.

792F MA MA Musicology
Duration: 1FT PMD
Entry Requirements: Interview required.

792P MA MA Musicology
Duration: 2.5PT PMD
Entry Requirements: Interview required.

791F MA MA Performance
Duration: 1FT PMD
Entry Requirements: Interview required.

791P MA MA Performance
Duration: 2.5PT Hon
Entry Requirements: Interview required.

620F PGDip Postgraduate Diploma in Composition
Duration: 1FT PMD
Entry Requirements: Interview required.

620P PGDip Postgraduate Diploma in Composition
Duration: 1.5PT PMD
Entry Requirements: Interview required.

601F PGDip Postgraduate Diploma in Performance
Duration: 1FT PMD
Entry Requirements: Interview required.

601P PGDip Postgraduate Diploma in Performance
Duration: 1.5PT PMD
Entry Requirements: Interview required.

R56 ROYAL COLLEGE OF MUSIC
PRINCE CONSORT ROAD
LONDON SW7 2BS
t: +44 (0)20 7591 4362 f: +44 (0)20 7591 4737
e: admissions@rcm.ac.uk
// www.rcm.ac.uk

851F ArtDip Artist Diploma in Opera
Duration: 2FT/1FT PMD
Entry Requirements: Interview required.

603F ArtDip Artist Diploma in Performance
Duration: 1FT Oth
Entry Requirements: Contact the institution for details.

300F BMus Bachelor of Music (Honours)
Duration: 4FT Hon
Entry Requirements: *GCE:* 120. Portfolio required.

940F DMus Doctoral Programme
Duration: 3FT/4FT Oth
Entry Requirements: Interview required.

940P DMus Doctoral Programme
Duration: 5PT/6PT Oth
Entry Requirements: Interview required.

420F GradDip Graduate Diploma in Vocal Performance
Duration: 1FT 0th
Entry Requirements: Contact the institution for details.

821F MComp Master of Composition
Duration: 2FT PMD
Entry Requirements: Interview required. Portfolio required.

705F MComp Master of Composition in Composition for Screen
Duration: 2FT PMD
Entry Requirements: Interview required.

822F MMus Fast-Track Master of Music in Composition
Duration: 1FT PMD
Entry Requirements: Interview required. Portfolio required.

802F MMus Fast-Track Master of Music in Performance
Duration: 1FT PMD
Entry Requirements: Interview required.

807F MMus Master of Music in Composition
Duration: 2FT PMD
Entry Requirements: Interview required. Portfolio required.

808F MMus Master of Music in Composition for Screen
Duration: 2FT PMD
Entry Requirements: Interview required. Portfolio required.

804F MMus Master of Music in Conducting
Duration: 2FT PMD
Entry Requirements: Interview required.

800F MMus Master of Music in Historical Performance
Duration: 2FT PMD
Entry Requirements: Contact the institution for details.

803F MMus Master of Music in Performance
Duration: 2FT PMD
Entry Requirements: Contact the institution for details.

805F MMus Master of Music in Piano Accompaniment
Duration: 2FT PMD
Entry Requirements: Contact the institution for details.

806F MMus Master of Music in Vocal Performance
Duration: 2FT PMD
Entry Requirements: Contact the institution for details.

801F MPerf Master of Performance
Duration: 2FT PMD
Entry Requirements: Contact the institution for details.

701F MPerf Master of Performance in Conducting
Duration: 2FT PMD
Entry Requirements: Interview required.

702F MPerf Master of Performance in Historical Performance
Duration: 2FT PMD
Entry Requirements: Contact the institution for details.

703F MPerf Master of Performance in Orchestral Performance
Duration: 2FT PMD
Entry Requirements: Contact the institution for details.

704F MPerf Master of Performance in Piano Accompaniment
Duration: 2FT PMD
Entry Requirements: Contact the institution for details.

850F MPerf Master of Performance in Vocal Performance
Duration: 2FT PMD
Entry Requirements: Contact the institution for details.

700P MSc Master of Science in Performance Science
Duration: 2PT PMD
Entry Requirements: Interview required.

706F MSc Master of Science in Performance Science
Duration: 1FT PMD
Entry Requirements: Interview required.

100F Non-award Gap Year Experience Programme
Duration: 1FT 0th
Entry Requirements: *GCE:* 120. Portfolio required.

102F Non-award Junior Year Experience Programme
Duration: 1FT 0th
Entry Requirements: *GCE:* 120. Portfolio required.

101F Non-award Semester Experience Programme
Duration: 0.5FT 0th
Entry Requirements: *GCE:* 160-240. Portfolio required.

R57 ROYAL NORTHERN COLLEGE OF MUSIC
124 OXFORD ROAD
MANCHESTER M13 9RD
t: +44 (0) 161 907 5260 f: +44 (0) 161 273 7611
e: admissions@rncm.ac.uk
// www.rncm.ac.uk

300F BMus BMus (Hons) Performance/Composition
Duration: 4FT Hon
Entry Requirements: *GCE:* AA-EE. *SQAH:* AAAA-CCCC. *SQAAH:*
AA-CC. *BTEC NC:* PP. *BTEC ND:* PPP. Interview required. Portfolio
required.

113F FdA Foundation Degree in Popular Music Practice (Session Musician)
Duration: 2FT Fdg
Entry Requirements: *GCE:* A-E. *SQAH:* AA-CC. *SQAAH:* A-C. *BTEC ND:* PPP. Interview required. Portfolio required.

399F GRNCM Joint Course
Duration: 4FT Hon
Entry Requirements: *GCE:* AAB. *SQAAH:* AAA-AAB. Interview
required. Portfolio required.

811F MMus MMus Chamber Music
Duration: 1FT PMD
Entry Requirements: Interview required. Portfolio required.

820F MMus MMus Composition
Duration: 2FT PMD
Entry Requirements: Interview required. Portfolio required.

823F MMus MMus Composition
Duration: 1FT PMD
Entry Requirements: Interview required. Portfolio required.

841F MMus MMus Orchestral Studies
Duration: 1FT PMD
Entry Requirements: Interview required. Portfolio required.

801F MMus MMus Solo Performance
Duration: 2FT PMD
Entry Requirements: Interview required. Portfolio required.

805F MMus MMus Solo Performance
Duration: 1FT PMD
Entry Requirements: Interview required. Portfolio required.

611F PGDip PGDip Chamber Music
Duration: 1FT PMD
Entry Requirements: Interview required.

620F PGDip PGDip Composition
Duration: 1FT PMD
Entry Requirements: Interview required. Portfolio required.

641F PGDip PGDip Orchestral Studies
Duration: 1FT PMD
Entry Requirements: Interview required.

601F PGDip PGDip Solo Performance
Duration: 1FT PMD
Entry Requirements: Interview required.

R58 ROYAL SCOTTISH ACADEMY OF MUSIC AND DRAMA
100 RENFREW STREET
GLASGOW G2 3DB
t: 0141 332 4101 f: 0141 332 8901
e: registry@rsamd.ac.uk
// www.rsamd.ac.uk

W310 BA BA (Hons) Contemporary Performance Practice
Duration: 4FT Hon
Entry Requirements: Interview required.

251F BA BA (Hons) Scottish Music - Piping
Duration: 4FT Hon
Entry Requirements: Interview required.

W410 BA BA Acting
Duration: 3FT Ord
Entry Requirements: Interview required.

200F BA BA Digital Film and Television
Duration: 3FT Ord
Entry Requirements: Interview required.

201F BA BA Modern Ballet
Duration: 3FT Ord
Entry Requirements: Interview required.

202F BA BA Musical Theatre
Duration: 3FT Ord
Entry Requirements: Interview required.

203F BA BA Technical and Production Arts (Applied Arts and Construction)
Duration: 3FT Ord
Entry Requirements: Interview required.

204F BA BA Technical and Production Arts (Management and Technology)
Duration: 3FT Ord
Entry Requirements: Interview required.

205F BA Technical and Production Arts (Design)
Duration: 3FT Ord
Entry Requirements: Interview required.

250F BAScotMus BA (Hons) Scottish Music
Duration: 4FT Hon
Entry Requirements: Interview required.

WX33 BEd BEd (Hons) Music
Duration: 4FT Hon
Entry Requirements: Interview required. Admissions Test required.

301F BMus Bachelor of Music (Hons) - Joint Principal Study
Duration: 4FT Hon
Entry Requirements: Interview required.

302F BMus Bachelor of Music (Hons) Composition
Duration: 4FT Hon
Entry Requirements: Interview required. Portfolio required.

303F BMus Bachelor of Music (Hons) Jazz
Duration: 4FT Hon
Entry Requirements: Interview required.

300F BMus Bachelor of Music (Hons) Performance
Duration: 4FT Hon
Entry Requirements: Interview required.

700F MA MA Classical and Contemporary Text (Acting)
Duration: 1FT PMD
Entry Requirements: Interview required.

701F MA MA Classical and Contemporary Text (Directing)
Duration: 1FT PMD
Entry Requirements: Interview required.

702F MA MA Musical Theatre (Musical Directing)
Duration: 1FT PMD
Entry Requirements: Interview required.

703F MA MA Musical Theatre (Performance)
Duration: 1FT PMD
Entry Requirements: Interview required.

893F MMus Master of Music (Accompaniment)
Duration: 2FT PMD
Entry Requirements: Interview required.

831F MMus Master of Music (Accompaniment) APEL
Duration: 1FT PMD
Entry Requirements: Interview required. Portfolio required.

891F MMus Master of Music (Composition)
Duration: 2FT PMD
Entry Requirements: Interview required. Portfolio required.

820F MMus Master of Music (Composition) APEL
Duration: 1FT PMD
Entry Requirements: Interview required. Portfolio required.

892F MMus Master of Music (Conducting)
Duration: 2FT PMD
Entry Requirements: Interview required.

840F MMus Master of Music (Conducting) APEL
Duration: 1FT PMD
Entry Requirements: Interview required. Portfolio required.

808F MMus Master of Music (Jazz)
Duration: 2FT PMD
Entry Requirements: Interview required.

807F MMus Master of Music (Jazz) APEL
Duration: 1FT PMD
Entry Requirements: Interview required. Portfolio required.

851F MMus Master of Music (Opera)
Duration: 2FT PMD
Entry Requirements: Interview required.

800F MMus Master of Music (Opera) APEL
Duration: 1FT PMD
Entry Requirements: Interview required. Portfolio required.

890F MMus Master of Music (Performance)
Duration: 2FT PMD
Entry Requirements: Interview required.

801F MMus Master of Music (Performance) APEL
Duration: 1FT PMD
Entry Requirements: Interview required. Portfolio required.

803F MMus Master of Music (Piano for Dance)
Duration: 2FT PMD
Entry Requirements: Interview required.

802F MMus Master of Music (Piano for Dance) APEL
Duration: 1FT PMD
Entry Requirements: Interview required. Portfolio required.

894F MMus Master of Music (Repetiteurship)
Duration: 2FT PMD
Entry Requirements: Interview required.

860F MMus Master of Music (Repetiteurship) APEL
Duration: 1FT PMD
Entry Requirements: Interview required. Portfolio required.

806F MMus Master of Music (Scottish Music)
Duration: 2FT PMD
Entry Requirements: Interview required.

805F MMus Master of Music (Scottish Music) APEL
Duration: 1FT PMD
Entry Requirements: Interview required. Portfolio required.

**R59 ROYAL WELSH COLLEGE OF MUSIC
AND DRAMA**
CASTLE GROUNDS
CATHAYS PARK
CARDIFF CF10 3ER
t: +44 (0)29 2039 1361 f: +44 (0)29 2039 1301
e: admissions@rwcmd.ac.uk
// www.rwcmd.ac.uk/howtoapply

200F BA (Hons) Acting
Duration: 3FT Hon
Entry Requirements: Interview required.

310F BMus Bachelor of Music (Honors) Jazz
Duration: 4FT Hon
Entry Requirements: Contact the institution for details.

300F BMus Bachelor of Music (Honours)
Duration: 4FT Hon
Entry Requirements: Interview required.

704F MA Acting for Stage, Screen & Radio
Duration: 1FT PMD
Entry Requirements: Interview required.

700P MA Arts Management
Duration: 2PT PMD
Entry Requirements: Contact the institution for details.

705F MA Arts Management
Duration: 1FT PMD
Entry Requirements: Contact the institution for details.

706F MA Brass Band Conducting
Duration: 2FT PMD
Entry Requirements: Contact the institution for details.

700F MA Composition
Duration: 2FT PMD
Entry Requirements: Contact the institution for details.

707F MA Creative Audio & New Media
Duration: 2FT PMD
Entry Requirements: Contact the institution for details.

701F MA Historical Performance
Duration: 2FT PMD
Entry Requirements: Contact the institution for details.

741F MA MA Choral Conducting
Duration: 2FT PMD
Entry Requirements: Contact the institution for details.

710F MA MA Jazz
Duration: 2FT PMD
Entry Requirements: Contact the institution for details.

752F MA MA Opera Performance
Duration: 2FT PMD
Entry Requirements: Interview required.

702F MA Music Performance
Duration: 2FT PMD
Entry Requirements: Contact the institution for details.

713F MA Musical Theatre
Duration: 1FT PMD
Entry Requirements: Contact the institution for details.

708F MA Orchestral Conducting
Duration: 2FT PMD
Entry Requirements: Contact the institution for details.

703F MA Orchestral Performance
Duration: 2FT PMD
Entry Requirements: Contact the institution for details.

709F MA Repetiteurship
Duration: 2FT PMD
Entry Requirements: Contact the institution for details.

711F MA Scenic Art & Construction for Stage & Screen
Duration: 2FT PMD
Entry Requirements: Contact the institution for details.

712F MA Theatre Design
Duration: 2FT PMD
Entry Requirements: Contact the institution for details.

809F MMus Brass Band Conducting
Duration: 1FT PMD
Entry Requirements: Contact the institution for details.

810F MMus Brass Band Conducting
Duration: 2FT PMD
Entry Requirements: Contact the institution for details.

811F MMus Choral Conducting
Duration: 1FT PMD
Entry Requirements: Contact the institution for details.

812F MMus Choral Conducting
Duration: 2FT PMD
Entry Requirements: Contact the institution for details.

802F MMus Composition
Duration: 1FT PMD
Entry Requirements: Contact the institution for details.

803F MMus Composition
Duration: 2FT PMD
Entry Requirements: Contact the institution for details.

813F MMus Creative Audio & New Media
Duration: 1FT PMD
Entry Requirements: Contact the institution for details.

814F MMus Creative Audio & New Media
Duration: 2FT PMD
Entry Requirements: Contact the institution for details.

801F MMus Historical Performance
Duration: 2FT PMD
Entry Requirements: Contact the institution for details.

804F MMus Historical Performance
Duration: 1FT PMD
Entry Requirements: Contact the institution for details.

805F MMus Music Performance
Duration: 2FT PMD
Entry Requirements: Interview required.

806F MMus Music Performance
Duration: 1FT PMD
Entry Requirements: Contact the institution for details.

815F MMus Orchestral Conducting
Duration: 1FT PMD
Entry Requirements: Contact the institution for details.

816F MMus Orchestral Conducting
Duration: 2FT PMD
Entry Requirements: Contact the institution for details.

807F MMus Orchestral Performance
Duration: 1FT PMD
Entry Requirements: Contact the institution for details.

808F MMus Orchestral Performance
Duration: 2FT PMD
Entry Requirements: Contact the institution for details.

817F MMus Repetiteurship
Duration: 1FT PMD
Entry Requirements: Contact the institution for details.

818F MMus Repetiteurship
Duration: 2FT PMD
Entry Requirements: Contact the institution for details.

611F PGDip Brass Band Conducting
Duration: 2FT PMD
Entry Requirements: Contact the institution for details.

612F PGDip Brass Band Conducting
Duration: 1FT PMD
Entry Requirements: Contact the institution for details.

613F PGDip Choral Conducting
Duration: 1FT PMD
Entry Requirements: Contact the institution for details.

614F PGDip Choral Conducting
Duration: 2FT PMD
Entry Requirements: Contact the institution for details.

603F PGDip Composition
Duration: 2FT PMD
Entry Requirements: Contact the institution for details.

604F PGDip Composition
Duration: 1FT PMD
Entry Requirements: Contact the institution for details.

615F PGDip Creative Audio & New Media
Duration: 2FT PMD
Entry Requirements: Contact the institution for details.

616F PGDip Creative Audio & New Media
Duration: 1FT PMD
Entry Requirements: Contact the institution for details.

605F PGDip Historical Performance
Duration: 2FT PMD
Entry Requirements: Contact the institution for details.

606F PGDip Historical Performance
Duration: 1FT PMD
Entry Requirements: Contact the institution for details.

607F PGDip Music Performance
Duration: 2FT PMD
Entry Requirements: Contact the institution for details.

608F PGDip Music Performance
Duration: 1FT PMD
Entry Requirements: Contact the institution for details.

617F PGDip Orchestral Conducting
Duration: 1FT PMD
Entry Requirements: Contact the institution for details.

618F PGDip Orchestral Conducting
Duration: 2FT PMD
Entry Requirements: Contact the institution for details.

609F PGDip Orchestral Performance
Duration: 1FT PMD
Entry Requirements: Contact the institution for details.

610F PGDip Orchestral Performance
Duration: 2FT PMD
Entry Requirements: Contact the institution for details.

619F PGDip Repetiteurship
Duration: 2FT PMD
Entry Requirements: Contact the institution for details.

620F PGDip Repetiteurship
Duration: 1FT PMD
Entry Requirements: Contact the institution for details.

T75 TRINITY LABAN CONSERVATOIRE OF MUSIC AND DANCE
KING CHARLES COURT
OLD ROYAL NAVAL COLLEGE
GREENWICH
LONDON SE10 9JF
t: +44 (0)20 8305 4444
e: admissions@trinitylaban.ac.uk
// www.trinitylaban.ac.uk

230F BA BA (Hons) Musical Theatre: Performance
Duration: 3FT Hon
Entry Requirements: Interview required.

300F BMus BMus (Hons) Performance
Duration: 4FT Hon
Entry Requirements: Admissions Test required.

310F BMus BMus (Hons) Performance Jazz Studies
Duration: 4FT Hon
Entry Requirements: Admissions Test required.

190F FPS Flexible Programmes of Study
Duration: 1FT Oth
Entry Requirements: Contact the institution for details.

801P MFA MFA Creative Practice (Music)
Duration: 2PT PMD
Entry Requirements: Contact the institution for details.

804F MFA MFA Creative Practice (Music)
Duration: 1FT PMD
Entry Requirements: Contact the institution for details.

800F MMus MMus (Performance) or (Composition)
Duration: 1FT PMD
Entry Requirements: Contact the institution for details.

800P MMus MMus (Performance) or (Composition)
Duration: 2PT PMD
Entry Requirements: Contact the institution for details.

802P MMus MMus Education Programme
Duration: 2PT PMD
Entry Requirements: Contact the institution for details.

805F MMus MMus Education Programme
Duration: 1FT PMD
Entry Requirements: Contact the institution for details.

803P MSc MSc in Performance Science
Duration: 2PT PMD
Entry Requirements: Contact the institution for details.

806F MSc MSc in Performance Science
Duration: 1FT PMD
Entry Requirements: Contact the institution for details.

602F PGA Postgraduate Advanced Diploma in Performance or Composition
Duration: 1FT PMD
Entry Requirements: Contact the institution for details.

602P PGA Postgraduate Advanced Diploma in Performance or Composition
Duration: 2PT PMD
Entry Requirements: Contact the institution for details.

600F PGDip Postgraduate Diploma (Performance, Composition, Jazz)
Duration: 1FT PMD
Entry Requirements: Contact the institution for details.

600P PGDip Postgraduate Diploma (Performance, Composition, Jazz)
Duration: 2PT PMD
Entry Requirements: Contact the institution for details.

DRAMA AND ACTING

A40 ABERYSTWYTH UNIVERSITY
WELCOME CENTRE, ABERYSTWYTH UNIVERSITY
PENGLAIS CAMPUS
ABERYSTWYTH
CEREDIGION SY23 3FB
t: 01970 622021 f: 01970 627410
e: ug-admissions@aber.ac.uk
// www.aber.ac.uk

W400 BA Drama & Theatre Studies
Duration: 3FT Hon
Entry Requirements: GCE: 300-320. IB: 32.

WW14 BA Drama & Theatre Studies/Fine Art
Duration: 3FT Hon
Entry Requirements: GCE: 300-320. IB: 32. Portfolio required.

WV41 BA Drama & Theatre Studies/History
Duration: 3FT Hon
Entry Requirements: GCE: 300-320. IB: 32.

LW24 BA Drama & Theatre Studies/International Politics
Duration: 3FT Hon
Entry Requirements: GCE: 300-320. IB: 32.

LWFK BA Drama & Theatre Studies/Politics
Duration: 3FT Hon
Entry Requirements: GCE: 300-320. IB: 32.

W401 BA Drama ac Astudiaethau Theatr
Duration: 3FT Hon
Entry Requirements: GCE: 300-320. IB: 32.

WWP4 BA Drama ac Astudiaethau Theatr/Astudiaethau Ffilm a Theledu
Duration: 3FT Hon
Entry Requirements: *GCE:* 300-320. *IB:* 32.

WVK1 BA Drama ac Astudiaethau Theatr/Hanes
Duration: 3FT Hon
Entry Requirements: *GCE:* 300-320. *IB:* 32.

VW24 BA Drama ac Astudiaethau Theatr/Hanes Cymru
Duration: 3FT Hon
Entry Requirements: *GCE:* 300-320. *IB:* 32.

WX43 BA Education/Drama & Theatre Studies
Duration: 3FT Hon
Entry Requirements: *GCE:* 300-320. *IB:* 32.

QW34 BA English Literature/Drama & Theatre Studies
Duration: 3FT Hon
Entry Requirements: *GCE:* 300-320. *IB:* 32.

RW14 BA French/Drama & Theatre Studies
Duration: 4FT Hon
Entry Requirements: *GCE:* 300-320. *IB:* 32.

GW14 BA Mathematics/Drama & Theatre Studies
Duration: 3FT Hon
Entry Requirements: *GCE:* 300-320. *IB:* 32.

W430 BA Performance Studies/Drama & Theatre Studies
Duration: 3FT Hon
Entry Requirements: *GCE:* 300-320. *IB:* 32.

W432 BA Scenography & Theatre Design/Drama & Theatre Studies
Duration: 3FT Hon
Entry Requirements: *GCE:* 300-320. *IB:* 32.

RW44 BA Spanish/Drama & Theatre Studies
Duration: 4FT Hon
Entry Requirements: *GCE:* 300-320. *IB:* 30.

VWF4 BA Welsh History/Drama & Theatre Studies
Duration: 3FT Hon
Entry Requirements: *GCE:* 300-320. *IB:* 32.

B20 BATH SPA UNIVERSITY
NEWTON PARK
NEWTON ST LOE
BATH BA2 9BN
t: 01225 875875 f: 01225 875444
e: enquiries@bathspa.ac.uk
// www.bathspa.ac.uk/clearing

WW4Y BA Creative Writing/Drama Studies
Duration: 3FT Hon
Entry Requirements: *GCE:* 220-300. *IB:* 24.

WW5K BA Dance/Drama Studies
Duration: 3FT Hon
Entry Requirements: *GCE:* 220-300. *IB:* 24. Interview required.

B80 UNIVERSITY OF THE WEST OF ENGLAND, BRISTOL
FRENCHAY CAMPUS
COLDHARBOUR LANE
BRISTOL BS16 1QY
t: +44 (0)117 32 83333 f: +44 (0)117 32 82810
e: admissions@uwe.ac.uk
// www.uwe.ac.uk

W4W8 BA (Hons) Drama with Creative Writing
Duration: 3FT Hon
Entry Requirements: Contact the institution for details.

C10 CANTERBURY CHRIST CHURCH UNIVERSITY
NORTH HOLMES ROAD
CANTERBURY
KENT CT1 1QU
t: 01227 782900 f: 01227 782888
e: admissions@canterbury.ac.uk
// www.canterbury.ac.uk

WW45 FdA Performing Arts 'International Only'
Duration: 4FT Fdg
Entry Requirements: Interview required.

C58 UNIVERSITY OF CHICHESTER
BISHOP OTTER CAMPUS
COLLEGE LANE
CHICHESTER
WEST SUSSEX PO19 6PE
t: 01243 816002 f: 01243 816161
e: admissions@chi.ac.uk
// www.chiuni.ac.uk

WW4N BA Performing Arts (Theatre Performance and Dance)
Duration: 3FT Hon
Entry Requirements: *GCE:* BBC-BCC. *SQAAH:* BBC-BCC. *IB:* 28.
BTEC NC: DD. *BTEC ND:* DMM. Interview required.

C99 UNIVERSITY OF CUMBRIA
FUSEHILL STREET
CARLISLE
CUMBRIA CA1 2HH
t: 01228 616234 f: 01228 616235
// www.cumbria.ac.uk

WW54 BA Dance Performance and Drama Performance
Duration: 3FT Hon
Entry Requirements: *GCE:* 280. *IB:* 30. *BTEC NC:* DD. *BTEC ND:* DMM. *OCR ND:* D Interview required.

D26 DE MONTFORT UNIVERSITY
THE GATEWAY
LEICESTER LE1 9BH
t: 0116 255 1551 f: 0116 250 6204
e: enquiries@dmu.ac.uk
// www.dmu.ac.uk

WW84 BA Creative Writing and Drama Studies
Duration: 3FT Hon
Entry Requirements: *GCE:* 260. *IB:* 28. *BTEC ND:* DMM.

E14 UNIVERSITY OF EAST ANGLIA
NORWICH NR4 7TJ
t: 01603 591515 f: 01603 458596
e: admissions@uea.ac.uk
// www.uea.ac.uk

WW84 BA Scriptwriting and Performance
Duration: 3FT Hon   CRB Check: Required
Entry Requirements: *GCE:* AAB. *SQAAH:* AAB. *IB:* 33. *BTEC NC:* DD. *BTEC ND:* DDD. Interview required. Portfolio required.

E42 EDGE HILL UNIVERSITY
ORMSKIRK
LANCASHIRE L39 4QP
t: 01695 657000 f: 01695 584355
e: study@edgehill.ac.uk
// www.edgehill.ac.uk

WW45 BA Dance and Drama with Physical Theatres
Duration: 3FT Hon
Entry Requirements: *GCE:* 280. *IB:* 26. *BTEC NC:* DD. *BTEC ND:* DMM. *OCR ND:* D *OCR NED:* M2 Interview required.

W490 BA Visual Theatre
Duration: 3FT Hon
Entry Requirements: *GCE:* 280. *IB:* 26. *BTEC NC:* DD. *BTEC ND:* DMM. *OCR ND:* D *OCR NED:* M2 Interview required.

E70 THE UNIVERSITY OF ESSEX
WIVENHOE PARK
COLCHESTER
ESSEX CO4 3SQ
t: 01206 873666 f: 01206 874477
e: admit@essex.ac.uk
// www.essex.ac.uk

W441 BA Acting and Contemporary Theatre
Duration: 3FT Hon
Entry Requirements: *GCE:* EE. *IB:* 24. *BTEC NC:* PP. *BTEC ND:* PPP. Interview required.

F66 FARNBOROUGH COLLEGE OF TECHNOLOGY
BOUNDARY ROAD
FARNBOROUGH
HAMPSHIRE GU14 6SB
t: 01252 407028 f: 01252 407041
e: admissions@farn-ct.ac.uk
// www.farn-ct.ac.uk

WW54 FdA Theatre, Dance and Film Acting
Duration: 2FT Fdg
Entry Requirements: Contact the institution for details.

H14 HAVERING COLLEGE OF FURTHER AND HIGHER EDUCATION
ARDLEIGH GREEN ROAD
HORNCHURCH
ESSEX RM11 2LL
t: 01708 462793 f: 01708 462736
e: HE@havering-college.ac.uk
// www.havering-college.ac.uk

54WW HNC Performing Arts (Dance/Drama)
Duration: 1FT HNC
Entry Requirements: Contact the institution for details.

45WW HND Performing Arts (Dance/Drama)
Duration: 1FT HND
Entry Requirements: Contact the institution for details.

H36 UNIVERSITY OF HERTFORDSHIRE
UNIVERSITY ADMISSIONS SERVICE
COLLEGE LANE
HATFIELD
HERTS AL10 9AB
t: 01707 284800
// www.herts.ac.uk

WW45 FdA Performing Arts
Duration: 2FT Fdg
Entry Requirements: *GCE:* 80. Interview required.

K84 KINGSTON UNIVERSITY

STUDENT INFORMATION & ADVICE CENTRE
COOPER HOUSE
40-46 SURBITON ROAD
KINGSTON UPON THAMES KT1 2HX
t: 0844 8552177 f: 020 8547 7080
e: aps@kingston.ac.uk
// www.kingston.ac.uk

WW84 BA Creative Writing and Drama
Duration: 3FT Hon
Entry Requirements: *GCE:* 300-360. *IB:* 30.

W8W4 BA Creative Writing with Drama
Duration: 3FT Hon
Entry Requirements: *GCE:* 300-360. *IB:* 30.

WW45 BA Dance and Drama
Duration: 3FT Hon
Entry Requirements: *GCE:* 300-360. *SQAH:* BBCCC. *SQAAH:* BBC.
BTEC ND: DDD. Interview required.

W5W4 BA Dance with Drama
Duration: 3FT Hon
Entry Requirements: *GCE:* 300-360. *SQAH:* BBCCC. *SQAAH:* BBC.
BTEC ND: DDD. Interview required.

W4W8 BA Drama with Creative Writing
Duration: 3FT Hon
Entry Requirements: *GCE:* 300-360. *SQAH:* BBCCC. *SQAAH:* BBC.
IB: 30. *BTEC ND:* DDD.

W4W5 BA Drama with Dance
Duration: 3FT Hon
Entry Requirements: *GCE:* 300-360. *SQAH:* BBCCC. *SQAAH:* BBC.
BTEC ND: DDD.

L39 UNIVERSITY OF LINCOLN

ADMISSIONS
BRAYFORD POOL
LINCOLN LN6 7TS
t: 01522 886097 f: 01522 886146
e: admissions@lincoln.ac.uk
// www.lincoln.ac.uk

WW45 BA Dance and Drama
Duration: 3FT Hon
Entry Requirements: *GCE:* 280. Interview required.

L46 LIVERPOOL HOPE UNIVERSITY

HOPE PARK
LIVERPOOL L16 9JD
t: 0151 291 3295 f: 0151 291 3444
e: admission@hope.ac.uk
// www.hope.ac.uk

WW54 BA Dance and Drama & Theatre Studies
Duration: 3FT Hon
Entry Requirements: *GCE:* 260-320. *IB:* 25.

L51 LIVERPOOL JOHN MOORES UNIVERSITY

KINGSWAY HOUSE
HATTON GARDEN
LIVERPOOL L3 2AJ
t: 0151 231 5090 f: 0151 231 3462
e: courses@ljmu.ac.uk
// www.ljmu.ac.uk

WW48 BA Drama and Creative Writing
Duration: 3FT Hon
Entry Requirements: *GCE:* 260. *IB:* 24. *BTEC NC:* DM. *BTEC ND:* DMM. Interview required.

M40 THE MANCHESTER METROPOLITAN UNIVERSITY

ADMISSIONS OFFICE
ALL SAINTS (GMS)
ALL SAINTS
MANCHESTER M15 6BH
t: 0161 247 2000
// www.mmu.ac.uk

W431 BA Contemporary Theatre and Performance
Duration: 3FT Hon
Entry Requirements: *GCE:* 240-280. *SQAH:* CCC. *SQAAH:* CC. *IB:* 28. Interview required.

WW54 BA Dance/Drama
Duration: 3FT Hon
Entry Requirements: *GCE:* 240-280.

WW84 BA Drama/Creative Writing
Duration: 3FT Hon
Entry Requirements: *GCE:* 240-280. *SQAH:* BBB. *SQAAH:* CC. *IB:* 28.

N36 NEWMAN UNIVERSITY COLLEGE, BIRMINGHAM
GENNERS LANE
BARTLEY GREEN
BIRMINGHAM B32 3NT
t: 0121 476 1181 f: 0121 476 1196
e: Admissions@newman.ac.uk
// www.newman.ac.uk

W4W8 BA Drama with Creative Writing
Duration: 3FT Hon
Entry Requirements: *Foundation:* Distinction. *GCE:* 260. *IB:* 24.
BTEC NC: MM. *BTEC ND:* DMM. *OCR ND:* M2 *OCR NED:* M2

N37 UNIVERSITY OF WALES, NEWPORT
ADMISSIONS
LODGE ROAD
CAERLEON
NEWPORT NP18 3QT
t: 01633 432030 f: 01633 432850
e: admissions@newport.ac.uk
// www.newport.ac.uk

W4W8 BA Applied Drama with Creative Writing
Duration: 3FT Hon
Entry Requirements: *GCE:* 260. *IB:* 24. Interview required.

N38 UNIVERSITY OF NORTHAMPTON
PARK CAMPUS
BOUGHTON GREEN ROAD
NORTHAMPTON NN2 7AL
t: 0800 358 2232 f: 01604 722083
e: admissions@northampton.ac.uk
// www.northampton.ac.uk

W8W4 BA Creative Writing/Drama
Duration: 3FT Hon
Entry Requirements: *GCE:* 260-280. *SQAH:* AAA-BBBB. *IB:* 24.
BTEC NC: DD. *BTEC ND:* DMM. *OCR ND:* D *OCR NED:* M2
Interview required.

W5W4 BA Dance/Drama
Duration: 3FT Hon
Entry Requirements: *GCE:* 260-280. *SQAH:* AAA-BBBB. *IB:* 24.
BTEC NC: DD. *BTEC ND:* DMM. *OCR ND:* D *OCR NED:* M2
Interview required.

W4W8 BA Drama/Creative Writing
Duration: 3FT Hon
Entry Requirements: *GCE:* 260-280. *SQAH:* AAA-BBBB. *IB:* 24.
BTEC NC: DD. *BTEC ND:* DMM. *OCR ND:* D *OCR NED:* M2
Interview required.

W4W5 BA Drama/Dance
Duration: 3FT Hon
Entry Requirements: *GCE:* 260-280. *SQAH:* AAA-BBBB. *IB:* 24.
BTEC NC: DD. *BTEC ND:* DMM. *OCR ND:* D *OCR NED:* M2
Interview required.

N77 NORTHUMBRIA UNIVERSITY
TRINITY BUILDING
NORTHUMBERLAND ROAD
NEWCASTLE UPON TYNE NE1 8ST
t: 0191 243 7420 f: 0191 227 4561
e: er.admissions@northumbria.ac.uk
// www.northumbria.ac.uk

WW84 BA Drama and Scriptwriting
Duration: 3FT Hon
Entry Requirements: *GCE:* 300. *SQAH:* BBBBC. *SQAAH:* BBC. *IB:* 26. *BTEC ND:* DMM. Portfolio required.

P63 UCP MARJON - UNIVERSITY COLLEGE PLYMOUTH ST MARK & ST JOHN
DERRIFORD ROAD
PLYMOUTH PL6 8BH
t: 01752 636890 f: 01752 636819
e: admissions@marjon.ac.uk
// www.ucpmarjon.ac.uk

W8W4 BA Creative Writing with Drama
Duration: 3FT Hon
Entry Requirements: *GCE:* 220.

W4W8 BA Drama with Creative Writing
Duration: 3FT Hon
Entry Requirements: *GCE:* 220.

R18 REGENTS BUSINESS SCHOOL, LONDON (REGENTS COLLEGE)
INNER CIRCLE, REGENT'S COLLEGE
REGENT'S PARK
LONDON NW1 4NS
t: +44(0)20 7487 7505 f: +44(0)20 7487 7425
e: exrel@regents.ac.uk
// www.regents.ac.uk/

W490 BA Acting and Global Theatre
Duration: 3FT Hon
Entry Requirements: *SQAH:* BBCC. *SQAAH:* CC.

R48 ROEHAMPTON UNIVERSITY
ERASMUS HOUSE
ROEHAMPTON LANE
LONDON SW15 5PU
t: 020 8392 3232 f: 020 8392 3470
e: enquiries@roehampton.ac.uk
// www.roehampton.ac.uk

WW84 BA Creative Writing and Drama, Theatre & Performance Studies
Duration: 3FT Hon
Entry Requirements: *GCE:* 300-340. *IB:* 26. *BTEC ND:* DDM. *OCR NED:* D2 Interview required.

WW45 BA Dance Studies and Drama, Theatre & Performance Studies
Duration: 3FT Hon
Entry Requirements: *Foundation:* Distinction. *GCE:* 280-340. *IB:* 25. *BTEC ND:* DMM. *OCR NED:* M2 Interview required.

R72 ROYAL HOLLOWAY, UNIVERSITY OF LONDON
ROYAL HOLLOWAY, UNIVERSITY OF LONDON
EGHAM
SURREY TW20 0EX
t: 01784 434455 f: 01784 473662
e: Admissions@rhul.ac.uk
// www.rhul.ac.uk

WW48 BA Drama and Creative Writing
Duration: 3FT Hon
Entry Requirements: *GCE:* AAB. *SQAH:* AAAAB. *SQAAH:* AAB. *IB:* 35.

S03 THE UNIVERSITY OF SALFORD
SALFORD M5 4WT
t: 0161 295 4545 f: 0161 295 4646
e: ug-admissions@salford.ac.uk
// www.salford.ac.uk

WW48 BA Drama and Creative Writing
Duration: 3FT Hon
Entry Requirements: Contact the institution for details.

S22 SHEFFIELD COLLEGE
THE SHEFFIELD COLLEGE
HE UNIT
HILLSBOROUGH COLLEGE AT THE BARRACKS
SHEFFIELD S6 2LR
t: 0114 260 2597
e: heunit@sheffcol.ac.uk
// www.sheffcol.ac.uk

WW45 FdA Performing Arts
Duration: 2FT Fdg
Entry Requirements: Contact the institution for details.

S64 ST MARY'S UNIVERSITY COLLEGE, TWICKENHAM
WALDEGRAVE ROAD
STRAWBERRY HILL
MIDDLESEX TW1 4SX
t: 020 8240 4029 f: 020 8240 2361
e: admit@smuc.ac.uk
// www.smuc.ac.uk

WW84 BA Drama and Creative and Professional Writing
Duration: 3FT Hon
Entry Requirements: *GCE:* 260. *SQAH:* BBBC. *IB:* 28. *BTEC NC:* DD. *BTEC ND:* MMM. *OCR ND:* D *OCR NED:* M3 Interview required.

W499 BA Drama and Physical Theatre
Duration: 3FT Hon
Entry Requirements: *GCE:* 260. *SQAH:* BBBC. *IB:* 28. *BTEC NC:* DD. *BTEC ND:* MMM. *OCR ND:* D *OCR NED:* M3 Interview required.

W400 BA Drama and Theatre Arts
Duration: 3FT Hon
Entry Requirements: *GCE:* 260. *SQAH:* BBBC. *IB:* 28. *BTEC NC:* DD. *BTEC ND:* MMM. *OCR ND:* D *OCR NED:* M3 Interview required.

S72 STAFFORDSHIRE UNIVERSITY
COLLEGE ROAD
STOKE ON TRENT ST4 2DE
t: 01782 292753 f: 01782 292740
e: admissions@staffs.ac.uk
// www.staffs.ac.uk

WW54 FdA Creative & Cultural Industries (Dance and Theatre Arts)
Duration: 2FT Hon
Entry Requirements: Interview required.

S84 UNIVERSITY OF SUNDERLAND
STUDENT HELPLINE
THE STUDENT GATEWAY
CHESTER ROAD
SUNDERLAND SR1 3SD
t: 0191 515 3000 f: 0191 515 3805
e: student.helpline@sunderland.ac.uk
// www.sunderland.ac.uk

WW45 BA Dance and Drama
Duration: 3FT Hon
Entry Requirements: *GCE:* 260-360. *BTEC NC:* DM. *BTEC ND:* MMM. *OCR ND:* D *OCR NED:* M3

W5W4 BA Dance with Drama
Duration: 3FT Hon
Entry Requirements: *GCE:* 260-360. *BTEC NC:* DM. *BTEC ND:* MMM. *OCR ND:* D *OCR NED:* M3

W4W5 BA Drama with Dance
Duration: 3FT Hon
Entry Requirements: *GCE:* 260-360. *BTEC NC:* DM. *BTEC ND:* MMM. *OCR ND:* D *OCR NED:* M3

U20 UNIVERSITY OF ULSTER
COLERAINE
CO. LONDONDERRY
NORTHERN IRELAND BT52 1SA
t: 028 7032 4221 f: 028 7032 4908
e: online@ulster.ac.uk
// www.ulster.ac.uk

W5W4 BA Dance with Drama
Duration: 3FT Hon
Entry Requirements: *GCE:* CCD. *IB:* 24. *BTEC NC:* MM. *BTEC ND:* MMM. Interview required.

W4W5 BA Drama with Dance
Duration: 3FT Hon
Entry Requirements: *GCE:* BBC. *IB:* 24. *BTEC NC:* DM. *BTEC ND:* DMM. Interview required.

W75 UNIVERSITY OF WOLVERHAMPTON
ADMISSIONS UNIT
MX207, CAMP STREET
WOLVERHAMPTON
WEST MIDLANDS WV1 1AD
t: 01902 321000 f: 01902 321896
e: admissions@wlv.ac.uk
// www.wlv.ac.uk

WW54 BA Dance and Drama
Duration: 3FT Hon   CRB Check: Required
Entry Requirements: *GCE:* 160-220. *IB:* 24. Interview required.

WW48 BA Drama and Creative Professional Writing
Duration: 3FT Hon   CRB Check: Required
Entry Requirements: *GCE:* 180. Interview required.

W76 UNIVERSITY OF WINCHESTER
WINCHESTER
HANTS SO22 4NR
t: 01962 827234 f: 01962 827288
e: course.enquiries@winchester.ac.uk
// www.winchester.ac.uk

WW45 BA Choreography & Dance and Drama
Duration: 3FT Hon
Entry Requirements: *Foundation:* Distinction. *GCE:* 260-300. *IB:* 25. *BTEC NC:* DD. *BTEC ND:* DMM. *OCR ND:* D *OCR NED:* M2

WWK5 BA Choreography & Dance and Contemporary Performance
Duration: 3FT Hon
Entry Requirements: *Foundation:* Distinction. *GCE:* 260-300. *IB:* 25. *BTEC NC:* DD. *BTEC ND:* DMM. *OCR ND:* D *OCR NED:* M2

WW48 BA Creative Writing and Drama
Duration: 3FT Hon
Entry Requirements: *Foundation:* Distinction. *GCE:* 260-300. *IB:* 25. *BTEC NC:* DD. *BTEC ND:* DMM. *OCR ND:* D *OCR NED:* M2

W80 UNIVERSITY OF WORCESTER
HENWICK GROVE
WORCESTER WR2 6AJ
t: 01905 855111 f: 01905 855377
e: admissions@worc.ac.uk
// www.worcester.ac.uk

WW48 BA Drama & Performance and Screen Writing
Duration: 3FT Hon
Entry Requirements: *GCE:* 240-260. *IB:* 24. *BTEC NC:* DD. *BTEC ND:* MMM. *OCR ND:* D *OCR NED:* M3

DIRECTING, PRODUCING AND STAGE MANAGEMENT

B25 BIRMINGHAM CITY UNIVERSITY
PERRY BARR
BIRMINGHAM B42 2SU
t: 0121 331 5595 f: 0121 331 7994
e: choices@bcu.ac.uk
// www.bcu.ac.uk

W450 BA Stage Management
Duration: 3FT Hon
Entry Requirements: *GCE:* 240. Interview required.

C35 CENTRAL SCHOOL OF SPEECH AND DRAMA, UNIVERSITY OF LONDON
EMBASSY THEATRE
64 ETON AVENUE
LONDON NW3 3HY
t: 0207 722 8183 f: 0207 722 4132
e: enquiries@cssd.ac.uk
// www.cssd.ac.uk

W451 BA Theatre Practice: Production Lighting
Duration: 3FT Hon
Entry Requirements: *GCE:* BBC. Interview required. Portfolio required.

W450 BA Theatre Practice: Theatre Lighting Design
Duration: 3FT Hon
Entry Requirements: *GCE:* BBC. Interview required. Portfolio required.

C99 UNIVERSITY OF CUMBRIA
FUSEHILL STREET
CARLISLE
CUMBRIA CA1 2HH
t: 01228 616234 f: 01228 616235
// www.cumbria.ac.uk

WJ49 FdA Lighting Design and Realisation
Duration: 2FT Fdg
Entry Requirements: Contact the institution for details.

W450 FdA Stage Management
Duration: 2FT Fdg
Entry Requirements: *Foundation:* Pass. *GCE:* C-cccc. *SQAH:* CC.
SQAAH: C. *IB:* 25. *BTEC NC:* MP. *BTEC ND:* PPP. Interview
required. Portfolio required.

E70 THE UNIVERSITY OF ESSEX
WIVENHOE PARK
COLCHESTER
ESSEX CO4 3SQ
t: 01206 873666 f: 01206 874477
e: admit@essex.ac.uk
// www.essex.ac.uk

**W450 BA Stage Management and Technical
Theatre**
Duration: 1FT Hon
Entry Requirements: Interview required.

**W453 FdA Stage Management and Technical
Theatre**
Duration: 2FT Fdg
Entry Requirements: *GCE:* E. *SQAH:* CCCC. *SQAAH:* CCC. *IB:* 24.
BTEC NC: PP. *BTEC ND:* PPP. Interview required. Admissions Test
required.

G70 UNIVERSITY OF GREENWICH
GREENWICH CAMPUS
OLD ROYAL NAVAL COLLEGE
PARK ROW
LONDON SE10 9LS
t: 0800 005 006 f: 020 8331 8145
e: courseinfo@gre.ac.uk
// www.gre.ac.uk

**W450 FdA Stage Management and Technical
Theatre (ALRA)**
Duration: 2FT Fdg
Entry Requirements: *GCE:* 60.

L23 UNIVERSITY OF LEEDS
THE UNIVERSITY OF LEEDS
WOODHOUSE LANE
LEEDS LS2 9JT
t: 0113 343 3999
e: admissions@leeds.ac.uk
// www.leeds.ac.uk

W450 BA Managing Performance
Duration: 3FT Hon
Entry Requirements: *GCE:* BBB. *SQAAH:* BBB. *IB:* 32.

W462 BA Performance Design
Duration: 3FT Hon
Entry Requirements: *GCE:* BBB. *SQAAH:* BBB. *IB:* 32. Interview
required.

**L48 THE LIVERPOOL INSTITUTE FOR
PERFORMING ARTS**
MOUNT STREET
LIVERPOOL L1 9HF
t: 0151 330 3000 f: 0151 330 3131
e: admissions@lipa.ac.uk
// www.lipa.ac.uk

**W450 BA Music, Theatre and Entertainment
Management**
Duration: 3FT Hon
Entry Requirements: *GCE:* 180. Interview required.

N30 NEW COLLEGE NOTTINGHAM
ADAMS BUILDING
STONEY STREET
THE LACE MARKET
NOTTINGHAM NG1 1NG
t: 0115 910 0100 f: 0115 953 4349
e: enquiries@ncn.ac.uk
// www.ncn.ac.uk

W450 FdA Theatre Arts (Technical Theatre)
Duration: 2FT Fdg
Entry Requirements: *GCE:* 120. Interview required.

N41 NORTHBROOK COLLEGE SUSSEX
LITTLEHAMPTON ROAD
WORTHING
WEST SUSSEX BN12 6NU
t: 0845 155 6060 f: 01903 606073
e: enquiries@nbcol.ac.uk
// www.northbrook.ac.uk

W490 FdA Prop Making and Special Effects
Duration: 2FT Fdg
Entry Requirements: Interview required. Portfolio required.

**W450 FdA Theatre Arts - Stage and
Production Management**
Duration: 2FT Fdg
Entry Requirements: *BTEC ND:* MMP. Interview required.

R51 ROSE BRUFORD COLLEGE
LAMORBEY PARK
BURNT OAK LANE
SIDCUP
KENT DA15 9DF
t: 0208 308 2600 f: 020 8308 0542
e: enquiries@bruford.ac.uk
// www.bruford.ac.uk

WG46 BA Creative Lighting Control
Duration: 3FT Hon
Entry Requirements: Contact the institution for details.

W450 BA Stage Management
Duration: 3FT Hon
Entry Requirements: *GCE:* 160-280.

R86 ROYAL WELSH COLLEGE OF MUSIC AND DRAMA (COLEG BRENHINOL CERDD A DRAMA CYMRU)
CASTLE GROUNDS
CATHAYS PARK
CARDIFF CF10 3ER
t: 029 2039 1361 f: 029 2039 1301
e: admissions@rwcmd.ac.uk
// www.rwcmd.ac.uk

W450 BA Stage Management
Duration: 3FT Hon
Entry Requirements: *GCE:* 240-360. Interview required.

THEATRE STUDIES

A44 ACCRINGTON & ROSSENDALE COLLEGE
BROAD OAK ROAD,
ACCRINGTON,
LANCASHIRE, BB5 2AW.
t: 01254 389933 f: 01254 354001
e: info@accross.ac.uk
// www.accrosshighereducation.co.uk/

W440 FdA Theatre and Performance
Duration: 2FT Fdg
Entry Requirements: *BTEC ND:* MMM. Interview required.

B06 BANGOR UNIVERSITY
BANGOR UNIVERSITY
BANGOR
GWYNEDD LL57 2DG
t: 01248 388484 f: 01248 370451
e: admissions@bangor.ac.uk
// www.bangor.ac.uk

Q3WX BA English with Theatre and Performance
Duration: 3FT Hon
Entry Requirements: Contact the institution for details.

B22 UNIVERSITY OF BEDFORDSHIRE
PARK SQUARE
LUTON
BEDS LU1 3JU
t: 0844 8482234 f: 01582 489323
e: admissions@beds.ac.uk
// www.beds.ac.uk

WQ43 BA English and Theatre Studies
Duration: 3FT Hon
Entry Requirements: *GCE:* 180-220. Interview required.

B32 THE UNIVERSITY OF BIRMINGHAM
EDGBASTON
BIRMINGHAM B15 2TT
t: 0121 415 8900 f: 0121 414 7159
e: admissions@bham.ac.uk
// www.bham.ac.uk

W440 BA Drama and Theatre Arts
Duration: 3FT Hon
Entry Requirements: *GCE:* AAB-ABB. *SQAH:* AABBB-ABBBB. *SQAAH:* AA-AB.

B72 UNIVERSITY OF BRIGHTON
209 MITHRAS HOUSE
LEWES ROAD
BRIGHTON BN2 4AT
t: 01273 644644 f: 01273 642607
e: admissions@brighton.ac.uk
// www.brighton.ac.uk

W4WD BA Performance and Visual Arts (Theatre)
Duration: 3FT Hon
Entry Requirements: *GCE:* BBC. *BTEC ND:* DMM. Foundation Course required. Interview required. Portfolio required.

B77 BRISTOL, CITY OF BRISTOL COLLEGE
ASHLEY DOWN CENTRE
ASHLEY DOWN ROAD
BRISTOL BS7 9BU
t: 0117 312 5211 f: 0117 312 5050
e: admissions@cityofbristol.ac.uk
// www.cityofbristol.ac.uk

WW54 FdA Dance Theatre Performance
Duration: 2FT Fdg   CRB Check: Required
Entry Requirements: *GCE:* 140.

B84 BRUNEL UNIVERSITY
UXBRIDGE
MIDDLESEX UB8 3PH
t: 01895 265265 f: 01895 269790
e: admissions@brunel.ac.uk
// www.brunel.ac.uk

W440 BA Theatre
Duration: 3FT Hon
Entry Requirements: *GCE:* BCC. *SQAAH:* BCC. *IB:* 29. *BTEC ND:* DDM.

W4WW BA Theatre and Creative Writing
Duration: 3FT Hon
Entry Requirements: *GCE:* BCC. *SQAAH:* BBC. *IB:* 30. *BTEC ND:* DDM.

WQ43 BA Theatre and English
Duration: 3FT Hon
Entry Requirements: *GCE:* BCC. *SQAAH:* BBC. *IB:* 30. *BTEC ND:* DDM.

WW46 BA Theatre and Film & TV Studies
Duration: 3FT Hon
Entry Requirements: *GCE:* BCC. *SQAAH:* BCC. *IB:* 29. *BTEC ND:* DDM.

WW42 BA Theatre and Games Design
Duration: 3FT Hon
Entry Requirements: *GCE:* BCC. *SQAAH:* BCC. *IB:* 29. *BTEC ND:* DDM.

C10 CANTERBURY CHRIST CHURCH UNIVERSITY
NORTH HOLMES ROAD
CANTERBURY
KENT CT1 1QU
t: 01227 782900 f: 01227 782888
e: admissions@canterbury.ac.uk
// www.canterbury.ac.uk

W440 BA Technical Theatre
Duration: 3FT Hon
Entry Requirements: *GCE:* 240. *IB:* 24. Interview required.

C30 UNIVERSITY OF CENTRAL LANCASHIRE
PRESTON
LANCS PR1 2HE
t: 01772 201201 f: 01772 894954
e: uadmissions@uclan.ac.uk
// www.uclan.ac.uk

W441 BA Contemporary Theatre and Performance
Duration: 3FT Hon
Entry Requirements: *GCE:* 260-300. *IB:* 26. Interview required.

W440 FdA Theatre and Performance
Duration: 2FT Fdg
Entry Requirements: *GCE:* 80. *SQAH:* CC.

C35 CENTRAL SCHOOL OF SPEECH AND DRAMA, UNIVERSITY OF LONDON
EMBASSY THEATRE
64 ETON AVENUE
LONDON NW3 3HY
t: 0207 722 8183 f: 0207 722 4132
e: enquiries@cssd.ac.uk
// www.cssd.ac.uk

W440 BA Theatre Practice: Performance Arts
Duration: 3FT Hon
Entry Requirements: *GCE:* BBC. Interview required. Portfolio required.

W441 BA Theatre Practice: Puppetry
Duration: 3FT Hon
Entry Requirements: *GCE:* BBC. Interview required. Portfolio required.

C55 UNIVERSITY OF CHESTER
PARKGATE ROAD
CHESTER CH1 4BJ
t: 01244 511000 f: 01244 511300
e: enquiries@chester.ac.uk
// www.chester.ac.uk

WW84 BA Creative Writing and Drama & Theatre Studies
Duration: 3FT Hon
Entry Requirements: *Foundation:* Pass. *GCE:* 260-300. *SQAH:* BBBB. *IB:* 28. *BTEC NC:* DM. *BTEC ND:* DMM.

C75 COLCHESTER INSTITUTE
SHEEPEN ROAD
COLCHESTER
ESSEX CO3 3LL
t: 01206 712777 f: 01206 712800
e: info@colchester.ac.uk
// www.colchester.ac.uk

W441 BA Technical Theatre
Duration: 3FT Hon
Entry Requirements: *GCE:* 80. Interview required.

W440 FdA Technical Theatre
Duration: 2FT Fdg
Entry Requirements: *GCE:* 80. Interview required.

C85 COVENTRY UNIVERSITY
THE STUDENT CENTRE
COVENTRY UNIVERSITY
1 GULSON RD
COVENTRY CV1 2JH
t: 024 7615 2222 f: 024 7615 2223
e: studentenquiries@coventry.ac.uk
// www.coventry.ac.uk

W440 BA Theatre and Professional Practice
Duration: 3FT/4SW Hon
Entry Requirements: *GCE:* CCC. *SQAH:* CCCCC. *IB:* 27. *BTEC ND:* MMM. *OCR NED:* M3 Interview required.

C93 UNIVERSITY FOR THE CREATIVE ARTS
FALKNER ROAD
FARNHAM
SURREY GU9 7DS
t: 01252 722441 f: 01252 892624
e: admissions@ucreative.ac.uk
// www.ucreative.ac.uk

W440 BA Creative Arts for Theatre & Film
Duration: 3FT Hon
Entry Requirements: *GCE:* 200. Interview required. Portfolio required.

C99 UNIVERSITY OF CUMBRIA
FUSEHILL STREET
CARLISLE
CUMBRIA CA1 2HH
t: 01228 616234 f: 01228 616235
// www.cumbria.ac.uk

W440 BA Performing Arts
Duration: 3FT Hon
Entry Requirements: *GCE:* 280. *IB:* 30. *BTEC NC:* DD. *BTEC ND:* DMM. *OCR ND:* D Interview required.

D39 UNIVERSITY OF DERBY
KEDLESTON ROAD
DERBY DE22 1GB
t: 01332 591167 f: 01332 597724
e: askadmissions@derby.ac.uk
// www.derby.ac.uk

KW14 BA Architectural Design and Theatre Arts
Duration: 3FT Hon
Entry Requirements: *Foundation:* Distinction. *GCE:* 260-300. *IB:* 28. *BTEC ND:* DMM. *OCR NED:* M2

NW24 BA Business Management and Theatre Arts
Duration: 3FT Hon
Entry Requirements: *Foundation:* Distinction. *GCE:* 260-300. *IB:* 28. *BTEC ND:* DMM. *OCR NED:* M2

MW24 BA Criminology and Theatre Arts
Duration: 3FT Hon
Entry Requirements: *Foundation:* Distinction. *GCE:* 260-300. *IB:* 28. *BTEC ND:* DMM. *OCR NED:* M2

WW45 BA Dance & Movement Studies and Theatre Arts
Duration: 3FT Hon
Entry Requirements: *Foundation:* Distinction. *GCE:* 260-300. *IB:* 28. *BTEC ND:* DMM. *OCR NED:* M2

NW64 BA Human Resource Management and Theatre Arts
Duration: 3FT Hon
Entry Requirements: *Foundation:* Distinction. *GCE:* 260-300. *IB:* 28. *BTEC ND:* DMM. *OCR NED:* M2

NW5K BA Marketing and Theatre Arts
Duration: 3FT Hon
Entry Requirements: *Foundation:* Distinction. *GCE:* 260-300. *IB:* 28. *BTEC ND:* DMM. *OCR NED:* M2

W440 BA Theatre Arts
Duration: 3FT Hon
Entry Requirements: *Foundation:* Merit. *GCE:* 240. *IB:* 26. *BTEC NC:* DD. *BTEC ND:* MMM. *OCR ND:* D *OCR NED:* M3 Interview required.

CW14 BA/BSc Biology and Theatre Arts
Duration: 3FT Hon
Entry Requirements: *Foundation:* Distinction. *GCE:* 260-300. *IB:* 28. *BTEC ND:* DMM. *OCR NED:* M2

QW34 BA/BSc English, Theatre Arts and Biology
Duration: 3FT Hon
Entry Requirements: *Foundation:* Distinction. *GCE:* 260-300. *IB:* 28. *BTEC ND:* DMM. *OCR NED:* M2

LW74 BA/BSc Geography and Theatre Arts
Duration: 3FT Hon
Entry Requirements: *Foundation:* Distinction. *GCE:* 260-300. *IB:* 28. *BTEC ND:* DMM. *OCR NED:* M2

FW64 BA/BSc Geology and Theatre Arts
Duration: 3FT Hon
Entry Requirements: *Foundation:* Distinction. *GCE:* 260-300. *IB:* 28. *BTEC ND:* DMM. *OCR NED:* M2

CW8K BA/BSc Psychology and Theatre Arts
Duration: 3FT Hon
Entry Requirements: *Foundation:* Distinction. *GCE:* 260-300. *IB:* 28. *BTEC ND:* DMM. *OCR NED:* M2

CW34 BA/BSc Zoology and Theatre Arts
Duration: 3FT Hon
Entry Requirements: *Foundation:* Distinction. *GCE:* 260-300. *IB:* 28. *BTEC ND:* DMM. *OCR NED:* M2

D52 DONCASTER COLLEGE
THE HUB
CHAPPELL DRIVE
SOUTH YORKSHIRE DN1 2RF
t: 01302 553610
e: he@don.ac.uk
// www.don.ac.uk

W441 BA Contemporary Performance Practice
Duration: 3FT Hon
Entry Requirements: *BTEC ND:* MPP.

E28 UNIVERSITY OF EAST LONDON
DOCKLANDS CAMPUS
UNIVERSITY WAY
LONDON E16 2RD
t: 020 8223 3333 f: 020 8223 2978
e: study@uel.ac.uk
// www.uel.ac.uk

L6W4 BA Cultural Studies with Theatre Studies
Duration: 3FT Hon
Entry Requirements: *GCE:* 200. *IB:* 24. *BTEC NC:* DM. *BTEC ND:* MMP. *OCR ND:* M1 *OCR NED:* P1

Q3WK BA English Literature with Theatre Studies
Duration: 3FT Hon
Entry Requirements: *GCE:* 200. *IB:* 24. *BTEC NC:* DM. *BTEC ND:* MMP. *OCR ND:* M1 *OCR NED:* P1

M1W4 BA Law with Theatre Studies
Duration: 3FT Hon
Entry Requirements: *GCE:* 240. *IB:* 28. *BTEC NC:* DD. *BTEC ND:* MMM.

WW5K BA Professional Dance and Musical Theatre
Duration: 3FT Hon
Entry Requirements: *GCE:* 200. *IB:* 24. *BTEC NC:* DM. *BTEC ND:* MMP. Interview required.

W442 BA Theatre Studies
Duration: 3FT Hon
Entry Requirements: *GCE:* 200. *IB:* 24. *BTEC NC:* DM. *BTEC ND:* MMP. Interview required.

W443 BA Theatre Studies (International)
Duration: 3FT Hon
Entry Requirements: *GCE:* 200. *IB:* 24. *BTEC NC:* DM. *BTEC ND:* MMP.

W444 BA Theatre Studies (International) Extended Degree
Duration: 4FT Hon
Entry Requirements: *GCE:* 80. *BTEC NC:* PP. *BTEC ND:* PPP.

W440 BA Theatre Studies - Extended
Duration: 4FT Hon
Entry Requirements: *GCE:* 40. *IB:* 24. Interview required.

W4L9 BA Theatre Studies with Communication Studies
Duration: 3FT Hon
Entry Requirements: *GCE:* 200. *IB:* 24. *BTEC NC:* DM. *BTEC ND:* MMP. *OCR ND:* M1 *OCR NED:* P1

W4W5 BA Theatre Studies with Dance: Urban Practice
Duration: 3FT Hon
Entry Requirements: *GCE:* 200. *IB:* 24. *BTEC NC:* DM. *BTEC ND:* MMP. *OCR ND:* M1 *OCR NED:* P1

W4X9 BA Theatre Studies with Education & Community Development
Duration: 3FT Hon
Entry Requirements: *GCE:* 200. *IB:* 24. *BTEC NC:* DM. *BTEC ND:* MMP. *OCR ND:* M1 *OCR NED:* P1

W4QJ BA Theatre Studies with English Literature
Duration: 3FT Hon
Entry Requirements: *GCE:* 200. *IB:* 24. *BTEC NC:* DM. *BTEC ND:* MMP. *OCR ND:* M1 *OCR NED:* P1

W4CP BA Theatre Studies with Sports & Exercise Science
Duration: 3FT Hon
Entry Requirements: *GCE:* 200. *IB:* 24. *BTEC NC:* DM. *BTEC ND:* MMP. *OCR ND:* M1 *OCR NED:* P1

B9WK BSc Health Promotion with Theatre Studies
Duration: 3FT Hon
Entry Requirements: *GCE:* 200. *IB:* 24. *BTEC NC:* DM. *BTEC ND:* MMP.

F33 UNIVERSITY COLLEGE FALMOUTH
WOODLANE
FALMOUTH
CORNWALL TR11 4RH
t: 01326213730
e: admissions@falmouth.ac.uk
// www.falmouth.ac.uk

W490 BA(Hons) Theatre
Duration: 3FT Hon
Entry Requirements: *GCE:* 220. *IB:* 24. Interview required.

G28 UNIVERSITY OF GLASGOW
THE UNIVERSITY OF GLASGOW
THE FRASER BUILDING
65 HILLHEAD STREET
GLASGOW G12 8QF
t: 0141 330 6062 f: 0141 330 2961
e: student.recruitment@glasgow.ac.uk
// www.glasgow.ac.uk

QWF4 MA Comparative Literature/Theatre Studies
Duration: 4FT Hon
Entry Requirements: *GCE:* AAA. *SQAH:* AAAA-AABB. *IB:* 36.

LW44 MA Public Policy/Theatre Studies
Duration: 4FT Hon
Entry Requirements: *GCE:* AAA. *SQAH:* AAAA-AABB. *IB:* 36.

LW34 MA Sociology/Theatre Studies
Duration: 4FT Hon
Entry Requirements: *GCE:* AAA. *SQAH:* AAAA-AABB. *IB:* 36.

RW4K MA Spanish/Theatre Studies
Duration: 5FT Hon
Entry Requirements: *GCE:* AAA. *SQAH:* AAAA-AABB. *IB:* 36.

W440 MA Theatre Studies
Duration: 4FT Hon
Entry Requirements: *GCE:* AAA. *SQAH:* AAAA-AABB. *IB:* 36.

WQ46 MA Theatre Studies/Latin
Duration: 4FT Hon
Entry Requirements: *GCE:* AAA. *SQAH:* AAAA-AABB. *IB:* 36.

VW64 MA Theology & Religious Studies/Theatre Studies
Duration: 4FT Hon
Entry Requirements: *GCE:* AAA. *SQAH:* AAAA-AABB. *IB:* 36.

G56 GOLDSMITHS, UNIVERSITY OF LONDON
GOLDSMITHS, UNIVERSITY OF LONDON
NEW CROSS
LONDON SE14 6NW
t: 020 7048 5300 f: 020 7919 7509
e: admissions@gold.ac.uk
// www.gold.ac.uk

W440 BA Drama and Theatre Arts
Duration: 3FT Hon
Entry Requirements: *GCE:* ABB. *SQAH:* BBBBB. *SQAAH:* BBB. *IB:* 32. *BTEC NC:* DD. *BTEC ND:* DDM. Interview required.

H54 HOPWOOD HALL COLLEGE
ROCHDALE ROAD
MIDDLETON
MANCHESTER M24 6XH
t: 0161 643 7560 f: 0161 643 2114
e: admissions@hopwood.ac.uk
// www.hopwood.ac.uk

W440 HND Performing Arts (Theatre in Education)
Duration: 2FT HND
Entry Requirements: Contact the institution for details.

H60 THE UNIVERSITY OF HUDDERSFIELD
QUEENSGATE
HUDDERSFIELD HD1 3DH
t: 01484 473969 f: 01484 472765
e: admissionsandrecords@hud.ac.uk
// www.hud.ac.uk

W440 BA Drama
Duration: 3FT Hon
Entry Requirements: *GCE:* 280. *IB:* 28. Interview required.

W442 BA Technical Theatre (Top-Up)
Duration: 1FT Hon
Entry Requirements: Interview required. Portfolio required. HND required.

W441 FdA Technical Theatre
Duration: 2FT Fdg
Entry Requirements: *GCE:* 120. Interview required.

H72 THE UNIVERSITY OF HULL
THE UNIVERSITY OF HULL
COTTINGHAM ROAD
HULL HU6 7RX
t: 01482 466100 f: 01482 442290
e: admissions@hull.ac.uk
// www.hull.ac.uk

Q3W4 BA English with Theatre & Performance
Duration: 3FT Hon
Entry Requirements: *GCE:* 240. *IB:* 26. *BTEC ND:* DMM.

WQ43 BA Theatre and English
Duration: 3FT Hon
Entry Requirements: **GCE:** 240. **IB:** 26. **BTEC ND:** DMM.

WWK5 BA Theatre and Performance
Duration: 3FT Hon
Entry Requirements: **GCE:** 240. **IB:** 24. **BTEC ND:** DMM.

H73 HULL COLLEGE
QUEEN'S GARDENS
HULL HU1 3DG
t: 01482 329943 f: 01482 598733
e: info@hull-college.ac.uk
// www.hull-college.ac.uk/HE

W441 BA Stage Management and Technical Theatre
Duration: 1FT Hon
Entry Requirements: Interview required. Admissions Test required. Portfolio required. HND required.

W440 FdA Stage Management and Technical Theatre
Duration: 2FT Fdg
Entry Requirements: **GCE:** 240. Interview required. Admissions Test required. Portfolio required.

L14 LANCASTER UNIVERSITY
THE UNIVERSITY
LANCASTER
LANCASHIRE LA1 4YW
t: 01524 592029 f: 01524 846243
e: ugadmissions@lancaster.ac.uk
// www.lancs.ac.uk

W440 BA Theatre Studies
Duration: 3FT Hon
Entry Requirements: **GCE:** ABB. **SQAH:** BBBBB. **SQAAH:** ABB. **IB:** 32. **BTEC ND:** DDM. Interview required.

L23 UNIVERSITY OF LEEDS
THE UNIVERSITY OF LEEDS
WOODHOUSE LANE
LEEDS LS2 9JT
t: 0113 343 3999
e: admissions@leeds.ac.uk
// www.leeds.ac.uk

QW34 BA English Literature & Theatre Studies
Duration: 3FT Hon
Entry Requirements: **GCE:** AAB. **SQAH:** AAAAB. **SQAAH:** AAB. **IB:** 35.

W440 BA Theatre & Performance
Duration: 3FT Hon
Entry Requirements: **GCE:** ABB. **SQAAH:** ABB. **IB:** 36.

L46 LIVERPOOL HOPE UNIVERSITY
HOPE PARK
LIVERPOOL L16 9JD
t: 0151 291 3295 f: 0151 291 3444
e: admission@hope.ac.uk
// www.hope.ac.uk

VW34 BA Art & Design History and Drama & Theatre Studies
Duration: 3FT Hon
Entry Requirements: **GCE:** 260-320. **IB:** 25.

M10 THE MANCHESTER COLLEGE
OPENSHAW CAMPUS
ASHTON OLD ROAD
OPENSHAW
MANCHESTER M11 2WH
t: 0800 068 8585 f: 0161 920 4103
e: enquiries@themanchestercollege.ac.uk
// www.themanchestercollege.ac.uk

W440 FdA Contemporary Theatre Practice
Duration: 2FT Fdg
Entry Requirements: **GCE:** 180. Interview required.

M95 MOUNTVIEW ACADEMY OF THEATRE ARTS
RALPH RICHARDSON MEMORIAL STUDIOS
KINGFISHER PLACE
CLARENDON ROAD
LONDON N22 6XF
t: 020 8881 2201 f: 020 8829 0034
e: enquiries@mountview.ac.uk
// www.mountview.ac.uk

W440 BA Technical Theatre
Duration: 2FT Hon
Entry Requirements: Interview required. Portfolio required.

N38 UNIVERSITY OF NORTHAMPTON
PARK CAMPUS
BOUGHTON GREEN ROAD
NORTHAMPTON NN2 7AL
t: 0800 358 2232 f: 01604 722083
e: admissions@northampton.ac.uk
// www.northampton.ac.uk

044W HND Theatre
Duration: 2FT HND
Entry Requirements: **GCE:** 120-140. **SQAH:** BC-CCC. **IB:** 24. **BTEC NC:** MP. **BTEC ND:** MPP. **OCR ND:** P1 **OCR NED:** P2 Interview required.

N41 NORTHBROOK COLLEGE SUSSEX
LITTLEHAMPTON ROAD
WORTHING
WEST SUSSEX BN12 6NU
t: 0845 155 6060 f: 01903 606073
e: enquiries@nbcol.ac.uk
// www.northbrook.ac.uk

W441 FdA Theatre Arts - Physical Theatre
Duration: 2FT Fdg
Entry Requirements: *BTEC ND:* MMP. Interview required.

N58 NORTH EAST WORCESTERSHIRE COLLEGE
PEAKMAN STREET
REDDITCH
WORCESTERSHIRE B98 8DW
t: 01527 572822 f: 01527 572901
e: admissions@ne-worcs.ac.uk
// www.ne-worcs.ac.uk

W441 FdA Technical Theatre
Duration: 2FT Fdg
Entry Requirements: *GCE:* 120. Interview required. Portfolio required.

P51 PETROC
OLD STICKLEPATH HILL
BARNSTAPLE
NORTH DEVON EX31 2BQ
t: 01271 338100 f: 01271 338121
e: he@petroc.ac.uk
// www.petroc.ac.uk

W401 FdA Theatre: Performance and Production
Duration: 2FT Fdg
Entry Requirements: *GCE:* EE.

Q25 QUEEN MARGARET UNIVERSITY, EDINBURGH
QUEEN MARGARET UNIVERSITY DRIVE
EDINBURGH EH21 6UU
t: 0131474 0000 f: 0131 474 0001
e: admissions@qmu.ac.uk
// www.qmu.ac.uk

WW46 BA Theatre and Film Studies
Duration: 4FT Hon
Entry Requirements: *GCE:* 300. *IB:* 30.

R12 THE UNIVERSITY OF READING
THE UNIVERSITY OF READING
PO BOX 217
READING RG6 6AH
t: 0118 378 8619 f: 0118 378 8924
e: student.recruitment@reading.ac.uk
// www.reading.ac.uk

QW34 BA English Literature and Film & Theatre
Duration: 3FT Hon
Entry Requirements: *GCE:* 300-340.

W440 BA Theatre Arts Education and Deaf Studies
Duration: 3FT Hon
Entry Requirements: *GCE:* 160.

R48 ROEHAMPTON UNIVERSITY
ERASMUS HOUSE
ROEHAMPTON LANE
LONDON SW15 5PU
t: 020 8392 3232 f: 020 8392 3470
e: enquiries@roehampton.ac.uk
// www.roehampton.ac.uk

W440 BA Drama, Theatre & Performance Studies
Duration: 3FT Hon
Entry Requirements: *Foundation:* Distinction. *GCE:* 280-340. *IB:* 25. *BTEC ND:* DMM. *OCR NED:* M2 Interview required.

R51 ROSE BRUFORD COLLEGE
LAMORBEY PARK
BURNT OAK LANE
SIDCUP
KENT DA15 9DF
t: 0208 308 2600 f: 020 8308 0542
e: enquiries@bruford.ac.uk
// www.bruford.ac.uk

WJ49 BA Performance Sound
Duration: 3FT Hon
Entry Requirements: Contact the institution for details.

R72 ROYAL HOLLOWAY, UNIVERSITY OF LONDON
ROYAL HOLLOWAY, UNIVERSITY OF LONDON
EGHAM
SURREY TW20 0EX
t: 01784 434455 f: 01784 473662
e: Admissions@rhul.ac.uk
// www.rhul.ac.uk

W440 BA Drama and Theatre Studies
Duration: 3FT Hon
Entry Requirements: *GCE:* AAB. *SQAH:* AAAAB. *SQAAH:* AAB. *IB:* 35.

S03 THE UNIVERSITY OF SALFORD
SALFORD M5 4WT
t: 0161 295 4545 f: 0161 295 4646
e: ug-admissions@salford.ac.uk
// www.salford.ac.uk

W440 BA Contemporary Theatre Practice
Duration: 3FT Hon
Entry Requirements: *GCE:* 280. *IB:* 28. *BTEC NC:* DD. *BTEC ND:* DMM. *OCR ND:* D *OCR NED:* M2 Interview required.

WW54 BA Physical & Dance Theatre
Duration: 3FT Hon
Entry Requirements: *GCE:* 260. *IB:* 28. *BTEC NC:* DD. *BTEC ND:* DMM. *OCR ND:* D *OCR NED:* M2 Interview required.

S18 THE UNIVERSITY OF SHEFFIELD
THE UNIVERSITY OF SHEFFIELD
9 NORTHUMBERLAND ROAD
SHEFFIELD S10 2TT
t: 0114 222 8030 f: 0114 222 8032
// www.sheffield.ac.uk

QW34 BA English and Theatre
Duration: 3FT Hon
Entry Requirements: *GCE:* AAB. *SQAH:* AAABB. *SQAAH:* AB. *IB:* 35. *BTEC ND:* DDD.

W440 BA Theatre and Performance
Duration: 3FT Hon
Entry Requirements: *GCE:* AAB. *SQAH:* AAABB. *SQAAH:* A. *IB:* 35. *BTEC ND:* DDD.

S51 ST HELENS COLLEGE
WATER STREET
ST HELENS
MERSEYSIDE WA10 1PP
t: 01744 733766 f: 01744 623400
e: enquiries@sthelens.ac.uk
// www.sthelens.ac.uk

W440 FdA Theatre and Performance
Duration: 2FT Fdg
Entry Requirements: *GCE:* 120. *IB:* 20. *BTEC NC:* PP. *BTEC ND:* PPP. Interview required.

S64 ST MARY'S UNIVERSITY COLLEGE, TWICKENHAM
WALDEGRAVE ROAD
STRAWBERRY HILL
MIDDLESEX TW1 4SX
t: 020 8240 4029 f: 020 8240 2361
e: admit@smuc.ac.uk
// www.smuc.ac.uk

W490 BA Drama and Applied Theatre
Duration: 3FT Hon
Entry Requirements: *GCE:* 260. *SQAH:* BBBC. *IB:* 28. *BTEC NC:* DD. *BTEC ND:* MMM. *OCR ND:* D *OCR NED:* M3 Interview required.

S72 STAFFORDSHIRE UNIVERSITY
COLLEGE ROAD
STOKE ON TRENT ST4 2DE
t: 01782 292753 f: 01782 292740
e: admissions@staffs.ac.uk
// www.staffs.ac.uk

WW84 BA Creative Writing and Theatre Studies
Duration: 3FT Hon
Entry Requirements: *GCE:* 180-220. *IB:* 24.

LW3K BA Ethics and Theatre Studies
Duration: 3FT Hon
Entry Requirements: *GCE:* 180-220. *IB:* 24.

VW24 BA International History and Theatre Studies
Duration: 3FT Hon
Entry Requirements: *GCE:* 180-220. *IB:* 24.

LW24 BA International Relations and Theatre Studies
Duration: 3FT Hon
Entry Requirements: *GCE:* 180-220. *IB:* 24.

WLK3 BA Theatre Studies and Crime Deviance and Society
Duration: 3FT Hon
Entry Requirements: *GCE:* 180-220. *IB:* 24.

WV41 BA Theatre Studies and Modern History
Duration: 3FT Hon
Entry Requirements: *GCE:* 180-220. *IB:* 24.

WW48 BA Theatre Studies and Scriptwriting
Duration: 3FT Hon
Entry Requirements: *GCE:* 180-220. *IB:* 24.

WLL3 BA Theatre Studies and Sociology
Duration: 3FT Hon
Entry Requirements: *GCE:* 180-220. *IB:* 24.

W441 BA Theatre Studies and Technical Stage Production
Duration: 3FT Hon
Entry Requirements: *GCE:* 180-220. *IB:* 24.

S85 UNIVERSITY OF SURREY
STAG HILL
GUILDFORD
SURREY GU2 7XH
t: +44(0)1483 689305 f: +44(0)1483 689388
e: ugteam@surrey.ac.uk
// www.surrey.ac.uk

W440 BA Theatre Studies
Duration: 3FT/4SW Hon
Entry Requirements: *GCE:* AAB-ABB. *SQAH:* BBBBC-BBBCC. *IB:* 34. *BTEC ND:* DDM.

T20 TEESSIDE UNIVERSITY
MIDDLESBROUGH TS1 3BA
t: 01642 218121 f: 01642 384201
e: registry@tees.ac.uk
// www.tees.ac.uk

W441 BA Performing Arts (Theatre)
Duration: 1FT Hon
Entry Requirements: Interview required.

W440 FdA Creating Theatre
Duration: 2FT Fdg
Entry Requirements: *GCE:* 80-100. *IB:* 24.

U20 UNIVERSITY OF ULSTER
COLERAINE
CO. LONDONDERRY
NORTHERN IRELAND BT52 1SA
t: 028 7032 4221 f: 028 7032 4908
e: online@ulster.ac.uk
// www.ulster.ac.uk

W440 BA Drama
Duration: 3FT Hon
Entry Requirements: *GCE:* BBC. *IB:* 24. *BTEC NC:* DM. *BTEC ND:* DMM. Interview required.

U65 UNIVERSITY OF THE ARTS LONDON
272 HIGH HOLBORN
LONDON WC1V 7EY
t: 020 7514 6000x6197 f: 020 7514 6198
e: c.anderson@arts.ac.uk
// www.arts.ac.uk

W440 BA Technical Effects for Performance
Duration: 3FT Hon
Entry Requirements: Interview required.

W20 THE UNIVERSITY OF WARWICK
COVENTRY CV4 8UW
t: 024 7652 3723 f: 024 7652 4649
e: ugadmissions@warwick.ac.uk
// www.warwick.ac.uk

R1W4 BA French with Theatre Studies
Duration: 4FT Hon
Entry Requirements: *GCE:* AAB. *SQAAH:* AA. *IB:* 36.

W440 BA Theatre and Performance Studies
Duration: 3FT Hon
Entry Requirements: *GCE:* AABb. *SQAAH:* AA. *IB:* 36. Interview required.

W67 WIGAN AND LEIGH COLLEGE
PO BOX 53
PARSONS WALK
WIGAN WN1 1RS
t: 01942 761605 f: 01942 760223
// www.wigan-leigh.ac.uk

W440 FdA Theatre Studies
Duration: 2FT Fdg
Entry Requirements: Interview required.

W75 UNIVERSITY OF WOLVERHAMPTON
ADMISSIONS UNIT
MX207, CAMP STREET
WOLVERHAMPTON
WEST MIDLANDS WV1 1AD
t: 01902 321000 f: 01902 321896
e: admissions@wlv.ac.uk
// www.wlv.ac.uk

W442 BA Performing Arts Management
Duration: 3FT Hon
Entry Requirements: *GCE:* 180.

W440 FdA Musical Theatre
Duration: 2FT Fdg
Entry Requirements: *GCE:* 100.

Y50 THE UNIVERSITY OF YORK
ADMISSIONS AND UK/EU STUDENT RECRUITMENT
UNIVERSITY OF YORK
HESLINGTON
YORK YO10 5DD
t: 01904 433539 f: 01904 433538
e: admissions@york.ac.uk
// www.york.ac.uk

W440 BA Writing, Directing and Performance
Duration: 3FT Hon
Entry Requirements: *GCE:* ABB. *SQAH:* AAABB. *IB:* 32. *BTEC ND:* DDM.

Y75 YORK ST JOHN UNIVERSITY
LORD MAYOR'S WALK
YORK YO31 7EX
t: 01904 876598 f: 01904 876940/876921
e: admissions@yorksj.ac.uk
// w3.yorksj.ac.uk

WW64 BA Film & Television Production (for international applicants only)
Duration: 4FT Hon
Entry Requirements: *GCE:* 240. *IB:* 24.

W401 BA Theatre (for international applicants only)
Duration: 4FT Hon
Entry Requirements: *Foundation:* Pass. *GCE:* 200-240. *IB:* 24.

WARDROBE AND MAKE UP

A66 THE ARTS UNIVERSITY COLLEGE AT BOURNEMOUTH (FORMERLY ARTS INSTITUTE AT BOURNEMOUTH)
WALLISDOWN
POOLE
DORSET BH12 5HH
t: 01202 363228 f: 01202 537729
e: admissions@aucb.ac.uk
// www.aucb.ac.uk

W451 BA Costume with Performance Design
Duration: 3FT Hon
Entry Requirements: *Foundation:* Pass. *GCE:* BBC. *IB:* 24. *BTEC NC:* DM. *BTEC ND:* DMM. *OCR ND:* M1 *OCR NED:* M1 Interview required. Portfolio required.

W453 BA Costume with Performance Design
Duration: 4FT Hon
Entry Requirements: *Foundation:* Pass. *GCE:* BBC. *IB:* 24. *BTEC NC:* DM. *BTEC ND:* DMM. *OCR ND:* M1 *OCR NED:* M1 Interview required. Portfolio required.

W45F BA Make Up For Media and Performance (Top-Up)
Duration: 1FT Hon
Entry Requirements: *Foundation:* Pass. *IB:* 24. *BTEC NC:* DM. *BTEC ND:* DMM. *OCR ND:* M1 *OCR NED:* M1 Interview required. Portfolio required.

W45G BA Make-Up for Media and Performance
Duration: 3FT Hon
Entry Requirements: Contact the institution for details.

B22 UNIVERSITY OF BEDFORDSHIRE
PARK SQUARE
LUTON
BEDS LU1 3JU
t: 0844 8482234 f: 01582 489323
e: admissions@beds.ac.uk
// www.beds.ac.uk

W901 FdA Specialist Make-up Design
Duration: 2FT Fdg
Entry Requirements: *GCE:* 80-120.

B25 BIRMINGHAM CITY UNIVERSITY
PERRY BARR
BIRMINGHAM B42 2SU
t: 0121 331 5595 f: 0121 331 7994
e: choices@bcu.ac.uk
// www.bcu.ac.uk

W2W4 BA Fashion Design with Design for Performance
Duration: 3FT Hon
Entry Requirements: *GCE:* 280. *IB:* 28. *BTEC ND:* DMM. Interview required. Portfolio required.

B41 BLACKPOOL AND THE FYLDE COLLEGE AN ASSOCIATE COLLEGE OF LANCASTER UNIVERSITY
ASHFIELD ROAD
BISPHAM
BLACKPOOL
LANCS FY2 0HB
t: 01253 504346 f: 01253 504198
e: admissions@blackpool.ac.uk
// www.blackpool.ac.uk

W455 BA Fashion and Costume for Performance
Duration: 3FT Hon
Entry Requirements: *GCE:* 120-360. *IB:* 24. *BTEC NC:* MP. *BTEC ND:* PPP. *OCR ND:* P2 *OCR NED:* P3 Interview required. Portfolio required.

B60 BRADFORD COLLEGE: AN ASSOCIATE COLLEGE OF LEEDS METROPOLITAN UNIVERSITY
GREAT HORTON ROAD
BRADFORD
WEST YORKSHIRE BD7 1AY
t: 01274 433008 f: 01274 433185
e: heregistry@bradfordcollege.ac.uk
// www.bradfordcollege.ac.uk/
university-centre

W453 BA Make-up Artistry & Special Make-up Effects
Duration: 1FT Hon
Entry Requirements: HND required.

W452 FdA Make-up Artistry & Special Make-up Effects
Duration: 2FT Fdg
Entry Requirements: *Foundation:* Pass. *GCE:* 60-80. *BTEC NC:* MM. *BTEC ND:* MMM. Interview required.

B94 BUCKINGHAMSHIRE NEW UNIVERSITY
QUEEN ALEXANDRA ROAD
HIGH WYCOMBE
BUCKINGHAMSHIRE HP11 2JZ
t: 0800 0565 660 f: 01494 605 023
e: admissions@bucks.ac.uk
// bucks.ac.uk

W232 FdA Costume for Stage and Screen
Duration: 2FT Fdg
Entry Requirements: *GCE:* 100-140. *IB:* 24. *BTEC NC:* MP. *BTEC ND:* PPP. *OCR ND:* P2 *OCR NED:* P3 Interview required.

C35 CENTRAL SCHOOL OF SPEECH AND DRAMA, UNIVERSITY OF LONDON
EMBASSY THEATRE
64 ETON AVENUE
LONDON NW3 3HY
t: 0207 722 8183 f: 0207 722 4132
e: enquiries@cssd.ac.uk
// www.cssd.ac.uk

W460 BA Theatre Practice: Costume Construction
Duration: 3FT Hon
Entry Requirements: *GCE:* BBC. Interview required. Portfolio required.

C71 CLEVELAND COLLEGE OF ART AND DESIGN
GREEN LANE
LINTHORPE
MIDDLESBROUGH TS5 7RJ
t: 01642 288888 f: 01642 288828
e: studentrecruitment@ccad.ac.uk
// www.ccad.ac.uk

W451 FdA Costume Construction for Stage and Screen
Duration: 2FT Fdg
Entry Requirements: *Foundation:* Pass. *GCE:* 100. Interview required. Portfolio required.

C99 UNIVERSITY OF CUMBRIA
FUSEHILL STREET
CARLISLE
CUMBRIA CA1 2HH
t: 01228 616234 f: 01228 616235
// www.cumbria.ac.uk

W451 FdA Costume
Duration: 2FT Fdg
Entry Requirements: *Foundation:* Pass. *GCE:* C-cccc. *SQAH:* CC. *SQAAH:* C. *IB:* 25. *BTEC NC:* MP. *BTEC ND:* PPP. Interview required. Portfolio required.

E58 EDINBURGH COLLEGE OF ART
EDINBURGH COLLEGE OF ART
LAURISTON PLACE
EDINBURGH EH3 9DF
t: 0131 221 6027 f: 0131 221 6039
e: enquiries@eca.ac.uk
// www.eca.ac.uk

W451 BA Performance Costume
Duration: 4FT Hon
Entry Requirements: *GCE:* 240. *SQAH:* BBBB. Foundation Course required. Interview required. Portfolio required. HND required.

G14 UNIVERSITY OF GLAMORGAN, CARDIFF AND PONTYPRIDD
ENQUIRIES AND ADMISSIONS UNIT
PONTYPRIDD CF37 1DL
t: 0800 716925 f: 01443 654050
e: enquiries@glam.ac.uk
// www.glam.ac.uk

W453 BA Costume Construction for Screen and Stage (Top-Up)
Duration: 1FT Hon
Entry Requirements: Contact the institution for details.

W451 FdA Costume Construction for Screen and Stage

Duration: 2FT Fdg

Entry Requirements: *Foundation:* Pass. *GCE:* BBC. *IB:* 24. *BTEC ND:* MMM. *OCR ND:* M1 *OCR NED:* P1 Interview required. Portfolio required.

G80 GRIMSBY INSTITUTE OF FURTHER AND HIGHER EDUCATION
NUNS CORNER
GRIMSBY
NE LINCOLNSHIRE DN34 5BQ
t: 0800 328 3631 f: 01472 315506/879924
e: headmissions@grimsby.ac.uk
// www.grimsby.ac.uk

W45A BA Historical and Performance Costume for Stage and Screen

Duration: 3FT Hon

Entry Requirements: Contact the institution for details.

W452 BA Special Effects Make-Up Design for TV, Film & Theatre

Duration: 3FT Hon

Entry Requirements: Contact the institution for details.

H36 UNIVERSITY OF HERTFORDSHIRE
UNIVERSITY ADMISSIONS SERVICE
COLLEGE LANE
HATFIELD
HERTS AL10 9AB
t: 01707 284800
// www.herts.ac.uk

W452 BA Character Creation and Technical Effects

Duration: 3FT Hon

Entry Requirements: *GCE:* 240. Interview required. Portfolio required.

W451 BA Special Effects

Duration: 3FT Hon

Entry Requirements: *GCE:* 240. Interview required. Portfolio required.

254W HND Specialist Make-up (Television and Film)

Duration: 2FT HND

Entry Requirements: Contact the institution for details.

H73 HULL COLLEGE
QUEEN'S GARDENS
HULL HU1 3DG
t: 01482 329943 f: 01482 598733
e: info@hull-college.ac.uk
// www.hull-college.ac.uk/HE

W451 FdA Costume Design and Interpretation

Duration: 2FT Fdg

Entry Requirements: *GCE:* 200. Foundation Course required. Interview required. Portfolio required.

L36 LEICESTER COLLEGE
FREEMEN'S PARK CAMPUS
AYLESTONE ROAD
LEICESTER LE2 7LW
t: 0116 224 2240 f: 0116 224 2190
e: msalotti@lec.ac.uk
// www.leicestercollege.ac.uk

W452 FdA Artistic Make Up and Special Effects

Duration: 2FT Fdg

Entry Requirements: *GCE:* 80. Interview required.

M10 THE MANCHESTER COLLEGE
OPENSHAW CAMPUS
ASHTON OLD ROAD
OPENSHAW
MANCHESTER M11 2WH
t: 0800 068 8585 f: 0161 920 4103
e: enquiries@themanchestercollege.ac.uk
// www.themanchestercollege.ac.uk

W453 FdA Design Media Make Up

Duration: 2FT Fdg

Entry Requirements: *GCE:* 120.

N41 NORTHBROOK COLLEGE SUSSEX
LITTLEHAMPTON ROAD
WORTHING
WEST SUSSEX BN12 6NU
t: 0845 155 6060 f: 01903 606073
e: enquiries@nbcol.ac.uk
// www.northbrook.ac.uk

W452 FdA Make Up & Hair for Theatre and Media

Duration: 2FT Fdg

Entry Requirements: *BTEC ND:* MMP. Interview required. Portfolio required.

W451 FdA Theatre Arts - Costume Design and Realisation for Theatre, Film and Television

Duration: 2FT Fdg

Entry Requirements: *BTEC ND:* MMP. Interview required. Portfolio required.

N91 NOTTINGHAM TRENT UNIVERSITY
DRYDEN BUILDINGG
BURTON STREET
NOTTINGHAM NG1 4BU
t: +44 (0) 115 848 4200 f: +44 (0) 115 848 8869
e: applications@ntu.ac.uk
// www.ntu.ac.uk/

W451 BA (Hons) Costume Design and Making
Duration: 3FT Hon

Entry Requirements: **GCE:** 240. **IB:** 28. **BTEC ND:** MMM. **OCR ND:** D Interview required. Portfolio required.

Q25 QUEEN MARGARET UNIVERSITY, EDINBURGH
QUEEN MARGARET UNIVERSITY DRIVE
EDINBURGH EH21 6UU
t: 0131474 0000 f: 0131 474 0001
e: admissions@qmu.ac.uk
// www.qmu.ac.uk

W451 BA Costume Design and Construction
Duration: 4FT Hon

Entry Requirements: **GCE:** 220. **IB:** 28. Interview required.

R51 ROSE BRUFORD COLLEGE
LAMORBEY PARK
BURNT OAK LANE
SIDCUP
KENT DA15 9DF
t: 0208 308 2600 f: 020 8308 0542
e: enquiries@bruford.ac.uk
// www.bruford.ac.uk

W451 BA Costume Production
Duration: 3FT Hon

Entry Requirements: **GCE:** 160-280.

S28 SOMERSET COLLEGE OF ARTS AND TECHNOLOGY
WELLINGTON ROAD
TAUNTON
SOMERSET TA1 5AX
t: 01823 366331 f: 01823 366418
e: enquiries@somerset.ac.uk
// www.somerset.ac.uk/student-area/
considering-a-degree.html

W45F BA Media Make-Up
Duration: 1FT Hon

Entry Requirements: Contact the institution for details.

W452 FdA Media Make-Up
Duration: 2FT Fdg

Entry Requirements: **GCE:** 160. **IB:** 24. **BTEC NC:** PP. **BTEC ND:** PPP. Interview required. Portfolio required.

S30 SOUTHAMPTON SOLENT UNIVERSITY
EAST PARK TERRACE
SOUTHAMPTON
HAMPSHIRE SO14 0RT
t: +44 (0) 23 8031 9039 f: + 44 (0)23 8022 2259
e: admissions@solent.ac.uk or ask@solent.ac.uk
// www.solent.ac.uk/

W453 BA Make Up & Hair Design for Music, Film & Photography
Duration: 3FT Hon

Entry Requirements: **Foundation:** Merit. **GCE:** 200. **SQAAH:** AC-DDD. **IB:** 24. **BTEC NC:** DM. **BTEC ND:** MMP. **OCR ND:** M1 **OCR NED:** P1 Interview required. Portfolio required.

S98 SWINDON COLLEGE
NORTH STAR AVENUE
SWINDON
WILTSHIRE SN2 1DY
t: 0800 731 2250 f: 01793 430503
e: studentservices@swindon-college.ac.uk
// www.swindon-college.ac.uk

W452 HND Production Arts (Media Make-Up)
Duration: 2FT HND

Entry Requirements: Interview required. Portfolio required.

U65 UNIVERSITY OF THE ARTS LONDON
272 HIGH HOLBORN
LONDON WC1V 7EY
t: 020 7514 6000x6197 f: 020 7514 6198
e: c.anderson@arts.ac.uk
// www.arts.ac.uk

W451 BA Costume for Performance
Duration: 3FT Hon

Entry Requirements: Foundation Course required. Interview required. Portfolio required.

W452 BA Make-up and Prosthetics for Performance
Duration: 3FT Hon

Entry Requirements: Interview required.

W65 WEST THAMES COLLEGE
LONDON ROAD
ISLEWORTH
MIDDLESEX TW7 4HS
t: 020 8326 2000 f: 020 8326 2001
e: info@west-thames.ac.uk
// www.west-thames.ac.uk/en/
higher-education/

W452 BA Specialist Makeup (top up)
Duration: 1FT Hon

Entry Requirements: Interview required. Portfolio required. HND required.

W451 FdA Costume in Practice
Duration: 2FT Fdg
Entry Requirements: *Foundation:* Pass. *GCE:* 40-120. *BTEC NC:*
MP. *BTEC ND:* MMP. Interview required. Portfolio required.

254W HND Specialist Makeup
Duration: 2FT HND
Entry Requirements: *Foundation:* Pass. *GCE:* 40-120. *BTEC NC:*
MP. *BTEC ND:* MMP. Interview required. Portfolio required.

W80 UNIVERSITY OF WORCESTER
HENWICK GROVE
WORCESTER WR2 6AJ
t: 01905 855111 f: 01905 855377
e: admissions@worc.ac.uk
// www.worcester.ac.uk

W453 BA Performance (Costume & Make-Up) (top-up)
Duration: 1FT Hon
Entry Requirements: Interview required. Portfolio required.

Y70 YORK COLLEGE
SIM BALK LANE
YORK YO23 2BB
t: 01904 770448 f: 01904 770499
e: CAU@yorkcollege.ac.uk
// www.yorkcollege.ac.uk

W452 FdA Media Make-up and Hair Design for Film, TV and Theatre
Duration: 2FT Fdg
Entry Requirements: Contact the institution for details.

Y80 YORKSHIRE COAST COLLEGE OF FURTHER AND HIGHER EDUCATION
LADY EDITH'S DRIVE
SCARBOROUGH
NORTH YORKSHIRE YO12 5RN
t: 01723 372105 f: 01723 501918
e: admissions@ycoastco.ac.uk
// www.yorkshirecoastcollege.ac.uk

W451 BA Costume
Duration: 3FT Hon
Entry Requirements: *GCE:* 160. Interview required. Portfolio required.

THEATRE AND STAGE DESIGN

A40 ABERYSTWYTH UNIVERSITY
WELCOME CENTRE, ABERYSTWYTH UNIVERSITY
PENGLAIS CAMPUS
ABERYSTWYTH
CEREDIGION SY23 3FB
t: 01970 622021 f: 01970 627410
e: ug-admissions@aber.ac.uk
// www.aber.ac.uk

W460 BA Scenography & Theatre Design
Duration: 3FT Hon
Entry Requirements: *GCE:* 300-320. *IB:* 32.

WQ43 BA Scenography & Theatre Design/English Literature
Duration: 3FT Hon
Entry Requirements: *GCE:* 300-320. *IB:* 32.

WW49 BA Scenography & Theatre Design/Performance Studies
Duration: 3FT Hon
Entry Requirements: *GCE:* 300-320. *IB:* 32.

A60 ANGLIA RUSKIN UNIVERSITY
BISHOP HALL LANE
CHELMSFORD
ESSEX CM1 1SQ
t: 0845 271 3333 f: 01245 251789
e: answers@anglia.ac.uk
// www.anglia.ac.uk

W461 BA Film, Television and Theatre Design
Duration: 3FT Hon
Entry Requirements: *GCE:* 260. *SQAH:* CCCC. *SQAAH:* BC. *IB:* 24.
Interview required. Portfolio required.

B25 BIRMINGHAM CITY UNIVERSITY
PERRY BARR
BIRMINGHAM B42 2SU
t: 0121 331 5595 f: 0121 331 7994
e: choices@bcu.ac.uk
// www.bcu.ac.uk

W460 BA Theatre, Performance and Event Design
Duration: 3FT Hon
Entry Requirements: *GCE:* 280. *IB:* 28. *BTEC ND:* DMM.
Interview required. Portfolio required.

G50 THE UNIVERSITY OF GLOUCESTERSHIRE
PARK CAMPUS
THE PARK
CHELTENHAM GL50 2RH
t: 01242 714503 f: 01242 714827
e: admissions@glos.ac.uk
// www.glos.ac.uk

QC38 BA/BSc English Language and Psychology
Duration: 3FT Hon
Entry Requirements: *GCE:* 280-300.

CQ83 BA/BSc English Literature and Psychology
Duration: 3FT Hon
Entry Requirements: *GCE:* 280-300.

H36 UNIVERSITY OF HERTFORDSHIRE
UNIVERSITY ADMISSIONS SERVICE
COLLEGE LANE
HATFIELD
HERTS AL10 9AB
t: 01707 284800
// www.herts.ac.uk

Q1C8 BSc English Language & Communication/Psychology
Duration: 3FT/4SW Hon
Entry Requirements: Contact the institution for details.

C8Q1 BSc Psychology/English Language & Communication
Duration: 3FT/4SW Hon
Entry Requirements: Contact the institution for details.

K12 KEELE UNIVERSITY
STAFFS ST5 5BG
t: 01782 734005 f: 01782 632343
e: undergraduate@keele.ac.uk
// www.keele.ac.uk

CTW7 BSc American Studies and Psychology
Duration: 3FT Hon
Entry Requirements: *GCE:* 300-320.

CQ83 BSc English and Psychology
Duration: 3FT Hon
Entry Requirements: *GCE:* 300-320.

K84 KINGSTON UNIVERSITY
STUDENT INFORMATION & ADVICE CENTRE
COOPER HOUSE
40-46 SURBITON ROAD
KINGSTON UPON THAMES KT1 2HX
t: 0844 8552177 f: 020 8547 7080
e: aps@kingston.ac.uk
// www.kingston.ac.uk

Q3C8 BA English Language & Communication with Psychology
Duration: 3FT Hon
Entry Requirements: *GCE:* 240-360. *IB:* 30.

QC38 BA English Language & Communications and Psychology
Duration: 3FT Hon
Entry Requirements: *GCE:* 240-360. *IB:* 30.

C8Q3 BA Psychology with English Language & Communication
Duration: 3FT Hon
Entry Requirements: *GCE:* 220-360. *IB:* 30.

C8R1 BSc Psychology with French
Duration: 3FT Hon
Entry Requirements: *GCE:* 220-360. *IB:* 24.

C8R4 BSc Psychology with Spanish
Duration: 3FT Hon
Entry Requirements: *GCE:* 220-360.

L14 LANCASTER UNIVERSITY
THE UNIVERSITY
LANCASTER
LANCASHIRE LA1 4YW
t: 01524 592029 f: 01524 846243
e: ugadmissions@lancaster.ac.uk
// www.lancs.ac.uk

CR81 BA French Studies and Psychology
Duration: 4SW Hon
Entry Requirements: *GCE:* AAB-ABB. *SQAH:* ABBBB-BBBBB. *SQAAH:* ABB.

CR82 BA German Studies and Psychology
Duration: 4SW Hon
Entry Requirements: *GCE:* AAB-ABB. *SQAH:* BBBBB. *SQAAH:* ABB.

CQ81 BA Linguistics and Psychology
Duration: 3FT Hon
Entry Requirements: *GCE:* AAB. *SQAH:* ABBBB. *SQAAH:* AAB. *IB:* 34.

CR84 BA Spanish Studies and Psychology
Duration: 4SW Hon
Entry Requirements: *GCE:* AAB-ABB. *SQAH:* BBBBB. *SQAAH:* ABB.

L46 LIVERPOOL HOPE UNIVERSITY
HOPE PARK
LIVERPOOL L16 9JD
t: 0151 291 3295 f: 0151 291 3444
e: admission@hope.ac.uk
// www.hope.ac.uk

CQ83 BA English Language and Psychology
Duration: 3FT Hon
Entry Requirements: *GCE:* 260-320. *IB:* 25.

M40 THE MANCHESTER METROPOLITAN UNIVERSITY
ADMISSIONS OFFICE
ALL SAINTS (GMS)
ALL SAINTS
MANCHESTER M15 6BH
t: 0161 247 2000
// www.mmu.ac.uk

QC38 BA English/Psychology
Duration: 3FT Hon
Entry Requirements: *GCE:* 240-280. *IB:* 28. *BTEC ND:* MMM.

CR89 BA/BSc Language(s)/Psychology
Duration: 3FT/4FT Hon
Entry Requirements: *GCE:* 300. *IB:* 30.

QC18 BA/BSc Linguistics/Psychology
Duration: 3FT Hon
Entry Requirements: *GCE:* 300. *IB:* 30.

N31 NEWHAM COLLEGE OF FURTHER EDUCATION
EAST HAM CAMPUS
HIGH STREET SOUTH
LONDON E6 6ER
t: 020 8257 4000 f: 020 8257 4325
e: admissions@newham.ac.uk
// www.newham.ac.uk

QC38 BA English and Psychology
Duration: 3FT Hon
Entry Requirements: Contact the institution for details.

Q3C8 BA English with Psychology
Duration: 3FT Hon
Entry Requirements: Contact the institution for details.

C8Q3 BSc Psychology with English
Duration: 3FT Hon
Entry Requirements: Contact the institution for details.

N36 NEWMAN UNIVERSITY COLLEGE, BIRMINGHAM
GENNERS LANE
BARTLEY GREEN
BIRMINGHAM B32 3NT
t: 0121 476 1181 f: 0121 476 1196
e: Admissions@newman.ac.uk
// www.newman.ac.uk

C8Q3 BA Psychology with English Literature
Duration: 3FT Hon
Entry Requirements: *Foundation:* Distinction. *GCE:* 280. *IB:* 25.
BTEC NC: MM. *BTEC ND:* DDM. *OCR ND:* M2 *OCR NED:* M2

CVQ3 BSc Psychology with English Language
Duration: 3FT Hon
Entry Requirements: *Foundation:* Distinction. *GCE:* 280. *IB:* 25.
BTEC NC: MM. *BTEC ND:* DDM. *OCR ND:* M2 *OCR NED:* M2

N38 UNIVERSITY OF NORTHAMPTON
PARK CAMPUS
BOUGHTON GREEN ROAD
NORTHAMPTON NN2 7AL
t: 0800 358 2232 f: 01604 722083
e: admissions@northampton.ac.uk
// www.northampton.ac.uk

Q3C8 BA English/Psychology
Duration: 3FT Hon
Entry Requirements: *GCE:* 260-280. *SQAH:* AAA-BBBB. *IB:* 24.
BTEC NC: DD. *BTEC ND:* DMM. *OCR ND:* D *OCR NED:* M2

R1C8 BA French/Psychology
Duration: 3FT Hon
Entry Requirements: *GCE:* 260-280. *SQAH:* AAA-BBBB. *IB:* 24.
BTEC NC: DD. *BTEC ND:* DMM. *OCR ND:* D *OCR NED:* M2

C8Q3 BA Psychology/English
Duration: 3FT Hon
Entry Requirements: *GCE:* 260-280. *SQAH:* AAA-BBBB. *IB:* 24.
BTEC NC: DD. *BTEC ND:* DMM. *OCR ND:* D *OCR NED:* M2

C8R1 BA Psychology/French
Duration: 3FT Hon
Entry Requirements: *GCE:* 260-280. *SQAH:* AAA-BBBB. *IB:* 24.
BTEC NC: DD. *BTEC ND:* DMM. *OCR ND:* D *OCR NED:* M2

O66 OXFORD BROOKES UNIVERSITY
ADMISSIONS OFFICE
HEADINGTON CAMPUS
GIPSY LANE
OXFORD OX3 0BP
t: 01865 483040 f: 01865 483983
e: admissions@brookes.ac.uk
// www.brookes.ac.uk

QC98 BA/BSc English Language and Communication/Psychology
Duration: 3FT Hon
Entry Requirements: Contact the institution for details.

QC38 BA/BSc English/Psychology
Duration: 3FT Hon
Entry Requirements: *GCE:* BBB.

RCC8 BA/BSc French Studies and Psychology
Duration: 4SW Hon
Entry Requirements: *GCE:* BBB.

P80 UNIVERSITY OF PORTSMOUTH
ACADEMIC REGISTRY
UNIVERSITY HOUSE
WINSTON CHURCHILL AVENUE
PORTSMOUTH PO1 2UP
t: 023 9284 8484 f: 023 9284 3082
e: admissions@port.ac.uk
// www.port.ac.uk

Q3C8 BA English with Psychology
Duration: 3FT Hon
Entry Requirements: *GCE:* 240-300. *IB:* 28. *BTEC NC:* DD. *BTEC ND:* DMM.

S18 THE UNIVERSITY OF SHEFFIELD
THE UNIVERSITY OF SHEFFIELD
9 NORTHUMBERLAND ROAD
SHEFFIELD S10 2TT
t: 0114 222 8030 f: 0114 222 8032
// www.sheffield.ac.uk

QC18 BSc Human Communication Sciences
Duration: 3FT Hon   CRB Check: Required
Entry Requirements: *GCE:* BBB. *SQAH:* AABBB. *IB:* 32. *BTEC ND:* DDM.

S36 UNIVERSITY OF ST ANDREWS
ST KATHARINE'S WEST
16 THE SCORES
ST ANDREWS
FIFE KY16 9AX
t: 01334 462150 f: 01334 463330
e: admissions@st-andrews.ac.uk
// www.st-andrews.ac.uk

CQ83 MA English-Psychology
Duration: 4FT Hon
Entry Requirements: *GCE:* AAA. *SQAH:* AAAB. *IB:* 36.

CR81 MA French-Psychology
Duration: 4FT Hon
Entry Requirements: *GCE:* AAA. *SQAH:* AAAB. *IB:* 36.

CR8C MA French-Psychology with Year Abroad
Duration: 5FT Hon
Entry Requirements: *GCE:* AAA. *SQAH:* AAAB. *IB:* 36.

CR82 MA German-Psychology
Duration: 4FT Hon
Entry Requirements: *GCE:* AAA. *SQAH:* AAAB. *IB:* 36.

CR8F MA German-Psychology with Year Abroad
Duration: 5FT Hon
Entry Requirements: *GCE:* AAA. *SQAH:* AAAB. *IB:* 36.

RC38 MA Italian and Psychology
Duration: 4FT Hon
Entry Requirements: *GCE:* AAA. *SQAH:* AAAB. *IB:* 36.

CR83 MA Italian-Psychology with Year Abroad
Duration: 5FT Hon
Entry Requirements: *GCE:* AAA. *SQAH:* AAAB. *IB:* 36.

S64 ST MARY'S UNIVERSITY COLLEGE, TWICKENHAM
WALDEGRAVE ROAD
STRAWBERRY HILL
MIDDLESEX TW1 4SX
t: 020 8240 4029 f: 020 8240 2361
e: admit@smuc.ac.uk
// www.smuc.ac.uk

QC38 BA/BSc English and Psychology
Duration: 3FT Hon
Entry Requirements: *GCE:* 240. *SQAH:* BBBC. *IB:* 28. *BTEC NC:* DM. *BTEC ND:* MMM. *OCR ND:* D *OCR NED:* M3 Interview required.

S72 STAFFORDSHIRE UNIVERSITY
COLLEGE ROAD
STOKE ON TRENT ST4 2DE
t: 01782 292753 f: 01782 292740
e: admissions@staffs.ac.uk
// www.staffs.ac.uk

CQ83 BSc English Literature and Psychology
Duration: 3FT Hon
Entry Requirements: *GCE:* 200-280. *IB:* 24. *BTEC NC:* DM.
BTEC ND: DMM.

S75 THE UNIVERSITY OF STIRLING
STIRLING FK9 4LA
t: 01786 467044 f: 01786 466800
e: admissions@stir.ac.uk
// www.stir.ac.uk

QC38 BA English Studies and Psychology
Duration: 4FT Hon
Entry Requirements: *GCE:* BBC. *SQAH:* BBBB. *SQAAH:* AAA-CCC.
IB: 32. *BTEC ND:* DDM.

CR89 BA Psychology and European Language
Duration: 4FT Hon
Entry Requirements: *GCE:* BBC. *SQAH:* BBBB. *SQAAH:* AAA-CCC.
IB: 32. *BTEC ND:* DDM.

S78 THE UNIVERSITY OF STRATHCLYDE
GLASGOW G1 1XQ
t: 0141 552 4400 f: 0141 552 0775
// www.strath.ac.uk

QC38 BA English and Psychology
Duration: 4FT Hon
Entry Requirements: *GCE:* ABB. *SQAH:* AAABB-AAAB. *IB:* 34.

RC18 BA French and Psychology
Duration: 5FT Hon
Entry Requirements: *GCE:* ABB. *SQAH:* AAABB-AAAB. *IB:* 34.

RC38 BA Italian and Psychology
Duration: 5FT Hon
Entry Requirements: *GCE:* ABB. *SQAH:* AAABB-AAAB. *IB:* 34.

CR84 BA Psychology and Spanish
Duration: 5FT Hon
Entry Requirements: *GCE:* ABB. *SQAH:* AAABB-AAAB. *IB:* 34.

S82 UNIVERSITY CAMPUS SUFFOLK (UCS)
WATERFRONT BUILDING
NEPTUNE QUAY
IPSWICH
SUFFOLK IP4 1QJ
t: 01473 338833 f: 01473 339900
e: info@ucs.ac.uk
// www.ucs.ac.uk

CQ83 BA English and Psychology
Duration: 3FT Hon
Entry Requirements: *GCE:* 280. *IB:* 28.

S84 UNIVERSITY OF SUNDERLAND
STUDENT HELPLINE
THE STUDENT GATEWAY
CHESTER ROAD
SUNDERLAND SR1 3SD
t: 0191 515 3000 f: 0191 515 3805
e: student.helpline@sunderland.ac.uk
// www.sunderland.ac.uk

Q1C8 BA English Language & Linguistics with Psychology
Duration: 3FT Hon
Entry Requirements: *GCE:* 260-360. *BTEC NC:* DM. *BTEC ND:*
MMM. *OCR ND:* D *OCR NED:* M3

Q3C8 BA English Studies with Psychology
Duration: 3FT Hon
Entry Requirements: *GCE:* 260-360. *IB:* 31. *BTEC NC:* DM.
BTEC ND: MMM. *OCR ND:* D *OCR NED:* M3

RC18 BA Modern Foreign Languages (French) and Psychology
Duration: 3FT Hon
Entry Requirements: *GCE:* 260-360. *IB:* 31. *BTEC NC:* DM.
BTEC ND: MMM. *OCR ND:* D *OCR NED:* M3

CR82 BA Modern Foreign Languages (German) and Psychology
Duration: 3FT Hon
Entry Requirements: *GCE:* 260-360. *IB:* 31. *BTEC NC:* DM.
BTEC ND: MMM. *OCR ND:* D *OCR NED:* M3

CR84 BA Modern Foreign Languages (Spanish) and Psychology
Duration: 3FT Hon
Entry Requirements: *GCE:* 260-360. *IB:* 31. *BTEC NC:* DM.
BTEC ND: MMM. *OCR ND:* D *OCR NED:* M3

CQ83 BA Psychology and Modern Foreign Language (English)
Duration: 3FT Hon
Entry Requirements: *GCE:* 260-360. *BTEC NC:* DM. *BTEC ND:*
MMM. *OCR ND:* D *OCR NED:* M3

C8R1 BA Psychology with Modern Foreign Languages (French)
Duration: 3FT Hon
Entry Requirements: *GCE:* 260-360. *BTEC NC:* DM. *BTEC ND:* MMM. *OCR ND:* D *OCR NED:* M3

C8R2 BA Psychology with Modern Foreign Languages (German)
Duration: 3FT Hon
Entry Requirements: *GCE:* 260-360. *BTEC NC:* DM. *BTEC ND:* MMM. *OCR ND:* D *OCR NED:* M3

C8R4 BA Psychology with Modern Foreign Languages (Spanish)
Duration: 3FT Hon
Entry Requirements: *GCE:* 260-360. *BTEC NC:* DM. *BTEC ND:* MMM. *OCR ND:* D *OCR NED:* M3

TC78 BA/BSc American Studies and Psychology
Duration: 3FT Hon
Entry Requirements: *GCE:* 260-360. *IB:* 31. *BTEC NC:* DM. *BTEC ND:* MMM. *OCR ND:* D *OCR NED:* M3

QC38 BA/BSc English Studies and Psychology
Duration: 3FT Hon
Entry Requirements: *GCE:* 260-360. *IB:* 31. *BTEC NC:* DM. *BTEC ND:* MMM. *OCR ND:* D *OCR NED:* M3

CQ81 BA/BSc Psychology and English Language/Linguistics
Duration: 3FT Hon
Entry Requirements: *GCE:* 260-360. *IB:* 32. *BTEC NC:* DM. *BTEC ND:* MMM. *OCR ND:* D *OCR NED:* M3

C8T7 BSc Psychology with American Studies
Duration: 3FT Hon
Entry Requirements: *GCE:* 260-360. *IB:* 32. *BTEC NC:* DM. *BTEC ND:* MMM. *OCR ND:* D *OCR NED:* M3

C8Q1 BSc Psychology with English Language/Linguistics
Duration: 3FT Hon
Entry Requirements: *GCE:* 260-360. *IB:* 32. *BTEC NC:* DM. *BTEC ND:* MMM. *OCR ND:* D *OCR NED:* M3

C8Q3 BSc Psychology with English Studies
Duration: 3FT Hon
Entry Requirements: *GCE:* 260-360. *IB:* 32. *BTEC NC:* DM. *BTEC ND:* MMM. *OCR ND:* D *OCR NED:* M3

C8QH BSc Psychology with Modern Foreign Languages (English)
Duration: 3FT Hon
Entry Requirements: *GCE:* 260-360. *BTEC NC:* DM. *BTEC ND:* MMM. *OCR ND:* D *OCR NED:* M3

S90 UNIVERSITY OF SUSSEX
UNDERGRADUATE ADMISSIONS
SUSSEX HOUSE
UNIVERSITY OF SUSSEX
BRIGHTON BN1 9RH
t: 01273 678416 f: 01273 678545
e: ug.applicants@sussex.ac.uk
// www.sussex.ac.uk

C8T7 BSc Psychology with American Studies
Duration: 4FT Hon
Entry Requirements: *GCE:* AAB. *SQAH:* AAABB. *IB:* 36. *BTEC NC:* DM. *BTEC ND:* DDD. *OCR ND:* D *OCR NED:* D1

U20 UNIVERSITY OF ULSTER
COLERAINE
CO. LONDONDERRY
NORTHERN IRELAND BT52 1SA
t: 028 7032 4221 f: 028 7032 4908
e: online@ulster.ac.uk
// www.ulster.ac.uk

Q3C8 BA English with Psychology
Duration: 3FT Hon
Entry Requirements: *GCE:* BCC. *IB:* 24. *BTEC NC:* DM. *BTEC ND:* DMM.

R9C8 BA European Studies with Psychology
Duration: 3FT Hon
Entry Requirements: *GCE:* CCC. *IB:* 24. *BTEC NC:* MM. *BTEC ND:* MMM. Interview required.

R1C8 BA French with Psychology
Duration: 3FT Hon
Entry Requirements: *GCE:* CCC. *IB:* 24. *BTEC NC:* MM. *BTEC ND:* MMM. Interview required.

R2C8 BA German with Psychology
Duration: 3FT Hon
Entry Requirements: *GCE:* CCC. *IB:* 24. *BTEC NC:* MM. *BTEC ND:* MMM. Interview required.

Q5C8 BA Irish with Psychology
Duration: 3FT Hon
Entry Requirements: *GCE:* BCD. *IB:* 24. Interview required.

R4C8 BA Spanish with Psychology
Duration: 4SW Hon
Entry Requirements: *GCE:* CCC. *IB:* 24. *BTEC NC:* MM. *BTEC ND:* MMM. Interview required.

W76 UNIVERSITY OF WINCHESTER
WINCHESTER
HANTS SO22 4NR
t: 01962 827234 f: 01962 827288
e: course.enquiries@winchester.ac.uk
// www.winchester.ac.uk

TC78 BA American Studies and Psychology
Duration: 3FT Hon
Entry Requirements: *Foundation:* Distinction. *GCE:* 260-300. *IB:* 25. *BTEC NC:* DD. *BTEC ND:* DMM. *OCR ND:* D *OCR NED:* M2

QC38 BA English Language Studies and Psychology
Duration: 3FT Hon
Entry Requirements: *Foundation:* Distinction. *GCE:* 260-300. *IB:* 25. *BTEC NC:* DD. *BTEC ND:* DMM. *OCR ND:* D *OCR NED:* M2

CQ83 BA English and Psychology
Duration: 3FT Hon
Entry Requirements: *Foundation:* Distinction. *GCE:* 260-300. *IB:* 25. *BTEC NC:* DD. *BTEC ND:* DMM. *OCR ND:* D *OCR NED:* M2

W80 UNIVERSITY OF WORCESTER
HENWICK GROVE
WORCESTER WR2 6AJ
t: 01905 855111 f: 01905 855377
e: admissions@worc.ac.uk
// www.worcester.ac.uk

QC38 BA/BSc English Literary Studies and Psychology
Duration: 3FT Hon
Entry Requirements: *GCE:* 240-300. *IB:* 24. *BTEC NC:* DD. *BTEC ND:* MMM. *OCR ND:* D *OCR NED:* M3

PSYCHOLOGY COMBINATIONS

A20 THE UNIVERSITY OF ABERDEEN
UNIVERSITY OFFICE
KING'S COLLEGE
ABERDEEN AB24 3FX
t: +44 (0) 1224 273504 f: +44 (0) 1224 272034
e: sras@abdn.ac.uk
// www.abdn.ac.uk/sras

CG84 BSc Behavioural Studies and Computing Science
Duration: 4FT Hon
Entry Requirements: *GCE:* BBB. *SQAH:* BBBB. *IB:* 30. *BTEC ND:* DDD.

CX81 BSc Behavioural Studies and Education (Primary)
Duration: 4FT Hon   CRB Check: Required
Entry Requirements: *GCE:* BBB. *SQAH:* BBBB. *IB:* 30. *BTEC ND:* DDD. Interview required.

GC48 BSc Computing Science and Psychology
Duration: 4FT Hon
Entry Requirements: *GCE:* 240. *SQAH:* BBBB. *SQAAH:* BCC. *IB:* 28. *BTEC ND:* MMM.

XC1V BSc Education (Primary) and Psychology
Duration: 4FT Hon   CRB Check: Required
Entry Requirements: *GCE:* BBB. *SQAH:* BBBB. *IB:* 30. *BTEC ND:* DDD. Interview required.

B170 BSc Neuroscience with Psychology
Duration: 4FT Hon
Entry Requirements: *GCE:* 240. *SQAH:* BBBB. *SQAAH:* BCC. *IB:* 28. *BTEC ND:* MMM.

LC68 MA Anthropology and Psychology
Duration: 4FT Hon
Entry Requirements: *GCE:* BBB. *SQAH:* BBBB. *IB:* 30. *BTEC ND:* MMM.

CX12 MA Behavioural Studies and Education (Primary)
Duration: 4FT Hon   CRB Check: Required
Entry Requirements: *GCE:* BBB. *SQAH:* BBBB. *IB:* 30. *BTEC ND:* MMM. Interview required.

CV15 MA Behavioural Studies and Philosophy
Duration: 4FT Hon
Entry Requirements: Contact the institution for details.

CL13 MA Behavioural Studies and Sociology
Duration: 4FT Hon
Entry Requirements: Contact the institution for details.

LC18 MA Economics and Psychology
Duration: 4FT Hon
Entry Requirements: *GCE:* BBB. *SQAH:* BBBB. *IB:* 30. *BTEC ND:* MMM.

XC18 MA Education (Primary) and Psychology
Duration: 4FT Hon   CRB Check: Required
Entry Requirements: *GCE:* BBB. *SQAH:* BBBB. *IB:* 30. *BTEC ND:* MMM. Interview required.

CM89 MA Legal Studies and Psychology
Duration: 4FT Hon
Entry Requirements: *GCE:* BBB. *SQAH:* BBBB. *IB:* 30. *BTEC ND:* MMM.

CN28 MA Management Studies and Psychology
Duration: 4FT Hon
Entry Requirements: *GCE:* BBB. *SQAH:* BBBB. *IB:* 30. *BTEC ND:* MMM.

VC58 MA Philosophy and Psychology
Duration: 4FT Hon
Entry Requirements: *GCE:* BBB. *SQAH:* BBBB. *IB:* 30. *BTEC ND:* MMM.

LC38 MA Psychology and Sociology
Duration: 4FT Hon
Entry Requirements: *GCE:* BBB. *SQAH:* BBBB. *IB:* 30. *BTEC ND:* MMM.

B1C8 MSci Neuroscience with Psychology with Industrial Placement
Duration: 5FT Hon
Entry Requirements: *GCE:* ABB. *SQAH:* AABB. *IB:* 32. *BTEC ND:* DDD.

A30 UNIVERSITY OF ABERTAY DUNDEE
BELL STREET
DUNDEE DD1 1HG
t: 01382 308080 f: 01382 308081
e: sro@abertay.ac.uk
// www.abertay.ac.uk

CL85 BA Mental Health and Counselling
Duration: 4FT Hon   CRB Check: Required
Entry Requirements: *GCE:* CC. *SQAH:* BBC. *IB:* 26. *BTEC NC:* DM. *BTEC ND:* MMP.

A40 ABERYSTWYTH UNIVERSITY
WELCOME CENTRE, ABERYSTWYTH UNIVERSITY
PENGLAIS CAMPUS
ABERYSTWYTH
CEREDIGION SY23 3FB
t: 01970 622021 f: 01970 627410
e: ug-admissions@aber.ac.uk
// www.aber.ac.uk

CV81 BA Psychology/History
Duration: 3FT Hon
Entry Requirements: *GCE:* 280. *IB:* 28.

CX83 BSc Psychology/Education
Duration: 3FT Hon
Entry Requirements: *GCE:* 280. *IB:* 28.

CG85 BSc Psychology/Information Technology
Duration: 3FT Hon
Entry Requirements: *GCE:* 280. *IB:* 28.

CM89 BScEcon Psychology/Criminology
Duration: 3FT Hon
Entry Requirements: *GCE:* 280. *IB:* 28.

CL81 BScEcon Psychology/Economics
Duration: 4FT Hon
Entry Requirements: *GCE:* 280. *IB:* 28.

CL82 BScEcon Psychology/International Politics
Duration: 3FT Hon
Entry Requirements: *GCE:* 280. *IB:* 28.

CN85 BScEcon Psychology/Marketing
Duration: 3FT Hon
Entry Requirements: *GCE:* 280. *IB:* 28.

CL8F BScEcon Psychology/Politics
Duration: 3FT Hon
Entry Requirements: *GCE:* 280. *IB:* 28.

A60 ANGLIA RUSKIN UNIVERSITY
BISHOP HALL LANE
CHELMSFORD
ESSEX CM1 1SQ
t: 0845 271 3333 f: 01245 251789
e: answers@anglia.ac.uk
// www.anglia.ac.uk

CL8H BSc Psychology and Criminology
Duration: 3FT Hon
Entry Requirements: *GCE:* 220. *SQAH:* AABC. *SQAAH:* AB. *IB:* 30.

A80 ASTON UNIVERSITY, BIRMINGHAM
ASTON TRIANGLE
BIRMINGHAM B4 7ET
t: 0121 204 4444 f: 0121 204 3696
e: admissions@aston.ac.uk
// www.aston.ac.uk

CN81 BSc Business and Psychology
Duration: 3FT/4SW Hon
Entry Requirements: *GCE:* 300-340. *SQAH:* ABBBB. *SQAAH:* ABB. *IB:* 33. *BTEC NC:* DM. *BTEC ND:* DDM. *OCR NED:* D2

B06 BANGOR UNIVERSITY
BANGOR UNIVERSITY
BANGOR
GWYNEDD LL57 2DG
t: 01248 388484 f: 01248 370451
e: admissions@bangor.ac.uk
// www.bangor.ac.uk

XC38 BA Astudiaethau Plentyndod/Seicoleg
Duration: 3FT Hon
Entry Requirements: *GCE:* 260-300. *IB:* 28.

CXV3 BA Childhood Studies/Psychology
Duration: 3FT Hon
Entry Requirements: *GCE:* 260-300. *IB:* 28.

MC98 BA Criminology & Criminal Justice and Psychology
Duration: 3FT Hon
Entry Requirements: *GCE:* 260-300. *IB:* 28.

CL84 BA Social Policy/Psychology
Duration: 3FT Hon
Entry Requirements: *GCE:* 260-300. *IB:* 28.

CL83 BA Sociology/Psychology
Duration: 3FT Hon
Entry Requirements: *GCE:* 260-300. *IB:* 28.

B20 BATH SPA UNIVERSITY
NEWTON PARK
NEWTON ST LOE
BATH BA2 9BN
t: 01225 875875 f: 01225 875444
e: enquiries@bathspa.ac.uk
// www.bathspa.ac.uk/clearing

NC18 BA/BSc Business & Management/Psychology
Duration: 3FT Hon
Entry Requirements: *GCE:* 220-300. *IB:* 24.

WC88 BA/BSc Creative Writing/Psychology
Duration: 3FT Hon
Entry Requirements: *GCE:* 240-280. *IB:* 24.

WC58 BA/BSc Dance/Psychology
Duration: 3FT Hon
Entry Requirements: *GCE:* 220-300. *IB:* 24. Interview required.

CW8L BA/BSc Drama Studies/Psychology
Duration: 3FT Hon
Entry Requirements: *GCE:* 220-300. *IB:* 24.

XC38 BA/BSc Education/Psychology
Duration: 3FT Hon   CRB Check: Required
Entry Requirements: *GCE:* 220-280. *IB:* 24.

WC68 BA/BSc Film & Screen Studies/Psychology
Duration: 3FT Hon
Entry Requirements: *GCE:* 220-300. *IB:* 24.

VC18 BA/BSc History/Psychology
Duration: 3FT Hon
Entry Requirements: *GCE:* 220-300. *IB:* 24.

PC98 BA/BSc Media Communications/Psychology
Duration: 3FT Hon
Entry Requirements: *GCE:* 220-300. *IB:* 24.

WC38 BA/BSc Music/Psychology
Duration: 3FT Hon
Entry Requirements: *GCE:* 220-300. *IB:* 24.

VC58 BA/BSc Philosophy & Ethics/Psychology
Duration: 3FT Hon
Entry Requirements: *GCE:* 220-300. *IB:* 24.

CV86 BA/BSc Psychology/Study of Religions
Duration: 3FT Hon
Entry Requirements: *GCE:* 220-300. *IB:* 24.

CC18 BSc Biology/Psychology
Duration: 3FT Hon
Entry Requirements: *GCE:* 220-300. *IB:* 24.

XC18 BSc Education/Psychology
Duration: 3FT Hon   CRB Check: Required
Entry Requirements: *GCE:* 220-300. *IB:* 24.

FC88 BSc Geography/Psychology
Duration: 3FT Hon
Entry Requirements: *GCE:* 220-300. *IB:* 24.

CL83 BSc Psychology/Sociology
Duration: 3FT Hon
Entry Requirements: *GCE:* 220-300. *IB:* 24.

B22 UNIVERSITY OF BEDFORDSHIRE
PARK SQUARE
LUTON
BEDS LU1 3JU
t: 0844 8482234 f: 01582 489323
e: admissions@beds.ac.uk
// www.beds.ac.uk

CL83 BSc Psychology and Criminal Behaviour
Duration: 3FT Hon
Entry Requirements: Contact the institution for details.

CM89 BSc Psychology and Criminology
Duration: 3FT Hon
Entry Requirements: *GCE:* 160-240. *SQAH:* BBC. *SQAAH:* BBC. *IB:* 30.

CB89 BSc Psychology, Counselling and Therapies
Duration: 3FT Hon
Entry Requirements: Contact the institution for details.

CL8H FdA Psychology and Crime
Duration: 2FT Fdg
Entry Requirements: Contact the institution for details.

B25 BIRMINGHAM CITY UNIVERSITY
PERRY BARR
BIRMINGHAM B42 2SU
t: 0121 331 5595 f: 0121 331 7994
e: choices@bcu.ac.uk
// www.bcu.ac.uk

MC98 BA Criminology and Psychology
Duration: 3FT Hon
Entry Requirements: *GCE:* 280. *IB:* 30. *BTEC ND:* DMM. *OCR NED:* M2

LC38 BA Sociology and Psychology
Duration: 3FT Hon
Entry Requirements: *GCE:* 260. *IB:* 25. *BTEC ND:* DMM. *OCR NED:* M2

B32 THE UNIVERSITY OF BIRMINGHAM
EDGBASTON
BIRMINGHAM B15 2TT
t: 0121 415 8900 f: 0121 414 7159
e: admissions@bham.ac.uk
// www.bham.ac.uk

F1C8 BSc Chemistry with Psychology
Duration: 3FT Hon
Entry Requirements: *GCE:* BBB. *SQAAH:* BBB-BBC.

G1C8 BSc Mathematics with Psychology
Duration: 3FT Hon
Entry Requirements: *GCE:* AAB-ABB. *SQAH:* AAAAB-AAABB.
SQAAH: AAB-ABB.

F1CV MSci Chemistry with Psychology
Duration: 4FT Hon
Entry Requirements: *GCE:* BBB. *SQAAH:* BBB-BBC.

B40 BLACKBURN COLLEGE
FEILDEN STREET
BLACKBURN BB2 1LH
t: 01254 292594 f: 01254 679647
e: he-admissions@blackburn.ac.uk
// www.blackburn.ac.uk

M1C8 LLB Law with Psychology
Duration: 3FT Hon
Entry Requirements: *GCE:* 220. *IB:* 26.

B44 UNIVERSITY OF BOLTON
DEANE ROAD
BOLTON BL3 5AB
t: 01204 903903 f: 01204 399074
e: enquiries@bolton.ac.uk
// www.bolton.ac.uk

CX83 BA/BSc Education Studies and Psychology
Duration: 3FT Hon
Entry Requirements: *GCE:* 260. Interview required.

MC18 BA/BSc Law and Psychology
Duration: 3FT Hon
Entry Requirements: *GCE:* 260. Interview required.

CB89 BSc Counselling & Psychology
Duration: 3FT Hon
Entry Requirements: *GCE:* 260. Interview required.

B54 BPP UNIVERSITY COLLEGE OF PROFESSIONAL STUDIES LIMITED
68-70 RED LION STREET
LONDON WC1R 4NY
t: +44 (0) 845 678 6868 f: +44 (0) 20 7404 1389
e: admissions@bpp.com
// www.bpplawschool.com/

NC18 BSc Business Studies with Psychology
Duration: 3FT Hon
Entry Requirements: Contact the institution for details.

1408 BSc Business Studies with Psychology (Accelerated)
Duration: 2FT Hon
Entry Requirements: Contact the institution for details.

MC18 LLB Law with Psychology
Duration: 3FT Hon
Entry Requirements: Contact the institution for details.

MCC8 LLB Law with Psychology (Accelerated)
Duration: 2FT Hon
Entry Requirements: Contact the institution for details.

B56 THE UNIVERSITY OF BRADFORD
RICHMOND ROAD
BRADFORD
WEST YORKSHIRE BD7 1DP
t: 0800 073 1225 f: 01274 235585
e: course-enquiries@bradford.ac.uk
// www.bradford.ac.uk

LC38 BA Sociology and Psychology
Duration: 3FT Hon
Entry Requirements: *GCE:* 180-220. *IB:* 24.

L1C8 BSc Economics with Psychology
Duration: 3FT Hon
Entry Requirements: *GCE:* 240-280. *IB:* 24.

CL83 BSc Psychology and Crime
Duration: 3FT Hon
Entry Requirements: *GCE:* 240. *IB:* 24.

C8B9 BSc Psychology with Counselling
Duration: 3FT Hon
Entry Requirements: *GCE:* 260. *IB:* 24.

B60 BRADFORD COLLEGE: AN ASSOCIATE COLLEGE OF LEEDS METROPOLITAN UNIVERSITY
GREAT HORTON ROAD
BRADFORD
WEST YORKSHIRE BD7 1AY
t: 01274 433008 f: 01274 433185
e: heregistry@bradfordcollege.ac.uk
// www.bradfordcollege.ac.uk/university-centre

CL85 BA Counselling and Psychology in Community Settings
Duration: 3FT Hon   CRB Check: Required
Entry Requirements: *GCE:* 100-140. *BTEC NC:* MP. *BTEC ND:* PPP. Interview required.

B78 UNIVERSITY OF BRISTOL
UNDERGRADUATE ADMISSIONS OFFICE
SENATE HOUSE
TYNDALL AVENUE
BRISTOL BS8 1TH
t: 0117 928 9000 f: 0117 925 1424
e: ug-admissions@bristol.ac.uk
// www.bristol.ac.uk

VC58 BSc Psychology and Philosophy
Duration: 3FT Hon
Entry Requirements: *GCE:* AAA-AAB. *SQAH:* AAAAA-AAABB. *IB:* 36.

B80 UNIVERSITY OF THE WEST OF ENGLAND, BRISTOL
FRENCHAY CAMPUS
COLDHARBOUR LANE
BRISTOL BS16 1QY
t: +44 (0)117 32 83333 f: +44 (0)117 32 82810
e: admissions@uwe.ac.uk
// www.uwe.ac.uk

M9C8 BSc (Hons) Criminology with Psychology
Duration: 3FT Hon
Entry Requirements: Contact the institution for details.

M1C8 BSc (Hons) Law with Psychology
Duration: 3FT Hon
Entry Requirements: Contact the institution for details.

C8M9 BSc (Hons) Psychology with Criminology
Duration: 3FT Hon
Entry Requirements: Contact the institution for details.

C8M1 BSc (Hons) Psychology with Law
Duration: 3FT Hon
Entry Requirements: Contact the institution for details.

C8L3 BSc (Hons) Psychology with Sociology
Duration: 3FT Hon
Entry Requirements: Contact the institution for details.

L3C8 BSc (Hons) Sociology with Psychology
Duration: 3FT Hon
Entry Requirements: Contact the institution for details.

B84 BRUNEL UNIVERSITY
UXBRIDGE
MIDDLESEX UB8 3PH
t: 01895 265265 f: 01895 269790
e: admissions@brunel.ac.uk
// www.brunel.ac.uk

LC68 BSc Psychology and Anthropology
Duration: 3FT Hon
Entry Requirements: *GCE:* BBB. *SQAAH:* BBB. *IB:* 32. *BTEC NC:* DM. *BTEC ND:* DDD.

LC6V BSc Psychology and Anthropology (4 year thin SW)
Duration: 4SW Hon
Entry Requirements: *GCE:* BBB. *SQAAH:* BBB. *IB:* 32. *BTEC NC:* DM. *BTEC ND:* DDD.

CL8H BSc Psychology and Sociology
Duration: 3FT Hon
Entry Requirements: *GCE:* BBB. *SQAAH:* BBB. *IB:* 32. *BTEC NC:* DM. *BTEC ND:* DDD.

CL83 BSc Psychology and Sociology (4 year Thin SW)
Duration: 4SW Hon
Entry Requirements: *GCE:* BBB. *SQAAH:* BBB. *IB:* 32. *BTEC NC:* DM. *BTEC ND:* DDD.

B90 THE UNIVERSITY OF BUCKINGHAM
YEOMANRY HOUSE
HUNTER STREET
BUCKINGHAM MK18 1EG
t: 01280 820313 f: 01280 822245
e: info@buckingham.ac.uk
// www.buckingham.ac.uk

N5C8 BSc Marketing with Psychology
Duration: 2FT Hon
Entry Requirements: *GCE:* 280. *IB:* 26. *BTEC NC:* DD. *BTEC ND:* MMM.

C8N1 BSc Psychology with Business & Management
Duration: 2FT Hon
Entry Requirements: *GCE:* 280. *IB:* 26. *BTEC NC:* DD. *BTEC ND:* MMM.

C8G5 BSc Psychology with Information Systems
Duration: 2FT Hon
Entry Requirements: *GCE:* 280. *IB:* 26. *BTEC NC:* DD. *BTEC ND:* MMM.

C8N5 BSc Psychology with Marketing
Duration: 2FT Hon
Entry Requirements: *GCE:* 280. *IB:* 26. *BTEC NC:* DD. *BTEC ND:* MMM.

C8P3 BSc Psychology with Media Communications
Duration: 2FT Hon
Entry Requirements: *GCE:* 280. *IB:* 26. *BTEC NC:* DD. *BTEC ND:* MMM.

B94 BUCKINGHAMSHIRE NEW UNIVERSITY
QUEEN ALEXANDRA ROAD
HIGH WYCOMBE
BUCKINGHAMSHIRE HP11 2JZ
t: 0800 0565 660 f: 01494 605 023
e: admissions@bucks.ac.uk
// bucks.ac.uk

CM89 BSc Psychology and Criminology
Duration: 3FT Hon
Entry Requirements: *GCE:* 240-280. *IB:* 25. *BTEC NC:* DD. *BTEC ND:* DMM. *OCR ND:* D *OCR NED:* M2

CL83 BSc Psychology and Sociology
Duration: 3FT Hon
Entry Requirements: *GCE:* 240-280. *IB:* 25. *BTEC NC:* DD. *BTEC ND:* DMM. *OCR ND:* D *OCR NED:* M2

C05 UNIVERSITY OF CAMBRIDGE
CAMBRIDGE ADMISSIONS OFFICE
FITZWILLIAM HOUSE
32 TRUMPINGTON STREET
CAMBRIDGE CB2 1QY
t: 01223 333 308 f: 01223 746 868
e: admissions@cam.ac.uk
// www.cam.ac.uk/admissions/
undergraduate/

L0C8 BA Politics, Psychology and Sociology
Duration: 3FT Hon
Entry Requirements: *GCE:* A*AA. *SQAAH:* AAA-AAB. Interview required.

C10 CANTERBURY CHRIST CHURCH UNIVERSITY
NORTH HOLMES ROAD
CANTERBURY
KENT CT1 1QU
t: 01227 782900 f: 01227 782888
e: admissions@canterbury.ac.uk
// www.canterbury.ac.uk

MC98 BA Applied Criminology and Psychology
Duration: 3FT Hon
Entry Requirements: *GCE:* 240. *IB:* 24.

M9C8 BA Applied Criminology with Psychology
Duration: 3FT Hon
Entry Requirements: *GCE:* 240. *IB:* 24.

M9CW BA Applied Criminology with Psychology 'International Only'
Duration: 4FT Hon
Entry Requirements: Interview required.

GC58 BA Business Computing and Psychology
Duration: 3FT Hon
Entry Requirements: *GCE:* 240. *IB:* 24.

G5C8 BA Business Computing with Psychology
Duration: 3FT Hon
Entry Requirements: *GCE:* 240. *IB:* 24.

GC4W BA Internet Computing and Psychology
Duration: 3FT Hon
Entry Requirements: *GCE:* 240. *IB:* 24.

G4CW BA Internet Computing with Psychology
Duration: 3FT Hon
Entry Requirements: *GCE:* 240. *IB:* 24.

LC28 BA Politics & Governance and Psychology
Duration: 3FT Hon
Entry Requirements: *GCE:* 240. *IB:* 24.

L2CV BA Politics & Governance with Psychology
Duration: 3FT Hon
Entry Requirements: *GCE:* 240. *IB:* 24.

C8G5 BA Psychology with Business Computing
Duration: 3FT Hon
Entry Requirements: *GCE:* 240. *IB:* 24.

C8GL BA Psychology with Internet Computing
Duration: 3FT Hon
Entry Requirements: *GCE:* 240. *IB:* 24.

C8LG BA Psychology with Politics & Governance
Duration: 3FT Hon
Entry Requirements: *GCE:* 240. *IB:* 24.

NC18 BA/BSc Business Studies and Psychology
Duration: 3FT Hon
Entry Requirements: *GCE:* 240. *IB:* 24.

GC4V BA/BSc Computing and Psychology
Duration: 3FT Hon
Entry Requirements: *GCE:* 240. *IB:* 24.

XC38 BA/BSc Early Childhood Studies and Psychology
Duration: 3FT Hon   CRB Check: Required
Entry Requirements: *GCE:* 240. *IB:* 24.

XC3V BA/BSc Education Studies and Psychology
Duration: 3FT Hon   CRB Check: Required
Entry Requirements: *GCE:* 240. *IB:* 24.

X3CW BA/BSc Education Studies with Psychology
Duration: 3FT Hon   CRB Check: Required
Entry Requirements: *GCE:* 240. *IB:* 24.

W6C8 BA/BSc Film, Radio & Television Studies with Psychology
Duration: 3FT Hon
Entry Requirements: *GCE:* 240. *IB:* 24.

CW81 BA/BSc Fine & Applied Arts and Psychology
Duration: 3FT Hon
Entry Requirements: *GCE:* 240. *IB:* 24.

W1C8 BA/BSc Fine & Applied Arts with Psychology
Duration: 3FT Hon
Entry Requirements: *GCE:* 240. *IB:* 24.

BC98 BA/BSc Health Studies and Psychology
Duration: 3FT Hon
Entry Requirements: *GCE:* 240. *IB:* 24.

NC58 BA/BSc Marketing and Psychology
Duration: 3FT Hon
Entry Requirements: *GCE:* 240. *IB:* 24.

CP83 BA/BSc Media and Communications and Psychology
Duration: 3FT Hon
Entry Requirements: *GCE:* 240. *IB:* 24.

P3C8 BA/BSc Media and Communications with Psychology
Duration: 3FT Hon
Entry Requirements: *GCE:* 240. *IB:* 24.

CW83 BA/BSc Music and Psychology
Duration: 3FT Hon
Entry Requirements: *GCE:* 240. *IB:* 24.

W3C8 BA/BSc Music with Psychology
Duration: 3FT Hon
Entry Requirements: *GCE:* 240. *IB:* 24.

CW86 BA/BSc Psychology and Film, Radio & Television Studies
Duration: 3FT Hon
Entry Requirements: *GCE:* 240. *IB:* 24.

C8MX BA/BSc Psychology with Applied Criminology
Duration: 3FT Hon
Entry Requirements: *GCE:* 240. *IB:* 24.

C8C1 BA/BSc Psychology with Biosciences
Duration: 3FT Hon
Entry Requirements: *GCE:* 240. *IB:* 24.

C8N1 BA/BSc Psychology with Business Studies
Duration: 3FT Hon
Entry Requirements: *GCE:* 240. *IB:* 24.

C8GK BA/BSc Psychology with Computing
Duration: 3FT Hon
Entry Requirements: *GCE:* 240. *IB:* 24.

C8X3 BA/BSc Psychology with Early Childhood Studies
Duration: 3FT Hon   CRB Check: Required
Entry Requirements: *GCE:* 240. *IB:* 24.

C8XJ BA/BSc Psychology with Education Studies
Duration: 3FT Hon   CRB Check: Required
Entry Requirements: *GCE:* 240. *IB:* 24.

C8W6 BA/BSc Psychology with Film, Radio & Television Studies
Duration: 3FT Hon
Entry Requirements: *GCE:* 240. *IB:* 24.

C8W1 BA/BSc Psychology with Fine & Applied Arts
Duration: 3FT Hon
Entry Requirements: *GCE:* 240. *IB:* 24.

C8FK BA/BSc Psychology with Forensic Investigation
Duration: 3FT Hon
Entry Requirements: *GCE:* 240. *IB:* 24.

C8V1 BA/BSc Psychology with History
Duration: 3FT Hon
Entry Requirements: *GCE:* 240. *IB:* 24.

C8N5 BA/BSc Psychology with Marketing
Duration: 3FT Hon
Entry Requirements: *GCE:* 240. *IB:* 24.

C8P3 BA/BSc Psychology with Media and Communications
Duration: 3FT Hon
Entry Requirements: *GCE:* 240. *IB:* 24.

C8W3 BA/BSc Psychology with Music
Duration: 3FT Hon
Entry Requirements: *GCE:* 240. *IB:* 24.

C8N8 BA/BSc Psychology with Tourism & Leisure Studies
Duration: 3FT Hon
Entry Requirements: *GCE:* 240. *IB:* 24.

N8C8 BA/BSc Tourism & Leisure Studies with Psychology
Duration: 3FT Hon
Entry Requirements: *GCE:* 240. *IB:* 24.

CC18 BSc Biosciences and Psychology
Duration: 3FT Hon
Entry Requirements: *GCE:* 240. *IB:* 24.

N1C8 BSc Business Studies with Psychology
Duration: 3FT Hon
Entry Requirements: *GCE:* 240. *IB:* 24.

B9C8 BSc Health Studies with Psychology
Duration: 3FT Hon
Entry Requirements: *GCE:* 240. *IB:* 24.

N5C8 BSc Marketing with Psychology
Duration: 3FT Hon
Entry Requirements: *GCE:* 240. *IB:* 24.

C8B9 BSc Psychology with Health Studies
Duration: 3FT Hon
Entry Requirements: *GCE:* 240. *IB:* 24.

C1C8 BSc/BA Biosciences with Psychology
Duration: 3FT Hon
Entry Requirements: *GCE:* 240. *IB:* 24.

G4CV BSc/BA Computing with Psychology
Duration: 3FT Hon
Entry Requirements: *GCE:* 240. *IB:* 24.

X3C8 BSc/BA Early Childhood Studies with Psychology
Duration: 3FT Hon CRB Check: Required
Entry Requirements: *GCE:* 240. *IB:* 24.

FC48 BSc/BA Forensic Investigation and Psychology
Duration: 3FT Hon
Entry Requirements: *GCE:* 240. *IB:* 24.

F4C8 BSc/BA Forensic Investigation with Psychology
Duration: 3FT Hon
Entry Requirements: *GCE:* 240. *IB:* 24.

CV81 BSc/BA History and Psychology
Duration: 3FT Hon
Entry Requirements: *GCE:* 240. *IB:* 24.

V1C8 BSc/BA History with Psychology
Duration: 3FT Hon
Entry Requirements: *GCE:* 240. *IB:* 24.

C20 UNIVERSITY OF WALES INSTITUTE, CARDIFF (UWIC)
ADMISSIONS UNIT
LLANDAFF CAMPUS
WESTERN AVENUE
CARDIFF CF5 2YB
t: 029 2041 6070 f: 029 2041 6286
e: admissions@uwic.ac.uk
// www.uwic.ac.uk

XC38 BA Educational Studies and Psychology
Duration: 3FT Hon CRB Check: Required
Entry Requirements: *GCE:* 260. *IB:* 24. *BTEC ND:* DMM. *OCR NED:* M2

C30 UNIVERSITY OF CENTRAL LANCASHIRE
PRESTON
LANCS PR1 2HE
t: 01772 201201 f: 01772 894954
e: uadmissions@uclan.ac.uk
// www.uclan.ac.uk

BC68 BA Deaf Studies and Psychology
Duration: 3FT Hon
Entry Requirements: *GCE:* 260-300. *SQAH:* ABBCC-BBBB. *SQAAH:* BBB-CCC. *IB:* 30. *BTEC ND:* DMM.

LC58 BA Health Studies and Psychology
Duration: 3FT Hon
Entry Requirements: *GCE:* 260-300. *SQAH:* ABBCC-BBBB. *SQAAH:* BBB-CCC. *IB:* 30. *BTEC ND:* DMM.

MC18 BA Law and Psychology
Duration: 3FT Hon
Entry Requirements: *GCE:* 260-300. *IB:* 28. *BTEC NC:* DM. *BTEC ND:* DMM. *OCR ND:* D *OCR NED:* M2

C8B1 BSc Forensic Psychology
Duration: 3FT Hon
Entry Requirements: *Foundation:* Distinction. *GCE:* 260-300. *SQAH:* BBBBC-BBCCC. *IB:* 30. *BTEC ND:* DMM. *OCR NED:* M2

CN81 BSc Psychology and Business
Duration: 3FT Hon
Entry Requirements: *GCE:* 260-300. *SQAH:* ABBCC-BBBB. *SQAAH:* BBB-CCC. *IB:* 30. *BTEC ND:* DMM.

CMV9 BSc Psychology and Criminology
Duration: 3FT Hon
Entry Requirements: *Foundation:* Distinction. *GCE:* 260-300. *SQAH:* BBBBC-BBCCC. *IB:* 30. *BTEC ND:* DMM. *OCR NED:* M2

CX83 BSc Psychology and Education Studies
Duration: 3FT Hon
Entry Requirements: *GCE:* 260-300. *IB:* 28. *BTEC NC:* DM. *BTEC ND:* DMM. *OCR ND:* D *OCR NED:* M2

CL85 BSc Psychology and Health Studies
Duration: 3FT Hon
Entry Requirements: *GCE:* 260-300. *SQAH:* ABBCC-BBBB. *SQAAH:* BBB-CCC. *IB:* 30. *BTEC ND:* DMM.

CM81 BSc Psychology and Law
Duration: 3FT Hon
Entry Requirements: **GCE:** 260-300. **SQAH:** ABBCC-BBBB. **SQAAH:** BBB-CCC. **IB:** 30. **BTEC ND:** DMM.

C55 UNIVERSITY OF CHESTER
PARKGATE ROAD
CHESTER CH1 4BJ
t: 01244 511000 f: 01244 511300
e: enquiries@chester.ac.uk
// www.chester.ac.uk

LC58 BA Counselling Skills and Psychology
Duration: 3FT Hon
Entry Requirements: **Foundation:** Pass. **GCE:** 260-300. **SQAH:** BBBB. **IB:** 28. **BTEC NC:** DM. **BTEC ND:** DMM.

WC48 BA Drama & Theatre Studies and Psychology
Duration: 3FT Hon
Entry Requirements: **Foundation:** Pass. **GCE:** 260-300. **SQAH:** BBBB. **IB:** 28. **BTEC NC:** DM. **BTEC ND:** DMM.

VC18 BA History and Psychology
Duration: 3FT Hon
Entry Requirements: **GCE:** 260-300. **SQAH:** BBBB. **IB:** 28. **BTEC NC:** DM. **BTEC ND:** MMP.

MC18 BA Law and Psychology
Duration: 3FT Hon
Entry Requirements: **Foundation:** Pass. **GCE:** 260-300. **SQAH:** BBBB. **IB:** 28. **BTEC NC:** DM. **BTEC ND:** DMM.

DC38 BSc Animal Behaviour and Psychology
Duration: 3FT Hon
Entry Requirements: **GCE:** 260-300. **SQAH:** BBBB. **IB:** 28. **BTEC NC:** DM. **BTEC ND:** MMM.

CC18 BSc Biology and Psychology
Duration: 3FT Hon
Entry Requirements: **GCE:** 260-300. **SQAH:** BBBB. **IB:** 28. **BTEC NC:** DM. **BTEC ND:** DDM.

MC98 BSc Criminology and Psychology
Duration: 3FT Hon
Entry Requirements: **Foundation:** Pass. **GCE:** 260-300. **SQAH:** BBBB. **IB:** 28. **BTEC NC:** DM. **BTEC ND:** DMM.

FC48 BSc Forensic Biology and Psychology
Duration: 3FT Hon
Entry Requirements: **GCE:** 260-300. **SQAH:** BBBB. **IB:** 24. **BTEC NC:** DM. **BTEC ND:** MMM.

FC88 BSc Geography and Psychology
Duration: 3FT Hon
Entry Requirements: **GCE:** 260-300. **SQAH:** BBBB. **IB:** 28. **BTEC NC:** DM. **BTEC ND:** MMM.

GC18 BSc Mathematics and Psychology
Duration: 3FT Hon
Entry Requirements: **GCE:** 260-300. **SQAH:** BBBB. **IB:** 24. **BTEC NC:** DM. **BTEC ND:** MPP.

FC78 BSc Natural Hazard Management and Psychology
Duration: 3FT Hon
Entry Requirements: **GCE:** 260-300. **SQAH:** BBBB. **IB:** 24. **BTEC NC:** DM. **BTEC ND:** MMM.

LC38 BSc Psychology and Sociology
Duration: 3FT Hon
Entry Requirements: **Foundation:** Pass. **GCE:** 260-300. **SQAH:** BBBB. **IB:** 28. **BTEC NC:** DM. **BTEC ND:** DMM.

C60 CITY UNIVERSITY
NORTHAMPTON SQUARE
LONDON EC1V 0HB
t: 020 7040 5060 f: 020 7040 8995
e: ugadmissions@city.ac.uk
// www.city.ac.uk

CP85 BA Journalism and Psychology (3 years or 4 year SW)
Duration: 3FT Hon
Entry Requirements: **GCE:** ABB. **IB:** 32.

LCH8 BSc Sociology/Psychology
Duration: 3FT Hon
Entry Requirements: **GCE:** BBB. **SQAH:** BBBBC. **IB:** 28. **BTEC ND:** DMM.

C78 CORNWALL COLLEGE
POOL
REDRUTH
CORNWALL TR15 3RD
t: 01209 616161 f: 01209 611612
e: he.admissions@cornwall.ac.uk
// www.cornwall.ac.uk

DC38 FdSc Animal Behaviour and Psychology
Duration: 2FT Fdg
Entry Requirements: **BTEC ND:** MMP. Interview required.

C85 COVENTRY UNIVERSITY
THE STUDENT CENTRE
COVENTRY UNIVERSITY
1 GULSON RD
COVENTRY CV1 2JH
t: 024 7615 2222 f: 024 7615 2223
e: studentenquiries@coventry.ac.uk
// www.coventry.ac.uk

CM89 BA Criminology and Psychology
Duration: 3FT/4SW Hon
Entry Requirements: **GCE:** BCC. **SQAH:** BCCCC. **IB:** 28. **BTEC ND:** DMM. **OCR NED:** M2

LC38 BA Sociology and Psychology
Duration: 3FT/4SW Hon
Entry Requirements: **GCE:** BCC. **SQAH:** BCCCC. **IB:** 28. **BTEC ND:** DMM. **OCR NED:** M2

CM82 BSc Psychology and Criminology
Duration: 3FT/4SW Hon
Entry Requirements: *GCE:* BBB. *SQAH:* BBBBC. *IB:* 28. *BTEC ND:*
DDM. *OCR NED:* M1

D26 DE MONTFORT UNIVERSITY
THE GATEWAY
LEICESTER LE1 9BH
t: 0116 255 1551 f: 0116 250 6204
e: enquiries@dmu.ac.uk
// www.dmu.ac.uk

L3C8 BA Applied Criminology with Psychology
Duration: 3FT Hon
Entry Requirements: *GCE:* 260. *IB:* 28. *BTEC NC:* DD. *BTEC ND:*
DMM. *OCR NED:* M2

X3C8 BA Education Studies with Psychology
Duration: 3FT Hon
Entry Requirements: *GCE:* 280. *IB:* 28. *BTEC ND:* DMM. *OCR NED:* M2

CN86 BA Human Resource Management and Psychology
Duration: 3FT/4SW Hon
Entry Requirements: *GCE:* 280. *IB:* 28. *BTEC ND:* DMM. *OCR NED:* M2 Interview required.

CM81 BA Law and Psychology
Duration: 3FT Hon
Entry Requirements: *GCE:* 280. *IB:* 28. *BTEC ND:* DMM. *OCR NED:* M2 Interview required.

CN85 BA Marketing and Psychology
Duration: 3FT/4SW Hon
Entry Requirements: *GCE:* 280. *IB:* 28. *BTEC ND:* DMM. *OCR NED:* M2 Interview required.

C8X3 BA Psychology with Education Studies
Duration: 3FT Hon
Entry Requirements: *GCE:* 280. *IB:* 28. *BTEC ND:* DMM. *OCR NED:* M2

CX83 BA/BSc Education Studies and Psychology
Duration: 3FT Hon
Entry Requirements: *GCE:* 280. *IB:* 28. *BTEC ND:* DMM. *OCR NED:* M2

F4C8 BSc Forensic Science with Psychology
Duration: 3FT Hon
Entry Requirements: *GCE:* 260. *IB:* 24.

C8L3 BSc Psychology with Applied Criminology
Duration: 3FT Hon
Entry Requirements: *GCE:* 280.

C8B9 BSc Psychology with Health Studies
Duration: 3FT Hon
Entry Requirements: *GCE:* 280.

D39 UNIVERSITY OF DERBY
KEDLESTON ROAD
DERBY DE22 1GB
t: 01332 591167 f: 01332 597724
e: askadmissions@derby.ac.uk
// www.derby.ac.uk

CW89 BA Creative Writing and Psychology
Duration: 3FT Hon
Entry Requirements: *Foundation:* Distinction. *GCE:* 260-300. *IB:* 28. *BTEC ND:* DMM. *OCR NED:* M2

MC28 BA Criminology and Psychology
Duration: 3FT Hon
Entry Requirements: *Foundation:* Distinction. *GCE:* 260-300. *IB:* 28. *BTEC ND:* DMM. *OCR NED:* M2

CM81 BA Law and Psychology
Duration: 3FT Hon
Entry Requirements: *Foundation:* Distinction. *GCE:* 260-300. *IB:* 28. *BTEC ND:* DMM. *OCR NED:* M2

PC38 BA Popular Culture & Media and Psychology
Duration: 3FT Hon
Entry Requirements: *Foundation:* Distinction. *GCE:* 260-300. *IB:* 28. *BTEC ND:* DMM. *OCR NED:* M2

CL8H BA Psychology and Sociology
Duration: 3FT Hon
Entry Requirements: *Foundation:* Distinction. *GCE:* 260-300. *IB:* 28. *BTEC ND:* DMM. *OCR NED:* M2

NC48 BA/BSc Accounting and Psychology
Duration: 3FT Hon
Entry Requirements: *Foundation:* Distinction. *GCE:* 260-300. *IB:* 28. *BTEC ND:* DMM. *OCR NED:* M2

KC1V BA/BSc Architectural Design and Psychology
Duration: 3FT Hon
Entry Requirements: *Foundation:* Distinction. *GCE:* 260-300. *IB:* 28. *BTEC ND:* DMM. *OCR NED:* M2

PC3V BA/BSc Broadcast Media and Psychology
Duration: 3FT Hon
Entry Requirements: *Foundation:* Distinction. *GCE:* 260-300. *IB:* 28. *BTEC ND:* DMM. *OCR NED:* M2

WC58 BA/BSc Dance & Movement Studies and Psychology
Duration: 3FT Hon
Entry Requirements: *Foundation:* Distinction. *GCE:* 260-300. *IB:* 28. *BTEC ND:* DMM. *OCR NED:* M2

VC18 BA/BSc History and Psychology
Duration: 3FT Hon
Entry Requirements: *Foundation:* Distinction. *GCE:* 260-300. *IB:* 28. *BTEC ND:* DMM. *OCR NED:* M2

LC28 BA/BSc International Relations & Global Development and Psychology
Duration: 3FT Hon
Entry Requirements: *Foundation:* Distinction. *GCE:* 260-300. *IB:* 28. *BTEC ND:* DMM. *OCR NED:* M2

WC88 BA/BSc Media Writing and Psychology
Duration: 3FT Hon
Entry Requirements: *Foundation:* Distinction. *GCE:* 260-300. *IB:* 28. *BTEC ND:* DMM. *OCR NED:* M2

CK82 BA/BSc Psychology and Property Development
Duration: 3FT Hon
Entry Requirements: *Foundation:* Distinction. *GCE:* 260-300. *IB:* 28. *BTEC ND:* DMM. *OCR NED:* M2

CW8K BA/BSc Psychology and Theatre Arts
Duration: 3FT Hon
Entry Requirements: *Foundation:* Distinction. *GCE:* 260-300. *IB:* 28. *BTEC ND:* DMM. *OCR NED:* M2

CC18 BSc Biology and Psychology
Duration: 3FT Hon
Entry Requirements: *Foundation:* Distinction. *GCE:* 260-300. *IB:* 28. *BTEC ND:* DMM. *OCR NED:* M2

CN8F BSc Business Management and Psychology
Duration: 3FT Hon
Entry Requirements: *Foundation:* Distinction. *GCE:* 260-300. *IB:* 28. *BTEC ND:* DMM. *OCR NED:* M2

FC68 BSc Geology and Psychology
Duration: 3FT Hon
Entry Requirements: *Foundation:* Distinction. *GCE:* 260-300. *IB:* 28. *BTEC ND:* DMM. *OCR NED:* M2

CN8P BSc Human Resource Management and Psychology
Duration: 3FT Hon
Entry Requirements: *Foundation:* Distinction. *GCE:* 260-300. *IB:* 28. *BTEC ND:* DMM. *OCR NED:* M2

CF87 BSc Psychology and Environmental Hazards
Duration: 3FT Hon
Entry Requirements: *Foundation:* Distinction. *GCE:* 260-300. *IB:* 28. *BTEC ND:* DMM. *OCR NED:* M2

CW83 BSc Psychology and Popular Music (Production)
Duration: 3FT Hon
Entry Requirements: *Foundation:* Distinction. *GCE:* 260-300. *IB:* 28. *BTEC ND:* DMM. *OCR NED:* M2

LC98 BSc Third World Development and Psychology
Duration: 3FT Hon
Entry Requirements: *Foundation:* Distinction. *GCE:* 260-300. *IB:* 28. *BTEC ND:* DMM. *OCR NED:* M2

CC38 BSc Zoology and Psychology
Duration: 3FT Hon
Entry Requirements: *Foundation:* Distinction. *GCE:* 260-300. *IB:* 28. *BTEC ND:* DMM. *OCR NED:* M2

D65 UNIVERSITY OF DUNDEE
NETHERGATE
DUNDEE DD1 4HN
t: 01382 383838 f: 01382 388150
e: contactus@dundee.ac.uk
// www.dundee.ac.uk/admissions/undergraduate/

CG81 BSc Mathematics and Psychology
Duration: 4FT Hon
Entry Requirements: *GCE:* BCC. *SQAH:* ABBB. *IB:* 30. *BTEC ND:* DMM.

CG84 BSc Psychology and Applied Computing
Duration: 4FT Hon
Entry Requirements: *GCE:* BCC. *SQAH:* ABBB. *IB:* 30. *BTEC ND:* DMM.

LNC0 MA Business Economics with Marketing and Psychology
Duration: 4FT Hon
Entry Requirements: *GCE:* BCC. *SQAH:* ABBB. *IB:* 30. *BTEC ND:* DMM.

CL87 MA Geography and Psychology
Duration: 4FT Hon
Entry Requirements: *GCE:* BCC. *SQAH:* ABBB. *IB:* 30. *BTEC ND:* DMM.

CV81 MA History and Psychology
Duration: 4FT Hon
Entry Requirements: *GCE:* BCC. *SQAH:* ABBB. *IB:* 30. *BTEC ND:* DMM.

CV85 MA Philosophy and Psychology
Duration: 4FT Hon
Entry Requirements: *GCE:* BCC. *SQAH:* ABBB. *IB:* 30. *BTEC ND:* DMM.

CL82 MA Politics and Psychology
Duration: 4FT Hon
Entry Requirements: *GCE:* BCC. *SQAH:* ABBB. *IB:* 30. *BTEC ND:* DMM.

T20 TEESSIDE UNIVERSITY
MIDDLESBROUGH TS1 3BA
t: 01642 218121 f: 01642 384201
e: registry@tees.ac.uk
// www.tees.ac.uk

W590 BA Dance
Duration: 3FT Hon   CRB Check: Required
Entry Requirements: *GCE:* 280. *IB:* 25. Interview required.

T85 TRURO AND PENWITH COLLEGE (FORMERLY TRURO COLLEGE)
TRURO COLLEGE
COLLEGE ROAD
TRURO
CORNWALL TR1 3XX
t: 01872 267122 f: 01872 267526
e: heinfo@trurocollege.ac.uk
// www.trurocollege.ac.uk

W500 FdA Dance
Duration: 2FT Fdg
Entry Requirements: *GCE:* 60. *IB:* 24. *BTEC NC:* PP. *BTEC ND:* PPP. Interview required.

U20 UNIVERSITY OF ULSTER
COLERAINE
CO. LONDONDERRY
NORTHERN IRELAND BT52 1SA
t: 028 7032 4221 f: 028 7032 4908
e: online@ulster.ac.uk
// www.ulster.ac.uk

W500 BA Dance
Duration: 3FT Hon
Entry Requirements: *GCE:* CCD. *IB:* 24. *BTEC NC:* MM. *BTEC ND:* MMM. Interview required.

W5Q5 BA Dance with Irish
Duration: 3FT Hon
Entry Requirements: *GCE:* 220. *IB:* 24. *BTEC NC:* MM. *BTEC ND:* MMM. Interview required.

W05 THE UNIVERSITY OF WEST LONDON
WALPOLE HOUSE
BOND STREET
EALING
LONDON W5 5AA
t: 0800 036 8888 f: 020 8566 1353
e: learning.advice@uwl.ac.uk
// www.uwl.ac.uk

W501 BA Dance (top-up)
Duration: 1FT Hon
Entry Requirements: Interview required. HND required.

WW45 BA Musical Theatre
Duration: 3FT Hon
Entry Requirements: *GCE:* 200. *IB:* 28. Interview required.

W541 BA (Hons) Ballet Education (Intensive)
Duration: 2FT Hon
Entry Requirements: *GCE:* 250. *IB:* 28. Interview required.

W500 FdA Dance
Duration: 2FT Fdg
Entry Requirements: *GCE:* 100. *IB:* 24. Interview required.

W08 WAKEFIELD COLLEGE
MARGARET STREET
WAKEFIELD
WEST YORKSHIRE WF1 2DH
t: 01924 789111 f: 01924 789281
e: courseinfo@wakefield.ac.uk
// www.wakefield.ac.uk

055W HND Performing Arts (Performance) Dance Pathway
Duration: 2FT HND
Entry Requirements: *GCE:* 240. Interview required.

W65 WEST THAMES COLLEGE
LONDON ROAD
ISLEWORTH
MIDDLESEX TW7 4HS
t: 020 8326 2000 f: 020 8326 2001
e: info@west-thames.ac.uk
// www.west-thames.ac.uk/en/ higher-education/

005W HND Dance
Duration: 2FT HND
Entry Requirements: *GCE:* 40-120. *BTEC NC:* MM. *BTEC ND:* MMP. Interview required.

W75 UNIVERSITY OF WOLVERHAMPTON
ADMISSIONS UNIT
MX207, CAMP STREET
WOLVERHAMPTON
WEST MIDLANDS WV1 1AD
t: 01902 321000 f: 01902 321896
e: admissions@wlv.ac.uk
// www.wlv.ac.uk

W500 BA Dance
Duration: 3FT Hon
Entry Requirements: *GCE:* 160-220. Interview required.

W76 UNIVERSITY OF WINCHESTER
WINCHESTER
HANTS SO22 4NR
t: 01962 827234 f: 01962 827288
e: course.enquiries@winchester.ac.uk
// www.winchester.ac.uk

VW4M BA Archaeology and Choreography & Dance
Duration: 3FT Hon
Entry Requirements: *Foundation:* Distinction. *GCE:* 260-300. *IB:* 25. *BTEC NC:* DD. *BTEC ND:* DMM. *OCR ND:* D *OCR NED:* M2

NW15 BA Business Management and Choreography & Dance Studies
Duration: 3FT Hon
Entry Requirements: *Foundation:* Distinction. *GCE:* 260-300. *IB:* 25. *BTEC NC:* DD. *BTEC ND:* DMM. *OCR ND:* D *OCR NED:* M2

LW55 BA Childhood,Youth & Community Studies and Choreography & Dance
Duration: 3FT Hon
Entry Requirements: *Foundation:* Distinction. *GCE:* 260-300. *IB:* 25. *BTEC NC:* DD. *BTEC ND:* DMM. *OCR ND:* D *OCR NED:* M2

W500 BA Choreography & Dance
Duration: 3FT Hon
Entry Requirements: *Foundation:* Distinction. *GCE:* 260-300. *IB:* 26. *BTEC NC:* DD. *BTEC ND:* DDM. *OCR ND:* D

WW58 BA Choreography & Dance and Creative Writing
Duration: 3FT Hon
Entry Requirements: *Foundation:* Distinction. *GCE:* 260-300. *IB:* 25. *BTEC NC:* DD. *BTEC ND:* DMM. *OCR ND:* D *OCR NED:* M2

WLN3 BA Choreography & Dance and Criminology
Duration: 3FT Hon
Entry Requirements: *Foundation:* Distinction. *GCE:* 260-300. *IB:* 25. *BTEC NC:* DD. *BTEC ND:* DMM. *OCR ND:* D *OCR NED:* M2

WXM3 BA Choreography & Dance and Education Studies
Duration: 3FT Hon
Entry Requirements: *Foundation:* Distinction. *GCE:* 260-300. *IB:* 25. *BTEC NC:* DD. *BTEC ND:* DMM. *OCR ND:* D *OCR NED:* M2

WX53 BA Choreography & Dance and Education Studies (Modern Liberal Arts)
Duration: 3FT Hon
Entry Requirements: *Foundation:* Distinction. *GCE:* 260-300. *IB:* 25. *BTEC NC:* DD. *BTEC ND:* DMM. *OCR ND:* D *OCR NED:* M2

WQ53 BA Choreography & Dance and English
Duration: 3FT Hon
Entry Requirements: *Foundation:* Distinction. *GCE:* 260-300. *IB:* 25. *BTEC NC:* DD. *BTEC ND:* DMM. *OCR ND:* D *OCR NED:* M2

WQ5H BA Choreography & Dance and English Language Studies
Duration: 3FT Hon
Entry Requirements: *Foundation:* Distinction. *GCE:* 260-300. *IB:* 25. *BTEC NC:* DD. *BTEC ND:* DMM. *OCR ND:* D *OCR NED:* M2

WN58 BA Choreography & Dance and Event Management
Duration: 3FT Hon
Entry Requirements: *Foundation:* Distinction. *GCE:* 260-300. *IB:* 25. *BTEC NC:* DD. *BTEC ND:* DMM. *OCR ND:* D *OCR NED:* M2

WW56 BA Choreography & Dance and Film & Cinema Technologies
Duration: 3FT Hon
Entry Requirements: *Foundation:* Distinction. *GCE:* 260-300. *IB:* 25. *BTEC NC:* DD. *BTEC ND:* DMM. *OCR ND:* D *OCR NED:* M2

WL5N BA Choreography & Dance and Health, Community & Social Care Studies
Duration: 3FT Hon   CRB Check: Required
Entry Requirements: Contact the institution for details.

WV51 BA Choreography & Dance and History
Duration: 3FT Hon
Entry Requirements: *Foundation:* Distinction. *GCE:* 260-300. *IB:* 25. *BTEC NC:* DD. *BTEC ND:* DMM. *OCR ND:* D *OCR NED:* M2

WW59 BA Choreography & Dance and Modern Liberal Arts
Duration: 3FT Hon
Entry Requirements: *Foundation:* Distinction. *GCE:* 260-300. *IB:* 25. *BTEC NC:* DD. *BTEC ND:* DMM. *OCR ND:* D *OCR NED:* M2

CW85 BA Choreography & Dance and Psychology
Duration: 3FT Hon
Entry Requirements: *Foundation:* Distinction. *GCE:* 260-300. *IB:* 25. *BTEC NC:* DD. *BTEC ND:* DMM. *OCR ND:* D *OCR NED:* M2

WL5H BA Choreography & Dance and Sociology
Duration: 3FT Hon
Entry Requirements: *Foundation:* Distinction. *GCE:* 260-300. *IB:* 25. *BTEC NC:* DD. *BTEC ND:* DMM. *OCR ND:* D *OCR NED:* M2

WNM8 BA Choreography & Dance and Sports Management
Duration: 3FT Hon
Entry Requirements: *GCE:* 260-300. *IB:* 24.

WL53 BA Choreography & Dance and Sports Studies
Duration: 3FT Hon
Entry Requirements: *Foundation:* Merit. *GCE:* 260-300. *IB:* 24. *BTEC NC:* DM. *BTEC ND:* MMP.

XWH5 BA Education Studies (Early Childhood) and Choreography & Dance Studies
Duration: 3FT Hon
Entry Requirements: *Foundation:* Distinction. *GCE:* 260-300. *IB:* 25. *BTEC NC:* DD. *BTEC ND:* DMM. *OCR ND:* D *OCR NED:* M2

LW25 BA Politics & Global Studies and Choreography & Dance
Duration: 3FT Hon
Entry Requirements: *Foundation:* Distinction. *GCE:* 260-300. *IB:* 25. *BTEC NC:* DD. *BTEC ND:* DMM. *OCR ND:* D *OCR NED:* M2

W80 UNIVERSITY OF WORCESTER
HENWICK GROVE
WORCESTER WR2 6AJ
t: 01905 855111 f: 01905 855377
e: admissions@worc.ac.uk
// www.worcester.ac.uk

005W HND Dance
Duration: 2FT HND
Entry Requirements: *GCE:* 60. *IB:* 24. *BTEC NC:* PP. *BTEC ND:* PPP.

W81 WORCESTER COLLEGE OF TECHNOLOGY
DEANSWAY
WORCESTER WR1 2JF
t: 01905 725555 f: 01905 28906
// www.wortech.ac.uk

54WW HNC Performing Arts
Duration: 1FT HNC
Entry Requirements: Contact the institution for details.

Y75 YORK ST JOHN UNIVERSITY
LORD MAYOR'S WALK
YORK YO31 7EX
t: 01904 876598 f: 01904 876940/876921
e: admissions@yorksj.ac.uk
// w3.yorksj.ac.uk

W500 BA Dance
Duration: 3FT Hon
Entry Requirements: *Foundation:* Pass. *GCE:* 200-240. *IB:* 24. Interview required.

W501 BA Dance (for international applicants only)
Duration: 4FT Hon
Entry Requirements: *Foundation:* Pass. *GCE:* 200-240. *IB:* 24. Interview required.

IMAGINATIVE WRITING AND SCRIPTWRITING

A40 ABERYSTWYTH UNIVERSITY
WELCOME CENTRE, ABERYSTWYTH UNIVERSITY
PENGLAIS CAMPUS
ABERYSTWYTH
CEREDIGION SY23 3FB
t: 01970 622021 f: 01970 627410
e: ug-admissions@aber.ac.uk
// www.aber.ac.uk

QW38 BA English Literature and Creative Writing
Duration: 3FT Hon
Entry Requirements: *GCE:* 300. *IB:* 28.

A60 ANGLIA RUSKIN UNIVERSITY
BISHOP HALL LANE
CHELMSFORD
ESSEX CM1 1SQ
t: 0845 271 3333 f: 01245 251789
e: answers@anglia.ac.uk
// www.anglia.ac.uk

WQ83 BA Writing and English Literature
Duration: 3FT Hon
Entry Requirements: *GCE:* 280. *SQAH:* BBBC. *SQAAH:* BC. *IB:* 28.

B06 BANGOR UNIVERSITY
BANGOR UNIVERSITY
BANGOR
GWYNEDD LL57 2DG
t: 01248 388484 f: 01248 370451
e: admissions@bangor.ac.uk
// www.bangor.ac.uk

W890 BA Creative and Professional Writing
Duration: 3FT Hon
Entry Requirements: Portfolio required.

Q3WL BA English Language with Creative Writing
Duration: 3FT Hon
Entry Requirements: *GCE:* 240-300. *IB:* 28.

Q3W4 BA English with Creative Writing
Duration: 3FT Hon
Entry Requirements: *GCE:* 240-300. *IB:* 28.

R1W8 BA French with Creative Writing
Duration: 4FT Hon
Entry Requirements: *GCE:* 240-260. *IB:* 28.

R2W8 BA German with Creative Writing
Duration: 4FT Hon
Entry Requirements: *GCE:* 240-260. *IB:* 28.

R4W8 BA Spanish with Creative Writing
Duration: 4FT Hon
Entry Requirements: *GCE:* 240-260. *IB:* 28.

B20 BATH SPA UNIVERSITY
NEWTON PARK
NEWTON ST LOE
BATH BA2 9BN
t: 01225 875875 f: 01225 875444
e: enquiries@bathspa.ac.uk
// www.bathspa.ac.uk/clearing

WW19 BA Art/Creative Writing
Duration: 3FT Hon
Entry Requirements: *Foundation:* Pass. *GCE:* 220-300. *IB:* 24.
Interview required.

NW19 BA Business & Management/Creative Writing
Duration: 3FT Hon
Entry Requirements: *GCE:* 220-300. *IB:* 24.

WW28 BA Ceramics/Creative Writing
Duration: 3FT Hon
Entry Requirements: *Foundation:* Pass. *GCE:* 220-300. *IB:* 24.
Interview required.

W800 BA Creative Writing
Duration: 3FT Hon
Entry Requirements: *GCE:* 220-300. *IB:* 24.

WX83 BA Creative Writing/Education
Duration: 3FT Hon   CRB Check: Required
Entry Requirements: *GCE:* 220-300. *IB:* 24.

WQ93 BA Creative Writing/English Literature
Duration: 3FT Hon
Entry Requirements: *GCE:* 220-300. *IB:* 24.

WW86 BA Creative Writing/Film & Screen Studies
Duration: 3FT Hon
Entry Requirements: *GCE:* 220-300. *IB:* 24.

WV91 BA Creative Writing/History
Duration: 3FT Hon
Entry Requirements: *GCE:* 220-300. *IB:* 24.

WP84 BA Creative Writing/Publishing
Duration: 3FT Hon
Entry Requirements: Contact the institution for details.

WV96 BA Creative Writing/Study of Religions
Duration: 3FT Hon
Entry Requirements: *GCE:* 220-300. *IB:* 24.

WWX2 BA Creative Writing/Textile Design Studies
Duration: 3FT Hon
Entry Requirements: *Foundation:* Pass. *GCE:* 220-300. *IB:* 24.
Interview required.

WW82 BA Creative Writing/Visual Design
Duration: 3FT Hon
Entry Requirements: *Foundation:* Pass. *GCE:* 220-300. *IB:* 24.
Interview required.

XW18 BA Education/Creative Writing
Duration: 3FT Hon   CRB Check: Required
Entry Requirements: *GCE:* 220-300. *IB:* 24.

WC91 BA/BSc Biology/Creative Writing
Duration: 3FT Hon
Entry Requirements: *GCE:* 220-300. *IB:* 24.

WF98 BA/BSc Creative Writing/Geography
Duration: 3FT Hon
Entry Requirements: *GCE:* 220-300. *IB:* 24.

WL84 BA/BSc Creative Writing/Health Studies
Duration: 3FT Hon
Entry Requirements: *GCE:* 220-300. *IB:* 24.

WV85 BA/BSc Creative Writing/Philosophy & Ethics
Duration: 3FT Hon
Entry Requirements: *GCE:* 220-300. *IB:* 24.

WC88 BA/BSc Creative Writing/Psychology
Duration: 3FT Hon
Entry Requirements: *GCE:* 240-280. *IB:* 24.

WL93 BA/BSc Creative Writing/Sociology
Duration: 3FT Hon
Entry Requirements: *GCE:* 220-300. *IB:* 24.

W802 FdA Professional Writing
Duration: 2FT Fdg
Entry Requirements: *GCE:* 160-200. *IB:* 24.

B22 UNIVERSITY OF BEDFORDSHIRE
PARK SQUARE
LUTON
BEDS LU1 3JU
t: 0844 8482234 f: 01582 489323
e: admissions@beds.ac.uk
// www.beds.ac.uk

W800 BA Creative Writing
Duration: 3FT Hon
Entry Requirements: *Foundation:* Pass. *GCE:* 200. *SQAH:* BCC.
SQAAH: BCC. *IB:* 24. *BTEC NC:* MM. *BTEC ND:* MPP. *OCR ND:*
M1 *OCR NED:* P1

PW38 BA Media Production (Scriptwriting)
Duration: 3FT Hon
Entry Requirements: *Foundation:* Pass. *GCE:* 200. *SQAH:* BCC.
SQAAH: BCC. *IB:* 24. *BTEC NC:* MM. *BTEC ND:* MPP. *OCR ND:*
M1 *OCR NED:* P1

B25 BIRMINGHAM CITY UNIVERSITY
PERRY BARR
BIRMINGHAM B42 2SU
t: 0121 331 5595 f: 0121 331 7994
e: choices@bcu.ac.uk
// www.bcu.ac.uk

QW38 BA English and Creative Writing
Duration: 3FT Hon
Entry Requirements: *GCE:* 280. *IB:* 25. *BTEC ND:* DMM.

B32 THE UNIVERSITY OF BIRMINGHAM
EDGBASTON
BIRMINGHAM B15 2TT
t: 0121 415 8900 f: 0121 414 7159
e: admissions@bham.ac.uk
// www.bham.ac.uk

Q3W8 BA English with Creative Writing
Duration: 3FT Hon
Entry Requirements: *GCE:* AAA-AAB. *SQAH:* AAABB. *SQAAH:* AAB-AA.

B40 BLACKBURN COLLEGE
FEILDEN STREET
BLACKBURN BB2 1LH
t: 01254 292594 f: 01254 679647
e: he-admissions@blackburn.ac.uk
// www.blackburn.ac.uk

W800 BA Writing for Creative Industries
Duration: 3FT Hon
Entry Requirements: *GCE:* 180.

B44 UNIVERSITY OF BOLTON
DEANE ROAD
BOLTON BL3 5AB
t: 01204 903903 f: 01204 399074
e: enquiries@bolton.ac.uk
// www.bolton.ac.uk

WW6V BA Animation & Illustration and Creative Writing
Duration: 3FT Hon
Entry Requirements: *GCE:* 240. Interview required. Portfolio required.

W800 BA Creative Writing
Duration: 3FT Hon
Entry Requirements: *GCE:* 240. Interview required.

QW38 BA Creative Writing and English
Duration: 3FT Hon
Entry Requirements: *GCE:* 240. Interview required.

WWD8 BA Creative Writing and Fine Arts
Duration: 3FT Hon
Entry Requirements: *GCE:* 240. Interview required. Portfolio required.

VW18 BA Creative Writing and Modern & Contemporary History
Duration: 3FT Hon
Entry Requirements: *GCE:* 240. Interview required.

B56 THE UNIVERSITY OF BRADFORD
RICHMOND ROAD
BRADFORD
WEST YORKSHIRE BD7 1DP
t: 0800 073 1225 f: 01274 235585
e: course-enquiries@bradford.ac.uk
// www.bradford.ac.uk

W800 BA Creative Writing
Duration: 3FT Hon
Entry Requirements: *GCE:* 180-220. *IB:* 24.

B84 BRUNEL UNIVERSITY
UXBRIDGE
MIDDLESEX UB8 3PH
t: 01895 265265 f: 01895 269790
e: admissions@brunel.ac.uk
// www.brunel.ac.uk

W800 BA Creative Writing
Duration: 3FT Hon
Entry Requirements: *GCE:* BBC. *SQAAH:* BBC. *IB:* 30. *BTEC ND:* DDM.

Q3W8 BA English with Creative Writing
Duration: 3FT Hon
Entry Requirements: *GCE:* BBC. *SQAAH:* BBC. *IB:* 30. *BTEC ND:* DDM.

WW28 BA Games Design and Creative Writing
Duration: 3FT Hon
Entry Requirements: *GCE:* BBC. *SQAAH:* BBC. *IB:* 30. *BTEC ND:* DDM.

C10 CANTERBURY CHRIST CHURCH UNIVERSITY
NORTH HOLMES ROAD
CANTERBURY
KENT CT1 1QU
t: 01227 782900 f: 01227 782888
e: admissions@canterbury.ac.uk
// www.canterbury.ac.uk

W800 BA Creative and Professional Writing
Duration: 3FT Hon
Entry Requirements: Interview required.

C20 UNIVERSITY OF WALES INSTITUTE, CARDIFF (UWIC)
ADMISSIONS UNIT
LLANDAFF CAMPUS
WESTERN AVENUE
CARDIFF CF5 2YB
t: 029 2041 6070 f: 029 2041 6286
e: admissions@uwic.ac.uk
// www.uwic.ac.uk

QW38 BA English & Creative Writing
Duration: 3FT Hon
Entry Requirements: *GCE:* 260. *IB:* 24. Interview required.

C30 UNIVERSITY OF CENTRAL LANCASHIRE
PRESTON
LANCS PR1 2HE
t: 01772 201201 f: 01772 894954
e: uadmissions@uclan.ac.uk
// www.uclan.ac.uk

W810 BA Film & Television Screenwriting
Duration: 3FT Hon
Entry Requirements: *GCE:* 240-260. *IB:* 28. *BTEC NC:* DD. *BTEC ND:* MMM. *OCR ND:* D *OCR NED:* M3

C55 UNIVERSITY OF CHESTER
PARKGATE ROAD
CHESTER CH1 4BJ
t: 01244 511000 f: 01244 511300
e: enquiries@chester.ac.uk
// www.chester.ac.uk

WQ83 BA Creative Writing and English
Duration: 3FT Hon
Entry Requirements: *Foundation:* Merit. *GCE:* 260-300. *SQAH:* BBBB. *IB:* 28. *BTEC NC:* DM. *BTEC ND:* DMM.

WV81 BA Creative Writing and History
Duration: 3FT Hon
Entry Requirements: *GCE:* 260-300. *SQAH:* BBBB. *IB:* 24. *BTEC NC:* DM. *BTEC ND:* MMM.

WR84 BA Creative Writing and Spanish
Duration: 4FT Hon
Entry Requirements: *GCE:* 240-280. *SQAH:* BBBB. *IB:* 24. *BTEC NC:* DM. *BTEC ND:* MMM.

QW38 BA English Language and Creative Writing
Duration: 3FT Hon
Entry Requirements: *GCE:* 260-300. *SQAH:* BBBB. *IB:* 24. *BTEC NC:* DM. *BTEC ND:* MPP.

C58 UNIVERSITY OF CHICHESTER
BISHOP OTTER CAMPUS
COLLEGE LANE
CHICHESTER
WEST SUSSEX PO19 6PE
t: 01243 816002 f: 01243 816161
e: admissions@chi.ac.uk
// www.chiuni.ac.uk

QW38 BA English & Creative Writing
Duration: 3FT Hon
Entry Requirements: *GCE:* BCC. *SQAH:* BBBB-BBBC. *SQAAH:* BCC. *IB:* 30. *BTEC ND:* DMM.

WV81 BA English & Creative Writing and History
Duration: 3FT Hon
Entry Requirements: *GCE:* BCC. *SQAH:* BBBB-BBBC. *SQAAH:* BCC. *IB:* 30. *BTEC ND:* DMM.

W8V6 BA English & Creative Writing and Theology & Religion
Duration: 3FT Hon
Entry Requirements: *GCE:* BCC. *SQAH:* BBBB-BBBC. *SQAAH:* BCC. *IB:* 30. *BTEC ND:* DMM.

W8V1 BA English & Creative Writing with History
Duration: 3FT Hon
Entry Requirements: *GCE:* BCC. *SQAH:* BBBB-BBBC. *SQAAH:* BCC. *IB:* 30. *BTEC ND:* DMM.

C85 COVENTRY UNIVERSITY
THE STUDENT CENTRE
COVENTRY UNIVERSITY
1 GULSON RD
COVENTRY CV1 2JH
t: 024 7615 2222 f: 024 7615 2223
e: studentenquiries@coventry.ac.uk
// www.coventry.ac.uk

QW38 BA English and Creative Writing
Duration: 3FT/4SW Hon
Entry Requirements: *GCE:* BCC. *SQAH:* BCCCC. *IB:* 28. *BTEC ND:* DMM. *OCR NED:* M2

C93 UNIVERSITY FOR THE CREATIVE ARTS
FALKNER ROAD
FARNHAM
SURREY GU9 7DS
t: 01252 722441 f: 01252 892624
e: admissions@ucreative.ac.uk
// www.ucreative.ac.uk

W803 BA Sports Journalism
Duration: 3FT Hon
Entry Requirements: *GCE:* 240. Interview required. Portfolio required.

C99 UNIVERSITY OF CUMBRIA
FUSEHILL STREET
CARLISLE
CUMBRIA CA1 2HH
t: 01228 616234 f: 01228 616235
// www.cumbria.ac.uk

QW38 BA English and Creative Writing
Duration: 3FT Hon
Entry Requirements: *Foundation:* Merit. *GCE:* 200. *IB:* 28. *BTEC NC:* DM. *BTEC ND:* MMP. *OCR ND:* M1 *OCR NED:* P1

QW3V DipHE English and Creative Writing
Duration: 2FT Dip
Entry Requirements: Contact the institution for details.

D26 DE MONTFORT UNIVERSITY
THE GATEWAY
LEICESTER LE1 9BH
t: 0116 255 1551 f: 0116 250 6204
e: enquiries@dmu.ac.uk
// www.dmu.ac.uk

WQ83 BA Creative Writing and English
Duration: 3FT Hon
Entry Requirements: *GCE:* 260. *IB:* 28.

QW38 BA Creative Writing and English Language
Duration: 3FT Hon
Entry Requirements: *GCE:* 260. *IB:* 28.

D39 UNIVERSITY OF DERBY
KEDLESTON ROAD
DERBY DE22 1GB
t: 01332 591167 f: 01332 597724
e: askadmissions@derby.ac.uk
// www.derby.ac.uk

NW48 BA Accounting and Creative Writing
Duration: 3FT Hon
Entry Requirements: *Foundation:* Distinction. *GCE:* 260-300. *IB:* 28. *BTEC ND:* DMM. *OCR NED:* M2

KW18 BA Architectural Design and Creative Writing
Duration: 3FT Hon
Entry Requirements: *Foundation:* Distinction. *GCE:* 260-300. *IB:* 28. *BTEC ND:* DMM. *OCR NED:* M2

KW1V BA Architectural Design and Media Writing
Duration: 3FT Hon
Entry Requirements: *Foundation:* Distinction. *GCE:* 260-300. *IB:* 28. *BTEC ND:* DMM. *OCR NED:* M2

PWJ8 BA Broadcast Media and Media Writing
Duration: 3FT Hon
Entry Requirements: *Foundation:* Distinction. *GCE:* 260-300. *IB:* 28. *BTEC ND:* DMM. *OCR NED:* M2

PW3W BA Broadcast Media, Creative Writing and Film & Television
Duration: 3FT Hon
Entry Requirements: *Foundation:* Distinction. *GCE:* 260-300. *IB:* 28. *BTEC ND:* DMM. *OCR NED:* M2

W800 BA Creative Writing
Duration: 3FT Hon
Entry Requirements: *Foundation:* Distinction. *GCE:* 260. *IB:* 28. *BTEC ND:* DMM. *OCR NED:* M2

WF86 BA Creative Writing and Geology
Duration: 3FT Hon
Entry Requirements: *Foundation:* Distinction. *GCE:* 260-300. *IB:* 28. *BTEC ND:* DMM. *OCR NED:* M2

WN86 BA Creative Writing and Human Resources Management
Duration: 3FT Hon
Entry Requirements: *Foundation:* Distinction. *GCE:* 260-300. *IB:* 28. *BTEC ND:* DMM. *OCR NED:* M2

WM81 BA Creative Writing and Law
Duration: 3FT Hon
Entry Requirements: *Foundation:* Distinction. *GCE:* 260-300. *IB:* 28. *BTEC ND:* DMM. *OCR NED:* M2

W890 BA Creative Writing and Media Writing
Duration: 3FT Hon
Entry Requirements: *Foundation:* Distinction. *GCE:* 260-300. *IB:* 28. *BTEC ND:* DMM. *OCR NED:* M2

WL83 BA Creative Writing and Sociology
Duration: 3FT Hon
Entry Requirements: *Foundation:* Distinction. *GCE:* 260-300. *IB:* 28. *BTEC ND:* DMM. *OCR NED:* M2

WC86 BA Creative Writing and Sport & Exercise Studies
Duration: 3FT Hon
Entry Requirements: *Foundation:* Distinction. *GCE:* 260-300. *IB:* 28. *BTEC ND:* DMM. *OCR NED:* M2

WV81 BA Creative Writing, English and History
Duration: 3FT Hon
Entry Requirements: *Foundation:* Distinction. *GCE:* 260-300. *IB:* 28. *BTEC ND:* DMM. *OCR NED:* M2

WX83 BA Education Studies and Creative Writing
Duration: 3FT Hon
Entry Requirements: *Foundation:* Distinction. *GCE:* 260-300. *IB:* 28. *BTEC ND:* DMM. *OCR NED:* M2

XW38 BA Education Studies and Media Writing
Duration: 3FT Hon
Entry Requirements: *Foundation:* Distinction. *GCE:* 260-300. *IB:* 28. *BTEC ND:* DMM. *OCR NED:* M2

QW38 BA English and Creative Writing
Duration: 3FT Hon
Entry Requirements: *Foundation:* Distinction. *GCE:* 260-300. *IB:* 28. *BTEC ND:* DMM. *OCR NED:* M2

QW3V BA English and Media Writing
Duration: 3FT Hon
Entry Requirements: *Foundation:* Distinction. *GCE:* 260-300. *IB:* 28. *BTEC ND:* DMM. *OCR NED:* M2

NW68 BA Human Resource Management and Media Writing
Duration: 3FT Hon
Entry Requirements: *Foundation:* Distinction. *GCE:* 260-300. *IB:* 28. *BTEC ND:* DMM. *OCR NED:* M2

MW18 BA Law and Media Writing
Duration: 3FT Hon
Entry Requirements: *Foundation:* Distinction. *GCE:* 260-300. *IB:* 28. *BTEC ND:* DMM. *OCR NED:* M2

NW58 BA Marketing and Media Writing
Duration: 3FT Hon
Entry Requirements: *Foundation:* Distinction. *GCE:* 260-300. *IB:* 28. *BTEC ND:* DMM. *OCR NED:* M2

WK82 BA Media Writing and Property Development
Duration: 3FT Hon
Entry Requirements: *Foundation:* Distinction. *GCE:* 260-300. *IB:* 28. *BTEC ND:* DMM. *OCR NED:* M2

JW98 BA Popular Music Production and Creative Writing
Duration: 3FT Hon
Entry Requirements: *Foundation:* Distinction. *GCE:* 260-300. *IB:* 28. *BTEC ND:* DMM. *OCR NED:* M2

WF87 BA/BSc Creative Writing and Environmental Hazards
Duration: 3FT Hon
Entry Requirements: *Foundation:* Distinction. *GCE:* 260-300. *IB:* 28. *BTEC ND:* DMM. *OCR NED:* M2

WL82 BA/BSc Creative Writing and International Relations & Global Development
Duration: 3FT Hon
Entry Requirements: *Foundation:* Distinction. *GCE:* 260-300. *IB:* 28. *BTEC ND:* DMM. *OCR NED:* M2

WG81 BA/BSc Creative Writing and Mathematics
Duration: 3FT Hon
Entry Requirements: *Foundation:* Distinction. *GCE:* 260-300. *IB:* 28. *BTEC ND:* DMM. *OCR NED:* M2

WL89 BA/BSc Creative Writing and Third World Development
Duration: 3FT Hon
Entry Requirements: *Foundation:* Distinction. *GCE:* 260-300. *IB:* 28. *BTEC ND:* DMM. *OCR NED:* M2

LW78 BA/BSc Geography and Media Writing
Duration: 3FT Hon
Entry Requirements: *Foundation:* Distinction. *GCE:* 260-300. *IB:* 28. *BTEC ND:* DMM. *OCR NED:* M2

FW68 BA/BSc Geology and Media Writing
Duration: 3FT Hon
Entry Requirements: *Foundation:* Distinction. *GCE:* 260-300. *IB:* 28. *BTEC ND:* DMM. *OCR NED:* M2

GW18 BA/BSc Mathematics and Media Writing
Duration: 3FT Hon
Entry Requirements: *Foundation:* Distinction. *GCE:* 260-300. *IB:* 28. *BTEC ND:* DMM. *OCR NED:* M2

WC88 BA/BSc Media Writing and Psychology
Duration: 3FT Hon
Entry Requirements: *Foundation:* Distinction. *GCE:* 260-300. *IB:* 28. *BTEC ND:* DMM. *OCR NED:* M2

WL8X BA/BSc Media Writing and Third World Development
Duration: 3FT Hon
Entry Requirements: *Foundation:* Distinction. *GCE:* 260-300. *IB:* 28. *BTEC ND:* DMM. *OCR NED:* M2

FW88 BSc Creative Writing and Geography
Duration: 3FT Hon
Entry Requirements: *Foundation:* Distinction. *GCE:* 260-300. *IB:* 28. *BTEC ND:* DMM. *OCR NED:* M2

E14 UNIVERSITY OF EAST ANGLIA
NORWICH NR4 7TJ
t: 01603 591515 f: 01603 458596
e: admissions@uea.ac.uk
// www.uea.ac.uk

T7W8 BA American Literature with Creative Writing with a Year Abroad
Duration: 4FT Hon   CRB Check: Required
Entry Requirements: *GCE:* ABB. *SQAAH:* ABB. *IB:* 32. *BTEC NC:* DD. *BTEC ND:* DDM.

Q3W8 BA English Literature with Creative Writing
Duration: 3FT Hon   CRB Check: Required
Entry Requirements: *GCE:* AAA. *SQAAH:* AAA. *IB:* 34. *BTEC NC:* DD. *BTEC ND:* DDD. Portfolio required.

E28 UNIVERSITY OF EAST LONDON
DOCKLANDS CAMPUS
UNIVERSITY WAY
LONDON E16 2RD
t: 020 8223 3333 f: 020 8223 2978
e: study@uel.ac.uk
// www.uel.ac.uk

WQ83 BA Creative & Professional Writing / English Literature
Duration: 3FT Hon
Entry Requirements: *GCE:* 200. *IB:* 24. *BTEC NC:* DM. *BTEC ND:* MMP.

W8Q3 BA Creative & Professional Writing with English Literature
Duration: 3FT Hon
Entry Requirements: *GCE:* 200. *IB:* 24. *BTEC NC:* DM. *BTEC ND:* MMP.

W8W2 BA Creative & Professional Writing with Illustration
Duration: 3FT Hon
Entry Requirements: *GCE:* 200. *IB:* 24. *BTEC NC:* DM. *BTEC ND:* MMP. *OCR ND:* M1 *OCR NED:* P1

WM89 BA Creative & Professional Writing/Criminology
Duration: 3FT Hon
Entry Requirements: *GCE:* 240. *IB:* 28. *BTEC NC:* DD. *BTEC ND:* MMM.

WN85 BA Creative & Professional Writing/Marketing
Duration: 3FT Hon
Entry Requirements: *GCE:* 200. *IB:* 24. *BTEC NC:* DM. *BTEC ND:* MMP.

W800 BA Creative and Professional Writing
Duration: 3FT Hon
Entry Requirements: *GCE:* 200. *IB:* 24. *BTEC NC:* DM. *BTEC ND:* MMP.

W801 BA Creative and Professional Writing (Extended)
Duration: 4FT Hon
Entry Requirements: *GCE:* 40. *IB:* 24.

X3W8 BA Education & Community Development with Creative & Professional Writing
Duration: 3FT Hon
Entry Requirements: *GCE:* 200. *IB:* 24. *BTEC NC:* DM. *BTEC ND:* MMP.

Q3W8 BA English Literature with Creative & Professional Writing
Duration: 3FT Hon
Entry Requirements: *GCE:* 200. *IB:* 24. *BTEC NC:* DM. *BTEC ND:* MMP.

NW18 BA International Business/Creative & Professional Writing
Duration: 3FT Hon
Entry Requirements: *GCE:* 200. *IB:* 24. *BTEC NC:* DM. *BTEC ND:* MMP. *OCR ND:* M1 *OCR NED:* P1

V000 BA Media & Creative Industries option - Creative and Professional Writing
Duration: 3FT Hon
Entry Requirements: *GCE:* 200. *IB:* 24.

W6W8 BA Photography with Creative & Professional Writing
Duration: 3FT Hon
Entry Requirements: *GCE:* 200. *IB:* 24. *BTEC NC:* DM. *BTEC ND:* MMP. *OCR ND:* M1 *OCR NED:* P1

GW58 BA/BSc Business Information Systems/Creative & Professional Writing
Duration: 3FT Hon
Entry Requirements: *GCE:* 200. *IB:* 24. *BTEC NC:* DM. *BTEC ND:* MMP. *OCR ND:* M1 *OCR NED:* P1

WL83 BA/BSc Creative & Professional Writing/Sociology (Professional Development)
Duration: 3FT Hon
Entry Requirements: *GCE:* 200. *IB:* 24. *BTEC NC:* DM. *BTEC ND:* MMP.

E42 EDGE HILL UNIVERSITY
ORMSKIRK
LANCASHIRE L39 4QP
t: 01695 657000 f: 01695 584355
e: study@edgehill.ac.uk
// www.edgehill.ac.uk

W800 BA Creative Writing
Duration: 3FT Hon
Entry Requirements: *GCE:* 280. *IB:* 26. *BTEC NC:* DD. *BTEC ND:* DMM. *OCR ND:* D *OCR NED:* M2

WQ83 BA Creative Writing and English Language
Duration: 3FT Hon
Entry Requirements: *GCE:* 280. *IB:* 26. *BTEC NC:* MM. *BTEC ND:* MMM. *OCR ND:* M2 *OCR NED:* M2

QW38 BA Creative Writing and English Literature
Duration: 3FT Hon
Entry Requirements: *GCE:* 280. *IB:* 26. *BTEC NC:* MM. *BTEC ND:* MMM. *OCR ND:* M2 *OCR NED:* M2

Q1W8 BA English Language with Creative Writing
Duration: 3FT Hon
Entry Requirements: *GCE:* 280. *IB:* 26. *BTEC NC:* DD. *BTEC ND:* DMM. *OCR ND:* M2 *OCR NED:* M2

Q2W9 BA English Literature with Creative Writing
Duration: 3FT Hon
Entry Requirements: *GCE:* 280. *IB:* 26. *BTEC NC:* DD. *BTEC ND:* DMM. *OCR ND:* M2 *OCR NED:* M2

Q3W8 BA English with Creative Writing
Duration: 3FT Hon
Entry Requirements: *GCE:* 280. *IB:* 26. *BTEC NC:* DD. *BTEC ND:* DMM. *OCR ND:* M2 *OCR NED:* M2

V1W8 BA History with Creative Writing
Duration: 3FT Hon
Entry Requirements: *GCE:* 280. *IB:* 26. *BTEC NC:* DD. *BTEC ND:* DMM. *OCR ND:* D *OCR NED:* M2

E70 THE UNIVERSITY OF ESSEX
WIVENHOE PARK
COLCHESTER
ESSEX CO4 3SQ
t: 01206 873666 f: 01206 874477
e: admit@essex.ac.uk
// www.essex.ac.uk

W800 BA Creative Writing
Duration: 3FT Hon
Entry Requirements: *GCE:* ABB. *SQAH:* AAAB. *IB:* 34.

W801 BA Creative Writing (Including Year Abroad)
Duration: 4FT Hon
Entry Requirements: Contact the institution for details.

F33 UNIVERSITY COLLEGE FALMOUTH
WOODLANE
FALMOUTH
CORNWALL TR11 4RH
t: 01326213730
e: admissions@falmouth.ac.uk
// www.falmouth.ac.uk

W890 BA(Hons) Creative Writing
Duration: 3FT Hon
Entry Requirements: *GCE:* 220. *IB:* 24. Interview required.

Q3W8 BA(Hons) English with Creative Writing
Duration: 3FT Hon
Entry Requirements: *GCE:* 220. *IB:* 24. Interview required.

G14 UNIVERSITY OF GLAMORGAN, CARDIFF AND PONTYPRIDD
ENQUIRIES AND ADMISSIONS UNIT
PONTYPRIDD CF37 1DL
t: 0800 716925 f: 01443 654050
e: enquiries@glam.ac.uk
// www.glam.ac.uk

WQ8H BA Creative Writing and English Language
Duration: 3FT Hon
Entry Requirements: *GCE:* BBC. *BTEC ND:* DMM.

W800 BA Creative and Professional Writing
Duration: 3FT Hon
Entry Requirements: *GCE:* BBC. *BTEC ND:* DMM.

G50 THE UNIVERSITY OF GLOUCESTERSHIRE
PARK CAMPUS
THE PARK
CHELTENHAM GL50 2RH
t: 01242 714503 f: 01242 714827
e: admissions@glos.ac.uk
// www.glos.ac.uk

W800 BA Creative Writing
Duration: 3FT Hon
Entry Requirements: *GCE:* 280-300.

QWH8 BA English Language and Creative Writing
Duration: 3FT Hon
Entry Requirements: *GCE:* 280-300.

QW38 BA English Literature and Creative Writing
Duration: 3FT Hon
Entry Requirements: *GCE:* 280-300.

VW18 BA History and Creative Writing
Duration: 3FT Hon
Entry Requirements: *GCE:* 280-300.

VWQ8 BA Religion, Philosophy & Ethics and Creative Writing
Duration: 3FT Hon
Entry Requirements: *GCE:* 280-300.

MW98 BA/BSc Criminology and Creative Writing
Duration: 3FT Hon
Entry Requirements: *GCE:* 280-300.

CW88 BA/BSc Psychology and Creative Writing
Duration: 3FT Hon
Entry Requirements: *GCE:* 280-300.

G53 GLYNDWR UNIVERSITY
PLAS COCH
MOLD ROAD
WREXHAM LL11 2AW
t: 01978 293439 f: 01978 290008
e: sid@glyndwr.ac.uk
// www.glyndwr.ac.uk

PW9V BA Broadcasting, Journalism and Creative Writing
Duration: 3FT Hon
Entry Requirements: *GCE:* 240.

WV81 BA Creative Writing and History
Duration: 3FT Hon
Entry Requirements: *GCE:* 240.

WQ83 BA English and Creative Writing
Duration: 3FT Hon
Entry Requirements: *GCE:* 240.

WP89 BA Media Communications and Creative Writing
Duration: 3FT Hon
Entry Requirements: *GCE:* 240.

G56 GOLDSMITHS, UNIVERSITY OF LONDON
GOLDSMITHS, UNIVERSITY OF LONDON
NEW CROSS
LONDON SE14 6NW
t: 020 7048 5300 f: 020 7919 7509
e: admissions@gold.ac.uk
// www.gold.ac.uk

Q3W8 BA English with Creative Writing
Duration: 3FT Hon
Entry Requirements: *GCE:* AAB. *SQAH:* ABBBB. *SQAAH:* ABB. *BTEC NC:* DD. *BTEC ND:* DDD. Interview required.

G70 UNIVERSITY OF GREENWICH
GREENWICH CAMPUS
OLD ROYAL NAVAL COLLEGE
PARK ROW
LONDON SE10 9LS
t: 0800 005 006 f: 020 8331 8145
e: courseinfo@gre.ac.uk
// www.gre.ac.uk

W801 BA Creative Writing
Duration: 3FT Hon
Entry Requirements: *GCE:* 280. *IB:* 24.

QW38 BA Creative Writing and English Literature
Duration: 3FT Hon
Entry Requirements: *GCE:* 280. *IB:* 24.

WV85 BA Creative Writing and Philosophy
Duration: 3FT Hon
Entry Requirements: *GCE:* 280. *IB:* 24.

Q3W8 BA English Literature with Creative Writing
Duration: 3FT Hon
Entry Requirements: *GCE:* 200. *IB:* 24.

WV8C BA Media Writing and History
Duration: 3FT Hon
Entry Requirements: *GCE:* 200. *IB:* 24.

W800 FdA Professional Writing
Duration: 2FT Fdg
Entry Requirements: Contact the institution for details.

G80 GRIMSBY INSTITUTE OF FURTHER AND HIGHER EDUCATION
NUNS CORNER
GRIMSBY
NE LINCOLNSHIRE DN34 5BQ
t: 0800 328 3631 f: 01472 315506/879924
e: headmissions@grimsby.ac.uk
// www.grimsby.ac.uk

W800 BA Professional Writing
Duration: 3FT Hon
Entry Requirements: *GCE:* 120-240. *BTEC NC:* MP. *BTEC ND:* PPP. Interview required.

H36 UNIVERSITY OF HERTFORDSHIRE
UNIVERSITY ADMISSIONS SERVICE
COLLEGE LANE
HATFIELD
HERTS AL10 9AB
t: 01707 284800
// www.herts.ac.uk

Q1W8 BA English Language & Communication with Creative Writing
Duration: 3FT Hon
Entry Requirements: *GCE:* 300.

Q3W8 BA English Literature with Creative Writing
Duration: 3FT Hon
Entry Requirements: *GCE:* 300.

WW68 BA Film and Television Fiction
Duration: 3FT Hon
Entry Requirements: *GCE:* 300. Interview required. Portfolio required.

V1W8 BA History with Creative Writing
Duration: 3FT Hon
Entry Requirements: *GCE:* 300.

V5W8 BA Philosophy with Creative Writing
Duration: 3FT Hon
Entry Requirements: *GCE:* 300.

H60 THE UNIVERSITY OF HUDDERSFIELD
QUEENSGATE
HUDDERSFIELD HD1 3DH
t: 01484 473969 f: 01484 472765
e: admissionsandrecords@hud.ac.uk
// www.hud.ac.uk

Q3WV BA English Language with Creative Writing
Duration: 3FT Hon
Entry Requirements: *GCE:* 280. *SQAH:* BBBB. *IB:* 28.

Q3WW BA English Literature with Creative Writing
Duration: 3FT Hon
Entry Requirements: *GCE:* 280. *SQAH:* BBBB. *IB:* 28.

Q3W8 BA English with Creative Writing
Duration: 3FT Hon
Entry Requirements: *GCE:* 280. *SQAH:* BBBB. *IB:* 28.

H72 THE UNIVERSITY OF HULL
THE UNIVERSITY OF HULL
COTTINGHAM ROAD
HULL HU6 7RX
t: 01482 466100 f: 01482 442290
e: admissions@hull.ac.uk
// www.hull.ac.uk

T7W8 BA American Studies with Creative Writing
Duration: 3FT Hon
Entry Requirements: *GCE:* 280-300. *IB:* 28. *BTEC ND:* DMM.

WT87 BA Creative Writing and American Studies
Duration: 3FT Hon
Entry Requirements: *GCE:* 280-320. *IB:* 30. *BTEC ND:* DDM.

WQ83 BA Creative Writing and English
Duration: 3FT Hon
Entry Requirements: *GCE:* 280-320. *IB:* 30. *BTEC ND:* DDM.

WW86 BA Creative Writing and Film Studies
Duration: 3FT Hon
Entry Requirements: *GCE:* 280-300. *IB:* 30. *BTEC ND:* DDM.

WV85 BA Creative Writing and Philosophy
Duration: 3FT Hon
Entry Requirements: *GCE:* 280-300. *IB:* 30. *BTEC ND:* DDM.

WV86 BA Creative Writing and Religion
Duration: 3FT Hon
Entry Requirements: *GCE:* 280-300. *IB:* 30. *BTEC ND:* DDM.

V5W8 BA Philosophy with Creative Writing
Duration: 3FT Hon
Entry Requirements: *GCE:* 280-300. *IB:* 28. *BTEC ND:* DMM.

K84 KINGSTON UNIVERSITY
STUDENT INFORMATION & ADVICE CENTRE
COOPER HOUSE
40-46 SURBITON ROAD
KINGSTON UPON THAMES KT1 2HX
t: 0844 8552177 f: 020 8547 7080
e: aps@kingston.ac.uk
// www.kingston.ac.uk

NW18 BA Business and Creative Writing
Duration: 3FT Hon
Entry Requirements: *GCE:* 280. *IB:* 30.

WL83 BA Creative Writing and Criminology
Duration: 3FT Hon
Entry Requirements: *GCE:* 220-360. *SQAH:* BBCCC. *SQAAH:* BBC. *IB:* 30.

WL81 BA Creative Writing and Economics (Applied)
Duration: 3FT Hon
Entry Requirements: *GCE:* 220-360. *IB:* 30.

WQ83 BA Creative Writing and English Language & Communications
Duration: 3FT Hon
Entry Requirements: *GCE:* 220-360.

WQV3 BA Creative Writing and English Literature
Duration: 3FT Hon
Entry Requirements: *GCE:* 220-360.

WV81 BA Creative Writing and History
Duration: 3FT Hon
Entry Requirements: *GCE:* 220-360. *IB:* 30.

WL82 BA Creative Writing and Human Rights
Duration: 3FT Hon
Entry Requirements: *GCE:* 220-360. *IB:* 30.

WLV2 BA Creative Writing and International Relations
Duration: 3FT Hon
Entry Requirements: *GCE:* 220-360. *IB:* 30.

WM81 BA Creative Writing and Law
Duration: 3FT Hon
Entry Requirements: *GCE:* 280.

WLW2 BA Creative Writing and Politics
Duration: 3FT Hon
Entry Requirements: *GCE:* 220-360.

WC88 BA Creative Writing and Psychology
Duration: 3FT Hon
Entry Requirements: *GCE:* 220-360.

W8N1 BA Creative Writing with Business
Duration: 3FT Hon
Entry Requirements: *GCE:* 280. *IB:* 30.

W8M9 BA Creative Writing with Criminology
Duration: 3FT Hon
Entry Requirements: *GCE:* 220-360. *SQAH:* BBCCC. *SQAAH:* BBC. *IB:* 30.

W8L1 BA Creative Writing with Economics (Applied)
Duration: 3FT Hon
Entry Requirements: *GCE:* 220-360. *IB:* 30.

W8Q1 BA Creative Writing with English Language & Communication
Duration: 3FT Hon
Entry Requirements: *GCE:* 220-360.

W8Q3 BA Creative Writing with English Literature
Duration: 3FT Hon
Entry Requirements: *GCE:* 220-360.

W8V1 BA Creative Writing with History
Duration: 3FT Hon
Entry Requirements: *GCE:* 220-360. *IB:* 30.

W8LG BA Creative Writing with Human Rights
Duration: 3FT Hon
Entry Requirements: *GCE:* 220-360. *IB:* 30.

W8LF BA Creative Writing with International Relations
Duration: 3FT Hon
Entry Requirements: *GCE:* 220-360. *IB:* 30.

W8M1 BA Creative Writing with Law
Duration: 3FT Hon
Entry Requirements: *GCE:* 280.

W8L2 BA Creative Writing with Politics
Duration: 3FT Hon
Entry Requirements: *GCE:* 220-360.

W8C8 BA Creative Writing with Psychology
Duration: 3FT Hon
Entry Requirements: *GCE:* 220-360.

M9W8 BA Criminology with Creative Writing
Duration: 3FT Hon
Entry Requirements: *GCE:* 220-320. *SQAH:* BBCCC. *SQAAH:* BBC. *IB:* 30.

L1W8 BA Economics (Applied) with Creative Writing
Duration: 3FT Hon
Entry Requirements: *GCE:* 220-320. *IB:* 24.

Q1W8 BA English Language & Communication with Creative Writing
Duration: 3FT Hon
Entry Requirements: *GCE:* 240-360.

Q3W8 BA English Literature with Creative Writing
Duration: 3FT Hon
Entry Requirements: *GCE:* 240-360.

V1W8 BA History with Creative Writing
Duration: 3FT Hon
Entry Requirements: *GCE:* 220-360. *IB:* 30.

L2WW BA Human Rights with Creative Writing
Duration: 3FT Hon
Entry Requirements: *GCE:* 220-360.

L2WV BA International Relations with Creative Writing
Duration: 3FT Hon
Entry Requirements: *GCE:* 220-360.

MW18 BA Law and Creative Writing
Duration: 3FT Hon
Entry Requirements: *GCE:* 280.

L2W8 BA Politics with Creative Writing
Duration: 3FT Hon
Entry Requirements: *GCE:* 220-360.

C8W8 BA Psychology with Creative Writing
Duration: 3FT Hon
Entry Requirements: *GCE:* 220-360.

L14 LANCASTER UNIVERSITY
THE UNIVERSITY
LANCASTER
LANCASHIRE LA1 4YW
t: 01524 592029 f: 01524 846243
e: ugadmissions@lancaster.ac.uk
// www.lancs.ac.uk

Q3WV BA English Language with Creative Writing
Duration: 3FT Hon
Entry Requirements: *GCE:* AAA-AAB. *SQAH:* ABBBB. *SQAAH:* AAB.

Q3W8 BA English Literature with Creative Writing
Duration: 3FT Hon
Entry Requirements: *GCE:* AAA-AAB. *SQAH:* ABBBB. *SQAAH:* AAB-ABB.

QW38 BA English Literature, Creative Writing and Practice
Duration: 3FT Hon
Entry Requirements: *GCE:* AAA-AAB. *SQAH:* ABBBB. *SQAAH:* AAB.

L24 LEEDS TRINITY UNIVERSITY COLLEGE (FORMERLY LEEDS TRINITY AND ALL SAINTS)
BROWNBERRIE LANE
HORSFORTH
LEEDS LS18 5HD
t: 0113 283 7150 f: 0113 283 7222
e: enquiries@leedstrinity.ac.uk
// www.leedstrinity.ac.uk

QW38 BA English and Writing
Duration: 3FT Hon
Entry Requirements: *GCE:* 220. *IB:* 24. *BTEC NC:* DD. *BTEC ND:* MMP.

L51 LIVERPOOL JOHN MOORES UNIVERSITY
KINGSWAY HOUSE
HATTON GARDEN
LIVERPOOL L3 2AJ
t: 0151 231 5090 f: 0151 231 3462
e: courses@ljmu.ac.uk
// www.ljmu.ac.uk

W800 BA Creative Writing
Duration: 3FT Hon
Entry Requirements: *GCE:* 260.

WW86 BA Creative Writing and Film Studies
Duration: 3FT Hon
Entry Requirements: *GCE:* 280.

WQ83 BA English and Creative Writing
Duration: 3FT Hon
Entry Requirements: *GCE:* 260.

L68 LONDON METROPOLITAN UNIVERSITY
166-220 HOLLOWAY ROAD
LONDON N7 8DB
t: 020 7133 4200
e: admissions@londonmet.ac.uk
// www.londonmet.ac.uk

W800 BA Creative Writing
Duration: 3FT Hon
Entry Requirements: *GCE:* 260. *IB:* 28. Portfolio required.

WQV3 BA Creative Writing and English Literature
Duration: 3FT Hon
Entry Requirements: *GCE:* 260. *IB:* 28. Portfolio required.

L75 LONDON SOUTH BANK UNIVERSITY
103 BOROUGH ROAD
LONDON SE1 0AA
t: 020 7815 7815 f: 020 7815 8273
e: enquiry@lsbu.ac.uk
// www.lsbu.ac.uk

W801 BA Creative Writing
Duration: 3FT Hon
Entry Requirements: *GCE:* 240. *IB:* 24. *BTEC NC:* DD. *BTEC ND:* MMM.

Q3W8 BA English with Creative Writing
Duration: 3FT Hon
Entry Requirements: *GCE:* 240. *IB:* 24. *BTEC NC:* DD. *BTEC ND:* MMM.

M40 THE MANCHESTER METROPOLITAN UNIVERSITY
ADMISSIONS OFFICE
ALL SAINTS (GMS)
ALL SAINTS
MANCHESTER M15 6BH
t: 0161 247 2000
// www.mmu.ac.uk

NW18 BA Business/Creative Writing
Duration: 3FT Hon
Entry Requirements: *GCE:* 240-280. *BTEC ND:* DMM.

WX83 BA Childhood & Youth Studies/Creative Writing
Duration: 3FT Hon
Entry Requirements: *GCE:* 240-280. *SQAH:* BBB. *SQAAH:* CC. *IB:* 28.

CW68 BA Coaching Studies/Creative Writing
Duration: 3FT Hon
Entry Requirements: *GCE:* 240-280. *BTEC ND:* DMM.

W800 BA Creative Writing
Duration: 3FT Hon
Entry Requirements: *GCE:* 240-280. *SQAH:* BBBCC. Interview required.

WX8H BA Creative Writing/Education Studies
Duration: 3FT Hon
Entry Requirements: *GCE:* 240-280. *BTEC ND:* DMM.

WC8P BA Creative Writing/Outdoor Studies
Duration: 3FT Hon
Entry Requirements: *GCE:* 240-280. *BTEC ND:* DMM.

WC8Q BA Creative Writing/Sport Development
Duration: 3FT Hon
Entry Requirements: *GCE:* 240-280. *BTEC ND:* DMM.

QW38 BA English and Creative Writing
Duration: 3FT Hon
Entry Requirements: *GCE:* 280. *IB:* 28. Interview required. Portfolio required.

WQ83 BA English/Creative Writing
Duration: 3FT Hon
Entry Requirements: *GCE:* 240-280. *IB:* 28. *BTEC ND:* DMM.

WW86 BA Film & Television Studies/Creative Writing
Duration: 3FT Hon
Entry Requirements: *GCE:* 240-280. *IB:* 28. *BTEC ND:* DMM.

NW38 BA Financial Management/Creative Writing
Duration: 3FT Hon
Entry Requirements: *GCE:* 240-280. *BTEC ND:* DMM.

MW28 BA Legal Studies/Creative Writing
Duration: 3FT Hon
Entry Requirements: *GCE:* 240-280. *BTEC ND:* DMM. Portfolio required.

WV85 BA Philosophy/Creative Writing
Duration: 3FT Hon
Entry Requirements: *GCE:* 240-280. *IB:* 28. *BTEC ND:* DMM.

WC88 BA Psychology/Creative Writing
Duration: 3FT Hon
Entry Requirements: *GCE:* 240-280. *IB:* 28. *BTEC ND:* DMM.

M80 MIDDLESEX UNIVERSITY
MIDDLESEX UNIVERSITY
THE BURROUGHS
LONDON NW4 4BT
t: 020 8411 5555 f: 020 8411 5649
e: enquiries@mdx.ac.uk
// www.mdx.ac.uk

WQ83 BA Creative Writing and English Literature
Duration: 3FT Hon
Entry Requirements: *GCE:* 200-300. *IB:* 28.

N36 NEWMAN UNIVERSITY COLLEGE, BIRMINGHAM
GENNERS LANE
BARTLEY GREEN
BIRMINGHAM B32 3NT
t: 0121 476 1181 f: 0121 476 1196
e: Admissions@newman.ac.uk
// www.newman.ac.uk

X3W8 BA Education Studies with Creative Writing
Duration: 3FT Hon
Entry Requirements: *Foundation:* Distinction. *GCE:* 260. *IB:* 24. *BTEC NC:* MM. *BTEC ND:* DMM. *OCR ND:* M2 *OCR NED:* M2

V1W8 BA History with Creative Writing
Duration: 3FT Hon
Entry Requirements: *Foundation:* Distinction. *GCE:* 260. *IB:* 24. *BTEC NC:* MM. *BTEC ND:* DMM. *OCR ND:* M2 *OCR NED:* M2

G5W8 BA IT with Creative Writing
Duration: 3FT Hon
Entry Requirements: *Foundation:* Distinction. *GCE:* 260. *IB:* 24. *BTEC NC:* MM. *BTEC ND:* DMM. *OCR ND:* M2 *OCR NED:* M2

C8W8 BA Psychology with Creative Writing
Duration: 3FT Hon
Entry Requirements: *Foundation:* Distinction. *GCE:* 280. *IB:* 25. *BTEC NC:* MM. *BTEC ND:* DDM. *OCR ND:* M2 *OCR NED:* M2

C6W8 BA Sports Studies with Creative Writing
Duration: 3FT Hon
Entry Requirements: *Foundation:* Distinction. *GCE:* 280. *IB:* 25. *BTEC NC:* MM. *BTEC ND:* DDM. *OCR ND:* M2 *OCR NED:* M2

V6W8 BA Theology with Creative Writing
Duration: 3FT Hon
Entry Requirements: *Foundation:* Distinction. *GCE:* 260. *IB:* 24. *BTEC NC:* MM. *BTEC ND:* DMM. *OCR ND:* M2 *OCR NED:* M2

L5W8 BA Working with Children Young People & Families with Creative Writing
Duration: 3FT Hon
Entry Requirements: *Foundation:* Distinction. *GCE:* 260. *IB:* 24. *BTEC NC:* MM. *BTEC ND:* DMM. *OCR ND:* M2 *OCR NED:* M2

N37 UNIVERSITY OF WALES, NEWPORT
ADMISSIONS
LODGE ROAD
CAERLEON
NEWPORT NP18 3QT
t: 01633 432030 f: 01633 432850
e: admissions@newport.ac.uk
// www.newport.ac.uk

VW68 BA Religious Studies and Creative Writing
Duration: 3FT Hon
Entry Requirements: *GCE:* 260. *IB:* 24.

Q3W8 BA/BSc English with Creative Writing
Duration: 3FT Hon
Entry Requirements: *GCE:* 260. *IB:* 24.

N38 UNIVERSITY OF NORTHAMPTON
PARK CAMPUS
BOUGHTON GREEN ROAD
NORTHAMPTON NN2 7AL
t: 0800 358 2232 f: 01604 722083
e: admissions@northampton.ac.uk
// www.northampton.ac.uk

N4W8 BA Accounting/Creative Writing
Duration: 3FT Hon
Entry Requirements: *GCE:* 260-280. *SQAH:* AAA-BBBB. *IB:* 24.
BTEC NC: DD. *BTEC ND:* DMM. *OCR ND:* D *OCR NED:* M2

N5WV BA Advertising/Creative Writing
Duration: 3FT Hon
Entry Requirements: *GCE:* 260-280. *SQAH:* AAA-BBBB. *IB:* 24.
BTEC NC: DD. *BTEC ND:* DMM. *OCR ND:* D *OCR NED:* M2

N1WV BA Business Entrepreneurship/Creative Writing
Duration: 3FT Hon
Entry Requirements: *GCE:* 260-280. *SQAH:* AAA-BBBB. *IB:* 24.
BTEC NC: DD. *BTEC ND:* DMM. *OCR ND:* D *OCR NED:* M2

N1W8 BA Business/Creative Writing
Duration: 3FT Hon
Entry Requirements: *GCE:* 260-280. *SQAH:* AAA-BBBB. *IB:* 24.
BTEC NC: DD. *BTEC ND:* DMM. *OCR ND:* D *OCR NED:* M2

W800 BA Creative Writing
Duration: 3FT Hon
Entry Requirements: *GCE:* 260-280. *SQAH:* AAA-BBBB. *IB:* 24.
BTEC NC: DD. *BTEC ND:* DMM. *OCR ND:* D *OCR NED:* M2

W8NA BA Creative Writing with Applied Management
Duration: 3FT Hon
Entry Requirements: *GCE:* 260-280. *SQAH:* AAA-BBBB. *IB:* 24.
BTEC NC: DD. *BTEC ND:* DMM. *OCR ND:* D *OCR NED:* M2

W8N4 BA Creative Writing/Accounting
Duration: 3FT Hon
Entry Requirements: *GCE:* 260-280. *SQAH:* AAA-BBBB. *IB:* 24.
BTEC NC: DD. *BTEC ND:* DMM. *OCR ND:* D *OCR NED:* M2

W8NM BA Creative Writing/Advertising
Duration: 3FT Hon
Entry Requirements: *GCE:* 260-280. *SQAH:* AAA-BBBB. *IB:* 24.
BTEC NC: DD. *BTEC ND:* DMM. *OCR ND:* D *OCR NED:* M2

W8C1 BA Creative Writing/Biological Conservation
Duration: 3FT Hon
Entry Requirements: *GCE:* 260-280. *SQAH:* AAA-BBBB. *IB:* 24.
BTEC NC: DD. *BTEC ND:* DMM. *OCR ND:* D *OCR NED:* M2

W8N1 BA Creative Writing/Business
Duration: 3FT Hon
Entry Requirements: *GCE:* 260-280. *SQAH:* AAA-BBBB. *IB:* 24.
BTEC NC: DD. *BTEC ND:* DMM. *OCR ND:* D *OCR NED:* M2

W8NF BA Creative Writing/Business Entrepreneurship
Duration: 3FT Hon
Entry Requirements: *GCE:* 260-280. *SQAH:* AAA-BBBB. *IB:* 24.
BTEC NC: DD. *BTEC ND:* DMM. *OCR ND:* D *OCR NED:* M2

W8G4 BA Creative Writing/Computing
Duration: 3FT Hon
Entry Requirements: *GCE:* 260-280. *SQAH:* AAA-BBBB. *IB:* 24.
BTEC NC: DD. *BTEC ND:* DMM. *OCR ND:* D *OCR NED:* M2

W8M9 BA Creative Writing/Criminology
Duration: 3FT Hon
Entry Requirements: *GCE:* 260-280. *SQAH:* AAA-BBBB. *IB:* 24.
BTEC NC: DD. *BTEC ND:* DMM. *OCR ND:* D *OCR NED:* M2

W8X3 BA Creative Writing/Education Studies
Duration: 3FT Hon
Entry Requirements: *GCE:* 260-280. *SQAH:* AAA-BBBB. *IB:* 24.
BTEC NC: DD. *BTEC ND:* DMM. *OCR ND:* D *OCR NED:* M2

W8Q3 BA Creative Writing/English
Duration: 3FT Hon
Entry Requirements: *GCE:* 260-280. *SQAH:* AAA-BBBB. *IB:* 24.
BTEC NC: DD. *BTEC ND:* DMM. *OCR ND:* D *OCR NED:* M2

W8NV BA Creative Writing/Events Management
Duration: 3FT Hon
Entry Requirements: *GCE:* 260-280. *SQAH:* AAA-BBBB. *IB:* 24.
BTEC NC: DD. *BTEC ND:* DMM. *OCR ND:* D *OCR NED:* M2

W8W6 BA Creative Writing/Film & Television Studies
Duration: 3FT Hon
Entry Requirements: *GCE:* 260-280. *SQAH:* AAA-BBBB. *IB:* 24.
BTEC NC: DD. *BTEC ND:* DMM. *OCR ND:* D *OCR NED:* M2

W8W1 BA Creative Writing/Fine Art Painting & Drawing
Duration: 3FT Hon
Entry Requirements: *GCE:* 260-280. *SQAH:* AAA-BBBB. *IB:* 24.
BTEC NC: DD. *BTEC ND:* DMM. *OCR ND:* D *OCR NED:* M2

W8R1 BA Creative Writing/French
Duration: 3FT Hon
Entry Requirements: *GCE:* 260-280. *SQAH:* AAA-BBBB. *IB:* 24.
BTEC NC: DD. *BTEC ND:* DMM. *OCR ND:* D *OCR NED:* M2

W8L4 BA Creative Writing/Health Studies
Duration: 3FT Hon
Entry Requirements: *GCE:* 260-280. *SQAH:* AAA-BBBB. *IB:* 24.
BTEC NC: DD. *BTEC ND:* DMM. *OCR ND:* D *OCR NED:* M2

W8V1 BA Creative Writing/History
Duration: 3FT Hon
Entry Requirements: *GCE:* 260-280. *SQAH:* AAA-BBBB. *IB:* 24.
BTEC NC: DD. *BTEC ND:* DMM. *OCR ND:* D *OCR NED:* M2

W8B1 BA Creative Writing/Human Bioscience
Duration: 3FT Hon
Entry Requirements: *GCE:* 260-280. *SQAH:* AAA-BBBB. *IB:* 24.
BTEC NC: DD. *BTEC ND:* DMM. *OCR ND:* D *OCR NED:* M2

W8L7 BA Creative Writing/Human Geography
Duration: 3FT Hon
Entry Requirements: *GCE:* 260-280. *SQAH:* AAA-BBBB. *IB:* 24.
BTEC NC: DD. *BTEC ND:* DMM. *OCR ND:* D *OCR NED:* M2

W8N6 BA Creative Writing/Human Resource Management
Duration: 3FT Hon
Entry Requirements: *GCE:* 260-280. *SQAH:* AAA-BBBB. *IB:* 24.
BTEC NC: DD. *BTEC ND:* DMM. *OCR ND:* D *OCR NED:* M2

W8L9 BA Creative Writing/International Development
Duration: 3FT Hon
Entry Requirements: *GCE:* 260-280. *SQAH:* AAA-BBBB. *IB:* 24.
BTEC NC: DD. *BTEC ND:* DMM. *OCR ND:* D *OCR NED:* M2

W8M1 BA Creative Writing/Law
Duration: 3FT Hon
Entry Requirements: *GCE:* 260-280. *SQAH:* AAA-BBBB. *IB:* 24.
BTEC NC: DD. *BTEC ND:* DMM. *OCR ND:* D *OCR NED:* M2

W8N2 BA Creative Writing/Management
Duration: 3FT Hon
Entry Requirements: *GCE:* 260-280. *SQAH:* AAA-BBBB. *IB:* 24.
BTEC NC: DD. *BTEC ND:* DMM. *OCR ND:* D *OCR NED:* M2

W8N5 BA Creative Writing/Marketing
Duration: 3FT Hon
Entry Requirements: *GCE:* 260-280. *SQAH:* AAA-BBBB. *IB:* 24.
BTEC NC: DD. *BTEC ND:* DMM. *OCR ND:* D *OCR NED:* M2

W8L5 BA Creative Writing/Social Care
Duration: 3FT Hon
Entry Requirements: *GCE:* 260-280. *SQAH:* AAA-BBBB. *IB:* 24.
BTEC NC: DD. *BTEC ND:* DMM. *OCR ND:* D *OCR NED:* M2

W8L3 BA Creative Writing/Sociology
Duration: 3FT Hon
Entry Requirements: *GCE:* 260-280. *SQAH:* AAA-BBBB. *IB:* 24.
BTEC NC: DD. *BTEC ND:* DMM. *OCR ND:* D *OCR NED:* M2

W8C6 BA Creative Writing/Sport Studies
Duration: 3FT Hon
Entry Requirements: *GCE:* 260-280. *SQAH:* AAA-BBBB. *IB:* 24.
BTEC NC: DD. *BTEC ND:* DMM. *OCR ND:* D *OCR NED:* M2

W8N8 BA Creative Writing/Tourism
Duration: 3FT Hon
Entry Requirements: *GCE:* 260-280. *SQAH:* AAA-BBBB. *IB:* 24.
BTEC NC: DD. *BTEC ND:* DMM. *OCR ND:* D *OCR NED:* M2

M9W8 BA Criminology/Creative Writing
Duration: 3FT Hon
Entry Requirements: *GCE:* 260-280. *SQAH:* AAA-BBBB. *IB:* 24.
BTEC NC: DD. *BTEC ND:* DMM. *OCR ND:* D *OCR NED:* M2

X3W8 BA Education Studies/Creative Writing
Duration: 3FT Hon
Entry Requirements: *GCE:* 260-280. *SQAH:* AAA-BBBB. *IB:* 24.
BTEC NC: DD. *BTEC ND:* DMM. *OCR ND:* D *OCR NED:* M2

Q3W8 BA English/Creative Writing
Duration: 3FT Hon
Entry Requirements: *GCE:* 260-280. *SQAH:* AAA-BBBB. *IB:* 24.
BTEC NC: DD. *BTEC ND:* DMM. *OCR ND:* D *OCR NED:* M2

N8WV BA Events Management/Creative Writing
Duration: 3FT Hon
Entry Requirements: *GCE:* 260-280. *SQAH:* AAA-BBBB. *IB:* 24.
BTEC NC: DD. *BTEC ND:* DMM. *OCR ND:* D *OCR NED:* M2

W6W8 BA Film & Television Studies/Creative Writing
Duration: 3FT Hon
Entry Requirements: *GCE:* 260-280. *SQAH:* AAA-BBBB. *IB:* 24.
BTEC NC: DD. *BTEC ND:* DMM. *OCR ND:* D *OCR NED:* M2

W1W8 BA Fine Art Painting & Drawing/Creative Writing
Duration: 3FT Hon
Entry Requirements: *GCE:* 260-280. *SQAH:* AAA-BBBB. *IB:* 24.
BTEC NC: DD. *BTEC ND:* DMM. *OCR ND:* D *OCR NED:* M2

R1W8 BA French/Creative Writing
Duration: 3FT Hon
Entry Requirements: *GCE:* 260-280. *SQAH:* AAA-BBBB. *IB:* 24.
BTEC NC: DD. *BTEC ND:* DMM. *OCR ND:* D *OCR NED:* M2

L4W8 BA Health Studies/Creative Writing
Duration: 3FT Hon
Entry Requirements: *GCE:* 260-280. *SQAH:* AAA-BBBB. *IB:* 24.
BTEC NC: DD. *BTEC ND:* DMM. *OCR ND:* D *OCR NED:* M2

V1W8 BA History/Creative Writing
Duration: 3FT Hon
Entry Requirements: *GCE:* 260-280. *SQAH:* AAA-BBBB. *IB:* 24.
BTEC NC: DD. *BTEC ND:* DMM. *OCR ND:* D *OCR NED:* M2

L7W8 BA Human Geography/Creative Writing
Duration: 3FT Hon
Entry Requirements: *GCE:* 260-280. *SQAH:* AAA-BBBB. *IB:* 24.
BTEC NC: DD. *BTEC ND:* DMM. *OCR ND:* D *OCR NED:* M2

N6W8 BA Human Resource Management/Creative Writing
Duration: 3FT Hon
Entry Requirements: *GCE:* 260-280. *SQAH:* AAA-BBBB. *IB:* 24.
BTEC NC: DD. *BTEC ND:* DMM. *OCR ND:* D *OCR NED:* M2

L9W8 BA International Development/Creative Writing
Duration: 3FT Hon
Entry Requirements: *GCE:* 260-280. *SQAH:* AAA-BBBB. *IB:* 24.
BTEC NC: DD. *BTEC ND:* DMM. *OCR ND:* D *OCR NED:* M2

M1W8 BA Law/Creative Writing
Duration: 3FT Hon
Entry Requirements: *GCE:* 260-280. *SQAH:* AAA-BBBB. *IB:* 24.
BTEC NC: DD. *BTEC ND:* DMM. *OCR ND:* D *OCR NED:* M2

N2W8 BA Management/Creative Writing
Duration: 3FT Hon
Entry Requirements: *GCE:* 260-280. *SQAH:* AAA-BBBB. *IB:* 24.
BTEC NC: DD. *BTEC ND:* DMM. *OCR ND:* D *OCR NED:* M2

N5W8 BA Marketing/Creative Writing
Duration: 3FT Hon
Entry Requirements: *GCE:* 260-280. *SQAH:* AAA-BBBB. *IB:* 24.
BTEC NC: DD. *BTEC ND:* DMM. *OCR ND:* D *OCR NED:* M2

L5W8 BA Social Care/Creative Writing
Duration: 3FT Hon
Entry Requirements: *GCE:* 260-280. *SQAH:* AAA-BBBB. *IB:* 24.
BTEC NC: DD. *BTEC ND:* DMM. *OCR ND:* D *OCR NED:* M2

L3W8 BA Sociology/Creative Writing
Duration: 3FT Hon
Entry Requirements: *GCE:* 260-280. *SQAH:* AAA-BBBB. *IB:* 24.
BTEC NC: DD. *BTEC ND:* DMM. *OCR ND:* D *OCR NED:* M2

C6W8 BA Sport Studies/Creative Writing
Duration: 3FT Hon
Entry Requirements: *GCE:* 260-280. *SQAH:* AAA-BBBB. *IB:* 24.
BTEC NC: DD. *BTEC ND:* DMM. *OCR ND:* D *OCR NED:* M2

N8W8 BA Tourism/Creative Writing
Duration: 3FT Hon
Entry Requirements: *GCE:* 260-280. *SQAH:* AAA-BBBB. *IB:* 24.
BTEC NC: DD. *BTEC ND:* DMM. *OCR ND:* D *OCR NED:* M2

C1W8 BSc Biological Conservation/Creative Writing
Duration: 3FT Hon
Entry Requirements: *GCE:* 260-280. *SQAH:* AAA-BBBB. *IB:* 24.
BTEC NC: DD. *BTEC ND:* DMM. *OCR ND:* D *OCR NED:* M2

G4W8 BSc Computing/Creative Writing
Duration: 3FT Hon
Entry Requirements: *GCE:* 260-280. *SQAH:* AAA-BBBB. *IB:* 24.
BTEC NC: DD. *BTEC ND:* DMM. *OCR ND:* D *OCR NED:* M2

B1W8 BSc Human Bioscience/Creative Writing
Duration: 3FT Hon
Entry Requirements: *GCE:* 260-280. *SQAH:* AAA-BBBB. *IB:* 24.
BTEC NC: DD. *BTEC ND:* DMM. *OCR ND:* D *OCR NED:* M2

N77 NORTHUMBRIA UNIVERSITY
TRINITY BUILDING
NORTHUMBERLAND ROAD
NEWCASTLE UPON TYNE NE1 8ST
t: 0191 243 7420 f: 0191 227 4561
e: er.admissions@northumbria.ac.uk
// www.northumbria.ac.uk

QW38 BA English Literature and Creative Writing
Duration: 3FT Hon
Entry Requirements: *GCE:* 320. *SQAH:* BBBBB. *SQAAH:* BBB. *IB:* 27.

N84 THE UNIVERSITY OF NOTTINGHAM
THE ADMISSIONS OFFICE
THE UNIVERSITY OF NOTTINGHAM
UNIVERSITY PARK
NOTTINGHAM NG7 2RD
t: 0115 951 5151 f: 0115 951 4668
// www.nottingham.ac.uk

W800 BA Creative and Professional Writing
Duration: 3FT Hon
Entry Requirements: *GCE:* BCC. *SQAAH:* BCC. *IB:* 28.

Q3W8 BA English with Creative Writing
Duration: 3FT Hon
Entry Requirements: *GCE:* AAB. *SQAAH:* AAB. *IB:* 36.

N91 NOTTINGHAM TRENT UNIVERSITY
DRYDEN BUILDINGG
BURTON STREET
NOTTINGHAM NG1 4BU
t: +44 (0) 115 848 4200 f: +44 (0) 115 848 8869
e: applications@ntu.ac.uk
// www.ntu.ac.uk/

Q3W8 BA English with Creative Writing
Duration: 3FT Hon
Entry Requirements: *IB:* 30. *BTEC NC:* DD. *BTEC ND:* DDM.

P60 UNIVERSITY OF PLYMOUTH
DRAKE CIRCUS
PLYMOUTH PL4 8AA
t: 01752 588037 f: 01752 588050
e: admissions@plymouth.ac.uk
// www.plymouth.ac.uk

WQ83 BA English and Creative Writing
Duration: 3FT Hon
Entry Requirements: *GCE:* 260. *IB:* 27. *BTEC ND:* DMM.

P63 UCP MARJON - UNIVERSITY COLLEGE PLYMOUTH ST MARK & ST JOHN
DERRIFORD ROAD
PLYMOUTH PL6 8BH
t: 01752 636890 f: 01752 636819
e: admissions@marjon.ac.uk
// www.ucpmarjon.ac.uk

W800 BA Creative Writing
Duration: 3FT Hon
Entry Requirements: *GCE:* 220.

W8Q1 BA Creative Writing with English Language & Linguistics
Duration: 3FT Hon
Entry Requirements: *GCE:* 220.

W8Q3 BA Creative Writing with English Literature
Duration: 3FT Hon
Entry Requirements: *GCE:* 220.

Q1W8 BA English Language & Linguistics with Creative Writing
Duration: 3FT Hon
Entry Requirements: *GCE:* 220.

Q3W8 BA English Literature with Creative Writing
Duration: 3FT Hon
Entry Requirements: *GCE:* 220.

P80 UNIVERSITY OF PORTSMOUTH
ACADEMIC REGISTRY
UNIVERSITY HOUSE
WINSTON CHURCHILL AVENUE
PORTSMOUTH PO1 2UP
t: 023 9284 8484 f: 023 9284 3082
e: admissions@port.ac.uk
// www.port.ac.uk

W800 BA Creative and Media Writing
Duration: 3FT Hon
Entry Requirements: *GCE:* 240-300. *IB:* 27. *BTEC NC:* DD. *BTEC ND:* DMM.

QW38 BA English and Creative Writing
Duration: 3FT Hon
Entry Requirements: *GCE:* 240-300. *IB:* 27. *BTEC NC:* DD. *BTEC ND:* DMM.

Q75 QUEEN'S UNIVERSITY BELFAST
UNIVERSITY ROAD
BELFAST BT7 1NN
t: 028 9097 3838 f: 028 9097 5151
e: admissions@qub.ac.uk
// www.qub.ac.uk

Q3W8 BA English with Creative Writing
Duration: 3FT Hon
Entry Requirements: Contact the institution for details.

R06 RAVENSBOURNE
6 PENROSE WAY
LONDON SE10 0EW
t: 020 3040 3500
e: info@rave.ac.uk
// www.rave.ac.uk

W810 BA Screenwriting
Duration: 3FT Hon
Entry Requirements: *Foundation:* Pass. *GCE:* AA-CC. *IB:* 28. *BTEC NC:* PP. *BTEC ND:* PPP. Interview required. Portfolio required.

W812 BA Screenwriting (Fast-Track)
Duration: 2FT Hon
Entry Requirements: Contact the institution for details.

W811 BA Screenwriting with Level 0
Duration: 4FT Hon
Entry Requirements: *Foundation:* Pass. *GCE:* A-E. *IB:* 28. *BTEC NC:* PP. *BTEC ND:* PPP. Interview required. Admissions Test required.

R18 REGENTS BUSINESS SCHOOL, LONDON (REGENTS COLLEGE)
INNER CIRCLE, REGENT'S COLLEGE
REGENT'S PARK
LONDON NW1 4NS
t: +44(0)20 7487 7505 f: +44(0)20 7487 7425
e: exrel@regents.ac.uk
// www.regents.ac.uk/

WW86 BA Screen Writing and Producing
Duration: 3FT Hon
Entry Requirements: *SQAH:* BBCC. *SQAAH:* CC.

R48 ROEHAMPTON UNIVERSITY
ERASMUS HOUSE
ROEHAMPTON LANE
LONDON SW15 5PU
t: 020 8392 3232 f: 020 8392 3470
e: enquiries@roehampton.ac.uk
// www.roehampton.ac.uk

W801 BA Creative Writing
Duration: 3FT Hon
Entry Requirements: *GCE:* 300-340. *IB:* 26. *BTEC ND:* DDM.
OCR NED: D2 Interview required.

WQ83 BA Creative Writing and English Literature
Duration: 3FT Hon
Entry Requirements: *GCE:* 300-340. *IB:* 26. *BTEC ND:* DDM.
OCR NED: D2 Interview required.

WV85 BA Creative Writing and Philosophy
Duration: 3FT Hon
Entry Requirements: *GCE:* 300-340. *IB:* 26. *BTEC ND:* DDM.
OCR NED: D2 Interview required.

WW68 BA Photography and Creative Writing
Duration: 3FT Hon
Entry Requirements: *GCE:* 300-340. *IB:* 26. *BTEC ND:* DDM.
OCR NED: D2 Interview required.

R72 ROYAL HOLLOWAY, UNIVERSITY OF LONDON
ROYAL HOLLOWAY, UNIVERSITY OF LONDON
EGHAM
SURREY TW20 0EX
t: 01784 434455 f: 01784 473662
e: Admissions@rhul.ac.uk
// www.rhul.ac.uk

QW38 BA English and Creative Writing
Duration: 3FT Hon
Entry Requirements: *GCE:* AAB. *SQAH:* AAAAB. *SQAAH:* AAB. *IB:* 35.

R90 RUSKIN COLLEGE OXFORD
WALTON STREET
OXFORD OX1 2HE
t: 01865 517832 f: 01865 554372
e: enquiries@ruskin.ac.uk
// www.ruskin.ac.uk

QW38 BA English Studies:Creative Writing & Critical Practice
Duration: 3FT Hon
Entry Requirements: Contact the institution for details.

W810 FdA Writing for Performance
Duration: 2FT Fdg
Entry Requirements: Contact the institution for details.

S03 THE UNIVERSITY OF SALFORD
SALFORD M5 4WT
t: 0161 295 4545 f: 0161 295 4646
e: ug-admissions@salford.ac.uk
// www.salford.ac.uk

W890 BA Comedy: Writing and Performance
Duration: 3FT Hon
Entry Requirements: Contact the institution for details.

QW38 BA English and Creative Writing
Duration: 3FT Hon
Entry Requirements: *GCE:* 260. *IB:* 31. *BTEC NC:* DD. *BTEC ND:* MMM. Interview required.

S21 SHEFFIELD HALLAM UNIVERSITY
CITY CAMPUS
HOWARD STREET
SHEFFIELD S1 1WB
t: 0114 225 5555 f: 0114 225 2167
e: admissions@shu.ac.uk
// www.shu.ac.uk

W800 BA Creative Writing
Duration: 3FT Hon
Entry Requirements: *GCE:* 300.

S30 SOUTHAMPTON SOLENT UNIVERSITY
EAST PARK TERRACE
SOUTHAMPTON
HAMPSHIRE SO14 0RT
t: +44 (0) 23 8031 9039 f: + 44 (0)23 8022 2259
e: admissions@solent.ac.uk or ask@solent.ac.uk
// www.solent.ac.uk/

WW48 BA Comedy - Writing and Performance
Duration: 3FT Hon
Entry Requirements: *Foundation:* Distinction. *GCE:* 240. *SQAAH:* AA-CCD. *IB:* 24. *BTEC NC:* DD. *BTEC ND:* MMM. *OCR ND:* D
OCR NED: M3 Interview required.

QW3V BA English and Screenwriting
Duration: 3FT Hon
Entry Requirements: *Foundation:* Distinction. *GCE:* 240. *SQAAH:* AA-CCD. *IB:* 24. *BTEC NC:* DD. *BTEC ND:* MMM. *OCR ND:* D
OCR NED: M3

QWH8 BA English and Screenwriting
Duration: 4SW Hon
Entry Requirements: *Foundation:* Distinction. *GCE:* 240. *SQAAH:* AA-CCD. *IB:* 24. *BTEC NC:* DD. *BTEC ND:* MMM. *OCR ND:* D
OCR NED: M3

W810 BA Screenwriting
Duration: 3FT Hon
Entry Requirements: *Foundation:* Distinction. *GCE:* 240. *SQAAH:* AA-CCD. *IB:* 24. *BTEC NC:* DD. *BTEC ND:* MMM. *OCR ND:* D
OCR NED: M3

W8Q3 BA Screenwriting with International Foundation Year
Duration: 4FT Hon
Entry Requirements: *GCE:* 240.

S64 ST MARY'S UNIVERSITY COLLEGE, TWICKENHAM
WALDEGRAVE ROAD
STRAWBERRY HILL
MIDDLESEX TW1 4SX
t: 020 8240 4029 f: 020 8240 2361
e: admit@smuc.ac.uk
// www.smuc.ac.uk

MW28 BA Business Law and Creative & Professional Writing
Duration: 3FT Hon
Entry Requirements: *GCE:* 240. *SQAH:* BBBC. *IB:* 28. *BTEC NC:* DM. *BTEC ND:* MMM. *OCR ND:* D *OCR NED:* M3 Interview required.

WN88 BA Creative & Profesional Writing and Tourism
Duration: 3FT Hon
Entry Requirements: *GCE:* 240. *SQAH:* BBBC. *IB:* 28. *BTEC NC:* DM. *BTEC ND:* MMM. *OCR ND:* D *OCR NED:* M3 Interview required.

WV86 BA Creative & Professional Writing and Theology & Religious Studies
Duration: 3FT Hon
Entry Requirements: *GCE:* 240. *SQAH:* BBBC. *IB:* 28. *BTEC NC:* DM. *BTEC ND:* MMM. *OCR ND:* D *OCR NED:* M3 Interview required.

W800 BA Creative and Professional Writing
Duration: 3FT Hon
Entry Requirements: *GCE:* 240. *SQAH:* BBBC. *IB:* 28. *BTEC NC:* DM. *BTEC ND:* MMM. *OCR ND:* D *OCR NED:* M3 Interview required.

QW38 BA English and Creative & Professional Writing
Duration: 3FT Hon
Entry Requirements: *GCE:* 240. *SQAH:* BBBC. *IB:* 28. *BTEC NC:* DM. *BTEC ND:* MMM. *OCR ND:* D *OCR NED:* M3 Interview required.

VW18 BA History and Creative & Professional Writing
Duration: 3FT Hon
Entry Requirements: *GCE:* 240. *SQAH:* BBBC. *IB:* 28. *BTEC NC:* DM. *BTEC ND:* MMM. *OCR ND:* D *OCR NED:* M3 Interview required.

NW28 BA Management Studies and Creative & Professional Writing
Duration: 3FT Hon
Entry Requirements: *GCE:* 240. *SQAH:* BBBC. *IB:* 28. *BTEC NC:* DM. *BTEC ND:* MMM. *OCR ND:* D *OCR NED:* M3 Interview required.

XW38 BA Physical & Sport Education and Creative & Professional Writing
Duration: 3FT Hon
Entry Requirements: *GCE:* 240. *SQAH:* BBBC. *IB:* 28. *BTEC NC:* DM. *BTEC ND:* MMM. *OCR ND:* D *OCR NED:* M3 Interview required.

CW68 BA/BSc Creative & Professional Writing and Sport Science
Duration: 3FT Hon
Entry Requirements: *GCE:* 240. *SQAH:* BBBC. *IB:* 28. *BTEC NC:* DM. *BTEC ND:* MMM. *OCR ND:* D *OCR NED:* M3 Interview required.

FW88 BA/BSc Geography and Creative & Professional Writing
Duration: 3FT Hon
Entry Requirements: *GCE:* 240. *SQAH:* BBBC. *IB:* 28. *BTEC NC:* DM. *BTEC ND:* MMM. *OCR ND:* D *OCR NED:* M3 Interview required.

BW4V BA/BSc Nutrition and Creative & Professional Writing
Duration: 3FT Hon
Entry Requirements: *GCE:* 240. *SQAH:* BBBC. *IB:* 28. *BTEC NC:* DM. *BTEC ND:* MMM. *OCR ND:* D *OCR NED:* M3 Interview required.

CW88 BA/BSc Psychology and Creative & Professional Writing
Duration: 3FT Hon
Entry Requirements: *GCE:* 240. *SQAH:* BBBC. *IB:* 28. *BTEC NC:* DM. *BTEC ND:* MMM. *OCR ND:* D *OCR NED:* M3 Interview required.

S72 STAFFORDSHIRE UNIVERSITY
COLLEGE ROAD
STOKE ON TRENT ST4 2DE
t: 01782 292753 f: 01782 292740
e: admissions@staffs.ac.uk
// www.staffs.ac.uk

W800 BA Creative Writing
Duration: 3FT Hon
Entry Requirements: *GCE:* 200-240. *IB:* 24.

WV81 BA Creative Writing and Modern History
Duration: 3FT Hon
Entry Requirements: *GCE:* 200-240. *IB:* 24.

WV85 BA Creative Writing and Philosophy
Duration: 3FT Hon
Entry Requirements: *GCE:* 200-240. *IB:* 24.

WL83 BA Creative Writing and Sociology
Duration: 3FT Hon
Entry Requirements: *GCE:* 180-220. *IB:* 24.

QWH8 BA English Literature and Scriptwriting
Duration: 3FT Hon
Entry Requirements: *GCE:* 200-240. *IB:* 24.

QW38 BA English and Creative Writing
Duration: 3FT Hon
Entry Requirements: *GCE:* 200-240. *IB:* 24.

LW38 BA Ethics and Creative Writing
Duration: 3FT Hon
Entry Requirements: *GCE:* 180-220. *IB:* 24.

LWH8 BA Ethics and Scriptwriting
Duration: 3FT Hon
Entry Requirements: *GCE:* 180-220. *IB:* 24.

VW28 BA International History and Creative Writing
Duration: 3FT Hon
Entry Requirements: *GCE:* 180-220. *IB:* 24.

VW2V BA International History and Scriptwriting
Duration: 3FT Hon
Entry Requirements: *GCE:* 200-240. *IB:* 24.

LW28 BA International Relations and Creative Writing
Duration: 3FT Hon
Entry Requirements: *GCE:* 180-220. *IB:* 24.

LW2V BA International Relations and Scriptwriting
Duration: 3FT Hon
Entry Requirements: *GCE:* 180-220. *IB:* 24.

VW18 BA Modern History and Scriptwriting
Duration: 3FT Hon
Entry Requirements: *GCE:* 200-240. *IB:* 24.

VW58 BA Philosophy and Scriptwriting
Duration: 3FT Hon
Entry Requirements: *GCE:* 200-240. *IB:* 24.

W890 BA Publication Design
Duration: 3FT Hon
Entry Requirements: *GCE:* 180-220. *IB:* 24. Interview required. Portfolio required.

W810 BA Scriptwriting
Duration: 3FT Hon
Entry Requirements: *GCE:* 200-240. *IB:* 24.

WL8H BA Scriptwriting and Sociology
Duration: 3FT Hon
Entry Requirements: *GCE:* 200-240. *IB:* 24.

S84 UNIVERSITY OF SUNDERLAND
STUDENT HELPLINE
THE STUDENT GATEWAY
CHESTER ROAD
SUNDERLAND SR1 3SD
t: 0191 515 3000 f: 0191 515 3805
e: student.helpline@sunderland.ac.uk
// www.sunderland.ac.uk

QW38 BA English and Creative Writing
Duration: 3FT Hon
Entry Requirements: *GCE:* 260-360.

P390 BA Scriptwriting: Film, Television and Radio
Duration: 3FT Hon
Entry Requirements: *GCE:* 260-360. *IB:* 30. *BTEC ND:* DMM.

S85 UNIVERSITY OF SURREY
STAG HILL
GUILDFORD
SURREY GU2 7XH
t: +44(0)1483 689305 f: +44(0)1483 689388
e: ugteam@surrey.ac.uk
// www.surrey.ac.uk

Q3W8 BA English Literature with Creative Writing (3 years)
Duration: 3FT Hon
Entry Requirements: *GCE:* 320.

Q3WV BA English Literature with Creative Writing (4 years)
Duration: 4SW Hon
Entry Requirements: *GCE:* 320.

W6W8 BA (Hons) Film Studies with Creative Writing (3 or 4 years)
Duration: 3FT/4SW Hon
Entry Requirements: *GCE:* ABB. *IB:* 34. *BTEC ND:* DDM.

T20 TEESSIDE UNIVERSITY
MIDDLESBROUGH TS1 3BA
t: 01642 218121 f: 01642 384201
e: registry@tees.ac.uk
// www.tees.ac.uk

Q3W8 BA English Studies with Creative Writing
Duration: 3FT Hon
Entry Requirements: *GCE:* 280. *IB:* 25.

T80 UNIVERSITY OF WALES TRINITY SAINT DAVID
COLLEGE ROAD
CARMARTHEN SA31 3EP
t: 01267 676767 f: 01267 676766
e: registrylc@trinitysaintdavid.ac.uk
// www.trinitysaintdavid.ac.uk/

W801 BA Creative Writing
Duration: 3FT Hon
Entry Requirements: *GCE:* 120-360. *IB:* 26. *BTEC NC:* MP. *BTEC ND:* PPP. Interview required.

QW38 BA Creative Writing and English
Duration: 3FT Hon
Entry Requirements: *GCE:* 120-360. *IB:* 26. *BTEC NC:* MP. *BTEC ND:* PPP. Interview required.

WV85 BA Creative Writing and Philosophy
Duration: 3FT Hon
Entry Requirements: Contact the institution for details.

U40 UNIVERSITY OF THE WEST OF SCOTLAND
PAISLEY
RENFREWSHIRE
SCOTLAND PA1 2BE
t: 0141 848 3727 f: 0141 848 3623
e: admissions@uws.ac.uk
// www.uws.ac.uk

WW68 BA Filmmaking and Screen Writing
Duration: 4FT Hon
Entry Requirements: *GCE:* BC-CC. *SQAH:* BBC. Interview required. Portfolio required.

W20 THE UNIVERSITY OF WARWICK
COVENTRY CV4 8UW
t: 024 7652 3723 f: 024 7652 4649
e: ugadmissions@warwick.ac.uk
// www.warwick.ac.uk

QW38 BA English Literature and Creative Writing
Duration: 3FT Hon
Entry Requirements: *GCE:* AAA. *SQAAH:* AA. *IB:* 38. Interview required.

W50 UNIVERSITY OF WESTMINSTER
2ND FLOOR
101 NEW CAVENDISH STREET,
LONDON W1W 6XH
t: 020 7911 5000 f: 020 7911 5788
e: course-enquiries@westminster.ac.uk
// www.westminster.ac.uk

QW38 BA English Language and Creative Writing
Duration: 3FT Hon
Entry Requirements: *GCE:* BBC. *SQAH:* BBCCC. *SQAAH:* BCC. *IB:* 30. *BTEC ND:* DMM. Portfolio required.

QW3V BA English Literature and Creative Writing
Duration: 3FT Hon
Entry Requirements: *GCE:* BBC. *SQAH:* BBCCC. *SQAAH:* BCC. *IB:* 30. *BTEC ND:* DMM. Portfolio required.

QW18 BA Linguistics and Creative Writing
Duration: 3FT Hon
Entry Requirements: *GCE:* BBC. *SQAH:* BBCCC. *SQAAH:* BCC. *IB:* 30. *BTEC ND:* DMM. Portfolio required.

W75 UNIVERSITY OF WOLVERHAMPTON
ADMISSIONS UNIT
MX207, CAMP STREET
WOLVERHAMPTON
WEST MIDLANDS WV1 1AD
t: 01902 321000 f: 01902 321896
e: admissions@wlv.ac.uk
// www.wlv.ac.uk

WQ83 BA Creative & Professional Writing and English
Duration: 3FT Hon
Entry Requirements: *GCE:* 160-220.

WL82 BA Creative Professional Writing and War Studies
Duration: 3FT Hon
Entry Requirements: *GCE:* 160-220.

QW38 BA English Language and Creative Professional Writing
Duration: 3FT Hon
Entry Requirements: *GCE:* 160-220.

VW58 BA Philosophy and Creative Professional Writing
Duration: 3FT Hon
Entry Requirements: *GCE:* 160-220.

W76 UNIVERSITY OF WINCHESTER
WINCHESTER
HANTS SO22 4NR
t: 01962 827234 f: 01962 827288
e: course.enquiries@winchester.ac.uk
// www.winchester.ac.uk

TWR8 BA American Studies and Creative Writing
Duration: 3FT Hon
Entry Requirements: *Foundation:* Distinction. *GCE:* 260-300. *IB:* 25. *BTEC NC:* DD. *BTEC ND:* DMM. *OCR ND:* D *OCR NED:* M2

VWK8 BA Archaeology and Creative Writing
Duration: 3FT Hon
Entry Requirements: *Foundation:* Distinction. *GCE:* 260-300. *IB:* 24. *BTEC NC:* DD. *BTEC ND:* DMM. *OCR ND:* D *OCR NED:* M2

NWC8 BA Business Management and Creative Writing
Duration: 3FT Hon
Entry Requirements: *Foundation:* Distinction. *GCE:* 260-300. *IB:* 25. *BTEC NC:* DD. *BTEC ND:* DMM. *OCR ND:* D *OCR NED:* M2

LW5V BA Childhood Youth & Community Studies and Creative Writing
Duration: 3FT Hon
Entry Requirements: *GCE:* 260-300. *IB:* 24.

WWL8 BA Contemporary Performance and Creative Writing
Duration: 3FT Hon
Entry Requirements: *Foundation:* Distinction. *GCE:* 260-300. *IB:* 25. *BTEC NC:* DD. *BTEC ND:* DMM. *OCR ND:* D *OCR NED:* M2

W800 BA Creative Writing
Duration: 3FT Hon
Entry Requirements: *Foundation:* Distinction. *GCE:* 260-300. *IB:* 26. *BTEC NC:* DD. *BTEC ND:* MMM. *OCR ND:* D

WL8J BA Creative Writing and Criminology
Duration: 3FT Hon
Entry Requirements: *Foundation:* Distinction. *GCE:* 260-300. *IB:* 25. *BTEC NC:* DD. *BTEC ND:* DMM. *OCR ND:* D *OCR NED:* M2

WX83 BA Creative Writing and Education Studies
Duration: 3FT Hon
Entry Requirements: *Foundation:* Distinction. *GCE:* 260-300. *IB:* 25. *BTEC NC:* DD. *BTEC ND:* DMM. *OCR ND:* D *OCR NED:* M2

WXW3 BA Creative Writing and Education Studies (Early Years)
Duration: 3FT Hon
Entry Requirements: *Foundation:* Distinction. *GCE:* 260-300. *IB:* 25. *BTEC NC:* DD. *BTEC ND:* DMM. *OCR ND:* D *OCR NED:* M2

WX8H BA Creative Writing and Education Studies (Modern Liberal Arts)
Duration: 3FT Hon
Entry Requirements: *Foundation:* Distinction. *GCE:* 260-300. *IB:* 25. *BTEC NC:* DD. *BTEC ND:* DMM. *OCR ND:* D *OCR NED:* M2

QW38 BA Creative Writing and English
Duration: 3FT Hon
Entry Requirements: *Foundation:* Distinction. *GCE:* 260-300. *IB:* 25. *BTEC NC:* DD. *BTEC ND:* DMM. *OCR ND:* D *OCR NED:* M2

WQ83 BA Creative Writing and English Language Studies
Duration: 3FT Hon
Entry Requirements: *Foundation:* Distinction. *GCE:* 260-300. *IB:* 25. *BTEC NC:* DD. *BTEC ND:* DMM. *OCR ND:* D *OCR NED:* M2

WN8W BA Creative Writing and Event Management
Duration: 3FT Hon
Entry Requirements: *GCE:* 260-300. *IB:* 24.

WW86 BA Creative Writing and Film & Cinema Technologies
Duration: 3FT Hon
Entry Requirements: *Foundation:* Distinction. *GCE:* 260-300. *IB:* 25. *BTEC NC:* DD. *BTEC ND:* DMM. *OCR ND:* D *OCR NED:* M2

VWC8 BA Creative Writing and History
Duration: 3FT Hon
Entry Requirements: *Foundation:* Distinction. *GCE:* 260-300. *IB:* 25. *BTEC NC:* DD. *BTEC ND:* DMM. *OCR ND:* D *OCR NED:* M2

WW8X BA Creative Writing and Modern Liberal Arts
Duration: 3FT Hon
Entry Requirements: *Foundation:* Distinction. *GCE:* 260-300. *IB:* 25. *BTEC NC:* DD. *BTEC ND:* DMM. *OCR ND:* D *OCR NED:* M2

WL82 BA Creative Writing and Politics & Global Studies
Duration: 3FT Hon
Entry Requirements: *Foundation:* Distinction. *GCE:* 260-300. *IB:* 25. *BTEC NC:* DD. *BTEC ND:* DMM. *OCR ND:* D *OCR NED:* M2

WL83 BA Creative Writing and Sociology
Duration: 3FT Hon
Entry Requirements: *Foundation:* Distinction. *GCE:* 260-300. *IB:* 25. *BTEC NC:* DD. *BTEC ND:* DMM. *OCR ND:* D *OCR NED:* M2

WNW8 BA Creative Writing and Sports Management
Duration: 3FT Hon
Entry Requirements: *GCE:* 260-300. *IB:* 24.

WC86 BA Creative Writing and Sports Studies
Duration: 3FT Hon
Entry Requirements: *Foundation:* Merit. *GCE:* 260-300. *IB:* 24. *BTEC NC:* DM. *BTEC ND:* MMP.

VW68 BA Creative Writing and Theology & Religious Studies
Duration: 3FT Hon
Entry Requirements: *Foundation:* Distinction. *GCE:* 260-300. *IB:* 25. *BTEC NC:* DD. *BTEC ND:* DMM. *OCR ND:* D *OCR NED:* M2

MW18 BA Law and Creative Writing
Duration: 3FT Hon
Entry Requirements: *Foundation:* Distinction. *GCE:* 260-300. *IB:* 25. *BTEC NC:* DD. *BTEC ND:* DMM. *OCR ND:* D *OCR NED:* M2

WNV8 DipHE Creative Writing and Event Management
Duration: 2FT Dip
Entry Requirements: *Foundation:* Pass. *GCE:* 260-300. *IB:* 20. *BTEC NC:* MP. *BTEC ND:* PPP.

W80 UNIVERSITY OF WORCESTER
HENWICK GROVE
WORCESTER WR2 6AJ
t: 01905 855111 f: 01905 855377
e: admissions@worc.ac.uk
// www.worcester.ac.uk

WW68 BA Animation and Screen Writing
Duration: 3FT Hon
Entry Requirements: *GCE:* 220-300. *IB:* 24. *OCR ND:* D Interview required. Portfolio required.

WW28 BA Creative Digital Media and Screen Writing
Duration: 3FT Hon
Entry Requirements: *GCE:* 220-300. *IB:* 24. *OCR ND:* D Interview required. Portfolio required.

WW6V BA Digital Film Production and Screen Writing
Duration: 3FT Hon
Entry Requirements: *GCE:* 220-300. *IB:* 24. *OCR ND:* D Interview required. Portfolio required.

QW3V BA English Language Studies and Screen Writing
Duration: 3FT Hon
Entry Requirements: *GCE:* 240-260. *IB:* 24. *BTEC NC:* DD. *BTEC ND:* MMM. *OCR ND:* D *OCR NED:* M3

QW38 BA English Literary Studies and Screen Writing
Duration: 3FT Hon
Entry Requirements: *GCE:* 240-300. *IB:* 24. *BTEC NC:* DD. *BTEC ND:* MMM. *OCR ND:* D *OCR NED:* M3

Y75 YORK ST JOHN UNIVERSITY
LORD MAYOR'S WALK
YORK YO31 7EX
t: 01904 876598 f: 01904 876940/876921
e: admissions@yorksj.ac.uk
// w3.yorksj.ac.uk

WQ83 BA Creative Writing and English Language
Duration: 3FT Hon
Entry Requirements: *GCE:* 200-240. *IB:* 24.

WQ8H BA Creative Writing and English Literature
Duration: 3FT Hon
Entry Requirements: *GCE:* 200-240. *IB:* 24.

Q3W8 BA English Literature with Creative Writing
Duration: 3FT Hon
Entry Requirements: *GCE:* 200-240. *IB:* 24.

PERFORMING ARTS

B22 UNIVERSITY OF BEDFORDSHIRE
PARK SQUARE
LUTON
BEDS LU1 3JU
t: 0844 8482234 f: 01582 489323
e: admissions@beds.ac.uk
// www.beds.ac.uk

W491 BA Theatre and Professional Practice
Duration: 3FT Hon
Entry Requirements: *GCE:* 160. Interview required.

B25 BIRMINGHAM CITY UNIVERSITY
PERRY BARR
BIRMINGHAM B42 2SU
t: 0121 331 5595 f: 0121 331 7994
e: choices@bcu.ac.uk
// www.bcu.ac.uk

W490 BA Community and Applied Theatre
Duration: 3FT Hon   CRB Check: Required
Entry Requirements: *GCE:* 240. *IB:* 28. *BTEC NC:* MM. *BTEC ND:* MMM. Interview required.

B50 BOURNEMOUTH UNIVERSITY
TALBOT CAMPUS
FERN BARROW
POOLE
DORSET BH12 5BB
t: 01202 524111
// www.bournemouth.ac.uk

W491 FdA Performing Arts: Contemporary Theatre
Duration: 2FT Fdg
Entry Requirements: *Foundation:* Distinction. *IB:* 24. Interview required.

B84 BRUNEL UNIVERSITY
UXBRIDGE
MIDDLESEX UB8 3PH
t: 01895 265265 f: 01895 269790
e: admissions@brunel.ac.uk
// www.brunel.ac.uk

WW49 BA Theatre and Sonic Arts
Duration: 3FT Hon
Entry Requirements: *GCE:* BCC. *SQAAH:* BCC. *IB:* 29. *BTEC ND:* DDM.

B92 BROOKSBY MELTON COLLEGE
MELTON CAMPUS
ASFORDBY ROAD
MELTON MOWBRAY
LEICESTERSHIRE LE13 0HJ
t: 01664 850850 f: 01664 855355
// www.brooksbymelton.ac.uk

094W HNC Community Theatre
Duration: 1FT HNC
Entry Requirements: Contact the institution for details.

C10 CANTERBURY CHRIST CHURCH UNIVERSITY
NORTH HOLMES ROAD
CANTERBURY
KENT CT1 1QU
t: 01227 782900 f: 01227 782888
e: admissions@canterbury.ac.uk
// www.canterbury.ac.uk

WQ43 BA Creative Arts
Duration: 3FT Hon
Entry Requirements: Interview required.

W490 BA Performing Arts
Duration: 3FT Hon
Entry Requirements: *GCE:* 240. *IB:* 24. Interview required.

C35 CENTRAL SCHOOL OF SPEECH AND DRAMA, UNIVERSITY OF LONDON
EMBASSY THEATRE
64 ETON AVENUE
LONDON NW3 3HY
t: 0207 722 8183 f: 0207 722 4132
e: enquiries@cssd.ac.uk
// www.cssd.ac.uk

W490 BA Drama, Applied Theatre and Education
Duration: 3FT Hon
Entry Requirements: *GCE:* BBB. Interview required.

W491 BA Theatre Practice: Stage Management
Duration: 3FT Hon
Entry Requirements: *GCE:* BBC. Interview required. Portfolio required.

W493 BA Theatre Practice: Technical and Production Management
Duration: 3FT Hon
Entry Requirements: *GCE:* BBC. Interview required. Portfolio required.

C64 CITY COLLEGE COVENTRY
SWANSWELL
50 SWANSWELL STREET
COVENTRY CV1 5DG
t: 0800 616 202 f: 024 7622 3390
e: courses@covcollege.ac.uk
// www.covcollege.ac.uk

194W HNC Performing Arts
Duration: 1FT HNC
Entry Requirements: Contact the institution for details.

C71 CLEVELAND COLLEGE OF ART AND DESIGN
GREEN LANE
LINTHORPE
MIDDLESBROUGH TS5 7RJ
t: 01642 288888 f: 01642 288828
e: studentrecruitment@ccad.ac.uk
// www.ccad.ac.uk

W490 BA(Hons) Entertainment Design Crafts
Duration: 3FT Hon
Entry Requirements: *Foundation:* Pass. *GCE:* 120. Interview required. Portfolio required.

C78 CORNWALL COLLEGE
POOL
REDRUTH
CORNWALL TR15 3RD
t: 01209 616161 f: 01209 611612
e: he.admissions@cornwall.ac.uk
// www.cornwall.ac.uk

W490 FdA Live Arts Performance
Duration: 2FT Fdg   CRB Check: Required
Entry Requirements: *GCE:* 80-120. *BTEC ND:* MMP. Interview required.

C99 UNIVERSITY OF CUMBRIA
FUSEHILL STREET
CARLISLE
CUMBRIA CA1 2HH
t: 01228 616234 f: 01228 616235
// www.cumbria.ac.uk

W493 BA Performance and Production top-up
Duration: 1FT Hon
Entry Requirements: Interview required. HND required.

D39 UNIVERSITY OF DERBY
KEDLESTON ROAD
DERBY DE22 1GB
t: 01332 591167 f: 01332 597724
e: askadmissions@derby.ac.uk
// www.derby.ac.uk

W490 BA Creative Expressive Therapies (Drama)
Duration: 3FT Hon   CRB Check: Required
Entry Requirements: *Foundation:* Merit. *GCE:* 180-200. *IB:* 26. *BTEC NC:* DM. *BTEC ND:* MMP. Interview required.

E28 UNIVERSITY OF EAST LONDON
DOCKLANDS CAMPUS
UNIVERSITY WAY
LONDON E16 2RD
t: 020 8223 3333 f: 020 8223 2978
e: study@uel.ac.uk
// www.uel.ac.uk

W4P9 BA Community Arts Practice with Communication Studies
Duration: 3FT Hon
Entry Requirements: *GCE:* 200. *IB:* 24. *BTEC NC:* DM. *BTEC ND:* MMP. *OCR ND:* M1 *OCR NED:* P1 Interview required.

W4X3 BA Community Arts Practice with Early Childhood Studies
Duration: 3FT Hon
Entry Requirements: *GCE:* 200. *IB:* 24. *BTEC NC:* DM. *BTEC ND:* MMP. *OCR ND:* M1 *OCR NED:* P1 Interview required.

W4Q3 BA Community Arts Practice with English Language
Duration: 3FT Hon
Entry Requirements: *GCE:* 200. *IB:* 24. *BTEC NC:* DM. *BTEC ND:* MMP. *OCR ND:* M1 *OCR NED:* P1 Interview required.

W4QH BA Community Arts Practice with English Literature
Duration: 3FT Hon
Entry Requirements: *GCE:* 200. *IB:* 24. *BTEC NC:* DM. *BTEC ND:* MMP. *OCR ND:* M1 *OCR NED:* P1 Interview required.

W4C6 BA Community Arts Practice with Sports & Exercise Science
Duration: 3FT Hon
Entry Requirements: *GCE:* 200. *IB:* 24. *BTEC NC:* DM. *BTEC ND:* MMP. *OCR ND:* M1 *OCR NED:* P1 Interview required.

Q3W4 BA English Literature with Community Arts Practice
Duration: 3FT Hon
Entry Requirements: *GCE:* 200. *IB:* 24. *BTEC NC:* DM. *BTEC ND:* MMP. *OCR ND:* M1 *OCR NED:* P1

NW84 BA Events Management /Community Arts Practice
Duration: 3FT Hon
Entry Requirements: *GCE:* 200. *IB:* 24. *BTEC NC:* DM. *BTEC ND:* MMP. *OCR ND:* M1 *OCR NED:* P1

NW64 BA Human Resource Management/Community Arts Practice
Duration: 3FT Hon
Entry Requirements: *GCE:* 200. *IB:* 24. *BTEC NC:* DM. *BTEC ND:* MMP. *OCR ND:* M1 *OCR NED:* P1

NW54 BA Marketing/Community Arts Practice
Duration: 3FT Hon
Entry Requirements: *GCE:* 200. *IB:* 24. *BTEC NC:* DM. *BTEC ND:* MMP. *OCR ND:* M1 *OCR NED:* P1

N2W4 BA Music Industry Management with Community Arts Practice
Duration: 3FT Hon
Entry Requirements: *GCE:* 200. *IB:* 24. *BTEC NC:* DM. *BTEC ND:* MMP. *OCR ND:* M1 *OCR NED:* P1

GW54 BA/BSc Business Information Systems/Community Arts Practice
Duration: 3FT Hon
Entry Requirements: *GCE:* 200. *IB:* 24. *BTEC NC:* DM. *BTEC ND:* MMP. *OCR ND:* M1 *OCR NED:* P1 Interview required.

B9W4 BSc Health Promotion with Community Arts Practice
Duration: 3FT Hon
Entry Requirements: *GCE:* 200. *IB:* 24. *BTEC NC:* DM. *BTEC ND:* MMP. *OCR ND:* M1 *OCR NED:* P1

E42 EDGE HILL UNIVERSITY
ORMSKIRK
LANCASHIRE L39 4QP
t: 01695 657000 f: 01695 584355
e: study@edgehill.ac.uk
// www.edgehill.ac.uk

WB49 BA Performance and Health
Duration: 3FT Hon CRB Check: Required
Entry Requirements: *GCE:* 280. *IB:* 26. *BTEC NC:* DD. *BTEC ND:*
DMM. *OCR ND:* D *OCR NED:* M2 Interview required.

E70 THE UNIVERSITY OF ESSEX
WIVENHOE PARK
COLCHESTER
ESSEX CO4 3SQ
t: 01206 873666 f: 01206 874477
e: admit@essex.ac.uk
// www.essex.ac.uk

W496 BA Acting and Community Theatre
Duration: 3FT Hon CRB Check: Required
Entry Requirements: *GCE:* 160. *IB:* 24. *BTEC ND:* MPP. Interview
required.

W494 BA Physical Theatre
Duration: 3FT Hon
Entry Requirements: *GCE:* EE. *SQAH:* CCCC. *SQAAH:* CCC. *IB:* 24.
BTEC NC: PP. *BTEC ND:* PPP.

W495 BA World Performance
Duration: 3FT Hon
Entry Requirements: *GCE:* 260. *SQAH:* BBBCC. *SQAAH:* BBC. *IB:*
28. *BTEC NC:* DM. *BTEC ND:* DMM. *OCR ND:* D

G70 UNIVERSITY OF GREENWICH
GREENWICH CAMPUS
OLD ROYAL NAVAL COLLEGE
PARK ROW
LONDON SE10 9LS
t: 0800 005 006 f: 020 8331 8145
e: courseinfo@gre.ac.uk
// www.gre.ac.uk

W490 FdA Creative Industries: Performing Arts
Duration: 2FT Fdg
Entry Requirements: Contact the institution for details.

H60 THE UNIVERSITY OF HUDDERSFIELD
QUEENSGATE
HUDDERSFIELD HD1 3DH
t: 01484 473969 f: 01484 472765
e: admissionsandrecords@hud.ac.uk
// www.hud.ac.uk

W490 BA Performance (Top-Up)
Duration: 1FT Hon
Entry Requirements: Interview required. HND required.

H72 THE UNIVERSITY OF HULL
THE UNIVERSITY OF HULL
COTTINGHAM ROAD
HULL HU6 7RX
t: 01482 466100 f: 01482 442290
e: admissions@hull.ac.uk
// www.hull.ac.uk

W490 BA Media Performance
Duration: 3FT Hon
Entry Requirements: *GCE:* 240. *IB:* 24. *BTEC ND:* DMM.

H73 HULL COLLEGE
QUEEN'S GARDENS
HULL HU1 3DG
t: 01482 329943 f: 01482 598733
e: info@hull-college.ac.uk
// www.hull-college.ac.uk/HE

WW14 FdA Visual Arts
Duration: 2FT Fdg
Entry Requirements: *GCE:* 80. Interview required. Portfolio
required.

K24 THE UNIVERSITY OF KENT
INFORMATION, RECRUITMENT & ADMISSIONS
REGISTRY
UNIVERSITY OF KENT
CANTERBURY, KENT CT2 7NZ
t: 01227 827272 f: 01227 827077
e: information@kent.ac.uk
// www.kent.ac.uk

WQ43 BA Drama & Theatre Studies and English Language & Linguistics
Duration: 3FT Hon
Entry Requirements: *GCE:* 320. *IB:* 33. *BTEC NC:* DD. *BTEC ND:*
DDM. *OCR ND:* D *OCR NED:* M1

L27 LEEDS METROPOLITAN UNIVERSITY
COURSE ENQUIRIES OFFICE
CITY SITE
LEEDS LS1 3HE
t: 0113 81 23113 f: 0113 81 23129
// www.leedsmet.ac.uk

W491 BA Contemporary Performance Practices
Duration: 1FT Hon
Entry Requirements: Contact the institution for details.

W492 BA Performance Arts
Duration: 1FT Hon
Entry Requirements: Interview required. HND required.

L48 THE LIVERPOOL INSTITUTE FOR PERFORMING ARTS
MOUNT STREET
LIVERPOOL L1 9HF
t: 0151 330 3000 f: 0151 330 3131
e: admissions@lipa.ac.uk
// www.lipa.ac.uk

W491 BA Community Drama
Duration: 3FT Hon
Entry Requirements: *GCE:* 180. Interview required.

M80 MIDDLESEX UNIVERSITY
MIDDLESEX UNIVERSITY
THE BURROUGHS
LONDON NW4 4BT
t: 020 8411 5555 f: 020 8411 5649
e: enquiries@mdx.ac.uk
// www.mdx.ac.uk

W490 FdA Inclusive Performance (Chicken Shed)
Duration: 2FT Fdg
Entry Requirements: Interview required.

N30 NEW COLLEGE NOTTINGHAM
ADAMS BUILDING
STONEY STREET
THE LACE MARKET
NOTTINGHAM NG1 1NG
t: 0115 910 0100 f: 0115 953 4349
e: enquiries@ncn.ac.uk
// www.ncn.ac.uk

W490 BA Theatre Arts (Top-up)
Duration: 1FT Hon
Entry Requirements: Interview required. HND required.

N37 UNIVERSITY OF WALES, NEWPORT
ADMISSIONS
LODGE ROAD
CAERLEON
NEWPORT NP18 3QT
t: 01633 432030 f: 01633 432850
e: admissions@newport.ac.uk
// www.newport.ac.uk

W490 BA Applied Drama
Duration: 3FT Hon
Entry Requirements: *GCE:* 260. *IB:* 24.

QW34 BA Applied Drama and English
Duration: 3FT Hon
Entry Requirements: *GCE:* 260. *IB:* 24. Interview required.

P60 UNIVERSITY OF PLYMOUTH
DRAKE CIRCUS
PLYMOUTH PL4 8AA
t: 01752 588037 f: 01752 588050
e: admissions@plymouth.ac.uk
// www.plymouth.ac.uk

WW46 BA Digital Performance Arts
Duration: 1FT Hon
Entry Requirements: HND required.

P80 UNIVERSITY OF PORTSMOUTH
ACADEMIC REGISTRY
UNIVERSITY HOUSE
WINSTON CHURCHILL AVENUE
PORTSMOUTH PO1 2UP
t: 023 9284 8484 f: 023 9284 3082
e: admissions@port.ac.uk
// www.port.ac.uk

W491 BA Drama and Performance
Duration: 3FT Hon
Entry Requirements: *GCE:* 240-300. *IB:* 25. *BTEC NC:* DD. *BTEC ND:* DMM. Interview required.

Q25 QUEEN MARGARET UNIVERSITY, EDINBURGH
QUEEN MARGARET UNIVERSITY DRIVE
EDINBURGH EH21 6UU
t: 0131474 0000 f: 0131 474 0001
e: admissions@qmu.ac.uk
// www.qmu.ac.uk

W490 BA Drama and Performance
Duration: 4FT Hon
Entry Requirements: *GCE:* 300. *IB:* 30.

S21 SHEFFIELD HALLAM UNIVERSITY
CITY CAMPUS
HOWARD STREET
SHEFFIELD S1 1WB
t: 0114 225 5555 f: 0114 225 2167
e: admissions@shu.ac.uk
// www.shu.ac.uk

W490 BA Performance and Professional Practice
Duration: 1FT Hon
Entry Requirements: HND required.

W491 BA Performance for Stage and Screen
Duration: 3FT Hon
Entry Requirements: *GCE:* 240.

N8W4 BSc Events Management with Arts & Entertainment (Top-up)
Duration: 1FT Hon
Entry Requirements: HND required.

S30 SOUTHAMPTON SOLENT UNIVERSITY
EAST PARK TERRACE
SOUTHAMPTON
HAMPSHIRE SO14 0RT
t: +44 (0) 23 8031 9039 f: + 44 (0)23 8022 2259
e: admissions@solent.ac.uk or ask@solent.ac.uk
// www.solent.ac.uk/

W490 BA Performance
Duration: 3FT Hon
Entry Requirements: *Foundation:* Distinction. *GCE:* 240. *SQAAH:*
AA-CCD. *IB:* 24. *BTEC NC:* DD. *BTEC ND:* MMM. *OCR ND:* D
OCR NED: M3 Interview required.

S32 SOUTH DEVON COLLEGE
LONG ROAD
PAIGNTON
DEVON TQ4 7EJ
t: 08000 380123 f: 01803 540541
e: highereducation@southdevon.ac.uk
// www.southdevon.ac.uk

WN48 FdA Drama, Performance and Arts Management
Duration: 2FT Fdg
Entry Requirements: Contact the institution for details.

S72 STAFFORDSHIRE UNIVERSITY
COLLEGE ROAD
STOKE ON TRENT ST4 2DE
t: 01782 292753 f: 01782 292740
e: admissions@staffs.ac.uk
// www.staffs.ac.uk

W491 BA Entrepreneurship for the Creative & Cultural Industries in Theatre Arts
Duration: 1FT Hon
Entry Requirements: Interview required. Portfolio required.

S74 STRATFORD UPON AVON COLLEGE
THE WILLOWS NORTH
ALCESTER ROAD
STRATFORD-UPON-AVON
WARWICKSHIRE CV37 9QR
t: 01789 266245 f: 01789 267524
e: college@stratford.ac.uk
// www.stratford.ac.uk

194W HND Performing Arts (Musical Theatre)
Duration: 2FT HND
Entry Requirements: Contact the institution for details.

S84 UNIVERSITY OF SUNDERLAND
STUDENT HELPLINE
THE STUDENT GATEWAY
CHESTER ROAD
SUNDERLAND SR1 3SD
t: 0191 515 3000 f: 0191 515 3805
e: student.helpline@sunderland.ac.uk
// www.sunderland.ac.uk

W490 FdA Performing Arts
Duration: 2FT Fdg
Entry Requirements: *GCE:* 80-220. *SQAH:* CCCC. *IB:* 22.
Interview required.

T20 TEESSIDE UNIVERSITY
MIDDLESBROUGH TS1 3BA
t: 01642 218121 f: 01642 384201
e: registry@tees.ac.uk
// www.tees.ac.uk

W493 BA Performing Arts
Duration: 1FT Hon
Entry Requirements: Interview required.

W490 FdA Performance and Events Production
Duration: 2FT Fdg
Entry Requirements: *GCE:* 80-100. *IB:* 24. Interview required.

W492 FdA Performing Arts
Duration: 2FT Fdg
Entry Requirements: *GCE:* 80-100. *IB:* 24. Interview required.

W76 UNIVERSITY OF WINCHESTER
WINCHESTER
HANTS SO22 4NR
t: 01962 827234 f: 01962 827288
e: course.enquiries@winchester.ac.uk
// www.winchester.ac.uk

LW5K BA Childhood, Youth & Community Studies and Contemporary Performance
Duration: 3FT Hon
Entry Requirements: *GCE:* 260-300. *IB:* 24.

LW3K BA Contemporary Performance and Criminology
Duration: 3FT Hon
Entry Requirements: *Foundation:* Distinction. *GCE:* 260-300. *IB:*
24. *BTEC NC:* DD. *BTEC ND:* DMM. *OCR ND:* D *OCR NED:* M2

QW3K BA Contemporary Performance and English Language Studies
Duration: 3FT Hon
Entry Requirements: *Foundation:* Distinction. *GCE:* 260-300. *IB:*
25. *BTEC NC:* DD. *BTEC ND:* DMM. *OCR ND:* D *OCR NED:* M2

NW8K BA Contemporary Performance and Event Management
Duration: 3FT Hon
Entry Requirements: *Foundation:* Distinction. *GCE:* 260-300. *IB:* 24. *BTEC NC:* DD. *BTEC ND:* DMM. *OCR ND:* D *OCR NED:* M2

WW64 BA Contemporary Performance and Film & Cinema Technologies
Duration: 3FT Hon
Entry Requirements: *Foundation:* Distinction. *GCE:* 260-300. *IB:* 24. *BTEC NC:* DD. *BTEC ND:* DMM. *OCR ND:* D *OCR NED:* M2

MW1K BA Contemporary Performance and Law
Duration: 3FT Hon
Entry Requirements: *Foundation:* Distinction. *GCE:* 260-300. *IB:* 25. *BTEC NC:* DD. *BTEC ND:* DMM. *OCR ND:* D *OCR NED:* M2

WW94 BA Contemporary Performance and Modern Liberal Arts
Duration: 3FT Hon
Entry Requirements: *Foundation:* Distinction. *GCE:* 260-300. *IB:* 25. *BTEC NC:* DD. *BTEC ND:* DMM. *OCR ND:* D *OCR NED:* M2

LW2K BA Contemporary Performance and Politics & Global Studies
Duration: 3FT Hon
Entry Requirements: *Foundation:* Distinction. *GCE:* 260-300. *IB:* 24. *BTEC NC:* DD. *BTEC ND:* MMM. *OCR ND:* D

WNKV BA Contemporary Performance and Sports Management
Duration: 3FT Hon
Entry Requirements: *Foundation:* Pass. *GCE:* 260-300. *IB:* 24. *BTEC NC:* DD. *BTEC ND:* MMP. *OCR ND:* D

VW63 BA Contemporary Performance and Theology & Religious Studies
Duration: 3FT Hon
Entry Requirements: *Foundation:* Distinction. *GCE:* 260-300. *IB:* 25. *BTEC NC:* DD. *BTEC ND:* DMM. *OCR ND:* D *OCR NED:* M2

W81 WORCESTER COLLEGE OF TECHNOLOGY
DEANSWAY
WORCESTER WR1 2JF
t: 01905 725555 f: 01905 28906
// www.wortech.ac.uk

094W HND Theatrical Make-Up and Costume
Duration: 2FT HND
Entry Requirements: *GCE:* 40.

PS